ATTACKS on the PRESS
in 2002

On the cover: A Chinese police officer pushes
an Al-Jazeera cameraman outside a German
government–run school where at least 15 suspected
North Korean asylum seekers were holed up
on September 3, 2002. *(AP/Greg Baker, staff)*

The publication of *Attacks on the Press in 2002*
is underwritten by a grant from Bloomberg.

CPJ
COMMITTEE
TO·PROTECT
JOURNALISTS

330 Seventh Avenue, 12th floor, New York, N.Y. 10001
Phone: (212) 465-1004 Fax: (212) 465-9568 e-mail: info@cpj.org
Web site: *www.cpj.org*

Founded in 1981, the Committee to Protect Journalists responds to attacks on the press world-wide. CPJ documents more than 500 cases every year and takes action on behalf of journalists and their news organizations, without regard to political ideology. Join CPJ and help promote press freedom by defending the people who report the news. To maintain its independence, CPJ accepts no government funding. We depend entirely on the support of corporations, foundations, and individuals.

The Associated Press, IDT, Lexis-Nexis, and Reuters provided electronic news and Internet services that were used to conduct research for this book.

AP Associated Press   **IDT**    **LEXIS·NEXIS** A member of the Reed Elsevier plc group   REUTERS

Editor: Susan Ellingwood
Deputy Editor: Amanda Watson-Boles
Design: FTK Media LLC

Attacks on the Press in 2002: A Worldwide Survey by the Committee to Protect Journalists
ISSN: 1078-3334
ISBN: 0-944823-22-X

iii

PREFACE

by Serge Schmemann

MANY REPORTERS FIND THEMSELVES IN A DILEMMA when the press comes under attack. Our pride, our institutional and tribal loyalties, all clamor for a retort. We may be the bearers of bad tidings, but we are not their cause. If the truth is inimical to you, we want to argue, assailing us will not alter it. But then the reporter's half of the brain pipes up. Our instinct is (or should be) to stay out of the fray, to remain impartial, not to become part of the story. If we claim the right to question those in authority, why should our power, our institutions, our work be above challenge and criticism? Why should we demand special treatment? And who better knows the failings of the press than we do? Above all, if we have become the news, have we not failed in our primary task of covering the news? These conflicting instincts often make us reluctant to write about the travails of our trade.

I think we would all agree that if we deliberately impose ourselves on a story, we have failed. But in many years of covering places such as the former Soviet Union and the Middle East, I have found that those reporters who are harassed, jailed, or killed are rarely those who chase after glory, danger, or ratings. Many of them are people who did not choose risky assignments but whose countries or beats were caught up in conflict, tyranny, or lawlessness. Telling the real story became dangerous, but they told it anyway because they believed they had to do so. *The Wall Street Journal*'s Daniel Pearl was not kidnapped and murdered because he was foolhardy or careless; he was in Pakistan because that was where the most important story in his beat was developing, and he was killed by extremists who hated him for being a journalist, for being an American, and for being a Jew.

"I don't consider myself a hero," said *Respublika* editor-in-chief Irina Petrushova, a soft-spoken mother who has been threatened, harassed, and attacked for writing about government corruption in Kazakhstan, after receiving a CPJ 2002 International Press Freedom Award. "Like hundreds of my colleagues in other countries around the world, I fear for myself and my sons. I am even more afraid that my children will have to live in a totally corrupt society. I fear they will have to lie, to offer bribes, to grovel in order to be successful in their lives. I fear the arbitrary rule of bureaucrats and police, who are not accountable to the people, and who are gradually turning Kazakhstan into an authoritarian state."

I was sitting next to Petrushova's husband as she spoke. "This will really make them angry," he whispered. "Will that make it worse for her?" I asked. "No! No! This is what they need to hear," he replied.

That brought me back to earlier years, when Petrushova's spiritual predecessors among Soviet dissidents would risk their freedom, and even their lives, to smuggle information to Western reporters, convinced that giving voice, or glasnost, to the realities of the Soviet regime was the ultimate weapon against its tyranny. Many of those dissenters were also unwilling heroes, people who had come to the painful conclusion that they had no moral choice but to tell the truth. In the end, it was former Soviet leader Mikhail Gorbachev's official embrace of glasnost—more than all the other weapons of the Cold War—that brought the communist system crashing down. And

Irina Petrushova of Kazakhstan delivering her acceptance speech at CPJ's 2002 International Press Freedom Awards dinner in the Grand Ballroom of the Waldorf-Astoria, New York City, November 27, 2002. (*CPJ Photo*)

however sad the revival of despotism across so much of the former Soviet empire may be, it is heartening that people such as Petrushova have not lost their voice.

More recently, I spent several months covering the Israeli-Palestinian conflict. In 2002, the West Bank ranked at the top of CPJ's list of the "worst places to be a journalist" based on the number of documented attacks on the press. The Israeli-Palestinian conflict is a very difficult story to cover because of the ardent passions that every report arouses among readers and viewers. Journalists are constantly accused of bias or of violating restrictions. Yet after watching so many reporters and cameramen surmount dangers, hatreds, and barriers day after day, I am convinced that the vast majority of them do so because that is the only way this story can be told, and because they believe it must be told. Their reports may infuriate one side or the other, but in the end, no one can claim ignorance of what is taking place in that sad and shattered land.

In the end, that is the answer to the dilemma. The response to those who killed Daniel Pearl, or to those who harass Irina Petrushova, is to ensure that the stories for which they suffered, their stories, get told—not out of vengeance or spite, but because they need to be told, because we ourselves need to hear them. That, ultimately, is our only real defense, and the real tribute we can pay to our colleagues.

Serge Schmemann is a member of *The New York Times'* editorial board. He has covered South Africa, the Soviet Union, Germany, post-Soviet Russia, and Israel. He was awarded a Pulitzer Prize in 1991 for his coverage of Germany's reunification.

| TABLE OF CONTENTS |

A total of 19 journalists were killed for their work in 2002, including three journalists each in **Colombia, Russia,** and the **West Bank**. That is the lowest number on record since CPJ began tracking the killings in 1985. Most were local journalists, murdered with impunity. (See page 354.)

Angered at the coverage of the murder trial of journalist Carlos Cardoso, which implicated her son, **Mozambique**'s first lady allegedly sent truckloads of chickens to the homes and offices of several journalists. (See page 27.)

In the **Philippines,** warlord politics, official corruption, and a breakdown in the justice system have contributed to the fact that 39 journalists have been murdered since democracy was restored there in 1986. All of these cases remain officially unsolved. (See page 182.)

Upset by a critical *Wall Street Journal Europe* article, **Romania**'s Defense Ministry sent a warning to several local newspapers that had republished the article. "Life is short," the ministry warned, "and your health has too high a price to be endangered by debating highly emotional subjects." (See page 255.)

Eritrea is Africa's foremost jailer of journalists. President Isaias Afewerki banned the entire independent press corps in September 2001, accusing them of "endangering national unity." Eighteen journalists were imprisoned without charge. When a group of them began a hunger strike in March 2002 to protest their detention, authorities moved the journalists to unknown sites and have held them incommunicado ever since. (See page 14.)

Three journalists in **Tajikistan** were conscripted into military service in retaliation for producing a talk show that criticized local military officials. After they were arrested and detained, military officials told them, "We'll show you how to present us on television." (See page 261.)

In the run-up to **China**'s 16th Communist Party Congress in November, propaganda officials issued guidelines to reporters listing 32 topics that were forbidden or to be covered with extra caution. On the list of forbidden topics: "Chinese eating dogs that Westerners breed." Among stories that must be reported with greater caution: "Reports on World Cup soccer," "restrictions on negative news," and "high-living consumer lifestyles." (See page 206.)

After the office of *Respublika*, a business weekly in **Kazakhstan**, was burned to the ground by Molotov cocktails, officials accused the paper's editor of starting the fire herself to help boost the publication's circulation. (See page 251.)

In April, **Israel** Defense Forces arrested three Palestinian journalists in the West Bank and held them for nearly six months without charge. (See page 309.)

A newscaster in **Gabon** was fired after stuttering through the name of President Denis Sassou-Nguesso, of the neighboring Republic of Congo, on live radio. Sassou-Nguesso is married to the daughter of Gabon's president. (See page 17.)

In **Saudi Arabia**, the Ministry of Information forced Muhammad Mukhtar al-Fal, editor of the daily *Al-Madina*, to resign after he published a poem criticizing the country's conservative judiciary as corrupt. (See page 321.)

The June murder of TV Globo investigative reporter Tim Lopes rocked **Brazil**, illustrating the dangers that journalists in that country face when covering organized crime. Lopes was brutally killed by drug traffickers while working on assignment in one of Rio de Janeiro's favelas, or shantytowns. (See page 93.)

When **The Gambia**'s president, Yahya Jammeh, was asked whether he would try to improve relations with the press by visiting media organizations, he replied, "Do you think you need to go into a toilet to know that it stinks?" (See page 17.)

According to the Federation of Nepalese Journalists, more than 130 journalists have been arrested in **Nepal** since the government introduced anti-terrorism legislation in November 2001 criminalizing contact with or support for the country's Maoist rebels. Sixteen journalists were in jail there at the end of 2002. (See page 176.)

The U.N. war crimes tribunal on Yugoslavia in **The Hague** announced a decision to limit compelled testimony from war correspondents in response to an appeal by former *Washington Post* reporter Jonathan Randal. The journalist, who had been subpoenaed to testify in the case of a former Bosnian-Serb housing minister facing charges of genocide, does not have to testify. (See page 277.)

In **Belarus**, three journalists who dared to write critical articles about President Aleksandr Lukashenko during the run-up to the September 2001 elections were sentenced to corrective labor for libeling the president, a criminal offense under Belarusian law. (See page 242.)

In **Chile**, a television commentator faces up to five years in jail for "disrespect" after he described the country's judiciary as "immoral, cowardly, and corrupt" for not providing compensation to a woman who had been imprisoned for a crime she did not commit. (See page 94.)

Islamic authorities in northern **Nigeria** issued a fatwa urging Muslims to kill a writer from the private daily *ThisDay* after her article about the Miss World pageant sparked deadly riots across the country. (See page 31.)

INTRODUCTION

by Ann Cooper

NINETEEN JOURNALISTS WERE KILLED BECAUSE OF THEIR WORK IN 2002, the lowest number since the Committee to Protect Journalists began recording the annual death toll in 1985.

One factor that set 2002 apart was an easing of conflict in some key regions. A year earlier, for example, 37 journalists were killed—eight of them while covering the war in Afghanistan. The relative quiet there, and the movement in 2002 toward peace in Sri Lanka, Angola, and elsewhere, reduced some of the risk faced by local journalists and foreign correspondents who cover violent conflicts. The West Bank was a dramatic exception; three journalists there were killed by gunfire from Israel Defense Forces, and several more were wounded.

But war is only one threat to journalists. Most of the 19 who died in 2002 were targeted in direct reprisal for their work, by Colombia's paramilitaries, by corrupt local officials in the Philippines, and by others who would silence journalists through intimidation and murder. At year's end, most of the killers in these 19 cases had not been brought to justice—a record of impunity that threatens press freedom worldwide.

For the second year in a row, the number of journalists in prison rose sharply. There were 136 journalists in jail at the end of 2002, a 15 percent increase from 2001 and a shocking 68 percent increase since the end of 2000, when only 81 journalists were imprisoned. For the fourth year in row, the world's leading jailer of journalists was China, which held 39 in prison; five of them were jailed in 2002. In Eritrea, where the government shut down the private press a week after the September 11, 2001, attacks, 18 journalists were in jail. In Nepal, where 16 journalists were incarcerated, the government justified its repressive actions as a necessary response to threats posed by "terrorist" Maoist rebels.

Until September 11, 2001, the number of journalists in prison had been on a downward trend—from 129 in 1997, to 118 in 1998, to 87 in 1999, and to a low of 81 at the end of 2000. Strong pressure from international organizations, the media, and governments worldwide, including the United States, was probably responsible for the decline. Countries that routinely jailed journalists were ostracized and often isolated. However, Nepal and Eritrea, both of which began their crackdowns on the press in late 2001, have largely escaped international criticism. Certainly, the stigma associated with jailing a journalist has faded.

International pressure, however, may have played a role in securing the early release of one of these imprisoned journalists at the beginning of 2003. Russian journalist Grigory Pasko was paroled for good behavior on January 23, after serving two-thirds of his four-year treason sentence. Pasko, who had been reporting for the Russian military newspaper *Boyevaya Vakhta* (Battle Watch) on environmental damage caused by the Russian navy, had been convicted of "treason in the form of espionage" for "intending" to give classified documents to Japanese news outlets. CPJ had campaigned intensely for Pasko's release.

Imprisonment is the most severe tactic routinely used by governments to suppress critical reporting. In hundreds of other cases, all documented in this book, journalists were assaulted, censored, harassed, or threatened, just for doing their jobs.

They were targeted for writing about government malfeasance: Irina Petrushova, editor of a business newspaper in Kazakhstan, was sent a funeral wreath and then a decapitated dog to discourage her from investigating financial corruption in the president's administration.

They were targeted for exposing the crime webs of ruthless drug lords: Television investigative reporter Tim Lopes of Brazil used a hidden camera to film the sexual exploitation of minors in a Rio de Janeiro slum but was caught by the slum's drug gang, beaten, executed with a sword, and burned.

They were targeted while working to expose the many threads of international terrorism: *Wall Street Journal* reporter Daniel Pearl, expecting to meet with the leader of a radical Islamic group in Pakistan, instead was kidnapped, accused of spying, killed, and his dismembered corpse was dumped in a shallow grave. His captors circulated the videotape of the beheading widely through the Internet to recruit others to take up arms against the United States and its allies.

Subsequent arrests and trials may lead to justice in the killings of Lopes and Pearl. Another murder trial, this one involving the grisly 2000 assassination of Mozambique's top investigative reporter, Carlos Cardoso, caused a sensation in 2002 with accusations of high-level plotting that even pointed a finger at the president's son. On January 31, 2003, a judge sentenced six men to lengthy prison terms for murdering Cardoso and vowed to push for a more thorough investigation into the crime.

But in most other cases, official investigations of journalists' murders are halfhearted or nonexistent. Two witnesses to the May 2002 murder of Edgar Damalerio, an editor and radio commentator in the Philippines, identified a local police officer as the killer, but officials have not yet charged him. (As this book was going to press, a judge in the Philippines ordered the officer's arrest.) Impunity is so standard in the Philippines, Colombia, and Russia that journalists there are resigned to losing several of their colleagues each year. Two died in the Philippines in 2002, while three Colombian journalists were murdered because of their work, and another three were killed in Russia.

And that's in addition to the three who were killed by Israeli gunfire in the West Bank, where foreign and local correspondents who covered that conflict—in particular Israel's March military offensive in the West Bank—reported that Israel Defense Forces fired at them despite the fact that they were clearly identified as journalists. Israel also detained several Palestinian journalists, holding three of them for several months before releasing them without charge. The attacks and arrests by Israel, along with pressures from the Palestinian National Authority, put the West Bank at the top of CPJ's list of the "10 Worst Places to Be a Journalist."

Israeli officials frequently justified their actions as necessary for national security. So did Russian authorities when they cracked down on the media during and after the October hostage crisis in which Chechen rebels seized a Moscow theater where some 700 people were attending a musical. The Russian government threatened or took action against the press for interviewing hostage-takers, publishing a photograph of a woman killed by the Chechens, and posting on the Web an interview with anguished relatives of some of the hostages. After security forces used a narcotic gas and stormed the theater—killing all the rebels and more than 120 civilians—the government became impatient with media outlets that questioned whether the death toll could have been kept lower. In November, protests by Russian journalists and international press freedom advocates managed to head off a set of amendments that would have fixed draconian new limits on media coverage of terrorism and terrorist activities, but journalists expect the government to continue debating restrictions in 2003.

The clear message, from both Israeli and Russian officials, was that in certain conflicts the media have little right to information, to the access they need to cover events, and little justification for questioning government actions. Such arguments have grown increasingly common, with political leaders in many parts of the world adopting the rhetoric of fighting terrorism to stifle independent reporting and opposition voices.

U.S. president George W. Bush's "war on terrorism," launched in the weeks after the September 11, 2001, attacks on the United States, gave impetus to the argument. Though the Bush administration has moved away from its strong warnings against the perils of dissent, other leaders wrap their repression in the anti-terrorism argument, even sometimes describing critical journalists as "terrorists.

The war on terrorism encourages repression of the media in another way. The United States, for example, has muted its criticism of human rights and press freedom abuses in countries that are strategically important to its military efforts, such as the states of Central Asia.

Eritrea has also gone largely uncriticized, despite a harsh crackdown in late 2001 that closed all independent media outlets and imprisoned 18 journalists. Several U.S. officials visited the country in 2002, in search of a possible site for an American Army base to be used for military action against Iraq. On one such visit in December, U.S. secretary of defense Donald Rumsfeld was asked about Eritrea's abysmal press freedom record. Eritrea, he answered, "is a sovereign nation, and they arrange themselves and deal with their problems in ways that they feel are appropriate to them."

That message left little hope that international pressure might push Eritrean president Isaias Afewerki to ease his ban on the private media—or even acknowledge where he has imprisoned journalists and opposition figures who are being held incommunicado.

No journalist's case drew as much international attention in 2002 as the kidnapping and murder of Daniel Pearl. In the wake of Pearl's death, journalist safety became a renewed priority for news organizations, particularly those in Europe and the United States that have substantial foreign reporting staffs and budgets to deploy them to conflicts all over the world. Many purchased bulletproof vests and sent their correspondents to hostile-environment training, usually week-long courses run by former military personnel to sensitize journalists to the risks they could face in a conflict zone.

The prospect of U.S. military action against Iraq prompted a new round of training, this time to prepare journalists for possible biological or chemical warfare. And the U.S. military offered "boot camp" courses to dozens of correspondents who could be "embedded" with American troops in the event of an invasion of Iraq.

As news organizations budgeted millions of dollars and negotiated with the U.S. military for access to the battlefield in the possible new conflict, a host of questions arose, among them: Would the Pentagon censor reports from the field, and how would U.S. troops regard free-lance journalists who were not accredited to travel with them? Along with journalist safety, press freedom in the potential new conflict zone was certain to be a top priority for journalists in 2003.

Ann Cooper is the executive director of the Committee to Protect Journalists. Before joining CPJ in 1998, she was a foreign correspondent for National Public Radio for nine years, serving as bureau chief in Moscow and Johannesburg.

OVERVIEW: AFRICA

by Yves Sorokobi

ALTHOUGH THE KENYA-BASED *EAST AFRICAN STANDARD*, one of Africa's oldest continuously published newspapers, marked its 100th anniversary in November, journalism remains a difficult profession on the continent, with adverse government policies and multifaceted economic woes still undermining the full development of African media.

At year's end, 26 journalists were in prison in Africa for their work: 18 in Eritrea, two each in Togo and the Democratic Republic of Congo, and one each in Guinea, Sierra Leone, Niger, and Ethiopia. This is a stark increase from the end of 2001, when 15 journalists were in African jails. The jump is attributable mainly to Eritrea's appalling record.

Also during 2002, overzealous riot police shot one journalist to death on January 12 in Uganda's capital, Kampala. Jimmy Higenyi was the only reporter killed in the line of duty in Africa in 2002, while 2001 was the first year in two decades when no journalists were killed there for their work. And despite Higenyi's death, the trend may last, with African rulers under increasing pressure from donors and civil-society groups to end impunity and aggressively track down journalists' murderers. This was the case, most recently, in Burkina Faso, where the December 1998 murder of editor Norbert Zongo unleashed waves of civil unrest; and in Mozambique, where widespread indignation over the botched investigation into the November 2000 killing of Carlos Cardoso, founding editor of the now defunct business daily *Metical*, could compromise the governing FRELIMO party's chances to retain power.

In 2002, African journalists continued to garner public support at home and abroad. This situation has compelled certain African leaders, such as Ethiopian prime minister Meles Zenawi, who has long dismissed Ethiopia's nonstate media as the "gutter press," to acknowledge their role as government watchdogs. The creation of regional infrastructures to deal with press freedom issues is also advancing, while the press is helping to establish democracy in Africa.

Radio broadcasting remains the most effective way to reach people in Africa. Radio's vital role in the flow of news and opinions has inspired media activists to intensify their lobbying of governments that still resist private broadcasting. In March, three years after Ethiopia passed a broadcast law, officials finally began issuing licenses to private radio station owners, leaving only three African countries—Angola, Eritrea, and Zimbabwe—with airwaves that are closed to private competition. Because of their curbs on the circulation of information and continued harassment and jailing of journalists, CPJ placed both Eritrea and Zimbabwe on its 2002 list of the "10 Worst Places to Be a Journalist."

On May 3, World Press Freedom Day, African journalists gathering in Pretoria, South Africa, endorsed the African Charter on Broadcasting, which was agreed upon at a global press freedom conference in May 2001. In October, the Banjul, Gambia–based African

Yves Sorokobi is CPJ's Africa program coordinator. **Adam Posluns** and **Wacuka Mungai** are the Africa program research associates at CPJ. They contributed substantially to the research and writing of this section. **The Freedom Forum** partly funded CPJ's missions to both Ethiopia and Eritrea.

Commission on Human and People's Rights added enforcing the broadcast charter to its roster of official activities. Aiming to serve as a blueprint for Africa's broadcast policies and laws, the charter focuses on airwave liberalization and the effects of globalization on the continent's emerging broadcast industry.

Also in October, the commission adopted a Declaration of Principles on Freedom of Expression, which stresses the "fundamental importance of freedom of expression as an individual human right, as a cornerstone of democracy and as a means of ensuring respect for all human rights and freedoms."

But some observers have serious reservations about how the commission, a nonjudicial body, will enforce these measures. The Declaration of Principles on Freedom of Expression, proposed by the anti-censorship group Article 19, for example, aims to serve as a benchmark for African governments' compliance with Article 9 of the 1986 African Charter on Human and People's Rights, which guarantees press freedom. But the declaration does not explain how its provisions can be enforced against delinquent governments. The declaration also aspires to boost free speech within the African Union (AU) and the New Partnership for Africa's Development (NEPAD) initiatives.

African heads of state, led by South African president Thabo Mbeki, developed NEPAD in 2001 to increase foreign investment in African countries. Tied to US$64 billion in promised investments from Western powers, NEPAD seeks to achieve a continent-wide growth rate of 7 percent by 2015 through democracy promotion and good governance. But in April, NEPAD's clause on good governance prompted an intense row between some African leaders and Western governments seeking to punish Zimbabwean president Robert Mugabe for his regime's illegal land seizures and repression of the opposition and independent press. Nigeria and South Africa, encouraged by Western NEPAD backers to force Zimbabwe to improve its human rights record, proved unwilling to confront President Mugabe.

Officially launched in July, the AU is the latest avatar of the Organization of African Unity (OAU), which led Africa's independence from colonial rule. Modeled after the European Union, the AU is expected to work on poverty alleviation and market development. According to a November World Bank report, strong evidence suggests that a free press can help reduce poverty and boost economic development. However, the AU's founding texts blatantly ignore the painful struggle of African journalists to secure more freedoms.

On August 12, CPJ wrote to AU secretary-general Amara Essy to voice concerns that the organization's constitution fails to protect press freedom. "The language of this new constitution marks a significant setback for press freedom and freedom of expression in Africa, both of which were enshrined in the constitution of the OAU, the precursor to the AU," CPJ wrote. At year's end, the AU had still not replied to CPJ's letter.

Meanwhile, the Internet continues to penetrate the continent slowly, despite restrictive laws hastily passed by many governments to control business and other opportunities connected to the technology. And African journalists and citizens appear eager to take advantage of the Internet. In February, a United Nations Development Program (UNDP) report concluded that Zimbabwe, with more than 100,000 citizens online, ranks among Africa's foremost Internet users, although a Post and Telecommunications Act empowers the government to intercept e-mails in the name of "national security." In December, Zimbabwean security agents accused journalist Lewis Machipisa of "spying for the BBC" after discovering an e-mail that he had allegedly sent to the British broadcaster, which has been banned from Zimbabwe since 2001. The accusation forced Machipisa to go into hiding.

According to the UNDP, 4 million Africans use the Internet regularly, with more than 50 percent of them in South Africa. "There are now 38 countries with 1,000 or more dial-up subscribers, but only 11 countries with more than 20,000 subscribers—Algeria, Botswana, Egypt, Kenya, Mauritius, Morocco, Nigeria, South Africa, Tunisia, Tanzania and Zimbabwe," the report said. The UNDP cited inadequate telecommunications infrastructure as the main hurdle to the Internet's further expansion.

There is hope, however, that more Africans will be able to join the global Internet community. On May 27, a group of African telecommunications experts gathered in Senegal's capital, Dakar, to launch a US$639 million undersea fiber-optic cable. The 26,448 kilometer (16,200 mile) cable links 10 African countries with Europe and Asia.

Yet despite the remarkable gains of recent years, press freedom in Africa remains quite vulnerable. In September, West African journalists hosted the 10th annual meeting of the International Freedom of Expression Exchange (IFEX) in Dakar. IFEX, with more than 50 members (including CPJ and several African journalist groups), coordinates international press freedom advocacy. In assessing IFEX's first decade of work, Cameroonian journalist Pius Njawe told the Dakar meeting that IFEX advocacy has forced some African governments to stop their most blatant repressions, such as sending police to close news outlets whose reporting angers authorities.

"But governments are quite clever," added Njawe. "They have turned to other forms of harassment." For example, instead of directly shuttering an offending newspaper, they now withhold advertising, creating financial hardship and sometimes even forcing a paper to close for lack of money. While there is a general consensus that the African press is freer than it was 10 years ago, "it's difficult for me to say," said Njawe. "In the past, the threat was an open threat. Now the threat is more subtle." ∎

ANGOLA

ON FEBRUARY 21, ANGOLA'S GOVERNMENT ANNOUNCED that its troops had killed Jonas Savimbi, who led the UNITA rebel group's fight for power in oil-rich Angola for more than 30 years. That same day, state television ran a special news program featuring Savimbi's corpse filmed from several angles with repeated close-ups of his neck, where the fatal bullet had entered. Many Angolans celebrated in the streets with fireworks, gunshots, and champagne, while others grappled with anxiety about the future.

In late March, war-weary UNITA fighters and the government of President José Eduardo dos Santos signed a peace accord. Angolan journalists cheered UNITA's surrender and began reporting on the rebels' demobilization and disarmament, as well as on the nationwide reconciliation effort. "Não Coragem" (Courageous Nation), a weekly public-affairs program on state television, won instant popularity inside and outside Angola when it was launched in May. The program broadcasts stories of citizens looking for relatives who disappeared during the decades-long conflict. By September, "Não Coragem" had aired the stories of 7,000 people, reuniting about 80 families, according to the BBC.

Law enforcement officials did not always welcome journalists' coverage of the reconciliation movement. On May 31, the Office of Criminal Investigations detained and interrogated Manuel Vieira, a correspondent from the Catholic-owned station Radio Ecclesia, in the southern Huila Province. For several hours, Veira was pressed to explain why he had chosen to report that government-built transit camps for demobilized UNITA fighters have curiously high death rates. He was warned against further disclosures and then released.

In January, the Provincial Court of Luanda ordered free-lance journalist Rafael Marques to pay US$950 to President dos Santos following the journalist's March 2000 conviction for defamation. The case against Marques stemmed from an article he had written blaming dos Santos for "the destruction of the country and the promotion of corruption."

At year's end, a Luanda court was considering a complaint filed by the Eduardo dos Santos Foundation against the private weekly *Agora*. The paper is accused of forgery and defamation for a November article it published claiming that two Angolan women arrested at the Rio de Janeiro airport in possession of US$1 million in cash were on assignment for the foundation. "It was with perplexity and profound indignation that we took notice of a matter deeply damaging to the image and objectives of the foundation," the chairman explained.

Angola's leaders have yet to present the draft of a new, more liberal, press law that was promised more than two years ago. Government officials say they are working on it, but journalists remain skeptical. While *Agora* regularly publishes editorials reminding the government of its promise, most Angolan journalists seem too busy making ends meet to monitor the authorities' long string of unfulfilled pledges.

BOTSWANA

THOUGH JOURNALISTS AND HUMAN RIGHTS OBSERVERS GENERALLY CONSIDER the independent press in Botswana free, the government proved in 2002 that it is unwilling to tolerate negative coverage from state media.

In mid-April, Minister of Presidential Affairs and Public Administration Daniel Kwelagobe berated reporters from the state-owned Botswana Television network (BTV) for insulting President Festus Mogae by broadcasting comments from Neo Mothlabane, leader of the opposition Botswana People's Party. Kwelagobe, who is also secretary-general of the ruling Botswana Democratic Party, warned the broadcaster to sanitize its reports. The minister's comments disturbed local journalists, who felt that such statements created a climate of government intimidation during a vital period of national debate about proposed constitutional amendments designed to protect the rights of minority tribes.

Kwelagobe also accused the private press of "sensationalism and lack of in-depth reporting on the ongoing tribal debate." According to the independent weekly *Mmegi*, Kwelagobe claimed that the state media act as "a tool for nation building," while the private media are "driven by business motives." Despite these criticisms, the government did not take any serious action against the private press in 2002.

Nevertheless, journalists for the state media experienced increased government pressure. On April 22, the popular Radio Botswana talk show "Live Line," which was to feature a discussion on the scope of news coverage by public-service media outlets, was canceled shortly before airtime. At around the same time, BTV general manager Oshinka Tsiang, who is known for his strong support of editorial independence, resigned because of government interference, according to local journalists. Despite government pledges not to meddle in BTV operations, Tsiang was the second BTV manager to quit within a year because of state interference, said local sources.

The political opposition also attacked the Botswanan press. During a rally in May, Botswana National Front politician David Mhiemang physically assaulted *Mmegi* news editor Stryker Motlaloso in reprisal for the paper's coverage of factionalism within the party.

However, there were some positive developments for the media in 2002. In September, jurisdiction over media issues—including media-government relations—was moved from Kwelagobe's Ministry of Presidential Affairs and Public Administration to the newly created Ministry of Communications, Science, and Technology. Journalists in Botswana were hopeful that the new ministry would be friendlier toward the press.

In late October, journalists and media-rights advocates established a press council to regulate the Botswanan media. The council will receive petitions from the public about the performance of members of the press and will be empowered to "adjudicate on such matters and apply appropriate remedies, including sanctions, where necessary, in order to promote an atmosphere of mutual trust and respect between the press and the public." This self-regulatory body is the Botswanan media's response to the government's Mass Media Communications Bill, which would establish a statutory press council with leaders appointed by the government. Local journalists have heavily criticized the bill, saying it is an attempt to muzzle the press and control editorial policy.

The government's resettlement of the San people in the Central Kalahari Game Reserve drew the attention of the international media in 2002. Authorities denied some journalists access to the San during the last stages of the resettlement, which many observers saw as a forced removal, and harassed reporters who were able to communicate with them.

BURKINA FASO

2002 WAS A PARTICULARLY TOUGH YEAR for President Blaise Compaoré, as accusations mounted that he is one of West Africa's most corrupt leaders and supports insurrection in neighboring Ivory Coast. Members of the media covering the corruption have been harassed, while the December 1998 murder of journalist Norbert Zongo remains unsolved.

In February, Denmark decreased aid to Burkina Faso from US$27 million to US$21 million after allegations surfaced that the country had violated a U.N. arms embargo. Citing U.N. evidence, the Danish government said that Burkina Faso's capital, Ouagadougou, had become the main transit point for weapons fueling wars in the region. Denmark also cited delays in the probe into the Zongo murder as another reason for the decision.

U.N. officials maintain that Compaoré and his Liberian counterpart, Charles Taylor, regularly contravene international law for personal gain. In October, a report in the French daily *Le Monde* supported allegations by the Ivoirian government that Compaoré had hosted, armed, and trained a group of discontented officers from the Ivoirian army. On September 19, these Ivoirian officers launched a bloody rebellion from their Burkina Faso base in a bid to topple their country's government. Compaoré later admitted his part in the coup attempt, to which European media have also tied Libyan leader Muammar Qaddafi.

In October, CPJ confirmed a *Le Monde* report that in late September, the rebel Ivoirian soldiers kidnapped veteran journalist Christophe Koffi, an Ouagadougou-based reporter for Agence France-Presse, and drove him to a village on the Lareda River, near the border with Ivory Coast. Koffi was released a week later, after rebel chief Ibrahim Coulibaly had accused him of spying for the Ivoirian government. Koffi was not injured during his captivity.

Koffi had earlier been detained on August 7 in connection with a Burkina Faso police inquiry into the August 1 murder of Balla Kéita, a self-exiled former Ivory Coast government minister. After Koffi's release the next day, police picked up Newton Ahmed Barry, editor-in-chief of the private monthly *L'Evénement*, and asked him about his contacts with Ivoirian journalists, as well as whether he worked for the Ivoirian government. Barry was held for two days before being released without charge.

As tensions between Burkina Faso and the Ivory Coast escalated, nationalistic hatred surged on both sides, most notably in the Ivory Coast, where more than 3 million Burkinabes work on coffee and cocoa plantations. On August 6, Burkina Faso border police detained and interrogated six Ivoirian reporters who were headed to Ouagadougou to cover Kéita's death.

After hotly contested legislative elections in May, President Compaoré's governing Congress for Democracy and Progress party saw its share of seats in Parliament shrink to 57 from 101 out of 111 total seats. Independent journalists and opposition leaders alike welcomed the results, saying they showed the population's dissatisfaction with Compaoré's rule.

On the evening of October 14, according to regional news reports, President Compaoré survived an assassination attempt that killed at least one senior Secret Service agent and maimed another. Unidentified attackers hurled an explosive at the presidential limousine as it drove down an Ouagadougou street, the reports said.

BURUNDI

PRESIDENT PIERRE BUYOYA'S GOVERNMENT REMAINED WARY of political opposition and critical press reports during 2002. Meanwhile, government attempts to identify war criminals following Burundi's eight-year civil war between the Tutsi-led regime and the Hutu-backed opposition stalled when peace talks collapsed again on November 7, and the conflict continued intermittently.

On January 14, Burundi's leaders banned the Hutu-owned private news wire service Net Press, which often criticizes the government, because its "subversive, defamatory, insulting, and deceptive" journalism "undermines national unity, order, security, and public morality," said officials. After press corps protests, the government lifted the ban on February 23.

Still, relations between the government and media remained strained in 2002. In February, President Buyoya traveled to New York to ask the U.N. Security Council to help end the killings and keep the peace process on track. But when violence erupted in various parts of the country throughout the year, a flurry of news reports questioned the regime's professed desire for peace.

Buyoya had supported independent radio stations, the country's most popular medium, since May 2001, when they favored Buyoya's attempts to crush a military coup. However, the president failed to condemn the March 6 police attack on Studio Ijambo reporter and

Associated Press stringer Aloys Niyoyita in the capital, Bujumbura. Police manhandled and detained Niyoyita while he was covering a rally by a group opposed to peace.

Buyoya also said nothing on May 17, when the official National Communication Council (NCC), which regulates media in Burundi, banned all news outlets from interviewing dissidents and rebel groups. The NCC's decision came after the Defense Ministry complained that the independent Radio Publique Africaine had harmed national security by airing details of a planned military operation. NCC president Jean-Pierre Manda later explained, "It was not possession of the information that was illegal, but its premature broadcast." A few months later, the NCC offered a similar argument when it banned the July issue of the private monthly *PanAfrika*, which the council said included "extremist and subversive" views. In an interview published in that *PanAfrika* edition, a former minister accused President Buyoya of being a dictator with policies that could "bury all Burundians alive."

Surprisingly, although official interference with free expression continued, in early June, the NCC reversed its usual policy of siding with the government by calling on authorities to stop the "harassment and intimidation" of journalists. The council accused the State Attorney's Office of violating press freedom with a news blackout on a police inquiry into the November 2001 killing of the head of the World Health Organization's local office.

CAMEROON

ON OCTOBER 10, THE INTERNATIONAL COURT OF JUSTICE RECOGNIZED Cameroon's rights to Bakassi, a Gulf of Guinea peninsula whose sizable offshore oil deposits Nigeria has long claimed. Nevertheless, Nigeria continued to assert its prerogative, reviving fears of an armed conflict along the 1,000 mile (1,600 kilometer) border between the two countries.

Covering the court ruling steered the Cameroonian media's attention from other pressing issues, such as the protracted secessionist campaign by the southwestern English-speaking provinces and the government's poor human rights record. Meanwhile, the state enlisted the press to buttress the government's case against Nigeria while continuing to harass and detain journalists.

On January 9, police imprisoned Georges Baongla, publisher of the private weekly *Le Démenti*, and seized the paper's computers on claims that Baongla had defrauded a Finance Ministry official of US$23,000. *Le Démenti* staff, however, say their boss was persecuted for articles the paper had published denouncing graft at the ministry. At year's end, Baongla had been released.

In March, authorities jailed Peter William Mandio, publisher of the private weekly *Le Front Indépendant*, for three days after his paper ran a story about several alleged illicit affairs between staff members at the Office of the President. Publisher Jacques Blaise Mvié, of the weekly *La Nouvelle Presse*, went into hiding to avoid similar reprisals after his paper reported the same allegations.

President Paul Biya's administration struggled to present itself as a democratic regime, even amid press reports that citizens had filed 127 complaints asking the Supreme Court to cancel the results of the June legislative and municipal elections, in which the ruling Cameroon's People Democratic Party (CPDM) increased its hold on Parliament. Under intense pressure, the court voided results for 17 out of 154 seats, ruling that the balloting was deeply flawed. The September by-elections were less controversial, landing the CPDM all but one of the contested seats and shrinking the opposition's share to 21 seats, down from 43.

Following the by-elections, the media began running vitriolic commentaries about Biya's foreign trips, including a 54-day vacation abroad, under headlines such as "President Gone AWOL" and "Biya Kidnaps Self, Or Has He Fled?" In response, Communications Minister Jacques Fame Ndongo lambasted the media's "slippery ethics," which he said amounted to "invasion of privacy likely to disturb public order." A few weeks later, when Biya returned to celebrate his 20th anniversary as president, *La Nouvelle Expression* ran an article titled "20 Years of Delusions," while *Le Renouveau* lamented that Cameroonians had just spent "20 years in confusion."

CENTRAL AFRICAN REPUBLIC

A YEAR AFTER A FAILED COUP, THE GOVERNMENT OF President Ange-Félix Patassé lifted a nationwide curfew in May. Five months later, in October, several hundred soldiers and civilians were killed in another coup attempt, led by disgruntled army general François Bozize, paralyzing the country for weeks. The Patassé regime prevailed with the help of more than 1,000 mercenaries from the Democratic Republic of Congo and a small fleet of Libyan fighter jets flown by Libyan pilots, who conducted bombing raids on the rebel-held town of Damara, 30 miles (50 kilometers) north of the capital, Bangui.

Most local journalists admitted that they refrained from criticizing the government's brutal reprisals against alleged Bozize supporters. The few reporters who did question Patassé's response received death threats or were harassed by regime supporters and officials. On November 14, six soldiers beat Joseph Benamse, a correspondent for The Associated Press and BBC radio, for alleged anti-Patassé bias. At around the same time, Maka Gbossokotto, publisher of the weekly *Le Citoyen* and one of the country's most outspoken government critics, told reporters that he had received several threats and that his telephone line was being tapped.

Foreign media also faced increased difficulties in 2002. On November 16, the government jammed the frequencies of the Pan-African radio station Africa Number 1 and the French government–owned Radio-France Internationale (RFI). According to local media, President Patassé found RFI's coverage of the coup attempt slanted in favor of the rebels. "If you continue, I will remove RFI from the FM dial in Bangui," Patassé warned, according to RFI's Web site. Communications Minister Gabriel-Jean Edouard Koyambounou denied any official interference with the broadcasters' frequencies, suggesting that "heavy rains or thunder" may have caused the jamming.

General Bozize's rebels also tormented news professionals, prompting widespread condemnation from journalists' groups. On November 15, three dozen Central African journalists called for the release of Prosper N'Douba, publisher of the weekly digest *Centrafrique-Presse* and a spokesperson for President Patassé, who was taken hostage by rebels on October 25. N'Douba was freed on December 3.

Meanwhile, a Bangui court sentenced former military ruler Gen. André Kolingba to death in absentia for "attacking state security." Kolingba, who is living abroad and is believed to have led the May 2001 attempted coup, ruled Central African Republic for 12 years before losing elections to Patassé in 1993. His sentencing came one day before the Central African Economic and Monetary Community Force, a regional peacekeeping force, deployed its first contingent of troops into the country. Observers expect that a number of journalists who fled the country during Kolingba's rule will return to the republic.

CHAD

AFTER THREE YEARS, CHAD'S BLOODY CIVIL WAR ENDED IN JANUARY, when the government of President Idriss Déby signed a peace accord with the rebel Movement for Democracy and Justice (MDJT). A month later, Parliament adopted a law granting MDJT members amnesty.

Despite the treaty, fighting continued sporadically, and the media remained tightly controlled by the government. Officials, anxious to keep the fragile truce with the MDJT, grew impatient with critical reporting on the situation. In February, the High Council of Communications (HCC), an official media regulatory body, suspended the independent radio station FM Liberté for three weeks for allegedly broadcasting "information likely to disrupt public order." The station had earlier aired reports on a student demonstration at a university in northern Cameroon during which several Chadians were injured.

Although officials promised "total transparency" during April parliamentary elections, the HCC banned all political programming on radio stations ahead of the poll. The council claimed that since it had been unable to effectively regulate the airtime that political parties receive for advertising, the ban was necessary to prevent unequal media access. But journalists charged that the ban actually favored the ruling Patriotic Salvation Movement (MPS) party. According to the private biweekly *N'Djamena Hebdo*, "Politics is now considered a fools' game … whose outcome is known in advance." Few seemed surprised by the MPS's electoral victory, which gave the party 110 of 115 parliamentary seats.

The bans on political programming and the election results confirmed for many journalists that the HCC—originally intended to be an independent authority promoting free access to the media—has become a government instrument for controlling information. The HCC ordered a similar ban on political programming ahead of the 2001 elections, during which President Déby sailed to victory.

With Chad's high illiteracy rate, radio is the country's most important medium. Although the government opened the audiovisual communications sector to private ownership in 1994, private stations have been unable to broadcast because the HCC keeps the licensing fee at US$4,000 per year—an astronomical sum in Chad, where the average annual income is US$200.

DEMOCRATIC REPUBLIC OF CONGO

IN LATE DECEMBER, WARRING PARTIES IN THE DEMOCRATIC REPUBLIC OF CONGO (DRC) sealed a power-sharing deal, while the last foreign troops backing government or rebel groups prepared to withdraw from the vast, mineral-rich Central African nation. The latest agreement calls for a unity government, ending a four-year civil war that has ruined the country and killed thousands.

The peace accord—reached after a series of on-again, off-again talks following the April inter-Congolese dialogue in Sun City, South Africa—keeps President Joseph Kabila in power for two more years. During this period, four vice presidents, from both the armed and unarmed opposition, will prepare for the DRC's first elections since independence in 1960. At year's end, treaty signatories were considering a new constitution that is expected to safeguard basic liberties, including freedom of speech and the press.

Hailed as a landmark by foreign observers, the treaty failed to impress many Congolese, including journalists, who have grown cynical of halfhearted attempts at peace. Many journalists in the DRC argue that any viable accord must include a pledge by politicians to respect reporters' rights. In the current context, however, such a promise seems unlikely. Although the overall number of attacks against journalists is decreasing as the war winds down, conditions remain tough. In 2002, most press abuses were perpetrated by the Kabila government and the two factions of the rebel Rally for Congolese Democracy (RCD), which controls the DRC's northeast.

On December 9, rebels from the Rwanda-backed RCD faction closed the offices of Radio Maendeleo, a community broadcaster in the northeastern town of Bukavu, and arrested the station's boss, Kizito Mushizi Nfundiko, and its chief of news programming, Omba Kamemgele. The rebels were apparently angered by a December 7 Radio Maendeleo newscast that included sound bites from citizens slamming the RCD's new tax regime, which they said hurts the region's already dismal economy. The journalists were released on December 11.

A few months earlier, on September 26, RCD rebels arrested several journalists from the private, South Kivu Province–based Radio Uvira after the province's vice governor took offense at a news program that called life conditions there "moribund."

In the capital, Kinshasa, government soldiers kidnapped human rights lawyer Sébastien Kayembe on October 15, burned his car, and took him to the outskirts of the city, where they beat and left him for dead in a gutter. Kayembe survived the attack, which came after he asked authorities to punish a prison guard accused of torturing two of Kayembe's clients, journalists Delly Bonsange and Raymond Kabala, of the daily *Alerte Plus*. The two were picked up in July for falsely reporting that Minister of Public Order and Security Mwenze Kongolo had been poisoned. The paper ran a correction the next day, but to no avail. In September, a Kinshasa court convicted them of "harmful accusations" and "falsification of a public document" and sentenced them to prison. Bosange was released on December 3; Kabala remains in jail, one of only two Congolese journalists still serving time at year's end, although three dozen were detained during 2002.

At the peak of the armed conflict two years ago, the DRC's Court of Military Order (COM), a secretive institution whose rulings cannot be appealed, became the primary enforcer of Article 78 of the 1996 Press Law, which prescribes death for reporters convicted of betraying the state in time of war, insulting the army, demoralizing the nation, or disseminating false news. Officials have pardoned some reporters convicted by the COM before they could be executed.

The COM will again make headlines in early 2003, when it will hear final arguments in the trial of 130 people accused of involvement in the January 2001 assassination of Joseph Kabila's father, then president Laurent-Désiré Kabila. All of the defendants, who include spouses, children, and relatives of the actual suspects, have pleaded not guilty. The verdicts were deferred until January 2003, and the media have been barred from most of the trial.

EQUATORIAL GUINEA

SINCE PRESIDENT TEODORO OBIANG NGUEMA MBASOGO TOOK CONTROL in a 1979 military coup, he and his ruling Democratic Party of Equatorial Guinea have governed one of Africa's most repressive regimes. The country's small press has been incessantly harassed and intimidated, while citizens have been fined for reading controversial publications. Obiang's landslide re-election victory in December ensured that the press freedom climate there would remain harsh.

As a former Spanish colony and Africa's only Spanish-speaking country, Equatorial Guinea is politically isolated from the rest of the continent. The government retains a virtual monopoly on all broadcast media. The president's son owns the only local private radio station—Radio Asonga—and its television affiliate. A handful of independent newspapers appear irregularly, due to high costs and government harassment, while all papers are subject to prior censorship by the Information Ministry. Authorities increasingly monitor telecommunications and Internet services. Under these circumstances, self-censorship pervades both the private and state media.

Despite allegations of widespread human rights abuses in 2002, on April 19, the Office of the U.N. High Commissioner for Human Rights ended the mandate of its special representative to Equatorial Guinea, who had been in the country since 1979. Surprisingly, the decision came after 144 opposition supporters had been arrested on charges of conspiracy to overthrow the government.

On May 18, the justice minister invited the public and international observers to attend the alleged conspirators' trial. However, the foreign affairs minister called initial reports about the proceedings from foreign journalists "distorted," claiming that they degraded the country's reputation. As a result, on May 21, two days before the trial began, Deputy Minister of Information Alfonso Nsue Mokuy implemented stricter press accreditation procedures for all foreign correspondents.

Meanwhile, journalists for the local private press attempting to cover the trial were harassed by authorities and had difficulty finding space in the courtroom because the state press was given priority seating. Rodrigo Angue Nguema, a correspondent for several foreign news organizations, was barred from covering the proceedings on two occasions, even though he was properly accredited. Local journalist and head of the Equatorial Guinea Press Association (ASOPGE), Pedro Nolasco Ndong, was also barred.

On May 3, authorities barred the independent newspaper *La Opinión* and ASOPGE from celebrating World Press Freedom Day. A few days later, Nsue Mokuy threatened to ban ASOPGE, accusing the press association of operating "like a parallel government that does not coordinate its activities with the [Information] Ministry."

Since ASOPGE was legalized in 1997, government officials have repeatedly harassed the organization and Nolasco Ndong. Last year, the mayor of the capital, Malabo, closed ASOPGE without explanation. It reopened after the Information Ministry intervened. In September, ASOPGE denounced an alleged government plan to remove the association's executive members and install state-controlled leaders. The government denied the allegation.

Nolasco Ndong fled the country in early July, following a series of threats related to articles he had published on the Internet in June describing the poor prison conditions of the 68 people who were sentenced to jail terms in the conspiracy trial. After the articles ran, state media described Nolasco Ndong as a "lowly journalist who publishes distorted and baseless information."

In early August, the Information Ministry and the U.N. Educational, Scientific, and Cultural Organization co-hosted a three-day seminar on "press freedom and the rule of law." At the opening ceremony, Prime Minister Candido Muatetema Rivas declared his wish "to offer more guarantees of free and accurate information" and announced the creation of a media studies faculty at the University of Equatorial Guinea. But he also reminded journalists to "respect the ethics of the profession so as not to abuse the rights of others."

Earlier in 2002, the government authorized the publication of *La Nación*, a new independent weekly owned by Nolasco Ndong. The information minister had rejected the publication's initial name—*La Liberación*—which, he said, "undermined the democratic principles" of President Obiang's regime. Since Nolasco Ndong went into exile, however, it is not clear whether the weekly is operating.

At the beginning of December, the United Nations sent Special Rapporteur on Freedom of Expression Ambeyi Ligabo to Equatorial Guinea at the government's invitation. The report on his mission is due in March 2003.

ERITREA

Eritrea was Africa's foremost jailer of journalists in 2002. The crackdown began in the summer of 2001 after a dozen senior officials and other members of the ruling elite signed public letters criticizing President Isaias Afewerki's dictatorial rule. The letters, which were leaked to the press, prompted a slew of editorials about human rights, democracy, and the border war with Ethiopia, which lasted from 1998 until 2000 and killed 19,000 Eritreans. On September 9, 2001, the weekly newspaper *Setit* printed an open letter to the president that sparked a full-blown political crisis. Days later, Afewerki launched a devastating clampdown on dissent, arresting top officials, banning the press, and jailing journalists and other critics.

The arrests of journalists continued in 2002, rising to 18 from 11 in 2001. To highlight this abysmal record, as well as the plight of Eritrea's journalists, CPJ honored imprisoned *Setit* editor Fesshaye "Joshua" Yohannes with a 2002 International Press Freedom Award.

But such efforts to highlight the country's disastrous human rights situation were seriously hampered by the U.S.-led "war on terrorism," which prompted a parade of American officials to visit Eritrea in 2002 to forge an anti-terror partnership. None of the visitors wanted to spotlight their potential partner's human rights record; U.S. officials were more interested in the possibility of opening an American Army base in Eritrea.

U.S. secretary of defense Donald Rumsfeld carefully skirted the issue of human rights when he came to Eritrea in December; when asked at a press conference in the capital, Asmara, about Eritrea's ban on the private press and the unlawful jailing of journalists,

Rumsfeld responded that Eritrea "is a sovereign nation and they arrange themselves and deal with their problems in ways that they feel are appropriate to them."

Eritrea, meanwhile, lobbied hard to lure the U.S. military, hiring the Washington-based lobbying firm Greenberg Traurig to make the case that Eritrea would be an excellent staging ground for a U.S.-led war against Iraq. The lobbying campaign, which costs the country $50,000 a month, was another sign to Eritreans that the government that had led them to joyous independence from Ethiopia 11 years ago is now out of touch and uninterested in dealing with such huge problems as joblessness, drought, and famine.

Meanwhile, two local employees of the U.S. Embassy in Asmara have remained jailed since their arrests in October 2001 for translating reports from the Eritrean press for the embassy. Eritrea's leaders insist that the two, along with journalists and political reformers, were working to destabilize Eritrea. They also accuse independent journalists of being paid by Ethiopian and other unidentified hostile forces—charges never verified but often used by officials to justify the September 2001 crackdown.

Eritrean leaders also continued their protracted diplomatic battles with several European countries, more than a year after Italian ambassador Antonio Bandini was deported for criticizing Afewerki's treatment of the opposition and the private press. In February, the Eritrean government said it was "dismayed by the unfair and unjustified resolution adopted by the European Parliament," which denounced the Eritrean Parliament's decision to maintain a ban on opposition parties and to delay general elections indefinitely.

Until early 2002, the jailed journalists were confined in dingy cells at Asmara's Police Station One. But on March 31, ten of them began a hunger strike to protest their continued detention without charge. In a message smuggled from inside the police station, the prisoners said they would refuse food until they were either released or charged and given a fair trial. Three days later, nine of them were transferred to an undisclosed detention facility. The 10th, Swedish national Dawit Isaac, was sent to a hospital, where he was treated for posttraumatic stress disorder allegedly resulting from torture in custody. His health status was unclear at year's end.

In July, a CPJ delegation visited Asmara to press for the journalists' freedom. The delegation—comprising CPJ board member Josh Friedman, Washington, D.C., representative Frank Smyth, and Africa program coordinator Yves Sorokobi—was the first human rights monitoring group to be allowed into Eritrea since the crackdown began. During CPJ's visit, the government admitted for the first time that it was holding journalists in secret detention facilities. However, in a July 18 meeting in his Asmara office, presidential spokesperson Yermane Gebremesken told CPJ that only "about eight" news professionals were being held. He declined to disclose their whereabouts, asserting that the crackdown was less draconian than the U.S. government's indefinite detention of Taliban and al-Qaeda fighters in Guantanamo Bay, Cuba.

The CPJ delegates also met with foreign diplomats and representatives of the U.N. peacekeeping mission in Asmara. Mission head Legweila Joseph Legweila told CPJ that he feels "sorry for the repression of journalists in Eritrea … but protecting free press is not part of the mission's mandate."

At around the same time, the Eritrean government began asking donors to help it prevent an impending famine, which the government blames on the border conflict with

Ethiopia and natural calamities. Relations with Ethiopia remain complex, with many Eritreans continuing to flee to their neighboring former colonial power. (Eritrea broke away from Ethiopia in 1991 after a 30-year armed struggle.)

The media implications of Eritrea's thorny relations with Ethiopia and the war of words that pitted Eritrean journalists against their Ethiopian colleagues during the border war were analyzed in a feature article in the fall/winter issue of CPJ's biannual magazine, *Dangerous Assignments*.

ETHIOPIA

IN EARLY DECEMBER, PRIME MINISTER MELES ZENAWI SURPRISED HIS DETRACTORS by inviting them to a series of debates on government policies and the future of the country. The organizer of the unprecedented forum, an independent association known as the Inter Africa Group, said the goal was to foster "the exchange of views between the government and other stakeholders" on matters of legitimate public interest. Government critics, most prominently the rebel Oromo Liberation Front (OLF), have dismissed the debates as a ploy to "refurbish the badly-damaged image" of the governing Ethiopian People's Revolutionary Democratic Front (EPRDF).

Ethiopian journalists, however, have welcomed the EPRDF's sudden openness and were hopeful that it would continue. At year's end, only one Ethiopian journalist, Tewodross Kassa, former editor-in-chief of the Amharic-language weekly *Ethiop*, was in prison for his work. Four other jailed journalists—Tamirate Zuma, Lubaba Said, Melese Shine, and Zegeye Haile—were released during 2002.

Nonetheless, Ethiopia's press corps remains wary of the Zenawi government. In late January, a joint delegation of the Ethiopian Free Press Journalists Association (EFJA) and the Media Institute of Southern Africa, a regional, nongovernmental press freedom group, marched to the headquarters of the Organization of African Unity, now known as the African Union (AU), in Ethiopia's capital, Addis Ababa, to deliver a petition urging the union to lobby member states to end attacks on press freedom in Ethiopia and Zimbabwe.

In July, a CPJ delegation conducted a five-day fact-finding mission to Ethiopia, which revealed that the government was planning undisclosed changes to its 10-year-old press law. While Information Minister Bereket Simon told CPJ that the new law would promote "constructive and responsible journalism," journalists argued that the statutes would lead to a crackdown and drive many media outlets out of business. But at year's end, journalists said that authorities appeared to have shelved the draft law.

Earlier in the year, the government released a code of ethics for reporters, which the EFJA dismissed as a book of restrictive "directives imposed on [journalists] by the rulers under the camouflage of a professional code of ethics." Authorities said the code was necessary because, they alleged, some independent newspapers are funded by "terrorist" groups and hostile foreign countries, namely the OLF and neighboring Eritrea. Ethiopia fought a border war with Eritrea from 1998 to 2000, following Eritrea's 30-year war for independence from Ethiopia, which ended in 1991.

Ethiopia's Broadcast Law was adopted in June 1999, but the government, citing lack of funds and qualified personnel, delayed creating the entity charged with implementing the law's provisions, the Ethiopian Broadcast Agency. That independent expert body, which will "ensure the expansion of high-standard, prompt and reliable broadcasting service which can contribute to the political, social, and economic development" of the country, finally opened its doors in July and received a long line of applicants, including the BBC and the local Addis Broadcasting Company (ABC), led by prominent economist and human rights activist Berhanu Nega. In an interview with the private *Addis Tribune*, Nega said that ABC had "no intention or any interest to oppose the government. We want to have responsible dialogue and reasoned discussion about our society."

Despite Ethiopian leaders' stated desire to improve relations with the media, old habits die hard. In October, the government accused the U.N. Mission in Ethiopia and Eritrea (UNMEE) of "leaking stories" to the media, arguing that the practice could undermine confidence in the peacekeeping mission. The charge came after UNMEE officials briefed reporters on a skirmish between armed Ethiopian militia and Indian peacekeepers.

GABON

PRESIDENT OMAR BONGO MAINTAINED HIS SOLID GRIP ON POWER in this small West African nation. Opposition and pro-democracy movements remained weak, while independent journalists, fearful of losing their jobs, softened their criticism of Bongo, who cultivates a cult of personality and uses widespread official bribery to secure his rule.

In early September, while local and foreign medical authorities struggled to suppress an outbreak of the deadly Ebola virus, the official National Communications Council (CNC), a state institution allegedly mandated to promote press freedom and ensure quality journalism, continued the crackdown on private media it began more than three years ago ahead of presidential elections.

After silencing the country's most outspoken newspapers—the satirical weekly *Gris Gris* and its sister paper, *La Griffe*—in 2001 for criticizing the president, the CNC hit more publications in 2002. On September 6, the CNC banned the weeklies *Gabaon* and *Misamu* after the papers reported on alleged government embezzlement schemes. Meanwhile, two other private weeklies, *Le Nganga* and *La Lowé*, received warnings for criticizing the prime minister.

The ruling Democratic Party controls all state institutions, including the judiciary and law enforcement, so bans and warnings from the CNC foster self-censorship among members of the media. Gabon's few remaining independent reporters, though privately indignant, are wary of speaking publicly about state interference in the press.

In 2002, state censors also strangled the broadcast media. On February 18, newscaster Edgard-Oumar Nziembi-Doukaga, of the Gabon-based Pan-African radio station Africa No. 1, was fired after he stuttered through the name of President Denis Sassou-Nguesso, of neighboring Republic of Congo, on air. Sassou-Nguesso, who is married to one of Bongo's daughters, enjoys close relations with Gabon's first family and government officials.

THE GAMBIA

THE GAMBIA'S RULING ALLIANCE FOR PATRIOTIC REORIENTATION AND CONSTRUCTION (APRC) won a landslide victory in mid-January parliamentary elections, capturing 52 of 55 seats in the National Assembly and cementing President Yahya Jammeh's rule. The main opposition parties boycotted the poll, alleging electoral fraud. Jammeh and the APRC used their renewed power to silence opposition voices and the independent media.

The government has justified its antagonistic relationship with journalists by accusing the independent press of being irresponsible and sensationalistic and of serving as the opposition's mouthpiece. In a January interview, Jammeh told the *Daily Observer*—a newspaper generally sympathetic to the APRC—that he was "not against the media," which he referred to as a "dead and rotten horse." The president said that the Gambian press was trying to please the international community by criticizing the government and spreading lies about him.

Journalists protest APRC accusations of bias, saying that the biggest obstacle for the independent media is the government's refusal to grant access to official information. Since ruling-party officials routinely refuse to be interviewed, journalists argue, opposition members receive more coverage. Members of the private media, however, acknowledge their shortcomings, saying that a lack of professional training leads to poor reporting.

At a Gambia Press Union (GPU) symposium in February, independent journalists called for the creation of an ethics regulatory body, composed of media professionals, and the establishment of a journalism school at the country's university to ensure greater professionalism and better training.

The APRC, however, took advantage of its virtual monopoly in the legislature to pass repressive legislation in late July that imposes a regulatory commission on the media. Jammeh signed the measure in early August. The law creates a commission that will establish a code of conduct for the private media, set standards of content and quality for published and broadcast materials, maintain a registry of all media practitioners and organizations, and adjudicate complaints against journalists and media organizations.

The commission can issue arrest warrants for journalists who ignore summonses and can also force journalists to reveal their sources. The commission will require all journalists and media organizations to obtain one-year renewable licenses, imposing a minimum fine of 5,000 dalasis (US$225) on those who do not. Journalists who fail to pay the fine can be suspended for nine months; media organizations can be suspended for three months.

The commission can also jail journalists for contempt for up to six months. Among the vague offenses listed in the act is the publication or broadcast of "language, caricature, cartoon or depiction, which is derogatory, contemptuous or insulting against any person or authority." While the government said the law would end sensationalistic journalism in the country, Gambian journalists and media-rights advocates heavily criticized the legislation, saying it was an attempt to muzzle the independent press.

State security forces also harassed journalists during 2002. National Intelligence Agency (NIA) officials arrested BBC correspondent Ebrimah Sillah in early July after he reported on tensions between The Gambia and neighboring Guinea-Bissau. NIA agents detained Pa Ousman Darboe, senior reporter for the private biweekly *The Independent*, for three days in early August for writing an article about the remarriage of the country's vice president. And Guy-Patrick Massoloka, a Congolese reporter for the Pan African News Agency, was held incommunicado without charge for nearly two weeks in late July. Authorities accused Massoloka of working with an unlicensed publication.

One of The Gambia's most popular radio stations, Citizen FM, remained closed throughout 2002. Authorities shuttered the station in 2001 for failing to pay back taxes—a pretext, said local journalists, to punish the broadcaster for airing critical news from independent sources in local languages. This claim was corroborated in 2002, when the station was prevented from opening even after it had paid all its tax arrears.

GHANA

ONE YEAR AFTER PRESIDENT JOHN AGYEKUM KUFUOR'S MEDIA-FRIENDLY GOVERNMENT repealed Ghana's criminal defamation law, the state imposed controls on reporting about interclan clashes in March, after a local tribal king and several of his supporters were killed during a feud between rival clans in the northern Dagbon region. Kufuor declared a state of emergency, which was still in effect at year's end, and the information minister announced that unless journalists were writing about official government-produced press releases, they were required to clear stories on the conflict in Dagbon with the ministry.

Initially, media outlets were divided over whether to obey these restrictions. In the end, however, most journalists largely ignored the rules and confronted little government censorship as a result.

Ghana has several private and state-owned publications, although most are based near the capital, Accra, and in Kumasi, a city in the central part of the country. In addition to two state-owned radio stations, there are more than a dozen private FM stations that operate by and large with little government interference.

The Ghana Journalists' Association, a media ethics committee created in 2001, successfully mediated several cases during 2002 that would ordinarily have gone to court. The committee heard complaints about the publication of pornography and corruption among journalists. It also heard a case brought in December 2001 by the Defense Ministry against the *Ghanaian Democrat*, which the ministry accused of repeatedly "packaging sensational stories about the Ghana Armed Forces." During the mediation, which both sides agreed was fair and balanced, editors complained about the difficulty of accessing military information, while the military promised to keep lines of communication open for members of the media.

In March, Margaret Amoakohene, a commentator and a lecturer at the School of Communications Studies of the University of Ghana, and Kweku Baako Jr., the editor-in-chief of the *Crusading Guide*, received death threats twice, both apparently in response to their critical stance against the family of Ghana's former president, Jerry Rawlings. Police investigations implicated Victor Smith, one of Rawlings' top aides. The case went to trial in July, and Rawlings denies any involvement in the threats. Smith maintains that while he "drafted some points" for an "open letter" to journalists who had criticized Rawlings, he did not conspire to attack anyone. The case was still in trial at year's end.

GUINEA

ON JUNE 30, ALMOST THREE-QUARTERS OF VOTERS CAST BALLOTS in parliamentary elections, which landed the ruling Unity and Progress Party 85 out of the National Assembly's 114 seats and further strengthened President Lassana Conté's long-standing hold on power. The country's usually feisty opposition leaders refrained from blaming their losses on voter manipulation, but some journalists alleged that the ruling party benefited from popular fears that the armed conflict in neighboring Liberia could spread to Guinea.

Guinean leaders and citizens appeared to show greater tolerance for press criticism in 2002 compared with previous years. However, on January 29, a presidential aide-de-camp interrogated Alcoumba Diallo, publisher of the private weekly *L'Aurore*, in an unsuccessful attempt to persuade the journalist to reveal his sources for an article alleging that the president's family owns some of the navy's ships.

Guinea's government and press corps joined forces to warn a wary population about the need to strengthen national security in the face of rebel insurgencies that continue to destabilize the West African region. In August, improved government-media relations moved Justice Minister Abou Camara to instruct police to stop arresting journalists for their work. At the same time, the minister said journalists should "voluntarily" respond to court summonses for press offenses. Camara said his goal was to "establish a partnership between the press and the Ministry of Justice."

In early September, while rebel attacks on Liberian towns intensified, Guinean soldiers harassed Nigerian radio reporter Funmi Olowofoyeku after she attempted to cross the border without a military escort. Soldiers held her equipment for several hours and then kept her from crossing into Liberia.

GUINEA-BISSAU

FOLLOWING AN ALLEGED COUP ATTEMPT IN LATE 2001, President Kumba Yala and his minority Social Renewal Party (PRS) government struggled to demonstrate to the international community their willingness to implement democratic reforms and restore stability to this impoverished West African country. But Guinea-Bissau plunged further into crisis, with Yala continuing to interfere with the judiciary and crack down on civil-society groups and the media.

In late May, the government announced that it had foiled the country's third alleged coup attempt in less than two years. Yala accused neighboring Gambia of supporting the insurgents, and in mid-June, authorities arrested Joao de Barros, owner and publisher of the independent daily *Correio da Guinea-Bissau*, for saying on a radio show that Yala's threats to "crush" the Gambian militarily were "pathetic." Nilson Mendonca, editor at the state-run Radio Difusão Nacional, was arrested a few days later after the station reported that Yala was going to apologize to Gambian authorities for his accusation. The political opposition, meanwhile, claimed that the president's threats prove that he is mentally unstable.

In December, the government banned the Portugal-based Radiotelevisão Portuguesa (RTP) after it aired a program about Gen. Ansumane Mane, who led an unsuccessful coup attempt against Yala's regime in 2000. The government claimed that RTP had broadcast "information that could tarnish the good image of Guinea-Bissau abroad and could foment anger within the country."

Despite repeated calls from the United Nations to work toward national reconciliation and good governance, authorities tolerated no criticism from civil-society groups. In early April, Attorney General Caetano Ntchama banned all media organizations from publishing any information from the Guinean League of Human Rights (LGDH)—an organization known for its criticism of Yala's party. The LGDH, which officials harassed throughout 2002, said the ban was an attempt to silence the group.

Opposition members continued to complain about ethnic bias in the government. In early August, Carlos Vamain, a host at the independent Radio Pidjiquiti, was summoned to the Attorney General's Office for allegedly making "defamatory" comments against the president. On his show, Vamain had accused Yala of "tribalism" for favoring members of his Balanta ethnic group in his government and military appointments. The journalist was fined 3 million CFA francs (US$4,500) for endangering "national unity."

Both the private and state-owned media suffer financial difficulties. In June, employees of the national printing press went on a 15-day strike, demanding 17 months of salary arrears and forcing all of the country's newspapers, which rely on the printing press, to cease publication. Two months later, workers for the national television broadcaster went on a two-week strike, demanding five months in salary arrears and better working conditions.

In a gesture designed to allay human rights concerns from the international community, the government allowed *Gazeta de Noticias* and *Diario de Bissau*—two private weeklies that the attorney general had banned in 2001—to resume publication in early 2002. Officials continued, however, to use licensing and registration requirements as a pretext to harass other media outlets and to threaten them with closure.

IVORY COAST

HOPES WERE HIGH IN JULY THAT IVORY COAST'S POLITICAL CRISIS WOULD END after a judge in the capital, Abidjan, confirmed that former prime minister Alassane Dramane Ouattara, the leader of the opposition Rally for Republicans (RDR), is an Ivory Coast citizen.

The controversy over Ouattara's citizenship has been at the heart of the country's ongoing unrest, which grew much worse in 1993, when then president Henri Konan Bédie sacked Ouattara as prime minister. Bédie concocted the concept of *Ivoirite* ("being a true Ivoirian") in response to anxieties caused by mass immigration from neighboring countries. In early August, the RDR joined the unity government of the current president, Laurent Gbagbo, to consolidate the national reconciliation initiated by Gbagbo in late 2001. But on September 19, disgruntled soldiers from Ivory Coast's Muslim north staged a mutiny. By year's end, the insurgency, also described by state media as a botched coup attempt and a "terrorist" attack, had turned into an active rebellion, effectively splitting the country in two.

The rebels, known as the Ivory Coast Popular Movement (MPCI), have demands similar to those of Ouattara's RDR, as well as the sympathy of the RDR's base constituency of Muslims and other northerners. At first, the MPCI advanced rapidly toward the capital, Abidjan, which is in the predominantly Christian and animist south. But troops sent to the Ivory Coast from France to protect Western and French interests in its former colony soon contained the rebels. The seeming collusion between the MPCI and the RDR, the only political party that did not condemn the rebellion, prompted state officials to accuse Ouattara, who later fled abroad, of attempting to destabilize the country. By December, the RDR leader was openly endorsing the MPCI's demands and asking for Gbagbo's resignation.

A number of death squads also became active in the confusion, killing mostly pro-opposition figures. Meanwhile, law enforcement officials detained and beat journalists suspected of anti-government bias, and Gbagbo's supporters destroyed the offices and equipment of pro-RDR news outlets.

CPJ and other international press freedom groups condemned the attacks on journalists, as did the Press Freedom and Media Ethics Observatory, the leading Ivoirian journalists' organization, which pleaded with "all insurgents, all militants and all young people, whatever their political affiliation, to show tolerance toward journalists and media houses." Communication Minister Sery Bailly also condemned the attacks, saying that "recourse to violence is retrogressive and reducing any organ or journalist to silence is a collective impoverishment."

But with suspicions running wild, Ivoirian journalists soon became embroiled in the civil strife, with reports and opinions in the press increasingly carrying religiously intolerant and xenophobic arguments. In December, the Paris-based International Federation of Human Rights Leagues said that it was collecting "evidence" likely to be used in international courts against the "Ivoirian hate media." Foreign observers, journalists, and diplomats concurred that local media had greatly contributed to the spread of anti-foreigner and anti-immigrant feelings that, coupled with the dispute over Ouattara's citizenship, had precipitated the explosion of deadly violence in this nation once noted for its political stability and economic success.

A large section of the pro-Gbagbo press corps has repeatedly accused foreign media of biased and insensitive reports that misrepresent the Ivory Coast, where an estimated 40 percent of the population is foreign-born. A September 22 editorial in the ruling Ivoirian Popular Front party daily, *Notre Voie*, for example, called the BBC, Radio-France Internationale (RFI), and Agence France-Presse "the other adversaries of the Ivory Coast" because they allegedly sympathize with the RDR and with the oppressed northern and Muslim people. That same day, the government jammed the broadcast signals of FM stations that relay programs from the BBC, RFI, and the Pan-African station Africa No 1. The head of the official National Audiovisual Committee, Jérome Diegou-Bailly, explained, "In a state of war, one must manage the information in order not to spread death and disruption among the population."

Almost 1,000 people have been killed since the start of the rebellion. Ivoirian authorities have blamed the conflict on Burkina Faso and Liberia, from where two rebel groups launched December attacks on towns along Liberia's border with the Ivory Coast. The French evening daily *Le Monde* first revealed credible information supporting the theory of foreign involvement in the Ivoirian crisis in an October 10 report accusing Burkina Faso of training and arming the rebels. Another French paper, the weekly *Le Canard Enchaîné*, later added that the rebels were partly financed by Libyan leader Col. Muammar Qaddafi, who then blamed the West for destabilizing the Ivory Coast "to exploit its riches."

KENYA

ON DECEMBER 30, OPPOSITION NATIONAL RAINBOW COALITION (NARC) LEADER Emilio Mwai Kibaki won Kenya's landmark presidential election with an enormous majority, replacing Daniel arap Moi, who, after 24 years in power, was barred by a new constitution from seeking another term. Because the elections were the toughest challenge ever to Kenya's ruling African National Union (KANU), in power since independence in 1963, the poll dominated the news.

Kibaki's NARC won 126 out of 210 seats in Parliament; Moi's KANU, now led by defeated presidential hopeful Uhuru Kenyatta, saw its share shrink to 63. A third party, the little-known Forum for the Restoration of Democracy–People, took 14 seats.

Politicians and the public complained about the election coverage, citing bias in both state-owned and independent media. According to a report by the independent Media Institute, which is based in the capital, Nairobi, KANU received a disproportionate amount of coverage on all television stations, but especially on the state-owned Kenya Broadcasting Corporation (KBC), the only station licensed to broadcast nationwide. Even after opposition politicians complained, KBC continued its pro-KANU coverage, blacking out opposition rallies and speeches.

KBC's long-standing role as a government mouthpiece endangered its employees in pro-opposition areas; the independent *Daily Nation* quoted an unnamed KBC source as saying, "We cannot send our equipment to the [opposition] rally and risk having it destroyed." His fears were well founded: KBC staffers were harassed, beaten, and assaulted on numerous occasions by rioting students and opposition-party supporters.

In a first for Kenya—and a coup for the independent Nation Television—all presidential candidates agreed to a series of live television appearances on a show called "Face the People," during which they answered questions from a studio audience. The candidates also agreed to the country's first-ever televised presidential debate, making Kenya the second country in Africa (after Ghana) to hold such an event. The debates were later canceled without explanation. The media also continued to use the Internet, with the two main dailies, *The Daily Nation* and the *East African Standard*, competing to update their Web sites with breaking news. In its annual financial report, issued in November, the Nation Media Group said the online edition of its flagship *Daily Nation* newspaper received more than 1 million hits per day.

In May, before the presidential campaign intensified, Attorney General Amos Wako once again introduced a controversial and repressive media bill in Parliament, the Statute Law (Miscellaneous Amendments) Bill. The measure, introduced in several incarnations since its initial appearance in 2000, has been met each time with hostility and fierce criticism from lawmakers, unions, and the press. The bill increases 100-fold the fee publishers must pay to insure against losses they may incur from libel or defamation suits, from 10,000 shillings (US$126) to 1 million shillings (US$12,605). Publishers who fail to post the fee face fines totaling 1 million shillings, a three-year jail sentence, or both. In addition, distributors and vendors of publications that have not paid the fee can be fined as much as 20,000 shillings (US$252), imprisoned for up to six months, or both. Publishers fear that these provisions will intimidate vendors into refusing to sell certain publications and could force several small newspapers to close.

President Moi signed the legislation on June 4. Claiming the bill violates Section 79 of the Kenyan Constitution, which guarantees freedom of expression, the local news agency Kenya Eye News Service immediately challenged the law and sought to bring the case before the Constitutional Court. The case remained pending at year's end.

The independent media faced other formidable enemies. In March, Cabinet minister Nicholas Biwott was awarded 20 million shillings (US$258,000) in a defamation suit he had filed against *The People* newspaper for publishing an article accusing him of corruption. Biwott has so far won four libel cases; the March ruling brought his total awards to 60 million shillings (US$773,000).

Meanwhile, the government admitted liability in the case of photojournalist Wallace Gichere, who was pushed out of a window by police officers in 1991 for allegedly writing damaging stories about Kenya for the foreign press. Gichere, who was paralyzed by the fall, sued the state for damages and went on a hunger strike to protest the government's lack of action on his case. On July 17, almost 10 years after the attack, Attorney General Wako said that although the government admitted liability, Gichere's claim for compensation was excessive. (Government sources say the journalist is asking for US$3.25 million.) Wako suggested that a court assess damages.

LIBERIA

DURING 2002, PRESIDENT CHARLES TAYLOR REPEATEDLY INVOKED the war against the rebel Liberians United for Reconciliation and Democracy (LURD) to clamp down on critical reporting. On February 8, he declared a state of emergency that broadened authorities' power to limit press freedom.

On June 24, Hassan Bility, editor-in-chief of the independent weekly *The Analyst*, was arrested on suspicion of collaborating with the LURD. In July, Bility was declared an "unlawful combatant," and on October 24, a five-member military tribunal recommended that he be considered a "prisoner of war." Despite several court rulings ordering the government to produce the journalist in court, Bility was not released until early December, when Liberian authorities remanded him into the custody of the U.S. Embassy in the capital, Monrovia. He left the country shortly after for an unknown destination.

Officials insist that Bility's arrest was not related to his work, but CPJ research shows that Liberian officials have consistently harassed *The Analyst* and its journalists. Four days after the government declared the state of emergency, police in Monrovia suspended the paper. Officials arrested the publisher and managing editor, Stanley Seakor, as well as reporters James Lloyd and Ellis Togba, for publishing a series of articles criticizing the state of emergency.

In a statement issued the same day, the Ministry of Information announced that anyone who commented on the state of emergency without official sanction would be "dealt with" under emergency laws. The journalists were released the next day, and the newspaper was allowed to resume publication. But *The Analyst* was closed again in April, when officials ordered it to cease publication "indefinitely" and police ransacked its offices.

Taylor interfered with the print media in other ways as well. He owns a 50 percent stake in the country's only printer, the Sabannoh Printing Press, and newspapers that use the company have complained of censorship, according to the Press Union of Liberia.

With Liberia's estimated 75 percent illiteracy rate, radio is the country's main source of news, and state interference in the medium has the biggest impact on Liberians' access to information. President Taylor banned the private Star Radio in 2000 and revoked the shortwave broadcast license for the Catholic Church–owned Radio Veritas in 2001 for alleged "anti-government reporting," leaving Kiss FM and Radio Liberia International, both of which the president owns, as the only stations with nationwide range.

Local private stations remain on the air, but they broadcast mainly music and religious programming. On his Kiss FM talk show, "Issues with the President," Taylor explained in early October that "the whole thing of broadcasting short wave is not a right. It is a privilege." However, in a surprise announcement in February, Taylor reissued Radio Veritas' license. In May, Taylor said his government would also ensure that the state-owned Liberia Broadcasting System is allocated a shortwave frequency before general elections, scheduled for October 14, 2003.

But the upcoming elections are already causing controversy. Early in 2002, after Taylor threatened to cancel the vote, the Press Union of Liberia lambasted him for attempting to keep himself in power unlawfully. Later in the year, on May 3, police banned events in Monrovia commemorating World Press Freedom Day.

MADAGASCAR

ON JANUARY 25, THE HIGH CONSTITUTIONAL COURT OF MADAGASCAR RULED THAT a runoff vote "within 30 days" would resolve the disputed December 2001 presidential election between longtime leader Didier Ratsiraka and Marc Ravalomanana, mayor of the capital, Antananarivo. Despite the ruling, however, both men declared themselves president and introduced their Cabinets to an impoverished populace, which they encouraged to take to the streets in support of their respective governments.

Caught in the middle, journalists felt the heat of the unusual political situation, with supporters on each side attacking media outlets suspected of editorial bias against the other. On February 2, Ratsiraka's Information Ministry seized broadcast equipment from the private FM 91 radio station, which is owned by a prominent Ravalomanana supporter, on the northern island of Nosy Be. Eighteen days later, pro-Ravalomanana high school students ransacked the offices of Amoron'i Mania Radio-Television, which Ratsiraka's prime minister owns.

By mid-February, with the country divided, the economy in tatters, and a rift widening in the military, the Indian Ocean island nation was on the brink of civil war. Individual journalists who attempted to report the news fairly were accused of partisanship. In the northern town of Diego Suarez, for example, supporters of both presidential contenders publicly threatened to kill journalist Narcisse Randriamirado, the correspondent for the private daily *Madagascar Tribune*.

Threats and violent assaults against the media continued throughout February, March, and April, forcing many reporters to go into hiding. On February 25, Malagasy State Radio and Television released a statement saying that its stations could not broadcast because Ratsiraka supporters had seized the outlet's equipment, including transmitters, and moved it to an undisclosed location. On April 8, the private Radio-Télévision Analamanga announced that it was canceling its news bulletin because of repeated phone threats.

In late April, the High Constitutional Court announced that Ravalomanana had won the runoff—with 51 percent of the ballots to Ratsiraka's 36—and declared Ravalomanana the country's new president. Ratsiraka fled to France. Despite threats of secession from embattled governors and hard-core elements of Ratsiraka's Association for Madagascar's Renaissance, the political situation gradually returned to normal, with no new attacks on media workers or news outlets reported from May through the end of 2002. On December 15, President Ravalomanana's Tiako I Madagasikara (I Love Madagascar) Party won more than half of the National Assembly's 160 seats in violence-free legislative elections involving 1,300 candidates from 40 political parties.

MALAWI

DURING 2002, THE BELEAGUERED MALAWIAN PRESS ENDURED THREATS and verbal attacks from President Bakili Muluzi and his ruling United Democratic Front (UDF), as well as physical abuse from party supporters, while local media outlets struggled to maintain editorial independence in the face of mounting financial difficulties.

The ruling party's ongoing attempt to amend the constitution to allow Muluzi to run for a third term has exacerbated antagonism between the government and the independent press. Though the UDF lost an early-July parliamentary vote to extend the president's term limit, the government reintroduced a third-term bill in the fall, drawing local and international criticism that the ruling party is preoccupied with retaining power instead of solving the country's social and economic ills.

In late May, several thousand UDF supporters besieged the offices of Blantyre Newspapers, publisher of the private *Daily Times* and the weekly *Malawi News*, to protest the papers' stances against the third-term bill. The crowd beat one journalist who attempted to record the license numbers of the vehicles that had ferried UDF partisans to the offices. The demonstration ended when Presidential Affairs Minister Dumbo Lemani ordered the protesters to disperse following a meeting with the newspapers' executive chair.

Also in late May, Muluzi banned all public demonstrations related to the third-term bill. But civil-society groups contended that since the government controls the country's most influential media—including the state-owned Malawi Broadcasting Corporation's two radio stations and the country's only domestic television station—anti–third-term campaigners had no choice but to demonstrate. According to local journalists, increased pressure from international donors later in 2002 forced the government to allow greater debate in state-controlled media, including opposition views, on the third-term issue.

During the last few years, Malawi's media have begun dividing along political lines. While opposition voices in the independent press have criticized the government for corruption and attempts to strengthen its rule, the UDF has increasingly used state and private media to promote its agenda. Several private publications, which local journalists say various UDF politicians bankroll, have emerged to attack the independent media. This so-called yellow gutter press, including *The Sun*, *The Malawi Standard*, and *Malawi Insider*, castigates anyone who criticizes UDF policy.

In October, the *Malawi Insider* and *The Malawi Standard* accused the National Media Institute of Southern Africa (NAMISA), a media rights group, of launching a war against media institutions and journalists for reporting that the proliferation of UDF-sponsored publications was part of the ruling party's attempt to promote Muluzi's third-term bid. According to *Malawi Insider, The Malawi Standard* said that NAMISA was engaged in character assassination, corruption, tribalism, and partisan politics.

Media-rights advocates say that because independent journalists often live in poverty, many of them have been lured to politicians' publications with better pay and then write whatever their patrons bid.

Religious differences—with Christian groups generally opposing the extension of Muluzi's tenure and many Muslims, a minority in the country, supporting a third term for the Muslim president—also play into media divisions, according to observers. In September, the Catholic Church complained to the Malawi Communications Regulatory Authority after Radio Islam aired programs during which callers criticized church policies. The church described the programs as "provocative and insulting," while church support-ers urged it to use its Radio Maria broadcaster to retaliate.

UDF Young Democrats physically attacked several journalists in 2002. In February, a group of Young Democrats abducted Mallick Mnela, of the independent weekly *The Chronicle*, and assaulted other *Chronicle* journalists after the paper published articles about infighting in the UDF.

Politicians continued to use litigation to stifle reporting on corruption. In early spring, Presidential Affairs Minister Lemani sued *The Chronicle* for damages after the paper quoted an opposition politician who alleged that the government's Anti-Corruption Bureau was failing to prosecute UDF leaders. It was the fifth lawsuit filed against *The Chronicle* in the last two years, in what journalists believe is a campaign to bankrupt the paper.

In a positive development, NAMISA launched a legal defense fund in October to sup-port journalists and media organizations facing litigation.

MOZAMBIQUE

MORE THAN A YEAR AFTER A CPJ MISSION TO MOZAMBIQUE found that the November 2000 murder of investigative reporter Carlos Cardoso had created "an atmosphere of fear" in the country's newsrooms, the independent press corps there appears to have regained confidence in its ability to denounce corruption and other ills. In the weeks before the trial of six suspects in the murder began in November, journalists in the capital, Maputo, reported the explosive news that Nymphine Chissano, a son of President Joaquim Chissano, was suspected of involvement in the assassination.

Mozambican journalists, along with CPJ and other foreign critics, have long believed that the investigation was flawed. A September 27 story in the private weekly *MediaFax* steered suspicions toward Nymphine Chissano. According to *MediaFax*, a man identified only as "Opa," or "Uapa," had told investigators that Cardoso was slain at the behest of "o filho do galo" (the son of the rooster), a code name that Opa claimed referred to Nymphine Chissano.

A day after the story was published, a truckload of chickens was delivered to the home of

Kok Nam, publisher of *Savana* newspaper, which is owned by MediaCoop, the same media cooperative that publishes *MediaFax*. The driver claimed that the chickens were a gift from the country's first lady, Marcelina Chissano, to Nam and Fernando Lima, the author of the article. Later that day, other chicken-laden trucks attempted to make deliveries to the home of *MediaFax* editor Marcelo Mosse and to the offices of MediaCoop.

The first lady denied any involvement in the incidents, stressing that both she and the president want to see justice done in the Cardoso case. Soon after, judicial authorities subpoenaed Nymphine Chissano, asking him to testify as a material witness, not as a suspect.

At year's end, it was not clear if the trial would solve the mysteries surrounding Cardoso's murder. Complicating matters, Anibal dos Santos Junior (commonly known as Anibalzhino), the man believed to have led the death squad that killed the journalist, escaped from a Maputo maximum-security jail on September 1, allegedly after prison guards received "orders from above" to let him leave. According to his mother, Anibalzhino is now in London and will return to tell "the whole truth" only if authorities guarantee his safety. He is being tried in absentia.

Of the five suspects present in court, two have confessed their parts in the killing, and most have accused Nymphine Chissano of masterminding the crime. Chissano denies involvement in the murder, although by the end of 2002, prosecutors were seriously considering opening a new case file in which he will be an official suspect.

Meanwhile, in September, after a yearlong deadlock threatened to delay the summer 2004 general elections, the ruling FRELIMO and the opposition RENAMO parties agreed to amend the country's election laws to allow the two parties to nominate 18 of the 19 members of the National Election Commission (CNE). The CNE chair will likely be an independent figure chosen by civil-society groups. With President Chissano not running for another term, the presidential contest will pit RENAMO leader Alfonso Dlakhama against Armando Gebuza, a hard-line FRELIMO nationalist who believes that the party has veered too far from its socialist roots.

NAMIBIA

IN A SURPRISE CABINET SHUFFLE IN LATE AUGUST, President Sam Nujoma appointed himself information and broadcasting minister in an effort, he said, to "tackle problems" at the state-owned Namibian Broadcasting Corporation (NBC), the country's largest news outlet.

The NBC, which has suffered from endemic corruption and mismanagement, made headlines all year with its deepening financial crisis. As politicians promised that "heads will roll" in a massive restructuring of the corporation, NBC staff wondered if their jobs depended on their political affiliation.

Many observers believe that the president's takeover of the information portfolio was also designed to tighten his grip on the state media to influence the public's opinion of his ruling South West African People's Organization (SWAPO). Nujoma's comments that the NBC was servicing the "enemy," and that "as journalists we all have to defend Namibia," matched his growing anti-colonialist rhetoric. Such statements also fueled fears that he would use his new position to exert direct influence over editorial content.

The president did not wait long to confirm these concerns. On September 30, Nujoma ordered the NBC to stop broadcasting foreign programs containing violence and sexual content—which, he said, "have a bad influence on the Namibian youth"—and instead to show programs that portray Namibia in a positive light. But Mocks Shivute, permanent secretary at the Ministry of Information and Broadcasting, called reports of Nujoma's interference in the NBC's daily operations "hearsay" and said that the president was acting as a "responsible father" by advising the broadcaster.

SWAPO officials, meanwhile, continued to antagonize the independent press, with government advertising and purchasing bans on *The Namibian*, the country's leading daily, remaining in place.

In early 2002, Prime Minister Hage Geingob accused *The Namibian*'s editor-in-chief, Gwen Lister, of "unpatriotic reporting" for criticizing his positive portrayal of Namibia at a symposium in the United States. Lister's writing, Geingob said, "smacks of deliberate efforts at derailing the important efforts we are making in showcasing our nation." Following the appearance of a cartoon depicting Nujoma as Zimbabwean president Robert Mugabe's attack dog in the September 6 edition of *The Namibian*, the SWAPO Party Youth League called for a ban on all insults to the president and threatened to take action to defend Nujoma.

In May, members of the media adopted a code of ethics drafted by media practitioners from both the private and state sectors. In addition, journalists appointed a new media ombudsman and created a media-monitoring project, which will focus on issues of bias. A government spokesperson praised the effort at self-regulation, saying it would help "normalize the often strained relations that existed between the media, government, and the public at large."

In February, the National Council Standing Committee on Foreign Affairs, Defense, and Security recommended several amendments to a draft defense bill, which many journalists have criticized for restricting free expression. Proposed changes include softening language that allows defense information to be disclosed if it is "in the public interest" and narrowing a restriction on publishing information that may endanger the safety of soldiers. A clause that makes it an offense to bring a military court into contempt, ridicule, or disrepute was changed only cosmetically, despite protests from press freedom advocates.

On October 30, CPJ released a special report titled "Undoing Press Freedom in Namibia," which details Nujoma's tense relationship with the Namibian media. In a November 4 press release, Shivute denied that Nujoma's takeover of the Information and Broadcast Ministry had hurt the Namibian press and said that the move was made solely to expedite reorganization at the NBC. Shivute called the CPJ report an attempt to "create news" and cast "disrepute nationally and in the international arena" on President Nujoma and his ruling party.

NIGER

IN EARLY AUGUST, A MILITARY UPRISING IN THE EASTERN DIFFA REGION by soldiers demanding salary arrears jeopardized Niger's fragile democracy. The mutiny was the first serious challenge to civilian rule since the election of President Mamadou Tandja in December 1999. Before that election, the country had experienced two coups in three years. Anxious to restore order and avoid instability, authorities used the insurgency as a pretext to crack down on the media and opposition voices.

Niger authorities have had a tense relationship with the country's emerging independent press during the first three years of democratic governance. Officials regard journalists as antagonists while at the same time seeking to enlist the media as partners in government attempts to institute reforms and foster social stability. In early January, President Tandja called for more responsible journalism, complaining that "the virtues of professionalism and impartiality, which are indispensable to the proper exercise of the profession, are lacking in certain sectors of the press." Tandja instructed journalists that they should avoid "amateurism, improvisation, rampant sensationalism, and inclination to slander."

Tandja's deep mistrust of the media was illustrated by his response to the Diffa uprising. During the mutiny, which lasted 10 days, Tandja issued an August 5 decree forbidding "the dissemination by any media of information or allegations liable to jeopardize national defense operations." Outlets violating the measure faced suspension, closure, or the seizure of their equipment. The decree further stipulated that persons involved in disseminating such reports would be considered accomplices in the mutiny and would be punished accordingly.

In the wake of the uprising, authorities used the decree to arrest Moussa Kaka, director of the private Radio Saraounia and local correspondent for Radio-France Internationale, and Boulama Ligari, the Diffa-based correspondent for the independent Radio Anfani. Though both journalists were accused of broadcasting false information in their reports on the uprising, the fact that they were arrested two weeks after the mutiny had ended led journalists in the capital, Niamey, to believe that the journalists' detentions were designed to harass and intimidate the press. Both men were eventually released without charge.

Local sources said that both foreign and local correspondents were called into the prime minister's office and told to temper their reports on the mutiny. Local human rights activist Amina Balla Kalto was accused of "taking sides" in the uprising and was arrested after she criticized the government for continuing to enforce the emergency decree, including press restrictions, weeks after the insurgency had been defeated. Another human rights activist, Bagnou Bonkoukou, was sentenced to a year in prison for "disseminating false information" after he challenged the official death toll in the mutiny during radio interviews. Both activists were detained under the August decree.

Authorities also used the country's harsh Press Law, which criminalizes several press offenses, to punish journalists who report negatively on high-ranking government officials. In May, police arrested Abdoulaye Tiémogo, publisher of the independent satirical weekly Le Canard Déchaîné, for accusing Prime Minister Hama Amadou of ethnic and regional bias in his nominations of top officials. Though acquitted on that charge, Tiémogo was sentenced in June to eight months in prison for "defamation" after his newspaper accused Amadou of attempting to bribe the parliamentary speaker to retain his premiership. It was the second time in eight months that Tiémogo had been sentenced to prison for defaming a public official.

Despite the draconian Press Law, Niger journalists say that lack of financial resources is the media's most serious problem. Journalists earn meager salaries, and the government is reluctant to advertise with media that criticize its policies. Poor distribution confines the print media to major urban centers, while small broadcast ranges limit radio stations—the most vital form of mass communication in a country with a 15 percent literacy rate—to regional audiences.

Nonetheless, authorities have helped promote the expansion of the country' s media, especially radio stations. In 2002, the government adopted a Communications Policy for National Development, which outlines a democratic approach to accessing information and advocates dialogue as an instrument to support development initiatives and to alleviate poverty. With the aid of international donors, authorities opened several community radio stations that provide rural and smaller urban populations with information on development needs.

NIGERIA

WITH PRESIDENTIAL ELECTIONS SCHEDULED FOR APRIL 12, 2003, Nigerian president Olusegun Obasanjo, who survived another impeachment vote in September, must boost his own popularity while maintaining peace in this restive nation, where ethnic and religious violence has left thousands dead in recent years. A retired army general, Obasanjo was elected in May 1999 elections that ended decades of military rule. Three years later, despite its remarkable expansion, the Nigerian press remains vulnerable to censorship and repression.

In November, Islamic leaders in the northern state of Zamfara called on Muslims to kill Isioma Daniel, a reporter with the private Lagos daily *ThisDay*. The edict, or fatwa, stemmed from a November 16 article by Daniel about the Miss World contest, scheduled to be held in Nigeria in December, in which she wrote that the Prophet Mohammed, were he alive, would not oppose Nigeria's hosting of the beauty pageant and might even choose a bride from among the contestants. The article sparked religious riots, during which more than 200 were killed. On November 20, hundreds of protesters set fire to *ThisDay*'s office in Kaduna State while chanting "Allahu Akbar" (God is great) and accusing Daniel of blasphemy. Although the paper retracted the story in several front-page apologies, Zamfara State deputy governor Mamuda Aliyu Shinkafi declared that the fatwa required "all Muslims, wherever they are, to consider the killing of the writer as a religious duty."

Daniel fled abroad soon after the rioting began, despite assurances from Nigeria's federal government that the fatwa would not be carried out. Speaking on behalf of federal authorities, Information Minister Jerry Gana said that Nigerian laws "do not provide for anyone who has done something like what *ThisDay* has done to be killed." But anxious to soothe Muslim ire, other state officials did threaten to punish *ThisDay*, although with less drastic actions. The Miss World contest, meanwhile, was moved to London.

A week after the incident, a Muslim vigilante group hired by the federal State Security Service to keep public order in Maiduguri, Borno State, in northeastern Nigeria, where Sharia (Islamic law) is in force, rounded up a dozen news vendors for selling tabloids considered offensive to Islamic tenets. The vendors were freed without charges. A Sharia court in Gusau, the capital of Zamfara State, imposed financial penalties on a group of newspaper vendors in August for selling magazines and calendars featuring nude women.

In January 2000, less than a year after the advent of democracy, Zamfara became one of the first Nigerian states to adopt Islamic law. Eleven more of Nigeria's 36 states have since followed suit, effectively dividing Nigeria into two bitterly antagonistic regions, a Muslim north and a mostly Christian south. Although northern regions have proven somewhat tolerant of diverse opinions in the press, journalists throughout the nation have been targeted for taking critical stances. In many cases, however, judicial authorities have defended members of the media. In early 2002, a magistrate court in Abakaliki, a town in the southeastern Ebonyi State, voided sedition charges against Emma Okeki-Ogo and Ogbonna Okorie, of *Ebonyi Times*, who were sued by the state governor, Sam Egwu, for a November 1999 article accusing him of reckless spending and of not being "a true Christian."

A dozen media lawsuits were still making their way through state and federal courts by late December, but Nigerian journalists said it was unlikely that authorities would jail reporters for work-related offenses, even though some prominent politicians spoke out in favor of such actions. In fact, according to local journalists, federal authorities now seem more willing to investigate cases of press attacks.

Despite these positive decisions, journalists and media activists remain critical of the federal and state legal systems, which are susceptible to corruption and influence peddling. In December, authorities in the west-central Kwara State became embroiled in a public tussle with Bukola Saraki, publisher of the weekly *National Pilot*, whose main office in Ilorin, the state's capital, was gutted by a terrorist bomb on November 15. Saraki has steadfastly objected to the regional commission created to investigate the blast, because he suspects that the commission is comprised of biased representatives of the state judicial system.

It remained unclear at year's end whether authorities would pursue the prosecution of a group of retired soldiers who had stormed the newsroom of the daily *Nigerian Tribune* in the federal capital, Abuja, and held some of the staff hostage for several hours. The soldiers claimed that a November 30 story describing them as "fake ex-service men" had compromised their pension payments. During their occupation of the paper's offices, the attackers demanded that the story's author identify himself, to no avail. In the end, an elite police squad had to rein in the angry veterans. No one was harmed in the incident.

In the face of such threats, Nigerian press freedom activists have intensified lobbying of lawmakers in both houses of Parliament. But partisan politicking in the upper house delayed the adoption of a bill that would improve work conditions and offer more protection for journalists. The measure, known as the Journalism Practice Enhancement Bill 2002, would also create a Media Practitioners Complaints Commission to deal with complaints against journalists and to take noncriminal disciplinary actions.

RWANDA

ALTHOUGH RWANDAN PRESIDENT PAUL KAGAME HAS BEEN IN POWER FOR NINE YEARS, in July, he canceled elections scheduled for 2003 because his government remains "in a transition phase." Despite almost a decade of rule, the Kagame administration has yet to draft a constitution that safeguards even basic freedoms.

As a result, journalists have few legal options when the government cracks down on the media. For example, media outlets have encountered stern retribution for covering Kagame's ongoing political fight with his one-time friend and ally former president Pasteur Bizimungu, who has been in jail since 1999 for "forming an ethnic-based political party." In late January, officials in the town of Butare arrested Laurien Ntezimana and

Didace Muremangingo, director and editor, respectively, of *Ubuntu*, a publication of the civil-society group Association Modeste et Innocente. The two men were questioned over *Ubuntu*'s suspected sympathies for Bizimungu and then released without charge.

The government maintains that the party Bizimungu attempted to create could have revived ethic hatred in Rwanda, where extremists from the majority Hutu tribe massacred almost 800,000 minority Tutsis in 1994. Hundreds of moderate Hutus were also slain during the genocide, which was supported and encouraged by the private Radio Télé des Mille Collines (RTLM) and the newspaper *Kangura*, among others. Hassan Ngeze, *Kangura*'s founding editor, is now on trial at a U.N. tribunal in Arusha, Tanzania, for his role in the slaughter. Also on trial are former RTLM director Ferdinand Nahimana and Jean-Bosco Barayagwiza, one of RTLM's founders. According to CPJ research, a total of 15 Rwandan journalists were killed during the genocide. It is unclear when the court will announce verdicts in the case, which has become known as the "media trial."

In June, the Rwandan Parliament passed a bill that, if approved by the Supreme Court and signed by President Kagame, will introduce greater media freedom by allowing private radio and television stations and news agencies to operate. The bill also creates a media council, staffed with members of the private press and government appointees, to establish and monitor a code of ethics for journalists.

In France, meanwhile, a court dismissed a defamation lawsuit filed by Kagame against Paris-based African journalist Charles Onana. His book, *Les Secrets Du Génocide Rwandais—Enquête Sur Les Mystères D'un Président* (The Secrets of the Rwandan Genocide—Investigation of the Mysteries of a President), charged that Kagame's ruling party, Le Front Patriotique Rwandais (Rwandan Patriotic Front), then a Tutsi guerrilla group, was responsible for shooting down the plane carrying the late Rwandan Hutu president Juvenal Habyarimana and his Burundian counterpart, Cyprien Ntaryamira. That incident is widely believed to have triggered the 1994 genocide. Onana said his book "derobes Kagame of the mask" he has been using to cover his involvement in the massacre.

SENEGAL

IN EARLY AUGUST, PRESIDENT ABDOULAYE WADE OFFERED A STUNNING APOLOGY to foreign donors who had hurriedly assisted the West African desert nation with US$23 million in emergency famine aid. The president had personally appealed for the money, but then rejected it and charged that the Senegalese media had misreported conditions in the drought-stricken countryside. After a three-day visit to the afflicted region, an angry Wade returned to the capital, Dakar—in what was an embarrassing incident for both the government and the press—to issue a statement that threats of famine had been exaggerated. The president sacked his press adviser over the incident, and Senegalese journalists conceded that they might have overstated the situation.

Until recently, Senegal was known as a beacon of free speech in West Africa. But in September, several Senegalese news professionals told CPJ that the current administration has jeopardized the country's free press. The local media, which have engaged in healthy competition with the state media since independence in 1960, suffered little censorship under the country's liberal founder, Léopold Sédar-Senghor, and his chosen heir, Abdou Diouf.

But, according to Senegalese journalists, the March 2000 election of Wade, who had been a member of the opposition, brought the press several new challenges. In fact, in the two years since Wade's election, 17 Senegalese journalists have been convicted of criminal press offenses or harassed or beaten by ruling-party supporters—while only 10 suffered such abuses between 1982 and March 2000.

Local journalists also charge that the Information Ministry, dismantled in 2000 and integrated into the Office of the President, has become President Wade's personal public relations office. And coverage of two issues in particular has proven tricky for Senegalese reporters: the president's links to the Islamic Mouride sect, to which he belongs, and his attempts to broker peace with the leaders of an armed insurgency in the lush southern Casamance Region.

Although Senegal is secular by law, Islamic brotherhoods have traditionally exerted tremendous influence on society and politics. Lately, these religious fraternities have extended their reach to media ownership, with some of Senegal's largest media companies, such as the Wal Fadjiri Group, now partially or entirely owned by prominent spiritual leaders or groups.

Non-Muslim journalists, such as Jean-Baptiste Sané of the state broadcaster Radio-Télé Senegal (RTS), say that Christians and other religious groups are given short shrift in the state media. Sané and other journalists also describe President Wade's appointment of a retired general and stalwart of the ruling Democratic Party to head the RTS as a government ploy to restrict access to information about the military campaign against the rebel Movement of Casamance Democratic Forces. On September 18, the rebels issued a threatening letter accusing a dozen journalists by name of unfairly criticizing the movement's cause.

SIERRA LEONE

WITH SIERRA LEONEANS STRUGGLING TO SAFEGUARD A FRAGILE PEACE after 10 years of civil war, the Independent Media Commission (IMC) moved to fulfill its mandate. The IMC, which the government established in 2001 and is staffed by mostly government appointees and a few media personalities, grants publication and broadcast licenses, monitors government-media relations, enforces a code of rules and conduct, and hears civil complaints against journalists and news outlets. By year's end, however, tensions between the IMC and the local press corps had increased, with the 11-member commission threatening court action against radio stations that owed overdue license fees of US$2,000. Station owners complained that the IMC deliberately ignores the bitter fact that because most broadcasters are community-based, they earn little from advertising. They also blamed the IMC for hampering the emergence of better-funded stations.

In fact, in late August, the IMC rejected a request by a coalition of civil-society movements to start a radio station based in the capital, Freetown, with a range extending across West Africa. IMC officials explained that approving West Africa Democracy Radio (WADR) would have endangered "national security and public safety." The IMC did not elaborate, but WADR proponents told reporters that approval had never been in doubt until a Liberian government delegation visited Freetown in mid-August. A Sierra Leonean government official admitted to CPJ that the delegation had conveyed Liberian leader Charles Taylor's "furious disapproval of any democracy-preaching" in the region.

In March, the IMC banned the private weekly *African Champion* for two months and demanded that Mohamed D. Koroma, the paper's publisher, temporarily quit practicing journalism because of his alleged lack of ethics. Koroma, who said he was being punished for an unflattering story about a son of President Ahmed Tejan Kabbah, ignored the ban, which the IMC did not enforce. But on August 31, IMC officials again banned Koroma from any "editorial function" in any local media and indefinitely closed *African Champion*.

Koroma was among a dozen reporters who ran for Parliament during the May general elections. Most failed, but one, *Standard Times'* Mohamed Kandeh Kakay, won a seat in voting that also secured another five-year term for President Kabbah. On August 15, CPJ released "Identity Crisis," a special report on the challenges facing Sierra Leone's media, including corruption and other unethical practices that have undermined their credibility.

Sierra Leonean news outlets and press corps are dangerously split along political lines, while reporters admit to taking bribes and using their news organizations to settle personal scores. In November, Paul Kamara, founding editor of the private daily *For Di People*, was sentenced to six months in prison for alleged defamation. Some of his colleagues think Kamara may be using his newspaper to launch a vendetta against prominent Appeals Court judge Tolla Thompson. The two men butted heads over the management of Sierra Leone's soccer association, which Thompson currently heads. In addition to being an editor, Kamara owns a popular soccer team. He remained in jail at year's end.

SOMALIA

SINCE THE 1991 OVERTHROW OF MAJ. GEN. MOHAMMED SIAD BARRE by forces loyal to warlord Mohammed Farah Aideed, historic clan rivals have threatened the unity of this country, once known for practicing multiparty democracy while military juntas and civilian despots controlled most other African countries. In the face of such chaos, the media, which had included opposition and independent newspapers under Siad Barre, quickly splintered into several small clan-run newsletters and low-watt radio stations. Independent journalism all but disappeared.

But in late 2000, when Abdikassim Salad Hassan was elected president of a transitional unity government, independent journalism began to re-emerge in Somalia, spearheaded by radio stations such as HornAfrik, which has won praise abroad for its relative fairness and objectivity in covering a messy political situation.

But the tenuous new order still faces difficulties, with various clan leaders increasingly challenging President Hassan's administration. The disappointing results of another round of negotiations in October—the 14th attempt at peace since 1991—proved that suspicion runs deep among Somalia's warring clans. Meanwhile, Somali journalists have endured growing hostility from political, religious, and tribal leaders in the country's four self-proclaimed independent or autonomous regions. In addition, the U.S.-mandated closure of the Al-Barakaat banking and telecommunications company in November 2001 for alleged terrorist ties has reduced the media's communications capabilities.

On February 12, unidentified gunmen raided Radio Mogadishu–Voice of the Somali Republic, which is operated by the National Transitional Government (TNG), whose authority is limited to the capital, Mogadishu. The attackers, armed with assault rifles and rocket-propelled grenades, took a transmitter and voice mixers, forcing the station off the air. Although the station eventually resumed broadcasting, the attack marked another serious blow to the TNG, whose shaky powers had already eroded in early April, when the Ethiopia-backed Southwestern Regional Government declared independence. That government, which is based in the town of Baidoa, controls a large swath of land and has also received the support of the Somali Reconciliation and Restoration Council, a coalition of local leaders opposed to the TNG.

In May, authorities in the northeastern autonomous region of Puntland suspended the broadcasting license of a relay station for the private Somali Broadcasting Corporation (SBC), which is based in Puntland's commercial capital, Bosaso. The suspension also affected the BBC's Somali-language service, which the SBC relays locally. In August, Puntland authorities banned local correspondents from reporting for the BBC's Somali service. Regional leaders justified both bans by alleging bias and partisanship among reporters.

In June, civil authorities and clan leaders in the self-declared northwestern republic of Somaliland, who appointed a new president in May, banned the establishment of private radio stations in the region, which has not yet adopted broadcasting regulations.

On September 30, Parliament passed a TNG-sponsored media bill that prohibits the publication of material that undermines Islam, national unity, the political system, or "the common interest of all Somalis" and forbids criticizing government officials or reporting on government secrets. Outraged, journalists in Mogadishu, which, despite years of conflict has a fairly active media, vowed to strike and black out any news about the TNG and Parliament until the legislation was withdrawn. Somali-run Web sites produced outside the country went on strike in solidarity.

On October 2, Mogadishu's two television stations, six daily newspapers, and six of seven local radio stations suspended operations in protest. That same day, President Hassan declined to sign the bill. Information Minister Abdirahman Ibbi said the president had created a committee of lawyers, journalists, and senior officials to study the journalists' grievances and had requested that their amendments be incorporated into the bill. At year's end, the measure was being redrafted.

SOUTH AFRICA

On September 27, in a landmark decision for press freedom in South Africa, a Johannesburg court dismissed a defamation lawsuit filed by Minister of Housing Sankie Mthembi-Mahanyele against the independent daily *Mail & Guardian* and its former editor Phillip van Niekerk. Van Niekerk and the *Mail & Guardian* had been sued over the paper's December 1998 "Report Card," a survey of the performance of government officials, which found that Minister Mthembi-Mahanyele was performing her duties poorly. Citing several low points in the minister's career, including a corruption scandal that emerged in 1997, the *Mail & Guardian* gave the housing minister a failing grade.

Even though the decision remained pending on appeal at year's end, van Niekerk and other South African journalists believe that President Thabo Mbeki's government is fighting a losing battle. "This ruling has extended the boundaries of press freedom in South Africa, bringing it more into line with South Africa's Constitution, one of the most progressive in the world," van Niekerk told CPJ. "This was an attempt by the government to harass the *Mail & Guardian* and silence criticism. If the appeal fails, a powerful weapon will have been removed from the government's armory." The decision to dismiss the lawsuit essentially overturned a 1975 decision barring the government from suing for defamation but allowing individual ministers to do so.

In March, President Mbeki's government announced the creation of a U.S.-style presidential press corps—the first of its kind in Africa. The press corps would have privileged access to the president, including the opportunity to attend on- and off-the-record briefings and accompany Mbeki on official trips. The idea arose from a meeting between the South African National Editors Forum (SANEF) and the government, during which SANEF raised concerns about the president's accessibility.

Journalists greeted the idea with enthusiasm, until they were required to complete an accreditation application, prepared by the National Intelligence Agency, asking them if they had ever sought psychiatric treatment, suffered from alcoholism or drug abuse, been divorced, or slept with someone of the same sex. In April, Intelligence Minister Lindiwe Sisulu issued a statement expressing "regret" over the questions and ordered that all questions deemed "insensitive" be removed. An interim press corps committee was formed to work with government agencies to refine the security-clearance procedure and formulate a code of conduct. No significant progress had been made by year's end, however.

In January, KwaZulu-Natal premier Lionel Mtshali appeared on Tim Modise's morning radio show on SABC-Safm and declared that his province would supply the anti-AIDS drug nevirapine to HIV-positive pregnant women at public health facilities. Mtshali's stance directly contradicted government requirements that the drug be tested at 18 designated pilot centers before public officials distribute it. Immediately after Modise's show, prominent journalist and AIDS activist Anita Allen filed a complaint with the Broadcasting Complaints Commission (BCC) accusing Modise of "sedition" and "supporting lawlessness" on the grounds that he had used his radio show to publicize public health policies that counter the government's. The BCC cleared Modise of any wrongdoing in early April.

On August 20, police detained Kerr Hoho, a researcher in the Eastern Cape Province legislature who, for almost two years, had allegedly published *Father Punch*, an illegal pamphlet featuring gossip, criticism, and corruption allegations against top legislative figures. Hoho's brief detention and subsequent 21-day suspension from work sparked a protest by the National Education Health and Allied Workers Union. Hoho's suspension was lifted on October 21, but he was charged with 10 counts of "criminal insult." In November, his lawyer asked the court to dismiss the criminal charges and filed a lawsuit against the legislature for 500,000 rands (US$ 55,800) because Hoho had been suspended before charges were formally filed against him. At year's end, judges were still hearing arguments in the case.

TANZANIA

LIKE MANY OF ITS EAST AFRICAN NEIGHBORS, Tanzania has been overwhelmed by the proliferation of pornographic tabloids. Since 1992, when the advent of multiparty politics fostered media liberalization, the number of privately owned newspapers has steadily increased to about 400.

Many of these publications are so-called leisure tabloids, which constantly stretch the boundaries of acceptability in this conservative republic. Gossipy articles filled with sexual innuendo continued to irritate authorities and the public alike during 2002, leading the prime minister's office to release a four-page statement threatening legal action against any publication that violates "professional ethics."

The publications, some of which are sold for very little money outside schools, divided the media community. Plagued by government accusations of extortion, blackmail, and bribery, members of the mainstream press continued to distance themselves from "pornographers." During 2002, the government shuttered nine publications because of pornographic content.

But mainstream journalists were not spared the government's wrath. The most controversial case involved George Maziku, a correspondent for the Kiswahili-language daily *Mwananchi*, who was accused of "contempt of Parliament" for an April 7 article alleging that some reforms proposed by the legislature were biased in favor of the ruling party, Chama Cha Mapinduzi. Maziku also criticized lawmakers for a bill that would allow them to "entertain" constituents, arguing that such legislation would foster corruption. Police detained and interrogated Maziku, releasing him without charge a few hours later. However, he was threatened with further legal action.

Meanwhile, the Media Council of Tanzania, which comprises academics, businesspeople, and prominent citizens chosen by journalists, continues to mediate between the press and the public. In 2002, the council called for the repeal of several laws that restrict press freedom, including the National Security Act, which essentially gives the government absolute power to define what information can be disclosed to the public, and the Broadcasting Services Act of 1993, which empowers the government to regulate the media.

The council was particularly outspoken on the Maziku case. In July, the director of public prosecutions said that he had "received Parliament's instructions to sue" Maziku and had forwarded the case to the director of criminal investigations. In response, the council, along with other free-speech defenders, lodged complaints, effectively blocking further prosecution of Maziku by year's end.

TOGO

THE TOGOLESE GOVERNMENT ATTEMPTED TO CREATE A VENEER OF OPENNESS and democracy by finally holding twice-postponed legislative elections, while President Gnassingbé Eyadéma and his ruling Rassemblement du Peuple Togolais (Rally of the Togolese People, or RPT) increasingly harassed the private press. Authorities' routine censorship of private publications, imprisonment of reporters, and attempts to impose new laws with even harsher penalties for press offenses further cemented Togo's reputation as one of the most repressive places for journalism in West Africa.

Since the January 2000 Press Law empowered the Interior Ministry to seize publications, authorities have been on a rampage. Police confiscated the print runs of several newspapers in 2002 for reasons ranging from publishing "offensive comments" to "undermining the authority of the state." All of the seizures resulted from articles criticizing the government.

Togolese journalists believe that the seizures were designed not only to censor coverage but also to drive critical publications out of business. Pro-opposition private newspapers survive almost entirely on sales because advertisers fear being associated with publications that criticize the government. Journalists' wages are also contingent on sales; when publications are seized, reporters often go unpaid. Even pro-government newspapers, which can derive nearly half their revenue from advertising, have trouble making ends meet. As a result, journalists from both sides of the media often accept bribes from officials in exchange for favorable coverage.

The Togolese press remains bitterly polarized between state and pro-government private media, which invariably support Eyadéma and the RPT, on the one hand, and the pro-opposition private media, which fiercely criticize the ruling party, on the other. This division is reflected in the organizations that represent journalists, with the Togolese Private Press Publishers Association comprising journalists from pro-opposition media, and the Private Press Editors Union comprising journalists from pro-government media. Local reporters say the split makes it difficult for journalists to coordinate to defend press freedom.

In February, the Interior Ministry shuttered the private Radio Victoire, claiming that the station's license had expired. Local sources said the station's news broadcasts and popular call-in programs, during which listeners frequently criticize the RPT, angered the government. In September, authorities jammed the signal for Radio-France Internationale (RFI) after the station aired comments critical of Eyadéma. In the run-up to October elections, meanwhile, Internet users were unable to access the news Web site *letogolais.com*, which is run by an editorial staff in Paris with correspondents based in Togo. Press freedom advocates said the site's independent editorial stance angered officials.

Authorities also chased, arrested, and imprisoned journalists in reprisal for their reporting on ruling-party scandals. *Le Scorpion* publication director Basile Agboh was jailed in June after his newspaper reported that Lt. Col. Ernest Gnassingbé, a son of President Eyadéma, had threatened Prime Minister Agbeyome Kodjo for not supporting the president. *Nouvel Echo* publication director Julien Ayi and editor Alphonse Nevamé Klu were sentenced to four months and six months in prison, respectively, and were ordered to pay hefty fines after the paper falsely reported that Eyadéma had illegally amassed a fortune that made him one of the world's wealthiest people. Newspaper editors regularly went into hiding to avoid arrest after their papers were seized, or when authorities summoned them.

Even senior RPT politicians were not immune from persecution for defying Eyadéma's rule. Prime Minister Kodjo had to flee the country after publishing a statement online criticizing Eyadéma's political and economic mismanagement of the country and accusing the president of rights abuses. Local sources said it was RFI's September interview with the erstwhile prime minister, during which Kodjo accused Eyadéma of wanting to extend his 35-year rule in upcoming presidential elections, that led officials to jam the broadcaster's signal.

In September, the RPT-dominated Parliament passed an amendment to the Press Code that compounds its already harsh punishments. The measure increases the penalty for "insulting the Head of State" from six months in prison to a "one- to five-year jail term with no parole and a fine of one to five million CFA francs [US$1,500 to $7,900]." Insulting the National Assembly speaker, the prime minister, or other government officials now draws jail terms of three months to two years. The penalty for defaming courts, tribunals, the armed forces, security forces, or other state bodies was increased from three months to three years in jail.

At the end of December, Parliament amended the constitution to allow Eyadéma to run for another term. Eyadéma, Africa's longest-serving head of state, had earlier promised to respect the constitution, raising hopes that he would step down ahead of 2003 presidential elections. Also in December, authorities arrested Sylvestre Djahlin Nicoué, publication director of the private *Citoyen du Courrier*, after the paper published an editorial suggesting that the Togolese people would rebel if democratic reforms were not instituted after the 2003 poll. Nicoué was charged with "inciting rebellion" and remained in jail at year's end.

UGANDA

UGANDA WAS THE ONLY COUNTRY IN AFRICA where a journalist was killed in 2002. Jimmy Higenyi, a student at the private journalism school United Media Consultants and Trainers, was shot by police while covering a rally of the opposition party Uganda People's Congress in the capital, Kampala, on January 12. The government had banned the gathering, and police officers trying to disperse the rally fired into the crowd, hitting Higenyi, who died instantly.

Despite Higenyi's death, Uganda continued to lead the region in the number of licensed and operating radio stations. Although not all of the more than 100 licensed stations were on the air, those that were broadcasting expanded beyond their urban bases to other parts of the country. New community-based stations were launched in 2002, including one geared to rural farmers that focuses on weather and the environment.

Call-in talk shows, dubbed *ekimeeza* (table talk), have become a regular, and immensely popular, feature of FM radio. The format is fairly uniform: Invited guests gather at a public place outside the studio—usually a pub or restaurant—and debate a topic selected by the moderator. Members of the public are encouraged to participate by either going to the venue or calling. In December, Information Minister Basoga Nsadhu declared *ekimeeza* illegal, saying broadcast licenses did not extend to bars. Radio stations ignored the ban and threatened to sue the state.

Pornography remained a source of concern across the country, with citizens and Parliament members decrying minors' easy access to it. The government interrogated two editors and the circulation manager of at least one newspaper, *Bukedde*, for nearly five hours over the publication of "seminude" photos of beauty contestants. No charges were filed, but Uganda's Penal Code prohibits "trafficking in obscenities."

Of more consequence for the media was the fallout from the country's 2001 presidential election. After nearly defeating President Yoweri Museveni in a bitterly disputed poll, Col. Kiiza Besigye fled the country, saying he feared for his life. From his self-imposed exile in the United States, Besigye became a regular guest on Uganda's popular call-in radio shows, during which he repeatedly accused Museveni's government of graft and vote rigging. During one notable interview with the Voice of Africa on August 17, Besigye threatened to resort to "untraditional" methods if his efforts to get fresh elections through constitutional means fail.

The backlash was immediate. On September 16, an official of Museveni's nonparty (all political parties are banned in Uganda) National Resistance Movement, Ofwono Opondo, warned radio stations against airing further interviews with Besigye and threatened them with prosecution under the new Anti-Terrorism Act of 2002, which was signed into law in May. The act, which empowers the Cabinet to designate an organization as terrorist, explicitly categorizes rebel groups as such. "Besigye has inadvertently declared war on the Government," Opondo stated, adding that anyone who helps Besigye "spread his propaganda … comes under suspicion of aiding terrorism, and the anti-terrorism law will apply." Those convicted of violating the act face up to 10 years' imprisonment or death by hanging.

On October 10, police officers raided the country's largest independent daily newspaper, *The Monitor*, manhandled staff, seized equipment, and then closed the publication for one week. The raid was prompted by a story about an army helicopter that had allegedly crashed in northern Uganda. Army spokesman Maj. Shaban Bantariza denied the report, and Information Minister Basoga Nsadhu accused the paper of promoting crimes by rebel groups.

Although it was closed, the paper continued to publish online. On October 17, the print version reappeared with a front-page apology to the government. That same day, Nsadhu announced that "the media has to be cautious" on "matters of national security." Soon after, the Kenyan Nation Newspaper group, which owns a majority share in *The Monitor*, announced plans to strengthen the paper's fact-finding and research procedures.

ZAMBIA

PRESIDENT LEVY MWANAWASA was inaugurated on January 2 amid opposition charges of fraudulent elections and editorial comments in the independent press that the new head of state was the "puppet" of his predecessor, Frederick Chiluba. The election controversy, power struggles, and financial scandals in the ruling Movement for Multiparty Democracy (MMD) dominated headlines in 2002.

Mwanawasa followed in Chiluba's footsteps early on by taking a hard line against the press. In late January, the government banned the media and public without explanation from witnessing the election of the parliamentary speaker. Independent journalists and opposition parliamentarians suspected that officials feared coverage of the controversial vote.

Mwanawasa, whose presidency remained fragile throughout 2002 while the opposition challenged the election results, proved unwilling to tolerate disrespect. In mid-February, he pressed "defamation of the president" charges against Fred M'membe, editor-in-chief of the independent daily *The Post*, and Dipak Patel, an opposition Parliament member, after *The Post* ran an article quoting Patel calling Mwanawasa a "cabbage." Patel's remark referred to Mwanawasa's alleged diminished mental capacities resulting from a near fatal car accident a decade ago.

Journalists and human rights groups persistently criticize the blatant pro-MMD bias in the state-owned media, alleging that the political opposition continues to be denied access to these organs. Opposition leader Anderson Mazoka contends that his constitutional right to free expression was violated when the Zambia National Broadcasting Corporation (ZNBC) refused to air a paid-for program in which Mazoka thanked Zambian voters after the elections. In early April, the Press Association of Zambia

(PAZA) vowed to uproot what it called "pocket journalism," or bribe-taking in exchange for favorable coverage. PAZA alleged that a group of journalists for the state-owned media had been paid in 2001 to spread political falsehoods to try to secure more MMD seats in the election.

Bribery extended to the private press as well. In late June, Reuters news agency suspended its Johannesburg-based correspondent, Buchizya Mseteka, following revelations that he had been receiving payments from Zambian intelligence services. News reports alleged that Mseteka had acted as an agent for members of the former Zambian government, used Reuters to run public relations campaigns for top African leaders, and received payments from African politicians to write positive stories about them.

Throughout 2002, Zambian journalists became entangled in MMD infighting, with Mwanawasa and his government pursuing former high-ranking officials from the Chiluba regime for corruption, while Chiluba and his associates attempted to discredit Mwanawasa's presidency. In early June, four journalists for the independent tabloid *The People* were jailed for three weeks on defamation charges when their paper ran a story alleging that Mwanawasa was suffering from Parkinson's disease. The journalists later apologized to the president when it was discovered that Mwanawasa's enemies in the MMD had duped them. Also in June, youth members of the MMD seized copies of private newspapers deemed critical of Mwanawasa from the streets of the capital, Lusaka, and then severely beat the vendors who had sold the publications. The papers had recently carried advertisements from patrons thought to be disaffected MMD members alleging that Mwanawasa's injuries from the car accident made him unfit to be president.

One positive development arose from the MMD's internal battles. In mid-July, the state dropped defamation charges against *The Post* editor Fred M'membe, reporter Bivan Saluseki, and two opposition politicians stemming from 2001 *Post* articles alleging that President Chiluba had been involved in a US$4 million graft scheme. The case was dropped when the court was unable to resolve whether or not presidential immunity could keep Chiluba from testifying.

In early November, the government rejected three bills—the Freedom of Information Bill, the Independent Broadcasting Authority Bill, and the Broadcasting Bill—drafted by the Zambia Independent Media Association and opposition members of Parliament. The MMD instead promoted its own bills. Journalists criticized the government's draft legislation, which gives Zambian security forces blanket exemptions from requests for information and allows the president to take over all broadcasters in a state of emergency.

In mid-November, the government postponed its legislation to consult with opposition members and media rights groups. Bt year's end, Parliament had approved the Independent Broadcasting Bill and the government's version of the Broadcasting Bill, both of which were awaiting the president's signature. Media rights advocates said amendments to the government's Broadcasting Bill, with allowances for a Parliament-approved ZNBC board and for the ZNBC to collect licensing fees without the intervention of the information minister, will allow the ZNBC to function more independently. The legislature suspended consideration of the Freedom of Information Bill while members debated some of its more contentious provisions.

ZIMBABWE

ZIMBABWEAN JOURNALISTS CONTINUE TO TOIL under extremely tough conditions, with government lawsuits and physical attacks by backers of the ruling ZANU-PF still regular occurrences. On August 28, unknown assailants blew up the newsroom of Voice of the People, which was founded by former employees of the official Zimbabwe Broadcasting Corporation. The private news outlet has been producing shows since June 2000 and usually airs its programs on Radio Netherlands and SW Radio, a Europe-based station opposed to President Robert Mugabe that can be heard on shortwave radio in Zimbabwe.

According to CPJ research, the August explosion is the fourth bomb attack on the independent media since January 2001, when a bomb gutted the printing presses of the *Daily News*, Zimbabwe's only independent daily newspaper, which has suffered two similar attacks since then.

On May 3, World Press Freedom Day, CPJ named Zimbabwe one of the world's 10 worst places to be a journalist, highlighting the harsh repression under President Mugabe and Information Minister Jonathan Moyo.

Earlier in the year, Mugabe had warned journalists that those who wrote "libelous" reports quoting unnamed sources "would be arrested." Addressing a gathering of church leaders who were pressing the president for a more liberalized media, the president said, "If these sources are reliable, let them be reliable enough to come and rescue you when you are arrested." And indeed, after the highly contentious and seriously flawed presidential elections on March 15—in which Mugabe faced the greatest threat ever to his 20-year rule from the opposition Movement for Democratic Change (MDC)—the state moved quickly to stifle independent reporting. Mugabe's first significant act after re-election was to sign the Access to Information and Protection of Privacy Act (AIPPA), by far the most repressive of the country's already draconian anti-media laws.

The controversial act, drafted in secret, criminalizes the publication of "falsehoods" and grants the government the right to decide who may or may not work as a journalist in Zimbabwe. Authorities say the bill will keep "dangerous elements" out of the country—a claim that was widely interpreted to mean foreign correspondents. The foreign press corps in Zimbabwe has been decimated during the last few years, since the Mugabe government accused Harare-based foreign journalists of being spies for the British government, Mugabe's most ardent critic. A few foreign reporters remain in Zimbabwe, but morale is low, and the dangers appear overwhelming.

With the president's explicit consent, the government turned its attention to the local media and arrested any journalist who dared author critical reports. Using the Public Order and Security Act (POSA), AIPPA, and the colonial-era Censorship and Entertainment Control Act, the state hauled more than a dozen journalists to court. The arsenal of legislation at the state's disposal meant that journalists could be charged with anything from defamation to publishing pornography to "engendering hostility against the president," which is illegal under POSA. The cases ranged from petty—Iden Wetherell, editor of the weekly *Zimbabwe Independent*, was arrested and questioned over a photograph he had published showing half-clad Amazonian men playing soccer—to shocking, such as the charge against Peta Thornycroft, correspondent for South Africa's

Mail & Guardian, who was accused of "inciting public disorder and violence" with an article she wrote alleging that ruling-party supporters were beating opposition members.

The most serious case involved the *Daily News* and U.S. journalist Andrew Meldrum. *Daily News* reporters Lloyd Mudiwa and Collin Chiwanza and editor-in-chief Geoff Nyarota were arrested with Meldrum in connection with an April 23 story by Mudiwa—later discovered to be inaccurate—stating that youths from the ruling ZANU-PF party had beheaded an opposition supporter. The *Daily News* published a front-page retraction of the story on April 30. Meldrum, a Zimbabwe-based correspondent for London's *Guardian* newspaper, wrote an article for that paper reporting on the fact that the story had appeared in the *Daily News* and was being widely discussed in Zimbabwe.

The article ran on the same day as the *Daily News* retraction, and *Guardian* editors later issued their own correction. Nyarota was detained and released pending the hearing of the case, but Mudiwa, Chiwanza, and Meldrum were arrested and kept in police custody for three days. All four journalists were charged with "abusing journalistic privilege" and "publishing false information" under AIPPA. The case against Chiwanza was dropped due to insufficient evidence. Meldrum, a permanent resident of Zimbabwe, was found not guilty but was immediately served with a deportation order requiring him to leave the country within 24 hours. He filed an appeal, his deportation was suspended, and the matter was referred to the Supreme Court. By year's end, no date had been set for a hearing, and Meldrum was free to remain and work in Zimbabwe. Mudiwa and Nyarota are currently free pending a decision on their cases.

Faced with all these legal challenges, journalists fought back. In May, the Foreign Correspondents Association filed suit with the Supreme Court contesting AIPPA's constitutionality. Although the case was filed under a certificate of urgency, the court declared the suit "not urgent," and at year's end, no hearing date had been set.

In August, the Independent Journalists Association of Zimbabwe also challenged sections of AIPPA, including the Media and Information Commission's power to compel journalists to register. On November 21, however, the Supreme Court upheld the government's right to register journalists. After initially refusing to comply with the registration requirement, independent journalists gave in but protested to the commission. In addition to paying a Z$6,000 (US$110) fee, journalists must complete detailed accreditation questionnaires.

In a letter to commission chair Tafataona Mahoso, Zimbabwe Union of Journalists secretary-general Luke Tamborinyoka wrote, "We do not know what this personal information is going to be used for," and he expressed fear that the form was an intelligence-gathering document disguised as an accreditation exercise. Mahoso dismissed the concerns and declined to change the questionnaires.

At year's end, a labor dispute at the *Daily News* threatened the paper's existence. The paper stopped publishing around December 20 after workers went on strike, demanding a more than 100 percent pay raise. On December 31, Nyarota, editor-in-chief and a CPJ 2001 International Press Freedom award recipient, was dismissed by the paper's board of directors. The *Daily News* resumed publication that same day. The reason for Nyarota's dismissal was murky but seemed to be both political and financial. What is clear is that after his dismissal, the government-controlled media began a smear campaign against Nyarota, and police attempted to arrest him. ∎

| CASES TABLE OF CONTENTS |

ANGOLA

JUNE 9

"Ponto de Vista"
CENSORED

Authorities in the eastern Angola town of Lunda-Norte banned the popular radio show "Ponto de Vista" (Point of View), which aired on Emissora Provincial da Lunda-Norte, a local affiliate of the Angolan state radio network.

Sources in Angola said that on June 6, the provincial director for social communications, Manuel Cambinda, told the program's host, Olavito de Assunção, that the program would be taken off the air for being "against the government." The program remained banned at year's end.

BOTSWANA

APRIL 19

Stryker Motlaloso, *Mmegi*
ATTACKED

Motlaloso, news editor for the independent weekly *Mmegi*, was assaulted by opposition Botswana National Front (BNF) politician David Mhiemang at a political rally in the capital, Gaborone.

According to sources at *Mmegi*, Mhiemang approached Motlaloso, who was covering the rally for the paper, and accused him of reporting negatively on BNF party activities. Mhiemang then punched Motlaloso in the eye and began insulting him. When Mhiemang drew a knife and threatened to stab the journalist, Motlaloso left.

Mmegi sources told CPJ that the paper's coverage of infighting among BNF factions, which many say hampers the party's ability to function effectively, had angered Mhiemang. On April 20, Motlaloso pressed assault charges against Mhiemang. By year's end, no progress had been made in the case.

BURKINA FASO

SEPTEMBER 20

Christophe Koffi, Agence France-Presse
IMPRISONED

Koffi, a reporter for Agence France-Presse, was kidnapped by Burkina Faso–backed rebel Ivoirian soldiers in Burkina Faso's capital, Ouagadougou, and driven to a village on Lareda River, near the border with Ivory Coast. The journalist, who was released a week later, said that during his captivity, rebel chief Ibrahim Coulibaly repeatedly accused him of being a spy for the Ivoirian government.

The rebel soldiers from Ivory Coast's Muslim north began fighting government troops on September 19 before agreeing to a cease-fire and peaceful negotiations in mid-October. They claim that southern Christians, who have ruled the country since independence from France in 1960, discriminate against Muslims. Veteran reporter Koffi, who was not injured during his ordeal, is from the south.

BURUNDI

JANUARY 14

Net Press
CENSORED

Net Press, a private, online news service, was banned by Minister of Communications Albert Mbonerrane. According to the PanAfrican News Agency, Mbonerrane said Net Press publishes "subversive, defamatory, insulting and deceptive" articles that "undermine national unity, order, security and public morality."

In a country that has been plagued by a drawn-out civil war between ethnic Hutus and Tutsis, Burundian sources report that Net Press has a reputation for spreading extremist Tutsi viewpoints. In November 2001, a Tutsi-dominated transitional government was installed to bring Burundi out of civil war. But Net Press has stridently rejected the peace process and the new government.

Local sources said, however, that both Hutu and Tutsi journalists protested the ban and also pressed Minister Mbonerrane to allow the media to regulate itself to address such issues. According to the United Nations Integrated Regional Information Networks, Mbonerrane lifted the ban on Net Press on February 23. The news agency began posting news again on its Web site on February 25.

MARCH 6

Aloys Niyoyita, Studio Ijambo, The Associated Press
HARASSED

Niyoyita, a reporter for Studio Ijambo, an independent broadcaster based in the capital, Bujumbura, and a stringer for The Associated Press (AP), was arrested while covering a protest by the dissident group Amasekanya.

That afternoon, government ministers were meeting at the Meridian Hotel in Bujumbura to inaugurate a nationwide awareness campaign for the Arusha peace accords, which were signed in August 2000. Niyoyita was covering a protest outside the hotel by Amasekanya, an ethnic Tutsi extremist group that opposes the accords and the transitional government of President Pierre Buyoya.

According to sources at Studio Ijambo, at about 4 p.m., police arrested Niyoyita, along with eight of the demonstrators, and seized

his camera and tape recorder. He protested, telling the officers that he was a journalist and not a demonstrator, but they did not release him.

Police drove the detainees to a gendarmerie station, where Niyoyita once again told officers that he was a journalist and showed them his press card. One of the officers took the card and tore it apart. Niyoyita and the other prisoners were then interrogated.

The journalist was able to contact his employers by cell phone from within the gendarmerie. He was released after about an hour, following several phone calls from both Studio Ijambo and the AP, and his equipment was returned to him. Sources at Studio Ijambo said that the guards had tried to take the negatives from his camera but could not because it was digital.

MAY 16

All Burundian journalists
CENSORED

At a meeting between government officials and journalists, Defense Minister Maj. Gen. Cyrille Ndayirukiye banned all media in the country from interviewing any rebels. Burundian sources said the ban came after local news outlets carried an interview with Agathon Rwasa, leader of the rebel National Liberation Front. In the interview, Rwasa denounced a government plot to assassinate him and threatened to take retaliatory actions against the regime in Bujumbura.

Government officials did not specify what penalties would be imposed on media that violated the ban. During the meeting, officials also discussed Radio Publique Africaine's continuing independent investigations into the November 2001 assassination of the World Health Organization representative in Burundi.

Authorities were angered that the station continued to investigate while police were still examining the case as well. Prosecutor General Gerard Ngendabanka said that the media were now prohibited from discussing criminal cases still under investigation. Both independent journalists and the National Communications Council, a state-run media regulatory body, protested the bans.

AUGUST 1

PanAfrika
CENSORED

The privately owned monthly *PanAfrika* was banned by the National Communication Council (NCC) for publishing a lengthy interview with a politician with extremist views, which the NCC said incited ethnic hatred. The Burundi Journalists Association immediately condemned the ban, arguing that *PanAfrika* must remain in print because it is the "only remaining privately owned newspaper that had resumed publication" in recent years. Government bans or financial problems have forced others out of print.

CAMEROON

MARCH 1

Peter William Mandio, *Le Front Indépendant*
Jacques Blaise Mvié, *La Nouvelle Presse*
HARASSED

Mandio, publisher of the Yaoundé-based private weekly *Le Front Indépendant*, was detained by police and questioned for several hours about an *Indépendant* article describing an extramarital affair between two unnamed officials at the Office of the President. Mandio was released on the evening of March 4 with orders to "remain accessible to the judiciary."

Meanwhile, Blaise Mvié, the publisher of the popular tabloid *La Nouvelle Presse*, went into hiding after he learned that police wanted to question him about a story in his publication that revealed the names of the officials allegedly having the affair and reported that they had occasional trysts inside presidential quarters. Mvié's colleagues at *La Nouvelle Presse* also claimed that their paper's offices were under police surveillance.

CHAD

FEBRUARY 11

FM Liberté
CENSORED

FM Liberté, a private radio station in the capital, N'Djamena, was suspended by the High Council on Communications (HCC), the state media supervisory body, for three weeks. HCC officials claimed that the popular station had violated broadcasting regulations by broadcasting "information likely to disrupt public order."

The previous week, FM Liberté had reported on a student rally at the University of Yaoundé in neighboring Cameroon, during which soldiers arrested and allegedly roughed up Chadian nationals. The news angered students at the Félix Eboué High School in N'Djamena, who took to the streets on February 4 to protest the enrollment of Cameroonian nationals in Chad's schools, looting and injuring several people. FM Liberté resumed normal programming at the end of the three-week ban, on March 4.

MARCH 30

All private radio stations
CENSORED

For the second time in 2002, the High

Council on Communications (HCC) banned "all political radio programs" on all of Chad's private, cooperative, and community radio stations during the run-up to the country's third round of parliamentary elections, which were held in March.

The HCC also warned that stations airing official campaign materials could be suspended "if the content is insulting or provocative, or contrary to provisions of the law and regulations in force." HCC officials told reporters that the move was intended to help the Electoral Commission track each political party's airtime on private radio stations to avoid "imbalances."

On April 20, the HCC lifted the ban and removed threats to suspend delinquent stations. The HCC had ordered a similar ban during the run-up to the presidential elections, which were held in May 2001.

DEMOCRATIC REPUBLIC OF CONGO

MARCH 7

Wema Kennedy, Radio Muungano
IMPRISONED

Kennedy, head of Radio Muungano, was arrested by rebels from the Congolese Rally for Democracy for announcing on the air that the rebel's chief was not at peace talks being held in Sun City, South Africa. Kennedy was reportedly freed a few days later.

MARCH 9

Raphael Paluku Kyana, Radio Rurale de Kanyabayonga
IMPRISONED

Kyana, director of community radio station Radio Rurale de Kanyabayonga, was arrested in Bunagana, a town located on the

DRC-Uganda border, by Immigration Department officials of the rebel Congolese Rally for Democracy (RCD). His captors accused him of traveling through rebel-held territory without authorization and confiscated his personal belongings.

Kyana was traveling to Nairobi for a training workshop at the All-African Council of Churches' Communications Training Center. Following this workshop, he planned to travel to Mbuji-Mayi, a Congolese town located in the area under the Kinshasa government's control, to attend a Congolese Community Radio Stations' Association meeting.

Journalists in the DRC are prohibited from entering RCD-controlled zones without authorization from rebel officials. According to Congolese sources, the restrictions have made it extremely difficult for journalists to cover events in the northern and eastern parts of the country during the 4-year-old conflict between the DRC and rebels backed principally by Rwanda and Uganda.

Following protests from local and international human rights organizations, Kyana was freed on March 14. His belongings and money were not returned to him upon his release. The following day, rebel agents attacked human rights activist Richard Muhindo Bayunda when he went to RCD authorities to protest Kyana's detention. Bayunda had refused to pay the rebels a bribe to stop them from re-arresting Kyana, and he had demanded that they return Kyana's belongings.

JUNE 7

Nyemabo Kalenga, La Tribune
HARASSED

Kalenga, publisher of the independent biweekly La Tribune, was detained for more than 10 hours at the National Intelligence Agency offices, where he was questioned about his sources for an article that had appeared in the May 9 edition of the paper about a financial scandal involving a Lebanese citizen residing in the capital, Kinshasa.

According to the local press freedom group Journaliste En Danger, Kalenga published a copy of a letter he had obtained from the Congolese foreign minister to the Lebanese ambassador asking him to intervene in the investigation into the business dealings of the Lebanese community in Kinshasa. Kalenga was released later that evening.

JUNE 19

Félix Kabuizi, *La Référence Plus*
HARASSED

Kabuizi, publication director of the independent Kinshasa daily *La Référence Plus*, was called in for questioning by members of the National Intelligence Agency (ANR) and interrogated for six hours about a June 18 *La Référence Plus* story that reported on the disappearance of seven leaders of a rebel movement in the eastern part of the country. The ANR agents warned Kabuizi not to write about such issues, claiming it could discourage former rebels now engaged in the peace process from returning to the country. The journalist was released later the same day.

JULY 11

Raymond Luaula, *La Tempête des Tropiques*
Bamporiki Chamira, *La Tempête des Tropiques*
HARASSED

Luaula and Chamira, publication direc-

tor and chief investigative reporter, respectively, for the independent daily *La Tempête des Tropiques*, and three other newspaper employees who are not journalists, were arrested and taken to the Special Services holding center in the capital, Kinshasa, where they were interrogated in connection with an article that had appeared in the July 10 edition of the paper. The article reported on a July 8 street confrontation between civilians and soldiers that had turned violent, resulting in four deaths and substantial material damage.

In addition, police seized the entire print run of the newspaper's July 11 edition. All five media workers were released the same evening on the condition that the paper print a correction to the story, which appeared on the front page of the next day's issue.

JULY 16

Arnaud Zajtman, BBC
CENSORED

Zajtman, the BBC's DRC correspondent, was banned from covering activities in the eastern part of the country, which is controlled by the rebel Congolese Rally for Democracy (RCD). In early July, Zajtman had obtained permission by e-mail from the RCD's information officer to enter the rebel-controlled territory. Zajtman says he was intending to research the story of Patrick Masunzu, a former RCD commander who has recently led an insurgency against the RCD command.

According to Zajtman, the e-mail letter of permission may have been sent without the consent of RCD president Adolphe Onusumba. On July 16, Zajtman received another e-mail from the RCD information officer denying him permission to enter the area under their control. The e-mail read, "Your offensive references to our president and the contempt and disrespect you have shown for our leadership oblige me to withdraw my permission."

Zajtman told CPJ that the ban most likely stemmed from a story he had filed for the BBC Africa service on May 26 about the massacre of about 200 people by RCD forces in Kisangani. Just before filing the report, Zajtman said he received a telephone call from Onusumba, who threatened to take Zajtman to court over the story. He also warned Zajtman that if the report were broadcast, he would see that the journalist is never allowed to report from rebel-controlled areas again.

JULY 19

Raymond Kabala, *Alerte Plus*
Delly Bonsange, *Alerte Plus*
IMPRISONED

Kabala, publication director of the independent Kinshasa daily *Alerte Plus*, was arrested by plainclothes police officers and detained at the provincial police department. The next day, he was transferred to Kinshasa's Penitentiary and Re-education Center (CPRK).

According to local sources, Kabala's arrest stemmed from a July 11 *Alerte Plus* article reporting that Minister of Public Order and Security Mwenze Kongolo had allegedly been poisoned. The newspaper learned that the information was false and published a correction the next day. According to the local press freedom group Journaliste En Danger (JED), Kabala claims that authorities repeatedly questioned him about the article's sources and tortured him during his detention.

On the afternoon of July 22, officers of the Kinshasa/Matete Appeals Court Prosecutor's Office arrested Bonsange, who had written the offending article. The journalist spent the

night in police custody, and authorities questioned him about the report the next day. He was later transferred to the CPRK.

On September 6, a Kinshasa court convicted Kabala and Bonsange of "harmful accusations," "writing falsehoods," and "falsification of a public document." Kabala was sentenced to 12 months in prison and fined US$200,000. Bonsange was sentenced to six months and fined US$100,000.

According to a JED representative who attended the court proceedings, the "falsification of a public document" conviction was based on the fact that the actual address of *Alerte Plus*'s office differs from the one listed in the paper.

On September 26, Bonsange was transferred to Kinshasa's General Hospital after a doctor found his blood sugar levels unusually high. The journalist told JED that, during the first days of his detention, officials had barred him from taking his diabetes medication and following his usual diet.

According to JED, on November 21, a Kinshasa appeals court ruled that the charge against Bonsange of "writing falsehoods" was unfounded but upheld the charge of "falsification of a public document." The journalist's six-month prison sentence was dropped, and he was released on December 3. He was, however, fined US$750. The court upheld the charges against Kabala but reduced his prison sentence from 12 to seven months. He remained in prison at year's end.

JULY 24

Radio Fraternité Buena Muntu
Radio Télévision Débout Kasaï
Radio Télé Inter Viens et Vois
CENSORED

Independent East Kasaï–based broadcasters Radio Fraternité Buena Muntu (RFBM), Radio Télévision Débout Kasaï (RTDK), and Radio Télé Inter Viens et Vois (RTIV) were banned from covering news about an opposition leader.

Justin Mpoyi, the National Intelligence Agency assistant director for East Kasaï Province, summoned Ghislain Banza, interim director general of RFBM; Didier Kabuya, marketing director of RTDK; and Kadima Mukombe Katende Didier, programming director of RTIV, to his office in Mbuji-Mayi. Mpoyi ordered the three to stop broadcasting news about Étienne Tshisekedi, president of the DRC's main opposition party, the Union Pour La Démocratie et Le Progrès Social.

According to the Congolese press freedom group Journaliste En Danger, the stations were forbidden to "quote the name of, refer to or broadcast pictures of Mr. Etienne Tshisekedi in any programs." The journalists were told that if they violated the ban they would be "punished with the utmost rigor of the law."

JULY 31

Achille Ekele N'Golyma, *Pot-Pourri*
IMPRISONED
Damien Baita, *Pot-Pourri*
HARASSED

N'Golyma and Baita, publisher and editor-in-chief, respectively, of the satirical weekly *Pot-Pourri*, were detained without a warrant by plainclothes detectives at a popular cafe in the capital, Kinshasa.

Both men were taken to the Public Prosecutor's Office, where Baita was released after an identity check. Officers told him they had mistaken him for Gogin Kifwakiou, a writer for the private weekly *Vision*.

N'Golyma remained in custody in connection with a criminal libel complaint filed

by opposition politician Joseph Olenghankoy. According to the local press freedom group Journaliste En Danger (JED), Olenghankoy had sued the paper over a July 23 article alleging that members of the politician's faction were arguing about the distribution of money that President Joseph Kabila had given to them. The paper accused Olenghankoy of taking most of the money.

State prosecutors later queried N'Golyma about his sources. After the journalist refused to reveal them, police manhandled him. JED activists who visited N'Golyma at a local pretrial detention center reported that he had sustained minor injuries to his left hand and chest. He was released on August 15 after state prosecutors dropped the case.

SEPTEMBER 13

Franklin Moliba-Sese, Radio Okapi
IMPRISONED

Moliba-Sese, a reporter for the United Nations–operated Radio Okapi, was arrested in the northwestern town of Gbadolite by fighters from the Movement for the Liberation of Congo (MLC), an armed rebel group opposed to the government of President Joseph Kabila. According to sources in the capital, Kinshasa, the MLC rebels detained Moliba-Sese in reprisal for a report he had recently filed about the poor living conditions of thousands of MLC child soldiers.

On September 14, MLC rebels in Gbadolite told representatives of the U.N. peacekeeping mission that Moliba-Sese was not under arrest but was being held so they could interview him. However, the U.N.'s Integrated Regional Information Networks reported on September 18 that the journalist had been transferred to a local jail.

Moliba-Sese was released on September

21 on the orders of the Gbadolite Public Prosecutor's Office. According to Radio Okapi, the MLC said that it detained Moliba-Sese because he had interviewed child soldiers without authorization and had divulged sensitive military information.

DECEMBER 9

Radio Maendeleo
CENSORED
Kizito Mushizi Nfundiko, Radio Maendeleo
Omba Kamengele, Radio Maendeleo
IMPRISONED

Agents from the Rassemblement Congolais Pour la Démocratie (Rally for Congolese Democracy, or RCD), the rebel movement that controls a large part of eastern DRC with the support of neighboring Rwanda, closed the offices of Radio Maendeleo, a community station run by local nongovernmental organizations in Bukavu, the major city of South Kivu Province.

All of the station's employees, as well as visitors to the station's library and Internet café, which is adjacent to the studio, were briefly detained while the rebels entered the station. The rebels arrested Radio Maendeleo director Nfundiko and news director Kamengele.

An RCD spokesperson explained that Radio Maendeleo was being indefinitely suspended for broadcasting political content, which the station's license prohibits. The rebels were apparently angered by a December 7 Radio Maendeleo broadcast that included sound bites from citizens criticizing the RCD's new tax regime. The RCD had declined an invitation to participate in the program. Mushizi and Kamengele were released on December 11. The station remained suspended at year's end.

DECEMBER 31

Kadima Mukombe, Radio Kilimandjaro
IMPRISONED
For full details on this case, see page 395.

ERITREA

JANUARY 6

Simret Seyoum, *Setit*
IMPRISONED
For full details on this case, see page 398.

FEBRUARY 15

Hamid Mohammed Said, Eritrean State Radio
Saadia, Eritrean State Television
Saleh Aljezeeri, Eritrean State Radio
IMPRISONED
For full details on this case, see page 398.

ETHIOPIA

JANUARY 25

Daniel Abraha, *Netsanet*
Zekerias Tesfaye, *Netsanet*
LEGAL ACTION
Tesfaye and Abraha, publisher and editor-in-chief, respectively, of the Amharic-language weekly *Netsanet*, were charged with criminal defamation.

The charges stem from a January 18 *Netsanet* article alleging that Sheik Mohammed al-Amoudi, a wealthy businessman and owner of the Sheraton hotel in the capital, Addis Ababa, has connections with Osama bin Laden, suspected mastermind of the September 11, 2001, attacks on the United States. The story also claimed that authorities had arrested al-Amoudi for questioning. After the article was published, a representative of the businessman phoned *Netsanet* and asked the paper to print a retraction of the story, but the paper refused. Al-Amoudi then lodged a complaint with police.

Plainclothes police officers detained Tesfaye while he was eating lunch with friends at an Addis Ababa hotel. Local sources say that Tesfaye had not responded to an earlier police summons for fear that he might be harassed. After making a statement to police, he was charged and then released on a 5,000 birr bail (US$600). On January 31, Abraha was also charged for the same article after he responded to a police summons. He was also released after paying a 5,000 birr (US$600) bail.

MARCH

Shimelis Asfaw, *Ethio-Time*
LEGAL ACTION

In early March, Asfaw, former editor-in-chief of the Amharic-language weekly *Ethio-Time*, appeared before an Addis Ababa court to face charges of "disseminating fabricated information about the government and its officials that could affect public opinion," the Ethiopian Free Press Journalists Association reported.

The charges stem from a July 2001 *Ethio-Time* article alleging that one general in the Ethiopian army had been dismissed from his post, while another general was being detained by police at a secret location. Asfaw was released on a 2,000 birr (US$250) bail, and a hearing was scheduled for May 29. By year's end, CPJ could not determine the status of the case.

MARCH 1

Kebebew Gebyehu Filate, *Tobia*
LEGAL ACTION

Filate, editor-in-chief of the independent

Amharic-language weekly *Tobia*, was charged under Press Proclamation No. 34 for "inciting violence" and "defamation." Both charges stem from a 2001 *Tobia* interview with Wondosen Lema, the vice administrator for a prison in the North Shoa Zone in central Ethiopia, according to local sources. In the articles, Lema alleged that human rights violations were rife in the region, and that the zone's justice minister, Dawit Argaw, was partly responsible for the region's poor administration. Filate appeared before an Addis Ababa court in early March. He was released on a 2,000 birr (US$250) bail.

MARCH 8

Wosonseged Gebre Amlake, *Ethiop*
LEGAL ACTION

Amlake, deputy editor-in-chief of the Amharic-language weekly newspaper *Ethiop* and the affiliated monthly *Ethiop* magazine, was called to court to face charges of "disseminating fabricated information that could affect public opinion," according to the Ethiopian Free Press Journalists Association.

The charges stem from a December 2001 *Ethiop* magazine article alleging that ethnic bias occurred during a personnel restructuring in the Ministry of Justice and in the police force, and that there was tension between police and the public prosecutor as a result. Amlake was released on bail of 2,000 birr (US$250). He was detained again in October in connection with the same article and was released a few days later on a 2,000 birr (US$250) bail. His case remained pending at year's end.

MARCH 15

Arega Wolde Kirkos Ayele, *Tobia*
LEGAL ACTION

Ayele, editor-in-chief of the independent,

Amharic-language weekly *Tobia*, appeared before an Addis Ababa court in mid-March to face criminal defamation charges that had been filed against him in December 1999. The charges stemmed from two articles about the state-owned Ethiopian Electric Power Corporation published in the summer of 1999. Local sources say the articles criticized the company's management and reported that some workers had complained that a non-Ethiopian had been appointed to the post of general manager. Ayele was released on a 1,000 birr (US$120) bail. His case has been adjourned until 2003.

MARCH 20

Melese Shine, *Ethiop*
IMPRISONED, LEGAL ACTION

Shine, editor-in-chief of the Amharic-language weekly *Ethiop*, appeared before an Addis Ababa court on March 20 to face two charges of violating Ethiopia's Press Proclamation, including "defaming the head of state" and "publishing an illegal article in collaboration with an outlaw."

The charges stem from two articles that appeared more than a year ago in *Ethiop*. Both stories were based on an interview with Col. Emiru Wonde, leader of an illegal opposition party, in which Wonde criticized Prime Minister Meles Zenawi and his Tigray People's Liberation Front. On March 26, Shine was granted bail of 10,000 birr (US$1,200). Unable to raise this sum, he remained in prison until June, when he was able to make bail.

MARCH 22

Berhanu Mamo, *Abyssinia*
LEGAL ACTION

Mamo, editor-in-chief of the defunct Amharic-language weekly *Abyssinia*,

appeared before an Addis Ababa court to face charges of violating the Ethiopian Press Proclamation by publishing an article that could incite ethnic conflict. The article, titled "Oromigna Speaking Generals Fall Under The Suspicion Ring of Tigrigna Speakers," appeared in 2001 in *Abyssinia*. Oromigna and Tigrigna are the languages spoken by two of Ethiopia's largest ethnic groups. Mamo was released on a 1,000 birr (US$120) bail. His case remained pending at year's end.

MARCH 26

Tsega Moges, *Zare New*
LEGAL ACTION

Moges, editor-in-chief of the Amharic-language weekly *Zare New*, was questioned by police about a press release printed in the February 23, 2002, issue of the paper from the Benishangul Liberation Front, a separatist ethnic group. The group's statement called on Ethiopians to fight the regime of Prime Minister Meles Zenawi. Moges was charged with inciting ethnic violence and released later that day on a 5,000 birr (US$620) bail pending trial.

APRIL 30

Asrat Wodajo, *Seife Nebelbal*
IMPRISONED, LEGAL ACTION

Wodajo, editor of the independent, Amharic-language weekly *Seife Nebelbal*, was jailed for failing to post bail after he was charged with publishing false information. The charge stemmed from an article Wodajo wrote that appeared in *Seife Nebelbal* in 1999 alleging that an official in the Oromia State regional administration had deserted his post and fled the country. Wodajo was released on May 23 after paying a 7,000 birr (US$800) bail.

MAY 17

Melese Shine, *Ethiop*
IMPRISONED, LEGAL ACTION

Shine, editor-in-chief of the Amharic-language weekly *Ethiop*, was jailed after failing to post bail for a charge of inciting the people to rebellion. The charge stemmed from a May 2001 article by Shine in which Abate Angore, secretary-general of the Ethiopian Teachers Association, criticized the government's handling of April 2001 student protests in the capital, Addis Ababa, during which more than 30 people were killed. Angore also said he believed that the government had a hand in provoking the riots.

The bail for the charge was 2,000 birr (US$250). At the time this charge was brought against him, Shine had already been in jail for nearly two months for failing to pay a 10,000 birr (US$1,200) bail from a previous charge. Shine was released from prison on June 25 after paying bail.

JULY 7

Tewodros Kassa, *Ethiop*
IMPRISONED

For full details on this case, see page 398.

JULY 17

Zegaye Haile, *Genanaw*
IMPRISONED

Haile, editor-in-chief of the private, Ahmaric-language paper *Genanaw*, was arrested and sentenced to an indefinite prison term for failing to post US$300 in bail after a prosecutor charged him with "distributing false information" in an article about prison conditions in the town of Nazareth. CPJ visited Zegaye in prison on July 25 during a mission to the country. He was released near the end of the year.

JULY 25

Wosen Seged Mersha, *St. George*
Almaz Yeheise, *St. George*
LEGAL ACTION

Mersha and Yeheise, reporter and deputy editor-in-chief, respectively, for the independent weekly *St. George*, were detained by police in the capital, Addis Ababa. *St. George*, a sports newspaper, is affiliated with the St. George football club, one of Addis Ababa's two main football teams. The arrests came after an April 10 article by Mersha criticized a referee who had officiated a game between the two teams in March for being biased. Police informed the two journalists that they were being charged with defamation and then released them after each had paid a 2,000 birr (US$250) bail.

DECEMBER 2

Henok Alemayhu, *Medina*
IMPRISONED, LEGAL ACTION

Alemayhu, publisher and editor of the private Amharic-language weekly *Medina*, was jailed after being unable to pay a 4,000 birr (US$500) bail. Alemayhu is charged with defamation in connection with an article that appeared in *Medina* in June. According to local sources, the article quoted an opinion piece from the Web site *ethiopiancommentator.com*, which is run by an Ethiopian in the diaspora, alleging that Prime Minister Meles Zenawi was involved in the May 2001 assassination of Kinfe Gebre-Medhin, Ethiopia's former security and intelligence chief and a close ally of Zenawi. The article also alleged that Zenawi was insane.

Sources in the capital, Addis Ababa, told CPJ that part of the basis for the lawsuit against Alemayhu was that *Medina* presented the article as a news item, not as commentary, as it had originally appeared on *ethiopi-ancommentator.com*. Alemayhu was released on December 4, after paying bail. His case was pending at year's end.

GABON

Misamu
Gabaon
CENSORED
Le Nganga
La Lowe
THREATENED

Misamu and *Gabaon*, two of Gabon's remaining independent weeklies, were banned for three months by the National Communication Council (NCC) for publishing content "that undermines confidence in the state and the dignity of those responsible for state's institutions."

Misamu was banned for reporting that because 3 billion CFA francs (US$4.4 million) had allegedly disappeared from the state's coffers, civil servants would not receive their September salaries. According to sources, *Gabaon* was silenced for "violently" criticizing Senate majority leader Georges Rawiri in an August 9 article, according to the NCC.

The NCC threatened two other weeklies, *Le Nganga* and *La Lowé*, with a similar ban, apparently for articles the council claimed undermined the prime minister's dignity.

THE GAMBIA

Pa Nderry Mbai, *The Point*
HARASSED

Mbai, a senior reporter for the independent publication *The Point*, which appears four times a week, was picked up by police detectives in the capital, Banjul, for an article he wrote in the June 19 edition of the paper alleging that police had mismanaged a bank loan, and that senior officers were using the funds to buy luxury items. As a consequence, the bank canceled the loan.

Mbai was taken to the inspector general of police's office, where he was interrogated for two hours and accused of publishing a biased report. Mbai told the inspector general that he had tried to contact all sides for comment. Gambian sources said that Mbai had contacted the police public relations officer, who confirmed the story but begged the journalist not to publish it because it would embarrass the police.

Mbai was released after Gambia Press Union president Demba A. Jawo vouched for his colleague's reporting. The inspector general warned Mbai to be careful in his future reports on the police.

Pa Ousman Darboe, *The Independent*
IMPRISONED
Alhaji Yorro Jallow, *The Independent*
HARASSED

Darboe, senior reporter for the Banjul-based biweekly *The Independent*, was arrested by National Intelligence Agency (NIA) officers and taken to NIA headquarters.

Darboe's arrest stemmed from an August 2 *Independent* article reporting that Gambian vice president Isatou Njie Saidy had married a schoolteacher in May. Saidy's aides denied the report, as did sources close to the schoolteacher, according to Agence France-Presse. Independent Gambian journalists told CPJ that the report was untrue. Sources in Banjul said the article offended Saidy because it reported that she had remarried less than a year after her previous husband's death, which violates local custom.

On August 3, *Independent* managing editor Jallow was called to NIA headquarters for questioning about the same article. He was interrogated for several hours and not allowed to meet with Darboe. Jallow was released that same day.

Darboe was repeatedly interrogated about his article's sources. On August 5, he was released but was told he would have to report back to NIA headquarters the following day. On August 6, he returned to the NIA and was only released after a relative signed a bail bond for him.

GHANA

MARCH 30

All media
CENSORED

The government imposed strict controls on reporting about interclan clashes in the northern Dagbon region of Ghana. Information Minister Jake Obetsebi-Lamptey stated that unless journalists were "reporting an official release from my office, [they] should clear any other news items on the Dagbon affair with the ministry."

Obetsebi-Lamptey was referring to events that occurred on March 25, when the king of Ghana's Dagomba tribe was killed in the town of Yendi in Dagbon, along with at least 25 of his supporters. Intense feuding between rival clans that had begun that day sparked the killings. On March 27, President John Kufuor declared a state of emergency. The Emergency Powers Act of 1994 allows the president to censor any news from or about the area affected by a state of emergency.

Defending the government's decision to impose controls on the media, Obetsebi-

Lamptey said various stations had broadcast news that was "highly inflammatory." In November, the government extended the state of emergency indefinitely. However, sources said that the media have for the most part ignored the restrictions, and that the government has not censored or punished the press in retaliation.

GUINEA

DECEMBER 19

Boubacar Yacine Diallo, *L'Enquêteur*
IMPRISONED

For full details on this case, see page 398.

GUINEA-BISSAU

APRIL 5

All Guinean media
CENSORED

Attorney General Caetano Ntchama issued an order to all print and broadcast media forbidding them to publish or broadcast any press releases or information from the Guinean League of Human Rights (LGDH). The LGDH is known for its criticism of the ruling Social Renewal Party. Authorities have repeatedly harassed LGDH members in a crackdown on civil-society groups that have criticized the government's human rights record.

LGDH vice president Joao Vaz Mane said the "imposition of censorship was another step by the attorney general ... to silence the LGDH." Local journalists called the ban illegal, saying it infringed on press freedom and deprived citizens of their constitutional right to disseminate their opinion through the press without restriction. The ban was lifted about two months later.

JUNE 17

Joao de Barros, *Correio da Guinea-Bissau*
IMPRISONED

De Barros, owner and publisher of the independent daily *Correio da Guinea-Bissau*, was arrested in the capital, Bissau, and taken to the central prison following an appearance on a talk show on the independent Radio Bombolom during which he criticized the government. According the Portuguese news agency LUSA, de Barros had been invited to comment on Parliament's recent rejection of new budget proposals submitted by the Social Renewal Party government.

De Barros said on air that recent rumors of coup plots against President Kumba Yala were designed to divert attention away from rampant government corruption. De Barros also called "pathetic" Yala's recent military threats against neighboring Gambia, which the president has accused of supporting insurgents in Guinea-Bissau. Interior Ministry official Baciro Dabo told the national radio station that de Barros was arrested both for his radio comments and for "other things," but he did not further clarify.

On June 18, de Barros began a hunger strike. He was released the next day, after police interrogated him about his comments on the radio, but was ordered to present himself to the Interior Ministry every 10 days.

JUNE 20

Nilson Mendonca, Radio Difusão Nacional
HARASSED

Mendonca, editor for the state-run Radio Difusão Nacional (RDN), was arrested by state security police in the capital, Bissau, the Portuguese news agency LUSA reported.

His arrest followed the broadcast of a news report earlier the same day on RDN during which Mendonca claimed that President Kumba Yala was going to apologize to Gambian authorities for having accused them of supporting insurgents who were planning a coup against him, and for having threatened to "crush" the Gambian militarily. Mendonca alleged that unnamed sources in the Foreign Ministry had said that Foreign Minister Filomena Tipote was going to fly to The Gambia with Yala's apology.

Tipote denied the report shortly after the broadcast, according to the Web site of the Portuguese public broadcaster Empresa Pública da Radiodifusão. Police branded the report "false information" and interrogated Mendonca about his sources. The journalist was released 24 hours later.

AUGUST 2

Carlos Vamain, Radio Pidjiquiti
HARASSED, LEGAL ACTION

Vamain, lawyer and host for the program "This Week's Salient Facts" on the independent Radio Pidjiquiti, was called by security forces for questioning in the capital, Bissau. Officials interrogated the journalist about allegedly "defamatory" comments he had made on air the previous week. On his show, Vamain said that "the problems of Guinea-Bissau cannot be resolved with tribalism." Vamain went on to accuse President Kumba Yala of favoring members of his Balanta ethnic group in his government and military appointments.

On August 5, Vamain was called in for questioning to the Attorney General's Office over the same comments. Vamain was told he was prohibited from leaving the country, and that he would have to report to authorities every Friday. On August 7, Vamain was fined 3 million CFA francs (US$4,500) for "endangering national unity." He was ordered to pay the sum by midnight on August 12. On August 13, after being summoned to the offices of the judicial police, Vamain took refuge in the U.N. office in Bissau. Local sources said that some time later the charges were inexplicably dropped, and Vamain left the U.N. offices.

DECEMBER 1

Radiotelevisão Portuguesa
CENSORED

Guinean authorities banned the Portuguese radio and television broadcaster Radiotelevisão Portuguesa (RTP) indefinitely after the station broadcast a November 30 program marking the second anniversary of the death of Gen. Ansumane Mane. The general was killed in late November 2000 while heading an unsuccessful coup against the government of President Kumba Yala. According to the Portuguese news agency LUSA, the program included coverage of an Amnesty International report calling for an inquiry into Mane's death.

In a press statement about the ban, the government said that RTP had broadcast "information that could tarnish the good image of Guinea-Bissau abroad and could foment anger within the country."

IVORY COAST

SEPTEMBER 9

Tassouman
Le Patriot
ATTACKED

The courtyard of the office building that houses two Abidjan dailies, *Le Patriot* and *Tassouman*, was raided by police.

That same day, *Tassouman* had published three articles reporting that bandits had robbed a vehicle belonging to Interior Minister Boga Doudou. Sources in the capital, Abidjan, said that after the paper appeared that morning, *Tassouman* received an anonymous call telling them the story was wrong. Shortly thereafter, the paper received a fax from Cabinet Director Alain Dogou inviting *Tassouman* editor Kone Satigui, as well as Généviève Kouassi and Beugré Mireille, the reporters who penned the stories, to his office for a meeting.

All three journalists went to Dogou's office, where he castigated them for publishing the articles. The minister then told the journalists that the stolen car belonged to Clotilde Ohouochi, minister of solidarity, health, and social security, and not to the interior minister.

While Satigui, Kouassi, and Mireille were at the meeting, about eight police officers entered the courtyard of the papers' building. The police asked journalists from both publications where the journalists responsible for the articles were. When the staff told the police that the reporters were out, the officers began beating the journalists. Though the police did not enter the offices of the two newspapers, they threw two canisters of tear gas into the courtyard before leaving.

Tassouman and *Le Patriot*, both owned by the same company, are aligned with the opposition Rally for Republicans and its leader, Alassane Dramane Ouattara. Sources said that the Interior Ministry later denied that it had ordered the police raid in reprisal for the articles and claimed instead that a group of unruly officers had acted without authority.

SEPTEMBER 21

Mamadou Keita, *Le Patriote*
ATTACKED

Keita, a reporter for the opposition daily *Le Patriote*, was attacked and severely injured by supporters of the ruling Ivoirian Popular Front (FPI) while covering an FPI rally. The journalist was later admitted to a hospital with wounds on his head and back.

OCTOBER 11

Alain Amontchi, Reuters TV
HARASSED

Reuters cameraman Amontchi was attacked by demonstrators outside the French Embassy in the capital, Abidjan, where he was covering a spontaneous rally of thousands of youth demanding that French officials hand over opposition leader Alassane Dramane Ouattara, whom soldiers had accused of mounting a bloody military uprising that broke out on September 19. Ouattara later left the Ivory Coast. The demonstrators heckled Amontchi, yelled slurs against the presence of foreign media in the country, and later damaged his recording gear. He suffered no serious injuries.

OCTOBER 16

Tassouman
Le Patriote
Abidjan Magazine
ATTACKED

A group of about 50 people looted and ransacked the offices of the private Mayama Media Group, publisher of three Ivory Coast pro-opposition newspapers, said several sources in the capital, Abidjan. The mob smashed computers and other equipment and damaged printing presses while chanting pro-government slogans. The newsrooms of *Le Patriote* and *Tassouman*, both daily newspapers, and the weekly *Abidjan Magazine* were destroyed. All three are close to the opposition Rally for Republicans, a party led by former prime minister Alassane Dramane Ouattara, whom some state officials suspect may be behind a bloody military uprising that began on September 19 in the northern part of the country.

No one was hurt in the attack since the news staff of the three papers—long accused by the government of working to destabilize the country with biased reporting—have been working from home since the crisis started. The military standoff has pitted a group of disgruntled soldiers from Ivory Coast's Muslim north against troops loyal to the government, which is mostly staffed by southern Christians.

OCTOBER 17

Radio Nostalgie
ATTACKED

The newsroom of the popular private broadcaster Radio Nostalgie, located in the business district of the capital, Abidjan, was raided by 20 armed men dressed in fatigues. The attackers scared off the station's security personnel and destroyed surveillance cameras before smashing computers and broadcast equipment. According to news reports, Radio Nostalgie owner, Hamed Bakayoko, estimated the losses at more than 200 million CFA francs (US$296,000).

The station had abruptly stopped airing news programs on the morning of September 19, when a bloody military uprising erupted in the northern part of the country. Some state officials have accused station owner Bakayoko, as well as leaders of the opposition Rally for Republicans (RDR), of which he is an outspoken member, of masterminding the rebellion. Bakayoko also holds controlling stakes in the private Mayama Media Group, which publishes three pro-RDR newspapers.

Gaël Mocaer, Radio France Outremer
IMPRISONED

Mocaer, an independent French filmmaker who was on assignment for the television division of the publicly funded French broadcaster Radio France Outremer, was detained by Ivoirian counterintelligence services when he arrived in the capital, Abidjan. Authorities did not explain why they arrested the journalist, who was in Abidjan to shoot a feature story on the bloody military crisis that erupted in the country on September 19. Mocaer was released without charge on the afternoon of October 23 and immediately left the country. When contacted by CPJ, the journalist declined to comment on the incident.

KENYA

JUNE 7

Weekly Citizen
CENSORED

Kenyan High Court judge Andrew Hayanga issued a temporary injunction forbidding the *Weekly Citizen*, a tabloid known for salacious reporting, and its vendors from continuing to distribute the June 3-9 issue until a libel suit filed by businessman Sunil Behal is heard and resolved, according to Kenyan news reports. The case remained pending at year's end.

AUGUST 9

Njehu Gatabaki, Finance
IMPRISONED

Gatabaki, publisher of the monthly maga-

zine *Finance*, was convicted of publishing an "alarming report" and sentenced to six months in jail by Senior Principal Magistrate Wanjiru Karanja. The case stemmed from a December 1997 report in the magazine alleging that President Daniel arap Moi was responsible for ethnic clashes that had plagued parts of Rift Valley Province in the early 1990s.

In her sentencing, Karanja called the article "irresponsible and alarming journalism" that "should and must be discouraged." Gatabaki was taken into custody after the sentencing. On August 12, he was transferred to a maximum-security prison outside the Kenyan capital, Nairobi. Gatabaki was pardoned and released on August 14 by presidential decree.

LIBERIA

MARCH 26

Jerome Dalieh, The News
Bill Jarkloh, The News
HARASSED

Dalieh and Jarkloh, editor-in-chief and acting editor, respectively, of the private daily *The News*, were detained by police for several hours at a station in the capital, Monrovia. The detention stemmed from an article in that day's edition of the paper calling for the establishment of a true democracy in Liberia and quoting a local political activist. Police interrogated the two editors for about an hour before releasing them. No charges were filed.

APRIL 25

The Analyst
HARASSED

Police shut down the independent newspaper *The Analyst* and ransacked the publication's offices in an early morning raid. According to an Associated Press (AP) report, Police Chief Paul Mulbah said the ban was permanent and refused to give reasons for the closure. "The paper is closed and will not print again. This is a government order," Mulbah told the AP. The police did not have a court order to shutter the publication. *The Analyst* had also been closed on February 12, after publishing articles that criticized the state of emergency, but was reopened a week later.

MAY 11

Emmanuel Mondaye, *Independent Inquirer*

IMPRISONED

Mondaye, a reporter for the *Independent Inquirer*, was arrested in the central town of Gbarnga by state security forces and driven to the National Police Headquarters in the capital, Monrovia, where his newspaper is based. He was held for three days and accused of violating media-related provisions of the nationwide state of emergency, which President Charles Taylor declared on February 8.

Mondaye had gone to Gbarnga to report on fighting between loyalist forces and the rebel Liberians United for Reconciliation and Democracy, which on May 9 attacked the town in a move to unseat President Taylor. Government troops overpowered the rebels three days later.

JUNE 24

Hassan Bility, *The Analyst*

IMPRISONED

Bility, a reporter at *The Analyst* newspaper, was arrested on suspicion of collaborating with the rebel group Liberians

United for Reconciliation and Democracy (LURD). On June 26, Minister of Information Reginald Goodridge told a press conference that Bility was in government custody. Soon after, Judge Winston O. Henries ordered the government to produce the journalist in court by July 1, and, even though he granted the government a two-day extension to comply, Bility was never presented. On July 9, Judge Henries ruled that the court had no jurisdiction over the accused since he was an "unlawful combatant" and said he should be tried before a military court.

According to several reports from news organizations and human rights groups, on July 25, the Court Martial Board, Liberia's military court, gave the government an August 7 deadline to produce Bility. However, the Ministry of National Defense later declared the writ "null and void," claiming that the individuals who issued the writ were not authorized to do so. Immediately after, the president of the Court Martial Board denied having issued the writ.

Bility was finally freed in early December, when Liberian authorities remanded him into the custody of the U.S. Embassy in the capital, Monrovia. He left the country shortly after for an unknown destination. Officials insist that Bility's arrest was not related to his work, but CPJ research shows that Liberian officials have consistently harassed *The Analyst* and its journalists. Four days after the government declared the state of emergency, police in Monrovia suspended the paper. Officials later arrested the publisher and managing editor, Stanley Seakor, as well as reporters James Lloyd and Ellis Togba, for publishing a series of articles that criticized the state of emergency.

DECEMBER 15

Throble Suah, *The Inquirer*
ATTACKED

Suah, a reporter for the independent daily *The Inquirer*, was severely beaten by armed security personnel in the capital, Monrovia. Officers stopped the journalist while he was walking home at night and asked him to identify himself. According to sources who later spoke to Suah, when he showed the officers his journalist ID card and told them that he works for *The Inquirer*, they said that journalists are "troublemakers," and that they were looking for reporters from several independent media outlets that authorities say criticize the government. The officers then beat Suah severely and threatened to kill him. He was later admitted to a local hospital with internal injuries. By year's end, none of the attackers had been identified.

MADAGASCAR

FEBRUARY 2

FM 91
ATTACKED

Private radio station FM 91, based on the northern island of Nosy Be, was closed by Lt. Col. Ancelin Coutiti, technical adviser to the information minister. The station's equipment was also confiscated. FM 91 is owned by a provincial councilor sympathetic to Marc Ravalomanana, former Antananarivo mayor and opposition leader who declared himself president on February 22, 2002, after disputed December 16, 2001, presidential elections.

FEBRUARY 17

Madagascar Broadcasting Service
ATTACKED

A Madagascar Broadcasting Service

(MBS) crew in Brickaville, a town east of the capital, Antananarivo, was attacked by supporters of then president Didier Ratsiraka. MBS is owned by Marc Ravalomanana, the former Antananarivo mayor and opposition leader who declared himself president on February 22, 2002, after disputed December 16, 2001, presidential elections.

FEBRUARY 20

Amoron'i Mania Radio-Television
ATTACKED

The offices of the Amoron'i Mania Radio-Television (ART) station in the town of Ambositra les Roses, south of the capital, Antananarivo, were raided by striking secondary school students. The students were protesting the station's coverage of the contested December 16, 2001, presidential elections, which they considered to be overly partisan. ART is owned by Tantely Andrianarivo, President Didier Ratsiraka's prime minister.

FEBRUARY 23

Madagascar Broadcasting Service
Radio TSIOKAVAO
Radio Vatovavy Mananjary
ART Ambositra
Malagasy State Radio and Television
ATTACKED

Four radio stations were attacked and destroyed as violence erupted over disputed presidential election results. Supporters of President Didier Ratsiraka allegedly attacked the offices of the Madagascar Broadcasting Service's (MBS) radio station in Fianarantsoa, some 90 miles (144 kilometers) south of the capital, Antananarivo. The station's facilities were set ablaze, seriously injuring three security guards.

MBS is owned by Marc Ravalomanana,

Antananarivo mayor and opposition leader who declared himself president on February 22, 2002, prompting embattled president Didier Ratsiraka to declare a state of emergency.

After the MBS station was attacked, Ravalomanana supporters ransacked and destroyed Radio TSIOKAVAO, a private, pro-government station. Radio Vatovavy Mananjary, owned by former cabinet minister Jacquit Simon, and station ART Ambositra, owned by Prime Minister Tantely Andrianarivo, were also attacked.

On February 25, Malagasy State Radio and Television released a statement saying that its stations could not broadcast because Ratsiraka supporters had seized the outlet's broadcast equipment, including transmitters, and moved it to an undisclosed location.

The conflict follows a hotly contested December 16, 2001, presidential poll between Ratsiraka and Ravalomanana. Ravalomanana claimed victory with 52 percent of the vote, but the Constitutional Court ruled that neither candidate had captured a clear majority and ordered a runoff. Ravalomanana rejected the ruling, and the second round of voting never occurred.

On February 22, Ravalomanana declared himself president; in response, Ratsiraka declared a state of emergency, which empowered the government to take control of public services and the media.

MALAWI

FEBRUARY 22

Mallick Mnela, *The Chronicle*
Rob Jamieson, *The Chronicle*
Quinton Jamieson, *The Chronicle*

Joseph Ganthu, *The Chronicle*
Kambani Bana, *The Chronicle*
ATTACKED

Offices of the independent weekly *The Chronicle* were attacked by members of the Young Democrats, a youth organization that supports President Bakili Muluzi's ruling United Democratic Front (UDF) party. The members threatened to destroy the office unless staffers handed Mnela, a junior reporter for the paper, over to them. When Mnela voluntarily came forward, the assailants bundled him into their car and left.

Reporters Quinton Jamieson and Ganthu followed them until the youth group's car stalled on the road. The reporters contacted the police, who forced the assailants to go to the nearby regional police station. Once there, police stood by as the youth group's regional director, Shaban Kadango, interrogated Mnela.

The Chronicle editor-in-chief Rob Jamieson arrived at the station with reporter Banda while the Young Democrats continued to harass Mnela. When the young cadres noticed that Banda was carrying a digital camera, they attacked him and stole the camera. Rob Jamieson, Quinton Jamieson, and Ganthu tried to intervene, but the Young Democrats began assaulting them as well. Police eventually broke up the melee and told all participants to go to the nearby Lilongwe police station to lodge their complaints. Mnela was then freed.

The Chronicle staff told CPJ they do not believe that the police, who are known to be sympathetic to the Young Democrats, will investigate the incident further.

Other sources at *The Chronicle* reported that the abduction most likely came in reprisal for two recent articles that Mnela had written alleging that the Young Democrats had split into two factions, one supporting UDF central region governor Uladi Mussa, and the other supporting former deputy minister Iqbal Omar. Less than a month before Mnela's abduction, clashes between the two rival factions led to several arrests.

Earlier in the week, members of the Young Democrats had attacked Mnela. The party's regional director Kadango explained to police that the scuffle related to a personal dispute between Mnela and one of the assailants over his girlfriend, but sources at *The Chronicle* dismissed Kadango's explanation as inaccurate and noted that during the attacks on their office, the assailants explicitly mentioned the paper's critical reporting on the UDF.

August 21

Bright Sonani, *Malawi News*
ATTACKED

Sonani, a senior reporter for the private *Malawi News*, was assaulted by three unidentified men, who accused the journalist of criticizing the government in his stories. The attackers knocked the journalist to the ground, beat him, and took his cell phone before fleeing. Local sources said that the journalist had recently written several critical stories that might have angered supporters of President Bakili Muluzi and the ruling United Democratic Front.

NIGER

May 17

Abdoulaye Tiémogo, *Le Canard Déchaîné*
Sanoussi Jackou, *La Roue de l'Histoire*
Abarad Mouddour, *La Roue de l'Histoire*
IMPRISONED

Tiémogo, publisher of the independent weekly *Le Canard Déchaîné*, was arrested in the capital, Niamey, for comments made on a May 11 radio show he hosted on Niamey's

private Tambara FM. Tiémogo had reportedly invited studio guests and listeners to voice their views on the country's embattled democratization process.

One of Tiémogo's guests, Sanoussi Jackou, an opposition leader and owner of the private weekly *La Roue de l'Histoire*, accused Prime Minister Hama Amadou of ethnic and regional bias in his nominations of high-ranking government officials. Several other government officials widely accused of corruption were also criticized during the broadcast.

On May 18, police arrested Jackou and Abarad Mouddour, *La Roue de l'Histoire*'s publisher. Both men were charged with defaming Prime Minister Amadou as well as Niger's minister of trade, Seini Oumarou. While Jackou's arrest was partially based on his on-air comments about the prime minister, police detained both him and Mouddour for an early May *La Roue de l'Histoire* article that accused the trade minister of not repaying huge loans he had taken from a state-operated bank that later went bankrupt. The article reportedly alleged that the minister's failure to pay off his debt directly contributed to the bank's collapse.

On May 21, all three journalists were transferred to Niamey's Civil Prison. On May 24, a judge in Niamey's Court of First Instance denied them bail.

Tiémogo, Jackou, and Mouddour were ultimately tried on May 28. While Tiémogo was acquitted for lack of evidence, the court convicted Jackou and Mouddour of criminal defamation and sentenced them to suspended four-month prison terms, coupled with fines of 100,000 CFA Francs (US$135) each. The court also sentenced Jackou and Mouddour to pay the plaintiffs a combined sum of 2 million CFA Francs (US$2,700) in damages.

JUNE 18

Abdoulaye Tiémogo, *Le Canard Déchaîné*
IMPRISONED

For full details on this case, see page 405.

AUGUST 23

Moussa Kaka, Radio Saraounia, Radio-France Internationale
HARASSED

Kaka, director of the private Niamey-based Radio Saraounia and a local correspondent for Radio-France Internationale, was arrested and detained at National Police Headquarters for about 10 hours. He was interrogated about his reports on the early August mutiny of soldiers in the southeastern part of the country.

Authorities were angered by Kaka's coverage of the mutiny, which they said could have endangered government forces. Niger journalists told CPJ that his detention was likely intended to harass and intimidate him since he was picked up nearly two weeks after loyalist forces had defeated the uprising and was never charged.

During the mutiny, President Mamadou Tanja banned the "propagation of information or allegations likely to be detrimental to the implementation of national defense operations." Media outlets were threatened with suspension or closure if they violated the ban, which also stipulated that individuals who disseminated false information would be punished.

AUGUST 26

Boulama Ligari, Radio Anfani
IMPRISONED

Ligari, Diffa-based reporter for the independent Radio Anfani, was arrested by police, who transferred him to a civilian prison the next day. According to Radio Anfani, Ligari had extensively covered the early August mutiny of soldiers in the southeast of the country. Local sources said that Ligari's comments on the insurgents angered the government. During his detention, Ligari was accused of broadcasting false information.

At the beginning of the mutiny, rebels occupied Radio Anfani's Diffa station, which they used to broadcast their demands. Niger journalists told CPJ that Ligari's detention was intended to harass and intimidate him since he was picked up more than two weeks after loyalist forces had defeated the uprising and was never charged. Ligari was released on August 29.

NOVEMBER 20

Ibrahim Manzo, *Le Canard Déchaîné*
IMPRISONED

Manzo, editor for the private satirical weekly *Le Canard Déchaîné*, and Cissé Omar Amadou, the paper's marketing director, were arrested by police and taken to police headquarters in the capital, Niamey.

Police summoned the *Le Canard Déchaîné* staffers after an article in the paper's most recent edition claimed that the army chief of staff had gone to police headquarters to demand the arrest of the leader of the opposition Nigerian Party for Democracy and Socialism, who had recently released a statement criticizing the country's leaders and accusing the army chief of staff of playing politics. The release asked the army commander to remain politically neutral.

Manzo and Amadou were released on November 24 without charge. Sources in Niger said that the journalists were released after they promised to publish a retraction of the story in the following edition of the paper, which they did.

NIGERIA

NOVEMBER 15

National Pilot
ATTACKED

An explosion destroyed the offices of the independent weekly *National Pilot* in Ilorin, the capital of Nigeria's west central Kwara State. Five people were seriously injured in the blast, which local sources suspect was politically motivated, including the paper's deputy editor-in-chief, Mudasiru Adewuyi.

The explosion occurred at approximately 12:30 p.m. on Friday, while the paper's staff was preparing its Monday edition. The blast caused the roof of the building to collapse, injuring five workers and destroying a substantial amount of equipment. The injured workers were taken to a local hospital. With printing assistance from the private daily *ThisDay*, which is based in the southwestern city of Lagos, *National Pilot* published that week's edition on Monday, November 18.

Dr. Bukola Saraki, a prominent local businessman and son of Nigeria's former senate leader, launched *National Pilot* in July. Known for its critical coverage of the local government, the newspaper has become one of the most popular in Kwara Sate.

Saraki called the attack "state terrorism against the press." He told CPJ that the attack followed a visit to the newspaper's offices earlier that week from local government officials who asked about sources for a front-page story in *National Pilot*'s previous edition that had mentioned a petition calling for an anti-corruption probe of Kwara State governor Muhammed Lawal, who is suspected of misappropriating funds.

When the newspaper's staff refused to cooperate, the officials threatened their lives, Saraki said.

Lawal denied state government involvement in the explosion, reported local newspapers, and instead accused *National Pilot* of mounting a "self-inflicted attack" to discredit his administration. Nigerian sources said that tension between Lawal and Saraki is mounting ahead of national elections, scheduled for spring 2003, in which Saraki is considering challenging Governor Lawal for his position.

Nigerian president Olesegun Obasanjo promised a federal police investigation into the attack, saying that the national government would deal with those responsible. Lawal, meanwhile, ordered state authorities to conduct an inquiry rather than leaving the investigation to federal police.

On November 18, Lawal inaugurated a seven-member panel of inquiry, composed of individuals from state security forces, a High Court judge, and a representative from the Nigerian Union of Journalists, to investigate the attack on *National Pilot*. Sources in Nigeria later said that Lawal told reporters that police had apprehended several suspects, who were taken to the capital, Abuja, for further questioning.

Political violence in Kwara State has been rising ahead of national elections. In August, a senior politician in the state from President Obasanjo's ruling People's Democratic Party (PDP) was murdered. Two months earlier, at least two people died in street fighting between supporters of the PDP and Lawal's All Nigeria Peoples Party.

NOVEMBER 20

ThisDay
ATTACKED

The Kaduna offices of the private daily

ThisDay were burned down by Muslim protesters who were angered by a news report the paper published about the Miss World pageant, which was scheduled to be held in Nigeria early in December. The protesters were reacting to a recent article in the paper that appeared to belittle Muslim concerns about the country's decision to host the beauty contest. The article said that the Prophet Mohammed probably would have chosen a wife from among the women competing. *ThisDay* later retracted the story and printed several front-page apologies for the comment.

News reports said that about 500 protesters, chanting "Allahu Akbar" (God is great), marched to the paper's offices in the early morning and set the building ablaze. Reuters quoted witnesses who said that the paper's staff was not in the office at the time. Local sources said that *ThisDay*'s staff went into hiding after the attack, while vendors in the area stopped selling the paper.

The last two years have seen violent clashes between Muslims and Christians across a dozen northern Nigerian states, all of which have recently adopted Sharia, or Islamic, law. Kaduna, in Kaduna State, is considered one of the most volatile cities in the region. Two years ago, more than 2,000 people died in violent interreligious clashes in the northern city.

NOVEMBER 26

Isioma Daniel, *ThisDay*
THREATENED
Simon Kolawole, *ThisDay*
IMPRISONED

Islamic authorities in the northern Nigerian state of Zamfara issued a fatwa urging Muslims to kill Daniel, a writer for the private daily *ThisDay*, whose November 16 article about the Miss World pageant sparked

deadly riots across the country. According to sources in the southern city of Lagos, the order to kill Daniel was passed early in the morning after a meeting between members of the Zamfara State government and representatives of at least 20 Islamic organizations.

Although the newspaper had retracted the story and issued several front-page apologies, Zamfara State deputy governor Mamuda Aliyu Shinkafi insisted that, "It is binding on all Muslims, wherever they are, to consider the killing of the writer as a religious duty."

Daniel, the style editor for the Lagos-based *ThisDay*, resigned from the paper and fled the country after repeatedly apologizing for the article, which Muslim leaders said belittled Muslim concerns about the country's decision to host the beauty contest. The journalist wrote that the Prophet Mohammed probably would have chosen a wife from among the women competing.

More than 200 people were killed in Kaduna State and in the federal capital, Abuja, where the pageant, later moved to London, was to take place. Violence erupted after Nigeria's Supreme Islamic Council declared in a statement that *ThisDay*'s article was a declaration of "total war against Islam" and called all Muslims to attack the paper.

On November 20, about 500 protesters, chanting "Allahu Akbar" (God is great), marched to the paper's Kaduna offices in the early morning and set the building ablaze. The next day, federal government spokesman Ufot Ekaette said that the publication had clearly exceeded the bounds of responsible journalism and would be punished "as provided by the law." So far, federal authorities have taken no action against the paper. The federal government also promised the fatwa against Daniel would not be enforced.

On November 23, secret police arrested

and questioned Kolawole, editor of *ThisDay*'s Saturday edition, about the offending article. Kolawole was released a few days later.

Zamfara was one of the first Nigerian states to adopt Islamic law, or Sharia, in January 2000. At least 11 more of Nigeria's 36 states followed suit, heightening tensions in the nominally secular federal republic, which is divided between a predominantly Muslim north and a mostly Christian south.

DECEMBER 18

Uche Maduemesi, *The Republican*
IMPRISONED

Maduemesi, publisher of the private weekly *The Republican*, was arrested by police in Enugu, a town in south-central Nigeria. In the paper's latest edition, an article had posed questions about the recent death of Enugu police commissioner Daniel Anyogo, suggesting that Anyogo might have been poisoned.

After a spate of recent apparent assassinations of prominent political and social figures in south and southeastern Nigeria, speculation has been rife that Anyogo's death was related to an investigation he was working on, local sources said.

Maduemesi was detained without charge for more than a week. Sources in Nigeria said he was released shortly before the end of the year, following protests from local human rights and civil-society groups.

RWANDA

JANUARY 26

Laurien Ntezimana, *Ubuntu*
Didace Muremangingo, *Ubuntu*
HARASSED, LEGAL ACTION

Ntezimana, publisher of the newsletter *Ubuntu*, and Muremangingo, editor-in-chief of the publication, were arrested on January 26 and 27, respectively, in the southern province of Butare and transferred to Butare Central Prison. Local judicial authorities said arrest warrants were issued over a matter related to their work but refused to elaborate.

However, CPJ sources said that Ntezimana has reportedly been questioned in the past about using the word *ubuyanja* in several articles. The word, which means "rebirth of strength" in Kinyarwanda, one of the country's official languages, also appears in the name of an outlawed political party founded by former Rwandan president Pasteur Bizimungu. The case was dropped on February 20 due to lack of evidence, and the two were released the following day.

JULY 23

Robert Sebufirira, *Umuseso*
Elly MacDowell Kalisa, *Umuseso*
Emmanuel Munyaneza, *Umuseso*
IMPRISONED, LEGAL ACTION

Sebufirira, Kalisa, and Munyaneza, all journalists with the independent weekly *Umuseso*, were sentenced to 30 days of "preventative detention" by a court in Rwanda's capital, Kigali.

The charges stemmed from a July 17 incident that took place at Bar Addis Ethiopian in the Kiyovu District of Kigali. Sebufirira, Kalisa, and Munyaneza arrived at the establishment after work and found a crowd gathered outside. When they went to investigate, they learned that the proprietor of the bar had called the police to deal with a rowdy patron who then attempted to resist arrest once the police arrived.

The patron identified himself as a member of the military and claimed that civilian police did not have the authority to arrest him. A fistfight ensued between the police and the patron, and some of the bystanders reportedly started shouting at the journalists to take note of the police and the soldier's conduct and make sure to report it in the newspaper.

The military police arrived soon after and promptly arrested the journalists, as well as the patron who had earlier fought the civilian police. The journalists were taken into custody and charged with assault, battery, and insulting a police officer.

Several eyewitnesses indicated that the journalists were not involved in any physical confrontation. Rather, they were simply observers. As Rwanda's only independent, Kinyarwanda-language publication, *Umuseso* has consistently criticized President Paul Kagame's administration and has written extensively about police misconduct.

The three journalists were released on August 7, on the condition that they remain in Kigali and report regularly to the police. However, it is unclear whether the charges against them have been dropped.

SIERRA LEONE

MARCH 11

African Champion
Mohamed D. Koroma, *African Champion*
CENSORED

The private daily newspaper *African Champion*, which is headquartered in the capital, Freetown, was suspended for two months by Sierra Leone's Independent Media Commission (IMC). Koroma, the daily's publisher, was barred from practicing journalism for the same period, but he defied the IMC order and printed the paper the next day. IMC officials took no action.

The IMC had justified the initial ban by arguing in a press release that Koroma and *African Champion* had published defamatory information that harshly criticized President Ahmed Tejah Kabbah's oldest son, who was allegedly involved in several dubious business dealings. The newspaper had also alleged that the president protected his son from police inquiries.

NOVEMBER 12

Paul Kamara, *For Di People*
IMPRISONED

For full details on this case, see page 407.

SOMALIA

MAY 23

Somali Broadcasting Corporation
CENSORED

Authorities in Somalia's self-declared autonomous region of Puntland suspended the broadcasting license of a substation of the privately funded Somali Broadcasting Corporation (SBC). The suspension ordered the SBC station in Puntland's commercial capital, Bosaso, closed and also affected the BBC's Somali-language service, which SBC-Bosaso broadcasts.

Puntland authorities declined to explain the move, but SBC station manager Ali Abdi Aware told foreign reporters that SBC-Bosaso was accused of violating Puntland's press laws, legislation many local reporters said they did not even know existed.

Other sources in Bosaso charged that the SBC was targeted for what the ruling authorities called its bias against Puntland leader, Col. Abdullahi Yusuf. The same sources also told the U.N.-affiliated Integrated Regional Information Networks that SBC-Bosaso was silenced for "supporting the interim government in Mogadishu and Jama Ali Jama [the former Puntland leader]" and having "a political agenda inimical to the Puntland state." Former leader Jama Ali Jama and Colonel Yusuf have been locked in a deadly power struggle since June 2001 over the right to rule the breakaway state of Puntland.

All private radio stations
CENSORED

Civil authorities and clan leaders in the self-declared Republic of Somaliland, which the international community does not recognize, banned the establishment of private radio stations. According to the U.N.-affiliated Integrated Regional Information Networks, Somaliland's Information Ministry justified the move by saying that the region had not yet adopted broadcasting regulations. The ministry also claimed that private radio stations, if allowed to operate in the region, could further destabilize the already shaky breakaway republic. Somaliland officials also demanded that all broadcasting equipment already in the region be surrendered to authorities. The ministry warned that delinquent prospective broadcasters would be prosecuted.

Ahmad Muhammad Kismayo, BBC
Muhammad Khalif Gir, BBC
CENSORED

Kismayo and Khalif Gir, both local correspondents for BBC's Somali service, were banned from reporting for the BBC by the Emergency Committee of Somalia's self-declared autonomous region of Puntland, the U.N.-affiliated Integrated Regional Information Networks (IRIN) reported.

Officials accused the two reporters of not being "objective in their reporting of events in the region" and urged the BBC "to bring in people who are objective and not engaged in political activity." Other sources told IRIN that the BBC reporters had been targeted for their perceived bias against Puntland's new leader, Abdullahi Yusuf, and sympathies for Jama Ali Jama, an ex-leader and Yusuf rival.

Abdirahman Isma'il Umar, *Wartire*
IMPRISONED

Umar, editor of the daily *Wartire*, was sentenced to four months in prison by a court in Hargeysa, the capital of the self-declared Republic of Somaliland, the official Radio Hargeysa reported.

Umar was found guilty of "misreporting" facts and of publishing "fabrications and baseless reports" in an article claiming that Somaliland president Dahir Riyale Kahin had, during a recent visit to Djibouti, signed a secret pact with Djiboutian president Ismael Omar Gelleh. Relations between Somaliland and Djibouti have been tense in the past, with authorities in Somaliland objecting to Djibouti's role in promoting Somalia's transitional government.

TOGO

Radio Victoire
CENSORED

Interior Ministry agents seized the broadcasting equipment of private station Radio Victoire, forcing it off the air. Management had received a letter from authorities two days earlier stating that the station's temporary broadcasting license was being canceled, and that it would have to cease broadcasting.

Togolese sources said that the High Authority for Audio-Visual Communications (HAAC), Togo's official media regulatory body, issues temporary licenses for six months to new stations that wish to begin broadcasting. If, at the end of the six-month period, the station is judged to have complied with Togo's media laws, then it may be issued a permanent broadcast license. Radio Victoire was issued its temporary license in late August 2001 and began broadcasting at that time.

In November 2001, the HAAC ordered Radio Victoire to cease broadcasting two news programs that it considered "controversial" and "defamatory." Sources in Lomé say the station was closed because its popular phone-in programs, during which callers criticized the ruling Rassemblement du Peuple Togolais (RPT) party, angered authorities. Though RPT cadres complained that the station never featured RPT officials, journalists at the station claimed that they frequently invited RPT members to attend but never received any response.

MARCH 25

Lucien Messan, *Le Combat du Peuple*
THREATENED, HARASSED

Messan, editor-in-chief of the private weekly *Le Combat du Peuple*, which is based in the capital, Lomé, received death threats from anonymous callers.

Shortly after *Le Combat du Peuple* ran a series of articles about corruption in the Togolese military in the March 18-22 edition, Messan was summoned to the office of Defense Minister Assani Tidjani. The minister asked Messan to reveal his sources for the stories, but the editor refused.

The March 25-29 edition of *Le Combat du Peuple* reported that Tidjani had asked Messan to reveal his sources. Shortly after that edition appeared, Messan began receiving death threats.

APRIL 4

La Tribune du Peuple
CENSORED

Police seized about 2,000 copies of the independent weekly *La Tribune du Peuple* from newsstands in the capital, Lomé. Interior Minister Sizing Walla, who ordered the seizure, accused *La Tribune du Peuple* of publishing "offensive comments" after the paper reported that two Togolese Armed Forces agents had assaulted a mechanic who was suspected of theft.

The following day, Walla summoned *La Tribune du Peuple* editor Siliadin Kodjo to the ministry. Fearing arrest, Kodjo went into hiding, and Pedro Amuzun, head of the Togolese Media Observatory and editor of the independent weekly *Crocodile*, went in his place.

Amuzun was taken to President Gnassingbé Eyadéma's office, along with the mechanic and the two soldiers named in the story. After Eyadéma questioned Amuzun and the mechanic to verify the report, he allowed them to leave. The two soldiers were subsequently dismissed from the army.

On April 10, police again confiscated copies of *La Tribune du Peuple*. One source in Lomé said the seizure likely resulted from the paper's reporting on the previous week's meeting at President Eyadéma's office.

APRIL 8

Motion d'Information
CENSORED

Police seized most copies of the independent, Lomé-based weekly *Motion d'Information* at the order of Interior Minister Sizing Walla. The order for the paper's seizure did not indicate any specific charge or refer to a particular article. However, Toukoula Amicet, the paper's editor-in-chief, said police told him that the article that prompted the seizure reported that several organizers of Togo's student union—Union Nationale des Etudiants Togolais (UNET)—had fled Togo for Benin in early February after police pursued them for their anti-government activism.

The article also said that the organizers are planning to ask the Office of the U.N. High Commissioner for Refugees to repatriate them to a country that has no extradition treaty with Togo. (The two principal organizers of UNET have been arrested repeatedly since August 2001.) The report went on to condemn President Gnassingbé Eyadéma's policies toward students.

APRIL 9

Le Regard
CENSORED

Police in Lomé, Togo's capital, confiscated nearly the entire print run of the private weekly *Le Regard* from newsstands. Sources said an article in the paper about Prime Minister Agbeyome Kodjo's recent appearance at a conference in Geneva sponsored by the Office of the U.N. High Commissioner for Human Rights prompted the seizure. The article criticized the commission's decision to halt the inquiry into an Amnesty International report alleging that hundreds of opposition supporters were killed following the 1998 presidential elections in Togo.

Fearing arrest, *Le Regard* editor Abass Derman Mikaila went into hiding following the seizure of his paper. Agents who confiscated the print run told Mikaila that he had

no right to comment on the decisions of the commission, said several sources in Lomé.

APRIL 16

Le Regard
Le Combat du Peuple
Motion d'Information
CENSORED

Copies of three private, Lomé-based weeklies—*Le Regard*, *Le Combat du Peuple*, and *Motion d'Information*—were seized from vendors by police on the order of Interior Minister Sizing Walla.

Le Regard was seized on April 16, while *Le Combat du Peuple* and *Motion d'Information* were seized on April 22. The seizures came after the papers reprinted a letter from Dahuku Péré, a member of the Togolese National Assembly for the ruling Rassemblement du Peuple Togolais (RPT) party and former president of the National Assembly, to RPT members. The letter criticized the party's methods and practices and called for reforms.

Though the letter was sent to a number of media outlets, only these three reprinted it, said sources in Lomé. When interviewed by Agence France-Presse, Walla called the newspapers' publication of the letter "a provocation."

JUNE 5

Basile Agboh, *Le Scorpion*
IMPRISONED
Maurice Atchinou, *Le Scorpion*
HARASSED

Agboh and Atchinou, publication director and editor-in-chief, respectively, of the independent weekly *Le Scorpion*, were arrested by police in the capital, Lomé. Their arrests stemmed from a June 3 *Le Scorpion* article alleging that Lt. Col. Ernest Gnassingbé, a son of President Gnassingbé Eyadéma, had issued death threats against Prime Minister Agbeyomé Kodjo.

On June 6, Agboh was charged with "attacking the honor" of Ernest Gnassingbé. As publication director of *Le Scorpion*, Agboh was found solely responsible for the paper's content, and Atchinou was released. Agboh was transferred to Lomé Civilian Prison to await trial.

The newspaper then printed an apology for the story in hopes of spurring Agboh's release, which came on August 16. Though he is currently free, Agboh could be tried at any time if prosecutors decide to pursue the case.

Police investigated other newspapers that had printed the same story, but no other journalists were arrested, most likely because *Le Scorpion* was the only publication to mention the president's son by name.

AUGUST 8

Julien Ayi, *Nouvel Echo*
Alphonse Nevamé Klu, *Nouvel Echo*
IMPRISONED

Ayi, publication director for the independent daily *Nouvel Echo*, was arrested and jailed at police headquarters in the capital, Lomé, on charges of "defamation of the president," and "disturbing public order." Alphonse Nevamé Klu, the paper's editor-in-chief, was likewise charged but went into hiding to avoid arrest.

The charges against the two journalists stemmed from an August 2 *Nouvel Echo* article claiming that President Gnassingbé Eyadéma had amassed a US$4.5 billion fortune, and that he is one of the world's 497 wealthiest people, according to a list published in the American financial magazine *Forbes*. The article also alleged that Faure Gnassingbé, a son of the president and a National Assembly member, had control over

the fortune and that the riches were "ill-gotten," the French news agency Agence France-Presse (AFP) reported.

On August 2, following the article's publication, the government informed the journalists that it was lodging a complaint with police against the newspaper. A government statement, meanwhile, verified that Eyadéma had not appeared on *Forbes*' list of 497 names. On August 3, the state television channel broadcast the *Forbes* list, pointing out that no Africans appeared in the document. When contacted by AFP, Interior Minister Sizing Walla said, "The publication of these lies is a way of inciting the population to rebellion."

Walla also said that when questioned by police before his arrest, Ayi had revealed that Claude Améganvi, a trade unionist and chair of the opposition Workers Party, was the article's source. Authorities arrested Améganvi, who faced the same charges as Ayi, on August 6. Though Améganvi also edits the trade union newspaper *Nyawo*, local journalists said his arrest was most likely not related to his journalistic activities.

On September 13, Ayi and Améganvi were convicted and sentenced to four months in prison and a fine of 100,000 CFA francs (US$150) each. Klu was sentenced in absentia to six months in prison and the same fine.

According to the news Web sites *Diastode.com* and *letogolais.com*, in early December, an appeals court extended Ayi and Améganvi's sentences by two months. *Nouvel Echo* has not appeared since early August.

NOVEMBER 5

Siliadin Kodjo, *La Tribune du Peuple*
HARASSED

Kodjo, managing editor of the independent weekly *La Tribune du Peuple*, a paper close to Togo's opposition, was arrested in the afternoon by a group of plainclothes police officers and taken to the central police station in the capital, Lomé.

Kodjo's arrest stemmed from an article in an early October edition of *La Tribune du Peuple* that denounced the government's suppression of a September 28 demonstration organized by the opposition Union of Forces for Change, which had informed the Interior Ministry of the rally in a September 19 letter.

Kodjo was released later that night, after the Togolese Media Observatory, a local media regulatory body, and other media groups intervened on his behalf. Authorities called him in again the next day but did not press charges. Local sources said that other journalists at *La Tribune du Peuple* began receiving anonymous threatening phone calls after the article ran.

NOVEMBER 18

Motion d'Information
CENSORED

Police seized all copies of the latest edition of the private weekly *Motion d'Information* from the offices of the newspaper's printer. The previous three editions of the paper had also been confiscated on orders from the Interior Ministry.

Authorities gave the paper's staff no explanation for the action, but the seizures followed the appearance of an article in the paper's October 21 issue that criticized Togo's late-October legislative elections, saying that results mattered little since the main opposition parties had boycotted the poll.

Local journalists said that *Motion d'Information*'s director was summoned to the interior minister's offices after the article ran. Fearing arrest, the director did not respond to the summons, and authorities began confiscating the newspaper. When the director finally went to the minister's office

in late November, the seizures stopped. *Motion d'Information* began to appear on newsstands again in late November.

NOVEMBER 20

L'Evénement
CENSORED, THREATENED

Early in the morning, police confiscated all copies of the private weekly *L'Evénement* from distribution centers and kiosks on the orders of Interior Minister Sizing Walla. Though the official seizure order did not specify a reason for the action, *L'Evénement* editor-in-chief Dimas Dzikodo said that the confiscation was linked to an article in that issue by two Ivoirian academics living in the United States that criticized Togolese president Gnassingbé Eyadéma's mediation of peace talks between the government of neighboring Ivory Coast and rebel groups, which have been waging an armed revolt since September. The authors called for more impartial methods of negotiation to resolve the crisis quickly.

Local sources said that the *L'Evénement* staff received several threats following the seizure of the edition carrying the contentious article.

DECEMBER 26

Sylvestre Djahlin Nicoué, *Courrier du Citoyen*
IMPRISONED

For full details on this case, see page 409.

UGANDA

JANUARY 12

Jimmy Higenyi, United Media Consultants and Trainers
KILLED

For full details on this case, see page 366.

James Akena, *New Vision*
Archie Luyimbazi, WBS Television
Andrew Mujema, WBS Television
HARASSED

Akena, of the state-owned daily newspaper *New Vision*, and Luyimbazi and Mujema, both from the television station WBS, were detained while covering a rally organized by the opposition Uganda Peoples' Congress. The government had banned the gathering, but the three were released after a few hours. During the same rally, one journalist, Jimmy Higenyi, was killed when the police violently dispersed the crowd.

JULY 25

Joseph Were, *The Monitor*
David Kibirige, *The Monitor*
Charles Onyango-Obbo, *The Monitor*
HARASSED

Onyango-Obbo, managing editor of the independent daily *The Monitor*; Were, an editor at the paper; and Kibirige, an investigative reporter at the paper, were summoned to appear at the police's Criminal Investigations Division.

On July 16, acting assistant inspector general of police E.N.B. Mbiringi ordered the journalists to be questioned about an April 4 story alleging that the Rwandan government had written a report accusing Uganda of training dissidents to fight the Rwandan government and had given a copy to the British government.

The news story directly contradicted a different report authored by the Rwanda/Uganda Joint Verification and Investigation Committee, a government-appointed body charged with defusing growing tensions between the two countries, both of which have accused the other of training and harboring rebel groups.

Were, Kibirige, and Onyango-Obbo

were interrogated for three hours on July 26 and released after signing statements. An officer informed them that police were continuing to investigate the matter, but the journalists had not been charged by year's end.

SEPTEMBER 16

All journalists
THREATENED

Director of information for Uganda's ruling National Resistance Movement, Ofwono Opondo, warned radio stations against airing interviews with Col. Kizza Besigye and threatened them with prosecution under the Anti-Terrorism Act of 2002, which was signed into law in May. The act, which empowers the Cabinet to designate an organization as terrorist, explicitly categorizes rebel groups as such.

After nearly defeating President Yoweri Museveni in a bitterly disputed poll, Besigye fled the country, saying he feared for his life. From his self-imposed exile in the United States, Besigye became a regular guest on Uganda's popular call-in radio shows, during which he repeatedly accused Museveni's government of graft and vote rigging. During one notable interview with the Voice of Africa on August 17, Besigye threatened to resort to "untraditional" methods if his efforts to get fresh elections through constitutional means fail, prompting Opondo's warning against further interviews.

"Besigye has inadvertently declared war on the Government," Opondo stated, adding that anyone who helps Besigye "spread his propaganda ... comes under suspicion of aiding terrorism, and the Anti-Terrorism Law will apply." Those convicted of violating the act face up to 10 years' imprisonment or death by hanging.

Radio Wa
ATTACKED

Catholic Church–owned Radio Wa, located on the outskirts of the town of Lira in northern Uganda, was attacked by rebels of the Lord's Resistance Army (LRA) in the early morning. According to news reports, the rebels used axes to break into the church complex, which houses the station. They then poured gas on the walls and set the church and radio station ablaze, killing two people.

Radio Wa director Rev. John Fraser, quoted in the state-owned daily *New Vision*, said that because the rebels headed straight for the studio after breaking into the complex, the station was the main target. Fraser also said that the station, which was destroyed in the fire, lost equipment worth about US$70,000.

Shortly before the attack, the station's staff, fearing that the LRA would target their studio, had asked for government protection. Though about a dozen troops were stationed outside the church before the attack, all but one fled when the rebels approached.

A source at the independent daily *Monitor* said that Radio Wa was probably not attacked for its coverage of the LRA, but that the group has voiced anger over how the Ugandan media in general portray them. The LRA has since threatened to hit other radio stations in the nearby town of Lira. The rebels, who are fighting to turn Uganda into a fundamentalist Protestant republic, have been battling the government for the last 16 years.

ZAMBIA

Charles Lwiindi, free-lance
ATTACKED

Lwiindi, a Zambian free-lance journalist, was attacked by opposition members, said sources in the capital, Lusaka. Lwiindi had gone to the home of United Party for National Development (UPND) president Anderson Mazoka to cover a meeting about the nomination of a UPND candidate for the upcoming parliamentary election of a National Assembly speaker. According to the BBC, several people at the meeting objected to Lwiindi's presence there, threw the journalist from the premises, and then assaulted him outside the house.

On April 27, Lwiindi died in a Lusaka hospital. Police arrested three UPND members in December, including party treasurer Tiens Kahenya, and charged them with murder, alleging that Lwiindi had died from injuries sustained during the January assault. Opposition members say the charges are political and aimed at tarnishing the party. Zambian journalists also claim that the charges are dubious since medical reports show that Lwiindi died of an unrelated illness that was suspected to be malaria.

Fred M'membe, *The Post*
LEGAL ACTION

M'membe, editor-in-chief of the independent daily *The Post*, was detained by police for about an hour after he came to Woodlands Police Station in the capital, Lusaka, in response to a summons. When his lawyers intervened, he was released on bond and charged with "defaming the President" under Section 69 of the Penal Code.

The charges stemmed from a January 25 *Post* article that featured a quote from opposition Forum for Democracy and Development member of Parliament Dipak Patel, who called newly elected president Levy Mwanawasa a "cabbage."

On February 27, Zambian director of

public prosecutions Mukelebai Mukelebai ordered the charges against M'membe dropped. Zambian sources speculated that President Mwanawasa asked that the charges be withdrawn since Patel had apologized to him for the remark.

FEBRUARY 14

Jerry Nkwendeenda, Mazabuka Community Radio
HARASSED

Nkwendeenda, a reporter for the independent Mazabuka Community Radio Station, was detained by police for about 30 minutes for allegedly interfering with police business.

At around 7 p.m., Nkwendeenda saw three police officers selling mealie-meal, government-subsidized cornmeal that serves as Zambia's staple food, outside of a shop. The journalist approached a buyer and asked why he was paying the police for food, and why the shop was open when its normal operating hours are 9 a.m. to 5 p.m. The police noticed Nkwendeenda asking questions and immediately grabbed him, took him into the shop, and confiscated his notebook. When Nkwendeenda identified himself as a reporter for the Mazabuka Community Radio Station, the police accused him of reporting "rubbish" and locked him in a small room at the back of the shop.

Earlier that day, Mazabuka Community Radio had carried a report on the sale of mealie-meal during which many callers complained of corruption in its distribution. According to Nkwendeenda, after the broadcast, the station lodged a complaint with the Mazabuka district administrator (DA) about corruption in the local distribution of mealie-meal.

While locked in the shop, Nkwendeenda phoned the DA to explain his situation. When the DA arrived shortly thereafter, two

of the three police officers fled. When the DA demanded to know on what charges Nkwendeenda was being held, the remaining officer told him the journalist had interfered with police business. The DA responded that the shop was not police property, and that the sale of mealie-meal was not official police business. He then demanded the reporter's release.

The police never filed charges against Nkwendeenda. The next day, Mazabuka Community Radio carried another report on corruption in mealie-meal sales, this time implicating the police and mentioning the incident that Nkwendeenda had witnessed.

FEBRUARY 24

Thomas Nsama, The Post
ATTACKED

Nsama, a reporter with The Post, was beaten by a group of supporters from the ruling Movement for Multiparty Democracy (MMD) party while covering an MMD convention at the Mulungushi International Conference Center in the capital, Lusaka.

The MMD supporters were pushing several vehicles, including one from The Post, that were parked in the conference center's driveway to create more room for the arrival of MMD party president and former head of state Frederick Chiluba and his entourage.

When the MMD supporters saw Nsama taking photographs of them lifting the cars, they charged at him. Before the attackers reached him, Nsama gave his camera to a photographer from the state-owned Zambia Daily Mail who ran with it to safety. The assailants then physically assaulted Nsama and left him on the ground.

Nsama said that police stationed nearby witnessed the incident and did not intervene. When the photographer later tried to report the attack at the local police station, police refused to file the complaint, claiming they were "too junior" to handle the case.

MAY 29

Emmanuel Chilekwa, *The People*
Shadreck Banda, *The People*
Kinsley Lweendo, *The People*
Jane Chirwa, *The People*
IMPRISONED, LEGAL ACTION

Chilekwa, managing editor of the independent weekly *The People*, went to police headquarters in response to a police "call-out" he had received the previous day and was informed that he was under investigation for defaming the president, a charge that is punishable by up to three years in prison under Article 69 of the Zambian Penal Code. The accusation stemmed from a *People* article alleging that President Levy Mwanawasa suffers from Parkinson's disease and implying that the illness renders him unfit to rule.

After interrogation, Chilekwa was released. On May 31, however, police detained and interrogated Chilekwa, Banda, assistant editor at *The People*, and Chirwa, a student reporter working for the paper. Zambian sources say Chilekwa and Banda were both physically harassed during their arrests. All three were released later that day.

On June 5, Chilekwa, Banda, Chirwa, and Lweendo, senior reporter for *The People*, were arrested and charged with defaming the president. In a June 7 court hearing, they pleaded not guilty, and Judge Frank Tembo postponed ruling on whether to grant the journalists bail. According to the Media Institute of Southern Africa, on June 17, Judge Tembo denied the journalists bail, arguing that cases of "defamation of the president" had recently increased. Journalists said the ruling confirmed their suspicion of political involvement in the case, because defamation is a bailable offense, and prosecu-

tors had not objected to bail being granted.

On June 27, a High Court judge granted the journalists bail. The four were freed later that day. On July 30, the charges against the journalists were dropped after they apologized to Mwanawasa. They admitted that they had not confirmed the story and said that the source of the article was a close associate of former president Frederick Chiluba. Mwanawasa has pushed for tough investigations into corruption allegations against Chiluba's administration.

JUNE 6

The Post
The People
Today
CENSORED

Youth members of the ruling Movement for Multiparty Democracy (MMD) confiscated copies of the independent daily *The Post* and the independent weeklies *The People* and *Today* from vendors in the capital, Lusaka. The youths then beat the vendors.

The MMD cadres accused the newspapers of carrying stories that criticized President Levy Mwanawasa. On June 4, members of the group issued a warning to journalists, vendors, and media owners to stop selling newspapers that had allegedly defamed Mwanawasa, Agence France-Presse reported.

Zambian journalists said that criticism of Mwanawasa had intensified in previous weeks. Internal divisions within the MMD led some party members, representing an anti-Mwanawasa faction, to buy advertisements in the independent daily *The Post* questioning Mwanawasa's mental state and his ability to lead. Four journalists from *The People* were arrested on June 5 and charged with defaming the president after they published an article alleging that Mwanawasa has Parkinson's disease.

ZIMBABWE

FEBRUARY 11

Daily News
ATTACKED

At about 3 a.m., two gasoline bombs were thrown from a moving vehicle at the Bulawayo bureau of the independent *Daily News*. No one was hurt in the explosion, and the office suffered only minor damage. A nearby building housing the Daily Press, a private printing business unrelated to the *Daily News*, was also bombed.

The attack followed a February 7 incident in which unidentified assailants plastered campaign posters for President Robert Mugabe's ZANU-PF party on the bureau's windows and outer walls. The individuals threatened to burn down the building if the posters were removed.

When *Daily News* editors called ZANU-PF headquarters to complain about the posters, party officials denied any involvement, claiming that some posters had been stolen from their offices.

FEBRUARY 25

Edwina Spicer, South African Broadcasting Corporation
Jackie Cahi, South African Broadcasting Corporation
HARASSED

Spicer, co-owner of the documentary and film production house Spicer Productions, and Cahi, a journalist at Spicer Productions, were arrested by police while working on a film for the South African Broadcasting Corporation. The two journalists were filming opposition Movement for Democratic Change leader Morgan Tsvangirai as he turned himself in to police to answer charges that he had plotted to assassinate President Robert Mugabe.

After filming Tsvangirai, the journalists headed back to their studio. On the way, police officers flagged them down and told them they had broken the law by filming in a restricted area—specifically by taping Tsvangirai's convoy as it passed Mugabe's official residence, the State House. Police took Spicer to Harare Central Police Station, and Cahi was told to follow in her car.

The two were detained and charged under the Protected Areas Act with "failing to comply with the direction as to movement or conduct in a protected area." The charges were dismissed the next day, and Spicer and Cahi were released.

FEBRUARY 28

The Associated Press
Sunday Times
Mail & Guardian
The Independent Newspapers Group
David Blair, *Daily Telegraph*
John Murphy, *The Baltimore Sun*
Sally Sara, Australian Broadcasting Service
Gorrel Espelund, *Sydsvenska Dagbladet*
CENSORED

Espelund, a reporter with the Swedish newspaper *Sydsvenska Dagbladet*; Sara, a journalist with the Australian Broadcasting Service; Murphy, with the U.S.-based *Baltimore Sun*; Blair, a journalist with the United Kingdom–based *Daily Telegraph*; other U.K.-based journalists and news organizations; and journalists from The Associated Press, South Africa's *Sunday Times*, *Mail & Guardian*, and the Independent Newspapers Group were barred from covering the March 9 and 10 presidential elections.

According to a February 26 report in the state-owned *The Herald*, at least 131 foreign journalists applied for accreditation to report on the poll, but only 72 were allowed to do so. *The Herald* asserted, "Accreditation has been restricted to those organizations considered not to have taken a biased position on land reform."

MARCH 25

Geoff Nyarota, *Daily News*
THREATENED, LEGAL ACTION

Zimbabwean information minister Jonathan Moyo threatened to prosecute Geoff Nyarota, editor-in-chief of the independent *Daily News*. In a letter to Nyarota, Moyo described a March 22 *Daily News* article as patently false. The article alleged that the African Caribbean Pacific–European Union (ACP-EU) Joint Parliamentary Assembly had adopted a resolution calling for fresh presidential elections in Zimbabwe.

A spokesperson for the ACP-EU confirmed the newspaper's report, but Moyo denied that any such resolution was passed and demanded that the paper print a retraction. Nyarota refused. He faces a fine of up to 100,000 Zimbabwean dollars (US$1,875) or up to two years in jail if found guilty. His case remained pending at year's end.

MARCH 27

Peta Thornycroft, *Daily Telegraph, Mail & Guardian*
IMPRISONED

Thornycroft, the Zimbabwe correspondent for South Africa's *Mail & Guardian* and Britain's *Daily Telegraph*, was arrested in the rural town of Chimanimani, 300 miles (480 kilometers) southeast of the capital, Harare. The journalist was investigating reports that supporters of the ruling ZANU-PF party were attacking members of the political opposition.

She was interrogated for five hours then accused of violating the Public Order and Security Act, which makes it an offense to

"publish or communicate false statements prejudicial to the state." The law specifically criminalizes statements that "incite or promote public disorder or public violence." Thornycroft faced five years in prison or a 100,000 Zimbabwean dollar fine (US$1,875) if charged and convicted. On March 31, Zimbabwean authorities, bowing to local and international criticism, released her without charge.

APRIL 15

Geoff Nyarota, *Daily News*
HARASSED

Nyarota, editor of the independent *Daily News* and the recipient of a 2001 CPJ International Press Freedom Award, was arrested and charged with abusing "journalistic privilege" and publishing false information under the Access to Information and Protection of Privacy Act.

The section of the act under which he was charged, 80(1)(a), stipulates that "a journalist shall be deemed to have abused his journalistic privilege and committed an offense if he falsifies or fabricates information and publishes falsehoods." Violators may be fined up to 100,000 Zimbabwean dollars (US$1,820) or jailed for up to two years.

The charges against Nyarota stem from an April 10 *Daily News* article about alleged vote rigging during the March presidential election. The newspaper reported Registrar General Tobaiwa Mudede's claim, made during a live radio and television broadcast by the Zimbabwe Broadcasting Corporation (ZBC), that election officials had collected 2.2 million valid votes—700,000 votes fewer than the number subsequently published by the state media.

In the article, the *Daily News* claimed to have a tape of the ZBC broadcast, but police did not ask Nyarota for that crucial evidence. The journalist was released after three hours. According to his lawyer, he may be summoned to face the charge in court at a later date but had not been called by year's end.

Dumisani Muleya, *Zimbabwe Independent*
Iden Wetherell, *Zimbabwe Independent*
LEGAL ACTION

Muleya, chief reporter for the independent business weekly *Zimbabwe Independent*, was arrested by the Criminal Investigations Department (CID) and charged with criminal defamation.

The charges stemmed form an April 12 article in which Muleya reported that the brother of first lady Grace Mugabe had asked her to intervene on his behalf in a business dispute. The story also quoted Lawrence Kamwi, Mugabe's spokesperson, as saying that the first lady recommended that her brother take up the matter with the relevant ministry.

Muleya was released the same day after police issued him a "warned and cautioned" statement. He was ordered to report to the Harare Central Police Station for fingerprinting on the morning of April 16.

On April 17, *Zimbabwe Independent* editor Iden Wetherell was arrested, also in connection with the story. He was released the next day. Although both journalists were released without charge, the police said they would "proceed by way of summons," meaning that the journalists can be summoned and charged at any time.

APRIL 30

Andrew Meldrum, *The Guardian*
Lloyd Mudiwa, *Daily News*
Collin Chiwanza, *Daily News*
IMPRISONED

Geoff Nyarota, *Daily News*
HARASSED

Mudiwa and Chiwanza, both staff writers at the privately owned *Daily News*, were arrested by Central Intelligence Division officers at their Harare office in the early morning. Meldrum, a U.S. citizen and permanent resident of Zimbabwe who covers the region for the London-based *The Guardian*, was taken into custody at his Harare home at around 5:40 a.m. on May 1.

All three reporters faced charges of "abusing journalistic privileges" and "publishing false information" in connection with an April 23 story, later discovered to be inaccurate, stating that youths from the ruling ZANU-PF party had beheaded an opposition supporter. The journalists faced up to two years in prison and fines of 100,000 Zimbabwean dollars (US$1,820).

The opposition Movement for Democratic Change (MDC), which provided the information to the journalists, initially claimed that a pro-government youth militia had decapitated Brandina Tadyanemhandu in Mashonaland West Province. The MDC also alleged that the militiamen had forced the victim's two daughters to watch the execution.

On April 30, after fact-checking determined that the story was inaccurate, the *Daily News* published a front-page retraction of the story. The paper also ran an MDC statement accusing the alleged victim's husband of fabricating the story in order to extort money from the party. (According to several Zimbabwe analysts, the MDC often makes small financial contributions to victims of political violence.)

Before the *Daily News* retraction was published, Meldrum filed the information in the article to *The Guardian*, which ran it as a front-page story on April 30. *The*

Guardian has since issued a statement acknowledging that the story was inaccurate.

On May 20, *Daily News* editor Nyarota was interrogated for several hours in connection with the same story before being released.

All three reporters were freed on May 2. Meldrum was acquitted on July 15 but was ordered to leave the country within 24 hours. He immediately filed an appeal against his deportation, which was heard on July 17. At the hearing, Justice Anele Matika suspended the deportation order and referred the matter to the Supreme Court. No date has been set for the hearing, and Meldrum is allowed to remain and work in Zimbabwe until the Supreme Court rules on his case. Charges against Chiwanza were dropped on May 7. Nyarota and Mudiwa appeared in court on October 28, and their case was postponed again until February 27, 2003.

MAY 6

Pius Wakatama, *Daily News*
LEGAL ACTION

Police arrested Wakatama, a reporter for the independent *Daily News*, at his home in the outskirts of the capital, Harare. Wakatama was charged on two counts of publishing false information and abusing journalistic privilege under the Access to Information and Protection of Privacy Act.

The charges stemmed from an article Wakatama wrote for the May 4 edition of the *Daily News* that expressed distress over the eviction of a white farming family from their property. The family had strongly opposed white minority rule under the former Rhodesian government and had supported the liberation movement. Zimbabwean officials denied that the farm was occupied.

Local sources say that Wakatama was also

charged because in the article he referred to a story about the beheading of an opposition Movement for Democratic Change supporter, which later proved to be false. Wakatama was issued a "warned and cautioned" statement before being released. He was the eighth journalist to be arrested under the Access to Information and Protection of Privacy Act since it was passed in March.

MAY 7

Assel Gwekwerere, *Daily News*
Aaron Ufumeli, *Daily News*
HARASSED

Gwekwerere, a reporter for the independent *Daily News*, and Ufumeli, a photographer for the paper, were briefly detained by the Criminal Investigations Department (CID) in the capital, Harare, after they tried to photograph the arrest of a man suspected of being involved in a multimillion dollar scandal.

Gwekwerere and Ufumeli were arrested outside a hotel, where they were waiting to take a photograph of the suspected criminal, for whom the police had set a trap. The two said the police, who thought the journalists were with the suspect, handcuffed them and drove them to Highlands Police Station for questioning. Ufumeli told CPJ that during the detention, the CID asked him to destroy the pictures he had taken. The journalists were released later that day without charge.

MAY 16

Bornwell Chakaodza, *The Standard*
Farai Mutsaka, *The Standard*
Fungayi Kanyuchi, *The Standard*
LEGAL ACTION

Chakaodza, editor of the independent Sunday weekly *The Standard*; entertainment editor Kanyuchi; and journalist Mutsaka, were arrested by officers from the Criminal Investigations Department for allegedly writing "falsehoods" about the military and the Zimbabwe Republic Police (ZRP).

In a May 12 article, Kanyuchi wrote that ZRP officers were extorting sex from arrested commercial sex workers as a condition of release from police custody. The story quoted Sergeant Mhondoro of Avondale Police Station as denying the allegations.

In the same edition of the weekly, Mutsaka had written a front-page story stating that the Zimbabwean government had acquired an assortment of anti-riot gear and military hardware from Israel. The story included a photograph of one of the riot vehicles the police had allegedly received. The reporter had contacted Home Affairs Minister John Nkomo, who refused to comment.

The three journalists were charged under the Access to Information and Protection of Privacy Act, which prescribes a fine of up to 100,000 Zimbabwean dollars (US$1,870) or a two-year jail sentence. On May 16, the journalists signed "warned and cautioned" statements and spent the night in police custody. They were released the following day. On December 5, the government dropped the charges against the three journalists.

MAY 28

Bornwell Chakaodza, *The Standard*
Fungayi Kanyuchi, *The Standard*
LEGAL ACTION

Chakaodza, editor of *The Standard*, and Kanyuchi, the paper's entertainment editor, were charged with violating the Access to Information and Protection of Privacy Act. The charges stem from a May 26 article by

Kanyuchi recounting his and Chakaodza's experiences in police cells, where they had been held overnight on May 16.

Police said that the journalist's description of the "blood-stained walls" in the cells was untrue and charged both Kanyuchi and Chakaodza with "publishing falsehoods." They both signed "warned and cautioned" statements and at year's end were awaiting a summons to appear in court.

MAY 30

Iden Wetherell, *Zimbabwe Independent*
LEGAL ACTION

Wetherell, deputy editor of the weekly *Zimbabwe Independent*, was arrested and questioned about a wire service photo published in the newspaper's May 17 issue of semi-naked Amazonian men wearing traditional clothes and playing soccer. Wetherell was subsequently charged under the censorship act for publishing pictures containing nudity.

According to Wetherell's lawyer, the charges were brought against the editor following a complaint from a deputy police commissioner in charge of personnel. However, such charges cannot proceed without the written consent of the Attorney General's Office, which had not consented at year's end. This is the second time Wetherell has been charged with violating the colonial-era censorship act. In March 2000, together with the Trevor Ncube, the publisher of the weekly, Wetherell was charged but never prosecuted.

JULY 4

Chris Gande, *Daily News*
LEGAL ACTION

Gande, Bulawayo-based correspondent for the independent *Daily News*, was arrested and charged under the Access to Information and Protection of Privacy Act for allegedly writing a false story. The June 29 article alleged that the government had not invited the family of late vice president Joshua Nkomo to attend a commemoration gala held in his memory.

Detectives from the Law and Order Section of the Criminal Investigations Department summoned Gande, who then signed a "warn and cautioned" statement. Gande said he stood by his story, saying that Nkomo's daughter, Thandi, had given him the information. She later recanted her story.

AUGUST 28

Voice of the People
ATTACKED

The offices of the private news production company Voice of the People (VOP), located in a suburb of the capital, Harare, were bombed.

According to several Zimbabwean and international reports, three men approached the VOP security guard outside the company headquarters at about 1 a.m. and told him not to struggle, warning him that "you don't want to die for something you know nothing about."

Two of the men then smashed the office's windows and threw what appeared to be bombs inside the building. Soon after, an explosion occurred and the entire building was demolished. Although no one was hurt, all of the company's equipment was destroyed.

VOP, which was founded by former employees of the state-owned Zimbabwe Broadcasting Corporation, is an independent production company that produces programs on community and political issues. To bypass Zimbabwe's tight media controls, the company sends their programs to a Radio Netherlands shortwave transmitter located in Madagascar, which broadcasts them across southern Africa. VOP was created during the run-up to the 1990 elections to counteract the state's monopoly of the press.

VOP's independent stance and large audience have angered the Zimbabwean government, which has accused the studio of "tarnishing" the country's image. In July, members of the Zimbabwean Police Force, accompanied by officers of the Broadcasting Authority of Zimbabwe, raided VOP's offices. They searched for a transmitter, broadcasting equipment, and other evidence that VOP was violating the Broadcasting Services Act of 2001, which bars stations from broadcasting without a license. The police did not find a transmitter but confiscated 133 tapes and files from the office, which they later returned.

The explosion is the fourth such attack on the independent media during the last two years. Since 2001, the *Daily News*, Zimbabwe's only independent daily newspaper, has been bombed three times. ■

OVERVIEW: THE AMERICAS

by Carlos Lauría

ECONOMIC AND POLITICAL TURMOIL THROUGHOUT LATIN AMERICA IN 2002 had profound implications for the region's press. Sharp decreases in advertising revenue bankrupted many media outlets, while the failure to consolidate democratic reforms left the media vulnerable to legal and physical assault. Five journalists were killed in Latin America in 2002 for their work.

The growing weakness of traditional political parties created another kind of danger for the media: In Venezuela, the press abandoned any show of neutrality and became a full-fledged political opposition. President Hugo Chávez Frías responded by increasing his already charged rhetoric against the media. In some cases, both Chávez supporters and opponents targeted reporters, photographers, and cameramen. During the April 11 coup, Jorge Ibraín Tortoza Cruz, a photographer for the daily 2001, was shot while covering violent clashes between opposition demonstrators and government supporters in the capital, Caracas. He later died from his wounds. In May, CPJ Americas program research associate Sauro González Rodríguez traveled to Caracas to investigate the situation and published a special report, titled "Cannon Fodder."

Three journalists were killed in Colombia, where leftist guerrillas and right-wing paramilitary forces routinely target the press. CPJ is still investigating the slayings of five other Colombian journalists whose deaths may have been related to their work. The government's failure to prosecute these crimes has led many journalists to leave the country, perpetuating a climate of impunity in which journalists are targeted with threats, intimidation, kidnapping, and murder.

After winning May presidential elections on a platform of security, anti-corruption, and zero tolerance for violence, Álvaro Uribe Vélez took office in August. Human rights and press freedom groups warned that his hard-line stance could create further abuses and predicted that the conflict would likely escalate. After investigative journalist Ignacio Gómez aired a story on a popular television news show linking Uribe to drug traffickers, the president argued "a free press is one thing, and a press at the service of straw men and shady deals is another thing."

Haitian journalists also continue to confront considerable danger, and several reporters went into exile. On December 25, two gunmen attacked the house of Michèle Montas, the news director of Radio Haïti-Inter, killing a security guard. Montas is the widow of Jean Léopold Dominique, a prominent journalist and radio station owner who was killed on April 3, 2000. Montas has harshly criticized the slow progress of the investigation into her husband's killing.

Carlos Lauría is CPJ's program coordinator for the Americas. CPJ's Americas program research associate, **Sauro González Rodríguez**, did extensive research and writing for this section. CPJ's deputy director, **Joel Simon**, Bogotá-based free-lance journalist **Michael Easterbrook**, and **Trenton Daniel**, a spring 2003 Pew International Journalism Fellow, also contributed to this section. **The Robert R. McCormick Tribune Foundation** provided substantial support for CPJ's work in the Americas in 2002. **The Tinker Foundation** is supporting CPJ's campaign to eliminate criminal defamation laws in the region.

In North America, the increasingly aggressive measures taken by the U.S. government to shield its activities from public scrutiny, including efforts to curtail the press's ability to obtain documents under the Freedom of Information Act, set a poor example for the rest of the hemisphere at a time when journalists in Latin America have made headway in their battle for greater government openness. In an important victory in June, Mexican president Vicente Fox signed the country's first freedom of information act, the Federal Law of Transparency and Access to Public Government Information.

Elsewhere, economic collapse fueled growing social crises. Argentina, South America's most enthusiastic convert to U.S.-supported free market policies, suffered currency devaluation, political turmoil, and riots in 2002. The collapse of Latin America's third-largest economy brought people to the streets to protest government actions, fomenting attacks against journalists who covered the demonstrations and exposed corruption among politicians and businessmen. All these factors have fostered a climate of fear in the run-up to the 2003 presidential elections.

While most of the political parties in the region are suffering from a loss of popular support, Brazil's democracy has matured, and its institutions have been fortified by the victory of Luiz Inácio Lula da Silva in the October presidential elections. But while journalists work in an atmosphere relatively free of government persecution, drug traffickers continue to threaten the press. The brutal murder of Tim Lopes, an award-winning investigative reporter with TV Globo, highlighted the serious risks that journalists face when covering organized crime.

The last decade of democratization in Latin America has not always fostered the legislative and judicial reforms necessary to institutionalize freedom of expression across the region. Many countries have colonial-era provisions known as *desacato* (disrespect) laws that penalize statements insulting the honor and dignity of public officials. Criminal defamation laws remain on the books in most countries despite a 2000 declaration by the Inter-American Commission on Human Rights (IACHR) that "[t]he protection of a person's reputation should only be guaranteed through civil sanctions in those cases in which the person offended is a public official...." This Washington, D.C.–based commission, which is the human rights monitoring body of the Organization of American States, has been an essential forum for defending freedom of expression in the Americas. In March, Argentine lawyer Eduardo A. Bertoni replaced Santiago A. Canton, who became IACHR executive director, as the commission's special rapporteur for freedom of expression.

While criminal defamation prosecutions are common throughout the region, Panama has perhaps Latin America's most pernicious legal environment for the press. Almost half of Panamanian journalists face criminal libel charges, the majority of them filed by public officials angered by the media's exposure of political corruption.

The excessive concentration of media ownership in a few powerful conglomerates also threatens press freedom and undermines pluralism. Assisted by liberalized and privatized markets, a handful of Latin American media groups—frequently tied to ruling political parties—have built prosperous multimedia empires, concentrating private interests at the expense of wider political and social goals. The lack of anti-monopoly legislation has made many journalists and press freedom groups pessimistic about the future. News coverage is often based on the ideological and economic views of media owners who see their outlets as a means to obtain political power. At the same time, the use of government advertising to reward or punish media outlets seriously affects independent journalism, thus damaging freedom of expression. ■

ARGENTINA

DESPITE A CATASTROPHIC ECONOMIC CRISIS IN ARGENTINA DURING 2002—including the default of US$141 billion in foreign debt, a sharp currency devaluation, and the banking system's collapse—the media remain free to report on matters of national importance.

Argentines, 50 percent of whom live below the poverty line, repeatedly filled the streets to protest the government's inability to cope with the failing economy. Media outlets have been hit hard as well. A free fall in both advertising revenue and circulation caused many small and medium-size publications to fold and also brought financial turmoil to some of the country's biggest publishing houses and radio and television stations.

According to Lauro Laiño, president of the publisher's association Asociación de Entidades Periodísticas Argentinas (Association of Argentine Journalistic Entities), the print media face an extremely difficult period because of increasing taxes and the higher costs of imported supplies brought on by the currency devaluation. He fears that the economic situation will eventually hurt the media's ability to cover news freely. "The freedom of the press cannot be guaranteed without freedom to print publications," he told CPJ.

Meanwhile, Editorial Perfil, Argentina's largest magazine publisher, filed for bankruptcy in December 2001 and at the same time petitioned a judge to annul the Argentine journalists' statute, which makes it difficult for companies to fire media professionals and requires employers to pay substantial compensation packages in cases of unfair dismissal. A judge ruled in the company's favor, and workers, fearing layoffs, called a strike, which ended 23 days later, after the Labor Department helped negotiate an agreement.

In a country pervaded with hopelessness and a complete lack of trust in democratic institutions, the press continues to play a vital role in uncovering corruption, denouncing police repression, and publicizing the stories of the country's most impoverished citizens. In September, María Mercedes Vázquez, a reporter for LT 7 Radio Corrientes, released transcripts of phone taps she had obtained revealing that several public officials may have been involved in a conspiracy to oust the governor of the northeastern Corrientes Province. Because of her reporting, on October 6, unidentified assailants threw a bomb at her house, but no one was injured. Previously, Vázquez received death threats and was beaten for her coverage of a political activist who was accused of looting businesses. The journalist has been under police protection since February.

CPJ documented an increasing number of attacks against journalists in 2002. At a rally for former president Carlos Saúl Menem on November 19, Menem supporters kicked and punched three journalists from the Buenos Aires TV station Canal 13. On November 23, a legislator from the southern province of Tierra del Fuego threatened and tried to attack a radio journalist after he criticized the lawmaker's work.

A bill to repeal Argentina's criminal defamation laws, which was developed by the press freedom organization PERIODISTAS, stalled in 2002 because Congress focused

THE AMERICAS |

most of its time on investigating the country's judiciary, which lawmakers have accused of rampant corruption. Taking advantage of the situation, politicians filed several criminal suits against reporters and columnists who have investigated corruption cases.

In mid-October, the Inter-American Commission on Human Rights (IACHR) agreed to review the case against the newsmagazine *NOTICIAS*, which the Supreme Court convicted on September 25, 2001, of violating former president Menem's right to privacy by reporting on his extramarital relationship with a former schoolteacher. The IACHR was still studying the case at year's end.

Another bill currently before Congress would add three articles to the Penal Code criminalizing the operation of small, community radio stations without broadcasting licenses. Many of these stations have been awaiting licenses for years, but the government has not responded to their requests. Some have remained on the air anyway. Politicians have at times used the stations during political campaigns, and many broadcasters receive or have received government advertising. If passed, the law could expose hundreds of broadcasters nationwide to prison sentences.

On December 17, Ernestina Herrera de Noble, owner of Grupo Clarín—one of South America's largest media conglomerates—was arrested for allegedly adopting two children illegally. The charges came during an ongoing investigation into adoption irregularities during Argentina's so-called Dirty War of the 1970s and 1980s, which killed more than 30,000 people. Some sources suspect that the arrest may have come in retaliation for Clarín's coverage of a scandal involving former president Menem, who was held under house arrest for five months for illegally selling arms to Croatia and Ecuador during his administration. Clarín called Herrera de Noble's detention "abusive, illegal, and politically motivated." CPJ continues to monitor the case.

On December 23, a former local police chief, Alberto Gómez, was sentenced to life in prison for organizing the kidnapping and murder of journalist José Luis Cabezas. Cabezas, a photographer for *NOTICIAS*, was found murdered on January 25, 1997, in the city of Pinamar, Buenos Aires Province, after having photographed a reclusive business tycoon thought to be the head of Argentina's mafia.

BOLIVIA

MILLIONAIRE MINING EXECUTIVE GONZALO SÁNCHEZ DE LOZADA was sworn in as president on August 6 and immediately announced emergency actions aimed at lifting South America's poorest nation out of an economic slump. But despite a four-year recession and widespread protests during 2002, the Bolivian press was able to cover the news with no major obstacles.

In February, police attacked several journalists in the central Bolivian city of Cochabamba during demonstrations by coca growers, who have been protesting for nearly two years a U.S.-backed eradication program that has destroyed most of Bolivia's crop. No one was seriously injured. But in a country where more that 60 percent of the population is indigenous, growing inequality and endemic corruption have caused increasing social instability. As a result, coca farmers in Chapare, the country's main coca-producing region, have verbally threatened and harassed some reporters because the farmers feel that journalists do not represent coca producers' interests in the mainstream press.

Meanwhile, roughly three-fifths of the Bolivian population is illiterate, according to the World Bank. That and high poverty are the prime reasons for print media's low circulation. But local journalists also worry that some businessmen and politicians exploit media outlets for their own interests, and that media ownership concentration is becoming a significant problem in Bolivia. For instance, Raúl Garafulic Gutiérrez, president of the multimedia group Illimani Comunicaciones, owns four newspapers—*La Razón*, *Extra*, *Opinión*, and *El Nuevo Día*—the ATB television network, and the Internet portal *Bolivia.com*. Garafulic is also the main shareholder in two telecommunications companies and is the president of a pension fund (AFP Previsión). Independent reporters have criticized Garafulic for buying 50 percent of the state-owned aviation company, Lloyd Aéreo Boliviano, in a secret sale, claiming that he used his media power to influence the purchase by giving it favorable coverage in *La Razón*.

By law, journalists in Bolivia must have a university degree and be registered with the National Registry of Journalists. But enforcement is far from strict, and numerous journalists work in the press without a degree. In Bolivia's largely privately owned media, most owners have personal ties to the business community, so journalists sometimes find it difficult to cover corporate malfeasance.

Government agencies are not required to release information to the public, and reporters often have trouble accessing certain information, such as budgets and public officials' travel expenses. During 2002, CPJ documented no prosecutions against journalists based on their reporting, but the Bolivian Penal Code provides strict sanctions for criminal defamation, including up to two years in prison.

BRAZIL

WORKERS PARTY (PT) CANDIDATE AND FORMER LABOR LEADER Luiz Inácio da Silva, known as Lula, won presidential elections in October, defeating the ruling coalition's candidate by a wide margin and becoming Brazil's first president not to come from the country's political and economic elite. In previous elections, the country's leading newspapers and television networks opposed Lula and his party. However, in the weeks leading up to the transfer of power, scheduled for January 2003, the press gave him and the PT more favorable coverage, prompting some commentators to speculate that ailing media companies want to improve relations with Lula to enlist his support for a possible financial bailout.

The June murder of Brazilian reporter Tim Lopes rocked the nation and illustrated the dangers that journalists in the country face when covering organized crime. Lopes, an award-winning investigative reporter with TV Globo, was brutally murdered by drug traffickers while working on assignment in one of Rio de Janeiro's favelas, or shantytowns.

CPJ continues to follow developments in the case of a second murdered journalist, Domingos Sávio Brandão Lima Júnior, the owner, publisher, and a columnist of the daily *Folha do Estado*. He was killed by hired gunmen in September.

While the Brazilian media work relatively free from government intervention, several judicial decisions have restricted the press's ability to disseminate news considered to be of public interest. Civil and criminal defamation lawsuits against journalists and media outlets have increased during the last several years, according to the publishers' group Associação

Nacional de Jornais (National Association of Newspapers). Too often, businessmen, politicians, and public officials pile up lawsuits against journalists to pressure them, strain their resources, and force them to halt their criticisms. Frequently, plaintiffs seek ridiculously high amounts of money as reparation for having suffered "moral damage." And judges more frequently admit such lawsuits in court and rule against journalists and media outlets.

For instance, in late October, Luís Nassif, a journalist with the daily *Folha de S. Paulo*, was convicted of defaming a construction company. The case stemmed from a September 2000 article in which Nassif reported on a high-court ruling against the company, which had sued a government-owned utility for damages. Bypassing the question of whether the journalist had intended to defame the company, the judge sentenced Nassif to three months in prison and ordered him to pay a fine worth 10 minimum salaries. The judge later commuted the sentence to community service work. At year's end, Nassif said he would appeal the sentence.

Members of the judiciary continued to interfere with the media by allowing prior censorship under the guise of protecting privacy and honor. Throughout 2002, judges granted injunctions banning the press from publishing any information about lawsuits involving politicians and public officials. In a decision that caused a widespread uproar, a judge ordered that copies of the October 24 edition of the Brasilia-based daily *Correio Braziliense* be searched and confiscated if the issue contained excerpts from conversations that were legally recorded by the police that the paper had obtained. These conversations allegedly implicated federal district governor Joaquim Roriz in acts of corruption. In addition, the judge ordered that a court official, accompanied by Roriz's lawyer, visit the paper's offices and monitor the editing process of the October 24 issue to ensure that no news about the tapes was published.

In December, the Senate's Justice and Constitution Committee passed a bill, known by its critics as the "gag law," to prohibit judicial and law enforcement officials from giving information to the press that could damage the reputation, honor, or privacy of any person under investigation. Violators face dismissal, hefty fines, up to two years' imprisonment, and a ban on holding a public job for three years. While the government insists that the bill seeks to prevent the premature disclosure of unsubstantiated allegations, many journalists fear the measure will inhibit press investigations of corruption, arguing that a person's reputation is already well protected under Brazilian law. The full Senate has not yet approved the bill.

CHILE

The administration of President Ricardo Lagos continued its efforts, begun in 2001, to repeal Chile's harsh criminal statutes for press offenses. In September, the government introduced a bill to amend several articles of the Penal Code and the Code of Military Justice that impose criminal penalties for "insulting the honor or dignity" of government authorities, members of Congress, senior judges, and members of the armed forces. Congress was still considering the legislation at the end of 2002.

Intense international pressure has pushed Chile to repeal these anachronistic "disrespect" statutes, which date from the colonial era, and bring its laws in line with international standards for freedom of expression. Some Chilean officials and legislators now say they are ready to renounce their special immunity from criticism provided under such statutes. "I am totally convinced that in a democracy, it is incumbent on us to accept criticism," said congressional deputy Víctor Barrueto. "We should leave behind legislation belonging to authoritarian countries."

However, because such laws are still on the books, Chilean journalists remain vulnerable. In January, TV commentator Eduardo Yáñez was charged with insulting the Supreme Court after he called Chile's justice system "immoral, cowardly and corrupt" during a panel debate on Chilevisión's talk show "El Termómetro." Yáñez was convicted on January 15 and appealed the decision to a superior court, which upheld the ruling in October. While he is currently free on bail, the journalist cannot leave the country without government permission. If sentenced, Yáñez faces up to five years in prison and a fine, according to Article 263 of Chile's Penal Code. He was awaiting sentencing at year's end.

A number of other restrictive statutes remain in effect. Chilean law allows the government to determine who is and isn't a journalist. And while legislation guarantees the right to protect sources, it restricts that right to "recognized" journalists, journalism students doing an internship, recent journalism graduates from accredited universities, publishers, editors, and foreign correspondents. The law also specifies that one must have a journalism degree to work as a spokesperson or journalist for state institutions.

However, some positive developments occurred on the legal front. In October, Congress passed legislation weakening the powers of the Film Classification Council to impose prior censorship on cinema. The bill restricts the council's authority to certify films for age group suitability and also eliminates police and military representation on the council. Previously banned films have now been authorized for public viewing.

On September 12, a group of 50 leading journalists founded the press freedom organization Periodistas por la Libertad de Expresión (Journalists for the Freedom of Expression) to defend their colleagues and to alert Chilean officials and the international community of any attacks against the media. The association follows a recent trend in Latin America— begun in the mid-1990s in Argentina, Colombia, and Peru—of journalists uniting to promote press freedom.

Alejandra Matus, a well-known investigative journalist and spokesperson for the group, told CPJ that members hope "to develop an information network that detects any attempt to censor or attack freedom of the press and denounce it publicly." Matus herself was a victim of one of Chile's most notorious defamation suits in 1999, when her muckraking exposé of the judiciary, *The Black Book of Chilean Justice*, was banned under the infamous State Security Law of 1958 and a judge issued a warrant for her arrest.

Matus secured political asylum in the United States in 1999 but returned to Chile in November 2001, after certain provisions of the law used to charge her were repealed and her book was allowed to circulate freely. She appealed her case to the Inter-American Commission on Human Rights, where it remains pending. The commission has the authority to order the Chilean government to award Matus damages.

During 2002, accessing government information remained problematic. In June, after the media harshly criticized President Lagos during a visit to a storm-ravaged region of the country, the government decided that, on future trips, only two media outlets, chosen by

THE AMERICAS

Lagos himself, would be allowed to accompany him. Following widespread criticism, however, the order was overturned. A similar situation involving the Chamber of Deputies, the lower house of Congress, occurred in July, when the press reported on legislators' frequent absences, nepotism, and refusals to disclose their salaries. As a result, the chamber restricted journalists' access to congressional buildings.

Radio in Chile is very opinionated and has a reputation for high-quality and diverse programming. State and private television usually avoid covering controversial issues, filling most news programs with reports on sports, crime, and entertainment.

The fact that only a few companies—notably COPESA and El Mercurio—own print-media outlets ensures a lack of pluralism and diversity in the media. However, some papers broke important stories in 2002. For example, in a report from the Santiago-based daily *La Nación*, a former Secret Police agent revealed that under the military dictatorship of Augusto Pinochet, he and his colleagues had been instructed to conceal information about people abducted during that time. Meanwhile, two other print-media outlets, *The Clinic* and *El Periodista*, and two Internet news sites, *El Mostrador* (*www.elmostrador.cl*) and *Primera Línea* (*www.primeralinea.cl*), continue to make strides in aggressive investigative reporting.

COLOMBIA

COLOMBIA'S CIVIL CONFLICT ONCE AGAIN TOOK A BRUTAL TOLL on the country's press, with journalists threatened, attacked, kidnapped, and murdered. At least three journalists were killed for their work in 2002, and CPJ continues to investigate the slayings of five others whose deaths may have been related to their reporting. At year's end, Colombia's overburdened justice system appeared far from solving any of these murders, perpetuating a climate of impunity that leaves the media wide open to attacks.

Leftist rebels and right-wing paramilitary fighters were blamed for most of the violence against the press in Colombia, which CPJ ranked as one of the 10 worst places to be a journalist in 2002. A three-year peace process with the country's largest rebel army collapsed in February, and in August, newly elected president Álvaro Uribe Vélez took power on promises to intensify the battle against armed groups.

Violence inhibited coverage of the 38-year-old conflict, which pits leftist rebels against the government and a right-wing paramilitary army. Journalists were often unable to do the reporting that would have provided more of the analysis and context needed to explain how the conflict has changed and the motives driving the various warring parties. Instead, most reports focused on casualty statistics, which are frequently based on only one anonymous military source.

The military was also criticized for allegedly feeding the press inaccurate information to enhance the perception that it is winning the battle. That became evident in September, when the media reported a claim by the head of Colombia's air force that 200 rebels had been killed in aerial bombardments. The report was later discredited when the military could not explain how it had calculated the figure and conceded that a body count had never been taken.

During 2002, journalists also became increasingly concerned that media owners threaten editorial independence. Two powerful business groups with ties to the political establishment own the television and radio networks with the largest reach in Colombia, RCN and Caracol. The perception among many Colombians that media owners and politicians comprise a single ruling class became even more widespread when, during the May presidential elections, Uribe picked a member of the family that owns the country's most influential daily newspaper to be his vice president.

These connections appear to have kept many journalists from reporting critically on sweeping economic reforms pushed through by Uribe after he became president and from examining questions raised during the elections about ties between drug gangs, Uribe, and his family. An exception was "Noticias Uno," a current-affairs program on the TV station Canal Uno, based in the capital, Bogotá. In April, the program ran a series produced by investigations director Ignacio Gómez on alleged links between Uribe and the Medellín drug cartel. After the reports aired, unidentified men began calling the news station, threatening to kill Gómez, news director Daniel Coronell, and Coronell's 3-year-old daughter, who was flown out of the country soon after the calls began. CPJ honored Gómez with an International Press Freedom Award in November.

Although guerrillas and paramilitaries were blamed for most of the attacks against the press and for two journalists' deaths in 2002, the groups don't appear to have been behind the murder of journalist Orlando Sierra. A deputy editor and columnist for *La Patria* newspaper in Colombia's coffee-growing region, Sierra had repeatedly denounced a group of powerful local political bosses, accusing them of looting public coffers, buying votes, and practicing nepotism. On January 30, he was walking to his office with his daughter when an assassin shot him in the head.

The killings in 2002, along with dozens of others in previous years, force journalists to take seriously the flood of death threats they receive. At least 26 journalists were threatened with death during 2002; ten of them fled the country.

The best known among them is Claudia Gurisatti, the nation's top television news anchorwoman, who left in February after receiving anonymous telephone calls warning of a plan to kill her. It wasn't clear who was behind the threats, but Gurisatti had fled Colombia once before when authorities warned that fighters with the Revolutionary Armed Forces of Colombia (FARC) were planning to kill her. In 2000, Gurisatti conducted one of the first live interviews in recent years with then paramilitary chief Carlos Castaño. Many Colombians say that Castaño's personable and charismatic performance during the interview helped the paramilitaries gain support among the country's middle class.

Murders and death threats were not the only methods that armed groups used to show their disdain for Colombia's press. FARC fighters reportedly dismantled a radio station, blew up the antenna and transmitter of two others, tried to fire a rocket into a television station, and kidnapped a reporter, apparently to force his paper to pay a ransom and publish a communiqué.

Rebels and government authorities also harassed the foreign press. As peace talks were unraveling in February, FARC fighters detained *Los Angeles Times* correspondent T. Christian Miller and his assistant, Mauricio Hoyos. In a separate incident days later, FARC fighters held Alain Kellert, a photographer from the French magazine *Marie Claire*. All three were released unharmed shortly after being picked up.

In September, President Uribe signed a sweeping security decree allowing the government to establish security zones to fight rebel and paramilitary combatants and requiring foreigners and the international press to get government permission to enter the zones. Some correspondents working in Colombia complained that the requirement was unnecessary, and in November, the country's Constitutional Court ruled that the press did not need government permission to enter the security zones.

Finally, in a development that may bode well for Colombia's press, the paramilitary United Self-Defense Forces of Colombia (AUC) declared an unlimited and unilateral cease-fire on December 1, vowing to end attacks against leftist rebels and suspected rebel collaborators. Though it is too early to tell if the cease-fire will hold, Colombian journalists hope it will mark the end of paramilitary-sponsored terror against the media.

COSTA RICA

INFORMATION ABOUT THE 2001 MURDER of journalist Parmenio Medina Pérez remains scarce. Although his killing heightened efforts to reform Costa Rica's outdated media laws, the legislative commission that was created to study such laws made no advances during 2002, while Costa Rican journalists continued to suffer from court interference.

Medina, host of the muckraking weekly radio program "La Patada" (The Kick), during which he repeatedly denounced political corruption, was shot and killed by unidentified assailants on July 7, 2001. In September 2002, President Abel Pacheco de la Espriella asked the judiciary to expedite the murder investigation and announced that if no advances were made, he would seek assistance from the U.S. Federal Bureau of Investigation (FBI).

On December 23, police arrested Colombia-born John Gutiérrez in Costa Rica's capital, San José, and held him in preventive detention in connection with the Medina case. Investigators believe that Gutiérrez, who has been a refugee in Costa Rica since 1999, might have acted as an intermediary in the murder. Gutiérrez denies the allegations. Police leaks to the press suggest that authorities are investigating four suspects and a businessman who allegedly paid the gunmen 10 million colones (US$28,000) to commit the crime. At year's end, the government decided it would not call on the FBI.

Costa Rican journalists have been reluctant to investigate the murder because they fear that publishing the results of their reporting could expose them to criminal defamation charges under the country's harsh Penal Code. CPJ published a report about Medina's killing, titled "The Silence," by Costa Rican journalist Montserrat Solano Carboni, on the one-year anniversary of his death.

The fear of being charged and punished is not unfounded. Mauricio Herrera Ulloa, a journalist for the San José–based daily *La Nación*, was convicted of defamation in 1999 for publishing information based on allegations made by European publications against former Costa Rican diplomat Félix Przedborski. A Costa Rican court ordered Herrera Ulloa to pay a fine equivalent to 120 days' wages, as well as the plaintiff's legal fees and 60 million colones (US$200,000) in damages. After numerous proceedings, Herrera Ulloa is still seeking an appeal. On October 28, the Inter-American Commission on Human Rights sent President Abel Pacheco's administration a report containing conclusions and recommendations about the Herrera Ulloa case and asking for a response in two months. By year's end, the government had not responded.

In September, a group of editors and members of the journalists' association Colegio de Periodistas (Association of Journalists) presented proposals to the legislative commission formed after Medina's murder to revise press laws. The commission established a subcommittee to study the proposals, but the subcommittee's report, which was released on November 7, disappointed Costa Rican journalists. They criticized the subcommittee for altering the journalists' suggestions in a way that left the legislation restrictive.

CUBA

THROUGHOUT 2002, SCORES OF JOURNALISTS in Cuba were harassed, detained, threatened with prosecution or jail, or had their freedom of movement restricted. Some had their reporting materials confiscated or their phone communications disrupted. Often, the government prevented journalists from covering opposition activities, turning reporters back or even forcing them to stay at their homes under surveillance. The state security agency also tried to tarnish the reputations of journalists and damage their relations with their families or colleagues. Occasionally, journalists' relatives were harassed or denied government services.

State repression continued to be more severe in the provinces, far from the scrutiny of the Havana-based foreign news bureaus and diplomatic corps. While some independent journalists fled the country to escape repression, others have stayed and continue to work under harsh conditions. Although independent news reports cannot circulate inside Cuba, where the government owns and controls all media outlets, independent journalists inform the Cuban community abroad and the world at large about local developments that the official press chooses to ignore.

Many foreign news outlets have correspondents in Havana, but it is hard to tell what effect their presence has had on the government's actions against the independent press. While foreign journalists can report on human rights abuses, the government has calculated that it can influence international coverage and derive some benefit by appearing to show tolerance. Nonetheless, the government often subjects foreign correspondents to subtle and not-so-subtle pressures. In the past, the government has accused foreign journalists of "spreading lies and insults against the Revolution" and has hinted that it might consider closing entire news bureaus rather than expelling individual reporters. Officials grant visas to foreign journalists selectively, excluding those from outlets deemed unfriendly, such as *The Miami Herald*. Most significantly, Cubans don't have access to foreign news about their own country.

In the single most important initiative ever to challenge the regime, a coalition of opposition groups in May submitted the Varela Project, a petition calling for the reform of laws that violate human rights and other constitutional rights, to Cuba's National Assembly. The country's constitution allows petitions with signatures from at least 10,000 eligible voters to be presented to the assembly for consideration. Varela Project organizers gathered more than 11,000 signatures and requested that five proposals, including one demanding the right to freedom of expression and the press, be submitted to a national referendum. In response, the government held its own petition drive in June to support a constitutional reform making Cuba's socialist system "irrevocable." While the government-backed reform was quickly adopted, the National Assembly has refused to consider the Varela Project, which has received widespread international support.

The Sociedad de Periodistas Manuel Márquez Sterling, which was founded in 2001 and is the most active of three organizations of independent journalists, continued its work in 2002 despite government intimidation. In March, the association was forced to suspend its journalism courses temporarily after members were blocked from the group's offices. The association condemned the harassment and vowed to continue the classes, changing schedules and choosing different locations to evade police surveillance. In late December, the association launched its magazine, *Revista de Cuba*, which features articles by independent journalists.

Journalist Bernardo Arévalo Padrón, imprisoned since 1997 for "disrespecting" President Fidel Castro and Cuban State Council member Carlos Lage in statements made to Miami-based radio stations, was transferred in July from a labor camp to the infamous maximum-security Ariza Prison. Arévalo Padrón remains in jail despite being eligible for parole since October 2000, and his health has suffered as a result of his prolonged incarceration. During a reporting trip to Cuba in May, CPJ board member and *Chicago Tribune* columnist Clarence Page visited the Sociedad de Periodistas Manuel Márquez Sterling and delivered medicine to Arévalo Padrón.

Carlos Alberto Domínguez, Léster Téllez Castro, and Carlos Brizuela Yera, three journalists who are also active members of opposition groups, have been imprisoned since early 2002. CPJ has concluded that these journalists were jailed for their human rights activism rather than for their journalistic work. A public prosecutor has asked a court to give Téllez Castro and Brizuela Yera six-year and five-year prison sentences, respectively. It is unclear whether any charges have been brought against Domínguez. All three have written letters from jail denouncing harsh prison conditions.

Concerned about the growing popularity of the quarterly magazine *Encuentro de la cultura cubana*, which is published by a group of Cuban exiles based in Madrid, Spain, the Cuban government in December accused the publication of being "a political operation of the U.S. government." The magazine provides a forum for cultural and political debate for Cubans from the island and abroad. Although it is banned in Cuba, copies are distributed by hand and are in great demand.

The government continues to deny exit permits to journalists who have obtained foreign visas to resettle abroad. Other journalists invited to conferences or seminars abroad have been told that they would be allowed to leave Cuba only if they promise never to return.

Jesús Joel Díaz Hernández, who received an International Press Freedom Award from CPJ in 1999 while imprisoned in Cuba, was finally presented with his award at the 2002 ceremony in November. Díaz Hernández was sentenced to four years in prison in 1999 for "dangerousness." He was released in 2001, after an intensive campaign by CPJ and other press freedom groups, and then moved to the United States.

DOMINICAN REPUBLIC

THE DOMINICAN REPUBLIC'S MEDIA DID NOT FACE SIGNIFICANT RESTRICTIONS in 2002 under President Hipólito Mejía. However, a bill designed to bring the country's press laws up to international standards and improve access to information stalled again in the Senate.

The measure, which would amend the 1962 Law of Expression and Dissemination of

Thought, was reintroduced in the Chamber of Deputies in late February and approved in March. President Mejía had first submitted the bill in September 2000, and the Senate passed it in July 2001, but the deadline for consideration in the Chamber of Deputies expired. In 2002, however, the measure originated in the Chamber of Deputies, which approved the legislation and passed it to the Senate for consideration. By year's end, that chamber had not yet voted on the measure, which means the bill might have to be resubmitted in 2003.

The bill addresses the right to free expression guaranteed under Article 8 of the Dominican Constitution. Local press organizations, newspaper executives, and legal experts proposed the new bill, which outlines the conditions under which access to state-held information should be granted. The bill does not, however, decriminalize defamation, which is punishable by fines and up to six months in prison.

In April, the Dominican press reported that the Colegio Dominicano de Periodistas (Dominican Association of Journalists, or CDP) was drafting a bill to reform Law 10-91, which authorized the group's foundation. At the time, CDP president Oscar López Reyes was quoted by the daily *Hoy* as saying that the CDP's proposed bill does not require journalists to register with the CDP to be able to practice journalism in the country. However, the measure does force journalists to have a university degree in journalism. (In a 1985 decision, the Costa Rica–based Inter-American Court of Human Rights found that such mandatory licensing laws violate the American Convention on Human Rights.)

In November, an appeals court annulled the sentences of three men who were convicted in 2000 of the 1975 murder of journalist Orlando Martínez Howley, on the grounds that procedural errors had been committed during their trial. The appeals court ordered an immediate retrial of the defendants. In August 2000, a judge sentenced retired air force general Joaquín Pou Castro and two accomplices to 30 years in prison and ordered them to pay a 5 million peso (US$300,000) fine for Martínez's murder. According to Martínez's family and friends, the journalist was killed because his reporting had angered then president Joaquín Balaguer. Balaguer, who was subpoenaed in 2000 but refused to testify because of his health, died in July 2002.

Meanwhile, investigations into the May 1994 disappearance of columnist and academic Narciso González remained stalled at year's end. González, a harsh critic of the Dominican government and the military, "disappeared" after he publicly criticized the tainted elections that brought Balaguer to power in 1992.

ECUADOR

PRESIDENT GUSTAVO NOBOA'S ADMINISTRATION, which has been in power since January 2000, was generally tolerant of criticism in 2002 and respected the work of the press, except for some incidents in which journalists were temporarily denied full access to the Palace of Government.

Following the current regional wave of disillusionment with traditional political parties in Latin America, on October 20, Ecuador's first round of general elections saw candidates from nontraditional parties—former army officer Lucio Gutiérrez and banana tycoon Álvaro Noboa (of no relation to the president)—advance to the runoff, where Gutiérrez emerged as the winner of the November 24 poll. According to Participación Ciudadana

Ecuador (Citizens' Participation Ecuador), a nongovernmental organization that monitored the electoral process, "while media coverage of all candidates has been acceptable, ... in the first round there were candidates who ... had a smaller presence in the news."

Some journalists praised the print media for maintaining relative independence from political parties but pointed out that powerful banking groups that control broadcasting outlets (and whose executives have been investigated or tried on corruption charges) have close ties to politicians. Other journalists noted that media owners, not the government, discouraged reporters from investigating the banking crisis that caused the collapse of several private banks in 2000 and cost taxpayers and account holders hundreds of millions of dollars.

Ecuadoran journalists confront some of the same pressures as their colleagues in the rest of Latin America, namely low salaries that make them more vulnerable to bribes, the threat of criminal defamation lawsuits, and difficulties accessing information held by state institutions, particularly the judiciary.

In 2002, Jorge Vivanco Mendieta, deputy editor and columnist at the Guayaquil daily *Expreso*, continued to fight criminal and civil defamation charges filed in July 2001 by Fernando Rosero, a parliamentary deputy from the Ecuadoran Roldosista Party. The charges stem from several *Expreso* articles by Vivanco criticizing army generals for not defending themselves against Rosero's allegations that they had purchased defective weapons from Argentina. In October, however, after numerous appeals by Rosero, the Supreme Court dismissed the criminal lawsuit. The appeals process in the civil lawsuit was continuing at year's end.

On September 30, newspaper owners proposed an access to information bill to President Noboa, who pledged to submit it to Congress. While the Ecuadoran Constitution guarantees access to information under Article 81, the country has no comprehensive law that establishes deadlines and procedures for disclosure or that punishes officials who refuse to comply.

On September 18, Congress approved a bill to reform the Law of Radio and Television Broadcasting. Article 1 of the measure recognizes the right of community radio stations run by Indian, Afro-Ecuadoran, and peasant organizations to raise funds through donations, paid announcements, and advertising. On September 30, Noboa vetoed the bill and sent it back to Congress because he objected to articles that could be used to restrict press freedom. On October 30, the Congress overrode Noboa's veto.

In February, the government imposed a state of emergency in the oil-producing provinces of Sucumbíos and Orellana after violent anti-government protests erupted there. The emergency decree called for the army to administer the region and restricted constitutional guarantees, including freedom of expression. As a result, Radio La Jungla, which the government accused of inciting the population to violence by telling people to engage in street protests and of issuing messages against the emergency decree, was temporarily shuttered. On March 4, the state of emergency was lifted and the station went back on the air.

EL SALVADOR

A DECADE AFTER EL SALVADOR'S LONG AND BITTER CIVIL WAR, the country's media remain polarized between conservative, pro-government groups and a small number of independent outlets.

TV DOCE, a television station recognized as one of the few independent voices during the brutal civil conflict, was derided in August by the pro-government, San Salvador–based daily *El Diario de Hoy* as a "communist advocate." The paper has also lambasted the local press freedom organization Asociación de Periodistas de El Salvador (Association of Salvadoran Journalists, APES) for having "no credibility" and has denounced the group's ethics code, which was created in 1999.

While politically divided, all Salvadoran journalists continue to labor under restrictive access to information laws, while the Penal Code, which went into effect in 1998, impedes coverage of the courts by giving individual judges the power to limit access to legal proceedings. During 2002, APES presented several proposals to reform statutes that inhibit press freedom, but the government considered none of them seriously.

In September, the Legislative Assembly approved a law reforming the government's auditing agency, the Court of Accounts. Currently, journalists have free access to audit reports as soon as they are submitted to the agency. With the reform, however, such reports will remain sealed until the auditing process is completed. Because the new law sets no time limits on the auditing process, documents could be sealed indefinitely. APES and Probidad, a nongovernmental anti-corruption organization, have both criticized the legislation.

On August 15, the assembly approved the National Defense Bill, which could have limited journalists' right to protect their sources. But in early September, following protests, President Francisco Flores returned the bill to the legislature, requesting that lawmakers revise the measure to conform to international agreements signed by El Salvador. The assembly approved a new version of the bill without the offending restriction on September 12.

Although CPJ documented no cases of journalists who were prosecuted or physically threatened in retaliation for their reporting in 2002, the government imposed advertising embargoes on media outlets that criticized the administration's policies.

Salvadoran journalists expressed concern that some media outlets censor their own journalists. Juan José Dalton, a columnist at the San Salvador–based daily *La Prensa Gráfica*, commended the July decision of a Florida jury that held two retired Salvadoran generals responsible for atrocities committed during the country's civil war and ordered the men to pay US$54.6 million to three torture victims. Dalton, however, criticized the Salvadoran government for not bringing those who tortured and murdered civilians during the war to justice. The paper canceled the column before publication, saying the article might "open wounds" and does not support El Salvador's "democratic stability."

GUATEMALA

RELATIONS BETWEEN THE GOVERNMENT AND MUCH OF THE PRESS remained hostile during 2002. Human rights groups continued to criticize President Alfonso Portillo Cabrera's administration for ignoring and postponing obligations that the Guatemalan state had agreed to under peace accords that ended the country's 36-year civil war in 1996.

Confrontation between Portillo's ruling Guatemalan Republican Front (FRG) and the nation's leading dailies—*Prensa Libre*, *Siglo Veintiuno*, and *elPeriódico*—escalated in 2002. While the president openly complained that the print media had joined an opposition campaign to overthrow his administration, the press accused Portillo of trying to discredit journalists and attacked the government for being corrupt and inefficient.

Members of the media in Guatemala still face intimidation and harassment for their work. The situation is even more difficult for provincial journalists, who are often pressured by local governors and mayors. Authorities have either failed to investigate several attacks against journalists or have not followed up on their own preliminary inquiries into the incidents. Moreover, local media are owned by a few economically powerful business groups, while several sectors of the population—particularly peasants and indigenous citizens—are excluded from the news agenda.

In January, Guatemala's Constitutionality Court temporarily suspended a law that requires all university graduates, including those with journalism degrees, to register with trade associations known as *colegios*. Many journalists and international press freedom organizations opposed the legislation, which was signed into law in December 2001.

Media tycoon Ángel González, a Mexican national and the brother-in-law of former Guatemalan minister of infrastructure, housing, and communications Luis Rabbé, has used his broadcasting empire to discredit newspapers that criticize the government. Through front companies, González owns all four of Guatemala's private television stations, which violates constitutional provisions against both monopolies and foreign ownership of the media. He has canceled two independent news programs and wields enormous influence over Guatemalan politics.

A bill on community media presented to the country's unicameral Congress in February remained stalled at year's end. In June, community radio organizations, which had helped draft the bill, denounced FRG attempts to extend the legislation's benefits to evangelical radio stations. According to the community groups, the move would allow the FRG, which has close ties to evangelical radio stations, to use them to disseminate partisan propaganda.

Under the Agreement on Identity and Rights of Indigenous Peoples—one of several peace agreements that the government and the former guerrillas signed under U.N. auspices—Guatemala is obligated to reform current broadcasting license laws to make frequencies available to the country's indigenous population. During 2002, however, the national telecommunications agency announced that it would auction the limited number of radio frequencies available to the highest bidders.

In October, the government submitted legislation to Congress that creates guidelines for accessing state information. The journalists' group Asociación de Periodistas de Guatemala (Association of Guatemalan Journalists) criticized the lack of debate and transparency surrounding the measure. At year's end, Congress was still discussing the bill.

Meanwhile, there was little progress in the case of radio journalist Jorge Mynor Alegría Armendáriz, who was murdered in September 2001 outside his home in the Caribbean port city of Puerto Barrios. Alegría hosted an afternoon call-in show that often discussed corruption and official misconduct. The man allegedly hired to kill Alegría remains in jail while awaiting trial.

HAITI

With President Jean-Bertrand Aristide under pressure from the international community and Haitian opposition groups to expedite political and economic reforms and to resolve a two-year-old electoral impasse that has stalled the flow of millions of dollars in aid, Haiti's embattled press corps vigilantly reported the news despite political unrest and a deteriorating economy.

Almost two years into his second term, Aristide continued to promise justice and dialogue with reporters and media owners. "I will do everything in my power so that journalists can do their jobs without interference, and I will make sure all the laws are respected," he told a group of journalists in January. But all too often, the government's actions contradicted the president's rhetoric.

Officials made only sluggish headway in two high-profile murder cases of journalists: Jean Léopold Dominique, Haiti's most outspoken broadcast journalist, whom an unidentified assassin gunned down in April 2000; and Brignolle Lindor, a radio broadcaster who was hacked to death by a machete-wielding mob in December 2001. In the Dominique case, examining magistrate Claudy Gassant fled to Florida in January after Aristide did not renew the judge's mandate to conduct the murder investigation. Prior to his departure, Gassant was threatened several times and had resigned on more than one occasion, fearing for his safety. Lawyer Bernard Saint-Vil replaced Gassant.

At year's end, with more than 80 people having been questioned and six suspects detained in the highly political investigation, two armed gunmen killed a bodyguard of Dominique's widow, Michèle Montas, outside Montas' home on December 25. Montas, who took over her husband's radio station after his murder and has used the airwaves to criticize the snail-like pace of the murder investigation, said the attack was an attempt on her life.

In the Lindor murder case, 10 men belonging to a "popular organization" known as "Asleep in the Woods" have been indicted, and two have been arrested. (Trial dates had not been set by year's end.) These popular organizations—informally called *chimères* (chimera) after the fire-breathing mythological creature—tend to comprise Aristide supporters, some of whom have even admitted to being on the state payroll. Popular organizations appear to be the most visible and viable obstacles for journalists, threatening and harassing members of the media at street demonstrations and accusing them of "working for the opposition."

Guyler Delva, a newspaper reporter who is also secretary-general of the Association of Haitian Journalists, said that during 2002, twenty-four journalists were threatened or assaulted by popular organizations, and 22 went into exile. Fearing attacks from these groups, journalists working for private media outlets often conceal their press badges. Seven radio reporters, including a station owner, went into hiding after they were threatened and an arson attack partially damaged one of their stations. The journalists told CPJ they believe that the popular organization the "Cannibal Army" attacked the station because of its coverage of an opposition protest, which drew several thousand, calling for Aristide's resignation.

In Haiti, where more than half of the population is illiterate and the price of a television surpasses the average yearly wage, radio is the primary medium, with some 200 stations on the air nationwide. Many stations are partisan and broadcast reports that serve the interests of either the government or its opponents, namely opposition parties and the private sector. Government officials tend to criticize private radio stations when their coverage does not support Aristide's ruling Fanmi Lavalas party or the president.

While private radio stations openly criticize Aristide's administration—and the state often cites such criticism to counter allegations of a pending dictatorship—they often fail to apply the same critical eye to civic organizations, opposition parties, and the private sector, whose paid advertisements help keep them afloat. Some journalists accept bribes and have been known to drop stories in exchange for money. There is virtually no investigative work because of the risks involved.

Still, even with its crumbling infrastructure, slumping economy, and legacy of dictatorship, Haiti enjoys a relatively free and resilient press—indeed, the Fourth Estate is one of the country's few functioning institutions. Despite paltry pay at radio stations, journalists there compete aggressively to scoop their competitors, and seasoned broadcasters don't shy away from asking government officials and foreign diplomats tough questions.

Although radio is the dominant medium, Haiti has two major dailies, *Le Nouvelliste* and *Le Matin*, and three partisan weeklies are distributed in both the United States and Haiti: the right-wing *Haïti-Observateur* and the leftist *Haïti Progrès* and *Haïti En Marche*. The 3-year-old *Haitian Times*, which is edited by former *New York Times* reporter Garry Pierre-Pierre and published in New York, aims to shed a nonpartisan light on current events in Haiti and in U.S.-based Haitian communities.

In June, CPJ Americas program coordinator, Marylene Smeets, and board members Franz Allina and Clarence Page visited Haiti as part of a solidarity mission to meet with journalists and to highlight the apparent rise in political violence there that has coincided with recent attacks on the press. During their three-day stay, the delegation met with media owners, government officials, foreign diplomats, local press associations, and journalists to discuss the Dominique case and other press freedom concerns, concluding the trip with a press conference. Having learned about the government's plan to form a legally enforceable code of ethics for the media, CPJ followed up with a letter to Haiti's secretary of state for communications, Mario Dupuy, requesting details about the proposed legislation and suggesting a dialogue to ensure that any law passed does not restrict press freedom. At year's end, no legislative action had been taken on the ethics code.

HONDURAS

THERE WERE SIGNS THAT THE PRESS FREEDOM CLIMATE improved this year under President Ricardo Maduro, of the National Party (PN), who took office on January 27. Maduro has shown more tolerance of criticism than his predecessor, Carlos Roberto Flores Facussé, and so far has not attempted to co-opt the press. However, some journalists cautioned that it was too early to tell whether Maduro's attitude amounted to a meaningful change.

The complex web of personal and business relations among media owners and political parties continues to compromise the independence of major media outlets. Former president Flores owns the daily *La Tribuna*, the mouthpiece of the opposition Liberal Party (PL). Jaime Rosenthal Oliva, a businessman and influential PL politician, owns the television channel Canal 11 and the daily *El Tiempo*. Businessman and PL politician Víctor Bendeck Ramírez controls Canal 13 and Radio Reloj.

On July 10, in a public announcement in *El Tiempo*, Canal 13 and Radio Reloj accused government officials of withdrawing advertising because of the stations' critical coverage of a secret trip by President Maduro to Italy in June.

In February, criminal charges were brought against Sandra Maribel Sánchez, director of two weekly radio programs broadcast on Tegucigalpa-based Radio América, by former comptroller general Vera Sofía Rubí. Rubí accused Sánchez of "intercepting phone calls and violating secrets" and of "illegally practicing journalism." (Under Honduran law, journalists must register in a trade association called a *colegio*. Sánchez graduated from journalism school but never registered with a *colegio*.)

The lawsuit against Sánchez came after she released the contents of an audiotape in January featuring a 1999 conversation between Rubí and then president of the Supreme Court of Justice, Oscar Armando Ávila Banegas. On the tape, Rubí and Ávila discuss trying to influence the outcome of several high-profile corruption cases. At the time of the disclosure of the tape, whose authenticity has not been questioned, Rubí was a nominee to the Supreme Court. In late January, however, a committee charged with approving the nominations rejected Rubí. As of October, her case against Sánchez was stalled, and Sánchez's colleagues were pressing for a ruling.

Meanwhile, Honduran journalists remain vulnerable to bribes and other economic pressures because of their low salaries. Investigative journalism is almost nonexistent. Defaming public officials is a criminal offense punishable by up to four years in prison (up to six years for defaming the president), according to Article 345 of the Penal Code.

MEXICO

TWO YEARS AFTER THE HISTORIC ELECTION OF VICENTE FOX, which ended 75 years of one-party rule in Mexico, the country is being governed somewhat more democratically. But in 2002, the president still faced urgent demands to break with the government's corrupt and secretive past in favor of transparency and public accountability.

On April 30, in response to pressure from civil society groups and the public, Congress unanimously passed the Federal Law on Transparency and Access to Public Information, which Fox signed in June. The law defines all government information as public and requires agencies to publish all information concerning their daily functions, including budgets, operations, staff, salaries, internal reports, and the awarding of contracts. The legislation grants citizens the right to request information that is not already public and allows them to appeal to the Federal Institute for the Access to Public Information an agency's decision to deny information. If that appeal is lost, citizens can take the case to court. The law also prohibits the government from withholding information regarding crimes against humanity or human rights violations under any circumstances.

Criminal libel laws still plague Mexico's journalists. In October, a judge filed arrest warrants against Oscar Cantú Murguía, owner and editor of the Juárez-based daily *Norte*, and seven of his journalists. Several months earlier, former mayor Manuel Quevedo Reyes, who now heads a real estate firm, had filed criminal libel charges against Murguía and his colleagues after a series of articles in the paper suggested that government officials had deliberately overvalued land that Reyes sold to the government. The warrants remained pending in a state court at year's end.

Although Fox promised to eliminate "all practices that get in the way of informing the public openly and truthfully," federal investigators still pressured journalists to reveal the sources of their stories. Since March, six reporters from the Mexico City daily *La Jornada*, as well as the news director of the daily *El Universal*, have been ordered to testify before investigators about sources for articles on a corruption scandal involving the public petroleum company Pemex. On December 3, the attorney general justified the investigation, saying it was not designed to attack journalists but rather to punish officials who leak classified information to the media.

Meanwhile, reporters covering high-crime areas, especially near the U.S.-Mexico border, which is rife with drug traffickers, still face danger. For example, in January, J. Jesús Blancornelas, co-editor of the Tijuana weekly *Zeta*, received an e-mail saying that a gunman based in the border city of Mexicali, in the northern state of Baja California, had orders to execute him. For years, Blancornelas has covered corruption and drug trafficking there and has received frequent threats because of his award-winning reports. The January threat was attributed to the Tijuana drug cartel, then headed by brothers Ramón and Benjamín Arellano Félix. In November 1997, the Arellano Félix brothers wounded Blancornelas in an attack. The journalist is currently under permanent protection by bodyguards from an army Special Forces unit.

Some Mexican politicians have tried to harass journalists by using the U.S. court system. On January 9, Dolía Estévez, the Washington, D.C., correspondent for the Mexican daily *El Financiero*, was ordered by a subpoena issued by the plaintiff's lawyer to hand over material related to a 1999 news article about the Hank family of Mexico, which has been linked to drug trafficking. The subpoena asked for all research materials used to prepare her article, including e-mail correspondence, tape recordings, calendar and appointment books, draft articles, and lists of U.S. government contacts. On March 19, a U.S. district judge granted Estévez's motion to quash the subpoena, noting that "the information sought by Plaintiffs appears to be nothing more than a fishing expedition." The plaintiffs appealed the ruling, and a hearing was scheduled for February 21, 2003.

In May, a three-judge appeals panel sentenced two men to 13-year prison terms for the 1998 murder of Philip True, a *San Antonio Express-News* (Texas) journalist who was killed while working on a story about the Huichols, an indigenous population that lives in a mountainous area stretching across Jalisco, Nayarit, and Durango states. The unanimous ruling overturned an August 2001 verdict that had acquitted the two men. The defendants' lawyers appealed the latest convictions, which remained pending at year's end.

NICARAGUA

ON JANUARY 10, PRESIDENT ENRIQUE BOLAÑOS GEYER of the ruling Constitutionalist Liberal Party (PLC) assumed office, promising to fight corruption. With strong popular and media backing, Bolaños took on PLC leader and former president Arnoldo Alemán, long suspected of malfeasance. In September, a judge found several of Alemán's associates and relatives guilty of corruption and sentenced them to prison. Alemán, who is a member of the National Assembly, escaped conviction because of immunity. On December 12, the assembly lifted Alemán's immunity, and on December 22, he was convicted of money laundering. At year's end, he remained under house arrest while awaiting trial on a host of other corruption charges.

Authorities have yet to enforce Law 372, which went into effect in April 2001 and requires all journalists to have authorization from the journalists' organization Colegio de Periodistas de Nicaragua (Association of Nicaraguan Journalists) to work in any media outlet. The Supreme Court of Justice is still considering a constitutional challenge to the law, which journalists and media owners filed in June 2001.

Asked about the most serious problems they face, Nicaraguan journalists cited job instability, low salaries, the lack of an ethics code, and the polarization and politicization of the media. They also complained about the lack of access to public information and the culture of secrecy that pervades the government.

Some journalists are concerned that the government favors giving advertisements to large media outlets supported by the Bolaños administration, hurting smaller news organizations without government ties. At the same time, a mounting economic crisis has forced officials to reduce state advertising. The daily *La Noticia*, which received generous government advertising during the Alemán administration despite its small circulation, folded in September, claiming it could not overcome its mounting debts and lack of private and government advertising.

A draft bill to improve access to government information, which Bolaños sent to the legislature in March, progressed little in 2002. At year's end, the legislation was stalled in the National Assembly.

PLC parliamentary deputies introduced two legislative proposals considered restrictive of press freedom that were withdrawn in October after protests from journalists. One, a bill to "regulate the crime of disrespect of State organs," proposed prison terms of up to five years for publicly offending government officials, according to local news reports.

The press saw the second proposal, the "law of civil protection of the right to a private life, family, honor, reputation, and image," as an attempt to block reporting on former PLC government officials under investigation for alleged involvement in corruption.

At the request of the Attorney General's Office, on October 11, the Nicaraguan Institute of Telecommunications (TELCOR) abruptly closed the radio station La Poderosa, claiming that its broadcasting license had not been properly registered and that it had acquired broadcasting equipment without paying import duties. Although La Poderosa was known as the mouthpiece of a PLC faction led by former president Alemán, journalists still protested the move. Many felt that the government did not attempt to exhaust other administrative sanctions or to bring charges against the station's owners and instead used technicalities to close the station. La Poderosa owners filed an injunction against TELCOR before the Managua Appeals Court, which ruled against TELCOR on October 25, restoring La Poderosa's license. However, the court ordered that the station remain shuttered until the Supreme Court considers the merits of another injunction filed by the station's owners against TELCOR. At year's end, the Supreme Court had not issued a ruling on the matter.

PANAMA

Since the U.S. invasion in 1991, Panama's three democratic administrations have pledged to repeal legislation that restricts press freedom. But little has been done, and officials seeking to silence critics or prevent exposure of corruption continue to harass the press with numerous "gag laws."

National and international pressure forced President Mireya Moscoso to approve a transparency law in January. The legislation is based on a proposal from the anti-corruption nongovernmental organization Transparency International and calls for fines of as much as 2,000 balboas (US$2,000) and the dismissal of government employees who do not release public information in a timely manner. In June, however, the government issued a decree that essentially annulled the law by attaching regulations that, among other things, exempt officials' salaries, benefits, bonuses, and travel expenses from public view. The regulations also require that those seeking information have some relationship to it—in effect barring the press and the public from taking advantage of the law. The People's Ombudsman Office challenged the decree in the Supreme Court, which had not ruled on the matter by year's end.

In March, the Communication and Transportation Commission of Panama's unicameral Legislative Assembly discussed a bill that would only recognize journalists who hold a university degree. The bill, which was still under consideration at year's end, would also create the Superior Council of Journalism, which would issue identification cards to journalists, accredit foreign correspondents, and sanction members of the media who violate journalistic ethics. On May 9, CPJ sent a protest letter to commission head Dennis Arce expressing concern that the proposal violates the standards established by the American Convention on Human Rights, which Panama ratified in 1978.

The proposed bill comes on top of an existing statute that requires all newsreaders at radio and television stations to be licensed. To get a license, newsreaders must hold a degree in a relevant field or attend an eight-month course at the University of Panama.

Annoyed by numerous reports documenting increased corruption, cronyism, and nepotism since President Moscoso took office, the government attempted to intimidate the media in 2002, accusing them of abusing press freedom. Authorities also established a new commission to evaluate existing press statutes without the participation of media representatives.

Panamanians use defamation laws liberally. More than 90 journalists in the country—almost half of the media's work force—have criminal libel or slander cases pending against them. And in 70 percent of those cases, public officials who felt their honor and dignity had been sullied filed the suits.

For example, after a February 1998 broadcast by Panamanian lawyer, columnist, and radio journalist Miguel Antonio Bernal on the news program "TVN Noticias," National Police director José Luis Sosa filed defamation charges against the journalist, claiming that his comments damaged the National Police's reputation. Under Panama's Penal Code, defamation carries a sentence of up to two years in prison.

Bernal was indicted on May 27, 1998, and later challenged the ruling. After numerous appeals, Judge Lorena Hernández acquitted him on May 29, 2002. The Attorney General's office appealed her decision, but the Second Superior Tribunal of Justice acquitted Bernal on October 27.

Although this case was a significant victory for press freedom in the country, Bernal has a grim view of the future. "I think I was acquitted because of the overwhelming international support my case has attracted," he said. In Panama, he added, "The judiciary, legislative, and executive branches of government are all hostile to the concept of free speech."

PARAGUAY

THE ADMINISTRATION OF PARAGUAYAN PRESIDENT LUIS GONZÁLEZ MACCHI, long paralyzed by accusations of corruption and incompetence, was facing an impeachment challenge at the end of 2002. Throughout the year, the media had criticized the president for trivializing public concerns about his administration. In early December, the Chamber of Deputies voted to impeach him. He will have to defend himself in 2003 should the Senate follow suit.

Meanwhile, the Paraguayan press continues to be divided among various political factions. Politicians and businessmen own media outlets and use them to advance their agendas. According to surveys by civil-society organizations, only about 8 percent of Paraguayans believe that the press is trustworthy. This public cynicism, combined with a recession, has drastically reduced circulation at most daily newspapers. Because of the economic crisis, foreign investors have bought some television stations, dropping news programs and replacing them with entertainment. Nonetheless, the broadcast media—particularly radio, which includes community stations—remain more diverse than other media.

As April 2003 elections approach, support for democracy in the country has fallen, while public acceptance of candidates with authoritarian agendas has risen. Some journalists believe that the media have contributed to the public's disenchantment with democracy by reporting rumors and gossip and manipulating and sensationalizing the news to benefit certain political parties.

A bill introduced in the Chamber of Deputies in August 2001 to improve access to public information remained stalled in 2002. Parliament member Rafael Filizzola, the journalists' union Sindicato de Periodistas del Paraguay (Union of Paraguayan Journalists), and other civil-society organizations drafted the legislation. According to some critics, the bill is flawed because it does not force private companies that offer public services to disclose information.

In a development that may have profound implications for press freedom and the campaign to decriminalize defamation in the Americas, in June, the Inter-American Commission on Human Rights (IACHR), the human rights body of the Washington, D.C.–based Organization of American States (OAS), took the case of Ricardo Canese—a former Paraguayan presidential candidate who was convicted of criminal defamation—to the Costa Rica–based Inter-American Court of Human Rights. This is the first time the court has agreed to hear a criminal defamation case.

The lawsuit against Canese dates back to August 1992, when he questioned then presidential candidate Juan Carlos Wasmosy about his ties to former Paraguayan dictator Alfredo Stroessner, who was deposed in a bloodless coup in 1989. In statements made to the local press, Canese said that Wasmosy, who went on to become president, was Stroessner's straw man in the construction partnership CONEMPA, which was awarded a contract to build the giant Itaipú hydroelectric power plant on the Paraguay-Brazil border. In October 1992, CONEMPA business partners whom Canese had not named in his statements sued him for libel and defamation. In March 1994, a judge sentenced Canese to four months in prison and ordered him to pay a US$7,500 fine. An appeals court rejected Canese's appeal in November 1997 but reduced his sentence to two months in prison and a US$600 fine. In May 2001, a Supreme Court panel dismissed Canese's appeal for review of the sentence.

The IACHR has asked the Inter-American Court to declare that Paraguay violated Canese's right to freedom of thought and expression, as well as other rights guaranteed by the American Convention on Human Rights. At the end of 2002, Paraguay's Supreme Court, fearing a ruling against the country, dismissed the case against Canese, though proceedings continue at the Inter-American Court.

In early November, after two television programs aired the contents of taped telephone conversations that allegedly showed that high-ranking government officials—including President González Macchi—were attempting to influence judicial decisions, the government's press office distributed a press release threatening to investigate broadcast media and possibly cancel their broadcasting concessions. Shortly after, the office sent out a second press release without the threat, apparently to forestall public criticism.

In late March, a court upheld the 25-year prison sentence of Milcíades Maylin, a local criminal convicted of the January 2001 murder of radio journalist Salvador Medina Velázquez. No motive was ever established, and Medina's relatives, who have received anonymous death threats, believe that the individuals who ordered the murder have not been brought to justice. They are pressing officials to reopen the case.

PERU

THE PERUVIAN PRESS CONTINUES TO RECOVER from the authoritarian and corrupt rule of Alberto K. Fujimori, who was Peru's president from 1990 until 2000, when a scandal forced him to resign and flee the country. During the last years of his regime, Fujimori managed to control much of the news agenda with the complicity of most broadcasting outlets. President Alejandro Toledo, whose 2001 election victory consolidated democracy and the rule of law in Peru, largely respects the media's work.

The government and the judiciary continue to investigate television executives and owners who had placed their media outlets at the service of Fujimori and his intelligence adviser, Vladimiro Montesinos. Using an array of tactics—million-dollar bribes, extortion, tax incentives, and manipulation of government advertising—Fujimori and Montesinos, along with compliant judges, dictated media coverage to secure Fujimori a third presidential term, which was widely considered unconstitutional, in April 2000. At the end of 2002, the cases of several television owners who had been charged in 2001 with embezzlement, influence peddling, and conspiracy to commit crimes were combined into one case and assigned to an anti-corruption judge. During 2002, these discredited media owners linked to Fujimori and Montesinos tried to use their outlets to denounce an alleged government campaign to muzzle journalists critical of Toledo.

A separate judicial investigation of several tabloid owners charged with embezzlement proceeded slowly in 2002. These businessmen had collaborated with the Fujimori regime to smear opposition politicians and independent journalists, especially from the dailies *El Comercio*, *La República*, and *Liberación*. Pro-Fujimori tabloids, known as the *prensa chicha*, reveled in publishing false allegations about those opposed to Fujimori. In 2001, a public prosecutor found that sufficient evidence exists that Fujimori's administration directly bankrolled the tabloids. Some of the owners remained under house arrest throughout 2002 while they were being investigated.

Although the press freedom climate has improved significantly in Peru, the Toledo administration came under fire in 2002 for showing intolerance to criticism and for demanding more favorable press coverage. Similarly, supporters of Toledo's Perú Posible party were implicated in several verbal and physical attacks against journalists.

In June, Congress passed the Law on Transparency and Access to Public Information, which is scheduled to go into effect on January 3, 2003. Though the media owners' group Consejo de la Prensa Peruana (Council of the Peruvian Press) and Peru's Ombudsman Office considered the legislation a step forward, they claimed that the exceptions under which access to public information may be denied—particularly those related to national security—are too broad and vague, giving the executive branch too much power to determine which information can remain secret on national security grounds. In September, representatives from the Ombudsman Office challenged the law in Peru's Constitutional Court, which had not ruled on the matter by year's end.

Journalist Javier Tuanama Valera, who was convicted during the Fujimori regime on charges of collaborating with terrorists, was granted a presidential pardon and was released from jail in November. After reviewing Tuanama's case, a government pardoning commission determined that there was insufficient evidence to convict him. Juan de Mata Jara Berrospi, who is serving a 20-year prison sentence, is now the only journalist still in jail on charges of collaborating with terrorists.

Also in November, Peruvian authorities captured an alleged member of the Shining Path Maoist guerrilla movement who they believe participated in the 1989 kidnapping and murder of *Tampa Tribune* reporter Todd Carper Smith. According to local reports, drug traffickers mistook Smith for a U.S. drug enforcement agent and ordered the Shining Path to abduct and execute him. Smith was in Peru on a working vacation to report on the guerrillas.

In November, the alleged head of the paramilitary death squad Grupo Colina, retired army major Santiago Martín Rivas, was captured and interrogated in connection with the 1992 kidnapping and murder of journalist Pedro Yauri Bustamante, director of the "Punto Final" news program on Radio Universal. Grupo Colina, which has been linked to several massacres and scores of other human rights abuses under the Fujimori regime, is allegedly behind Yauri's killing. The journalist's program frequently denounced abuses committed by the military.

UNITED STATES

THE U.S. GOVERNMENT TOOK AGGRESSIVE MEASURES IN 2002 to shield some of its activities from press scrutiny. These steps not only reduced access for U.S. reporters but had a global ripple effect, with autocratic leaders citing U.S. government actions to justify repressive policies.

While access to U.S. forces in Afghanistan improved somewhat in 2002, journalists who encountered U.S. troops in the field did not always receive a friendly reception. In

THE AMERICAS |

February, U.S. soldiers detained *Washington Post* reporter Doug Struck at gunpoint and prevented him from investigating reports of civilian casualties. In late August, U.S. Special Forces involved in the hunt for Osama bin Laden confiscated film from *New York Times* photographer Tyler Hicks and also forced him to erase images from his digital camera. Some U.S. journalists worry that these actions bode ill for coverage of a possible military invasion of Iraq, although the Defense Department has pledged to "embed" journalists with U.S. forces and has even provided journalists with special training designed to allow them to accompany forces safely.

In some cases, the restrictive measures extended to more mundane reporting inside the United States. In March, U.S. military police handcuffed Fox News cameraman Gregg Gursky and confiscated his videotape. Gursky was on Pentagon property when he filmed Virginia police pulling over a pickup truck outside the Pentagon. Although Gursky had Defense Department credentials, officials claimed he needed a security escort to film on Pentagon property. The next day, officials returned the tape to Fox.

In September, Washington police detained at least five reporters covering demonstrations against the International Monetary Fund and the World Bank. One of the journalists, Larry Towell of Magnum photo agency, told CPJ that police ignored press passes and seized the journalists without warning. They were held in a detention center for several hours before being released without charge.

The U.S. government also took measures to limit coverage of internal policy debates. New Justice Department guidelines instituted in October give government agencies wide latitude to reject public requests made under the 1966 Freedom of Information Act. Attorney General John Ashcroft said the Bush administration would support withholding documents as long as "a sound legal basis" for doing so exists. The administration of Bush's predecessor, Bill Clinton, withheld documents only if disclosure was deemed "harmful."

The Homeland Security Bill passed in November imposes criminal penalties on government employees who disclose information about "critical infrastructure"—including communications, transportation, and health—voluntarily provided to the government by private companies. The Washington, D.C.–based Reporters Committee for Freedom of the Press charged that the provision was inserted at the behest of businesses and could prevent the public from receiving timely information about threats to public health and welfare.

Journalists were also denied access to deportation hearings for hundreds of immigrants detained in the aftermath of the September 11, 2001, attacks. In August, the 6th Circuit Court of Appeals, in Cincinnati, ruled that the automatic closure of these proceedings violates the First Amendment, noting that, "The only safeguard on this extraordinary governmental power is the public, deputizing the press as the guardian of their liberty." Immigration hearings are now open in that court's jurisdiction but are closed in the rest of the country. The issue may eventually go before the Supreme Court.

The government imposed tight restrictions on coverage of U.S. military detainees at Camp Delta in Guantanamo Bay, Cuba. The camp is shrouded in a green tarp, making it impossible to photograph it from a distance. Journalists who are given access face a number of restrictions and are always accompanied by an escort. Secrecy is so pervasive that the U.S. government did not respond to allegations from the Qatar-based, Arabic-language satellite network Al-Jazeera that one of its cameramen was among the detainees. In a September 27 letter to U.S. secretary of defense Donald Rumsfeld, CPJ also requested information about the alleged detention of the journalist. By year's end, Rumsfeld had not responded.

CPJ did receive a response to a January 31 letter sent to Rumsfeld requesting information about the circumstances surrounding the November 13, 2001, missile attack on Al-Jazeera's Kabul, Afghanistan, offices. In its February 26 reply, the Pentagon said the building was a "known al-Qaeda facility" but provided no evidence to support that contention. CPJ continues to investigate the incident.

A CPJ report released on the anniversary of the September 11, 2001, attacks expressed concern that authoritarian governments have appropriated the rhetoric of the "war on terror" to justify press freedom restrictions in their countries. The report, titled "Looking Forward, Looking Back," noted that governments in Eritrea, Russia, and Zimbabwe have labeled journalists who criticize those regimes as "terrorists."

Aside from access to information issues, other troubling legal developments in 2002 affect U.S. journalists. Although Texas free-lancer Vanessa Leggett—who was jailed for five months in 2001 for refusing to turn over her research to federal prosecutors—was released in early January, publisher David W. Carson and editor Ed Powers of *The New Observer* in Kansas were convicted in July of criminal defamation, a state misdemeanor that can result in up to a year in prison. The paper had falsely reported that the mayor of one county actually lived in another. In November, the journalists were sentenced to fines and probation; they are appealing their convictions. CPJ has long maintained that journalists should never be jailed for their work and has campaigned worldwide against criminal defamation laws. While criminal libel prosecutions are extremely rare in the United States, many states still have such laws on the books.

U.S. journalists and media outlets were also subject to legal proceedings outside the United States in 2002. In December, the U.N. International War Crimes Tribunal for the former Yugoslavia ruled that former *Washington Post* reporter Jonathan Randal, who had been subpoenaed in the trial of a former Bosnian official accused of genocide, did not have to testify in the case. The decision stated that war correspondents could not be compelled to testify unless "the evidence sought is of direct and important value in determining a core issue in the case ... and cannot reasonably be obtained elsewhere." CPJ worked with lawyers and journalists around the world to support Randal's case.

The Hague tribunal's ruling, however, only extends to war correspondents, not all journalists. The issue of compelled testimony could re-emerge as the international legal system expands, particularly with the establishment of the International Criminal Court (ICC), which is scheduled for 2003. The ICC will have the authority to try individuals accused of crimes against humanity and war crimes.

The growing threat of international legal action also came into play when Australia's High Court ruled in December that an Australian businessman could pursue a defamation case in Australia against the U.S.-based company Dow Jones because of an article published in the business magazine *Barron's* and posted on its Web site. Dow Jones, which owns *Barron's*, argued that the case should have been pursued in the United States, where the magazine is published.

The early 2002 abduction and murder of *Wall Street Journal* reporter Daniel Pearl forced U.S. foreign correspondents to confront their own vulnerabilities. They did so by

THE AMERICAS |

re-evaluating their routines and enrolling in increasingly popular journalist security courses.

In May, CPJ Washington, D.C., representative Frank Smyth testified before the U.S. Senate and called on the Central Intelligence Agency (CIA) to refrain from using non-U.S. journalists as spies. The CIA has been barred since the 1970s from using U.S. journalists as spies except in extraordinary circumstances, but the ban does not apply to foreign journalists. In his testimony, Smyth noted that, "The perception—or even the rumor—that a local journalist works with the CIA would obviously put him or her at considerable risk." The policy also endangers U.S. journalists by creating the impression that all journalists are potential spies; Daniel Pearl's captors falsely accused him of working for both U.S. and Israeli intelligence.

Partly in response to Pearl's killing, CPJ launched a new journalist security program in 2002 to provide journalists with authoritative and practical information about security, including safety equipment, hostile-environment training, health and life insurance, post-traumatic stress counseling, and field tips from veteran correspondents. CPJ will publish a journalist security handbook in the spring of 2003.

While journalists working inside the United States face relatively little physical risk, in October, Los Angeles police charged a man with threatening *Los Angeles Times* reporter Anita M. Busch, who was working on a story about an extortion plot against actor Steven Seagal. Convicted drug offender Alexander Proctor allegedly told an FBI informant that a private detective working for Seagal had hired him to threaten Busch. Proctor allegedly broke her car window and left a package containing a dead fish with a rose in its mouth along with a sign reading "Stop." Another journalist, *Vanity Fair* reporter Ned Zeman, was threatened at gunpoint in August while working on the same story.

URUGUAY

WHILE PRESS FREEDOM IS GENERALLY RESPECTED IN URUGUAY, the current economic crisis has damaged the media's diversity and independence. Journalists also continue to struggle to obtain government information, even as lawmakers consider legislation to expand access to it.

Under President Jorge Batlle's government, direct pressures against journalists and the press have diminished as compared with previous administrations. But according to the journalists' association Asociación de la Prensa Uruguaya (Association of the Uruguayan Press), the protracted economic crisis has forced news organizations to fire many journalists. Some of those who remain employed have resorted to self-censorship to avoid losing their jobs.

In a country where many publications depend almost exclusively on government advertising, journalists and media owners remain concerned that state agencies and enterprises continue to withhold advertising from critical media outlets, while rewarding those that provide favorable coverage. Several news organizations have closed during the last two years, and journalists speculate that more may soon fold, further limiting the diversity of views.

In October, the Chamber of Deputies approved a right to information bill that was first introduced in 1996. The measure, which the Senate was considering at year's end, would guarantee access to government documents, as well as the right to access, without a court order, public records containing information about oneself. Such legislation is urgently needed in Uruguay, where government agencies are notorious for refusing to provide even basic information to the public. Some journalists doubt that the Senate will pass the law quickly, faulting both politicians for their lack of interest and journalists' organizations for not raising awareness about the legislation's importance.

Radio broadcasters have long been divided over the issue of community stations; currently, dozens of them operate without permits, despite having applied for them years ago. While commercial stations claim that community stations interfere with their frequencies, community broadcasters argue that they cannot afford to buy frequencies, which are granted through auctions. In October 2001, the country's telecommunications regulatory agency, URSEC, convened talks on the issue. In November 2002, URSEC sent a proposal to the executive aimed at creating a legal framework in which community stations can operate. Officials were still considering the proposal at year's end.

Uruguay still has several laws that restrict freedom of expression, including *desacato* (disrespect) statutes, which criminalize insulting public officials. In addition, several articles in the Penal Code and the Uruguayan Press Law prescribe prison terms for defamation, though CPJ has not documented any recent cases of journalists jailed under these provisions.

VENEZUELA

DURING 2002, A WORSENING POLITICAL CRISIS brought Venezuela to the brink of collapse and threatened to derail democracy there. As the degradation of state institutions continued, society's extreme polarization and intolerance multiplied the risks for journalists.

Throughout the year, President Hugo Chávez Frías and his supporters accused the local press of distorting facts and under-covering his administration's achievements. On Chávez's weekly radio and TV program, "Aló, Presidente," he often lambasted the media. In addition, he used *cadenas*—his nationwide simultaneous radio and television broadcasts—to counter the private media's news coverage, which was heavily biased toward the opposition. Spurred by the president's discourse, government supporters harassed and attacked news crews.

The private media continued to plunge into the political arena, unabashedly promoting the agenda of opposition parties while ignoring professionalism and balance. Because opposition parties in Venezuela are either discredited or divided, the media have stepped in to fill the vacuum, becoming an extremely powerful source of government opposition.

Events in April underscored the dangers for journalists covering the political crisis. On April 11, following three days of opposition protests, the government pre-empted broadcasts from local television stations for a message from President Chávez. During the address, private stations split the screen to continue covering the protests. Upset by this decision, Chávez ordered the stations closed and accused them of conspiring to overthrow his government. At around midnight that day, Chávez was ousted, and Pedro Carmona, president of the country's most powerful business group, was appointed to head the new, military-backed Cabinet. But news of the coup resulted in protests by Chávez supporters, and within 48 hours, military officers loyal to Chávez had reinstated him. At least six photographers were shot and wounded while covering the violent clashes that preceded the April 11 coup. One of them, Jorge Ibraín Tortoza Cruz, an 11-year veteran of the Caracas daily *2001*, died from his wounds on April 11.

In the days following Chávez's ouster, the four main private TV channels featured scant coverage of pro-Chávez demonstrations. Venezuelans had to rely on CNN and Colombian and Spanish channels received by cable or satellite for news about the protests. Many foreign and local journalists alleged that private media executives had colluded to impose a news blackout, heeding instructions given by Carmona. But the executives claimed that they could not cover the story for fear that Chávez supporters, who had harassed several media outlets earlier in the year, would attack their staff or offices. Yet several local journalists pointed out that the events could have been covered without exposing journalists to unnecessary risks. Moreover, during previous political crises and instability, Venezuelan journalists did not stop providing the public with information.

During Carmona's brief tenure, security forces at his command harassed journalists working for pro-government community media, while the state-run television station, Venezolana de Televisión (VTV), was taken off the air on the evening of April 11 after being occupied by police forces that had joined the coup. VTV remained shuttered until April 13, when government supporters took it over and brought it back on the air.

Concerned about the effects of the April 11 events on journalists, CPJ sent a fact-finding mission to Venezuela in May. With information gathered from members of the media and human rights organizations during the trip, CPJ published a report in August titled "Cannon Fodder" describing the polarized and politicized environment in which Venezuelan journalists work. In more than a dozen interviews with CPJ, journalists said they were caught in the middle of the struggle between Chávez and media owners.

In early December, during an opposition-led general strike that paralyzed key sectors of the country, including the oil industry, government supporters attacked and harassed several journalists and private media outlets. In what looked like coordinated actions rather than spontaneous protests, pro-government demonstrators surrounded other private news offices. State security forces, meanwhile, assaulted reporters and photographers or impeded their work. Most private newspapers joined the strike and did not circulate for several days.

By the end of 2002, with the opposition strike extended indefinitely, both private and state media completely abandoned all pretense of objectivity and balance, offering propaganda in place of news and possibly undermining prospects for an Organization of American States–sponsored negotiated settlement to the crisis.

The government did not take firm action to investigate the numerous attacks against journalists and media outlets in 2002. The Public Prosecutor's Office had little to show for its investigations into the attacks, including Tortoza's killing. Often, journalists filed complaints with authorities, who never completed the initial investigations. The government's failure to conduct thorough inquiries reinforced the impunity that has long prevailed in Venezuela and encouraged those who perpetrate assaults on journalists. Similarly, officials did not comply consistently with the Inter-American Commission on Human Rights' precautionary measures requiring the government to, among other orders, protect threatened media outlets and prevent attacks against journalists. ■

| CASES TABLE OF CONTENTS |

ARGENTINA

SEPTEMBER 17

Thomas Catan, *The Financial Times*
LEGAL ACTION

Catan, the Buenos Aires correspondent for the U.K.-based newspaper *The Financial Times*, had his phone records subpoenaed by a federal judge. The records could have potentially revealed the sources the journalist had used for a story about alleged bribes requested by Argentine legislators.

On August 20, 2002, Catan, citing unnamed bankers and diplomats he had interviewed, reported that Argentine legislators had solicited bribes from foreign banks operating in Argentina as a condition for stalling a bill that, among other things, would have reinstated a 2 percent tax on interest and commissions for a failed health scheme for bank workers. Foreign banks have strongly opposed the tax because they could reportedly lose hundreds of millions of dollars.

A federal investigation into the bribery allegations was launched in early September, and Federal Judge Claudio Bonadío called Catan to testify. In his September 17 testimony, Catan said that four sources, whom he refused to identify, supported his story. Judge Bonadío asked the journalist to give his phone number, without explaining why it was necessary. As Catan finished his testimony, however, the journalist was told that his phone records would likely be subpoenaed.

After learning that on September 18 Judge Bonadío had ordered the State Intelligence Office (SIDE) to provide him with Catan's phone records, the journalist appealed the order to a higher court, claiming that the decision violated Article 43 of the Argentine Constitution, which protects the "secrecy of the sources of journalistic information."

In early October, Judge Bonadío rejected a request by Public Prosecutor Guillermo Marijuan to return the phone records to the journalist with a note stating that they had not been used in the investigation. Instead, the judge gave the phone records to the SIDE.

On October 28, the Federal Chamber, to which Catan had appealed Judge Bonadío's decision to take the phone records, ruled in favor of Catan, concluding that it was unnecessary to reveal Catan's sources to gather evidence since the information could be obtained by other means. The court also declared that Judge Bonadío's order "constituted an unreasonable restriction on freedom of expression and, therefore, [was] illegitimate." The ruling further instructed Bonadío to recover the phone records from SIDE and destroy them in the presence of Catan or his lawyers.

In late October, Catan left Argentina for Great Britain, where he continues working for *The Financial Times*.

OCTOBER 6

María Mercedes Vázquez, LT 7 Radio Corrientes
ATTACKED, THREATENED

A group of unknown assailants hurled a homemade bomb at the home of Vázquez, a reporter with LT 7 Radio Corrientes, in the northeastern province of Corrientes. No one was injured, according to local press reports. In September, Vázquez had released transcripts of phone taps she obtained revealing that several public officials may have been involved in a conspiracy to oust the governor of Corrientes.

That was the third time in eight months that Vázquez was attacked or threatened in retaliation for her reporting. The journalist has been under permanent police protection since February, when she received death threats for her reporting on a corrupt judge. In one of the anonymous calls, answered by Vázquez's elder daughter, the caller described how the journalist would be killed. Two months later, two individuals stopped Vázquez in the street and beat her, telling her not to talk about a political activist wanted by police in connection with several crimes.

OCTOBER 26

Alberto Recanatini, Indymedia Argentina
Tomás Eliaschev, Indymedia Argentina
ATTACKED

Eliaschev and Recanatini, reporters for Indymedia Argentina, an international alternative media outlet, were attacked by police while covering a protest in the capital, Buenos Aires. The protestors were calling for the release of 30 activists arrested during a Greenpeace Argentina demonstration.

In an attempt to disperse the crowd, the police fired rubber bullets and tear gas. Eliaschev told CPJ that when the police realized that they were being filmed, they shot rubber bullets at the journalists and tried to destroy their equipment. Although Recanatini was hit by three bullets and Eliaschev sustained six shots to his legs, neither was seriously injured. The journalists filed a complaint before judge Wilma López. At year's end, the judge had taken no action on the case.

BRAZIL

MAY 23

Brazilian media
LEGAL ACTION, CENSORED

A Brazilian judge granted an injunction banning the country's media from publishing any information about the administrative-disciplinary proceedings against Judge Renato Mehana Khamis, of the Regional Labor Tribunal of São Paulo State.

São Paulo State Court of Justice judge Zélia Maria Antunes Alves granted the injunction requested by Judge Khamis—who faces administrative-disciplinary proceedings for alleged sexual harassment—which bars the Brazilian media from circulating any information related to the case. According to Brazilian news reports, a lower-court judge in the city of São Paulo had earlier denied the injunction.

JUNE 3

Tim Lopes, TV Globo
KILLED

For full details on this case, see page 355.

SEPTEMBER 19

Lúcio Flávio Pinto, Jornal Pessoal
LEGAL ACTION

Lúcio Flávio, a free-lance journalist based in Belém, the capital of the northern state of Pará, faced several criminal and civil lawsuits because of his reporting. The journalist writes the column "Carta da Amazônia" (Letter from the Amazon) for the São Paulo–based daily O Estado de S. Paulo and is the publisher and editor of the small, Belém-based monthly Jornal Pessoal.

The charges stem from a series of articles that the journalist published in Jornal Pessoal in 1999 and 2000 denouncing the illegal appropriation of timber-rich land in the Amazon rain forest by companies controlled by Cecílio do Rego Almeida, owner of the construction company CR Almeida, and his sons. The journalist also reported that the Pará Land Institute, a government agency that manages the land belonging to Pará State, and federal prosecutors were trying to cancel land titles that Almeida and his sons had bought and registered in collusion with corrupt judicial officials.

Lúcio Flávio supported his allegations with data from Brazil's Ministry of Agrarian Development. In interviews with the Brazilian press, Cecílio do Rego Almeida has denied that the land is public property. In 1996, federal and state authorities filed a lawsuit to try to recover the land. A court decision is still pending.

Cecílio do Rego Almeida filed a criminal defamation lawsuit and two civil lawsuits against Lúcio Flávio. According to legal documents that were made available to CPJ, the businessman alleges that the journalist's articles offended him and requests monetary compensation for "moral damages."

Pará State judge João Alberto Paiva has also filed criminal and civil lawsuits against the journalist. The charges stem from an editorial in which Lúcio Flávio heavily criticized the judge for granting an injunction that restored temporary control of the land contested by Brazilian authorities to a company controlled by Cecílio do Rego Almeida.

An award-winning journalist, Lúcio Flávio has received numerous threats in the past for his critical reporting on a variety of subjects, including drug trafficking, environmental devastation, and political and corporate corruption.

SEPTEMBER 30

Domingos Sávio Brandão Lima Júnior,
Folha do Estado
KILLED (MOTIVE UNCONFIRMED)
For full details on this case, see page 368.

CHILE

JANUARY 15

Eduardo Yáñez Morel, free-lance
LEGAL ACTION
Yáñez, a regular panelist on Chilevisión's

debate show "El Termómetro," was detained overnight after proceedings were initiated against him for "disrespecting" the Supreme Court. Yáñez was released on bail and faces up to five years in prison.

The complaint stemmed from a November 27, 2001, episode of the show in which Yáñez called the judiciary "immoral, cowardly, and corrupt" for not compensating a woman who had been imprisoned for a crime she did not commit. Yáñez, a businessman and environmental activist, also said the judiciary had shown "little manliness" in failing to apologize for the incident.

On November 30, 2001, the Supreme Court asked its then president, Hernán Álvarez, to file a criminal complaint accusing Yáñez of "disrespect." In early January 2002, the judge in charge of the case, Juan Manuel Muñoz Pardo, gave the parties 10 working days to reach a settlement. But the Supreme Court's new president, Mario Garrido Montt, repeatedly refused to meet with Yáñez, who wanted to offer his apologies.

On January 15, 2002, Judge Muñoz initiated proceedings against Yáñez, and the panelist was detained overnight. The next day, the Santiago Appeals Court confirmed Judge Muñoz's decision to grant Yáñez a 100,000 peso (US$150) bail.

The Inter-American Commission on Human Rights then interceded on Yáñez's behalf, asking the Chilean government to provide it with information on the case. In May, Yáñez told CPJ that although his lawyers had filed repeated requests, Judge Muñoz refused to give them a copy of the summons from the Supreme Court.

Yáñez's lawyers appealed the case to a superior court, which upheld the conviction on October 29. While he is currently free on bail, the journalist cannot leave the country without government permission. If sentenced, Yáñez faces up to five years in prison and a fine, according to Article 263 of Chile's Penal Code. He was awaiting sentencing at year's end.

COLOMBIA

JANUARY 20

Claudia Gurisatti, RCN Televisión
THREATENED

Gurisatti, a popular anchorwoman and talk show host at RCN Televisión, fled Colombia for the United States for the second time in one year after receiving death threats. The 28-year-old journalist told CPJ that, beginning on January 20, an unknown man called her several times at her office in Bogotá, Colombia's capital, to warn her of a plot against her life. She left Colombia on February 4.

During several calls, the man told Gurisatti that a group of people were watching her closely and had spent thousands of dollars on an elaborate plan to kill her. When Gurisatti asked him if he was a member of a leftist guerrilla army or a right-wing paramilitary group, which have been fighting in a 38-year civil conflict, he refused to answer.

As host of RCN Televisión's evening news and a nightly news show called "La Noche" (The Night), Gurisatti has interviewed leaders of both guerrilla and paramilitary groups, as well as officials involved in alleged corruption.

In January 2001, Gurisatti left Colombia for Miami after government authorities said members of the nation's largest guerrilla army, the Revolutionary Armed Forces of Colombia (FARC), were trying to kill her. Gurisatti returned in June 2001 and later said she doubted the rebels wanted to assas-

sinate her. In December 2002, the journalist, who is working for RCN Televisión from the United States, told CPJ that she has no immediate plans to return to Colombia.

JANUARY 23

Marco Antonio Ayala Cárdenas, *El Caleño*
KILLED (MOTIVE UNCONFIRMED)

For full details on this case, see page 369.

JANUARY 31

Caracol Televisión
ATTACKED

A car bomb exploded before dawn near Caracol Televisión studios in the capital, Bogotá, shattering windows but causing no serious damage or injuries. About 65 pounds of dynamite were packed into a red four-wheel-drive vehicle and detonated at 4:30 a.m. on a residential street behind the office, where the network broadcasts its news programs, authorities said. The explosion also blew out windows in surrounding buildings and homes.

Bogotá mayor Antanas Mockus blamed the attack on the nation's largest guerrilla army, the Revolutionary Armed Forces of Colombia (FARC). But Caracol news director, Gonzalo Guerra, said it was premature to assign blame and denied police reports that the network had received threats prior to the explosion. The blast came on the heels of dozens of attacks allegedly perpetrated by the FARC against the nation's infrastructure, security forces, and civilians.

FEBRUARY 1

Orlando Sierra Hernández, *La Patria*
KILLED

For full details on this case, see page 356.

FEBRUARY 5

Alfonso Pardo, *Voz*
THREATENED

Pardo, a columnist for the Communist Party newspaper *Voz*, accused army officials of making threatening phone calls to him. Pardo said he was in the southern town of Pasto, Nariño Department, when he received two calls on his cell phone on the morning of February 5. The calls came just hours before he was to talk with authorities from the Attorney General's Office about death threats he received last year from a right-wing paramilitary army.

According to Pardo, the first caller—whom he described as a man with a thick regional accent—said: "Son of a bitch, are you going to comply?" Pardo said a different man called 15 minutes later and said: "Is that clear?" An investigator from the Attorney General's Office who traced the numbers said they belonged to three officials from the army's 18th Brigade with the last names Parra, Roldón, and Hernández, said Pardo.

Col. Alberto Ruiz, a spokesman for the 18th Brigade, based in the eastern department of Arauca, said he did not know the names. "This is the first time we've heard of the case, but it's a supremely grave charge and it will oblige us to initiate an investigation immediately," Ruiz said. Colombia's military has long been accused of collaborating with the paramilitary United Self-Defense Forces of Colombia (AUC) against leftist rebels, who are waging a decades-long insurgency.

A wing of the paramilitary army known as the Southern Liberators Front sent a letter to news organizations in Pasto in November 2001 accusing Pardo and three other journalists of working with the rebels. The letter said they would be executed if they didn't quit their jobs and leave the area within two days. Last year, paramilitary

fighters allegedly assassinated Pardo's friend and colleague at *Voz*, Flavio Bedoya.

The Interior Ministry's Program for the Protection of Journalists and Social Communicators gave Pardo money to hire a bodyguard, but he left the country shortly after the threats.

FEBRUARY 19

T. Christian Miller, *The Los Angeles Times*
Mauricio Hoyos, *The Los Angeles Times*
HARASSED

Miller, a journalist with *The Los Angeles Times*, and his Colombian assistant, Hoyos, were detained by the leftist guerrilla group Revolutionary Armed Forces of Colombia (FARC) for 24 hours near the village of Bututo on the border of Putumayo and Caquetá departments.

They were released unharmed on February 20, just hours before then Colombian president Andrés Pastrana Arango suspended peace talks with the FARC.

The guerrillas detained the Colombia-based journalist and his assistant when the two men walked into a rebel encampment swarming with more than 200 fighters from the FARC's 49th Front.

Miller and Hoyos had come to interview the rebels about a U.S. helicopter that had been downed in the region by FARC ground fire while conducting a drug-fumigation mission in January. Although the crew escaped unharmed, five Colombian police officers died trying to defend the helicopter after it crashed. No Americans were on board.

Shortly after the journalists arrived at the camp, a subcommander told them that they should not have come to a conflict zone and said they were being detained both for their own safety and so rebels could verify that they were journalists. FARC members confiscated their wallets, cell phones, and notebooks and took them to a shack in a jungle clearing nearby. Both men said they were never threatened or physically abused.

On the afternoon of February 20, the group's commander, Héctor Ramírez, apologized for the inconvenience and freed them. After their belongings were returned, Ramírez took them to see the helicopter nearby.

FEBRUARY 23

Alain Kellert, *Marie Claire*
HARASSED

Kellert, a photographer with the French magazine *Marie Claire*, was detained by the Revolutionary Armed Forces of Colombia (FARC) while covering a story about internationally known Colombian presidential candidate Ingrid Betancourt.

Kellert and others were riding in a vehicle with Betancourt when the leftist FARC rebels stopped them inside the rebel army's former safe haven in southern Colombia, said Adair Lamprea, Betancourt's logistics director, who was driving.

Betancourt was on her way to the main town inside the safe haven to show solidarity with its residents. Days earlier, on February 20, the Colombian government had ended a three-year peace process with the FARC and ordered the military to retake the Switzerland-sized safe haven.

Moments after rebels forced Betancourt's vehicle to stop, a young FARC fighter stepped on a land mine nearby. Other rebels then commandeered the vehicle, placed the badly wounded fighter inside, and drove off in search of medical treatment with Kellert, Betancourt, and the others forced to remain inside, said Lamprea.

About an hour later, rebels abducted Betancourt and her campaign manager, Clara Rojas, from the vehicle and drove them off in separate trucks. By year's end, they had not been freed.

The remaining detainees—Kellert, Lamprea, and Mauricio Mesa, a cameraman hired by the campaign—were driven for another three hours to a rebel camp, where the wounded fighter was whisked away.

The rebels gave the three men Gatorade, rice, and fish and released them at around 7 p.m., about five hours after they were detained. They were forced to walk back to the nearest town, Florencia, and spent part of the night sleeping on the side of the road. They arrived in Florencia at around 8 a.m. the next morning. Lamprea said he and the others were treated well and were never threatened or physically abused. Kellert returned to France two days later, Lamprea said.

FEBRUARY 28

Onda Zero
ATTACKED

Onda Zero, a radio station based in the southern town of Acevedo, Huila Department, was forced to close by leftist guerrillas, who accused the station of serving government interests.

Some 10 fighters from the Revolutionary Armed Forces of Colombia (FARC) threatened to blow up the station and then took a transmitter, antennas, and other equipment valued at US$12,500, said director José Vicente Rodríguez.

A journalist at the station, Divier Alexander López, fled the region the next day in fear of his life. Neither he nor anyone else at the station had previously been threatened. "They argued that they were taking us out because we were working for the government," said Rodríguez. "I don't know what reasons they have for saying that."

Rodríguez denied FARC accusations that Onda Zero, which employs eight people, was working for the government. The station serves nine townships and began broadcasting 11 years ago. Seventy percent of its 16 hours of daily programming is popular music. The rest is devoted to educational programs, said sources at the station. Rodríguez said he would raise money to buy new equipment if the rebels refuse to return the transmitter and other equipment.

The radio station is located near the border of the safe haven that the Colombian government ceded to the FARC in 1998. On February 20, the government suspended peace talks with the FARC and launched a military operation to retake the area. In the weeks after negotiations collapsed, the FARC blew up electrical towers in Huila Department.

MARCH 1

Jairo Lozano, *El Tiempo*
Juan Carlos Giraldo, RCN Televisión
Julia Navarrete, Caracol Televisión
Jairo Naranjo, RCN Radio
Hernando Marroquín, Caracol Radio
Marilyn López, "Noticias Uno"
José Antonio Jiménez, TV Hoy
THREATENED

Lozano, a reporter for the daily *El Tiempo*; Giraldo, a senior correspondent for RCN Televisión; Navarrete, a correspondent for Caracol Televisión; Naranjo, a correspondent for RCN Radio; Marroquín, a correspondent for Caracol Radio; López, a correspondent for the news program "Noticias Uno"; and Jiménez, a former correspondent for now defunct TV Hoy, were threatened with death and given three days to leave the country. All have covered high-profile criminal investigations for major Colombian media outlets.

A message typed on a card used to request a Catholic prayer for the dead accused the journalists of being "gossipy sons-of-bitches who with their lies have led the Attorney General's Office to screw around with our people." RCN Televisión received the first letter on March 1. Caracol Televisión received an identical letter three days later.

The Attorney General's Office is investigating the threats, said agency spokesperson Carolina Sánchez. By year's end, investigators had yet to determine who was responsible.

The message, a copy of which was obtained by CPJ, warned that the journalists and their families would be considered military targets if they did not leave the country within 72 hours. The note was signed "Death Commando" and included an image of Jesus. Four of the seven journalists told CPJ that the threats came from "a criminal organization" but declined to elaborate. The other journalists could not be reached for comment.

All seven journalists had covered high-profile drug investigations for their news organizations. The letter that arrived at Caracol Televisión on March 4 was addressed to Navarrete, who covers the Attorney General's Office. She has received four previous threats and attributes a minor heart attack she suffered in February to work-related stress.

Hours after opening the letter, Navarrete was heading home in a chauffeur-driven company car from her office in the capital, Bogotá, when a vehicle with its headlights on high beam raced up from behind and tailed her car. The pursuer sped away after Navarrete's driver pulled into a police checkpoint.

The Interior Ministry's Program for the Protection of Journalists and Social Communicators provided the journalists with bodyguards. At least three of them went into hiding within Colombia, but they had returned to their homes by year's end.

MARCH 21

Fernando Garavito, *El Espectador*
THREATENED

Garavito, columnist for the Bogotá-based newspaper *El Espectador*, fled Colombia after a series of events that made him fear for his life. The journalist, who writes a Sunday column for the paper, left Colombia for the United States on March 21.

In a series of columns, Garavito criticized the right-wing United Self-Defense Forces of Colombia (AUC) and described the then front-running presidential candidate Álvaro Uribe as an ultraright candidate whose election would be dangerous for the country. (Uribe won the May 26 poll.) Garavito told CPJ that his problems began soon after the columns appeared.

On February 19, the AUC published a communiqué about the Colombian press on its Web site. Signed by paramilitary leaders Salvatore Mancuso and Carlos Castaño, the communiqué accused local columnists of having "poisonous spirits" and mentioned Garavito by name. Soon after, people began calling Garavito at home and work and hanging up before speaking. Meanwhile, strangers called Garavito's friends to ask about the journalist.

On the morning of March 18, two men claiming to represent an organization to protect journalists entered the Sergio Arboleda University campus in the capital, Bogotá, where Garavito teaches. The two men wanted to know Garavito's teaching schedule and his home telephone number. They also asked to know what newspaper he worked for. Garavito, 57, went into hiding the next day. He fled the country on March 21.

Garavito has been a columnist for *El Espectador* since 1998 and plans to continue writing from exile. In the past, he has used his column to criticize not only the paramilitaries but also leftist guerrillas and the Colombian government. The three sides are entangled in a 38-year-old civil conflict.

APRIL 4

Carlos José Lajud, Citytv
THREATENED

Lajud, television reporter with the Bogotá-based station Citytv, received a death threat after reporting extensively on the country's left-wing guerrilla movement. On April 4, Lajud received a letter at the Citytv offices. "Our sincere condolences ... for the death of Carlos Lajud," read the note, a copy of which was obtained by CPJ.

The letter referred to Lajud as a "gossipy son-of-a-bitch," accused the journalist of serving the interests of Colombia's ruling class, declared him and his family "military targets," and demanded that he leave the country within three days.

Since February, Lajud has produced some 20 investigative reports claiming that the Revolutionary Armed Forces of Colombia (FARC) and the smaller National Liberation Army (ELN) have established armed cells in Bogotá. Lajud detailed the organizational structures of these new urban guerrilla groups, showed how they bought explosives, and revealed that one cell had opened a clandestine clinic to treat its wounded, the journalist told CPJ.

The letter was the most serious of several threats against Lajud that began in late February, just three days after his reports on the new urban guerrilla groups began to air. On February 27, strangers began calling Lajud and his wife, Patricia Busigo, at their home and describing their daily routines. In March, at a park near the television station, an unknown man grabbed Lajud by the arm, said he had a "big mouth," and predicted he would "disappear."

Lajud claims not to know the source of the threats, but the Interior Ministry's Program for the Protection of Journalists and Social Communicators gave the journalist a bodyguard. In May, the Canadian government granted the journalist and his wife asylum. The couple left Colombia in July. Lajud is the son of the late radio journalist Carlos Alfonso Lajud Catalán. In 1993, Catalán was shot and killed after he publicly accused a local mayor of corruption.

APRIL 6

Adriana Aristizábal, RCN Televisión
Andrés Reina, RCN Televisión
HARASSED

Aristizábal, an RCN Televisión correspondent, and Reina, her cameraman, were detained, along with driver Joaquín Gómez, by fighters from the Revolutionary Armed Forces of Colombia (FARC) in the small town of Pulí, where they had traveled to report on a guerrilla attack. The town is in Cundinamarca Department, about 60 miles (96 kilometers) east of the capital, Bogotá.

The journalists were leaving the town when about 10 FARC combatants stopped them, ordered them to exit their car, and said they would be used as human shields so the military would not fire at the rebels, said Aristizábal. The rebels then took their car, a camera, film, and other personal belongings, including money and identification cards. Four hours later, the fighters stopped a passing car and ordered the driver to take the journalists.

Aristizábal said the rebels refused to return the journalists' equipment or belongings and insulted them repeatedly. Aristizábal has worked for RCN Televisión, Colombia's largest television station, for four years. She covers the Ministry of Defense and often works in combat zones.

APRIL 12

Héctor Sandoval, RCN Televisión
KILLED

For full details on this case, see page 357.

RCN Televisión
ATTACKED

A rocket exploded near the studios of RCN Televisión in the capital, Bogotá. Local authorities said the station was intentionally targeted. The blast destroyed a brick wall surrounding the offices of a telephone company located less than 13 yards (12 meters) from the station in an industrial neighborhood in south Bogotá, said Sgt. Alberto Cantillo, a spokesperson for the city's police department.

The rocket was fired at a range of less than 330 yards (300 meters) from the station by a man who was driven to the area on the back of a motorcycle, Cantillo said. No one was injured in the attack, which authorities blamed on the leftist Revolutionary Armed Forces of Colombia (FARC). RCN's sprawling facility contains executive offices as well as television and news studios, said Rocío Arias, executive producer of RCN Televisión news.

APRIL 15

Mauricio Bayona, El Tiempo, Citytv
THREATENED

Bayona, a sports editor at El Tiempo newspaper and Citytv television station who has written frequently about links between drug gangs and professional soccer, fled Colombia on April 15 after secret police learned of a plot to kill him. He returned to Colombia on May 15.

The journalist said agents from the Department of Administrative Security told him that a drug boss in southwestern Valle

Department had paid the equivalent of US$25,000 to have him assassinated. The agents said the attack was being planed from Modelo Prison in the capital, Bogotá.

Bayona, his colleagues, and his parents then began receiving calls from unidentified men who said that the journalist would be killed if he continued to write columns denouncing the influence of drug traffickers in Colombia's professional soccer leagues.

The 37-year-old journalist, who has been sports editor at *El Tiempo* and Citytv in Bogotá for two years, said he returned "because I love my work." The government has given him two bodyguards.

APRIL 22

Daniel Coronell, "Noticias Uno"
Ignacio Gómez, "Noticias Uno"
THREATENED

Coronell, news director of "Noticias Uno," a current affairs program on the Bogotá TV station Canal Uno, and his 3-year-old daughter were threatened with death by unidentified men.

Coronell received threatening calls on his cell phone, home phone, and office phone after he aired an investigative report examining possible links between the country's leading presidential candidate and drug traffickers. The journalist reported the threats to police and on April 24 sent his daughter out of the country with relatives.

The report that Coronell aired revealed that a helicopter seized during a notorious 1984 cocaine bust was registered to an aerial photography business co-owned by presidential front-runner Álvaro Uribe Vélez's father. The segment also reported that in 1981, Colombia's civil aviation department granted an operating license for the helicopter in one day, although the normal waiting time was up to 20 working days. Uribe headed the department when the license was approved.

Less than two weeks before the report aired, Gómez, director of investigations at "Noticias Uno," received some 15 threats—many of them death threats—by telephone at his home in Bogotá.

The day after the report was broadcast, a man called Coronell's office three times and told the secretary that Coronell would be killed. At 11 p.m. that night, a man called Coronell from an unregistered telephone number and said, "We're going to kill you, son-of-a-bitch." At 9:30 a.m. the following morning, another man called Coronell on his cell phone and threatened to kill his daughter. The journalist told CPJ that he does not know who is responsible for the threats.

APRIL 28

Manuel Benavides, *Diario del Sur*
THREATENED

Benavides, a correspondent for the daily newspaper *Diario del Sur*, based in southwestern Nariño Department, fled the region with his wife and son after paramilitary fighters accused him of being friendly with rival leftist guerrillas and threatened to kill him.

Benavides, 54, said the threats stemmed from an article he wrote in April criticizing the armed forces for failing to respond quickly when guerrillas from the leftist Revolutionary Armed Forces of Colombia (FARC) attacked a village near Benavides' home. Three-days later, a man who identified himself as a member of the paramilitary United Self-Defense Forces of Colombia (AUC) called Benavides at his home and accused him of being a friend of the guerrillas because the journalist had criticized the armed forces. The guerrillas are fighting the government and the paramilitary army in a civil conflict that began 38 years ago.

In May, Benavides said he was traveling from his home in San Pablo to Pasto, the departmental capital, when paramilitary fighters detained him at a roadblock. After the militia commander identified Benavides, he said that the journalist would be declared a "military target" if he did not leave Nariño.

Benavides said he was detained at four other paramilitary roadblocks during the following two weeks, and that paramilitary members repeated the threat each time they identified him. He said he reported the threats to the local public prosecutor's office and to a human rights official on May 17.

Benavides has covered fighting in Nariño as a free-lance correspondent for the 4,000-circulation newspaper for 14 years. Paramilitary fighters and guerrillas are battling for control of lucrative drug crops in the region. Benavides went into hiding on July 12.

APRIL 30

Astrid María Legarda Martínez, RCN
Televisión
`THREATENED`

Legarda, a correspondent who covers Colombia's civil conflict for independent RCN Televisión, learned that the nation's largest rebel army, the Revolutionary Armed Forces of Colombia (FARC), was planning to kill her. The journalist heard about the alleged plan from a source in a high-security prison in the capital, Bogotá. Legarda went into hiding soon after and fled Colombia on July 3.

MAY 2

Edgar Buitrago Rico, Revista Valle 2000
`THREATENED`

Buitrago, founder and director of the Cali-based monthly *Revista Valle 2000*, received repeated death threats. The journalist received two threats by e-mail on May 2. In June, armed men mistook the magazine's advertising salesman for Buitrago, forced him into a vehicle, and threatened to kill him before realizing their mistake and freeing him.

Buitrago fled to Bogotá in early August but returned to Cali three weeks later after running out of money. On August 21, Buitrago requested assistance from the Interior Ministry's Program for the Protection of Journalists and Social Communicators to relocate to the capital, Bogotá.

The latest threat appeared in late August in a letter sent to the local press and politicians in Cali. It accused Buitrago of publishing lies in support of Cali's mayor, whom Buitrago has backed publicly because of the mayor's stance against corruption.

The letter warned that Buitrago and 10 other people would be declared "military targets" unless they left the city immediately. The note was signed by the Committee for the Rescue of Cali.

The journalist launched the magazine *Revista Valle 2000* in 1998 as a publication dedicated to investigating and denouncing cases of political corruption in Valle del Cauca Department, whose capital is Cali.

Death threats in recent years have forced four of Buitrago's volunteer correspondents to resign. Before starting the magazine, Buitrago was subdirector at the daily *El Caleño* and a reporter for the daily *El País*, both based in Cali.

On September 17, CPJ sent a letter to Colombia's interior minister, Fernando Londoño Hoyos, supporting the journalist's request for financial assistance to relocate for his safety. The ministry later granted him funds.

MAY 8

Carlos Pulgarín, Universidad de La
Sabana
César Mauricio Velásquez, Universidad
de La Sabana
Alejandro Santos, *Semana*
THREATENED
Francisco Tulande, RCN Radio
ATTACKED, THREATENED

Pulgarín, a journalism professor at the
Universidad de La Sabana, a private university in the capital, Bogotá, was approached
by two men as he was walking toward the
bus stop to go to work, the journalist told
CPJ. One of the men grabbed him by the
arm and the other patted him on the shoulder in a seemingly friendly manner. They
were not visibly armed.

The men told Pulgarín that it was a lovely
day and that he had better enjoy it, because
he did not have many days left to live. They
told him to convey the same message to
Velásquez, the dean of the Universidad de La
Sabana's department of social communication and journalism. Before leaving in a red
all-terrain vehicle, the men told Pulgarín that
they knew where his family lived.

A similar car had followed Velásquez in
April, Pulgarín said. One of the men who
threatened Pulgarín resembled the driver of
the vehicle that had tailed Velásquez.

The threats to Pulgarín and Velásquez were
the latest in a series of warnings directed at
four local journalists beginning on March 19.
That day, a man who identified himself as a
retired army sergeant called Velásquez's office
twice and told his secretary that there was a
plan under way to kill Tulande, deputy director of RCN Radio; Santos, editor of the news
magazine *Semana*; and Pulgarín.

On April 8, the same man called again
and told Velásquez's secretary that the
attack was imminent and that Velásquez was
also a target. The man said the four journalists were considered "enemies of Colombia"
because of their work but did not elaborate.

Velásquez notified authorities and the
other journalists about the alleged plot. The
Interior Ministry's Program for the Protection
of Journalists and Social Communicators provided him with a bodyguard.

While none of the journalists know why
they were threatened, Santos said *Semana*'s
participation in a collaborative media investigation into the shooting death earlier this year
of journalist Orlando Sierra is one possible
motive. On March 3, *Semana* and six other
prominent Colombian newspapers and news
magazines published the results of a joint
investigation concluding that local politicians
may have ordered Sierra's murder because he
had frequently accused them of corruption.

Pulgarín fled Colombia on May 14. Death
threats have forced the journalist to flee
Colombia on several occasions since 1999. All
the threats apparently resulted from his exposés
of violence perpetrated by Colombia's guerrillas, paramilitaries, and government forces.

Pulgarín said that the men who accosted
him on May 8 had harassed him on several
previous occasions. The first incident took
place outside his apartment building in
2001. On that occasion, the two men were
armed and identified themselves as members
of a right-wing paramilitary organization.

They demanded that Pulgarín leave
Colombia and renounce journalism. Pulgarín
subsequently quit his job (he was working at
the Bogotá daily *El Tiempo* at the time) and
left the country. When he returned to
Colombia in September 2001, the journalist
said, the same two men accosted him and
repeated their threats. On March 14, 2002,
his birthday, Pulgarín received a phone call
from an unidentified man who said, "*Sapo*
[informer], son-of-a-bitch, enjoy it because
it's your last year."

MAY 16

Nidia Álvarez Mariño, *Hoy Diario del Magdalena*
HARASSED
Ramón Vásquez Ruiz, *Hoy Diario del Magdalena*
IMPRISONED, THREATENED

Álvarez and Vásquez, both of the Santa Marta–based daily *Hoy Diario del Magdalena,* and their driver, Vladimir Revolledo Cuisman, were abducted by the leftist Revolutionary Armed Forces of Colombia (FARC) in Magdalena Department, in northern Colombia, said Mónica Pimienta, an editor at the paper. Álvarez was freed unharmed the next morning, but the rebels did not free Vásquez and the driver until May 24.

The reporters were traveling to a town south of Santa Marta to cover a local court case and satanic cults when they unknowingly drove into a rebel roadblock near Ciénaga, about 420 miles (670 kilometers) from the capital, Bogotá. The rebels kidnapped nine other people in addition to the reporters and the driver.

On May 23, the founder and director of *Hoy Diario del Magdalena,* Ulilo Acevedo, told CPJ that the FARC had sent the paper a communiqué on May 18 demanding that the newspaper print the statement and pay the equivalent of US$500,000 to secure the release of Vásquez and Revolledo. He said that the communiqué analyzed the current political situation in Colombia and lambasted the paramilitary armies. Acevedo feared that a rival right-wing paramilitary army could retaliate against the daily newspaper for publishing the statement. On May 24, the FARC freed Revolledo and Vásquez, who told CPJ that the rebels had dropped their demands.

Vásquez also told CPJ two unidentified men called him three times on his cell phone just hours after the FARC freed him. The men accused the journalist of collaborating with the group that abducted him, alleging the 52-year-old reporter had staged the kidnapping with the help of the FARC, presumably for economic gain. Vásquez denied the charge.

Although the men did not make specific threats, Vásquez said he reported the calls to the local Prosecutor's Office and fears for his life. A spokesman for the Prosecutor's Office in Magdalena Department declined to say whether authorities were investigating the threats or if they had received the complaint.

Vásquez said the nation's smaller rebel group, the National Liberation Army (ELN), kidnapped him five years ago while he was working for a newspaper in the nearby city of Barranquilla and held him for eight days. Both rebel groups have been fighting the government and a rival paramilitary army for the last 38 years.

JUNE 6

Oscar Javier Hoyos Narváez, Radio Súper
KILLED (MOTIVE UNCONFIRMED)

For full details on this case, see page 369.

JUNE 28

Efraín Varela Noriega, Radio Meridiano-70
KILLED

For full details on this case, see page 357.

JULY 9

Anyela Muñoz, *El Vocero*
THREATENED

Muñoz, owner of the weekly *El Vocero,* was accosted by two unidentified gunmen on a street in Barrancabermeja, an oil-refining town in the northeastern department of Santander. The men told her that if that week's issue of her paper were published, someone would die.

This threat followed a statement by a commander of the Bloque Central Bolívar unit of the rightist paramilitary army United Self-Defense Forces of Colombia (AUC) that was directed at journalists in Barrancabermeja. "You either stop playing with the pain of the community, or it will be our sad obligation to execute someone so you know the pain of the people," said the commander in a July 8 interview with the daily *Vanguardia Liberal*, which is based in the Santander Department capital, Bucaramanga.

Barrancabermeja is a hotbed of violence in Colombia's 38-year-old civil conflict, which pits two of the country's main leftist rebel armies against the AUC and the Colombian military.

On the same day that Muñoz was threatened, she and journalists from other media outlets met to discuss the matter and subsequently published a communiqué denouncing the threats. *El Vocero* appeared on newsstands with the headline, "Yes to the Press."

Following a national and international outcry, the commander who made the declaration backed down from the threats. According to a CPJ source, however, Barrancabermeja journalists are still wary of the situation.

JULY 12

Mario Prada Díaz, *Horizonte del Magdalena Medio*
KILLED (MOTIVE UNCONFIRMED)
For full details on this case, see page 370.

JULY 13

El Nuevo Día
ATTACKED
Elisabeth Obando, a newspaper salesper-

son for the daily *El Nuevo Día*, and her friend were pulled off a bus and shot by unidentified gunmen along a roadside in the town of Playarrica in Tolima Department, authorities said.

Obando was taken to a hospital, where she died the next day, said *El Nuevo Día* director Antonio Melo. He said that during the last four years, the 40-year-old Obando had sold copies of the newspaper from her shop in the nearby town of Roncesvalles. Police in Playarrica identified the other victim as Angela Bríñez, 23, who worked in Roncesvalles for the department's Human Rights Office.

In September 2001, the 10,000-circulation newspaper began publishing articles accusing local members of the Revolutionary Armed Forces of Colombia (FARC) of seizing privately owned land as part of an illegal land reform policy. Following the reports, the local FARC commander publicly threatened reprisals against Obando if she continued selling the newspaper, said Melo. Obando stopped selling it in March.

JULY 23

Jairo Orlando Guzmán, "Noticias Uno"
THREATENED
Guzmán, a news cameraman for "Noticias Uno," a current-affairs program on the Bogotá TV station Canal Uno, and his family fled Colombia for the United States following a series of death threats that began last year. Guzmán, 42, said the threats started in March 2001, when a Catholic prayer card traditionally used to honor the dead arrived at his house with a bullet and a painting of a red crucifix inside.

The next month, Guzmán's 16-year-old son answered a telephone call from a man who told him to tell his father to stop being a "gossiper" and recommended that they leave the country. Later the same day, the son said a second man called with another message for his father: "We're going to hit him where it hurts the most," the caller reportedly said. Guzmán's 21-year-old daughter said she received two similar threats on June 2. Guzmán, along with his wife and two children, left Colombia on July 23, said Nubia Sánchez, subdirector of the private company that produces "Noticias Uno."

Guzmán began working as a cameraman for the program 11 years ago and has reported on both leftist rebels and rival paramilitaries in Colombia's ongoing civil conflict. Guzmán reported the threats to the Attorney General's Office and police, but he does not know who is behind them.

JULY 29

Rodrigo Ávila, Caracol Televisión
Radio Meridiano-70
THREATENED

Ávila, a Caracol Televisión correspondent, and Radio Meridiano-70 received e-mail messages from paramilitary fighters accusing members of the press and media owners in Arauca Department of flouting justice and warning that they could be declared military targets. The Arauca Liberators Block of the paramilitary United Self-Defense Forces of Colombia (AUC) signed the letter.

Paramilitary leaders announced before the July 29 threat that the AUC was disbanding because they no longer had control over their fighters. The AUC is now fighting under the banner of Peasant Self-Defense Forces of Córdoba and Urabá.

A month before, on June 28, presumed paramilitary fighters in Arauca shot and killed Radio Meridiano-70 owner Efraín Varela, who, days before his death, had alerted listeners to the presence of paramilitary fighters in the departmental capital.

Ávila, Caracol's correspondent in Arauca,

said he received at least 10 threats by telephone in mid-July and hired a bodyguard with financial help from a private human rights group in Colombia. He said repeated requests for protection from the previous government and the new government of President Álvaro Uribe Vélez, who took office on August 7, have gone unanswered. Evelyn Varela, manager of Meridiano-70 and Efraín Varela's daughter, said she reported the e-mail message to local authorities, who have not responded.

AUGUST 6

Iván Noguera, El Tiempo
Héctor Fabio Zamora, El Tiempo
HARASSED

Noguera and Zamora, correspondent and photographer, respectively, for the daily El Tiempo, along with their driver, were detained by the Revolutionary Armed Forces of Colombia (FARC) and freed two days later. About 10 FARC fighters forced the men out of their vehicle outside the town of Mistrató in western Colombia.

The men had traveled there from their office in nearby Pereira, the capital of Risaralda Department, to report on local indigenous groups that have been caught in the middle of fighting between leftist rebels and rival paramilitary fighters in the region, said Noguera.

The rebels marched them for two hours through the mountains to a farmhouse, where they were held for two nights before being released early on August 8. Although the rebels robbed the newspaper's Toyota truck and confiscated five rolls of film, Noguera said he and his colleagues were not mistreated. The FARC did not explain why the men were being detained but complained to them that Colombia's press is slandering the 17,000-strong rebel army and kowtowing to the army, Noguera said.

OCTOBER 28

José Eli Escalante, La Voz de Cinaruco
KILLED (MOTIVE UNCONFIRMED)

For full details on this case, see page 370.

NOVEMBER 19

La Opinión
ATTACKED

Two unidentified men placed a 66 pound (30 kilogram) bomb in front of the offices of the daily newspaper *La Opinión* in northeastern Colombia. Police later destroyed the bomb.

Two men arrived at *La Opinión* offices in the city of Cúcuta shortly after midnight and asked two security guards to carry a briefcase inside the building, news editor Ángel Romero told CPJ. The guards refused. Minutes later, the men placed the briefcase in front of the office, which also houses the newspaper's printing press, and fled in a van, said Romero.

The guards called the police, who discovered a bomb inside the briefcase and destroyed it shortly before dawn, said a spokesperson for the Norte de Santander Department police.

Police said it wasn't clear who was responsible for the foiled attack. Fighters from Colombia's two largest leftist rebel armies and rival right-wing paramilitary groups are all active in the region. The outlaw groups are fighting in a 38-year-old civil conflict.

Romero said no one had recently threatened the 15,000-circulation newspaper. In March 1993, fighters from the leftist National Liberation Army (ELN) shot and killed *La Opinión* publisher Eustorgio Colmenares.

DECEMBER 1

Gimbler Perdomo Zamora, Panorama Estéreo
KILLED (MOTIVE UNCONFIRMED)

For full details on this case, see page 371.

DECEMBER 9

Radio Caracol
ATTACKED

Presumed members of the Revolutionary Armed Forces of Colombia (FARC) blew up a Radio Caracol antenna and transmitter near the town of Cúcuta, in northeastern Colombia, knocking one radio station off the air but causing no injuries.

A day after the explosion, a man named Rubén Zamora, who identified himself as a FARC commander, called the local newspaper *La Opinión* and claimed responsibility for the attack, according to a reporter at the paper. The reporter told CPJ that the man said his fighters attacked Radio Caracol because "the capitalist media doesn't agree with the changes the FARC wants to make."

The 33 pound (15 kilogram) bomb was placed directly under the antenna, which is located near a farmhouse about 9 miles (14 kilometers) from Radio Caracol's offices in Cúcuta, and was detonated at 10:15 p.m., said Radio Caracol general manager Javier Rojas. The explosion, which destroyed the antenna and transmitter, caused about US$90,000 worth of damage, according to Rojas.

Radio Caracol operates five stations in Cúcuta that broadcast news, music, and sports. The destroyed antenna and transmitter served two of those stations: Caracol Básica, which broadcasts news and opinion; and Radio Reloj, which broadcasts primarily music but also news and sports. Radio Caracol is using another antenna to continue broadcasting Caracol Básica, but Radio Reloj remained off the air at the end of 2002, said Rojas.

A spokesman for the police in Norte de Santander Department, of which Cúcuta is the capital, said authorities were still investigating the attack. He had no knowledge of the call that the alleged FARC commander reportedly made to *La Opinión*.

CUBA

JANUARY 17

Omar Rodríguez Saludes, Nueva Prensa Cubana
HARASSED

Rodríguez Saludes, 36, director of the independent news agency Nueva Prensa Cubana, was arrested by police after covering a meeting between several well-known dissidents and a Spanish official. The journalist was arrested at about 6 p.m. outside the Spanish Embassy, in the municipality of Habana Vieja, where several opposition leaders met with Josep Antoni Duran Lleida, secretary-general of Catalonia's ruling party, Convergencia i Unió (Convergence and Union). After the meeting, Rodríguez Saludes tried to interview the dissidents but was arrested by the police.

The journalist was handcuffed and taken to a police station, where a state security officer interrogated him about his work. The officer called Rodríguez Saludes' writing "counterrevolutionary," according to the independent news agency CubaPress. Sources in Cuba told CPJ that the journalist was released around 11:45 p.m. the same day. Some of the dissidents who attended the earlier meeting waited for him outside the police station until his release.

FEBRUARY 27

Andrew Cawthorne, Reuters
Alfredo Tedeschi, Reuters
ATTACKED

Police and state security agents attacked Reuters journalists Tedeschi and Cawthorne with batons while they covered an incident in front of the Mexican Embassy in the capital, Havana. A group of Cuban citizens had used a bus to crash into the gates of the embassy in hopes of seeking asylum, according to international news reports.

Police chased, beat, and detained several onlookers who had congregated outside the embassy. The two journalists were caught in the fray: Tedeschi, a cameraman, was beaten to the ground by police, and his camera was taken. Cawthorne, Reuters' Cuba correspondent, was beaten on the arm and back.

Although violent attacks against journalists in Cuba are unusual, Reuters reported that police and state security agents aggressively moved foreign media workers away from the scene, calling them "sons of bitches." Plainclothes state security agents and police with dogs later cordoned off an area of several blocks around the embassy, banning access to journalists and passers-by.

The gate crash was prompted by rumors that Mexico had offered to grant asylum to all Cubans who wanted to leave the country. As a result, hundreds of Cubans gathered outside the embassy to seek information. Mexican chargé d'affaires Andrés Ordóñez later met with foreign journalists and denied that Mexico had changed its immigration policy toward Cuba.

MARCH 4

Léster Téllez Castro, Agencia de Prensa Libre Avileña
HARASSED
Jesús Álvarez Castillo, CubaPress
ATTACKED, LEGAL ACTION

Álvarez Castillo, correspondent for the independent news agency CubaPress in the central province of Ciego de Ávila, was attacked by state security forces. Álvarez Castillo told CPJ that at about 11 a.m., he and a colleague, Téllez Castro of the independent news agency Agencia de Prensa Libre Avileña, were on their way to cover a demonstration by the human rights organization Fundación Cubana de Derechos Humanos (FCDH) in the city of Ciego de Ávila when Interior Ministry officers stopped them and turned them back.

The journalists then went to a post office nearby and called a colleague. While they were on the phone, State Security Department (DSE) officers arrived and told the journalists they were under arrest. As Téllez Castro started shouting, "Long live human rights!" and anti-government slogans, an officer held him from behind, while another officer applied a chokehold to Álvarez Castillo and dragged him to the officers' car. Both journalists were taken to the local DSE headquarters.

As Álvarez Castillo exited the car in front of the DSE headquarters, he fainted and was taken to a hospital. Téllez Castro was released soon after arriving at the DSE headquarters. At the hospital, X-rays revealed that Álvarez Castillo had a sprained neck. Meanwhile, at around 1 p.m., several journalists and FCDH activists gathered at the hospital to inquire about Álvarez Castillo's condition and to protest the attack. The group included Téllez Castro, who is also the organizing secretary of the FCDH, and Carlos Brizuela Yera, a reporter with the independent news agency Colegio de Periodistas Independientes de Camagüey who is also active in the organization.

The protesters were charged with "public disorder" and other offenses for allegedly physically blocking access to a hallway inside the hospital. They were arrested by police and taken to the Technical Department of Investigations (DTI). At around 2 p.m.,

Álvarez Castillo was discharged from the hospital and also brought to DTI headquarters, where he was held until 6:30 p.m. During that time, he was told to describe the beating incident and his statements were videotaped.

On March 11, the police transferred the hospital protesters, which included Brizuela Yera, to a detention center in the eastern province of Holguín. Téllez Castro was moved to a facility in the central province of Cienfuegos. In April, Téllez Castro was transferred to Canaleta Prison, in Ciego de Ávila, while Brizuela Yera was moved to a prison in Holguín. All of the hospital protesters have been charged and are facing stiff sentences, but the Ciego de Ávila public prosecutor cited the past criminal records of Téllez Castro and Brizuela Yera in seeking prison sentences of six and five years, respectively, for the two men. Téllez Castro had previously served six years for armed robbery; Brizuela had been convicted of assaulting a police officer.

Local authorities have called Álvarez Castillo to testify against his colleagues charged for protesting his attack. In early August, officials charged him with perjury, a crime punishable by six months to eight years in prison. The cases remained pending at year's end.

MARCH 21

Sociedad de Periodistas Manuel Márquez Sterling
HARASSED

The Sociedad de Periodistas Manuel Márquez Sterling (SPMMS), an association of independent journalists, was forced to suspend its journalism courses temporarily after its members were blocked from entering the association's offices.

At about 1 p.m., several Department of State Security (DSE) officers stopped

journalists Jorge Olivera Castillo, Dorka
Céspedes Vila, Omar Rodríguez Saludes,
Adolfo Fernández Sainz, Aimée Cabrera
Álvarez, and Pedro Pablo Álvarez before
they reached the SPMMS offices, which are
located in the municipality of Playa in the
capital, Havana. Journalists Ricardo
González Alfonso, Carmelo Díaz
Fernández, Víctor Manuel Domínguez, and
Álida Viso Bello, who were already inside,
were forced to postpone the classes.

On March 22, the SPMMS issued a communiqué condemning the crackdown.
Members have vowed to continue the
courses and have changed class schedules
and locations to overcome DSE surveillance.

MAY 3

Juan Carlos Garcell Pérez, Agencia de
Prensa Libre Oriental
HARASSED

Garcell Pérez, a journalist with the independent news agency Agencia de Prensa
Libre Oriental in the eastern province of
Holguín, was detained twice and beaten
by police, according to the journalists' association Sociedad de Periodistas Manuel
Márquez Sterling, of which Garcell Pérez is
a local representative.

At around 7 p.m. on May 3, when
Garcell Pérez was interviewing a patient's
mother at a hospital in the town of Sagua de
Tánamo, a police officer grabbed him and
took him to the local police station. He was
released an hour later, but an officer hit him
twice during the detention.

Later the same day, at around midnight,
eight police officers arrived at the journalist's house, detained him, and searched his
home for two hours. The officers confiscated several books on journalism, as well
as personal documents. Garcell Pérez was
released at 1 p.m. the next day. He was

fined, and the police registered him as a
person with "high criminal potential."

JULY 11

Juan Carlos Garcell Pérez, Agencia de
Prensa Libre Oriental
HARASSED

Garcell Pérez, a journalist with the independent news agency Agencia de Prensa
Libre Oriental in the eastern province of
Holguín, was detained at the Holguín
train station as he returned from the capital, Havana, according to the Sociedad
de Periodistas Manuel Márquez Sterling,
of which Garcell Pérez is a local representative. A police officer and two state
security agents searched his belongings
and took him to the Holguín Police Station,
where he was interrogated, held for two
hours, and threatened with charges of violating Law 88, which mandates prison
terms of up to 20 years for anyone found
guilty of "ruining internal order" and
"destabilizing the country."

The agents asked the journalist about a
fax machine he had bought in Havana and
about books on journalism and office materials he was given while visiting the U.S.
Interests Section in Havana.

JULY 30

Ángel Pablo Polanco, Noticuba
IMPRISONED

Polanco, 60, director of the independent
news agency Noticuba, was detained at
around 11:30 a.m. by plainclothes state security agents who came to his apartment, in
the Havana municipality of Diez de Octubre,
according to Polanco's wife.

The security agents, who said they were
looking for "illegal items," searched the
apartment until 8:30 p.m., confiscating

several electronic appliances, including a fax machine and a cordless phone, documents, books, money, and Polanco's passport.

The security agents did not have a warrant, but they arrested Polanco, who is handicapped and can barely walk, and demanded that he leave with them. When he refused, the officers lifted him, carried him away, and forced him into a car.

The journalist, who was released on August 3, told the independent journalists' association Sociedad de Periodistas Manuel Márquez Sterling that the authorities charged him with instigating others to commit the crimes of "contempt for authority" and "insulting the nation's symbols."

Polanco is now required to report bimonthly to a local police station while police continue an investigation. His confiscated items have not been returned to him. In the past, Polanco has filed news reports for the Miami-based Web sites Nueva Prensa Cubana and Cubanet. More recently, his reports have been broadcast back to Cuba over Miami-based, U.S. government–funded Radio Martí.

NOVEMBER 10

Pablo Pacheco, Cooperativa Avileña de Periodistas Independientes
THREATENED, HARASSED

Pacheco, a journalist with the independent news agency Cooperativa Avileña de Periodistas Independientes (CAPI), based in the central province of Ciego de Ávila, was harassed and threatened by police.

The journalist, accompanied by his wife and his son, was filming a rodeo tournament in the town of Jicotea at around 5 p.m. when he saw several police officers beating two women. As Pacheco attempted to videotape the incident, officers grabbed the camera, arrested the journalist, and took him to the

Jicotea Police Station, where he was held for 45 minutes. The police then took him to the Ciego de Ávila police headquarters, where he arrived at around 7 p.m.

At the Ciego de Ávila police headquarters, police insulted Pacheco and threatened to imprison him. The journalist was told he wasn't under arrest, but that they needed to erase the material he had recorded because he could send it abroad "to discredit the Revolution," according to the journalist. Pacheco remained at the police station for four hours, until the police returned the camera to him with the erased tape.

GUATEMALA

APRIL 10

David Herrera, free-lance
ATTACKED, THREATENED

Herrera, a free-lance journalist, was kidnapped and threatened by four unidentified assailants, apparently in retaliation for his work with Gerry Hadden, the Mexico, Central America, and Caribbean correspondent for U.S.-based National Public Radio (NPR). Herrera works as a free-lancer for NPR, among other international news organizations. A week earlier, Herrera and Hadden had been covering several sensitive stories, including recent murders blamed on government forces.

According to an account that Hadden provided to CPJ, Herrera arrived at the offices of Enlaces, a consortium of free-lance journalists in downtown Guatemala City, at around 10:30 a.m. on April 10. As Herrera was exiting a truck that Hadden had rented for the week, he noticed four men loitering in the area, at least two of whom were carrying automatic pistols. The men approached Herrera and pushed him into the truck.

The assailants asked Herrera, "Where is

the material?" apparently referring to the recordings and documents the journalists had gathered during the week. Herrera emptied his pockets and handed over his belongings, but they repeated their question and searched the truck. The assailants told Herrera that they were going to kill him, and one cocked his gun.

Herrera was later released and filed a police report. Although he suffered no physical injuries, he was in shock and checked into a private clinic, where he stayed for a few days. On April 16, Herrera filed a complaint with the office in the Public Ministry that investigates crimes against journalists. He went into exile the next day.

JUNE 7

Abner Guoz, *elPeriódico*
Marielos Monzón, Emisoras Unidas
Ronaldo Robles, Emisoras Unidas
Rosa María Bolaños, *Siglo Veintiuno*
THREATENED

Guoz, a reporter with the daily *elPeriódico*; Monzón and Robles, hosts of the morning radio program "En Perspectiva," broadcast on the radio station Emisoras Unidas; and Bolaños, a reporter with the daily *Siglo Veintiuno*, received death threats from a group that may be linked to far-right extremists.

In late May, various human rights organizations and media outlets received a fax that referred to meetings that human rights organizations had recently held with a United Nations representative about abuses in Guatemala. The fax, which was addressed to the "enemies of the motherland" and was signed by an unknown group that called itself "True Guatemalans," threatened the four journalists and seven human rights activists. The note called human rights activists the

"scum of society," accused them of damaging Guatemala's image, and warned that should their denunciations have any effect on the country, the activists "would have to pay for it with their blood."

Radio journalists Monzón and Robles had extensively covered the meetings with the U.N. representative and, according to Robles, devoted the June 3 edition of "En Perspectiva" to a special report on threats against human rights activists. Guoz regularly covers the official residence of the Guatemalan president for *elPeriódico* but has also reported on the issue of land redistribution. Bolaños, who was abroad at the time of the threats, said that she did not know why she was mentioned in the fax, and that she had not received threats before. Bolaños regularly covers the Congress, the Supreme Electoral Tribunal, and political affairs.

In several meetings with the U.N. representative, human rights activists expressed their concerns about the escalation of threats against them and other personnel involved in investigations into human rights violations that took place during Guatemala's civil war, which officially ended in 1996. Observers attribute the threats to right-wing paramilitary or clandestine groups with alleged links to the military and the police.

HAITI

JANUARY 22

Roosevelt Benjamin, Signal FM
Evelyne Dacelus, Signal FM
Carl Dieudonné, Signal FM
Jean-Claudy Saint-Cyr, Signal FM
ATTACKED

Signal FM journalists Benjamin, Dacelus, Dieudonné, and Saint-Cyr were traveling in the radio's staff bus, clearly marked as a

Signal FM vehicle, to cover a conference in southern Haiti when the driver of a car from the president's National Palace attempted to run the bus off the road and aimed a machine gun at the passengers, said Benjamin. The bus driver then lost control of the vehicle and crashed into another car. The man driving the National Palace car left the scene after the accident. The journalists were not injured and returned to Signal FM to report the incident, said Benjamin. He told CPJ that the National Palace car appeared to have been waiting for them.

That evening, the National Palace Press Service issued a communiqué calling the alleged attack on the reporters "pure invention" and denied that the vehicle and the driver were from the palace. Two days later, however, in response to protests from Haitian media and human rights associations, National Palace spokesperson Jacques Maurice called Signal FM and acknowledged the attack.

According to Signal FM and several witnesses, Franz Gabriel, who is also President Jean-Bertrand Aristide's helicopter pilot, was seen driving the National Palace car during the attack. Signal FM asked the National Palace to make a public statement regarding these reports but had not received a response by year's end.

JULY 15

Israel Jacky Cantave, Radio Caraïbes
ATTACKED

Cantave, a journalist with Radio Caraïbes, which is based in Haiti's capital, Port-au-Prince, and his cousin, Frantz Ambroise, were abducted by unidentified assailants and found a day later tied and blindfolded on the side of a road. From the hospital where both men were taken, Cantave, 28, gave CPJ an account of what

happened to him and his cousin after they left the radio station when Cantave had finished his 10 p.m. news broadcast on July 15.

Cantave said that on the way home, he and his cousin realized that a red jeep was following them. A stop at a gas station failed to shake off their pursuer, and before long another vehicle—a pickup truck whose color they could not distinguish—banged into their car, forcing them to stop.

When Cantave and Ambroise climbed out of the car, two masked men asked them at gunpoint which of the two was Cantave. When the journalist identified himself, the assailants told him they were going to kill him. Cantave said that four armed men were in the pickup truck, but that he could not tell how many were in the jeep. All assailants were masked.

Cantave and Ambroise were then forced into one of the vehicles. The assailants tied the hands of both men, gagged them, blindfolded them, and took them to a house, where they were held for about 24 hours.

Cantave said that he was interrogated, kicked, and beaten repeatedly, and that his assailants made him listen to his mother, who was pleading for her son's life on the Port-au-Prince station Radio Kiskeya. "It's the last time you're going to hear your mother's voice," the journalist quoted the perpetrators as saying. Cantave said that it was clear that his assailants were aware and concerned about the fact that a search for the journalist was under way. Throughout his interrogation, Cantave could hear the cries of Ambroise, who was being beaten repeatedly with a stick.

They were then forced back into a car— still blindfolded with their hands tied—and dumped along the side of a road. Passers-by heard Cantave's cries for help and brought the two men to a local police station, where they were then taken to a hospital. Cantave said that he thinks his reports on a variety of sensitive subjects for Radio Caraïbes caused the abduction and assault.

NOVEMBER 21

Esdras Mondélus, Radio Étincelle
Henry Fleurimond, Radio Étincelle
Renais Noël Jeune, Radio Étincelle
Jean Niton Guérino, Radio Étincelle
Gédéon Présandieu, Radio Étincelle
René Josué, Signal FM
Jean-Robert François, Radio Métropole
Guyler Delva, Association of Haitian Journalists
THREATENED, ATTACKED

Journalists from four privately owned media outlets—Mondélus, Jeune, Présandieu, and Guérino, of Radio Étincelle; Fleurimond, of Radio Kiskeya; Josué, of Signal FM; and François, of Radio Métropole—based in Gonaïves, a seaside town northwest of Haiti's capital, Port-au-Prince, went into hiding after receiving menacing telephone calls and verbal threats for covering opposition protests in Gonaïves and the northern city of Cap-Haïtien, CPJ sources said.

On November 28, unidentified attackers opened fire outside a provincial hotel while a group of radio journalists was meeting with the local press freedom organization Association of Haitian Journalists (AHJ) and police officials to discuss how to improve security conditions for journalists, Delva, AHJ director, told CPJ. No one was killed in the attack, but it remained unclear at year's end how many people may have been injured.

According to the journalists, the threats and the attack came from a group loyal to President Jean-Bertrand Aristide that was angered by the journalists' coverage of both a student march in Gonaïves and a November 17 rally in the northern city of Cap-Haïtien that had drawn thousands.

NOVEMBER 25

Radio Étincelle
ATTACKED, THREATENED

Unidentified assailants set fire to Radio Étincelle's studio, damaging a generator and other equipment. The station's director and owner, as well as three of its reporters, went into hiding. The attack came after the station had suspended broadcasting on November 21 in the face of threats from militants of the Popular Organization for the Development of Raboteau, a heavily armed populist group commonly known as the "Cannibal Army." The group accused the station of "working for the opposition" and threatened to burn the station's studio, CPJ sources said. The militants were angered over the station's coverage of both a student march in Gonaïves and an opposition rally in the northern city of Cap-Haïtien that had drawn thousands.

DECEMBER 25

Michèle Montas, Radio Haïti-Inter
ATTACKED

At around 5:30 p.m., a few minutes after Montas, news director of Port-au-Prince–based Radio Haïti-Inter, had returned to her home in Pétionville, a suburb of Port-au-Prince, two heavily armed gunmen appeared on foot. As the assailants tried to enter her home, two security guards shut the gate. The gunmen then opened fire, killing security guard Maxim Séide. Neither Montas nor the second bodyguard was injured in the attack.

Montas is the widow of Jean Léopold Dominique, a renowned journalist and radio station owner, who was gunned down at Radio Haïti-Inter on April 3, 2000. Montas has run the station since then, anchoring the daily newscast.

As the gunmen fled on foot, police cordoned off the area outside Montas' house to investigate. At year's end, no arrests had been made. Montas has criticized the slow investigation into her husband's killing.

MEXICO

JANUARY 10

J. Jesús Blancornelas, *Zeta*
THREATENED

Blancornelas, co-editor of the Tijuana weekly *Zeta*, received an anonymous, threatening e-mail, apparently in connection to his reports on drug trafficking.

He publicized the threats on January 15 in his weekly column "Conversaciones Privadas" (Private Conversations), which is carried by *Zeta* as well as more than 20 other Mexican dailies. According to Blancornelas, the message said that a gunman based in the border city of Mexicali, in the northern state of Baja California, had orders to execute him.

For years, Blancornelas has covered corruption and drug trafficking there and has received frequent threats because of his award-winning reports. These latest threats were attributed to the Tijuana drug cartel, headed by the brothers Ramón and Benjamín Arellano Félix. On February 10, Ramón Arellano Félix was shot dead by Mexican law enforcement officials, while Benjamín Arellano Félix was apprehended on March 9 and sent to a maximum-security prison.

The journalist told CPJ that he did not file a complaint about the threat because he does not trust the local authorities, who he believes may have ties to drug traffickers. In November 1997, the Arellano Félix brothers wounded Blancornelas in an attack, and Luis Valero Elizaldi, his friend and bodyguard, was killed. The journalist is currently under permanent protection by bodyguards from an army Special Forces unit.

FEBRUARY 1

Isabel Arvide, free-lance
LEGAL ACTION

Arvide, a journalist and author, was charged with criminal defamation by Osvaldo Rodríguez Borunda, owner of Editora Paso del Norte, a publishing company that owns the dailies *El Diario de Chihuahua* and *El Diario de Juárez*, both based in the northern state of Chihuahua. Rodríguez Borunda also requested 50 million pesos (US$5,000,000) in "moral damages."

Judge Armando Rodríguez Gaytán of the Second Penal Court in the district of Morales, Chihuahua, in north central Mexico, confirmed to CPJ that Arvide was charged with criminal defamation. According to Mexico's Criminal Code, Arvide faces six months to two years in prison if convicted.

Chihuahua State police arrested Arvide on Friday, August 19, at the airport in Chihuahua City as she was boarding a flight for Mexico City. She was released more than 24 hours later, after paying a bail of 100,000 Mexican pesos (US$10,000).

The charges stemmed from a June 2, 2001, article by Arvide that appeared on the journalist's own Web site, *www.isabelarvide.com*, and in the Mexico City–based daily *Milenio*. In the article, Arvide accused Rodríguez Borunda of being involved in drug trafficking and money laundering.

Arvide has written many exposés about drug traffickers, corruption, and violence. She also wrote the book *Muerte en Juárez* (Death in Juarez). She was in Chihuahua covering a tour of the region by the national director of the Institutional Revolutionary Party when she was arrested at the Chihuahua airport.

Arvide maintains that the arresting authorities failed to properly identify themselves or to clarify the charges against her at the time of arrest. Judge Rodríguez had issued the warrant for her arrest on June 16. A court rejected an injunction she filed challenging the arrest warrant and the imprisonment order, and at year's end, her case was ongoing.

Arvide, who lives in Mexico City, is currently free on bail but must appear before a Chihuahua court every 15 days and sign a court record, she told CPJ. She also needs authorization to leave the country.

NICARAGUA

OCTOBER 22

La Prensa
ATTACKED, THREATENED

Tirso Moreno, a former commander of the right-wing contras, attacked the offices of the Managua daily *La Prensa* and took several journalists and other personnel hostage. He surrendered to the police nearly two hours later.

Moreno, who appeared to be drunk and nervous, entered *La Prensa*'s offices wielding a handgun at around 3:30 p.m., according to *La Prensa*. After threatening a security guard at gunpoint, Moreno forced him to give up his handgun. He then went into the paper's newsroom, where some employees escaped, but at least 18 were trapped.

Once inside, Moreno blamed *La Prensa* for the death of former president Arnoldo Alemán's eldest son, who had just died in an accident at the Alemán family ranch. After, Moreno went outside and fired several shots at security guards. Back in the newsroom, Moreno told his hostages that if the police attempted a rescue, there would be "a bloodbath."

Moreno demanded to speak to several religious and political figures, but attempts to contact them were unsuccessful. Finally,

two police officers entered the newsroom with Moreno's consent and convinced him to surrender. Moreno was then taken to the Department of Criminal Investigations headquarters.

On October 24, criminal proceedings began against Moreno, who was charged with several counts of assault, kidnapping, death threats, attempted homicide, endangering others, and violating property. On November 4, a judge found Moreno guilty of kidnapping and endangering others but dismissed the remaining charges. Under the Penal Code, he faces a maximum sentence of five and three years in prison, respectively, for the two crimes. *La Prensa*'s lawyers said they would appeal the decision, claiming the evidence also proved the other charges.

PERU

MARCH 26

Mabel Cáceres Calderón, *El Búho*
THREATENED, LEGAL ACTION

Cáceres, editor of the biweekly publication *El Búho*, which is based in the southern city of Arequipa, received death threats that appeared to be related to *El Búho*'s stories on corruption and nepotism at a local university.

At around 11:30 a.m., Cáceres arrived at the engineering sciences library of the Universidad Nacional de San Agustín (UNSA), where she works in the afternoon, and was given a package that had arrived for her in the mail. Noticing that the package lacked a return address, she called her family, who in turn called the police. Police bomb disposal experts opened the box and found a bull's testicles with a threatening note, according to a report by the Lima-based press freedom organization Instituto Prensa y Sociedad.

That same afternoon, Cáceres filed an official complaint with the Arequipa Police Department, which has opened an investigation into the case.

In a series of articles published in November and December 2001, *El Búho* claimed that certain university employees had received payments for unspecified services and complained that it was impossible to know the salary of UNSA's rector, Rolando Cornejo Cuervo. In late November 2001, the university television station, TV UNSA, broadcast a two-hour program in which Cáceres was referred to as a "rat" that needed to be "exterminated," the journalist told CPJ. At around the same time, a flyer containing insulting references to the journalist's private life began circulating throughout the university.

Cáceres was first threatened on January 29, when she received an envelope with an anonymous note that read, "We know it's you." Enclosed in the envelope were clippings of a January 27 article in the national daily *OJO* announcing that, at the request of an Arequipa congressman, the General Comptroller's Office would investigate allegations of corruption at UNSA.

In December 2001, the rector of UNSA filed a criminal defamation lawsuit against Cáceres. After the lawsuit was dismissed in mid-February 2002, Cornejo filed an appeal, which the Supreme Court of Justice is currently considering. The rector filed two other criminal defamation lawsuits, but they were dismissed for lack of evidence.

The harassment of Cáceres stopped after the Public Prosecutor's Office began investigating the rector in connection with the threats, the journalist told CPJ. At year's end, a judge was considering whether to recommend the rector's prosecution. Cáceres, meanwhile, relaunched *El Búho* in October.

OCTOBER 24

Juan Carlos Masías, Frecuencia Latina
Elizabeth Rubianes, América TV
Jorge Castañeda, América TV
ATTACKED
Juan Carlos Sánchez, Radio Comas
ATTACKED, THREATENED

Police attacked several journalists who were trying to cover an event in front of the Congress building in Peru's capital, Lima.

At around noon, former government official Mauricio Diez Canseco, accompanied by 150 supporters, arrived at the Congress building determined to enter the facility and find congressman Jorge del Castillo, whom Diez had challenged to a fistfight. As Diez was giving statements to the press, the police, who had orders to prevent the crowd from entering the Congress building, charged the protesters and journalists with water cannons and tear gas grenades.

Several minutes later, as the journalists sought to obtain comments from a police commander about the use of water cannons and tear gas against them, the police assaulted them. Sánchez, a reporter for "La Grúa Radial" program, broadcast by Lima-based station Radio Comas, was hit in the head with a stick by two police officers, leaving his face and head bloodied. Masías, a cameraman with television station Frecuencia Latina, was roughed up and hit in the head with a stick by an officer. Masías suffered a contusion and required five stitches. Rubianes, a reporter for television station América TV, and her cameraman, Castañeda, were slightly injured after a tear gas grenade thrown by police exploded next to them.

To protest the police assault, journalists went to the entrance of the Congress building and placed their microphones, tape recorders, cameras, and press credentials on the floor.

On October 28, Sánchez said he had received anonymous phone threats on his cell phone, apparently in retaliation for statements he had made that he would file a complaint against the Ministry of the Interior and the police because of the attacks.

In an October 30 report, the Ministry of the Interior claimed that Sánchez had thrown a "sharp object" at police officers, and that Masías was beaten after he pushed through a police cordon to interview a police commander. The report, however, conceded that the police response was unnecessary and disproportionate. The Lima-based press freedom organization Instituto Prensa Y Sociedad said that some journalists may have reacted violently, but only after the police attacked them. The journalists filed a complaint with the police, who were still investigating the case at year's end.

UNITED STATES

MARCH 18

Gregg Gursky, Fox News
HARASSED

Gursky, a cameraman with Fox News, was on the property of the U.S. Department of Defense headquarters, known as the Pentagon, when he filmed Virginia police pulling over a pickup truck outside the Pentagon. Military police stopped the journalist and asked for his tape. They also told Gursky that he needed a security escort to film on Pentagon property.

When the journalist refused to hand over the tape, he was frisked, handcuffed, and arrested for disobeying a police officer. Once the military police had confiscated Gursky's tape, they removed his handcuffs and allowed him to go free. Fox News officials were quoted as saying that Gursky had security clearance and credentials to film on Pentagon property.

Generally, journalists need permission to shoot footage on Pentagon property and have to be accompanied by an escort while doing so. On the afternoon of March 20, the Defense Department returned the tape to the Fox News bureau in Washington, D.C., but officials did not disclose whether the tape had been copied or used in any investigation, Fox News reported.

JULY 17

Edgar H. Powers Jr., *The New Observer*
David W. Carson, *The New Observer*
LEGAL ACTION

Carson and Powers, publisher and editor, respectively, of the Kansas-based, free-circulation monthly *The New Observer*, as well as Observer Publications Inc., were found guilty of seven counts of criminal defamation.

The case stemmed from a November 2000 *New Observer* article alleging that Carol Marinovich, mayor of the Unified Government of Wyandotte County, Kansas City, Kansas, and her husband, Wyandotte County District Court judge Ernest Johnson, did not live in Wyandotte County but in an affluent county nearby. By law, the mayor and the judge are required to live in the county where they hold public office. The paper's allegation proved to be false.

Though special prosecutor David Farris had not decided whether to seek jail terms, Carson and Powers faced fines and prison time of up to one year each. Defense attorney Mark Birmingham announced that he would ask the judge to set aside the verdict or he would file an appeal, The Associated Press reported.

In a November 12 hearing, Carson and Powers asked a judge to grant them a new trial or dismiss the case, claiming the guilty verdict against them was tainted by

THE AMERICAS

juror misconduct. However, three days later, the judge ruled that no such juror misconduct had occurred. On November 27, the judge sentenced Carson and Powers to one year of unsupervised probation and fined them US$3,500 each. All but US$700 for each was suspended, and payment was to be delayed pending an appeal of the case. In mid-December, Carson and Powers filed an appeal before the Kansas Court of Appeals, which remained pending at year's end.

SEPTEMBER 27

Larry Towell, Magnum
Stephany Moore, United Press International
Nick Roberts, *U.S. News and World Report*
Michael Bruno, *Washingtonpost.com*
Christina Pino-Marina, *Washingtonpost.com*
Robin Bell, IndyMedia
Matthew Bradley, IndyMedia
HARASSED

Towell, a photographer with Magnum photo agency; Moore, a writer with United Press International; Roberts, a photographer with the weekly *U.S. News and World Report*; Bruno and Pino-Marina, writers at *Washingtonpost.com*; and Bell and Bradley, free-lance writers with IndyMedia, were arrested in Washington, D.C., while covering demonstrations where hundreds had gathered to protest the annual meetings of the World Bank and International Monetary Fund.

According to the journalists, police officers in riot gear surrounded about 500 people, demonstrators as well as journalists, and arrested all of them. Although the journalists were accredited, they told CPJ that officers said the journalists were being

arrested because they were not carrying press passes issued periodically by the Washington, D.C., Metropolitan Police. The journalists with IndyMedia said they were arrested even though both were wearing their Washington, D.C., Metropolitan Police press passes.

Towell, a veteran photographer, was wearing various press credentials around his neck. But a senior police officer arrested the journalist after asking if he had a D.C. police press pass. Bruno and Pino-Marina wrote on *Washingtonpost.com* that they "were grabbed forcefully by police officers in riot gear, handcuffed and led to Metrobus No. 8771 with 34 protesters and an indignant United Press International reporter."

The police released all the journalists about four hours later without charge. D.C. Metropolitan Police spokesperson Joseph Gentile declined to comment on the arrests due to pending civil litigation involving the department and some of the arrested journalists.

VENEZUELA

JANUARY 7

El Nacional
THREATENED, HARASSED

About 100 supporters of President Hugo Chávez Frías' Fifth Republic Movement (MVR) surrounded the offices of the Caracas daily *El Nacional* for two hours in an apparent attempt to prevent the paper from publishing the next day's issue.

For the duration of the siege, the paper's employees could not leave the building for fear of being attacked by the protesters. Some demonstrators shouted, "Tell the truth or we will burn you," and many were armed with baseball bats and sticks, according to local news reports.

On January 10, *El Nacional* filed a complaint with the Washington, D.C.–based Inter-American Commission on Human Rights (IACHR). The next day, the IACHR asked the Venezuelan government to adopt precautionary measures designed to guarantee the physical safety of *El Nacional*'s staff and uphold their right to freedom of expression. Venezuelan authorities agreed to adopt the measures and have opened an investigation into the incident.

JANUARY 20

Mayela León, Globovisión
Jorge Manuel Paz, Globovisión
Jhan Bernal, Globovisión
Luisana Ríos, Radio Caracas Televisión
`ATTACKED`

A team from the television channel Globovisión, including reporter León, cameraman Paz, and assistant Bernal, was attacked by a crowd of President Hugo Chávez Frías supporters while covering a broadcast of his weekly radio and television program, "Aló, Presidente," in the Caracas neighborhood of 23 de Enero. The mob surrounded Globovisión's van, kicking and rocking the vehicle and hurling insults. After soldiers intervened, the Globovisión journalists left without finishing their reporting assignment. A Radio Caracas Televisión team led by reporter Ríos was also manhandled during the broadcast, according to local press reports.

On January 29, Globovisión asked the Washington, D.C.–based Inter-American Commission on Human Rights (IACHR) to grant precautionary measures in favor of the journalists who were assaulted. On January 30, the IACHR sent a letter asking that the Venezuelan government adopt the measures, and Venezuelan authorities agreed to do so.

JANUARY 31

Así es la Noticia
`ATTACKED, THREATENED`
Ibéyise Pacheco, *Así es la Noticia*
Marianela Salazar, *Así es la Noticia*
Patricia Poleo, *Así es la Noticia*
Marta Colomina, *Así es la Noticia*
`THREATENED`

Two men on a motorcycle launched a homemade explosive device at the entrance of the daily *Así es la Noticia*, part of the publishing house CA Editora El Nacional, which also owns the daily *El Nacional*. The attackers fled after throwing flyers that accused *Así es la Noticia* editor Pacheco and journalists Salazar, Poleo, and Colomina of orchestrating a campaign against "the process of change." The explosion shattered the glass entrance door but caused no injuries.

Ten minutes after the attack, an unidentified caller said that another bomb would go off in the building's parking lot, and employees were evacuated from the building. The police arrived minutes later but did not find a bomb. In statements quoted by *El Nacional*, Rafael Vargas, minister of the presidential secretariat, called the explosive device "practically, a match box." The Ministry of Interior and Justice has since assigned police to protect the paper's facilities and staff.

Pacheco told *El Nacional* that she had received several anonymous phone threats on the night before the attack. The caller told her that her house and her newspaper would be raided. The threats came one day after Pacheco, Salazar, Poleo, and Colomina had made public a video showing Venezuelan military officials and Revolutionary Armed Forces of Colombia (FARC) guerrillas discussing the release of a kidnapped Venezuelan citizen with alleged links to Colombian paramilitaries. The video suggested close collaboration between the Venezuelan military and the FARC.

FEBRUARY 21

Carlos Pérez, Televén
Juan Carlos Toro, Televén
Carlos Toro, Televén
ATTACKED

Cameraman Pérez, camera assistant Carlos Toro, and reporter Juan Carlos Toro, members of a Televén TV news crew, were attacked while covering an anti-government protest by students at Central University of Venezuela (UCV).

About 50 supporters of President Hugo Chávez Frías, led by political activist Lina Ron, attacked crowds of students who were congregating on the UCV campus to stage a protest against the government. The attackers included students who, in March 2001, had attempted a violent takeover of UCV aimed at installing a pro-government administration.

The attackers, reportedly members of the so-called Bolivarian Circles, which are neighborhood committees supported by the government, also threw stones and pipes at Televén's vehicle, wounding Carlos Toro in the head, the Caracas daily *El Universal* reported. Juan Carlos Toro and Pérez took Carlos Toro to a clinic, where he was treated and later released.

The attackers also threw stones and bottles at the vehicles of private TV channels Venevisión and Globovisión, whose news crews had to leave the scene, according to Venezuelan news reports. At the request of UCV's rector, Giuseppe Giannetto, the Attorney General's Office filed charges against Ron and other attackers in late February. Ron was awaiting trial at year's end.

APRIL 11

Jorge Ibraín Tortoza Cruz, *2001*
KILLED

For full details on this case, see page 366.

Jonathan Freitas, *TalCual*
Jorge Recio París, free-lance
Enrique Hernández, Venpres
Luis Enrique Hernández, *Avance*
Miguel Escalona, *El Carabobeño*
ATTACKED

Freitas, a photographer with the newspaper *TalCual*; Recio, a free-lance photographer; Enrique Hernández, a photographer with the state news agency Venpres; and Luis Enrique Hernández, a photographer with the newspaper *Avance*, were attacked while covering violent clashes between opposition demonstrators and government supporters near the Miraflores Presidential Palace. Escalona, a photographer with the daily *El Carabobeño*, was attacked later the same day.

Freitas told CPJ that a bullet passed through his arm and lodged in his cell phone, which was in his vest pocket. According to Freitas, the shot came from the direction of government supporters. A police officer immediately took the journalist to the José María Vargas Hospital, where he was treated and released the same day.

Recio, who was hit in the back with a bullet, told the daily *TalCual* that the bullet came from an area where some Caracas Metropolitan Police officers were standing. The journalist was taken to the José María Vargas Hospital, where he underwent emergency surgery. He remained paralyzed from his chest down at year's end, but doctors are hopeful he will be able to walk again.

Enrique Hernández was injured by a bullet that grazed his abdomen, and he was later hit in the head with a stone. He was treated for minor injuries and returned to work the next day. Luis Enrique Hernández, brother of Enrique Hernández, was hit with two bullets, one in the stomach and one in the kidney. He was taken to the José María Vargas Hospital, where he underwent surgery and had one kidney removed. The journalist was released from the hospital on April 22.

Escalona was attacked by unidentified individuals later that evening while he was taking pictures of the Miraflores Presidential Palace from Urdaneta Avenue. The attackers surrounded him, took his camera, and hit him in the head with a bat, according to *El Carabobeño*. Escalona was hospitalized and has since recovered.

The clashes came on the third day of a nationwide strike that led to a short-lived coup that ousted President Hugo Chávez Frías on April 11. He returned to power on April 14.

TV Caricuao
Radio Catia Libre
Catia TV
Venezolana de Televisión
HARASSED

In the hours that followed the April 11 coup that briefly unseated President Hugo Chávez Frías from power, several Caracas-based community media outlets and the state-run television station, Venezolana de Televisión, were harassed.

At around midnight on April 11, Chávez was ousted and Pedro Carmona, president of the powerful business association Fedecámaras, was appointed by some sectors of the opposition to head a new, military-backed Cabinet. However, news of Chávez's ouster resulted in more protests, this time by his supporters, and within 48 hours, military officers loyal to Chávez had reinstated him.

During Carmona's brief tenure, police raided several community media outlets, according to sources in Venezuela. Community media outlets, which covered the April 11

events, are mostly pro-Chávez. The police raids were carried out without court orders.

On April 12, about 12 police officers from the Technical Judicial Police raided the facilities of the community television station TV Caricuao. After the officers said that they were searching for weapons, station director Jesús Blanco let them in. When they found a military jacket belonging to station employee José Calles, they arrested him and took him away. Calles was released later the same day.

That afternoon, police officers from the Caracas Metropolitan Police raided the offices of the community radio station Radio Catia Libre. The police forced the door open and subdued station employee Leopoldo Monsalve. While the station's offices were ransacked, police interrogated Monsalve, pointing a gun at him. Monsalve was taken away and released about two hours later.

Also on the afternoon of April 12, Metropolitan Police officers surrounded the offices of the community television station Catia TV and blocked the entrance for two hours. During this time, no one was allowed to enter or leave.

Under Carmona, the state-run television station, Venezolana de Televisión, was taken off the air on the evening of April 11 after being occupied by police forces that had joined the coup. The station remained shuttered until April 13, when it was taken over by government supporters who brought it back on the air.

J U L Y   9

Globovisión
ATTACKED

Globovisión, a 24-hour news channel, was attacked with a grenade. At around 1:10 a.m., unidentified individuals in a car launched a grenade above a wall and into the parking lot of a building that houses Globovisión offices. The explosion partially damaged seven vehicles and the building's entrance, but no one was injured.

After gathering evidence and performing tests, the police confirmed that the explosion had resulted from a fragmentation grenade of the type used by the military, Globovisión said. No one has claimed responsibility for the attack. Interior Minister Diosdado Cabello called the action "a terrorist act" and promised to investigate the case.

The motive behind the attack remains unclear. Some opposition leaders blamed the government, which has often lashed out against the media, particularly Globovisión. Government officials, however, claimed that the incident was aimed at sabotaging an ongoing visit by former U.S. president Jimmy Carter, who had agreed to mediate in the political crisis engulfing Venezuela.

JULY 31

Gabriel Osorio, *Primicia*
ATTACKED

Osorio, a photographer with the weekly *Primicia*, published by the company CA Editora El Nacional, which owns the daily *El Nacional*, was attacked in the capital, Caracas.

At around 3:30 p.m., as Osorio was heading toward the Supreme Court of Justice building after covering violent clashes between pro-government and opposition demonstrators, a group of government supporters began yelling at him, accusing the journalist of being a spy. The men surrounded Osorio, and when he identified himself as a journalist from *El Nacional*, they beat him up and threw him on the ground. After Osorio reached for a metal pipe to defend himself, the attackers left.

Noticing that his equipment had been stolen, Osorio went after the assailants to try to recover it. One of the attackers told Osorio that he would be shot if he did not leave. The journalist left the area with minor bruises and cuts. In addition, he lost his camera, a flash, lenses, film, and his cell phone.

In October, Osorio told CPJ that no one had been detained for the attack despite the fact that the Public Prosecutor's Office had a video recording of the incident. Osorio added that the prosecutor had not contacted him in connection with the investigation.

SEPTEMBER 21

Rossana Rodríguez, Globovisión
Felipe Lugo, Globovisión
Wilmer Escalona, Globovisión
ATTACKED, THREATENED

Rodríguez, a TV reporter with the 24-hour news channel Globovisión; Lugo, a cameraman; and Escalona, an assistant, were attacked by government supporters while they were on their way to an assignment in the capital, Caracas. According to Globovisión, when the journalists drove by Urdaneta Avenue, near the Miraflores Presidential Palace, attackers surrounded their car, which was marked with the Globovisión logo, and beat Escalona, threatened him with a handgun, and forced him to hand over the car keys. Rodríguez was threatened with a broken bottle. The three were then forced out of the car, which the attackers took, along with a camera and a tripod.

Rodríguez took refuge nearby in the Vice President's Office, where she contacted Globovisión. Meanwhile, Lugo and Escalona ran into Lina Ron, a leader of a pro-government organization, who agreed to help them and escorted them to a bridge where the news crew recovered their car and equipment. A videotape was not returned, however.

Later that day, municipal police detained

Luis Cortez in connection with the attack. The next day, Cortez appeared in court, where Franco Arquímedes, the leader of a pro-government group, arrived, apologized for the incident, and accepted responsibility for the attack. Cortez was later released.

OCTOBER 19

Unión Radio
ATTACKED

At around 12:00 a.m., unidentified attackers in a moving vehicle threw a small explosive device at the offices of the radio station Unión Radio, located in the eastern section of the capital, Caracas. The explosion caused minor material damage to the building and an adjacent house. The attack occurred two days before the opposition started a nationwide strike calling for President Hugo Chávez Frías' resignation.

According to Unión Radio management, several of the station's journalists have received threatening phone calls during the last three years because of their coverage, but it is unclear why the station was attacked. Authorities have opened an investigation into the bombing, but there had not been any progress by year's end.

NOVEMBER 4

Héctor Castillo, *El Mundo*
Mauricio Muñoz Amaya, Associated
Press Television News
ATTACKED
Pedro Rey, *Notitarde*
HARASSED

Castillo, a photographer for the Caracas daily *El Mundo*, told CPJ that he was beaten at around 12 p.m. near the offices of the National Electoral Council while covering demonstrations during a nationwide strike.

After Castillo took a picture of a govern-ment supporter who was setting off fire-works, the man became angry and attempted to grab his camera. When Castillo resisted, 10 to 15 men surrounded him, threw him to the ground, and kicked him several times. The men also stole his lens and flash. Castillo was able to escape after Rey, a pho-tographer for the daily *Notitarde*, and Desirée Santos Amaral, a parliamentary deputy for the ruling party, intervened. Castillo sustained injuries to his head and legs, went to a local hospital for treatment, and was released a few hours later. Rey told CPJ that, when he intervened to help Castillo, someone stole his flash and a gas mask he carried for protection.

Muñoz, an Associated Press Television News (APTN) cameraman from El Salvador, was hit with a 9 mm bullet in the chest at around 12:30 p.m. while he stood filming behind a row of riot police, APTN reporter Fernando Jáuregui told CPJ. Because Muñoz was wearing a bulletproof vest, he only suffered minor bleeding and a bruise in the chest. Muñoz was taken to local a hospital, where he stayed for three days. Muñoz then returned to Peru, where he lives. It is unclear whether he was tar-geted, or who fired the shot. The Public Prosecutor's Office has opened an investiga-tion into the shooting, but no progress had been reported by year's end.

NOVEMBER 19

Eduard Escalona, Venezolana de
Televisión
Zaida Pereira, Venezolana de Televisión
ATTACKED, HARASSED

Escalona, a cameraman for Venezolana de Televisión (VTV), and Pereira, a reporter for the channel, were attacked while trying to cover an opposition demonstration in Plaza Francia Square, in the Caracas neighborhood of Altamira. They were preparing to broad-cast a report when journalist Arturo Vilar, who was working as press officer for a group of rebellious military officers, approached them. (In October, the officers had turned the Plaza Francia Square and the nearby Four Seasons Hotel into their base of operations.) Vilar then blocked Pereira and Escalona's access to the area.

As Pereira protested and Escalona began filming, Vilar began beating Escalona. Other opposition supporters joined Vilar and took Escalona's camera, which had recorded part of the assault. The camera was returned 30 minutes later without the tape and on the condition that Pereira and Escalona leave the scene. The journalists returned to VTV's offices and gave an interview denouncing the attack.

DECEMBER 3

Fernando Malavé, *2001*
Rafael Fuenmayor, CMT
José Antonio Dávila, CMT
Luis Alfonso Fernández, Venevisión
Aymara Lorenzo, Globovisión
ATTACKED

On the second day of a nationwide strike called by opponents of President Hugo Chávez Frías, National Guard troops attacked several journalists while they covered an opposition demonstration near the Caracas headquarters of the state oil company, PDVSA.

The security forces fired rubber bullets and threw tear gas grenades at journalists and other civilians. Malavé, a photographer with the Caracas daily *2001*, was arguing with guards who were preventing him from taking photos when one guard shot him with a rubber bullet. Although he was wear-ing a bulletproof vest, Malavé suffered a serious wound to his ribs that required surgery at a local hospital.

In another attack, security forces kicked Fuenmayor, a reporter with the Caracas-based TV channel CMT. Dávila, a CMT technician, was hit with rubber bullets in the neck, face, and back after a guard shot him. He was treated in an ambulance parked nearby and returned to work immediately.

Troops also hit Fernández, a reporter with the Caracas-based TV channel Venevisión, with a blunt-edged sword and threw a tear gas grenade at him. Lorenzo, a reporter with the news channel Globovisión, was beaten as well.

National Guard generals and government officials justified their actions by claiming that the journalists had attacked National Guard troops, despite evidence that the opposite had occurred. On December 4, the Public Prosecutor's Office and the People's Ombudsman Office publicly criticized the National Guard's actions.

DECEMBER 4

José Rodríguez, *El Impulso*
Clara Reverol, Televén
Martín Urteaga, *El Informador*
Julio Torres, Venevisión
Gustavo Escalona, Venevisión
Cristian Rodríguez, Promar TV
José Barreto, Promar TV
Yelina Torrealba, Telecentro
Miguel Ángel López, Telecentro
Erika Paz, RCTV
Samuel Sotomayor, RCTV
ATTACKED

Several journalists were attacked by government supporters in the city of Barquisimeto, in northeastern Lara State. The journalists were covering an opposition protest when government supporters began throwing bottles and stones at the journal-ists and the protesters.

José Rodríguez, a photographer for the

Barquisimeto daily *El Impulso*, was hit on the head with a sharp object and suffered from a concussion. Reverol, a reporter with the Caracas-based TV channel Televén, was hit on the forehead. Urteaga, a photographer for the Barquisimeto daily *El Informador*, was hit on the head. Torres and Escalona, two cameramen with the TV channel Venevisión, were also hit on the head. Cristian Rodríguez, a reporter for the Barquisimeto-based TV channel Promar TV, was kicked in the abdomen, while Barreto, her cameraman, had the lens of his camera smashed. Torrealba, a reporter for the Barquisimeto TV channel Telecentro, and López, his cameraman, were beaten. Paz, a reporter with the Caracas-based TV channel RCTV, was beaten, while Sotomayor, her cameraman, was beaten and had his camera kicked and destroyed.

According to local news reports, the police stood by during the incident.

DECEMBER 9

Globovisión
TVS
Televisora Regional del Táchira
Venezolana de Televisión
ATTACKED

A week after the beginning of a nationwide strike called by the opposition, several regional television stations were attacked by supporters of President Hugo Chávez Frías.

In the evening, scores of government supporters broke into the studios of the 24-hour news channel Globovisión in the city of Maracaibo, in northwestern Zulia State. They ransacked the offices, destroying or damaging furniture, computers, cameras, television monitors, and other audio and video equipment. According to Globovisión, a pro-government radio station had called on government supporters to occupy Globovisión's facilities. The police arrived only after the attack was finished.

Government supporters twice attacked the offices of the television station TVS, in the city of Maracay, Aragua State, about an hour west of the capital, Caracas. They broke several windows but pulled back after the police arrived. Then, after the police left, government supporters returned and continued to ransack the facilities. The attackers also knocked down an antenna, taking the station off the air.

In the Andean Táchira State, government supporters partially destroyed the offices of the television station Televisora Regional del Táchira, spraying walls with graffiti, shattering glass windows, and destroying video equipment.

Also in the evening hours, unidentified attackers on motorcycles, presumably opposition supporters, fired several shots at the Caracas offices of the state-run television station Venezolana de Televisión. No one was injured.

Organization of American States secretary-general César Gaviria, who was in Caracas mediating talks between the opposition and the government, condemned all attacks against private and state-run media. ∎

CHAIN POLICE
GOONS NOT PRES

LAHORE PRESS CLUB

OVERVIEW: ASIA

by Sophie Beach

THE VICIOUS MURDER OF *WALL STREET JOURNAL* REPORTER Daniel Pearl in Pakistan focused international attention on the dangers faced by journalists covering the U.S. "war on terror," yet most attacks on journalists in Asia happened far from the eyes of the international press. In countries such as Bangladesh and the Philippines, reporters covering crime and political corruption were as vulnerable to attack as those reporting on violent insurgency. Seven journalists were killed in 2002 for their work in Asia.

Most murders occur in countries where weak governments or corrupt law enforcement agencies ensure that violent attacks on the press go unpunished. Yet journalists also endure excessive government interference, with authorities utilizing legal or political pressures to silence critical media reports. Several governments exploit national security legislation to harass and imprison members of the media, and Asia ended 2002 with far more journalists in jail than any other region of the world.

Physical assaults against journalists were most common in countries facing political instability or localized conflict, including Bangladesh and the Philippines. The southwestern region of Bangladesh along the border with India, where violent guerrilla groups and criminal gangs are active, remains especially dangerous for journalists. One journalist was killed there in 2002, and another was kidnapped and is feared dead. CPJ gave a 2002 International Press Freedom Award to Tipu Sultan, a Bangladeshi journalist who was almost killed in January 2001 after a savage beating by a gang he identified as followers of a local politician.

While Muslim insurgent groups, including the Abu Sayyaf, continue to pose a danger to journalists in the fractious southern Philippines, the biggest threat in 2002 came from corrupt local officials and criminals, who routinely attack members of the media for reporting on their activities. Two reporters were assassinated in the Philippines in 2002, apparently in reprisal for their exposés on corruption and crime. Thirty-nine journalists have been murdered in the Philippines since the return to democracy there in 1986, but no one has yet been convicted in any of these slayings.

In Afghanistan, a nascent local press has gained strength following the overthrow of the repressive Taliban regime. However, Afghan journalists still endure political pressures and the threat of violence, especially in areas beyond the capital, Kabul, that are controlled by autocratic warlords or plagued by factional fighting. With a weak central government, no effective law enforcement agencies, and no international peacekeeping force outside Kabul, regional warlords operate with impunity, and several journalists who reported on abuses by ruling officials in 2002 were harassed, detained, or tortured. Foreign journalists operate with relative freedom, although the U.S. military tightly restricts reporting on its operations in the country.

Physical attacks against journalists decreased in Indonesia, where political tensions

Sophie Beach, senior research associate for Asia, along with **Kavita Menon**, a senior program coordinator who is responsible for Asia, researched and wrote this section. **A. Lin Neumann**, Asia program consultant, also made substantial contributions to this section.

eased overall. However, violent unrest continues in places such as Aceh and Irian Jaya, where separatist movements are active. Visiting reporters still must secure special visas to enter Indonesia, and authorities sometimes restrict media access to these conflict areas. Though resident foreign correspondents are generally free to do their jobs, one journalist was refused an extension of his visa after reporting on human rights abuses allegedly committed by Indonesian authorities in Aceh and East Timor.

Access restrictions that had prevented substantial coverage of the civil war in Sri Lanka were finally relaxed in early 2002, just before the government and the rebel Liberation Tigers of Tamil Eelam (LTTE) signed a cease-fire agreement. However, even as peace talks were under way to end the bloody, 19-year-old conflict, LTTE rebels and state security officials still threatened journalists with violent reprisal for their reporting.

A spate of attacks against local journalists in India-controlled Kashmir highlighted the dangers of reporting on the conflict there. Amid increased tensions between Pakistan and India, which have competing claims of sovereignty over Kashmir, pressure on the media intensified during the run-up to state legislative assembly elections in the fall. Journalists reporting on communal violence in the western state of Gujarat, during which rampaging mobs killed more than 1,000 Muslims, were targeted not only by the mobs but also by police who did not want evidence of their complicity in the attacks documented.

Daniel Pearl's murder by Islamic militants sent a chilling signal to reporters attempting to cover the activities of terrorist networks across Asia. However, journalists were more commonly threatened and harassed by governments fearful that reports of terrorist activity in their back yards could damage international relations and discourage foreign investment. In Malaysia, officials delayed distribution of foreign publications that reported on the existence of terrorist networks in the country. In Pakistan, local journalists covering the sensitive issue of the military government's failure to curb radical militant groups complained of intensified surveillance and harassment by state intelligence agencies. And in Bangladesh, the government arrested several journalists at the end of 2002 for anti-state activities, described in one government statement as the "malicious intent of portraying Bangladesh as an Islamic fanatical country."

In 2002, Asian leaders used the threat of imprisonment more than ever before to punish journalists for unwelcome reporting. Governments most often exploited legislation designed to safeguard national security to crack down on their critics in the media—a tactic that linked Asia's most repressive regimes, including China and Vietnam, with the region's democracies, including Bangladesh, Nepal, and Taiwan. While the international community remained largely silent about many of these abuses, there seemed to be a growing sense that security concerns trump civil liberties.

Asia's authoritarian governments have long used national security legislation to jail journalists, and such laws are the primary reason that in 2002 Asia led the world in the number of imprisoned journalists, with 78 behind bars in the region out of a world total of 136. In China, where laws against subversion have been used routinely to silence critical writers, five new arrests brought the total number of imprisoned journalists to 39, making China the world's leading jailer of journalists for the fourth year in a row.

The Internet has become a way for citizens in authoritarian countries such as China, Vietnam, and Laos to escape state censorship and publish with relative freedom. In response, governments increasingly use national security laws to imprison writers who publish critical reports online. For the last two years, the majority of new arrests of Chinese journalists were in response to writings published on the Internet. In an ongoing cat-and-mouse game, Chinese Internet users in 2002 frequently managed to protest and evade government controls. In response, authorities have implemented sophisticated new technologies to monitor users' online activities and control online content.

The Vietnamese government seems be following in China's footsteps: The number of imprisoned journalists in Vietnam jumped from two in 2001 to seven in 2002. This drastic increase reflects a disturbing new strategy by Vietnam's leaders of using national-security charges against those who publish online news reports and opinions that are banned from the tightly controlled official media. In recent years, most Vietnamese journalists on CPJ's imprisoned list have been under an administrative order that provides for indefinite house arrest without due process.

The most spectacular abuse of press freedom under the guise of protecting national security occurred in Nepal, where a violent uprising by Maoist rebels prompted the Nepalese government to declare a state of emergency and introduce sweeping anti-terrorism legislation in November 2001. While these measures were intended to quell the bloody conflict, the government's tactics also precipitated an ongoing crisis for the media. The state of emergency, which was lifted in August 2002, suspended constitutional guarantees of press freedom and other civil rights. Meanwhile, hundreds of journalists were detained under the broad provisions of the anti-terrorism ordinance, which allows for the arrest of anyone "in contact with" or "supportive of" the rebels and remained in effect as this book went to press.

In both Taiwan and Hong Kong, government attempts to exploit national security concerns to limit reporting were thwarted by free media, which aired heated public debates on the issue. The Hong Kong government's plan to draft anti-subversion legislation provoked widespread outrage internationally and throughout the region, with journalists and press freedom advocates fearing that the laws would threaten Hong Kong's status as a bastion of free expression in Asia. A diverse and international group—including lawyers, journalists, bankers, librarians, and legislators—that coalesced to protest the legislation will no doubt keep up the pressure when the government issues a draft law in early 2003.

In Southeast Asia, governments continue to interfere in the media through a combination of legal and financial pressures. The announcement that longtime Malaysian prime minister Mahathir Mohamad will resign in 2003 is not expected to improve the repressive climate for the press there. His designated successor is likely to continue the legal coercion and ownership restrictions that have been in effect there for 25 years. Meanwhile, the Thai government of Thaksin Shinawatra has used similar tactics to curb one of the region's freest media by banning foreign news reports and domestic radio broadcasts that criticize official policy. Thai journalists reported numerous instances throughout 2002 of backdoor political and financial pressure being applied against the media. ■

ASIA

AFGHANISTAN

IN MANY OBVIOUS WAYS, PRESS CONDITIONS IN AFGHANISTAN in 2002 were far better than the year before, when virtually no local independent media outlets operated, and eight journalists were killed covering the U.S.-led military offensive that ended the repressive rule of the Taliban regime. During 2002, Afghan journalists produced some 150 publications in the capital, Kabul, alone. The one journalist who lost his life in Afghanistan in 2002, New Zealand free-lancer Alastair McLeod, died in a car accident.

However, such statistics do not capture the complexities of reporting in the country. Local journalists were more vulnerable than foreign correspondents to political pressures and violence, with dangers most acute in areas outside Kabul that tend to be controlled by autocratic regional warlords or plagued by factional fighting. With warlords in control, security could not be guaranteed for those who dared to exercise the right to free expression.

In Herat, for instance, a province famous as the cultural and intellectual center of Afghanistan, Ismail Khan, the local governor and one of the country's most powerful warlords, tolerated no independent publications. Under his rule, "Herat has remained much as it was under the Taliban: a closed society in which there is no dissent, no criticism of the government, no independent newspapers ... and no respect for the rule of law," wrote Human Rights Watch in a report on freedom of expression in western Afghanistan that was released in November.

The most famous case of abuse was the detention and torture of Mohammad Rafiq Shahir, the editor of *Takhassos*, an influential newsletter published by Herat's Professional Shura, an association of intellectuals, lawyers, doctors, and other professionals that has been outspoken about the need for reforms in Afghanistan. In late May, intelligence agents in Herat abducted Shahir and detained him for two days, tying him up and beating him, according to Human Rights Watch. He was also taken to a nearby graveyard and threatened at gunpoint.

In December, a Herat-based journalist was forced to go into hiding after Ismail Khan publicly criticized him for "giving reports against us and against our country." Similarly, a free-lance journalist who had been based in the northern city of Mazar-i-Sharif was forced into hiding after reporting on mass graves of hundreds of Taliban prisoners who had allegedly died in the custody of forces loyal to Gen. Abdul Rashid Dostum, one of Afghanistan's most ruthless warlords. Colleagues said that the journalist fled after he was abducted and badly beaten, allegedly by Dostum's men. This journalist, like many others who have endured violence and harassment, wanted to remain anonymous so that he would be able to return to work.

In such a volatile environment, with a weak central government and no independent, effective law enforcement agencies, the role of the international community in monitoring abuses and intervening when necessary was paramount. That was one theme discussed at September's International Seminar on Promoting Independent and Pluralistic Media in Afghanistan, a meeting in Kabul hosted by the country's Information and Culture Ministry. At the meeting, the deputy information minister endorsed a declaration listing a series of reforms needed: to include the right of free speech and free media in Afghanistan's new constitution; to begin a thorough review of the legal system's effects on the media, including the criminal prosecution of journalists; and to suspend licensing provisions for publications. In a letter addressed to President Hamid Karzai following the conference, CPJ added that his government must take swift action against political leaders, military commanders, and others who attempt to bully the press.

Foreign correspondents operated with relative freedom in Afghanistan, though Western journalists risked being targeted in areas hostile to the United States and allied forces. *Toronto Star* correspondent Kathleen Kenna was seriously injured in March when a grenade was thrown at her car near Gardez, in the eastern Paktia Province, where she was covering the U.S.-led military offensive there, known as Operation Anaconda. The incident occurred shortly after two gunmen nearby were overheard discussing whether to take a group of foreign journalists hostage, according to *The Washington Post*.

In March, the British-led International Security Assistance Force announced a credible threat from an unidentified source to kidnap foreign journalists in Afghanistan. And in April, U.S. military officials in Afghanistan announced "credible threats of violence against coalition service members, citizens, and journalists" in the form of pamphlets circulating in eastern Paktia advertising a bounty of up to US$100,000 for the body of any Westerner.

The U.S. military continued to closely restrict coverage of military operations in Afghanistan and at least twice during the year forcibly prevented journalists from reporting in an area under its control.

In another case, U.S. Special Forces arrested a Pakistani journalist, Hayat Ullah Khan, a stringer for various publications, and his companions, all natives of Pakistan's tribal areas, in Paktika Province in July on suspicion of being associated with al-Qaeda. The group was detained for four days, until the military was able to verify their identities.

BANGLADESH

FOR BANGLADESHI JOURNALISTS, COVERING CRIME AND CORRUPTION can be as dangerous as reporting in a war zone. Journalists regularly endure vicious attacks, and since 1998, five Bangladeshi journalists have been killed in reprisal for their work.

All of the five murdered journalists were based in towns along the country's southwestern frontier with India—a crime-ridden area rife with guerrilla groups, gunrunners, and smuggling syndicates. The latest victim, crime reporter Harunur Rashid, was killed by gunmen on March 2 as he was riding his motorcycle to work in Khulna District. Another crime reporter from the same district went missing after armed men kidnapped him in early July, and colleagues believe that he, too, may have been killed.

Nationwide, 2002 saw a near total collapse of law and order in Bangladesh. The magnitude of the crisis became clear in mid-October, when Prime Minister Khaleda Zia ordered the army to aid police in a major anti-crime drive, resulting in rampant human rights abuses. According to police and news reports, more than 10,000 people were detained during the three-month operation, and 44 died—either in custody or after their releases—from injuries sustained while in detention. By early November, about 46,000 soldiers were engaged in the crackdown, which opposition leader Sheikh Hasina, who was prime minister until October 2001, characterized as "undeclared martial law."

Zia's clampdown did little to address the fact that many of those involved in crime are themselves police, political-party activists, and elected officials. The politicization of law enforcement agencies, combined with political corruption, has heightened the risks for journalists, who often have no recourse when they are targeted for their work.

One of the most famous cases of a journalist attacked for reporting on a politician's criminal misdeeds is that of Tipu Sultan, a winner of CPJ's 2002 International Press Freedom Award. Sultan was nearly killed in January 2001 when a gang he identified as followers of a local politician in the town of Feni savagely beat him. His assault received international attention and was one of several cases the Zia government promised to prosecute. (The politician, who allegedly ordered the attack, is a member of the main opposition Awami League and has since fled the country.) Sultan has recovered and is back at work, but no progress was made this year in bringing his assailants to justice.

Political partisans and gangs associated with Zia's Bangladesh Nationalist Party (BNP), the lead partner in the coalition government, were responsible for a number of attacks on members of the media during 2002. For example, journalists reporting on violent clashes between police and student demonstrators at Dhaka University at the end of July were targeted by activists associated with the BNP's youth wing who were unhappy with media coverage of the unrest, as well as by police, who apparently did not want the press to document their use of force to suppress the demonstrations.

The four-party ruling coalition that came to power at the end of 2001 includes the Islamist party Jamaat-i-Islami and the more militant Islami Oikya Jote. The presence of religious extremists among the country's top leadership signaled trouble for journalists who upheld Bangladesh's secular traditions.

In August, a religious group linked to the Islami Oikya Jote called for the arrest of anyone involved with a play staged in the town of Faridpur about sex trafficking, and cases were filed against at least 32 people. Police arrested the playwright, as well as two journalists identified as supporters of the drama group. Several Hindu journalists received death threats, and a group armed with machetes and axes attacked one reporter after he publicly criticized the protestors.

In October, *Time* magazine reported that Taliban and al-Qaeda fighters from Afghanistan had sought refuge in Bangladesh. In the report, *Time* noted that "the Bangladeshi government typically reacts with fury to reports of Jihadi camps or fundamentalism within its borders." Foreign Secretary Shamser Mobin Chowdhury called the report "irresponsible and malicious" and suggested it was part of "an orchestrated campaign designed to malign the country's international image as a liberal democratic country." However, the government did not ban the magazine, perhaps because of its earlier, bungled attempt to censor the *Far Eastern Economic Review*.

The April 4 edition of the *Review* featured a cover story branding Bangladesh a "Cocoon of Terror" and warning that "rising fundamentalism and religious intolerance are threatening secularism and moderate Islam." The Information Ministry declared the publication, sale, reprinting, and preservation of the issue illegal. The Hong Kong–based magazine, which ordinarily has a very small readership in Bangladesh, did not appear on newsstands but was accessible online. The piece was also widely distributed via e-mail. In the end, the story reached a larger audience than it would have had the government ignored the report.

In November, authorities detained two U.K.-based filmmakers working on a documentary for Channel 4's "Unreported World" series and accused them of sedition. The Home Ministry said that the journalists were arrested for their "malicious intent of portraying Bangladesh as an Islamic fanatical country." They were released after 16 days and were deported to Britain after signing a statement agreeing not to use any of their footage from Bangladesh. Bangladeshi journalists Priscilla Raj and Saleem Samad, who had worked for the Channel 4 team as interpreter and fixer, respectively, were also detained and charged with involvement in "anti-state activities." According to local sources, both journalists were tortured in custody. Raj was released on bail in December, and Samad was freed on January 18, 2003.

Nonetheless, Bangladesh has managed to sustain a diverse and aggressive local press. This does not apply, however, to the broadcast media, which continue to be dominated by state-run Bangladesh Television and its radio counterpart, Bangladesh Betar. At the end of August, Ekushey Television (ETV), the country's only private channel that is not broadcast via cable or satellite, was closed after Bangladesh's Supreme Court ruled that the station's license had been obtained improperly and was therefore invalid. BNP leaders had accused ETV of supporting the opposition Awami League, but the station was widely regarded as a professionally run, independent news organization.

BURMA

DEMOCRACY LEADER AUNG SAN SUU KYI'S RELEASE from 19 months of house arrest on May 6 did nothing to improve conditions for the media in one of the world's most repressive countries. More than seven months after the Nobel Peace Prize laureate was freed with the help of a U.N. special rapporteur, the ruling State Peace and Development Council had not fulfilled its promise to open a dialogue with Suu Kyi.

The generals who oversee all aspects of life in Burma, including the press, barred local newspapers from printing stories about Suu Kyi's release, despite the fact that it made headlines worldwide. "What has changed since she was let out? Nothing," said Aung Zaw, editor of the respected Thailand-based exile magazine *The Irrawaddy*.

Around the time of Suu Kyi's release, the government began allowing foreign reporters relatively free access to the country, although limits on the number of visas allowed for international correspondents were reimposed later in the year. In October, the regime barred the press corps traveling with Australian foreign minister Alexander Downer, the first Australian foreign minister to visit the country in two decades, from the capital, Rangoon.

Newspapers, magazines, and all other media in Burma (which the current military government renamed Myanmar after crushing a pro-democracy revolt in 1988) are either state-owned or subject to harsh censorship through the official Press Scrutiny Board. Burmese rely on shortwave Burmese-language broadcasts from the BBC, Voice of America, Radio Free Asia, or the Democratic Voice of Burma, based in Norway, for uncensored information. However, those caught listening to such broadcasts can be arrested.

The only Internet access in the country is through a partially state-owned company, Bagan Cybertech, which in the last year was allowed for the first time to offer prohibitively expensive public access to a heavily restricted Burmese "intranet." This service provides about 900 carefully selected Web sites, none of them containing news or access to the rest of the world, through Web-based e-mail. The government announced in September that it would allow the company to open a handful of Internet—or, more properly, "intranet"—cafés in Rangoon and Mandalay.

The litany of news topics that the Burmese people are not allowed access to includes everything from social issues, like widespread poverty and a burgeoning AIDS epidemic, to human rights developments, such as allegations that Burmese army troops have been involved in the systematic rape of ethnic minorities in northern areas of the country. News coverage in the country is generally devoid of political developments, with the exception of ribbon-cutting ceremonies and official government announcements.

A border conflict with neighboring Thailand reportedly led the regime to issue an order in May barring mention of Thailand or Thai products in the Burmese press. The exile group Burma Media Association (BMA) reported that the fashion magazine *Beauty* was banned in October for carrying advertisements from a Thai company. BMA noted that the ban has damaged the Burmese private media, which rely heavily on their prosperous neighbor for advertising revenue. In July, the government forbade 15 Thai journalists from visiting Burma, accusing them of "damaging bilateral relations, causing disunity among ethnic minorities and belittling [government] policies."

When the architect of Burma's retreat from the modern world, Gen. Ne Win, died in December at the age of 91, the event was also absent from the press. The former dictator held power for 26 years, starting with a coup in 1962. Ne Win imposed a reclusive, authoritarian form of socialism that impoverished what was once one of the richest countries in Asia. At the time of his death, he was under house arrest. Ne Win's son-in-law and three of his grandsons were arrested in March 2002 for allegedly plotting to overthrow the current government. The stunning arrests, a subsequent trial, convictions, and pending death sentences against the supposed plotters all went unreported in Burma.

Although the government claims to have released more than 600 political prisoners in the last two years, the regime still holds at least nine journalists in jail. The best known of these is U Win Tin, 72, who has been imprisoned since 1989 and is in poor health. Sources in Burma have told CPJ that his long detention is due not only to his influence as one of the country's leading journalists and intellectuals, but also to his role as a close adviser to Suu Kyi.

CAMBODIA

WHILE CAMBODIA'S MANY BOISTEROUS NEWSPAPERS ARE GENERALLY FREE from official sanction, the broadcast media remain captive to the political interests of Prime Minister Hun Sen and his allies. Because Cambodia has a low literacy rate and poor newspaper distribution outside the capital, Phnom Penh, the press there will not be completely free until restrictions on radio and television are lifted.

The government, the military, and the two parties in the ruling coalition, the Cambodia People's Party (CPP) and the National United Front for a Neutral, Peaceful, Cooperative, and Independent Cambodia, dominate the broadcast media. The opposition

Sam Rainsy Party has been trying in vain for several years to obtain a broadcast license.

During local elections on February 3, opposition parties ran full slates of candidates, but the broadcast media virtually froze out opposition candidates. A European Union (EU) mission reported that state TV devoted most of its coverage to the government and the CPP, leaving opposition parties with almost nothing. "Coverage by private Cambodian TV showed a similar bias," according to the EU. In addition, the National Election Commission canceled a series of broadcast roundtables, which were to give equal time to eight parties in the elections, before the poll.

Cambodia has some 200 Khmer-language newspapers, most of them aligned with political parties and published in Phnom Penh. A press law requires newspapers to be licensed and allows the government to suspend or cancel licenses; national security considerations, meanwhile, limit constitutional guarantees of free speech. Still, even pro-government papers frequently criticize officials, sometimes in harsh language. Given the highly politicized environment, journalists have had trouble organizing for their own protection. There are six different and competing press associations, which are seldom able to work together for a common goal.

Without an effective press freedom group, Cambodian journalists are vulnerable to legal harassment. In September, Hun Sen intervened to release two journalists from the daily pro-government newspaper *Chakraval* who were arrested and charged for allegedly defaming two senior police officials. In May, Dam Sith, editor of the opposition newspaper *Khmer Conscience*, was convicted of libel and defamation for criticizing Cambodia's Prince Norodom Ranariddh and the National Assembly, which the prince leads. Ranariddh, a former government foe, is now Hun Sen's chief coalition partner. "It is our impression that this shows the judge is more intent on doing politics than finding justice," said Pen Samithy, the president of the Club of Cambodian Journalists.

In April, another opposition newspaper was ordered to pay a businessman and two military officers nearly US$20,000 in a defamation suit, though the parties later settled the case without damages being awarded. In 2001, Foreign Minister Hor Namhong sued the American-owned, English-language *Cambodia Daily* for defamation after it printed two stories alleging that he had once run a Khmer Rouge prison camp. The case was under appeal at year's end.

2002 marked the 10th anniversary of one of the most interesting and independent newspapers in Asia, the *Phnom Penh Post*. Started by an American couple after the United Nations restored a measure of peace to the country in 1992, the biweekly *Post* has been an important source of in-depth stories and analysis since its inception and has also served as a training ground for Cambodian journalists.

CHINA

During the run-up to the 16th Communist Party Congress, which was held in November and marked the first orderly transfer of power in the party's history, China's leaders used the national media to launch a propaganda blitz reminiscent of Chairman Mao's days. Throughout 2002, officials issued strict new guidelines to prevent any independent reporting that reflected negatively on the party. Authorities also cracked down on the Internet, utilizing innovative new technologies to curb online speech. As in the past, journalists who overstepped boundaries faced censorship, harassment, demotion, or even arrest.

Still, China's media persevered. With local publications relying more on the market for revenue, Chinese journalists are becoming increasingly professional and aggressive in their reporting. One unfortunate consequence is that more journalists have been attacked in reprisal for their work, especially in the provinces, where corrupt local officials often act like warlords. In early January, three reporters for local papers in eastern Shandong Province were interrogated and beaten by security officials inside the local Propaganda Bureau offices after reporting on villagers' anti-corruption protests. While Chinese journalists increasingly report on violent attacks against their colleagues, there is no legal recourse to protect their rights or protest such treatment.

In January, the Dalian Intermediate Court formally sentenced journalist Jiang Weiping, a CPJ 2001 International Press Freedom award recipient, to eight years in prison. Jiang was arrested in December 2000 after writing a series of articles for the Hong Kong monthly *Qianshao* (Frontline) revealing corruption scandals in northeast China. Although U.S. government and U.N. officials have demanded Jiang's release, there has been no progress in his case. Jiang is one of 39 journalists now imprisoned in China, making it the world's leading jailer of journalists for the fourth year in a row.

Official corruption is just one of many topics that the propaganda bureaucracy bans journalists from independently investigating. As the Communist Party contends with escalating social problems—including unemployment, widening income gaps between rural and urban areas, an impending AIDS crisis, and rampant corruption—authorities have tried to maintain an image of stability by controlling information. When laid-off workers in the industrial northeast staged massive protests this spring, for example, officials stifled news of the unrest, restricting foreign and domestic journalists' access to the region.

But AIDS activist and Web site publisher Wan Yanhai, together with several domestic and foreign journalists, defied tight reporting restrictions to expose a health crisis in central Henan Province, where thousands of peasants acquired HIV after selling their blood in official blood-collection stations. In August, authorities held Wan for almost a month on suspicion of "leaking state secrets" after he posted a government report online documenting the spread of AIDS in Henan. An international outcry over Wan's arrest helped mobilize awareness of China's AIDS crisis, and at the end of the year, the government announced plans to mount a long-overdue public service campaign to educate the population about the risks of HIV and AIDS.

Corporations and other targets of journalists' investigative exposés found new ways in 2002 to punish journalists through China's legal system. Several high-profile libel suits were filed against publications for their aggressive reporting on corporate scandals and other topics. In June, the influential financial weekly *Caijing* (Finance and Economics) lost a libel suit brought by a Shenzhen real estate corporation for a report exposing the company's fraudulent accounting practices. The court ordered the magazine to pay 300,000 yuan (US$36,200) in damages. *Caijing*'s editor, Hu Shili, stood by the story, saying, "We felt we had a responsibility to tell the truth to the public."

Government efforts to control information have faced a formidable challenge with the rapid spread of the Internet, which now has almost 58 million users in China. Authorities have devoted massive resources to blocking Web sites, filtering e-mail, and monitoring Internet users' online activities to block "subversive" content. Following a deadly fire in June at an unlicensed Internet café in the capital, Beijing, authorities launched a nationwide crackdown on the businesses, permanently closing more than 3,000 cafés and requiring others to install filtering software on their computers before reopening. While the government often justifies Internet censorship as an anti-pornography effort, a study released in December by Harvard University's Berkman Center for Internet and Society demonstrated that Chinese authorities block many more news and political sites than those with sexually explicit content.

In 2002, the government announced new regulations mandating that Internet service providers censor their own sites or risk being closed. Hundreds of domestic companies, universities, government agencies, and other organizations acquiesced, signing a voluntary and vaguely worded pledge to block any information that "may jeopardize state security and disrupt social stability." The U.S.-based Yahoo! corporation also signed the pledge, prompting widespread international protest from free speech advocates.

Large segments of the urban, educated population who now rely on the Internet for daily work or personal use have become increasingly outspoken against government censorship of the Web. The Declaration of Internet Citizens' Rights, which had gathered more than 1,000 signatures from academics, Web site publishers, and everyday Internet users by the end of 2002, challenged the constitutionality of Internet restrictions. A government decision to block access to the Google search engine in August sparked online protests. After two weeks, officials restored access to the site.

While trying to maintain control over an increasingly independent-minded domestic press, the government also continues to control the activities of foreign journalists by issuing strict regulations governing reporting and by harassing those who don't comply. Local sources who speak to foreign journalists often risk harassment or imprisonment. In December, authorities sentenced Li Lan, a Hunan Province rice farmer, to one year in jail on charges of "malicious slander" after she spoke with a *New York Times* reporter for a story about rural lawlessness.

As the 16th Communist Party Congress began in Beijing on November 7, almost 800 foreign journalists swarmed the city, eager to cover what the government called the most open meeting in the party's history. But they were disappointed to find most proceedings closed to journalists, except for a few carefully scripted meetings. To learn what was happening, reporters were reduced to chasing delegates while they took rest room breaks.

Although Chinese newspapers featured bright red headlines lauding the congress, the news was almost devoid of any real information about the transfer of power appointing Vice President Hu Jintao to succeed President Jiang Zemin as the party's general secretary. In the spring, propaganda officials had issued a document asking journalists to create a "correct ideological atmosphere" during the congress and listing 32 restricted topics, including Taiwan's political status, religious minorities, and independent media. Nervous editors told several of China's most aggressive journalists not to report to work during the meetings. "My boss told me to take a month off," one journalist told the *South China Morning Post*. The authorities "do not want any bad news," said the journalist.

For China's journalists, the power transition doesn't offer much reason for optimism.

Shortly after the congress ended, the editor of *Shenzhen Weekly* newsmagazine was fired for publishing a satirical piece about a mock press conference in which a journalist is reprimanded for referring to Hu Jintao as a "puppet" of President Jiang Zemin.

FIVE YEARS AFTER HONG KONG'S RETURN TO CHINESE SOVEREIGNTY, the debate over the future of free expression in the territory rages on. While several prominent journalists publicly condemned their colleagues for practicing self-censorship, the government moved forward with plans to draft anti-subversion legislation, which many observers view as a direct threat to Hong Kong's free and lively media. Nevertheless, local papers continue to publish stories that would be banned from the mainland press, including reports about Chinese politics, Taiwan's political status, and pro-democracy activism in China.

Just before the July 1 anniversary of Hong Kong's handover to China, government officials announced plans to proceed with anti-subversion legislation as required under Article 23 of the Basic Law, the territory's constitution. Article 23 mandates that Hong Kong enact, "on its own," statutes outlawing sedition, subversion, secession, and the theft of state secrets. In September, the Security Bureau issued a Consultation Document on the legislation and called for comment during a three-month public consultation period.

A diverse range of groups—including CPJ, the Hong Kong Bar Association, the U.S. Chamber of Commerce, banking officials, librarians, and numerous individual journalists, lawyers, legislators, and religious figures—protested the proposed laws, expressing concern that they would chill free speech and the free flow of information in Hong Kong. Press freedom advocates said that the enactment of such laws would discourage journalists from covering topics that Beijing considers politically sensitive, including the banned spiritual group Falun Gong and independence movements in the Tibet and Xinjiang autonomous regions.

In December, CPJ submitted a response to the government stating that the proposed legislation should not be enacted because it exceeds the requirements of Article 23 and poses a grave threat to press freedom. Chinese vice premier Qian Qichen, who has pushed Hong Kong to enact the measures, did little to quell concerns when he publicly stated that anyone who opposes the legislation must "have the devil in their hearts." The government plans to finalize draft legislation by February 2003.

The April dismissal of Jasper Becker, the *South China Morning Post*'s veteran Beijing bureau chief, was one in a series of incidents that brought the issue of self-censorship into the public spotlight. *Post* editors said that Becker was fired for "insubordination," while Becker, who has written prolifically about Chinese politics and social problems, claimed that his dismissal was part of a larger management effort to "make the coverage more pro-China." The incident reignited an ongoing public debate in Hong Kong about the extent of political influence on editorial decisions. During a fact-finding mission to Hong Kong in September, CPJ found that while there has been little direct government interference in the media since 1997, political and corporate interests often subtly influence editorial decisions, helping foster a climate of excessive caution.

In interviews with CPJ, several Hong Kong journalists acknowledged a trend among their colleagues of less aggressive reporting on China. While some blamed it on a lack of interest from the Hong Kong public, others pointed to more complicated reasons. "At our paper, when we need to cut space, we cut China coverage first," one editor at a major Chinese-language daily told CPJ. "Other papers think that if they cover China less, they'll get in less trouble.... The media's not trying to dig out stories anymore."

EAST TIMOR

A DECADES-LONG STRUGGLE FOR INDEPENDENCE ENDED ON MAY 20, when the U.N. Transitional Authority for East Timor (UNTAET) formally handed power to East Timor's first elected government, making the tiny half-island state the first new nation of the millennium. A fledgling press has emerged from the destruction that followed the territory's vote for independence from Indonesia in 1999, and now the country has two daily newspapers, a handful of weeklies, and seven small private radio stations. Indonesia, which annexed East Timor in 1975 following the collapse of Portuguese colonial rule, did not tolerate an independent press.

East Timor's dominant media outlet is the national radio service established by the United Nations in 1999, Radio UNTAET, renamed Radio Timor Lorosae after independence. Roughly modeled on the BBC, the station was intended to become a blueprint for a public broadcaster independent of the government. But for most of 2002, the service was mired in controversy, funding problems, and charges of political interference. U.N. officials failed to establish an independent broadcasting authority, and instead the ruling Fretilin Party of Prime Minister Mari Alkatiri pushed through legislation in May giving the new government control over management of the station after independence.

The move was disquieting, given accusations throughout the April presidential election campaign that Fretilin Party activists already had begun trying to influence reporters at Radio UNTAET. Following independence, sources at the service told CPJ that Fretilin interference was pervasive at the station.

The constitution approved by the National Assembly in March falls short of making press freedom absolute, leaving the right to free expression subject to several legal provisions. There will likely be numerous court battles in the future as legislators draft press, libel, and broadcast regulation laws.

By and large, however, private media outlets in East Timor—all of which are small, financially struggling, and mostly confined to the capital, Dili—say they have so far been free to report without fear of political retribution.

In November, East Timorese authorities indicted two Indonesian military officers for the September 1999 murder of Dutch journalist Sander Thoenes. A reporter for the *Financial Times* and the *Christian Science Monitor*, Thoenes was one of two journalists killed in the violence that followed East Timor's August 30, 1999, vote for independence from Indonesia (see page 172). As pro-Jakarta militias went on a rampage with support from the Indonesian military, journalists were deliberately targeted in an apparent effort to ensure that there would be no witnesses to the atrocities. The indictments put the onus on Indonesia either to prosecute the two accused, who were also charged with 16 additional counts of "crimes against humanity" stemming from the 1999 carnage, or extradite them to East Timor.

In early December, Dili's usual calm was shattered by two days of rioting that left two

ASIA

dead from police gunfire and scores injured. The prime minister's house, government buildings, and some foreign-owned businesses were burned during the unrest, which exposed political rifts in the new nation.

FIJI

FIJI'S DIVERSE AND ENERGETIC MEDIA HAVE REMAINED STRONG despite ongoing political instability in the country. Tensions between indigenous Fijians and the ethnic Indian population dominate political and social life and are often played out in the media, which include several English- and Hindi-language newspapers, the partially privatized Fiji TV, and two major radio broadcasters that operate English-, Fijian-, and Hindi-language channels.

Two years after a failed coup by businessman George Speight, who claimed to be fighting for the rights of indigenous Fijians, the battle for power has moved from the streets to the courtroom. In February, Speight was sentenced to life in prison for treason, and legal proceedings against other coup participants dragged on throughout the year. Meanwhile, the opposition Indo-Fijian Labour Party, which was ousted during the 2000 uprising, directly challenged the legitimacy of Prime Minister Laisenia Qarase's government. The party brought a court case against Qarase, an ethnic Fijian, claiming he had failed to abide by constitutional requirements to form a multiethnic coalition government after narrowly winning general elections in August 2001. The High Court ruled in favor of the Indo-Fijian Labour Party, and the case is slated to go before the Supreme Court in 2003.

Members of the local media told CPJ that they were able to report on these sensitive court proceedings without significant interference, and that violent attacks and harassment against journalists had declined under the Qarase administration. Nevertheless, some officials launched verbal attacks on the media for exposing social or political problems. Qarase dedicated three pages of an official speech to criticizing Fiji TV, calling the station "eager beavers famous for its spin and bias." In August, a senator who is also a Methodist minister, responded to media reports of financial irregularities in the church by calling journalists "agents of some powerful foreign agencies, agents of evil planning against Christianity." A week later, on the Senate floor, another legislator blamed journalists for the breakdown of Fijian society. "They are indeed Satan's agents and forces," he said. "They are mad crazy loonies and crazy people."

Ofa Swann, a member of the opposition New Labour Party, called on her colleagues in Parliament to stop using their positions to lambaste the country's journalists. She also advocated raising journalists' salaries, an issue of major concern for those in the media industry. "The media can be both convenient and annoying," she said. "However, they are there for a reason, and they are not just there for politicians."

INDIA

INDIA IS FAMOUS FOR BEING THE WORLD'S LARGEST DEMOCRACY, but government actions in 2002 to curb the press indicate a growing intolerance among the country's leadership. Many journalists say the ruling Hindu nationalist Bharatiya Janata Party (BJP) seems to target its critics in the media as a matter of policy—and largely gets away with it.

In the western state of Gujarat, police and political activists were responsible for a series of physical assaults against journalists covering the violence that swept the state after a Muslim mob attacked a train carrying Hindu activists in late February. The ensuing reprisal attacks left more than 1,000 Muslims dead and tens of thousands homeless. When journalists reported that much of the violence against Muslims was organized and sponsored by police and activists associated with Hindu nationalist groups, including the BJP, Gujarat's chief minister, Narendra Modi, lashed out. Modi, himself a BJP leader, accused the press of "making attempts to project Gujarat as a violent and disturbed state" and conspiring "to remove people's faith from the elected government."

Journalists who covered the violence were vulnerable not only to the rage of unruly mobs but also to harassment and assault by police who did not want evidence of their complicity in the attacks publicized. Police in Rajkot, a city in Gujarat, beat Sudhir Vyas, a reporter from the national *Times of India*, while he attempted to cover the unrest. "They said, 'Why are you here? Have you come to report on what we are doing?'" Vyas told CPJ. "They knew I was seeing what they allowed others to do."

In June, the government threatened to expel *Time* magazine's New Delhi bureau chief, Alex Perry, after he wrote an article questioning Prime Minister Atal Behari Vajpayee's fitness to lead the country during heightened tension on the subcontinent. Though officials interrogated Perry about alleged visa infractions, they took no further action.

Less than a month later, the government forced Al-Jazeera correspondent Nasir Shadid to leave India. "Al-Jazeera is replacing its correspondent," External Affairs Ministry spokeswoman Nirupama Rao said, according to The Associated Press. "This is a decision the government of India makes." Shadid's colleagues in the capital, New Delhi, said the journalist had angered officials with his reporting, particularly on attacks against Muslims in Gujarat and on the conflict in Kashmir, a mostly Muslim territory claimed by both India and Pakistan.

Iftikhar Gilani, the New Delhi bureau chief for the Jammu-based newspaper *Kashmir Times*, suffered the worst state harassment. The government accused him of possessing classified documents and jailed him for seven months under the Official Secrets Act, a draconian, colonial-era law.

Journalists working in strife-torn Kashmir continue to endure physical assault, threats, and harassment, and in 2002 the number of attacks against the press increased there. Militant groups fighting against Indian rule were believed to have perpetrated the most serious of these assaults, including three separate incidents in which journalists were shot and one in which a grenade hit a reporter's home. Tensions ran high in the run-up to controversial state legislative assembly elections held in September and October. Militant groups had threatened to assassinate anyone who supported the elections, which they believe conferred undue legitimacy on the Indian government. The United Jihad Council, a Pakistan-based organization representing about 14 militant groups in Kashmir, issued a threat against the press hours before a prominent editor was shot: "Mujahideen (warriors) are aware of the black sheep among journalists and warn them to mend their ways." Nine journalists have been killed in Kashmir since civil war erupted there in 1989, according to CPJ research.

Separatist insurgencies in India's northeastern states, especially in Manipur and Assam, also endangered journalists. In October, ethnic Kuki militants kidnapped two journalists in

Manipur State to protest the media's "poor coverage" of the United Kuki Liberation Front. Just two days after the journalists were released, reporter Yambem Meghajit Singh was found dead in Imphal, Manipur's capital. His colleagues say they do not know what motivated the killing. And in Assam, police threatened to arrest journalist Lachit Bordoloi and accused him of ties to the rebel United Liberation Front of Assam after he wrote about police corruption.

Though covering India's conflict areas was obviously dangerous, even ordinary reporting on crime or political infighting occasionally sparked violent reprisal. One editor was murdered in the northern state of Haryana after reporting on sexual abuse and other crimes allegedly committed by a local religious sect. A crime reporter in the neighboring state of Uttar Pradesh was also murdered in 2002, though the motive behind his killing remained unconfirmed at year's end. In the southern state of Tamil Nadu, meanwhile, a political gang armed with wooden batons assaulted several journalists working for a newspaper that had published an unflattering cartoon of the group's leader.

INDONESIA

SEPARATIST REBELLIONS, A DETERIORATING ECONOMY, AND POLITICAL INTRIGUE combined to keep Indonesia on edge for much of 2002. But despite the many challenges and tensions facing the country, the press remained substantially free and hung on to most gains made since 1998, when decades of dictatorship ended with the ouster of then president Suharto.

The October 12 terrorist bombing on the resort island of Bali, which claimed nearly 200 lives, highlighted the increasing divide between foreign press's treatment of Indonesia's terrorism crisis and the approach taken by the local media. While Western news organizations have been quick to outline the details of a terrorist network in the country, many observers were disturbed by domestic news reports, even in the mainstream press, claiming that the attack was the work of a foreign country intent on seizing Indonesia's natural resources or discrediting Islam. Some local newspapers even asserted that the U.S. government had participated in the attack.

In September, Muslim cleric Abu Bakar Ba'asyir threatened *Time* magazine with a libel suit for running a story in which U.S. intelligence sources identified him as a terrorist leader. Indonesian authorities later arrested Ba'asyir and charged him with plotting several terrorist actions.

There was little progress on the legislative front during 2002. Nearly three years of debate about the future of Indonesia's electronic media ended in November with the passage of a landmark broadcasting regulatory bill. The measure had been long delayed because reformers and industry representatives sought to establish an accountable, independent regulatory mechanism for radio and television that would reverse the legacy of central control left by Suharto's regime.

Unfortunately, closed-door negotiations between lawmakers and government representatives produced a bill establishing a flawed National Broadcasting Commission, whose members are appointed by the government. In addition, the bill leaves control of frequency allocation in the hands of a government ministry, allowing for substantial political interference in broadcast content and regulation.

CPJ and a number of local and international advocacy organizations opposed the bill, but its passage still brought a measure of relief to some in the Indonesian media who had been operating in a chaotic regulatory environment since the dismantling of Suharto-era controls in 1998. The respected Alliance of Independent Journalists urged the media to work with the new broadcasting commission to make it responsive to the press.

Other Suharto-period laws remain in effect. Foreign reporters, for example, are still required to obtain special journalist visas. Failure to do so can result in deportation and criminal prosecution. Police in the restive northwestern province of Aceh arrested and jailed Scottish journalist and academic Lesley McCulloch in September for allegedly violating the terms of her tourist visa. Authorities had threatened to file espionage charges against McCulloch for possessing documents and photographs related to the Free Aceh Movement, the rebel group battling the Indonesian government for control of the province. McCulloch, who says she was on vacation visiting friends in Aceh, was ultimately charged under Indonesia's immigration law for "activities incompatible with tourist visas," which is punishable by up to five years in prison.

During her trial, which began in late November, McCulloch told reporters that Indonesian authorities were harassing her because of articles she had written about human rights abuses in Aceh. On December 30, 2002, an Aceh court found McCulloch guilty, and the judge in the case accused her of endangering national security. She was sentenced to five months in jail, including time served awaiting trial, and was expected to be released early in 2003.

Indonesian authorities use visa restrictions to monitor and control the activities of visiting reporters, resulting in discrimination against nonresident foreign correspondents. Resident journalists, both foreign and local, face no formal restrictions on their movement in the country and are generally free to visit conflict areas such as Aceh and Irian Jaya, where another separatist rebellion is under way. Immigration authorities, however, frequently stamp restrictions into journalist visas barring them from conflict areas.

Even resident foreign journalists sometimes draw fire from authorities. In March, veteran Australian correspondent Lindsay Murdoch of the *Sydney Morning Herald* was banned from working in the country. Indonesian authorities refused to renew his working visa, offering no explanation. Murdoch, who was based in the capital, Jakarta, for three years and won numerous awards for his reporting, told CPJ that he was banned because his aggressive reporting on human rights abuses had angered the military.

In November, East Timorese prosecutors indicted two Indonesian soldiers for the 1999 murder of *Financial Times* reporter Sander Thoenes, who was killed in the aftermath of East Timor's vote for independence from Indonesia. The two soldiers, Maj. Jacob Sarosa and Lt. Camilo dos Santos, were both members of Battalion 745, which has been implicated in numerous rights abuses in East Timor. Observers doubt that the two officers, both of whom reportedly remain on active duty, will be extradited to face trial in East Timor. Meanwhile, efforts to prosecute the Thoenes murder in Indonesia have stalled. In June, a spokesman for the Attorney General's Office in Jakarta claimed that there was not enough evidence to pursue the case. A month later, Indonesian prosecutors promised to reopen the investigation, but there was no discernible progress by year's end.

Corruption continued to plague the local media. Since the restoration of press freedom, some journalists, especially in rural areas, have used their press credentials to extort

ASIA

money from local authorities and businesses. Conversely, many companies will pay journalists to cover press conferences. In October, provincial authorities in Riau, on the island of Sumatra, announced a scheme to give every journalist in the province a no-interest housing loan. According to the *Jakarta Post*, only members of the reform-minded Alliance of Independent Journalists refused the offer.

LAOS

ALTHOUGH LAOS IS AN INCREASINGLY POPULAR DESTINATION for budget travelers, it is not a very hospitable place for journalists. The ruling Communist Lao People's Revolutionary Party, which brooks no dissent, owns all of the country's media outlets.

In late 2001, Laotian officials announced that the one-party Parliament would consider a Mass Media Bill permitting private ownership of some media for the first time since the communist regime came to power in 1975. The bill would also create a regulatory body to control the media and ensure enforcement of official policies. By the end of 2002, no action had been taken on the legislation, although Laotian journalists privately expressed hope that its eventual passage would open up at least some democratic space for their profession.

In March, the ruling party predictably swept elections for the 109 seats in the National Assembly, with Radio Vientiane reporting that 99 percent of eligible voters had cast ballots. Most candidates ran unopposed, and no outside observers were allowed to monitor the elections.

Internet use is slowly spreading in Laos, with privately owned cybercafés dotting popular tourist centers in the capital, Vientiane, and in Luang Prabang, to the north of the capital. In July, the official National Internet Control Committee announced that it had installed Internet filters to block unwanted information. "Like other societies, we want to protect our youth and vulnerable citizens from bad stuff such as pornography and dissident Web sites that post false information about governments," committee executive director Maydom Chanthanasinh told Thailand's *The Nation* newspaper. Internet cafés that try to bypass the filters can be fined or have their business licenses revoked. In October, the government opened its first Internet center, in Vientiane, offering cheaper Web access than private cybercafés.

Foreign journalists, who must obtain special visas to visit the country, are also required to pay for the services of an official "escort" during their stays. Most government information is secret, and Laotian officials seldom grant interviews.

It is virtually impossible, however, for the government to block all access to foreign news sources, especially given Laos' close proximity to—and heavy economic reliance on—Thailand. Thai radio and television can be heard in much of Laos, and there is enough similarity between the nations' languages that most Laotians can easily understand Thai broadcasts. Cable television is expensive but available through satellite, and viewers with access can watch CNN, the BBC, and other international news channels.

MALAYSIA

STRICT LICENSING LAWS, SELF-CENSORSHIP, AND PERVASIVE POLITICAL INFLUENCE dominate the press in Malaysia. Under the country's severe Internal Security Act, journalists are also subject to indefinite detention without charge, as well as harsh libel penalties. The ruling National Front coalition and corporations allied with the government of Prime Minister Mahathir Mohamad control all major newspapers and broadcast outlets, ensuring a substantial degree of official influence over news published in the country. The only exception is the Internet, which has so far remained censorship-free. The courageous online newspaper *Malaysiakini* is the only truly independent source of information in the country.

Traditionally strained relations between the foreign media and the Malaysian government continued in 2002, with authorities blocking the distribution of three U.S. newsmagazines—*Newsweek*, *Time*, and the *Far Eastern Economic Review*—in January and February, apparently because the government considered some stories "inaccurate and untrue," including reports on alleged links between the al-Qaeda terrorist network and groups in Malaysia. "It is unfair on the part of the correspondent to give views without checking the facts," Deputy Home Minister Chor Chee Heung told *The Star* newspaper in explaining the actions. Under Malaysian law, authorities are required to screen foreign publications prior to their distribution in the country.

Some officials accused the Western press of conspiring against Malaysia. In May, hard-liner Datuk Zainuddin Maidin, then parliamentary secretary at the Information Ministry, reacted to a local seminar held on World Press Freedom Day (May 3) by saying, "The big problem faced by the Asian countries now after the end of the cold war is the infiltration by subversive elements from the developed countries through their media and the use of local journalists to carry out the agenda of Western media imperialism." Zam, as he is known in Malaysia, then accused journalists from the Philippines and Thailand of trying to influence Malaysia on behalf of the West. In November, Zam was promoted to the even more influential post of deputy information minister.

On May 3, the Home Ministry suspended the Malay-language tabloid *Perdana Sari* for three months for alleging that a leading member of Mahathir's United Malay National Organization party is a lesbian.

Ethnic Malays comprise about 60 percent of the population, with Chinese and Indians accounting for the rest. Until recently, Chinese-language papers were more independent than Malay and English media outlets, perhaps because of the inordinate economic clout of the Chinese minority. In 2001, the Malaysian Chinese Association, a member of the ruling coalition, took over Nanyang Press Holdings, which publishes Malaysia's two leading Chinese dailies, sparking fears that the previously independent Chinese press would follow in the timid footsteps of the rest of the Malaysian media. A new independent Chinese-language daily, *The Oriental Daily News*, published only one issue, on September 29, before the Home Ministry suspended the publication's permit without explanation. The suspension was lifted in early December, but it was not clear when the new daily would publish again. Observers linked the suspension to political pressure: Large numbers of journalists had left the Nanyang group to join the new paper, according to press reports.

In June, Mahathir tearfully announced that, after 21 years, he would resign as prime minister and cede the post to his deputy, Abdullah Badawi. The resignation is expected to become effective in late 2003, but observers doubt that it will result in a better environment for the press. In fact, some journalists say the situation has already deteriorated. Since

ASIA |

the announcement, aides to the future prime minister have begun ordering newspapers to increase their coverage of Badawi. "We are told now to put his picture on the front page and what to say about him. The instructions are very clear," an editor told CPJ.

Since 1998, mainstream journalists have been pushing the government to repeal the repressive Printing Presses and Publications Act (PPPA) of 1984—which allows the government to license and close newspapers—in favor of a self-regulatory, nongovernmental media council. Meanwhile, the conservative, private Malaysian Press Institute has drafted a plan for a media council that does not lift the PPPA and instead creates a semigovernmental body with additional powers to control the media.

In early January, management at *The Sun* daily newspaper fired 41 journalists after a story ran alleging that police had foiled an assassination plot against Mahathir. Observers suspect that the government was behind the layoffs and believe that the story was an excuse to rid *The Sun* of a number of independent-minded journalists, some of whom had worked on the piece. Government officials denied involvement in the incident. The financially ailing paper eventually laid off 256 more employees before being sold to a new company and relaunched as a free publication in April. Wrongful termination lawsuits filed by several former employees remain pending.

NEPAL

POLITICAL TURMOIL AND AN INTENSIFIED MAOIST INSURGENCY severely strained Nepal's young democracy and profoundly challenged the country's independent media. In November 2001, the government, then led by Prime Minister Sher Bahadur Deuba, imposed a state of emergency, introduced a sweeping anti-terrorism ordinance, and called out the army to counter the mounting threat posed by Maoist rebels. Each of these actions had serious repercussions for the press in 2002. Under the state of emergency, in effect until late August, press freedom and other civil liberties were suspended. The anti-terrorism ordinance—formally known as the Terrorist and Disruptive Activities (Control and Punishment) Ordinance and commonly referred to as TADO—identifies the Maoist faction of the Communist Party of Nepal (CPN-M) as a terrorist group and allows for the arrest of anyone "in contact with" or "supportive of" the rebels. More than 100 journalists were detained during 2002 under these broad provisions, which remain in force. The government also introduced reporting guidelines, banning anything "likely to create hatred against [the] Royal Nepal Army, police, and civil servants, and lower their morale and dignity."

The crisis prompted CPJ to send a mission to Nepal from May 20 to June 6 to talk with journalists, human rights activists, and government officials to identify the major challenges facing the Nepalese press. In meetings with the prime minister and the information minister, CPJ representatives expressed concern about press freedom abuses that accompanied the government's crackdown on the Maoist rebellion—specifically protesting the illegal detention of journalists and their alleged torture by authorities.

The drastic actions, which, according to Prime Minister Deuba, were taken to maintain Nepal's democracy, actually made it more vulnerable. In June, Deuba, facing opposition to his plan to extend the state of emergency, abruptly dissolved Parliament and scheduled new elections for November. But in early October, when he proposed postponing the elections, citing security concerns, King Gyanendra surprised everyone by dismissing Deuba and his Cabinet and taking executive powers for himself. (Gyanendra was crowned in June 2001 after his brother King Birendra and eight other relatives were shot dead by Crown Prince Dipendra, who then killed himself.)

Nepal is supposed to be a constitutional monarchy, with the king limited to a largely ceremonial role and real power resting with the prime minister and the Parliament. But the country's experiment with democracy is only 12 years old, and some say that recent gains could be easily overturned.

More than 7,000 people have been killed during the Maoists' six-year insurgency, according to government figures released at the end of October. However, journalists say these numbers are almost impossible to verify independently. Since the army began counterinsurgency operations in November 2001, the government has not provided regular briefings or access to conflict areas. After the imposition of TADO, the Maoist leadership went deep underground and severed already limited contacts with most mainstream journalists. Many reporters themselves became skittish about seeking interviews with Maoist cadre for fear of arrest.

The Maoist rebels, who model their movement after Peru's Shining Path, have declared a People's War to topple Nepal's constitutional monarchy. They were increasingly hostile to members of the media in 2002, mounting three alarming attacks against journalists during the year—including the murder of editor Nava Raj Sharma. Maoist rebels kidnapped Sharma, editor of a local paper in remote Kalikot District, in June. He was found dead in mid-August, his body badly mutilated. Maoists claimed responsibility for the murder, posting flyers in the area saying that Sharma was killed because he was a government spy. In separate incidents, rebels kidnapped two other journalists, both of whom worked for state-run Radio Nepal. One of them, Demling Lama, managed to escape and later described being tortured and threatened at gunpoint. The other journalist, Dhan Bahadur Rokka Magar, remained missing at year's end.

State security forces committed the vast majority of abuses against journalists. Of the scores of journalists who have been detained since November 2001, most have no connection to the Maoist movement, and most were released after relatively short periods of detention. Journalists were targeted for various reasons—for reporting on Maoists or for expressing views considered supportive of the rebel movement, but also for reporting that had nothing to do with the insurgency. However, of the 16 journalists who remain in prison, most were working for pro-Maoist publications.

A member of the government's Nepal Human Rights Commission told CPJ that, of the thousands of people arrested under TADO, "there are very few cases in which a charge sheet is produced." He said that due process rights tend to be ignored, and that people "are just 'disappeared.'"

The most notorious case of abuse was the alleged killing of journalist Krishna Sen, editor of the daily *Janadisha* and former editor of the weekly *Janadesh*, both publications often referred to as mouthpieces of the Maoist rebel movement. Sen was arrested on May 20 and was reportedly killed in police custody. The government denied responsibility for Sen's disappearance, claiming that no security agencies had any record of having detained

ASIA

him. Officials also said that Sen should not be considered a journalist since they believe he is a central committee member of the CPN-M. The government, however, has never proved its allegations against him in a court of law.

The mass arrests have, not surprisingly, fostered self-censorship in the Nepalese press. Many journalists told CPJ they do not report on civilian casualties and other human rights abuses for fear of reprisal.

Despite all the pressures, at year's end, local media still featured critical coverage of authorities, including the views of those opposed to the king's government takeover and reporting on alleged rights abuses by the army. This is especially significant because the palace and the army, neither of which normally tolerate outside scrutiny, have tradition-ally been taboo subjects for the press. But with the king in charge and the army taking the lead role in curbing the insurgency, independent coverage of their activities was more crucial than ever.

At the end of October, the national English-language daily *Kathmandu Post* obtained a letter from King Gyanendra directing his newly appointed prime minister "to make necessary changes in the laws" to curb "yellow journalism." The king's order came after a local film actress committed suicide because a tabloid published her nude photograph with an article claiming that she had been a prostitute. While most media organizations condemned the story as an ethical breach, journalists also feared that the palace might use the scandal as an excuse to further restrict the press.

NORTH KOREA

SHORTLY AFTER U.S. PRESIDENT GEORGE W. BUSH arrived in South Korea's capital, Seoul, in February 2002 for a state visit, the North Korean state news agency, KCNA, reported a miracle: that a cloud in the shape of a Kimjongilia, the flower named after the country's leader, Kim Jong Il, had appeared over North Korea. "Even the sky above the Mount Paektu area seemed to be decorated with beautiful flowers," KCNA said. The piece was a whimsical effort to trump news of Bush's visit to the other side of the divided Korean peninsula, according to *The New York Times*.

North Korean propaganda has its lighter side, but the effects of the government's absolute control over news and information are extremely serious. This had become obvious by the end of 2002, when a tense standoff developed between the United States and North Korea over Pyongyang's alleged admission to maintaining a secret nuclear weapons pro-gram. With so little information available about the exact status of North Korea's nuclear capabilities, diplomats and analysts around the world were left parsing the bellicose rhetoric of state media accounts for signs of Pyongyang's intentions. A single phrase broadcast by Pyongyang Radio on November 17 initially seemed to make the stunning revalation that North Korea already has nuclear weapons, though translators said the line may have indi-cated only that the country is "entitled to have weapons." The difference lay in one syllable.

One of the last totalitarian states in the world, North Korea uses the media to foster a cult of personality around Kim Jong Il and his deceased father, Kim Il Sung, the country's "eternal leader." The local media tend to ignore the country's gravest problems—such as the devastating famine that began in the mid-1990s and has cost as many as 2 million lives. State media instead demonize Pyongyang's enemies, especially the United States, which has been called "the empire of the devil." President Bush returned the favor in 2002, casting North Korea as part of an "axis of evil" along with Iran and Iraq.

North Korea has opened up to a degree, experimenting with market reforms, tourism promotion schemes, and diplomatic overtures after decades of Stalinist rule and isolationism that strengthened the country's reputation as the "Hermit Kingdom." Foreign journalists visited the country in 2002, mostly as part of the press corps accompanying visiting dignitaries, who included Russian president Vladimir Putin and Japanese prime minister Junichiro Koizumi.

Foreign correspondents also received visas to North Korea during the highly touted Arirang festival, a celebration marking the birthday of Kim Il Sung, which began on April 29 and lasted more than two months. Arirang, the centerpiece of the government's bid to promote tourism, featured performances six days a week by thousands of dancers, gymnasts, soldiers, and other performers. "For the ... months of Arirang, the Hermit Nation is inviting the world in," wrote Jonathan Watts in the British newspaper *The Guardian*. "Even journalists are being welcomed into the country and allowed a freedom of movement that was hardly imaginable a year ago." However, correspondents still complained of being closely watched and restricted by government minders.

And not all journalists were welcome. In September, during the Koizumi visit, North Korea refused to grant a visa to a reporter from the conservative, staunchly anti-communist South Korean newspaper *Chosun Ilbo*. The reporter had been chosen by lottery to join the 120-person press corps accompanying Koizumi, according to the South Korean news agency Yonhap. *Chosun*, one of the South's leading dailies, has repeatedly angered the North Korean leadership with its denunciations of Pyongyang, and North Korea routinely denies access to *Chosun* reporters.

PAKISTAN

PAKISTANI JOURNALISTS HAVE LONG NAVIGATED A TREACHEROUS COURSE, threatened by militant groups, criminal gangs, political bosses, and powerful intelligence agencies, but the rest of the world scarcely noticed these dangers until the assassination of American reporter Daniel Pearl. Months after Pearl's murder, another journalist was killed in Pakistan: Shahid Soomro. Like Pearl, Soomro was killed in volatile Sindh Province, but he was the victim of local politicos angered by his reporting on their abuse of power.

Pearl, the South Asia bureau chief for the U.S.-based *Wall Street Journal*, was kidnapped and killed in the port city of Karachi while reporting on links between Pakistani militant groups and the al-Qaeda terrorist network. In the days following Pearl's abduction, his captors sent e-mail messages containing photographs of the journalist, as well as a series of demands addressed to the U.S. government. The first message accused Pearl of being an American spy, while another sent days later branded him an agent of the Israeli intelligence agency Mossad. U.S. officials confirmed his brutal murder on February 21, after receiving a digital videotape documenting his beheading.

Many Pakistani journalists strongly condemned Pearl's kidnappers. Local press organizations issued statements in support of Pearl, and several newspapers published editorials calling for his safe release. That an American journalist working for a powerful news organization could be so easily targeted sent tremors through the local press corps and discouraged serious investigations into matters such as militant groups active inside Pakistan.

However, the Pakistani press—which includes everything from religious-party organs to scandal sheets to sober political journals—largely holds its own under the military government led by Gen. Pervez Musharraf. While self-censorship is widespread, the tenacity of the local media is remarkable. Pakistani journalists have long endured routine surveillance and harassment by state intelligence agencies, especially the Inter-Services Intelligence, which the army controls, and these pressures have intensified under Musharraf's rule.

Working without the protections offered by democratic institutions, many journalists avoid publicizing state-sponsored harassment for fear of reprisals. One of the country's leading newspapers sent a private letter to General Musharraf after two of its correspondents complained of harassment and threats from intelligence officials. The letter, a copy of which CPJ obtained, urged Musharraf to order an inquiry into the matter but also explained that the newspaper "does not want to generate a public controversy through its publications ... when there is a dire need for greater harmony in the country to meet the external threat."

One U.S. journalist, Elizabeth Rubin, who attempted to escape her military minders while traveling in Azad Kashmir, the Pakistan-controlled section of the disputed Himalayan territory, said that as soon as she left the area, intelligence agents interrogated her sources. Authorities detained one of these sources, a Kashmiri, for nearly two months. Intelligence agents held another man, a refugee who had fled from Indian-controlled Kashmir and had worked with Rubin as a guide and translator, incommunicado for 10 days. He was repeatedly interrogated and accused of working to tarnish Pakistan's image. A local journalist who had worked with Rubin as a fixer, meanwhile, nearly lost his job at an Urdu-language daily that was under government pressure to dismiss him.

While the military government did not undertake a sweeping crackdown on the media, several actions belied its avowed commitment to press freedom. Shaheen Sehbai, the former editor of *The News* newspaper, resigned in March, citing government interference with the publication's editorial content. From the United States, Sehbai began publishing an online newspaper, *The South Asia Tribune*, which frequently criticizes the military regime. With Sehbai out of the country and out of reach, police harassed and arrested several members of his family on spurious charges, including armed robbery.

During the run-up to Musharraf's broadly criticized April referendum, which extended his presidency for five years, the general frequently accused the press of unfairly attacking his record. In August, Musharraf introduced a series of new media ordinances, which were billed as reform measures but may be used to limit press freedom. The All Pakistan Newspaper Society, a powerful organization of the country's publishers, criticized the new laws, calling them "illegitimate, unethical, and unconstitutional." Under these laws, defamation remains a criminal offense, and publishing without a government license is punishable by imprisonment. One ordinance mandates the creation of a Press Council, chaired by a government appointee, with the power to ban publications and issue other punitive sanctions.

The press laws were announced at around the same time that Musharraf unilaterally introduced a number of constitutional amendments to strengthen his powers and give the military a permanent role in governance. All these steps came in advance of the October parliamentary elections, which were supposed to usher in a shift to a civilian government. The new prime minister, however, is a Musharraf ally, and ultimate power appears to remain with the general and his army.

Although no party won an absolute majority in the elections, a coalition of hard-line Islamist parties won control of two key provinces along the Afghan border, North West Frontier Province (NWFP) and Baluchistan Province. This religious alliance, the Muttahida Majlis-i-Amal (MMA), adamantly opposes U.S. presence in the region, especially U.S. operations in the border areas, where al-Qaeda and Taliban members are believed to have found refuge after fleeing Afghanistan.

In the past, religious parties have not tolerated the press. One journalist who had worked in Peshawar, in NWFP, was forced into exile in 1999 after the Jamiat Ulema-i-Islam, a powerful religious party that now belongs to the MMA, organized large-scale demonstrations calling for his assassination. The journalist had angered local religious leaders by reporting on allegations of sexual harassment of children at Muslim seminaries in the area. In 2001, religious parties in NWFP organized a series of protests against journalists working for the Peshawar-based *Frontier Post* newspaper, which had accidentally published a letter that was considered blasphemous. Local authorities responded by arresting seven journalists for blasphemy, which is punishable by death. At the end of 2002, one of these journalists, Munawwar Mohsin, remained in prison.

Reporting along the Afghan border is difficult and dangerous. Non-Pakistanis are required to obtain permission before traveling to the Federally Administered Tribal Areas, over which the central government exercises little control, but foreign journalists were generally denied access to the area in 2002. This made reporting on the nature and extent of U.S. military activity in the region almost impossible. Journalists based in the tribal areas are vulnerable to pressure from local administrators, who wield unchecked power under laws dating from the British colonial period. Members of the media also face threats and harassment from heavily armed segments of the public. In 2002, one local journalist received death threats after filming footage along the border areas for a U.S. documentary about the search for al-Qaeda members. He was accused of working as a U.S. informant.

PAPUA NEW GUINEA

JOURNALISTS IN PAPUA NEW GUINEA, who had faced harassment and violence during the administration of former prime minister Mekere Morauta, viewed the August election of Sir Michael Somare, a former journalist, positively. Nevertheless, continued violence reminded observers how far the country is from reaching political and social stability.

Throughout the year, the Papua New Guinea Media Council, a self-regulatory membership group, conducted a nationwide campaign to expose and eradicate corruption, a longtime scourge on national politics and society. While this effort helped expose several major cases, one journalist was targeted for her investigative reporting. When Robyn Sela, a reporter for the country's largest daily, the *Papua New Guinea Post-Courier*, went to military barracks in the capital, Port Moresby, to cover a story about the secretary of defense, who is under investigation for corruption, a soldier told her that if she continued writing about the case, "We will shoot you dead." Sela went into hiding for a brief period. No arrests had been made in the incident by year's end.

Eliminating corruption was a major issue during the national elections, which began in mid-June. The voting was troubled from the beginning, with almost 3,000 candidates from 43 parties running for 109 seats. The polling period, which was scheduled to last for two weeks, was extended by more than a month following widespread reports of voter intimidation, fraudulent voting, stolen ballot boxes, and general chaos, during which at least 25 people were killed. Groups of armed men reportedly intimidated voters in Port Moresby and other urban centers. In the Highlands provinces, where violence is rampant and armed candidates and their supporters controlled voting sites, journalists often employed bodyguards.

On August 5, Somare was elected after candidates from his party won the majority in Parliament. Voters were hopeful that Somare, who was Papua New Guinea's first prime minister after it gained independence from Australia in 1975 and served again in the 1980s, would help bring political and economic stability to the country, which has been so politically unstable that no prime minister has served a full five-year term since independence.

Foreign journalists, especially Australians, were prevented from reporting on the elections when officials failed to process entry visas, a common tactic to deny access to the country. The government has long blamed foreign journalists for reporting negatively about Papua New Guinean society and has made it difficult for them to enter the country. Only five foreign journalists were granted permission to enter, while reporters from major Australian media outlets, including the Australian Broadcasting Corporation, the *Sydney Morning Herald*, and the *Courier-Mail*, were barred. After the elections, the Media Council began working with the new administration to ease restrictions on foreign journalists, but no discernible progress had been made by year's end.

Off the east coast on the island of Bougainville, which has been fighting for independence for 10 years, a nascent media began to emerge after an August 2001 agreement granted the region autonomy. In May, EM-TV, the nation's only television broadcaster, restarted transmission to the island for the first time since the conflict began.

PHILIPPINES

RAUCOUS AND UNINHIBITED, THE PHILIPPINE PRESS CONTINUES to be one of Asia's freest. There are few government controls on the media, newspapers do not have to be licensed, and broadcasters are largely left alone. The private Association of Philippine Broadcasters regulates itself, unlike in many other Asian countries, where the government performs this function.

Unfortunately, freedom does not always translate into safety or respect for journalists, especially in rural areas. Thirty-nine journalists have been murdered in the Philippines since democracy was restored there in 1986, making the country one of the most perilous in the world for members of the media. No one has been convicted in any of the murders.

On the evening of May 13, journalist Edgar Damalerio was gunned down in full view of the local police station in Pagadian City, a port town on the southern island of Mindanao. An award-winning radio commentator and newspaper reporter, Damalerio frequently criticized police abuses and political corruption. Two witnesses to the murder came forward and identified a local police officer as the killer, but months after the slaying, prosecutors and local officials were still dragging their feet. In August, a third witness in the case was murdered in an ambush near Pagadian City. At year's end, the alleged assailant remained free, while the witnesses and Damalerio's family feared for their lives.

Officials in the capital, Manila, responded to pleas for justice by promising to move the investigation forward, but their efforts yielded few results. A CPJ investigation into the murder found evidence that local political pressure was delaying the prosecution of the alleged assailant.

In August, an unidentified gunman murdered journalist Sonny Alcantara, a publisher and cable-television commentator in the town of San Pablo, 50 miles (80 kilometers) south of Manila, as he was driving a motorcycle to his office. Local police and the journalist's colleagues believe that Alcantara was murdered because of his reporting, which had angered local officials.

Journalists also faced dangers while covering the conflict between the government and Muslim separatist rebels in Mindanao. Armed men in a rebel-infested area of Mindanao detained a reporter and a cameraman from the Philippine's GMA television network for six days in October. Philippine military authorities, meanwhile, mistakenly identified reporter Bernadette Tamayo as a member of the rebel Abu Sayyaf group in July by putting her picture in a wanted poster circulated in Mindanao. The military later apologized.

In recent years, journalists covering Abu Sayyaf have frequently been kidnapped by the group, which uses ransom payments to finance its activities. In January, cable-television reporter Arlyn de la Cruz disappeared in the jungles of southern Mindanao while searching for the Abu Sayyaf guerrillas holding U.S. hostages Gracia and Martin Burnham. De la Cruz, who has had frequent contact with the Abu Sayyaf, was later reportedly kidnapped by a competing armed group. She was released after nearly four months in captivity, after well-known Philippine senator and television celebrity Loren Legarda brokered her release.

While the constitution and national law guarantee press freedom, some local mayors seem undeterred when it comes to harassing radio stations. Local mayors closed two stations owned by the national Bombo Radyo network, one in Mindanao and another on the island of Luzon, in February over supposed business-permit violations. The Luzon station, in the town of Cauayan, was shuttered after the mayor sent armed men to take it over. The station remained off the air for several months before legal action reversed the order. A similar incident in October resulted in the closure of a locally owned radio and television station in Lucena City, south of Manila.

In all three cases, station owners claimed that the mayors were retaliating for the news outlets' critical coverage of the local administrations. "It seems they are using their local muscle to fight us," said an executive at Bombo Radyo. "It is their way of challenging press freedom."

SINGAPORE

IN APRIL, FOR THE FIRST TIME IN 10 YEARS, SINGAPORE'S GOVERNMENT acknowledged the need to relax controls over media. In an effort to promote the country as an international arts and culture hub, officials also launched a review of the country's stringent censorship policies, which regulate licensing and all media content, including on Singapore-based Web sites. The Censorship Review Panel, comprised of 22 members, including artists, journalists, government officials, business leaders, and academics, met in May and is expected to publish a report on its findings in early 2003.

Yet reform is still far from becoming reality. The censorship code forbids any publications that "erode the core moral values of society [or] subvert the nation's security or stability," and journalists are still subject to expensive fines or lawsuits if they overstep government limits on reporting. In June, a Mandarin-language radio station was fined 15,000 Singapore dollars (US$8,000) for violating the Singapore Broadcasting Authority's Radio Programme Standards and Censorship Code after a reporter injected into her reading of the news "unwarranted" personal remarks about a variety of topics, including the conflict in the Middle East, Chinese immigrants in Singapore, and an announcement by U.S. officials that they reserve the right to use nuclear weapons in an international conflict.

Following the implementation in 2001 of regulations requiring Web sites with political content to register with the government, officials continued to crack down on the Internet in 2002. In July, Muslim activist Zulfikar Mohamad Shariff left Singapore for Australia after the government began investigating him for criminal defamation because articles published on his Web site, *Fateha.com*, criticized government officials and Ho Ching, the newly appointed director of Temasek Holdings, a government-owned investment company. Ho is also daughter-in-law of elder statesman Lee Kuan Yew.

Despite such threats to online speech, citizens have become increasingly bold in using online forums, including one operated by the *Straits Times* daily, to critique government policies. *Sintercom*, an online news site that closed in 2001 after refusing to register with the government, has been revived by anonymous editors who have been able to evade government regulations by keeping their identities and locations secret.

Even international media giants are not immune to the government's legal pressures. After officials accused the U.S.-based financial news service Bloomberg of defamation because of an article on Bloomberg's Web site that described Ho Ching's appointment to Temasek as nepotism, the company issued a statement saying that "these allegations are false and completely without foundation. We unreservedly apologize." The company also agreed to pay damages to the government and removed the story from the Web site before the case even went to court.

In August, print journalists received another legal blow when the High Court ruled that reporters do not have the right to protect confidential sources in civil cases if the court decides the documents are "relevant" to the proceedings. The controversial ruling came from a libel case brought by a door manufacturer against the Singapore daily *Business Times*, which had reported about the company's financial difficulties. The plaintiff requested that the court order the newspaper to turn over the reporter's notes and article drafts, but the court ultimately did not request the journalist's documents because they were judged irrelevant to the case.

Of the two major media companies in Singapore, one, Media Corp., is fully government-owned, while the other, Singapore Press Holdings, has close ties to the ruling

People's Action Party. In 2002, the government's Economic Review Committee recommended raising the ceiling on foreign investment in the media—which had previously been capped at 5 percent—to 20 percent as part of an effort to develop and diversify the domestic news business.

SOLOMON ISLANDS

DESPITE A HOSTILE POLITICAL AND ECONOMIC ATMOSPHERE, the Solomon Islands' small but tenacious media have managed to pursue controversial stories, including exposés of official misconduct and links between the government and ethnic militias. In 1998, a violent conflict erupted after indigenous residents of Guadalcanal, the archipelago's largest island, formed the Isatabu Freedom Movement (IFM) to force out migrants from neighboring Malaita Island—who in turn created the Malaita Eagle Force (MEF). Although the warring militias signed a peace deal in 2000, they have mostly reneged on pledges to disarm and still hold tremendous power. Militants from both groups have been responsible for violent threats against journalists who report on their activities.

Prime Minister Sir Allan Kemakeza was elected in December 2001, in the first parliamentary elections since the MEF's failed coup attempt in 2000. But the new government, which includes former militia members, has done nothing to improve the security situation or the impoverished economy. Instead, Kemakeza and others in his administration have publicly blamed the media for these problems, and throughout 2002, officials were directly involved in violent attempts to intimidate journalists.

Soon after his inauguration, Kemakeza lashed out at the media, accusing the public radio broadcaster, Solomon Islands Broadcasting Corporation (SIBC), of damaging the government's international reputation by regularly publishing "inaccurate" reports.

In January, Economic Reform Minister Daniel Fa'afunua and his armed supporters forced the country's only daily newspaper, the *Solomon Star*, to pay the minister US$1,000 compensation for an article that they claimed had insulted him. The government has failed to arrest any of the armed men, and the minister is still in his post. Soon after the incident, Foreign Minister Alex Bartlett, a former member of the MEF, issued a public statement calling on journalists to be patriotic and refrain from reporting negatively on the government or its leaders.

In May, a group of police officers stormed SIBC's offices, destroying equipment and assaulting two employees in retribution for a report about disagreements within police ranks, according to SIBC general manager Johnson Honimae. Despite a formal complaint filed by SIBC, the responsible officers remain on the job.

The dire economic situation also imperils the press. SIBC, the nation's most popular media outlet, has received none of its designated funding from Parliament for two years in a row, despite repeated requests from SIBC management, and is operating at a loss. The print media have been hit hard by a decrease in advertising revenue. The *Solomon Star*, for example, was forced to cut its number of pages by almost half to conserve funds.

Still, some journalists remain optimistic about press freedom on the islands. SIBC's Honimae says that the social and political chaos "has made journalists stronger by encouraging them to get to the truth."

ASIA |

SOUTH KOREA

PRESIDENT KIM DAE JUNG, WINNER OF THE NOBEL PEACE PRIZE IN 2000 for his efforts to reconcile with North Korea, spent his final year in office politically isolated and unloved. His unpopularity came partly from the constant hammering he took from the country's major media outlets, which oppose his "Sunshine Policy" of engagement with the North, as well as his administration's decision in 2001 to hit news organizations with extensive audits.

South Korean journalists and political observers continued to debate whether the tax audits constituted a government ploy to silence critics. In 2001, authorities arrested three top newspaper executives—Bang Sang Hoon, president and owner of *Chosun Ilbo*; Kim Byung Kwan, principal owner and honorary chairman of *Dong-A Ilbo*; and Cho Hee Joon, controlling shareholder of *Kookmin Ilbo*—on charges of tax evasion and embezzlement. The three publishers, who were convicted and sentenced to jail in 2002, were also ordered to pay fines totaling more than 13 billion won (US$11 million) combined. All three men remained free on bail pending what is likely to be a lengthy appeals process. Other media executives were also tried during 2002, but Bang, Kim, and Cho received the heaviest sentences.

While the administration denies that the massive tax probe was politically motivated, some newspaper executives say it was no coincidence that the media companies most critical of President Kim and his Sunshine Policy were those hardest hit by the audits. On the other hand, many journalists and civil-society groups strongly support the tax probe, arguing that the domestic media business is rife with corruption and needs a complete structural overhaul.

Chosun Ilbo, the country's largest-circulation daily, maintained its position that the administration had unfairly used the tax probes to target critical media but pledged to reform its business practices "through financial independence via transparent management." In the end, the tax audits and subsequent prosecutions did nothing to blunt the media's often sharp criticism of the president and his administration's failings.

A probe into alleged corruption in South Korea's sports and entertainment industry also had implications for journalists. In July, the Seoul District Prosecutor's Office announced the arrest of Lee Chang Se, a former editor of a leading sports daily and "one of the most powerful figures in entertainment journalism," according to the *Korea Times*. Lee was charged with having pocketed about 22 million won (US$19,000) in bribes during the previous six years. Prosecutors also questioned many journalists about the receipt of so-called PR expenses in exchange for writing favorable stories. A television program director, an entertainment-industry executive, and a singer and her manager were among those arrested during the crackdown.

Although President Kim had made battling corruption a top priority of his administration, he was disgraced when two of his sons were convicted of bribery. "It was more than disappointment," Kim said of his sons' arrests, speaking to a group of foreign journalists. "It was the biggest misfortune of my life."

The scandals and bitter political feuding contributed to the defeat of the pro-government Millennium Democratic Party during legislative by-elections in August. With the conservative, staunchly anti-communist Grand National Party in control of the National

Assembly, it was unlikely that legislators would try to abolish or amend South Korea's draconian National Security Law, which has been used to jail people for publishing and distributing material that favors North Korea.

Three journalists arrested under the National Security Law in 2001 were convicted in 2002, though they were all given suspended jail terms. All three, however, spent more than three months in jail while their trial was under way. In a letter to CPJ justifying their arrests, the Justice Ministry said the journalists were jailed for publishing "journalistic material benefiting the enemy" by praising the North Korean regime. Among the alleged offenses cited were the journalists' contacts with members of a Japan-based, pro–North Korea group.

Relations with North Korea were the primary focus of the December 19 presidential elections, in which the Millennium Democratic Party's Roh Moo Hyun narrowly defeated Lee Hoi Chang of the Grand National Party. Roh, a former human rights lawyer and democracy activist, promotes engagement with Pyongyang and has called for a more "equal" relationship with the United States. Anti-U.S. sentiment flared after two American soldiers were acquitted in a U.S. military court for killing two Korean teenagers in a June road accident.

SRI LANKA

A CEASE-FIRE AGREEMENT SIGNED IN FEBRUARY BY THE GOVERNMENT and the rebel Liberation Tigers of Tamil Eelam (LTTE) ushered in a period of relative calm in Sri Lanka after 19 years of war. The LTTE has been fighting for an independent homeland for the country's ethnic Tamil community, which has suffered discrimination from the Sinhalese majority. The brutal conflict has claimed more than 60,000 lives, displaced more than 1 million people, and devastated the economy. The Sri Lankan media, which are generally outspoken and aggressive, carried extensive debates about the ongoing peace talks.

Reporting on Sri Lanka's civil war was extremely difficult, not only because of periodic censorship but also because the government generally prevented journalists from traveling to areas in the north and east of the country, where fighting was most intense. But on February 11, a week-and-a-half before the cease-fire agreement was signed, the government issued a statement declaring that the Defense Ministry would no longer require prior approval for travel to the northern Jaffna peninsula and "uncleared areas" under rebel control. Officials reopened the A-9 highway, the key road linking Jaffna to the south, in April and began allowing daily flights to Jaffna in June.

The highway opened just in time for nearly 300 journalists to make the journey to LTTE-held territory for an April 10 press conference with the reclusive head of the rebel movement, Vellupillai Prabhakaran—his first in 12 years. Journalists faced elaborate security screenings, and the LTTE banned satellite phones and live broadcast transmissions, ostensibly to prevent government forces from finding Prabhakaran's exact location.

The LTTE has not tolerated critics in the past. Some political and human rights observers said the group exerted even more pressure on journalists and other members of civil society during the cease-fire period because the LTTE was able to operate openly, even in government-controlled areas.

ASIA

Violence, and the threat of violence, is frequently used to silence the media in Sri Lanka, and attacks against journalists are generally committed with impunity. However, the Sri Lankan press won an important victory this year, when two air force officers were sentenced in February to nine years in prison for their role in a nighttime raid on the home of Iqbal Athas, a well-known defense correspondent for the English-language weekly *The Sunday Times* and a 1994 recipient of CPJ's International Press Freedom Award. The raid, which occurred in February 1998, came in reprisal for a series of exposés on military corruption that Athas had written. Trial proceedings in the case had been repeatedly postponed and began in earnest only in May 2001, after CPJ sent letters protesting the delays to Sri Lanka's attorney general and justice minister.

Relations between the government and the press deteriorated under the leadership of President Chandrika Kumaratunga, who remains in power though her party lost control of Parliament in December elections. Kumaratunga has imposed censorship restrictions, particularly during political or military crises, and has used Sri Lanka's criminal defamation laws to harass journalists. Two of the country's leading editors were sentenced to jail in 2000 for allegedly defaming the president. In each case, the court issued a suspended sentence, but the threat of imprisonment remains. In August 2002, the Supreme Court overturned the conviction of one of these editors, Sinha Ratnatunga of *The Sunday Times*.

Prime Minister Ranil Wickremasinghe, who was elected in December 2001, promised to improve the climate for the media. Soon after taking office, he discussed legal reforms with the country's three leading media organizations—the Editors Guild, the Free Media Movement, and the Newspaper Society of Sri Lanka. His Cabinet approved draft legislation to repeal the criminal defamation law in April, and in mid-June, Parliament unanimously voted to do so.

TAIWAN

TAIWAN'S FREE AND FEISTY MEDIA CONTINUED TO REPORT AGGRESSIVELY on everything from sensitive political issues to colorful celebrity scandals despite several high-profile government efforts to rein in controversial reporting.

Taiwan's strained relationship with mainland China, which considers Taiwan a renegade province, ensured that national security would remain a highly controversial topic. Balancing press freedom with national security concerns became the focus of a heated public debate in Taiwan after officials cracked down on two publications for articles that allegedly revealed government secrets.

In March, authorities raided the offices of *Next* (Yi Chou-kan) magazine and tried to prevent distribution of an article that revealed details of secret bank accounts allegedly used by former president Lee Teng-hui's government to buy influence abroad. Prosecutors charged reporter Shieh Chung-liang, the article's author, with endangering national security. (Shieh, a veteran investigative journalist, was a 1997 recipient of CPJ's International Press Freedom Award.) Huang Ching-lung, editor-in-chief of the Chinese-language daily *China Times* (Chung-kuo Shih-pao), was also charged in March with endangering national security after his paper ran a story based on the same official documents.

In response to a protest letter from CPJ criticizing the government's use of national security charges against journalists, President Chen Shui-bian—himself a former magazine editor and political prisoner—wrote to CPJ executive director Ann Cooper, stating that "the essence of democracy should never be quelled under the pretext of national security, nor should the flag of national security be used as a cover for undermining press freedom." The initial frenzy over the case abated after prosecutors could not determine whether official documents used by *Next* and the *China Times* were in fact classified. Legal proceedings against Shieh and Huang have stalled, although the charges against them still stand.

The case highlighted journalists' concerns that the government abuses the "state secret" label by applying it to any issue that could be politically embarrassing. In the wake of the controversy, the Cabinet rushed to approve the pending National Secrets Protection Law, which may help clarify official standards by delineating three categories of confidential material. The Legislative Yuan, the government's lawmaking body, rejected the same bill in 2001, and it is scheduled to be passed in January 2003.

A draft Government Information Disclosure Bill, which would obligate all major government bodies to disclose information requested by the public, was also submitted to the Legislative Yuan. The measure would exempt information protected under the state secrets law.

While Taiwan's diverse press—which includes more than 300 Chinese- and English-language newspapers, several commercial and public broadcasting stations, and a major national news agency—has distinguished itself with its political reporting, it has also developed a reputation for tabloid-style exposés on crime, celebrities, and politicians. Lurid and aggressive reporting on several celebrity scandals in 2002 inspired Justice Minister Chen Ding-nan to declare that Taiwan's media had abused their freedom and created a "dictatorship of the press."

In April, the Taipei District Court ruled against the weekly *The Journalist* (Hsin Hsin-wen Chou-kan) in a libel suit brought in 2000 by Vice President Annette Lu after the magazine reported that Lu had provided information to editors about a romantic affair between President Chen and an aide. Lu denied the story and asked for an apology from the magazine. The court's ruling declared that *The Journalist*'s report was "fictitious" and ordered the editor, Lee Ming-chun, to publish a 400-word correction in major newspapers and to personally read a clarification to be broadcast over major television and radio networks during prime-time hours for three consecutive days.

In October, a group of at least 10 men stormed the offices of *Next* and destroyed equipment in apparent retribution for the publication's reporting on a criminal gang called the Sun. Soon after the attack, media outlets in Taiwan received a fax signed by the leader of the Sun declaring that, "*Next* has dared to provoke the Sun and myself and should be warned that we vow to drive the magazine from Taiwan." Despite the incident, which was the second violent attack on the magazine in less than two years, *Next* owner Jimmy Lai plans to launch a Taiwan version of his popular Hong Kong tabloid *Apple Daily* next spring.

THAILAND

DURING 2002, THAILAND'S REPUTATION AS A REGIONAL HAVEN of constitutionally guaranteed free expression was frequently assaulted by the country's powerful prime minister, Thaksin

ASIA

Shinawatra, and his political allies. The government booted radio and television programs off the air, threatened Thai journalists with financial investigations and foreign reporters with expulsion, and engaged in angry exchanges with the press.

Problems began to surface in January after the Dow Jones–owned *Far Eastern Economic Review* published a short article about tensions between Thaksin and the country's revered monarch, King Bumibol Adulyadej. Police banned the issue and threatened to expel the magazine's two Bangkok correspondents, claiming that the pair had violated Thailand's tough lèse majesté laws, which forbid public discussion of internal palace issues and ban critical commentary about the royal family. The royal palace did not publicly complain about the article, and many observers believe the magazine's frequently harsh criticism of Thaksin motivated the action. The move sparked local and international outcry, and eventually the magazine issued an apology. The government later backed down and allowed the journalists to remain in the country.

The *Economist* magazine, meanwhile, avoided a formal ban by withholding an issue from Thailand in early March, after authorities announced they would review the contents. The issue carried an article analyzing the thorny relations between the palace and the prime minister.

In the aftermath of the incidents, the government also acted against the local press. Officials pulled the outspoken and independent Nation Multimedia Group's news program from a government-owned radio station in March because a show included commentary criticizing the government's moves against the *Far Eastern Economic Review* correspondents. The Nation Multimedia Group later pulled all political commentary from its cable news channel, Nation TV, to protest what it called government interference.

Just days later, *The Nation* newspaper, which the Nation Multimedia Group also owns, reported that local bankers had received a letter from the government's Anti-Money Laundering Office (AMLO), a body created to investigate drug dealers and other criminals, asking for the financial records of journalists from *The Nation* and another critical daily, the *Thai Post*. The Administrative Court quickly issued an injunction calling the probe illegal and ordering the AMLO to suspend the investigations. At the same time, some 1,000 Thai journalists sent a petition to Parliament calling for legislators to defend press freedom.

Also in March, an executive of *Naew Na*, a Thai-language daily, told a Senate committee that Thaksin himself had asked the newspaper to drop the column of staunch government critic Prasong Soonsiri. The newspaper refused, and the executive told the committee that as a result, the publication had lost advertising revenue from several state-owned enterprises. Other editors told CPJ that the government frequently withholds advertising from critics and awards lucrative advertising contracts to favored media outlets.

Thaksin, who is also one of the country's richest tycoons, sought to distance himself from these controversies, telling reporters he had nothing to do with expelling reporters or attacking the press through the AMLO.

One of the media's few victories during 2002 came in September, when Thailand's Central Labor Court ruled in favor of 21 employees of iTV—the country's sole privately owned television channel—who were dismissed in 2001. The workers, most of whom are journalists, had complained that iTV, which had been sold to a company controlled by Thaksin's family, was slanting its coverage to favor Thaksin, who was then running for office. After airing their complaints publicly, the journalists were fired. The court ordered the employees reinstated with back pay.

A 1997 reform constitution called for the privatization of the country's radio and television frequencies, almost all of which are held by the military or government agencies, but there was no progress in 2002 toward liberalization of the broadcast media. In addition, Thailand continued to use harsh criminal defamation laws against journalists and editors. In August, Chaisiri Samuddhavanij, a columnist at the *Manager Daily*, was convicted of libeling former foreign minister Surin Pitsuwan in a January 2000 article. The journalist, who had alleged that Surin was involved in attacks by Burmese dissident groups in Thailand, was sentenced to three months in jail but was freed on bail pending an appeal.

Meanwhile, lawmakers have failed to make any commitment to repeal the 1941 Printing Act, an outdated and unconstitutional law that allows authorities to close media outlets.

VIETNAM

IN AN EFFORT TO CONTAIN PUBLIC DISSATISFACTION WITH OFFICIAL CORRUPTION and a lack of political reform, Vietnam's government tightened its already stringent control over the media during 2002. Writers were detained, harassed, placed under tight surveillance, or arrested for expressing independent viewpoints, while authorities targeted those who use the Internet to distribute independent news or opinions.

In January, the government launched a crackdown on free expression by instructing police to confiscate and destroy prohibited publications. At the same time, officials escalated surveillance of several well-known dissidents, retired Lt. Gen. Tran Do and Nguyen Thanh Giang among them, and placed writer Bui Minh Quoc under house arrest for "possessing anti-government literature," including his own writing.

Quoc was one of several writers targeted by the government for criticizing land and sea border agreements between China and Vietnam, which were signed as part of a rapprochement following the 1979 war between the two countries. Quoc and others criticized the government for agreeing to border concessions without consulting the Vietnamese people. Sensitivities over the issue were heightened in late February, when Chinese president Jiang Zemin visited Vietnam as part of a bilateral reconciliation effort.

Just before President Jiang arrived, authorities arrested law school graduate Le Chi Quang for writing several critical articles, including one titled, "Beware of Imperial China." His arrest demonstrated the efficiency of the state's Internet controls: Cybercafé owners and Internet service providers (ISPs) are required by law to monitor customers' activities and prevent distribution of "harmful" material, including any unsanctioned political reporting. Officials at a popular ISP notified public security officials that Quang had used a specific Internet café in the capital, Hanoi, to communicate with "reactionaries" living abroad, and on February 21, more than 30 police officers arrived at the café and arrested Quang. Writers Nguyen Vu Binh, Tran Khue, and Pham Hong Son were also arrested or harassed for their writings about the border agreements, as well as for disseminating their opinions online.

While Internet use in Vietnam is still limited by expense and poor telecommunications infrastructure, the number of people online jumped to 1.3 million in 2002 from 300,000 in 2001. An increasing number of people use the Internet to express their opinions and to dis-

ASIA

tribute information prohibited in the traditional media. In August, authorities shut the domestic Web site *www.ttvonline.com*, which had become a popular forum for posting articles and comments that criticized government policy. In explaining the closure, a government spokesperson said the site had posted "articles and messages that promote Nazism, violence, a multi-party political system, and ideological pluralism." In November, the Hanoi People's Court sentenced Le Chi Quang to four years in prison, sending an additional message to the burgeoning Internet generation that publishing critical viewpoints online will not be tolerated.

The government owns all of the country's print and broadcast media outlets and issues strict reporting guidelines. While the official media are usually a mere conduit for government policy, in June, local journalists played a very important role in investigating and exposing a corruption scandal that linked several high-level government officials with Nam Cam, the leader of an underground criminal gang. The government at first displayed a rare willingness to tolerate this independent, investigative reporting but soon cracked down on the coverage. In an interview with an official newspaper, a propaganda official said that all reporters had been instructed not to "expose secrets, create internal divisions, or hinder key propaganda tasks" while covering the scandal. By year's end, more than 100 people had been arrested in the case, including several vice ministers and other high-ranking officials.

Throughout 2002, the government maintained its stringent control over foreign journalists in the country. Foreign reporters must receive formal permission before conducting interviews or traveling outside Hanoi and are frequently lambasted in the official press for supporting "hostile forces" overseas. As the Nam Cam corruption scandal broke, the government refused all interview requests about the case from foreign correspondents. These journalists often must take additional precautions in their reporting since Vietnamese citizens who have contact with them—either as sources, translators, or assistants—are often harassed.

Overseas media are among the only sources of independent information in the country, but because of tight government controls, very few Vietnamese citizens can access such news. Vietnamese-language shortwave radio broadcasts from services including the U.S. government–sponsored Radio Free Asia and the BBC are a crucial information source, although these broadcasts are routinely blocked. In June, Prime Minister Phan Van Khai signed a decree reaffirming that only government officials, state-run media organizations, and foreign businesses and residents are allowed to access international television programs transmitted by satellite into Vietnam. In recent years, however, Vietnamese citizens have ignored the ban, turning to such satellite broadcasts for independent news coverage.

Advocates of free expression in Vietnam lost an influential voice in August, when dissident Lt. Gen. Tran Do died of multiple ailments at the age of 79. Do, a decorated war veteran and the former head of the Culture and Ideology Department, was expelled from the Communist Party in 1999 after he began to call openly for multiparty democracy. During his last years, Do was under tight surveillance and his writings were banned. In a three-part memoir, which police confiscated from him in 2001, he wrote, "Our present life, it seems, is less and less like what we dreamed of building, and more and more like what we had spent time overthrowing." At his official eulogy, a government spokesman said that Do had made important contributions to the party but had "made mistakes and errors in his final years." ■

| CASES TABLE OF CONTENTS |

AFGHANISTAN

FEBRUARY 10

Doug Struck, *The Washington Post*
THREATENED

Struck, a correspondent for *The Washington Post*, was threatened by American soldiers and barred from reporting near the site of a U.S. missile strike that may have killed a group of civilians. Struck says that although he identified himself as a reporter for *The Washington Post*, the soldiers trained an M-16 rifle on him for about 15 to 20 minutes. The soldiers, after conferring with superiors over the radio, refused to let him go to a nearby village, where the three men killed in the missile attack had lived. When Struck asked what would happen if he continued toward the village, according to the reporter, the soldier's commander said, "You would be shot." The commander refused to identify himself.

On February 12, U.S. Defense Department officials rejected Struck's claim that American soldiers had threatened to shoot the journalist. "To believe that a U.S. serviceman would knowingly threaten, especially with deadly force, another American is hard for me to accept," Rear Adm. John Stufflebeam, deputy operations director for the Joint Chiefs of Staff, said during a press briefing. Rear Adm. Craig Quigley, a Pentagon spokesperson, said that the soldier's words to Struck were: "For your own safety, we cannot let you go forward. You could be shot in a firefight." *The Washington Post* stood by Struck's account.

MARCH 4

Kathleen Kenna, *Toronto Star*
Hadi Dadashian, free-lance
Bernard Weil, *Toronto Star*
ATTACKED

Kenna, a correspondent for the *Toronto Star* newspaper, suffered serious leg injuries when unidentified assailants threw a grenade into her car. Kenna was traveling with her husband, free-lance photographer Hadi Dadashian; *Star* photographer Bernard Weil; and an Afghan driver on the main road from Kabul to Gardez, in eastern Paktia Province. None of the other passengers were hurt.

The incident occurred shortly after two gunmen nearby were overheard discussing whether to take a group of foreign journalists hostage, according to *The Washington Post*. It was not clear whether the two incidents were related, but on March 6, the international peacekeeping force in the capital, Kabul, reported a credible threat to kidnap foreign journalists.

Weil told the *Toronto Star* that one man threw a rock at the car from the left side, and then an explosion from an unidentified object hit the right side, where Kenna was sitting. Two Agence France-Presse journalists who were ahead of them on the same road helped transport Kenna to a U.S. medical compound in Gardez. She was later moved to Uzbekistan, then Turkey, and, finally, to the Landstuhl Regional Medical Centre in Germany. In early March, U.S.-led troops had engaged in intensive ground and air battles against Taliban and al-Qaeda fighters in eastern Afghanistan.

MARCH 6

Foreign journalists
THREATENED

The British-led international peacekeeping force in Afghanistan's capital, Kabul, warned reporters of a credible threat to kidnap foreign journalists. "Information about threats come and go all the time, but this is the first one assessed as credible enough to pass on to journalists," said Lt. Col. Neal Peckham of the International Security Assistance Force (ISAF), according to CNN. Peckham said that the kidnap plans concerned journalists in Kabul. However, an ISAF press officer said the threat was not specific to any region of Afghanistan, according to the Agence France-Presse news agency.

The ISAF advised journalists to "maintain extra vigilance and consider their movements." ISAF officials said that the threat appeared to be related to the recent U.S.-led offensive against Taliban and al-Qaeda fighters in eastern Paktia Province.

APRIL 5

Western journalists
THREATENED

U.S. military officials told journalists that Taliban and al-Qaeda fighters had distributed leaflets in eastern Afghanistan offering bounties to local villagers for the killing or capture of American soldiers or other Westerners, including journalists. Officials said the leaflets offered US$50,000 for the body of a Westerner and US$100,000 for a Westerner who is alive. "We continue to receive credible threats of violence against coalition service members, citizens and journalists," Maj. Bryan Hilferty told reporters at Bagram Air Base, according to *The New York Times*.

American military officials said that the leaflets advertising the bounty were distributed in Paktia Province, near the Pakistani border, where Taliban and al-Qaeda fighters were believed to have strong support.

APRIL 10

Ebadullah Ebadi, *Boston Globe*
ATTACKED

Ebadi, a translator and assistant working for the *Boston Globe*, was attacked by Afghan fighters working with U.S. Special Forces in Sarobi District, about 45 miles (70 kilometers) east of the capital, Kabul. The assault occurred

within view of the U.S. soldiers, who did not intervene to stop the beating, according to an account published by the *Globe*.

The incident occurred when Ebadi and *Globe* reporter Indira A.R. Lakshmanan approached a convoy of about 10 vehicles carrying U.S. Special Forces and Afghan fighters loyal to Jalalabad commander Hazrat Ali. A group of the Afghan fighters blocked the pair from continuing toward the U.S. soldiers.

According to the *Globe* report, "as an interview request was being delivered to the American soldiers, one of the U.S. forces gestured toward a young Afghan soldier, who sprinted toward the visitors and roughly shoved the *Globe*'s translator. The soldier unlatched the safety on his rifle while other soldiers began punching the *Globe* translator in the face and kicking him. Another soldier slapped Ebadi, knocking off his glasses, while the first soldier beat him with his rifle. The incident ended when another soldier stopped the beating."

A U.S. Special Forces officer, who identified himself only as Steve, approached the two journalists immediately after the incident and "said the soldiers were reluctant to give interviews," the *Globe* reported. He claimed not to know about the assault on Ebadi.

An Afghan commander, who identified himself as Hazrat Ali's deputy, apologized on behalf of the principal assailant and offered to beat him publicly. When Ebadi refused the offer, the deputy commander admonished his troops for "beating a guest, instead of just preventing him from reaching the Americans," according to the *Globe*.

MAY 27

Mohammad Rafiq Shahir, *Takhassos*
ATTACKED, THREATENED

Intelligence agents in the western city of Herat arrested Shahir, editor of *Takhassos*, an

ASIA |

influential newsletter published by Herat's Professional Shura, an association of intellectuals, lawyers, doctors, and other professionals established in early 2002 to discuss issues related to Afghanistan's reconstruction. Shahir and his group have been outspoken about reforms needed in Afghanistan, including in Herat Province, which is ruled by governor and warlord Ismail Khan.

Shahir's detention occurred during the run-up to the loya jirga meeting held in the capital, Kabul, in June to select a new national government. The editor, who was a delegate to the meeting, was bound, whipped, and beaten while in custody, according to Human Rights Watch (HRW). He says agents took him to a nearby graveyard and held him at gunpoint, warning that, "We could leave you right here." HRW reported that the agents who made the arrest work with Amniat-e Mille, the national intelligence agency. Ismail Khan reportedly controls the Amniat office in Herat.

Shahir was released two days later, but bruises and cuts were still visible when he went to the loya jirga. Journalists and human rights activists noted that after the editor's detention, the content of *Takhassos* changed markedly, with the newsletter no longer criticizing the government.

One Herat resident told HRW that the arrest of Shahir, a prominent citizen, prompted widespread self-censorship. "After Shahir was imprisoned," the resident said, "people went quiet and no one is daring to say anything against [Ismail Khan]."

JULY 3

Hayat Ullah Khan, *Ausaf, The Nation*
IMPRISONED

Hayat Ullah, a Pakistani journalist who reports for the national dailies *Ausaf* and *The Nation*, was detained by U.S. Special Forces when he crossed into Afghanistan along with four companions. Soldiers arrested the group, who were not carrying any travel documents, on suspicion that they were associated with the al-Qaeda terrorist network.

All five detainees are natives of Pakistan's tribal areas. Although security along the border had increased in the previous months due to U.S. concerns that al-Qaeda and Taliban forces were in the area, local tribespeople are generally accustomed to traveling freely across the porous frontier.

Hayat Ullah says he approached a group of Afghan soldiers in the Barmal area of Paktika Province and began interviewing them about reports that a U.S. military base nearby had recently been attacked. The Afghan soldiers then radioed to U.S. forces, and two Americans, not in uniform, arrived on the scene. Hayat Ullah says the men were likely members of the U.S. Special Forces, which have been active in the area.

According to Hayat Ullah, the Americans accused him and his companions of involvement with al-Qaeda. He says he told them he was a professional journalist on assignment for the U.S. television network ABC and also gave them contact information for his editors at *Ausaf* and *The Nation*, who could verify his credentials. He also suggested contacting CPJ's office in New York.

Hayat Ullah, who speaks English, says the soldiers ignored his repeated requests to check his background. Instead, soldiers took Hayat Ullah and his four companions into custody, placing bags over their heads and tying their hands behind their backs with a special plastic binding used by the U.S. military in place of handcuffs. Soldiers also confiscated Hayat Ullah's equipment, including a digital video camera, digital cassettes, a still camera, film, several notebooks, and his address book. (All belongings were eventually returned, except the videotapes and the film.)

Hayat Ullah says that he was initially

held with the other detainees but was moved within hours to a small, unventilated room, where he was kept in solitary confinement.

U.S. soldiers interrogated him twice in a 24-hour period, during which time he says he was denied food, water, and rest. Hayat Ullah says that his head was covered and his hands tied throughout his four-day detention. He said that during one interrogation, officers threatened repeatedly to shoot him if he did not provide information about al-Qaeda operations in the area. When one officer accused him of having phone numbers for Taliban leaders, Hayat Ullah said, "I told him every journalist tries to get the numbers of these types of leaders."

U.S. military officials did contact ABC staff in Kabul and Washington, D.C., but could not confirm that Hayat Ullah was working for ABC. Sources at ABC said there was some confusion because Hayat Ullah was commissioned as a stringer, through an intermediary, to shoot video in Pakistan's tribal areas, not Afghanistan. U.S. military officials also contacted the U.S. Embassy in Pakistan to determine Hayat Ullah's connection to *Ausaf* and *The Nation*.

Hayat Ullah and his companions were finally released on July 7, after Pakistani journalists alerted the U.S. Consulate in Peshawar to the mistake. Upon their return to Pakistani territory, Hayat Ullah and his companions were briefly detained and threatened with prosecution by an officer from the local security force in South Waziristan, who accused the group of working as American spies.

AUGUST 23

Tyler Hicks, *The New York Times*
HARASSED
The New York Times
CENSORED

Hicks, a photographer for *The New York Times*, was briefly detained and questioned by U.S. Special Forces while he was on assignment

in eastern Afghanistan, near the U.S. military base in Asadabad. According to a *New York Times* story datelined August 23 and published on August 28, the Special Forces unit "demanded that the photographer clear his photographs from his digital camera and hand over a roll of exposed film, saying photographs of them could compromise their mission." Not all the pictures were deleted, and the *Times* published one of the surviving photographs of the Special Forces unit on the front page of the newspaper. The *Times* article was about U.S.-led efforts in Afghanistan and neighboring Pakistan to find Osama bin Laden and others associated with his al-Qaeda terrorist network.

SEPTEMBER 5

Abdul Qadir Qaumi, Bakhtar Information Agency
Ahmad Zia, Bakhtar Information Agency
Abdul Halem, Bakhtar Information Agency
ATTACKED

Qaumi, a photographer for the government-controlled Bakhtar Information Agency (BIA), and Zia and Halem, both BIA reporters, were injured while reporting on a bomb attack in downtown Kabul, the capital. The car bomb, which killed at least 30 people and wounded about 170, detonated minutes after a smaller explosion had lured crowds, and journalists, to the area. BIA journalists, whose offices are nearby, were the first on the scene. Qaumi suffered several serious shrapnel wounds in his back.

BANGLADESH

FEBRUARY 5

Shahriar Kabir, free-lance
ATTACKED
Explosions from several homemade

ASIA

bombs rocked the area surrounding the Chittagong Press Club, where journalist Kabir was attending a reception to celebrate his release on bail. One bystander was killed in the attack, and several others were injured. Kabir was not harmed.

Kabir, a documentary filmmaker, regular contributor to the national Bengali-language daily *Janakantha*, and author of several books about Bangladesh's war for independence, had been arrested on November 22, 2001, for "anti-state activities." Officials arrested him at the Dhaka International Airport upon his return to Bangladesh from India, where he had interviewed minority Bangladeshi Hindus who fled there following attacks against their community after the October 1, 2001, parliamentary elections. Kabir was released on bail on January 20, 2002.

A newly formed group called the Action Committee to Resist a Traitor had declared that Kabir was not welcome in Chittagong, and about 300 members of this committee held demonstrations outside the press club during the reception, according to local and international press reports. Kabir has been a longtime opponent of Islamic fundamentalism and has previously come under attack by religious extremists.

MARCH 2

Harunur Rashid, *Dainik Purbanchal*
KILLED

For full details on this case, see page 354.

APRIL 3

Far Eastern Economic Review
CENSORED

The government banned the April 4 edition of the Hong Kong–based weekly *Far Eastern Economic Review* because the cover story, "Bangladesh: Cocoon of Terror,"

described the country as besieged by "Islamic fundamentalism, religious intolerance, militant Muslim groups with links to international terrorist groups, a powerful military with ties to the militants, the mushrooming of Islamic schools churning out radical students, middle-class apathy, poverty and lawlessness."

The Information Ministry called the article a "malicious report" that would "create hatred and division among the people of Bangladesh." On April 3, the ministry declared the publication, sale, reprinting, and preservation of the magazine illegal, according to Bangladeshi and international news reports. While the April 4 edition was not available on newsstands in the country, people in Bangladesh were able to access it online.

The government responded to the article's claims in a letter to the *Review* that ran in its April 11 edition. Shafi Ahmed, the Bangladeshi consul general in Hong Kong, wrote, "Your description of Bangladesh as a Cocoon of Terror is at best a figment of someone's wild imagination. …Your article could only be described as being motivated, if not by malicious intentions, then by reasons best known to you."

Prime Minister Khaleda Zia, when addressing Parliament on the issue, blamed the opposition Awami League for sponsoring the *Review* story and claimed that "vested quarters at home and abroad are trying to tarnish the country's image by spreading untrue, misleading, and malicious information."

APRIL 9

M.A. Faisal, *Daily Runner*
ATTACKED

Faisal, a reporter for the Jessore-based *Daily Runner*, was assaulted by a gang of men who approached him near the Tala Government College in southern Satkhira District. The assailants hit Faisal in the head and used a hammer to break his leg, according to the Dhaka-based organization Media Watch.

Faisal was attacked around noon on the day the *Runner* published an article about the intimidation of participants in a public bidding process in Tala, a subdistrict of Satkhira. While Faisal was recovering in the hospital, Altaf Hossain, a local leader of the Bangladesh Nationalist Party (BNP), visited the journalist and told him, "I warned you not to report on that issue, now look at what has happened as a result," according to a report in the *Runner*. Hossain also warned Faisal against writing future articles that could anger his party "boys," an apparent reference to the youth wing of the BNP, known as the Jubo Dal, an organization whose members often assault journalists and opposition supporters.

Hossain did not publicly deny newspaper accounts reporting on his involvement in the incident. An editor from the *Runner* said that no charges were filed, although the police had registered a complaint identifying the assailants by name.

APRIL 20

Nashir Uddin, *Prothom Alo*
ATTACKED, THREATENED
M. Sadeq, free-lance
ATTACKED

Nashir Uddin, Comilla-based correspondent for the national Bengali-language daily *Prothom Alo*, and Sadeq, a free-lance photographer on assignment for *Prothom Alo*, were assaulted and detained by a group led by local activists associated with the Bangladesh Nationalist Party (BNP), the lead partner in the country's coalition government.

The two were attacked in the village of Krishnapur, Comilla District, when they went there to report on the destruction of 24 homes, allegedly by supporters of a local Parliament member from the BNP. At around 9:30 a.m. on April 20, dozens of men, led by BNP activists, looted and burned property that was at the center of a land dispute between two families. Nashir Uddin and Sadeq arrived in Krishnapur at around 12:30 p.m. and began interviewing witnesses and taking photographs of the damage.

According to Nashir Uddin, a group of men responsible for the attack arrived on the scene and threatened to kill the journalists if they published news of the incident. The gang pushed the journalists, confiscated their film, and then detained them in a room in the Krishnapur Government Primary School for three hours. The men released the journalists after they promised not to report on the incident.

Nashir Uddin said that among those who threatened and harassed the journalists were Anwar Hossain, a leader of the local youth wing of the BNP and nephew of Abu Taher, a local Parliament member representing the BNP from Barura Subdistrict; Abdur Rahim, a local BNP leader from the village of Bhateswar; and Bahar, a BNP leader from the village of Paduarpar.

On April 21, the Comilla Press Club organized a protest condemning the attack on the journalists and demanded that the assailants be punished. The same day, Abdullah Hel Baki, the additional district magistrate of Comilla, visited Krishnapur, prepared a report for the local deputy commissioner about the arson attack, and filed a case on behalf of the victims—including the two journalists—with the Comilla police. No progress in the case had been reported by year's end.

Despite action taken at the district level, police in Barura Subdistrict have failed to take up any of the cases related to the arson attack. Meanwhile, Nashir Uddin continued to receive threats. On April 24, Amiruzzaman Amir, a municipal leader of the BNP, told Nashir Uddin that if he continued to write about

ASIA

Barura, he would "face the consequences." The journalist said he has also received several anonymous death threats over the phone.

MAY 3

Azadul, *Daily Runner*
Delwar Hossain, *Dainik Purbanchal*
Shaikh Ahsanul Karim, *Manavzamin*
Rezaul Karim, *Ittefaq*
Babul Sarder, *Janakantha*
S.M. Tajuddin, *Dainik Prabartan*
THREATENED

Azadul, of the *Daily Runner*; Hossain, of the daily *Dainik Purbanchal*; Shaikh Ahsanul Karim, of the daily *Manavzamin*; Karim, of the daily *Ittefaq*; Sarder, of the daily *Janakantha*; and Tajuddin, of the daily *Dainik Prabartan*, filed a complaint with police alleging that Sheikh Wahiduzzaman Dipu, joint secretary of the Bangladesh Nationalist Party (BNP) in Bagerhat District, threatened to have the journalists killed for accusing him of criminal activities. The journalists said armed men associated with the BNP were seen patrolling in front of their homes. Dipu also threatened to blow up the Bagerhat office of *Dainik Purbanchal*, according to the police report. The BNP is the party of Prime Minister Khaleda Zia.

MAY 28

Nazmul Imam, *Manavzamin*
ATTACKED

Imam, the Kushtia correspondent for the national Bengali-language daily *Manavzamin*, was attacked at around 1:30 a.m. while on his way home. According to several Bangladeshi and international news reports, about five men brandishing knives stopped Imam's rickshaw. Imam gave them his wallet and cell phone. When he then tried to run away, one of the men shouted, "Catch the journalist."

The assailants attacked Imam, slicing off his right thumb and stabbing him repeatedly in his arms, back, and waist, said news reports. After the attackers fled the scene, passers-by took Imam to a local hospital. On May 30, he was transferred to a hospital in the capital, Dhaka.

Imam, who has reported on drug smugglers and other criminal groups, has been targeted for attack before. In May 2001, a group of knife-wielding men stopped Imam's vehicle and ordered him to follow them, according to Bangladeshi news reports. Imam escaped unharmed after running to a nearby police station.

JULY 5

Shukur Hossain, *Anirban*
MISSING

Hossain, a crime reporter for the Khulna-based newspaper *Anirban*, was kidnapped from his home in Ula, a village near the town of Dumuria, Khulna District, at around midnight by a group of about 35 armed men. His colleagues fear that he may have been killed. Police suspect that the assailants belong to the outlawed Biplobi Communist Party, one of several guerrilla groups active in the southwest of the country.

Hossain was last seen alive on the banks of the Ghangrail River, according to the national English-language newspaper *The Daily Star*. Two villagers who were in the area at the time reported that shots were fired, but police could not confirm whether Hossain was killed.

JULY 10

Iqbal Hossain, *Prothom Alo*
ATTACKED

Hossain, a reporter for the national Bengali-language daily *Prothom Alo*, was abducted while bathing in a river in

Keraniganj, a town just outside the capital, Dhaka. His assailants tortured him for several hours and used rocks to crush the bones in his hands, according to a *Prothom Alo* editor. He was later found by a roadside and taken to a hospital in Dhaka.

Hossain filed a complaint with police identifying three members of the Jubo Dal, the youth wing of the Bangladesh Nationalist Party, as the assailants. Police told The Associated Press that the Jubo Dal denied responsibility for the attack.

AUGUST 3

Syed Farroque Ahmed, *Pubali Barta*
KILLED (MOTIVE UNCONFIRMED)

For full details on this case, see page 368.

NOVEMBER 25

Zaiba Malik, free-lance
Bruno Sorrentino, free-lance
IMPRISONED, EXPELLED
Priscilla Raj, free-lance
Saleem Samad, Reporters Sans Frontières
IMPRISONED

Malik, Sorrentino, Raj, and Samad, all free-lance journalists, were detained while working on a documentary for Britain's Channel 4 "Unreported World" series. Reporter Malik, director and cameraman Sorrentino, and Raj, a free-lance Bangladeshi journalist working for the documentary team as an interpreter, were taken into custody on November 25 along with their driver, Misir Ali.

Malik, who is British, and Sorrentino, who was traveling on an Italian passport, were arrested at the Benapole border crossing en route to India. Raj and Ali, who are both Bangladeshi nationals, were picked up in Rajbari District on their way back to the capital, Dhaka. Ali was released the same

day. Samad, a free-lance Bangladeshi reporter who worked as a fixer for the Channel 4 team, went into hiding after his colleagues' arrest but was found and detained by police on November 29.

The journalists were arrested for alleged involvement in "clandestine activities as journalists with an apparent and malicious intent of portraying Bangladesh as an Islamic fanatical country," said a statement issued by the Bangladeshi government, according to the Agence France-Presse news agency. They were accused of sedition, which is punishable by death in Bangladesh.

On December 11, authorities released Malik and Sorrentino and deported them to Britain. The two journalists signed a statement saying they would not produce any reports from their footage gathered in Bangladesh and "expressing regret for the unfortunate situation arising since their arrival in Bangladesh."

Raj was released on December 23, while Samad was not freed until January 18, 2003, four days after the High Court in Dhaka had ordered his release. Both Raj and Samad say they were tortured in police custody. Raj said her interrogators used electric shocks to compel her to give evidence against her colleagues, and Samad said an officer beat his knees repeatedly with a wooden baton when he denied police accusations.

DECEMBER 8

Shahriar Kabir, free-lance
IMPRISONED

For full details on this case, see page 375.

Muntasir Mamun, free-lance
IMPRISONED

For full details on this case, see page 376.

ASIA

DECEMBER 13

Enamul Hoque Chowdhury, Bangladesh
Sangbad Sangstha
`IMPRISONED`

For full details on this case, see page 376.

BURMA

JULY 12

Kavi Chongkittavorn, *The Nation*
Thepchai Yong, *The Nation*
Suparak Kanchanakhundee, *The Nation*
Suvit Suvitsawad, *Siam Rath*
Wassana Nanuam, *Bangkok Post*
Trirat Sunthornprapat, *The Daily News*
Sorakon Ayulyanonda, *Mathichon Daily*
Yeow Thala Lom, *Mathichon Daily*
Lom Pianthit, *Thai Rath*
Maha Sethi, *Khao Sod*
Sai Phubua
Mon Krithula
Anchalee Pairirak
`CENSORED`

Burma's military junta, the State Peace and Development Council (SPDC), announced that it had banned 13 Thai journalists and a historian from the country. Labor Minister Tin Win said that they had been banned for writing anti-junta articles and "belittling" government policies, according to the *Bangkok Post*.

According to the Bangkok-based Thai Journalists Association, the blacklist includes: Chongkittavorn, Yong, and Kanchanakhundee, of the daily *The Nation*; Suvitsawad, of the daily *Siam Rath*; Nanuam, of the daily *Bangkok Post*; Sunthornprapat, of *The Daily News*; Ayulyanonda and Lom, of *Mathichon Daily*; Pianthit, of the daily *Thai Rath*; Sethi, of the newspaper *Khao Sod*; Phubua, Krithula, and Pairirak, whose affiliations are unknown; and Dr. Charnvit Kasetsiri, a Thai historian.

The Burmese junta, which tightly restricts the foreign media's access to the country, has maintained a blacklist of Thai and other foreign journalists for years. The announcement of the most recent blacklist came amid heightened tensions between Burma and Thailand after the SPDC blamed Thailand for aiding ethnic Shan rebels who had attacked a Burmese military base in May.

CHINA

JANUARY

Xu Zerong, free-lance
`IMPRISONED, LEGAL ACTION`

Sometime in January, the Shenzhen Intermediate Court sentenced Xu to 10 years in prison on charges of "leaking state secrets" and to an additional three years on charges of committing "economic crimes."

On June 24, 2000, Xu, an associate research professor at the Institute of Southeast Asian Studies at Zhongshan University in Guangzhou, was arrested and held incommunicado for more than a year before his trial in August 2001. He has written several free-lance articles about China's foreign policy and co-founded a Hong Kong–based academic journal, *Zhongguo Shehui Kexue Jikan* (China Social Sciences Quarterly). Xu is a permanent resident of Hong Kong.

Chinese officials have said that the "state secrets" charges against Xu stem from his use of historical materials for his academic research. In 1992, Xu photocopied four books published in the 1950s about China's role in the Korean War, which he then sent to a colleague in South Korea, according to a letter from the Chinese government to St. Antony's College, Oxford University. (Xu earned his Ph.D. at St. Antony's College, and since his arrest, college personnel have actively researched and protested his case.) The Security Committee of the People's Liberation Army in Guangzhou later determined that these documents should be labeled "top secret."

The "economic crimes" charges are related to the "illegal publication" of more than 60,000 copies of 25 books and periodicals since 1993, including several books about Chinese politics and Beijing's relations with Taiwan, according to official government documents.

Some observers believe that the charges against Xu are more likely related to an article he wrote for the Hong Kong–based *Yazhou Zhoukan* (Asia Weekly) newsmagazine revealing clandestine Chinese Communist Party support for Malaysian communist insurgency groups. Xu was arrested only days before the article appeared in the June 26, 2000, issue. In the article, Xu accused the Chinese Communist Party of hypocrisy for condemning the United States and other countries for interfering in China's internal affairs by criticizing its human rights record. "China's support of world revolution is based on the concept of 'class above sovereignty' ... which is equivalent to the idea of 'human rights above sovereignty,' which the U.S. promotes today," Xu wrote.

Xu's family has filed an appeal, which was pending at press time. They have not been allowed to visit him since his arrest in 2000.

JANUARY 5

Zhao Jingqiao, *Jinan Shibao*
Lu Yanchuan, *Jinan Shibao*
Yang Fucheng, *Shandong Qingnian*
ATTACKED, HARASSED

Zhao and Lu, both reporters for the daily *Jinan Shibao* (Jinan Times), and Yang, a reporter for *Shandong Qingnian* (Shandong Youth magazine) were beaten by security officials inside the local Propaganda Bureau offices in Ningyang County, Shandong Province, after they reported on anti-corruption protests by villagers, according to Chinese press reports.

The three journalists, who are based in Jinan, the provincial capital, had traveled to Ximeng Village in Ningyang County to investigate complaints that the local Communist Party secretary had beaten villagers who protested against his corrupt behavior. As the journalists were leaving the village at about 4:00 p.m., the Ningyang County deputy propaganda chief, Ji Weijian, called and asked them to come by his office, according to a report in *Jinan Shibao*.

On their way to Ji's office, Yang received a phone call from his editor, who told him to return to Jinan immediately because the Ningyang Public Security Bureau had been ordered to track down the journalists. As the journalists turned the car around to return home, seven or eight police cars pulled them over. After Yang, Zhao, and Lu called Ji Weijian for assistance, he arrived on the scene and asked the reporters to accompany him back to his office.

At the Propaganda Bureau offices, Ji and another local official questioned the journalists and confiscated their notebooks and tape recorders. At about 8:00 p.m., plainclothes security officers entered the offices and demanded that the journalists leave with them. When Zhao, Lu, and Yang refused, the officers began to beat and kick them.

After about 20 minutes, the officers forced the reporters into a police car and drove them to the local precinct. There, they were separated and interrogated for several hours. They were released at midnight only after Zhao and Lu's colleagues from *Jinan Shibao* arrived on the scene. Upon their release, the reporters were taken to the hospital, where they were treated for various injuries. Zhao was diagnosed with a severe concussion.

After the incident was reported in the domestic media, Ji Weijian denied that it had happened. On January 8, when a reporter from the state news agency, Xinhua, questioned him about the beatings, he replied, "We [propaganda officials] and reporters are one family. How could we beat them? In fact, when they stopped by the bureau offices, we gave them tea and took them out to dinner."

JANUARY 24

Wang Daqi, *Shengtai Yanjiu*
IMPRISONED

For full details on this case, see page 391.

JANUARY 25

Jiang Weiping, free-lance
IMPRISONED, LEGAL ACTION

The Dalian Intermediate Court formally sentenced free-lance journalist Jiang to eight years in prison on charges including "inciting to subvert state power" and "illegally providing state secrets overseas." This judgment amended an earlier decision to sentence Jiang to nine years.

On December 4, 2000, Jiang was arrested after publishing a number of articles in the Hong Kong magazine *Qianshao* (Frontline), a monthly Chinese-language magazine focusing on mainland affairs, revealing corruption scandals in northeastern China.

Jiang wrote the *Qianshao* articles, which were published between June and September 1999, under various pen names. His coverage exposed several major corruption scandals involving high-level officials. Notably, Jiang reported that Shenyang vice mayor Ma Xiangdong had lost nearly 30 million yuan (US$3.6 million) in public funds gambling in Macau casinos. Jiang also revealed that Liaoning provincial governor Bo Xilai had covered up corruption among his friends and family during his years as Dalian mayor.

Soon after these cases were publicized in *Qianshao* and other Hong Kong media, authorities detained Ma. He was accused of taking bribes, embezzling public funds, and gambling overseas and was executed for these crimes in December 2001. Ma's case was widely reported in China and used as an example in the government's ongoing fight against corruption. However, in May 2001, Jiang was indicted for "revealing state secrets."

The Dalian Intermediate Court held a secret trial in September 2001. In January 2002, when the court announced Jiang's sentence, he proclaimed his innocence and told the court that the verdict "trampled on the law," according to CPJ sources. He has since appealed the verdict, but the case remained pending at year's end.

According to CPJ sources, Jiang has a serious stomach disorder and has been denied medical treatment. Jiang's wife and daughter have not been allowed to see or speak with him in the two years since his arrest. His wife, Li Yanling, has been repeatedly interrogated and threatened since her husband's arrest. In March 2002, the local Public Security Bureau brought her in for questioning and detained her for several weeks.

An experienced journalist, Jiang had worked until May 2000 as the northeastern China bureau chief for the Hong Kong paper *Wen Hui Bao*. He contributed free-lance articles to *Qianshao*. In the 1980s, he worked as a Dalian-based correspondent for Xinhua News Agency.

In November 2001, CPJ honored Jiang with its annual International Press Freedom Award. In February 2002, CPJ sent appeals to President Jiang Zemin from almost 600 supporters—including CBS anchor Dan Rather, civil rights leader Jesse Jackson, and former U.S. ambassador to China Winston Lord—demanding Jiang's unconditional release. That month, President Bush highlighted Jiang's case in meetings with Jiang Zemin during a state visit to China. No progress had been made in his case by the end of 2002.

FEBRUARY 9

All foreign journalists
CENSORED

The Foreign Affairs Office of the Chaoyang District municipal government in the capital, Beijing, issued a directive to local Communist Party committees, government offices, and businesses outlining the proper procedures for giving interviews to foreign journalists, including topics that are off-limits and procedures for reporting "illegal" interviews.

The document, titled "On Strengthening the Management of Interviews by Foreign Reporters," stated that interviewees must "actively uphold the dignity of the state, observe regulations regarding foreign affairs ... and strictly guard secrets of the party and state." After being interviewed, individuals must submit a report to the district Foreign Affairs Office.

The document also requires employees to prevent foreign reporters from conducting interviews about sensitive issues, including, "Falun Gong, democracy activists, private residences, the courts, religion, human rights or family planning policies." If foreign reporters conduct "illegal" interviews, employees must report them immediately to Public Security or Foreign Affairs offices. Authorities may then confiscate journalists' notes, audio equipment and cameras, according to the document.

Most foreign reporters in Beijing are based in diplomatic compounds in Chaoyang District. The government has issued a number of regulations governing the activities of foreign reporters, which are enforced to varying degrees. This directive was issued to tighten control over domestic and foreign reporters during the run-up to the 16th Communist Party Congress, which was held in November. Authorities often harass or detain domestic sources who speak with foreign reporters about sensitive topics.

FEBRUARY 16

Chu Wai-kit, TVB
ATTACKED, HARASSED
Wong Chun-mei, TVB
Cheung Chi-fai, South China Morning Post
HARASSED

Chu, a cameraman for TVB; Wong, a reporter for TVB; and Cheung, a reporter for the *South China Morning Post*, were assaulted by Macau police while covering a demonstration against Chinese National People's Congress chairman Li Peng's visit to the territory.

As Chu filmed police deporting Hong Kong–based democracy activist Leung Kwok-hung from the Macau ferry terminal, police warned the journalist to stop, according to the Hong Kong Journalists Association (HKJA). When Chu ignored the warning, several officers grabbed him and briefly detained him in a separate room. Chu claims police beat him and broke his camera.

Police grabbed TVB reporter Wong and dragged her away when she tried to intervene and help Chu, according to local and international press reports. Police also took Cheung and forced him into an office, where he was questioned for 45 minutes.

On February 17, Macau police issued a statement acknowledging that they had detained Chu and Cheung but denying that they had assaulted the journalists or damaged any equipment. The Macau government rejected a request from TVB and HKJA for an independent investigation into the incident, declaring instead that that they would carry out an internal inquiry. Macau, a former Portuguese colony 40 miles (64 kilometers) west of Hong Kong, reverted to Chinese rule in December 1999.

MARCH 24

Yang Wei, *Beijing Times*
ATTACKED

Yang, a photographer for the *Beijing Times* (Jinghua Shibao), was beaten while working undercover to investigate reports of mismanagement and unfair pricing at Beijing property management company Zhongchuang. The investigation focused on Zhongchuang's management of the Shiliu Yuan Estates in Beijing's Fengtai District.

On March 24, after discovering that Yang was a journalist, several Zhongchuang staff members beat him up, according to local news reports. Yang was taken to the Chaoyang Hospital, where he was treated for a damaged eardrum. He was released from the hospital on March 26.

Immediately following the beating, police detained four suspects. All four were released without charge on March 27, the *Beijing Times* reported. While officers at the Fengtai District precinct pledged to resolve the case, little progress had been made by year's end.

APRIL 15

Australian Broadcasting Corporation
CENSORED

The Chinese government blocked the Web site of the Australian Broadcasting Corporation (ABC), Australia's national broadcaster, according to ABC . On April 23, after the Web site had been unavailable for more than a week, ABC officials lodged a complaint with the Ministry of Foreign Affairs and the Public Security Bureau. The government gave no formal response, although the Foreign Ministry told ABC they were investigating the complaint. On April 25, access to the site was restored after ABC officials met with Chinese government representatives.

Chinese censors routinely block the Web sites of major international news agencies, including *The New York Times*, BBC, and CNN. However, the ABC site had previously been accessible inside China, and network officials said the block was most likely related to a May visit to Australia by the Dalai Lama, the exiled Tibetan spiritual leader whom the Chinese government considers a separatist.

APRIL 25

Fung Siu-wing, *Ming Pao*
Butt Kwong-lai, Cable TV
Chong Chi-chung, Cable TV
HARASSED

Fung, a photographer with the Chinese-language daily *Ming Pao*, and Butt, a cameraman with Hong Kong's Cable TV, were harassed by Hong Kong police while covering the officers' removal of mainland Chinese immigrants protesting for the right to remain in Hong Kong.

Police grabbed Fung as he photographed officers breaking up the demonstration. Officers then dragged him away and handcuffed him for about 15 minutes, according to international reports. Police also handcuffed Butt and verbally harassed reporter Chong, also with Cable TV. Officials then forced the journalists and several of their colleagues to report on the demonstrations from a designated area in a remote corner of the park.

On April 26, Butt and Chong filed a formal complaint against the police. A police spokesperson responded that all complaints would be investigated but that, "There is absolutely no question of police trying to limit press freedom," according to the *South China Morning Post*.

JUNE

All journalists
CENSORED

In the run-up to the 16th Communist Party

Congress, which was held in November, the Central Propaganda Bureau issued a directive to local propaganda offices outlining 32 restricted topics, according to international news reports. Provincial or regional propaganda offices oversee all publications within their territory.

The directive divided the restricted topics into three categories: those that cannot be reported at all; those that must be reported with extra caution; and those that must originate from the official Xinhua News Agency. The list of forbidden topics included Taiwan's political independence; China's media policies; recognition of private property rights; and religion among ethnic minorities. Topics that must be reported with greater caution included citizens' complaints against authorities; private business owners who become wealthy; individuals who fight corruption; rural unrest; and the impact of China's World Trade Organization membership on domestic industries.

JUNE 3

Jiang Xueqin, free-lance
IMPRISONED, EXPELLED

Authorities detained free-lance reporter Jiang, a Chinese-born Canadian citizen, in Daqing, Heilongjiang Province, while he was filming labor unrest for the U.S.-based Public Broadcasting Service (PBS). On June 5, Jiang flew to Canada after being deported from China.

A police official in Daqing told Agence France-Presse that Jiang had "made illegal video recordings and violated the law." However, authorities did not clarify which law Jiang had violated and did not file formal charges against him before his deportation.

Throughout the spring of 2002, tens of thousands of unemployed workers in Daqing staged massive protests against layoffs and the government's failure to deliver welfare

benefits. The Chinese government banned domestic and foreign reporters from covering the unrest, which also erupted sporadically in several other Chinese cities. The protests were the largest in China since the 1989 pro-democracy demonstrations.

Jiang has written for *The Nation*, the *Christian Science Monitor*, and the *Far Eastern Economic Review*. He also contributed to a June 17 cover story in *Time* magazine's Asia edition on China's unemployment problem.

JUNE 15

The Economist
CENSORED

Domestic distribution of the June 15 edition of *The Economist*, which contained an in-depth survey of the country, an editorial titled "Set China's Politics Free," as well as articles that mentioned grassroots democracy, labor unrest, political reform, and other sensitive topics, was banned by the Chinese government.

On June 14, *The Economist*'s circulation director for Asia-Pacific called China National Publications, a government-owned company with exclusive rights to distribute foreign publications in the country, to ask whether the issue would be distributed. According to international news reports, on June 19, the company responded that "the issue was not legal to distribute."

About 3,100 copies of *The Economist* are distributed in mainland China every week. An official at the magazine told reporters that all mainland subscribers had received the June 15 edition, but that all 1,000 copies for sale at hotel newsstands were banned.

International publications such as *The Economist* are commonly only distributed at newsstands in China's luxury hotels, and only foreign residents are permitted to subscribe. Authorities often rip out *Economist* articles about China before distributing the magazine, but this is the first time an entire issue has been banned, said the *South China Morning Post*.

JULY 1

BBC World
CENSORED

Government officials blocked the encrypted signal that transmits BBC World television news broadcasts through the Sinosat 1 satellite. The Chinese government did not offer the BBC any formal explanation for the suspension of broadcasts, according to BBC sources in London. However, the suspension followed a report on BBC World about the banned spiritual group Falun Gong that was broadcast repeatedly on June 30 and July 1.

On July 5, a spokesman for the China International Television Corporation, which regulates foreign programming in the country, told Agence France-Presse that "some programs of the BBC infringed rules on the transmission of foreign programs in China." He did not clarify which program had offended the government, or which rules had been broken.

BBC World has been broadcast into China via satellite since January 2001. However, because government censors tightly control both foreign and domestic news, the broadcasts are only available in some hotel rooms and in the homes of foreign residents. The majority of Chinese citizens do not see BBC World.

JULY 9

Tao Haidong, free-lance
IMPRISONED

For full details on this case, see page 391.

JULY 19

Zhang Wei, *Shishi Zixun, Redian Jiyao*
IMPRISONED

For full details on this case, see page 392.

AUGUST

Chen Shaowen, free-lance
IMPRISONED

For full details on this case, see page 392.

AUGUST 1

All Internet publishers
LEGAL ACTION, CENSORED

The "Interim Regulations on Management of Internet Publishing," which were promulgated jointly by the State Administration of Press and Publishing and the Ministry of Information Technology, went into effect. The regulations outline topics that are forbidden on online news sites, including reports that "harm national unity, sovereignty or territorial integrity"; "reveal state secrets, endanger national security, or damage national honor or interests"; or "disturb the social order or damage social stability." They also outlaw news "advocating cults or superstition," which could cover any reports about the banned spiritual group Falun Gong.

The Chinese government routinely uses charges of "revealing state secrets" and "endangering national security" to prosecute individuals who publish independent news and opinion. By the end of 2002, fifteen individuals were imprisoned in China for publishing or distributing information online.

During the last few years, the Chinese government has issued a series of regulations limiting online content and holding Internet service providers and Web site publishers responsible for censoring their sites.

The latest regulations outline specific penalties, including fines, for online publications that publish illegal content.

Online publishers must designate an editor to examine news content and determine if it violates the new rules. Web sites must also indicate on their front page that the relevant government office has approved the site. Web publishers must report any offending content to the State Administration of Press and Publishing in the capital, Beijing, or to the administration's regional offices. Operators of Web sites that do not abide by the new rules will face penalties including heavy fines, confiscation of equipment, and closure.

Soon after the regulations were announced in July, Web users inside China initiated a campaign protesting the new rules and demanding freedom of expression on the Internet. One petition, titled "Declaration of Web Citizens' Rights," called for freedom of expression, freedom of information, and freedom to organize online. More than 1,000 free-lance writers, Web publishers, and other Internet users—including well-known Beijing-based writers Liu Xiaobo and Yu Jie—signed the statement.

AUGUST 24

Wan Yanhai, AIDS Action Project
IMPRISONED

Wan, coordinator of the AIDS Action Project (Aizhi Xingdong) and publisher of the group's Web site, disappeared while attending a film screening in the capital, Beijing. On August 28, Wan's wife, Su Zhaosheng, who is studying in Los Angeles, filed a missing-persons report with the Beijing Public Security Bureau. In early September, public security agents informed Wan's colleagues in Beijing that they were holding him on suspicion of "leaking state secrets," according to Su.

He was not formally charged, and authorities did not inform Wan's friends or family where he was being held.

On September 20, Wan was released, after international organizations, including CPJ, campaigned vigorously on his behalf. China's official news agency, Xinhua, as quoted by Agence France-Presse, said that Wan was released after "confessing to his crimes and agreeing to cooperate with police in the investigation." Xinhua stated that an official from the State Information Office "revealed that Wan had delivered some illegally acquired interior classified documents … to overseas individuals, media sources, and Web sites on August 17, 2002."

The accusations appear to be tied to a government report documenting the spread of AIDS in Henan Province, which Wan posted on his Web site. Wan, a former employee of the Ministry of Health, started the AIDS Action Project in 1994 to raise awareness about HIV/AIDS in China and support the rights of AIDS victims. Notably, his reporting for the project's Web site has exposed an AIDS epidemic in Henan Province, where huge numbers of peasants acquired the disease after selling their blood at government-supported clinics. The United Nations has predicted that 10 million people in China could be infected with HIV during the next eight years.

In June 2002, Beijing authorities had shut the offices of the AIDS Action Project. After that, several of Wan's employees were called in for questioning, and Wan was followed by plainclothes police officers, according to Su Zhaosheng. The Web site (*www.aizhi.org*) remained accessible.

The Chinese government strictly censors reporting on AIDS, and Chinese and foreign journalists who investigate the topic have faced harassment or detention. Because of this, Wan Yanhai's Web site was one of the only independent sources of information in China about the disease. Wan was also an outspoken opponent of new Internet regulations, enacted on August 1, that require publishers of all China-based Web sites to register with the government and censor their content or risk being closed.

SEPTEMBER 1

Yeo Shi-dong, *Chosun Ilbo*
HARASSED

Just after midnight, seven police officers forcibly entered Yeo's office, which is based in his family's Beijing residence, according to a report by Yeo, a Korean citizen and Beijing bureau chief for the South Korean daily *Chosun Ilbo*. The officers questioned Yeo, searched his home and office, and confiscated documents including his passport, journalist identification card, and government certificate of residency.

Police accused Yeo of failing to properly notify the local police when he moved into the residence on June 18. According to his report, Yeo had notified the Foreign Ministry of his move, as required by Chinese law.

Yeo has written extensively about China's accelerated efforts to prevent North Korean refugees from seeking asylum in foreign countries by entering embassies in China. As part of the crackdown, officials have prevented journalists from reporting on the defection attempts, which have been occurring regularly since March. Authorities appear to have focused their efforts on South Korean journalists, who are especially active in reporting on the defections.

NOVEMBER 7

Liu Di, free-lance
IMPRISONED

For full details on this case, see page 393.

INDIA

FEBRUARY 28

Sudhir Vyas, *Times of India*
ATTACKED

Vyas, a reporter for the national daily *Times of India*, was physically assaulted by police in Rajkot, in the western state of Gujarat, while trying to go to the city's commercial center to cover massive rioting. Vyas was traveling on a scooter clearly marked as a press vehicle and also showed his press credentials to the officers. "They knew I was a journalist," Vyas told CPJ. "They said, 'Why are you here? Have you come to report on what we are doing?' They knew I was seeing what they allowed others to do" during the riots. About four officers assaulted Vyas, beating him with wooden batons. He says he sustained a hairline fracture to his right elbow, which he had raised to protect his head, and also suffered severe blows to his back.

The assault on Vyas was typical of attacks against journalists reporting on the communal violence that swept Gujarat following the burning of a train carrying Hindu activists, which left 59 people dead. That incident, which occurred on February 27, triggered a wave of reprisal attacks largely targeting the state's Muslim minority. Journalists reported that much of the violence directed against Muslims was organized and sponsored by police and political activists associated with Hindu nationalist groups, including the Bharatiya Janata Party, which is the ruling party in Gujarat and the leading partner in India's national coalition government.

APRIL 7

Pranav Joshi, New Delhi Television
Harsh Shah, *The Indian Express*
Harshal Pandya, Eenadu Television

Dhimant Purohit, Aaj Tak
Sanjeev Singh, New Delhi Television
Amit Dave, *Jansatta*
Ketan Trivedi, *Gujarat Samachar*
Gautam Mehta, *Gujarat Samachar*
Kalpit Bachech, *Times of India*
ATTACKED

Police in the Ahmedabad, the state capital of Gujarat, assaulted several journalists who were covering the officers' attempts to restore order at a peace meeting disrupted by a group of Hindu nationalists. Police, failing to control the mob, turned on journalists documenting the scene. Joshi, a cameraman for New Delhi Television, was among the most seriously injured. Police hit him over the head, knocking him unconscious, and continued beating him until a senior officer intervened. Joshi was rushed to a hospital for treatment.

Others injured included Shah, a photographer for the national newspaper *The Indian Express*; Pandya, a reporter for the private broadcaster Eenadu Television; Purohit, a correspondent for the private news channel Aaj Tak; Singh, a reporter for New Delhi Television; Dave, a photographer for the newspaper *Jansatta*; Trivedi, a reporter for the newspaper *Gujarat Samachar*; Mehta, a photographer for *Gujarat Samachar*; and Bachech, a photographer for the national daily *Times of India*.

The incident occurred at the historic Sabarmati Ashram, founded by Mohandas K. Gandhi, the leader of India's nonviolent movement for independence. Peace activists had convened the meeting at the ashram to discuss recent communal violence in Gujarat. The gathering was interrupted by protests led by the youth wing of the Bharatiya Janata Party, the ruling party in Gujarat and the leading partner in India's coalition government.

In an editorial headlined "Savaging the Journalist," *The Indian Express* reported that the attack on journalists was the culmination of a "systematic anti-media campaign" spon-sored by the state government, which had garnered negative press coverage for official complicity in violence that largely targeted the Muslim minority community.

APRIL 14

Paritosh Pandey, *Jansatta Express*
KILLED (MOTIVE UNCONFIRMED)

For full details on this case, see page 371.

APRIL 18

Ehsan Fazili, *The Tribune*
ATTACKED

A grenade exploded outside the Srinagar residence of Fazili, a correspondent covering Jammu and Kashmir for the regional, English-language daily *The Tribune*. Srinagar is the summer capital of Jammu and Kashmir State, where separatists have been fighting against Indian rule since 1989.

Fazili told CPJ that the grenade appeared to have been planted by a teenage boy who had entered his office minutes before the explosion asking permission to use a water tap. The journalist said he became suspicious when he heard some activity on the other side of the house. Just as he went outside to investigate, the young man fled but also warned him to move away from the house. Fazili escaped the blast with only a few splinter injuries on his back.

A separatist militant group later claimed that the grenade was not intended for Fazili. Local journalists said they perceived the attack as a warning to the Srinagar press corps—many of whom live and work in the same neighborhood.

MAY 29

Zafar Iqbal, *Kashmir Images*
ATTACKED

Iqbal, a journalist for the Srinagar,

Kashmir-based, English-language daily *Kashmir Images*, was seriously injured after being shot by three unidentified assailants, according to journalists in Kashmir and Indian news reports. At about 3:00 p.m., three gunmen entered the Srinagar offices of *Kashmir Images* and asked for Iqbal. After speaking with the journalist for several minutes, one of them took out a gun and shot him in the leg and neck. The assailants fled the scene and have not been caught by police.

Iqbal is an editor and reporter at *Kashmir Images*, a publication known for supporting the Indian government. Local journalists believe Iqbal may have been targeted because of a front-page story he wrote in the May 29 issue about the Indian army's efforts to help an impoverished family. His colleagues told reporters that the assailants discussed the story with Iqbal before shooting him.

Journalists are regularly targeted for violent attack in Indian-administered Kashmir, where Muslim separatists and Indian security forces are fighting for control of the region. The shooting came amid escalating tensions between India and Pakistan over the disputed territory.

JUNE 9

Iftikhar Gilani, *Kashmir Times*
IMPRISONED

For full details on this case, see page 399.

JUNE 21

Alex Perry, *Time*
HARASSED

Perry, New Delhi bureau chief for *Time* magazine, was threatened with expulsion after he wrote an article questioning Prime Minister Atal Behari Vajpayee's fitness to the lead the country during a time of heightened tension on the subcontinent. Though officials

repeatedly summoned Perry for questioning over alleged visa infractions, in the end, no further action was taken.

The controversial article prompted small demonstrations, including one in Pune, a city in Maharashtra State, that was led by members of Vaypayee's Bharatiya Janata Party during which a pile of *Time* magazine copies was burned. *Time* magazine also hired armed security guards after *The Pioneer*, a conservative newspaper, published Perry's home address along with a scathing critique of his article.

JULY 7

Nasir Shadid, Al-Jazeera
EXPELLED

Shadid, New Delhi correspondent for the Arabic-language satellite channel Al-Jazeera, was expelled from the country. "Al-Jazeera is replacing its correspondent," External Affairs Ministry spokeswoman Nirupama Rao said, as quoted by The Associated Press. "This is a decision the government of India makes."

Though Al-Jazeera denied that it was under pressure to replace Shadid, the journalist's colleagues in New Delhi said he had been pressured for some time over his reporting on abuses committed against India's Muslim community. Shadid "has been asked to leave India because of his reporting on Kashmir and Gujarat," said S. Venkat Narayan, president of the Foreign Correspondents Club of South Asia. The government is extremely sensitive about reports of government complicity in attacks against the Muslim minority community in Gujarat and also keeps close watch of reporting on the disputed Kashmir region.

JULY 10

Shahid Rashid, *State Reporter*
ATTACKED

Rashid, editor of the Urdu-language daily

State Reporter, was shot by masked gunmen as he rode his scooter to the newspaper office in the Chanapora area of Srinagar, the summer capital of India's Jammu and Kashmir State. Both Pakistan and India claim the disputed territory of Kashmir.

Local residents took Rashid to the S.M.H.S. Hospital in Srinagar, where he underwent surgery. Rashid had bullet wounds in his neck and arm, a hospital spokesperson told Agence France-Presse. Journalists in Srinagar were not sure what motivated the shooting but noted that violent attacks against the media appeared to be on the rise.

JULY 30

Dinamalar
Saravana Kumar, *Dinamalar*
Raja, *Dinamalar*
Pakkiri Samy, *Dinamalar*
ATTACKED

The office of the Tamil-language newspaper *Dinamalar*, located in Thanjavur, a city in the southern Indian state of Tamil Nadu, was attacked by about six people armed with wooden sticks. The gang destroyed office equipment and furniture and assaulted employees who attempted to stop them.

The journalists most seriously injured were Kumar, a subeditor, and Raja, a reporter, both of whom were taken to Thanjavur Medical College Hospital for treatment. Samy, a subeditor, suffered minor injuries. Also hurt were several staffers including Murugan, the office manager, who was also hospitalized; Raman, a computer operator; and Thanga Rajan, an office assistant.

According to sources at the newspaper, the journalists recognized their assailants as members of Dravida Kazhagam, a nationalist organization that promotes the advancement of the Dravidian ethnic group in Tamil Nadu. The news editor at the paper told CPJ that

the attack was likely motivated by a July 26 political cartoon that depicted Dravida Kazhagam's leader as a rat to be chased out of the house of Tamil Nadu's chief minister.

SEPTEMBER 17

Ghulam Mohammed Sofi, *Srinagar Times*
ATTACKED

Sofi, a prominent editor in Srinagar, the summer capital of India's Jammu and Kashmir State, was shot and wounded by two unidentified gunmen. The two young men entered the offices of Sofi, editor of the popular Urdu-language daily *Srinagar Times*, at about 6:30 p.m. and opened fire. Sofi's bodyguard attempted to block an assailant and was shot in the thigh. Sofi was briefly hospitalized for a bullet injury to his right hand.

The attack on Sofi was one of several violent incidents that occurred in Jammu and Kashmir as polling for state legislative elections began. Some militant organizations fighting for independence for Kashmir or accession to neighboring Pakistan had threatened to assassinate those who participated in or supported the elections, which they believe confer legitimacy on Indian rule. India and Pakistan have competing claims over the disputed territory of Kashmir. The *Srinagar Times* is an independent newspaper that supported the state elections.

Sofi told CPJ that his newspaper has been attacked nine times since 1989, when fighting between the government and insurgents in Muslim-majority Kashmir flared into civil war. However, this was the first time that he came face-to-face with his assailants. "We don't know who is behind this attack," Sofi said. "But the attackers have failed to fulfill their objective," he added, noting that he had spent some time at his offices the day after the attack.

ASIA

The United Jihad Council, a Pakistan-based organization representing about 14 militant groups active in Kashmir, released a threatening statement only hours before the attack on Sofi. "Mujahideen (warriors) are aware of the black sheep among journalists and warn them to mend their ways," said the statement, according to The Associated Press.

OCTOBER 8

Iboyaima Laithangbam, *The Hindu*
Yumnam Arun, free-lance
MISSING

Laithangbam, a reporter for the national English-language newspaper *The Hindu*, and Arun, a free-lancer reporting for the regional monthly *Eastern Panorama*, were kidnapped by ethnic Kuki militants in India's conflict-ridden Manipur State. Abducted in an ambush in Chandel District on the road that leads from the state capital, Imphal, to the Burmese border, the two were released safely on October 10, in the town of Palel. A driver and fellow passenger kidnapped along with the journalists were held separately and released on October 12.

In a brief account of his detention published in the October 11 edition of *The Hindu*, Laithangbam said that members of the United Kuki Liberation Front (UKLF), one of many insurgent groups fighting in India's fractious northeastern states, abducted the journalists. "The outfit's 'commander,' Lt. Mingthang, told us that we were being taken to protest 'poor coverage' of the UKLF activities," Laithangbam wrote. He said the rebels warned that they would target any newspaper that did not publish their press releases, and that journalists may be captured again in the future.

On the day of their capture, the two journalists were forced to march for about four hours through forested mountains and were held overnight in a tribal village where the UKLF had set up a temporary camp, according to Laithangbam. The next day, they were taken to another village, where they were again forced to spend the night. Although the two were not physically harmed, the rebels stole a digital camera, tape recorder, pocket radio, and money.

OCTOBER 13

Yambem Meghajit Singh, Northeast Vision
KILLED (MOTIVE UNCONFIRMED)

For full details on this case, see page 372.

NOVEMBER 21

Ram Chander Chaterpatti, *Poora Sach*
KILLED

For full details on this case, see page 358.

INDONESIA

JANUARY 10

Persatuan Wartawan Indonesia
ATTACKED

A bomb exploded at the office of Persatuan Wartawan Indonesia, or the Indonesian Journalists Association, in Lhokseumawe, in northern Aceh Province. The bomb caused no injuries but damaged the basement of the two-story building, according to the Indonesian news agency Antara. No one claimed responsibility for the attack. Journalists reporting in restive Aceh Province, which is located at the western tip of the Indonesian archipelago, are often subject to violent reprisals from separatist rebels and security forces. The civil war in Aceh began in 1976 and is one of Asia's longest-running, and least reported, conflicts.

MARCH 10

Lindsay Murdoch, *The Sydney Morning Herald, The Age*
EXPELLED

Murdoch, an award-winning reporter for the Australian newspapers *The Sydney Morning Herald* and the Melbourne-based *The Age*, was refused a renewal of his work visa, effectively banning him from continuing as a correspondent in the capital, Jakarta. This action was taken to punish Murdoch for writing stories that criticize government policies, local sources said.

Murdoch had applied to renew his work visa on December 10, 2001. Wahid Supriyadi, the spokesman for the Foreign Ministry, had earlier sent a fax to the *Herald* suggesting that the paper send a new correspondent to replace Murdoch. Subsequently, Murdoch's application was denied.

After Murdoch's editors visited the Foreign Ministry several times, he was granted a three-month extension of his visa, which expired on March 10. Supriyadi told Murdoch that an "interdepartmental committee" had recommended that he not be granted a new work visa. Supriyadi also told Murdoch that the committee had mentioned two stories as being particularly objectionable.

The first was a May 14, 2001, piece about an incident in which Indonesian soldiers in the restive province of Aceh murdered a baby in front of his mother. The other was a series of articles in 2001 that uncovered evidence that East Timorese children, separated from their families during the violence following the territory's 1999 vote rejecting Indonesian rule, had been sent to orphanages in Indonesia and were being held against their parents' will. According to CPJ research, Indonesian authorities did not deny that these incidents occurred.

JULY 1

Cahyo Paksi Priambodo, *Sinar Harapan*
Indra Sholihin, *detik.com*
M. Sholeh, *Media Indonesia*
Saptono, Antara
ATTACKED

Cahyo, a photographer for the daily *Sinar Harapan*; Sholihin, of the online newsmagazine *detik.com*; Sholeh, of the daily *Media Indonesia*; and Saptono, of the state news agency Antara, were beaten by police while covering security forces who were trying to disperse a crowd of student demonstrators protesting in front of the parliamentary compound in the capital, Jakarta.

Cahyo told the Antara news agency that he was taking pictures of "student-police brawls ... when suddenly someone kicked my head from behind and beat me up. I was shouting that I was a journalist while holding up my camera, but they continued beating me," he said. Police also confiscated Cahyo's camera, though they later returned it after his colleagues protested.

The next day, the House of Representatives' Commission on Defense and Foreign Affairs issued a statement condemning the assault on journalists and asking the police chief to punish the officers responsible. "Should the police continue resorting to violence like that, the House would not approve their request for more budget," said commission vice chairman Effendi Choirie of the National Awakening Party.

About 300 student demonstrators had demanded a special legislative probe into allegations that Parliament speaker Akbar Tandjung was involved in channeling US$4.5 million in government funds to his powerful Golkar Party. Police used water cannons and batons to break up the protest, according to The Associated Press.

SEPTEMBER 11

Lesley McCulloch, free-lance
IMPRISONED
For full details on this case, see page 399.

NOVEMBER 29

All broadcast journalists
LEGAL ACTION
The House of Representatives passed a landmark broadcast bill establishing a National Broadcasting Commission (KPI), which is empowered to revoke broadcast licenses and censor broadcasters over a variety of vaguely defined content restrictions. The commission answers to the Office of the President.

In essence, the KPI will be a quasi-governmental agency that can punish but not issue regulations, according to critics who have studied the law closely. The commission, for example, will issue recommendations on the granting of licenses, but the government retains veto power. Another provision creates a corps of investigators—in effect an ill-defined "broadcast police force"—to enforce potential violations of content restrictions on advertising and programming. It is unclear whether these investigators will come under the purview of the KPI or government agencies.

Broadcasters complain that the law will inhibit investment and planning by calling for a "tryout period" of six months to one year, during which time a new license could be revoked arbitrarily. This clause could severely inhibit the independence of broadcast journalists, who may censor themselves to curry favor with government regulators. The bill also bans commercial advertising by so-called community broadcasters. This could result in community broadcasters being unable to generate sufficient revenue to sustain their operations.

Members of the Indonesian Press and Broadcasting Society (MPPI) have called some provisions in the bill "monstrous." According to MPPI executive director Leo Batubara, "the final draft of the broadcasting bill marks the return of the era of repression."

MALAYSIA

JANUARY 24

Time
Far Eastern Economic Review
Newsweek
CENSORED
In late January and February, the Malaysian government delayed the distribution of *Time, Newsweek,* and the *Far Eastern Economic Review* because the three magazines published reports linking Malaysia to international terrorist activities. Distribution of five issues of the *Far Eastern Economic Review* was delayed, beginning on January 24.

Four issues of *Newsweek,* starting with the February 4 edition, were also delayed. That edition cited FBI reports calling Malaysia a "primary operational launchpad for the September 11 attacks" on New York City and Washington, D.C. Authorities also blocked distribution of four issues of *Time* magazine in February. The February 11 issue reported on alleged financial links between Malaysia and Osama bin Laden's al-Qaeda network.

The Home Ministry has the power to approve all foreign publications for distribution. On February 28, Deputy Home Minister Chor Chee Heung told *The Star* newspaper that distribution of the publications had been delayed due to "inaccurate and untrue reporting." Distribution was restored in March.

SEPTEMBER 30

Oriental Daily News
CENSORED
Oriental Daily News (ODN), a new, inde-

pendent Chinese-language daily, was able to publish only one issue, on September 29, before the Home Ministry suspended its publishing permit without explanation. Observers linked the suspension to political pressure.

In 2001, Nanyang Press Holdings, which publishes *Nanyang Siang Pau* and *China Press*, Malaysia's two leading Chinese dailies, was taken over by the Malaysian Chinese Association (MCA), a member of the government's ruling coalition, sparking fears that the previously independent Chinese press would follow in the timid footsteps of the rest of the Malaysian media. Large numbers of journalists left the Nanyang Group and joined *ODN*, according to press reports.

ODN's suspension was lifted in early December, still with no explanation for the actions. The daily's second issue was published on January 1, 2003. *ODN* management and individual newspaper vendors complained that employees of papers affiliated with the MCA had warned vendors against selling *ODN*.

NEPAL

DATE UNKNOWN

Ambika Timsina, *Janadesh*
KILLED (MOTIVE UNCONFIRMED)
For full details on this case, see page 372.

JANUARY 1

Debram Yadav, *Blast Times, Jana Aastha*
IMPRISONED
For full details on this case, see page 404.

JANUARY 5

Sharad K.C., Radio Nepal
HARASSED
Sharad, a reporter for the government-controlled Radio Nepal and local stringer for

the BBC, was detained by security forces in the midwestern town of Nepalgunj. Officers picked him up at the offices of Radio Nepal and took him to nearby army barracks, where he was detained for nearly two hours, according to the Center for Human Rights and Democratic Studies, a Kathmandu-based press freedom group.

After his release, Sharad told reporters that uniformed soldiers had blindfolded him and taken him away in a van. Following the imposition of a sweeping anti-terrorism ordinance in November 2001 that criminalized any contact with or support for the Maoist rebels, security officials frequently detained and harassed journalists.

JANUARY 19

Bijay Raj Acharya, Srijanashil Prakashan
IMPRISONED
Acharya, head of Srijanashil Prakashan publishing house, was detained by police. Soon after his detention, Acharya was brought to a military camp, where his hands and feet were tied and he was repeatedly tortured with electric shocks during a two-day interrogation, according to CPJ sources in Nepal.

Police originally detained Acharya for his suspected connections with *Janadesh*, a weekly with close links to the rebel Maoist movement. However, soon after the journalist's arrest, police admitted that their information was incorrect, according to the Center for Human Rights and Democratic Studies (CEHURDES) in the capital, Kathmandu. Nonetheless, Acharya remained in custody until March 19. No formal charges were ever filed against him, according to CEHURDES.

On November 28, Acharya was among some 14 journalists who filed lawsuits against the government claiming compensation for being illegally detained.

JANUARY 23

Posh Raj Poudel, *Chure Sandesh*
Suresh Chandra Adhikari, *Chure Sandesh*
IMPRISONED

Police arrested Poudel, executive editor of the newspaper *Chure Sandesh*, in the capital, Kathmandu, along with his colleague Adhikari, the paper's editor-in-chief. Police initially detained them at the Hanuman Dhoka Police Detention Center in Kathmandu but later transferred them to southern Chitwan District, along the Indian border. *Chure Sandesh* was a pro-Maoist newspaper published from Chitwan.

On November 26, 2001, the government declared a state of emergency and issued sweeping anti-terrorism legislation that criminalized any contact with or support for Maoist rebels. Two days later, police raided the offices of *Chure Sandesh*, as well as the home of the weekly's publisher, where they seized documents and copies of the paper, according to the Kathmandu-based Center for Human Rights and Democratic Studies.

Adhikari was released on November 8, but Poudel remained imprisoned at Bharatpur Jail in Chitwan at year's end.

MARCH 3

Gopal Budhathoki, *Sanghu Weekly*
IMPRISONED

Budhathoki, editor of the newspaper *Sanghu Weekly*, went missing while riding his motorcycle home from work in the capital, Kathmandu. Budhathoki has frequently covered alleged abuses of power by the Nepalese army, including financial irregularities in the purchase of military helicopters, according to local sources. On March 6, Prime Minister Sher Bahadur Deuba announced that the army had detained Budhathoki for publishing reports that "encouraged and raised morale of the Maoists," according to local press accounts. The announcement came only after a flurry of inquiries from legislators and media organizations about the journalist's status.

Budhathoki was among scores of journalists arrested after November 26, 2001, when the government introduced a sweeping anti-terrorism ordinance that criminalized any contact with or support for Maoist rebels.

Budhathoki, who is also a leading activist with the Federation of Nepalese Journalists, was held incommunicado for 23 days. In May, during a CPJ mission to Nepal, Budhathoki described the circumstances of his arrest. He said that, late on the night of March 3, he was tailed while riding home on his motorcycle, just around the corner from his office in the Bag Bazaar area of Kathmandu. A van cut him off and forced him to a stop. A group of officers in plainclothes exited the van and ordered him to come with them.

Budhathoki says that they identified themselves as army officers and told him, "Our chief is looking for you." They covered his head with a black cloth and took him to another location. He says he was questioned repeatedly about publishing an article that criticized the army's commander-in-chief for failing to pay proper tribute to soldiers killed in a battle with Maoist rebels. Budhathoki says that on the day he was released, March 26, an officer warned him, "Don't write anything that will demoralize the army."

On November 28, Budhathoki was among some 14 journalists who filed lawsuits against the government claiming compensation for being illegally detained.

MARCH 16

Shyam Shrestha, *Mulyankan*
IMPRISONED

Shrestha, editor of the leftist monthly

Mulyankan, was detained at the Tribhuvan International Airport in the capital, Kathmandu. He was on his way to New Delhi, India, to participate in a conference on the conflict between Maoist rebels and the Nepalese government, local sources said.

Shrestha is a well-known journalist and political activist. He was arrested along with Mahesh Maskey, a medical doctor and officer in the Intellectuals' Solidarity Group, a Nepalese human rights organization, and Pramod Kafle, a human rights activist.

On March 17, Prime Minister Sher Bahadur Deuba confirmed that Shrestha, Maskey, and Kafle had been detained but would not give any explanation for their arrest. Military sources told local media that the three were being held in army headquarters in Kathmandu. Their families were not allowed to see them in detention. On March 27, all three men were released after an officer warned them that journalists should not criticize the army, according to an account by Shrestha.

After his release, Shrestha told the *Kathmandu Post* that during his detention, officers repeatedly interrogated him and accused him of supporting the Maoist rebels. "They flung every possible obscene word at me. They said that press did not have right to comment on defense and foreign policy," he said.

In addition to his work as a journalist, Shrestha had helped mediate negotiations between the government and Maoist leaders. Those talks broke down in November 2001, when the Maoists violated a cease-fire agreement and increased violent attacks. In response, the government imposed a state of emergency and introduced a sweeping anti-terrorism ordinance that criminalized any contact with or support for the Maoist rebels. Many journalists were arrested under the ordinance's broad provisions.

On November 28, Shrestha was among some 14 journalists who filed lawsuits against the government claiming compensation for being illegally detained.

APRIL 5

Demling Lama, Radio Nepal, *Himalaya Times*
ATTACKED, MISSING

Lama, a correspondent in Sindhupalchok District for both Radio Nepal and the national Nepali-language daily *Himalaya Times*, was kidnapped by more than a dozen armed Maoist rebels who entered his house during the early morning, ordered him from his bed, and took him away, according to Nepalese press reports. He managed to escape from his captors two days later.

After his release, Lama described his ordeal to a local journalist. Lama said his kidnappers accused him of crimes against their "People's War" for broadcasting news for government-controlled Radio Nepal about a group of rebels who had surrendered to authorities. The journalist's captors later accused him of being a government spy. Lama said he was threatened with a knife and with a loaded gun, and that at one point he was taken to a remote area of the forest and beaten with a pipe. Months after his escape, Lama said he remained threatened and avoided travel outside the district headquarters.

MAY 6

Bhim Sapkota, *Narayani Khabar Weekly, Adarsha Samaj*
IMPRISONED

For full details on this case, see page 404.

MAY 19

Shiva Tiwari, *Janadisha*
Bharat Sigdel, *Janadisha*
IMPRISONED

For full details on this case, see page 405.

ASIA |

MAY 20

Krishna Sen, *Janadisha*
Atindra Neupane, *Janadisha*
Sangeeta Khadka, *Jana Ahwan*
IMPRISONED

For full details on this case, see page 405.

MAY 23

Tara Neupane, *Sanghu*
HARASSED

At around 3:30 p.m., plainclothes officers arrived at the Kathmandu district office of the Federation of Nepalese Journalists (FNJ) and took Neupane into custody. He was held overnight at the Kathmandu Valley Police Station at Ratna Park, according to the FNJ.

Neupane, a columnist for the Nepali-language weekly *Sanghu*, is a veteran journalist who writes mainly about economic and political affairs, said local sources. The reason for his arrest is unknown, but Nepalese officials have targeted *Sanghu* journalists in the past. The weekly's editor, Gopal Budhathoki, was detained briefly in December 2001 and then for more than three weeks in March 2002.

Sanghu is a political tabloid that generally supports the policies of the mainstream Communist Party of Nepal (United Marxist-Leninist), a legal political party. Neupane was among the more than 100 journalists who were detained under the broad provisions of an anti-terrorism ordinance introduced in November 2001 that allowed for the arrest of anyone suspected of supporting the outlawed Maoist rebels.

MAY 24

Rewati Sapkota, *Rajdhani*
IMPRISONED

Sapkota, a reporter for the national Nepali-language daily *Rajdhani*, was detained by police at his home at around 4:30 p.m. Just as he was preparing to leave for his evening shift at the office, plainclothes police officers came to his house and told him to come outside to meet someone. When he went outside, a uniformed police officer introduced himself as the older brother of one of Sapkota's colleagues at *Rajdhani* and insisted that the reporter accompany him. Sapkota did not recognize the officer but later identified him as Subinspector Komal Manandhar of the Kamal Pokhari Police Station in the capital, Kathmandu.

Upon Manandhar's insistence, Sapkota reluctantly went with the officer in his police van and was taken to the Kamal Pokhari station. Sapkota says that after about a half-hour, he was taken to the Mahendra Police Club, where he was blindfolded after a senior police officer admonished the junior officer, "Why haven't you covered his eyes? You're supposed to cover his eyes!"

Sapkota told CPJ he was then taken somewhere and seated on a couch until another officer yelled that he should be made to sit on the floor. He says he was moved to the floor and had his wrists bound with rope. Sapkota was interrogated about the stories he writes and about his sources. Officers had seized his address book and questioned him about his contacts.

The officers questioned him about suspected Maoist leaders, but they also asked him about the background of certain lawyers and journalists, including Yadu Devkota, a journalist at *Spacetime Daily*, and Gunaraj Luitel, a journalist at *Kantipur*.

Sapkota says that at one point during the interrogation, he was ordered to straighten his legs. He told CPJ that it felt as if two people were standing on his knees and beating him with wooden sticks—known locally as *lathis*. He says his captors caned him on the soles of his feet, thighs, and head.

He said after several hours of torture and

questioning, he was taken by van to another location. When his blindfold was finally removed, he discovered he was being held at Kathmandu's Hanuman Dhoka Police Station.

Sapkota told CPJ that he was only physically tortured on the first day, but that he was threatened during subsequent interrogations. "If you don't tell the truth, you'll die," he quoted an officer as saying. After protests by the Federation of Nepalese Journalists, Sapkota was released on May 28.

On November 28, Sapkota was among some 14 journalists who filed lawsuits against the government claiming compensation for being illegally detained.

Mina Sharma Tiwari, *Eikyavaddatha*
Binod Tiwari, *Eikyavaddatha*
IMPRISONED

On May 24, security forces arrested Mina Sharma Tiwari, editor of the newspaper *Eikyavaddatha*, from her home in the capital, Kathmandu. According to an account of her imprisonment, which she wrote after her release more than five months later, security forces covered her head with a black cloth, forced her into a vehicle, and took her to an unknown location.

On May 28th, army personnel raided *Eikyavaddatha*'s offices, seizing documents, computers, a printer, and a fax machine. They arrested Binod Tiwari, who is Mina Sharma's nephew and the paper's assistant editor. Authorities arrested the two journalists under the provisions of a sweeping anti-terrorism ordinance introduced in November 2001 that allowed for the arrest of anyone suspected of supporting the outlawed Maoist rebels.

Eikyavaddatha, which means solidarity, is a leftist publication that supports many of the declared aims of the rebel movement. Both Mina Sharma and Binod were reportedly tortured in custody. Mina Sharma says she was transferred several times during her detention

and that she was tortured with electric shocks and threatened that she would be forced to dig a trench for her body. Binod was held at the Sorakhutte Police Station in Kathmandu but was taken repeatedly to army headquarters in Tundikhel, according to the human rights group Amnesty International. Binod was released in sometime July, and Mina Sharma was released on November 5.

JUNE 1

Nava Raj Sharma, *Kadam*
KILLED

For full details on this case, see page 359.

AUGUST 1

Dhan Bahadur Rokka Magar, Radio Nepal
MISSING

Rokka Magar, a newsreader for the Kham Magar–language service of Radio Nepal, was abducted by Maoist rebels while traveling by bus to the town of Surkhet, where he works. Rebels intercepted the bus near Jaluki, a Maoist-controlled village near the borders of Western Rolpa and Pyuthan districts, and kidnapped several passengers, including Rokka Magar and a representative from the British charity the Gurkha Welfare Trust.

It was not clear why the Maoists targeted certain passengers, but rebels generally view journalists working for state-run Radio Nepal as government agents. Colleagues fear that Rokka Magar may therefore be particularly vulnerable to severe harassment and torture. He was still missing at year's end.

AUGUST 4

Kishor Shrestha, *Jana Aastha*
HARASSED

Shrestha, editor of the Nepali-language

ASIA

221

weekly newspaper *Jana Aastha*, was briefly detained by police. CPJ believes Shrestha's arrest was intended to silence his newspaper's reporting on the case of Krishna Sen, a pro-Maoist editor who, according to *Jana Aastha*, was allegedly killed in police custody.

At around 5 p.m., eight plainclothes police officers arrived at the *Jana Aastha* office in the capital, Kathmandu, according to Shrestha. He said the officers did not produce an arrest warrant and then forcibly dragged him from his office when he refused to accompany them.

Superintendent of Police Ram Chandra Khanal told the national daily *Kathmandu Post* later that evening that Shrestha had been arrested "for the news that appeared in *Jana Aastha*'s last edition" and threatened to charge him with either defamation or for violating the Public Offenses Act. The article in question alleged that Khanal was involved in illegal activities unrelated to the Sen case.

The next day, Shrestha was released without charge following protests led by the Federation of Nepalese Journalists. As a condition of his release, he was required to sign a statement apologizing for using "an objectionable adjective inadvertently" to describe Khanal, according to the *Kathmandu Post*.

However, Shrestha told CPJ that the threat of the defamation charge was only the pretext for his arrest. He said that during his detention, an interrogating officer warned him to stop reporting on the Krishna Sen case since *Jana Aastha*'s allegations of police misconduct had "created many problems" for the police.

In a June 26 article, *Jana Aastha* had reported that Sen, former editor of the pro-Maoist newspapers *Janadesh* and *Janadisha*, was tortured and killed in police custody. Authorities, who had arrested Sen on May 20, accused him of being among the senior leaders of the Maoist movement and of commanding rebel operations in Kathmandu. *Jana Aastha*'s account of his alleged killing,

which was based on confidential sources and never independently confirmed, caused a scandal in Nepal.

NOVEMBER 3

Dinesh Chaudhari, *Spacetime Daily*
IMPRISONED

For full details on this case, see page 405.

NOVEMBER 12

Tikaram Rai, *Aparanha*
IMPRISONED

Rai, editor of the Nepali-language daily *Aparanha,* was arrested in the capital, Kathmandu, after his newspaper published an article accusing a senior police officer of bribery. *Aparanha* had recently reported that police officer Basanta Kuwar had received bribes for issuing driver's licenses, pocketing some 16 million rupees (US$205,000), said the Agence France-Presse news agency. Kuwar said the report amounts to character assassination and filed a criminal complaint under Nepal's Public Offense Act, according to The Associated Press news agency (AP).

Rai was detained at Kathmandu's Hanuman Dhoka District Police Office, according to the Federation of Nepalese Journalists. A police officer told the AP that the journalist could be held for up to 10 days for questioning. However, Rai was released on bail on November 14 after protests from local and international press freedom groups, including CPJ.

PAKISTAN

DATE UNKNOWN

Daniel Pearl, *The Wall Street Journal*
KILLED

For full details on this case, see page 359.

APRIL 14

A.R. Shuja, *Khabrain*
Tahir Rasheed, *Khabrain*
Tasneem, *Khabrain*
Ibrahim Lucky, Online Lahore
Mian Aslam, *Business Report*
Mehtabuddin Nishat, *Ghareeb*
Sarfraz Sahi, *Insaaf*
Malik Naeem, *Parwaz*
Ashfaq Jahangir, *Parwaz*
Naseer Cheema, *Current Report*
Muhammad Bilal, *Current Report*
Hamid Raza, *Juraat*
Ramzan Nasir, *Tehrik*
Mayed Ali, *The News*
Roman Ihsan, *Jang*
Nasir Butt, *Pakistan*
Ziaullah, *Pakistan*
Khalid, *Pakistan*
Mian Saeef, *Ausaf*
Jawed Saddiqui, *Musawat*
Saeed Qadri, *Din*
Mian Rifaat Qadri, News Network International
Jawed Malik, *Soorat-i-Hal*
ATTACKED

Police in Faisalabad, Punjab Province, assaulted a group of journalists during a rally staged to promote an upcoming referendum to prolong the presidency of General Pervez Musharraf for five more years. Dozens of journalists had walked out of the rally to protest hostile remarks by Punjab governor Khalid Maqbool, who accused the Pakistani media of undermining General Musharraf's referendum campaign "by publishing fake reports." As the journalists left the rally, which was held at the Iqbal Stadium in Faisalabad, baton-wielding police officers assaulted them.

According to a report in the newspaper *Dawn*, at least 23 journalists were injured, including:

- Shuja, Rasheed, and Tasneem (full name unavailable), of the newspaper *Khabrain*;
- Lucky, of the news agency Online Lahore;
- Aslam, of the newspaper *Business Report*;
- Nishat, of the newspaper *Ghareeb*;
- Sahi, of the newspaper *Insaaf*;
- Naeem and Jahangir, of the newspaper *Parwaz*;
- Cheema and Bilal, of the newspaper *Current Report*;
- Raza, of the newspaper *Juraat*;
- Nasir, of the newspaper *Tehrik*;
- Ali, of the daily *The News*;
- Ihsan, of the daily *Jang*;
- Butt, Ziaullah, and Khalid (full names unavailable), of the newspaper *Pakistan*;
- Saeef, of the newspaper *Ausaf*;
- Saddiqui, of the daily *Musawat*;
- Saeed Qadri, of the daily *Din*;
- Mian Rifaat Qadri, of the Pakistani news agency News Network International; and
- Malik of the newspaper *Soorat-i-Hal*.

Members of the public also assaulted some journalists after Governor Maqbool, a retired lieutenant general, warned that "the public could take revenge on [journalists] if they did not desist from wrong reporting," according to *Dawn*. Maqbool then led the crowd in chanting "Shame!" against the press, prompting the journalists to walk out.

MAY 10

Amardeep Bassey, *The Sunday Mercury*
IMPRISONED

Bassey, investigations editor for the British newspaper *The Sunday Mercury*, and his two Pakistani guides, Naoshad Ali Afridi and Khitab Shah Shinwari, were arrested at the Torkham border crossing, near Peshawar, on their way back into Pakistan from Afghanistan. Pakistani officials told journalists that Bassey, a British citizen, was being held on suspicion of espionage.

An Interior Ministry official told The Associated Press that Bassey had failed to obtain an exit visa before leaving Pakistan. Bassey, Afridi, and Shinwari were first held in Landi Kotal, a Pakistani town at the mouth of the Khyber Pass. They were later transferred to a detention center in Peshawar, where they were interrogated by members of Pakistan's Inter-Services Intelligence agency (ISI) and other state security agencies, according to local and international news reports.

The British Foreign Office said that Bassey was one of five accredited journalists on an April trip to Afghanistan sponsored by the British government, but that he was working independently at the time of his arrest. Pakistani officials told local journalists that they were suspicious of Bassey because of his Indian descent. An activist with the independent Human Rights Commission of Pakistan who visited Bassey in detention said the journalist was accused of spying for neighboring India. Authorities also claimed that Bassey's watch, which includes a built-in digital camera, raised suspicions that he was acting as a spy.

Indian journalists and journalists of Indian origin are rarely granted visas to report in Pakistan. Once the country , they are generally subject to intense scrutiny by Pakistan's intelligence services. On May 25, after finding no evidence of criminal wrongdoing, local authorities issued a deportation order for Bassey and forwarded it to the Interior Minister's office. However, authorities did not release Bassey until June 6 and offered no explanation for the delay. His guides were released without charge on July 10.

AUGUST 20

Shaheen Sehbai, *The South Asia Tribune*
HARASSED, LEGAL ACTION
Police in Rawalpindi filed a First Information Report (FIR) against Sehbai,

editor of the online weekly *South Asia Tribune*, accusing him of criminal acts allegedly committed in February 2001. The complaint was made by Khalid Mahmud Hekazi, who is, according to Sehbai, a civilian employee who works at the Pakistani army's general headquarters in Rawalpindi. Hekazi was formerly married to a cousin of Sehbai's, whom he recently divorced.

The FIR states, among other things, that Sehbai threatened to rob Hekazi at his home at gunpoint, and names Sehbai's wife, as well as several nieces and nephews, as complicit in these crimes. Sehbai and his wife live in the United States and were therefore in no danger of arrest. However, police began harassing Sehbai's relatives, even arresting several of them as alleged "accomplices." *The South Asian Tribune* has written critically about Pakistan's military government.

Sehbai had previously worked as editor of the national English-language daily *The News*, one of Pakistan's most influential newspapers. He resigned from *The News* on March 1, alleging government interference with the editorial content of the paper.

OCTOBER 20

Shahid Soomro, *Kawish*
KILLED
For full details on this case, see page 361.

PAPUA NEW GUINEA

OCTOBER 4

Robyn Sela, *Papua New Guinea Post-Courier*
THREATENED
Sela, a reporter for the *Papua New Guinea Post-Courier*, was verbally assaulted by a soldier during a visit to the Murray military

barracks in the capital, Port Moresby. The threat apparently stemmed from an exposé Sela wrote about Fred Punangi, the secretary of the Defense Department, who is being investigated on charges of improper conduct.

A military officer dressed in civilian clothes grabbed Sela as she entered a car to leave the Murray barracks. According to Sela's account, reported in the *Post-Courier*, "He grabbed me by the forearm and shook me a few times, then he said, 'You better stop writing stories about Mr. Punangi.'" The soldier then pointed two fingers at her temple and said, "If you continue, and if we find you somewhere, we will shoot you dead."

The man then drove away. Military police have acknowledged that a soldier was responsible for the threat and are investigating the incident. The *Post-Courier*, which media magnate Rupert Murdoch owns, is Papua New Guinea's largest newspaper.

PHILIPPINES

FEBRUARY 9

All journalists
THREATENED

The Philippine military warned journalists of threats from Abu Sayyaf, an armed group active in the southern Philippines that U.S. and Philippine officials have linked to Osama bin Laden's al-Qaeda network, which is accused of masterminding the September 11, 2001, attacks on the United States.

More than 600 U.S. troops arrived in early 2002 on the southern island of Basilan to help the Philippine army in its efforts to crush the Abu Sayyaf, which claims to be fighting for a separate Islamic state. On February 9, Capt. Harold Cabunoc, who commands Philippine Scout Ranger troops operating on Basilan, warned all foreign journalists about the risk of kidnapping by

the Abu Sayyaf and advised them against traveling to the island alone. More than 100 journalists were in Zamboanga City on the island of Mindanao, near Basilan, to cover joint military exercises by Philippine and U.S. troops.

Philippine officials say three foreign reporters escaped kidnapping attempts, according to local press reports. On February 8, free-lance journalists Christopher Johnson, a Canadian, and Urban Hamid, a French national, were boarding a ferry to Basilan when two men approached them, saying they were soldiers sent to escort the journalists to the island. Johnson and Hamid became suspicious and reported the encounter to local military authorities, who denied having sent an escort.

In a similar incident, on February 11, two unidentified men approached Japanese journalist Jun Ida, Manila bureau chief for the Tokyo-based newspaper *Mainichi*, just after he arrived in Basilan. The men offered to guide Ida to Abu Sayyaf hideouts, according to local news reports. Ida declined the offer and reported it to the authorities. Philippine military authorities claimed the incidents were kidnapping attempts by members of the Abu Sayyaf, said local press reports. These claims have not been independently verified.

In his February 9 announcement, Captain Cabunoc asked foreign journalists to notify the military before arriving on Basilan to report on the military exercises. In 2000, Abu Sayyaf guerrillas kidnapped a total of 15 journalists during a hostage crisis on the island of Jolo, near Basilan. Most of the journalists were released after their news organizations paid hefty ransoms to the kidnappers. Local journalists have expressed concern that those events set a precedent and encouraged rebel groups to kidnap journalists as a source of revenue.

ASIA

FEBRUARY 12

Bombo Radyo
ATTACKED, CENSORED

The private broadcaster Bombo Radyo, in the city of Cauayan, was forcibly closed by a group of armed men on the orders of the local mayor's office. The men cut the radio station's power lines and padlocked its fuse boxes. Mayor Caesar Dy said the managers had failed to get the proper operating permit from the city government. However, the station manager claimed that the closure stemmed from news reports that had criticized the mayor.

MAY 13

Edgar Damalerio, *Zamboanga Scribe,*
DXKP Radio
KILLED

For full details on this case, see page 364.

MAY 22

Bombo Radyo
ATTACKED

A bomb exploded at about 1 a.m. at the entrance of the private broadcaster Bombo Radyo, in Cagayan de Oro City, on the southern island of Mindanao. According to local news reports, no one was injured in the attack, but the blast caused superficial damage to the exterior of the building. The attack did not affect the radio station's ability to broadcast.

Bombo Radyo is known for its coverage of local crime and official corruption. Station manager Jun Albino told Agence France-Presse that the attack came either in retaliation for his station's reporting or because of a rivalry with another radio station. No group claimed responsibility for the bombing, and police have not named any suspects.

In preceding months, several bomb explosions struck the island of Mindanao, where separatist Muslim guerrilla groups have been battling the Philippine army. Journalists in the region are frequently targets of violent attacks.

JULY 9

Bernadette Tamayo, *People's Journal*
THREATENED

Tamayo, a veteran military correspondent with the *People's Journal* newspaper, announced to the media that military intelligence officials on the southern island of Mindanao had issued a poster mistakenly identifying her as a member of the Abu Sayyaf guerrilla group. The poster included a photograph of Tamayo and advertised a 1 million peso (US$20,000) bounty for her life.

Tamayo told CPJ that the error could be fatal, especially in the strife-torn southern region, where the Philippine military has declared an all-out war against the guerrillas. Tamayo's picture was taken with members of the Abu Sayyaf in May 2000 when she was conducting an interview for her newspaper.

Tamayo criticized military officials for failing to corroborate the information in the poster and not checking her identity. "It was haphazard and dangerous," Tamayo told CPJ. She said that although military officials have cleared her of any involvement with the guerrilla group , she remains concerned that she may be harmed if she returns to Mindanao. Abu Sayyaf guerrillas have been involved in kidnap-for-ransom activities in southern Mindanao and have also been targeted by Philippine army units being trained by the U.S. military.

AUGUST 22

Sonny Alcantara, "Quo Vadis San Pablo," *Kokus*
KILLED

For full details on this case, see page 364.

Gilbert Ordiales, GMA
Carlo Lorenzo, GMA
MISSING

Lorenzo and Ordiales, a reporter and cameraman, respectively, for the television network GMA, were held captive on the southern island of Jolo, Sulu Province, for five days before being released unharmed on October 3. The journalists were in Jolo to report on rebel groups in the region, according to Philippine and international news reports. Before the men disappeared, they had made arrangements to interview three Indonesian fishermen being held hostage by rebels on the island.

On October 4, in an account published on the Web site of the *Philippine Daily Inquirer*, Lorenzo said that soldiers held them up once they arrived in the village of Kagay on September 28. "I thought they were our protectors," Lorenzo told the *Inquirer*. But then "they started to open our bags. They took my cell phone, calling cards, notebooks, tape recorders and the handy camera." According to the *Inquirer*, Lorenzo said the soldiers left them in the custody of local villagers, who later freed them.

Lorenzo later retracted his statement, saying that he did not know if the men who had held them up were in fact members of the military. GMA issued a statement saying that, "Lorenzo never directly implicated the military in his and Ordiales' abduction." The *Inquirer* stood by its original story. Julie Alipala, the reporter who wrote the article, received several threatening messages because of the story.

In October, police on Jolo Island arrested Hadja Jarma Mohammed Imran, a military informant who had helped Lorenzo and Ordiales arrange the interviews, on kidnapping charges, according to CPJ sources in the Philippines. She denied the allegations. Three activists with the Islamic separatist group

Moro National Liberation Front (MNLF) and the GMA crew were also called as witnesses in court proceedings, which are expected to begin in early 2003.

During 2002, the Philippine army escalated efforts to fight several rebel groups in Sulu Province. The armed group Abu Sayyaf, which claims to be fighting for a separate Islamic state, has sought refuge in Sulu since 2001, when the military waged an intensive campaign—with assistance from U.S. troops—against the group's former stronghold of nearby Basilan Island. The MNLF, which also advocates an independent Muslim state, signed a peace agreement with the government in 1996, but a breakaway rebel faction is still active in the province.

SINGAPORE

All journalists
LEGAL ACTION

High Court judge Choo Han Teck ruled that reporters do not have the right to protect confidential sources in civil cases if the court decides the documents requested are "relevant" to the proceedings. In a ruling published in the *Law Academy Digest*, Judge Choo said that journalists do not have the "privilege of exemption" if the court orders disclosure, according to Singaporean and international press reports.

The court issued the controversial ruling during a libel case brought by a door manufacturer against the Singapore daily *Business Times*, which had reported about the company's financial difficulties. The plaintiff requested that the court order the newspaper to turn over the reporter's notes and article drafts, but the court ultimately did not request the journalist's documents because they were judged irrelevant to the case.

ASIA

SOLOMON ISLANDS

JANUARY 24

Solomon Star
THREATENED, HARASSED

A group of about eight men, some of whom were armed, entered the *Solomon Star* offices in the capital, Honiara, and demanded that the paper pay "compensation" to a government official for a report published in the January 22 edition. That day's paper carried a news story, an editorial, and a letter to the editor about an unnamed drunken government official who had allegedly assaulted a taxi driver. Agence France-Presse later identified the official as Economic Reform Minister Daniel Fa'afunua.

Solomon Star's publisher, John Lamani, and associate editor Ofani Eremae refused to pay. The men then brought them to Fa'afunua, who told Lamani and Eremae that he was angered by the reports and demanded Sol$5,000 (US$1,000) as compensation, according to the Fiji-based Pacific Islands News Association (PINA). Lamani and Eremae paid the money.

Before they left the meeting, Fa'afunua warned the two journalists that if the *Solomon Star* published any more reports about him, they would be in trouble, according to PINA. By year's end, police had made no arrests in the case.

SRI LANKA

FEBRUARY 15

Frederica Jansz, *The Sunday Leader*
THREATENED

Jansz, an investigative reporter for the Colombo-based weekly *The Sunday Leader*, received a letter threatening her for her reporting on Sri Lankan security forces. In the letter, which was typed and written in English, the writer(s) "promise[s] to destroy me if I

continue to write, adding that acid will be too kind a treatment," Jansz told CPJ by e-mail.

Jansz filed a complaint with the Mirihana Police Department in Colombo, and local media reported on the threat. Following the reports, military spokesman Brig. Sanath Karunaratne called her to apologize and to offer army assistance. However, Jansz said that she could not be sure "if this letter is merely a hoax or a genuine threat." She told CPJ that she writes on a broad range of subjects, including investigative articles on the security forces, but also on politics and social issues.

JUNE 25

Ponnuthurai Sathsivanandam,
Virakesari
THREATENED

Sathsivanandam, a stringer for the Tamil-language newspaper *Virakesari*, went into hiding after his home in the northeastern town of Mutur was attacked. Mutur, which is just south of the major port city Trincomalee, was one of several places in the northeast where violent clashes between Muslims and Tamils had erupted during the spring. The attack on Sathsivanandam's home followed an interview he had given earlier in the day with the BBC's Tamil service describing the unrest.

Sathsivanandam told the BBC that he believed the attack came in reprisal for his on-air statements. Sathsivanandam is, like most Tamils, a member of Sri Lanka's Hindu minority. Muslims make up about 8 percent of the country's population. Sri Lanka is dominated by ethnic Sinhalese, who are mostly Buddhist.

AUGUST 8

Thinakkathir
Kodeeswaran Rushangan, *Thinakkathir*
ATTACKED

At around 11 p.m., a group of about 10

masked men raided the office of *Thinakkathir*, a Tamil-language daily newspaper published in the eastern city of Batticaloa. The gang assaulted several members of the night staff, including the newspaper's editor, Rushangan, and seized valuable office equipment, including computers, printers, tape recorders, and cameras, according to an official complaint filed by *Thinakkathir*. They also set fire to documents in the newspaper's editorial room and library.

The intruders left abruptly, "in military style, at the blow of a whistle," according to the *Thinakkathir* account, and drove off in a van with the stolen equipment. Newspaper management estimated they lost about 1.2 million rupees (US$12,500).

Journalists at the paper believe that a division of the Liberation Tigers of Tamil Eelam (LTTE), a rebel group that has been fighting for an independent homeland for Sri Lanka's ethnic Tamil minority for nearly two decades, committed the attack. The LTTE agreed to a cease-fire with the Sri Lankan government in February, but some human rights observers say the group has increased pressure on journalists and other critics during sensitive peace negotiations.

Manoranjan Rajasingam, *Thinakkathir*'s chief editor and managing director, wrote an open letter claiming that a section of the LTTE in Batticaloa was responsible for the attack and calling on the LTTE leadership to "take immediate action to guarantee the freedom of the press." Rajasingam claimed that the paper had received threats in response to recent political columns.

Thinakkathir filed complaints with police, the LTTE, and the Sri Lankan Monitoring Mission, the government body charged with investigating violations of the cease-fire agreement.

TAIWAN

MARCH 20

Shieh Chung-liang, *Next*
HARASSED, LEGAL ACTION
Next
ATTACKED

The offices of the weekly *Next* (Yi Chou-kan) were raided by government officers after authorities accused the magazine of endangering national security by publishing an article revealing details of secret bank accounts that former president Lee Teng-hui's government allegedly used to fund international lobbying efforts and to pay various countries to maintain diplomatic relations with Taiwan. Investigators also searched the magazine's printing plant and the home of Shieh, the journalist who wrote the article. The article, titled, "Lee Teng-hui Illegally Used 3.5 Billion Taiwan Dollars," appeared in the March 21 edition of the magazine.

Police confiscated about 160,000 copies of the issue, according to sources at *Apple Daily*, *Next*'s Hong Kong–based sister publication. Despite the raid, copies of the magazine were available on newsstands that evening, according to news reports. The National Security Bureau issued a statement declaring that officials had conducted the raid and confiscation to "protect national security and ... the interests and safety of our international friends and relevant officials." In response, *Next* executive editor Pei Wei told reporters that the public had a right to know about the secret accounts.

On March 26, High Court prosecutors questioned Shieh during the investigative stage of legal proceedings against him, but the journalist refused to divulge the source for his story. *Next*, a popular, tabloid-style news magazine, is published by Next Media Ltd., which is owned by Hong Kong media tycoon Jimmy Lai.

ASIA

In a related case, Huang Ching-lung, editor of the Chinese-language daily *China Times* (Chung-kuo Shih-pao), was charged with endangering national security based on a similar article about the secret government funds that ran in the March 20 edition of that paper.

In a March 20 letter to President Chen, CPJ expressed concern that *Next* was accused of "endangering national security" for reporting on a topic of legitimate public concern.

On March 26, President Chen responded to CPJ executive director Ann Cooper, stating his belief that "the essence of democracy should never be quelled under the pretext of national security, nor should the flag of national security be used as a cover for undermining press freedom." On April 1, CPJ replied to President Chen's letter, urging him to ensure that charges of endangering national security are not misused in any of the legal proceedings against Shieh, Huang, or other journalists.

Legal proceedings against Shieh stalled after prosecutors were unable to determine whether official documents used in *Next*'s reporting were in fact classified, but the charges against him still stand.

MARCH 21

Huang Ching-lung, *China Times*
LEGAL ACTION

Huang, editor-in-chief of the Chinese-language daily *China Times* (Chung-kuo Shih-pao), was charged in March with endangering national security after his paper ran a story on secret bank accounts used by former President Lee Teng-hui's government to buy influence abroad. The article appeared in the March 20 edition of the paper. Because an anonymous reporter wrote the story, the government charged Huang, according to sources at *China Times*.

The article, based on classified government documents, revealed that in 1994, former president Lee authorized the use of US$11 million from the secret funds to pay the South African government, then led by President Nelson Mandela, to extend diplomatic relations with Taiwan for three years. In 1997, South Africa officially cut diplomatic ties with Taiwan when it established diplomacy with China.

On March 20, the National Security Bureau issued a statement declaring that, "We protest the daily's move and plan to embark on litigation in court." Officials at the newspapers immediately agreed to turn over relevant documents to the police, so authorities did not attempt to censor the publication, according to international press reports.

That day, police raided the offices and confiscated copies of the weekly *Next* (Yi Chou-kan) magazine, which had published a similar article based on the same official documents. Shieh Chung-liang, the journalist who wrote the *Next* magazine article, was accused of endangering national security and ordered not to leave the country.

On April 1, CPJ wrote to President Chen Shui-ban, urging him to ensure that charges of endangering national security are not misused in any of the legal proceedings against Shieh, Huang, or other journalists. Legal proceedings against Huang stalled after prosecutors were unable to determine whether official documents used in the *China Times* reporting were in fact classified, but the charges against him still stand.

OCTOBER 6

Next
ATTACKED, THREATENED

At about 1 p.m. at least 10 men stormed the *Next* (Yi Chou-kan) offices in the capital, Taipei, destroying office equipment and carrying away two computers. Three security guards were injured when they tried to stop the assailants. *Next*, a popular, tabloid-style weekly magazine, is owned by Hong Kong media tycoon Jimmy Lai.

Pei Wei, the magazine's editor-in-chief, has linked the attack to *Next*'s reporting on a criminal group called the Sun. According to a report in the *Apple Daily*, a Hong Kong–based sister publication of *Next*, the assailants were wearing black T-shirts with Chinese characters meaning "the Sun Group" written on the back, an apparent reference to the Sun branch of the Heaven's Way Alliance, an underground criminal group.

On October 8, media outlets in Taiwan received a faxed letter signed by a leader of the Sun claiming responsibility for the attack. The letter stated that, "*Next* has dared to provoke the Sun and myself and should be warned that we vow to drive the magazine from Taiwan," said a report in the *China Times Evening News*. On October 22, police arrested 17 alleged members of the Sun Group on suspicion of carrying out the attack.

THAILAND

JANUARY 8

Far Eastern Economic Review
CENSORED

The January 10 issue of the *Far Eastern Economic Review* was banned because of an article about the strained relationship between King Bhumibol Adulyadej and Prime Minister Thaksin Shinawatra. Maj. Gen. Treethos Ronlitthiwichai, the chief of a police department that oversees press affairs, issued the order banning the sale and distribution of the January 10 edition of the weekly magazine, according to news reports. In banning the issue, which had already been on sale in Thailand since January 4, police officials cited a 1941 Publishing Act, which permits censoring statements or articles that "might lead to social and national disorder."

The article in question was a one-paragraph item in the magazine's "Intelligence" section that commented upon reported tensions between the prime minister's office and the Thai Royal Palace. Much of the information was based on a public speech given by the king on his birthday on December 5. The content of the speech, which was widely perceived to be critical of Thaksin, was reported in the Thai press.

FEBRUARY 22

Shawn Crispin, *Far Eastern Economic Review*
Rodney Tasker, *Far Eastern Economic Review*
HARASSED, LEGAL ACTION

Thai immigration authorities threatened to expel two foreign correspondents from the Hong Kong–based *Far Eastern Economic Review* (FEER) on the grounds that they endanger national security. Crispin, the magazine's bureau chief, and correspondent Tasker, who is also president of the Foreign Correspondents' Club of Thailand, received an official notice revoking their visas dated February 22, the same day that Thai-language newspapers carried stories saying that the police had placed the two reporters on a blacklist. The magazine's publisher, Philip Revzin, and editor-in-chief, Michael Vatikiotis, were also named in the blacklist circulated to Thai media outlets.

The action stemmed from a January 10 item in the *FEER* that discussed tensions between Thailand's venerated King Bhumibol Adulyadej and the prime minister's office. The article was largely based on public comments the king had made that were seen as critical of the government. Officials banned the January 10 issue from being sold in Thailand. The magazine presented a formal appeal to Thai immigration officials on

February 25 in Bangkok, and Crispin and Tasker were allowed to stay in the country.

Thaksin was quoted in the Thai press as saying he knew nothing of the order to expel the journalists. But on February 25, the U.S. ambassador to Thailand, Darryl Johnson, raised the issue with the prime minister in very forceful terms, according to the U.S. Embassy.

Interior Minister Purachai Piemsomboon, who must formally sign any deportation order, told reporters that it was purely an immigration issue. "This matter has nothing to do with prime minister's personal anger over *FEER*," Purachai told The Associated Press. "Please do not speculate that the government has ordered the police to do such kind of thing."

MARCH 4

Nation Multimedia Group
CENSORED

A Defense Department official ordered Smart Bomb, the company that licenses airtime on FM 90.5, to discontinue programming produced by the Nation Multimedia Group. The order went into effect the next day. Deputy Prime Minister Chavalit Yongchaiyudh, who is also the defense minister, claimed that the Nation Multimedia Group's radio programs had "unreasonably criticized the government."

FM 90.5 is owned by the Defense Department, which gives private companies the right to license airtime. (Most Thai broadcast outlets remain in the hands of the army and government agencies, a legacy from years of military dictatorship.) These companies, in turn, hire third parties to produce the actual programming. The Nation Multimedia Group supplied eight hours of daily programming to FM 90.5. The group, which also owns the English-language daily *The Nation* and the Thai-language business daily *Krungthep Turakij*, is one of the largest independent media organizations in the country.

The order followed the previous week's broadcast on FM 90.5 of an interview with Prasang Soonsiri, a leading critic of the current government. In the interview, Prasang criticized the government's reaction to an article in the January 10 *Far Eastern Economic Review* that discussed tensions between Prime Minister Thaksin Shinawatra and the venerated King Bhumibol Adulyadej. The administration banned circulation of the January 10 edition of the *Review* and subsequently issued a deportation order for the magazine's two Bangkok-based correspondents.

The interview with Prasang Soonsiri also aired on Nation Channel, which the Nation Multimedia Group produces for the private television station UBC 8. However, the broadcast of the interview was interrupted. While station officials cited unspecified technical problems, the Nation Multimedia Group issued a statement blaming political interference. In the statement, the group announced that it would cease all political coverage and commentary on Nation Channel pending assurances that its "political news production will be free from all forms of interference, directly or indirectly."

JUNE 28

Ma Tin Win, *New Light of Myanmar*
Maung Maung, *New Light of Myanmar*
HARASSED

Burmese journalists Ma Tin Win, a columnist for the official daily *New Light of Myanmar*, and Maung Maung, an editor at the paper, were banned from entering Thailand by Thai foreign minister Surakiat Sathirathai. The Thai government deemed a series of articles Ma Tin Win had written about the history of Thailand's monarchy to be "insulting," according to Thai news reports. The ban came amid tense relations between the two countries, which worsened in May when Burma's military junta, the State Peace and Development Council, blamed Thailand for aiding ethnic Shan rebels who had attacked a Burmese military base that month.

VIETNAM

JANUARY 7

Ha Sy Phu, free-lance
IMPRISONED, HARASSED

Police searched the home of Nguyen Xuan Tu, a scientist and political essayist better known by his pen name, Ha Sy Phu, and confiscated his computer. Ha Sy Phu has been under house arrest in Dalat, Lam Dong Province, since May 2000. The raid came during a period of escalating harassment of dissidents in Vietnam. Authorities cut phone lines and maintained tight surveillance over numerous dissidents, including Ha Sy Phu.

JANUARY 8

Nguyen Khac Toan, free-lance
IMPRISONED

For full details on this case, see page 416.

Tran Do, free-lance
Nguyen Thanh Giang, free-lance
HARASSED, CENSORED
Tran Khue, free-lance
Nguyen Thi Thanh Xuan, free-lance
Vu Cao Quan, free-lance
CENSORED

The government issued a decree instructing police to confiscate and destroy publications that do not have official approval. An announcement of the decree, signed by Vice Minister of Culture and Information Nguyen Khac Hai, appeared in newspapers in Vietnam on January 8, according to CPJ sources. The new decree established formal nationwide regulations tightening restrictions on prohibited

publications, including those that express dissenting political viewpoints.

According to The Associated Press, a government official named several publications that were targeted for confiscation, including the memoirs of Lt. Gen. Tran Do, Vietnam's most famous dissident. Tran Do's three-part memoirs include his thoughts on the future of the country, as well as an analysis of the 9th Party Congress, held in April 2001. In June 2001, police confiscated 15 photocopies of Part 3 from Tran Do. Part 2 was published overseas, also in 2001, and has been widely distributed on the black market in Vietnam.

Also banned were *Dialogue 2000* and *Dialogue 2001*, hard-copy editions of an Internet publication started in 1999 by Ho Chi Minh City–based scholars Tran Khue and Nguyen Thi Thanh Xuan. The editions featured articles by both writers advocating political reform. Also confiscated were "Meditation and Aspiration," an essay by dissident geophysicist Nguyen Thanh Giang, and "A Few Words Before Dying," an essay by Haiphong-based dissident Vu Cao Quan.

The decree accompanied an escalation in the harassment of Vietnamese dissidents. In preceding days, the phone lines of several dissidents had been cut, while Lt. Gen. Tran Do and Nguyen Thanh Giang had come under heightened surveillance. In August 2002, Tran Do died of multiple ailments at the age of 79.

JANUARY 14

Bui Minh Quoc, free-lance
IMPRISONED

For full details on this case, see page 417.

FEBRUARY 21

Le Chi Quang, free-lance
IMPRISONED

For full details on this case, see page 417.

MARCH 8

Tran Khue, free-lance
IMPRISONED, HARASSED

Seven police officers entered and searched the home of free-lance journalist Tran Khue, also known as Tran Van Khue, in Ho Chi Minh City and confiscated his computer equipment and several documents, according to CPJ sources. On March 10, Tran Khue sent a message via cell phone to a friend indicating that he was in danger. Immediately after the message was sent, all means of communication with Tran Khue were cut.

According to CPJ sources, police searched Tran Khue's house for materials relating to an open letter that he had sent to Chinese president Jiang Zemin during Jiang's visit to Vietnam in late February. The letter, which was distributed over the Internet, protested recent border accords between the two countries. Tran Khue has been under house arrest since October 2001, when he and other dissidents tried to legally register the National Association to Fight Corruption.

On December 29, 2002, about 20 security officials came to Khue's home and detained him for meeting with Hanoi-based democracy activist Pham Que Duong and his wife. The officers also confiscated his computer and computer disks. The day before, Duong was arrested at the Ho Chi Minh City train station as he was returning to Hanoi. A government official stated that the two men had been "caught red-handed while carrying out activities that seriously violate Vietnamese laws." She said that Khue and Duong will be tried but did not clarify on what charges or when.

MARCH 27

Pham Hong Son, free-lance
IMPRISONED

For full details on this case, see page 418.

JUNE 20

All journalists
CENSORED

Nguyen Khoa Diem, head of the Communist Party's Central Ideology and Culture Board, declared that the media were no longer permitted to report on a high-profile corruption case involving a well-known criminal gang.

Several high-ranking government officials and police officers were implicated for accepting bribes from the gang, led by notorious mob boss Truong Van Cam (also known as Nam Cam). Tran Mai Hanh, secretary-general of the Vietnam Journalists Association, was removed from the Communist Party Central Committee after authorities accused him of lobbying for Nam Cam's release from re-education camp in the 1990s. By July, almost 100 people had been arrested in the scandal.

The domestic media initially played a very important role in investigating and exposing the case. While the government at first displayed a rare willingness to tolerate this independent, investigative reporting, they eventually cracked down on the coverage.

On June 20, in an interview with *Phap Luat* (Law) newspaper, Diem said that the Ideology and Culture Board had instructed the media not to "expose secrets, create internal divisions, or hinder key propaganda tasks" while reporting on the scandal, according to Vietnamese and international news reports.

SEPTEMBER 25

Nguyen Vu Binh, free-lance
IMPRISONED

For full details on this case, see page 418. ■

OVERVIEW: EUROPE AND CENTRAL ASIA

by Alex Lupis

WHILE SOME GOVERNMENTS IN CENTRAL ASIA AND EASTERN EUROPE are taking small steps forward regarding the media, 2002 was another dismal year for press freedom in much of the region. In some countries, a growing concern about Western public opinion resulted in a shift from blatant attacks to more subtle, covert tactics to control national media, and a lack of public information and state accountability continued to haunt the majority of the region.

Nowhere was this absence seen more starkly than in Russia, where conflict in the southern region of Chechnya became nearly impossible for the media to cover. The Kremlin maintained its information embargo on Chechnya, severely restricting the ability of Russian and foreign correspondents to report independently on the war's devastation. Journalists were required to travel with police escorts, which, along with the fear of being kidnapped by Chechen rebels, made it difficult to meet and speak with ordinary citizens.

Reporting in Russia was not only difficult, but it was also often dangerous. In 2002, three journalists were killed there because of their work—bringing the total number killed during the last 10 years to 37. Moreover—as seen by the shocking June 2002 acquittal of six suspects who had confessed to various elements of the 1994 murder of journalist Dmitry Kholodov—perpetrators are almost never punished, fostering a culture of impunity in the country.

In October, the sheer level of violence in Russia hit the world stage when a group of heavily armed Chechen rebels seized some 700 people in a Moscow theater, demanding that Russian troops pull out of Chechnya. The three-day crisis had a disastrous effect on the media. As local journalists scrambled to cover the situation and provide the public with information about what was happening in the theater, the Kremlin panicked, and the Media Ministry threatened news outlets that reported on the hostage-takers' demands and the government's sloppy response. The ministry temporarily closed the private Moscow television station Moskoviya for allegedly promoting terrorism and threatened to shut down the Web site of independent Moscow-based Ekho Moskvy radio station for posting the transcript of a telephone interview with a hostage-taker.

After President Vladimir Putin ordered security forces to use a narcotic gas and storm the theater—a move that resulted in more than 120 civilian deaths—the Kremlin set its sights on a number of media outlets whose coverage had criticized the decision. The government pressured the television network NTV, unsuccessfully, to fire host and deputy head of news Savik Shuster for broadcasting an interview with anguished relatives of some of the hostages. Kremlin officials succeeded in pressuring authorities in the autonomous republic of Tatarstan to dismiss Irek Murtazin, director of the republic's television station, for hosting a talk show where participants criticized the Kremlin's domestic policies and called for an end to the war in Chechnya. Even Russian embassies

Alex Lupis is CPJ's program coordinator for Europe and Central Asia. **Olga Tarasov**, who is CPJ's Europe and Central Asia research associate, contributed substantially to the research and writing of this section. CPJ interns **Ana Andjelic**, **Jimmy Manuel Wong**, **Lidija Markes**, and **Aijan Mukanbektalieva** assisted in researching and documenting the cases.

throughout Europe went on the offensive, publicly criticizing German ARD television, Czech Television, and the Turkish media for their coverage of the hostage crisis.

While the Kremlin tried to maintain a democratic veneer over its elaborate authoritarian policies, other countries didn't even bother with appearances. In Turkmenistan, Belarus, and Kazakhstan, draconian regimes continued to use violence and criminal prosecution to squelch unwanted voices. The ongoing repression of journalists in these nations intensified regional instability by denying citizens access to the most basic information about their countries. Press restrictions also prevented citizens from expressing their frustration, exposing official corruption, and encouraging political participation.

Meanwhile, elsewhere in Central Asia, government leaders were busy showing the United States that they support the Americans in their "war on terror." That had some positive effects on press freedom, with stronger U.S. diplomatic and military engagement encouraging authorities in Tajikistan and Uzbekistan to take some concrete steps toward liberalization. For instance, Tajik president Imomali Rakhmonov granted Asia-Plus news agency a broadcasting license in July, while Uzbekistan's president, Islam Karimov, authorized the release of journalist Shodi Mardiev from prison in January, allowed for the registration of the country's first human rights organization, and announced the end of prior censorship.

While these steps were often merely diplomatic overtures rather than changes in policy (for instance, in Uzbekistan, responsibility for censorship was transferred from the government to editors, who are unlikely to risk publishing something that offends authorities), journalists saw the moves as small victories. Nonetheless, members of the media were frustrated that the United States did not push more aggressively for press freedom reforms. In Tajikistan, Uzbekistan, and Kyrgyzstan, whose president, Askar Akayev, has also been emboldened by the growing number of U.S. troops stationed in the country, authorities have used the threat of international terrorism to curb political dissent and suppress independent and opposition media. In fact, Uzbekistan's president continued to view imprisonment as an acceptable means of silencing the media; at year's end, at least three journalists remained incarcerated in that country's brutal penal system in retaliation for their reporting.

In Ukraine, the killings and beatings of journalists and state-ordered closings of media outlets gave way to covert pressure and government directives. In the run-up to March parliamentary elections, President Leonid Kuchma violated press freedom and censored the media by denying his political opponents media access and turning influential state and private news outlets that supported him into government mouthpieces. Journalists in the capital, Kyiv, reported receiving explicit instructions from the president's administration prescribing subjects to be covered and how to report them. The instructions were distributed to all television stations and large newspapers by a representative from Kuchma's office who, when questioned about them, said they were merely "suggestions."

Such methods also prevailed in Yugoslavia, where politicians have forsaken the brutal methods of former Yugoslav president Slobodan Milosevic but have, nonetheless, sought to preserve other levers of power over the press through carefully leaked information and public smear campaigns. Prime Minister Zoran Djindjic shut down the Information Ministry, replacing it with the Communications Bureau and installing propaganda chief Vladimir "Beba" Popovic as its head. Popovic proceeded to discredit Djindjic rivals by leaking secret police files to media outlets loyal to the prime minister. In some cases, Popovic bullied journalists and editors for criticizing Djindjic. For example, in mid-September, Popovic was accused of organizing a smear campaign in the local media wrongfully accusing radio B92 editor-in-chief Veran Matic of illegally privatizing the station. Two media outlets allied with Djindjic, TVBK and TV Pink, gave the story prime-time news coverage. B92 is Belgrade's most popular radio station, and local journalists said the campaign was an attempt to punish the outlet for maintaining an independent editorial policy and diluting the government's influence over the broadcast media.

On a more positive note, elsewhere in Europe, the possibility of membership in the European Union (EU) and NATO sometimes gave a boost to press freedom. Eager for the security guarantees of NATO and EU agricultural and economic subsidies, the Czech Republic, Hungary, Romania, Slovakia, and Slovenia gradually worked toward Western ideals of democracy to comply with the legal reforms necessary for membership. In their desire to put their recent communist past behind them and integrate culturally and politically with the West, these countries moved to adopt democratic media regulations and laws. For instance, Slovakia suspended parts of its criminal defamation statute, making it more difficult for an individual to file a criminal libel suit against a journalist. Some countries, notably Romania, used threats and intimidation to suppress critical reporting that could jeopardize the country's bid to join NATO.

But the concern about presenting a democratic face to curry favor with the EU and NATO during the application processes may have been an optimistic sign for press freedom in the Czech Republic. In July, Czech authorities were quick to investigate and prevent the assassination of Sabina Slonkova, a reporter for the Prague daily *Mlada Fronta Dnes*. Slonkova was the target of a hit man who had been hired by a former high-level government official about whom she had written critically. ∎

ALBANIA

DESPITE SOME MODEST MEDIA-RELATED REFORMS implemented by Parliament in 2002, Albania's contentious political scene and economic underdevelopment continue to make the country a relatively chaotic and difficult place for the independent press. Journalists face government harassment, criminal libel lawsuits, arbitrary dismissal by politicized owners, and limited access to basic government information, particularly when investigating official corruption and organized crime. Furthermore, low professional standards, an editorial emphasis on sensationalism, and the financial influence of political parties over many media outlets mean that journalists have little credibility with the public.

The media and the ruling Socialist Party enjoyed a more cooperative relationship during the first half of 2002, but when Fatos Nano was appointed prime minister in July, he took a tougher stance, instructing ministers to order their staffs to stop speaking with the press.

Blatant intimidation and violent attacks against journalists are less common than they were in the 1990s, when war was blazing in neighboring Kosovo and the Albanian government was reeling from a national scandal over failed pyramid schemes. However, in October, several independent media outlets faced politically motivated financial inspections and government pressure to dismiss journalists for their critical reporting. Financial

EUROPE AND CENTRAL ASIA |

239

inspectors investigated the offices of the independent daily *Koha Jone* and the independent Gjeli Vizion television station shortly after both outlets criticized Prime Minister Nano for alleged abuse of power. Also in October, Arban Hasani, editor-in-chief of the independent television station Arberia, and Enton Abilekaj, news director of the independent TeleNorba Shqiptare television station, were both fired for criticizing the government's response to devastating September floods.

The Parliament pressed ahead with reforming the broadcast media. On September 30, legislators appointed Artur Zheji, a political analyst from Arberia television, to head the public broadcaster, Albanian Radio and Television. He will be responsible for addressing significant financial and managerial problems at the outlet. On November 7, Parliament approved amendments to the Law on Public and Private Radio and Television to create a legal framework for issuing licenses and to develop a strategy to improve government oversight of broadcast media.

ARMENIA

IN THE RUN-UP TO PRESIDENTIAL ELECTIONS SCHEDULED FOR 2003, President Robert Kocharian, who is seeking another term, muzzled dissenting voices in the press and called for more compliant media coverage of government policies. As a result, journalists continued to face criminal prosecution, attacks, and censorship. Meanwhile, poor economic conditions drove some members of the press to ignore journalistic standards and sell their skills to the highest bidder—even if that meant being a mouthpiece for a powerful politician or businessman.

2002 began with controversy. On February 7, the executive branch approved and sent to Parliament a vague legislative proposal called the Law on Mass Information, which would increase state control of the media. Local journalists immediately decried the measure, which, among other things, would introduce licensing procedures and make it easier to suspend a publication. On March 1, several leading Armenian publications launched a protest against the proposal. By the end of the month, the Justice Ministry had submitted a revised draft law that remedied some of the more contentious points in the legislation. The wording remained vague, however, and protests against the draft law continued. At year's end, the legislation was still being discussed.

In another legislative development, on October 23, Parliament adopted the Law on Freedom of Information, which would regulate access to government information. However, politicians, journalists, and press freedom organizations all said the draft was flawed, and it was sent back to committee for review.

In February, the National Council on Television and Radio (NCTR), whose members are appointed by the president, announced a frequency tender, as prescribed by the 2000 Press Law. The NCTR awarded the frequency for A1+, an independent television channel known for its criticism of Kocharian, to a company that allegedly has government ties. A1+ was forced off the air at midnight on April 2. Armenian and international press freedom and human rights groups protested the NCTR's decision, calling it a politically motivated attack on the media. Tens of thousands of demonstrators in Armenia's capital, Yerevan, rallied to A1+'s defense on April 5. The protests continued throughout the month. A1+'s management embarked on a futile legal battle, petitioning the Economic Court to block the tender, citing procedural violations. The court ruled against the channel on April 25. The company unsuccessfully appealed in May, and again in June.

In late April, the independent Noyan Tapan television station sued the NCTR in an effort to retain its broadcasting frequency, which the NCTR had granted to another television company in the April 2 tender. But in May, the Economic Court ruled against this station, too, and the Appeals Court rejected the channel's appeal in July. A group of private citizens also sued the NCTR, claiming that its decisions against A1+ and Noyan Tapan television violated their right to information. The court rejected this lawsuit on September 2, and again in late November.

The NCTR continued to obstruct Noyan Tapan's pursuit of a frequency. On November 8, the council refused to accept Noyan Tapan's entry in a future broadcasting license tender. The television company protested, and in December, the Economic Court ruled in Noyan Tapan's favor, obliging the NCTR to accept the station's candidacy within three days. The NCTR appealed the ruling. At year's end, the case was pending.

The controversy surrounding the frequency tenders, along with the proposed Law on Mass Information, caused the National Press Club, an Armenian press freedom organization, to name President Kocharian an "Enemy of the Press."

In a stark reminder of the security risks journalists face for reporting on sensitive subjects, free-lance reporter Mark Grigorian suffered serious injuries when a grenade was thrown at him in Yerevan on October 22. Grigorian had been working on a highly sensitive article about the 1999 attack on the Parliament, which left several politicians—including the prime minister—dead. The journalist, who suffered injuries to his head and chest, underwent surgery and was released from the hospital six days after the attack.

AZERBAIJAN

DESPITE PROCLAIMING A COMMITMENT TO DEMOCRACY and offering some financial aid to the beleaguered press, President Heydar Aliyev's relationship with the media remained tense in the run-up to presidential elections scheduled for October 2003. During 2002, independent and opposition outlets struggled to overcome official harassment and economic hardship, while the government passed flawed media legislation.

Amendments to the Media Law abolishing registration and licensing restrictions for the print media, approved by the Parliament in December 2001, came into effect in March, making publications less vulnerable to government harassment. But the proposed Law on Television and Radio Broadcasting caused a commotion in the spring over provisions creating a National Broadcasting Council, whose nine members are appointed by the president. The council has the authority to license and regulate private broadcasters and can also petition courts to suspend an outlet's license for up to two months if it violates broadcasting laws. Despite strong international and domestic objections, the law took effect in early October.

Also in October, Parliament passed the Law on Public Television and Radio Broadcasting, which creates a public broadcaster. Under the law, the National Broadcasting Council and the broadcaster's general director, who is also appointed by the president, will administer the new state outlet. The government will fund the broadcaster until 2010, when it will begin collecting fees from subscribers.

A far more direct effort to control the media came in August, when the government introduced the Rules for Preventing the Disclosure of State Secrets in Media, which requires all media to submit information to the Interdepartmental Commission for the Protection of State Secrets before publication. Under the policy, the commission had seven days to determine if the information contains state secrets, rendering media outlets unable to publish information quickly. The regulations do not define what constitutes a state secret, and journalists say that that almost any information could be censored. The commission was also granted the authority to impel journalists to reveal their sources. These rules were highly criticized for violating press freedom and access to information. As a result, they were redrafted, shortening the commission's review period to 48 hours and guaranteeing the protection of sources.

Aliyev's December 2001 decree providing financial assistance to independent and opposition media outlets triggered a drawn-out process. In March 2002, the state allocated US$3.5 million for low-interest loans to these media outlets, which were required to submit business plans and collateral to acquire the funds. Despite repeated pledges to distribute the credits and ease collateral requirements, government efforts to approve applications and establish an allocation scheme moved slowly throughout 2002. Moreover, many journalists were concerned about possible discrimination and the stiff penalties imposed for failing to repay the state loans—three to 15 years in prison.

Meanwhile, the government continued its efforts to reassert the Azeri language. In late September, Parliament passed the Law on Use and Protection of the Azeri Language, which requires Azeri to be used in official work and on television broadcasts. Although the law's effect on the media was unclear at year's end, some journalists were concerned about losing viewers because most middle-aged and senior Azerbaijanis are educated in Russian and not Azeri.

Azerbaijan's journalists continue to participate in regional efforts to promote cooperation with their colleagues in neighboring Armenia. The two countries have failed to reach an agreement on the status of the self-declared Republic of Nagorno-Karabakh, a breakaway region of ethnic Armenians in Azerbaijan supported by the Armenian government. Nagorno-Karabakh continues to function independent of Azerbaijani authorities. In June, the region's self-declared Parliament passed a draft law on television and radio broadcasting that abolishes local authorities' monopoly on broadcasters and creates a public station.

BELARUS

IN MAY 2002, CPJ NAMED BELARUS one of the world's 10 worst places to be a journalist, highlighting the stifling repression of Europe's most authoritarian regime. The rest of the year brought more bad news for the country's besieged but strong-willed private media, with President Aleksandr Lukashenko tightening his grip on power while the economy floundered. Using a broad arsenal of weapons, Lukashenko carried out an unprecedented assault against the independent and opposition press.

Though criminal libel laws have been in effect since 1999, officials used the statutes for the first time in 2002, specifically targeting those journalists who had dared to criticize Lukashenko's successful, but controversial, fall 2001 re-election. Three journalists with independent newspapers—Mikola Markevich and Paval Mazheika of *Pahonya* and Viktar Ivashkevich of *Rabochy*—received corrective labor sentences for libeling the president in pre-election articles. At year's end, all three were serving their terms.

During the second half of 2002, criminal cases were launched against an opposition politician for libeling the president in a published statement; against a woman for distributing anti-Lukashenko flyers; and against a journalist with the daily *Belarusskaya Delovaya Gazeta* for criticizing Belarus' prosecutor general. Meanwhile, a former lawyer for the mother of disappeared cameraman Dmitry Zavadsky received a one-and-a-half-year prison sentence for libeling the prosecutor general.

In September, the Belarusian Association of Journalists, a prominent local nongovernmental organization, launched a campaign to repeal criminal libel clauses and even submitted a proposal to the Chamber of Representatives, the Parliament's lower house. The legislators, however, voted against placing the proposal on the agenda.

Politically motivated civil libel lawsuits, with exorbitant fines, also debilitated the media during 2002. In August, the independent newspaper *Nasha Svaboda* was convicted of libeling the chairman of the State Control Committee and fined 100 million Belarusian rubles (US$55,000). Unable to pay, the publication was forced to close.

Local journalists told CPJ about more subtle financial pressures used to harass the independent press. During an October research mission to Belarus, CPJ found that non-state media face financial discrimination. For example, according to local journalists, government officials pressure some advertisers not to buy space in publications that criticize Lukashenko and his regime. Government officials also regularly encourage companies to pull advertising and threaten them with audits should they fail to do so.

State publications received subsidies and other financial breaks that helped them weather escalating costs in 2002. The Belarusian postal service, Belpochta, which distributes almost all of the country's print media, increased newspaper delivery rates. That charge fell only on independent outlets, as did a new 5 percent tax levied in September by the Minsk City Council of Deputies.

In 2002, several independent newspapers—including *Belaruskaya Maladzyozhnaya*, *Rabochy*, *Den*, and *Tydnyovik Mahilyouski*—unable to shoulder the financial burdens, halted operation. In June, lack of money forced the private radio station Radyjo Racyja off the air.

Meanwhile, Lukashenko moved to strengthen state television—already an official mouthpiece. He announced the creation of the Second National Channel (BT-2), to join the existing First National Channel (ONT), as well as measures to bolster Stolichnoye Televideniye (Capital Television). Lukashenko also reduced the amount of broadcast time allocated for the hugely popular Russian television networks, ostensibly for financial reasons. But observers say the government has been displeased with Russian television, which frequently portrays Lukashenko and his administration negatively.

The July 2000 disappearance of Russian cameraman Zavadsky continues to evoke local and international outrage and serve as a chilling reminder of the scope of human rights abuses in Belarus. Although two former members of Belarus' elite Almaz special

EUROPE AND CENTRAL ASIA

forces unit were convicted in 2002 of kidnapping the journalist, state prosecutors failed to investigate allegations that senior government officials may have been involved. In hopes of finding the mastermind behind the disappearance, the Zavadsky family has appealed the convictions. Although their appeal was initially rejected, the Prosecutor General's Office reopened the Zavadsky case in December.

BOSNIA AND HERZEGOVINA

BOSNIA AND HERZEGOVINA'S LIVELY MEDIA REPORTED ON NUMEROUS corruption and political scandals in 2002, from bomb threats against the U.S. Embassy in the capital, Sarajevo, to the government's involvement in weapons sales to Iraq. The astonishing number of scandals reflected fragile government institutions and the existence of two ministates within the country: Republika Srpska and the Federation. Rampant lawlessness fostered widespread fraud, human trafficking, and drug smuggling. It also kept journalists there vulnerable to a broad array of harassment and abuses, including threatening phone calls and letters, politically motivated tax inspections, retaliatory lawsuits, and physical assaults.

Impunity for attacks against journalists remained the norm in 2002. For example, despite local and international pressure, no progress was reported in the Republika Srpska police investigation into the October 1999 assassination attempt against Zeljko Kopanja, editor of the daily *Nezavisne Novine*, who lost both legs when a bomb blew up his car. Kopanja had just published several articles about Serbian war crimes.

The internationally run Office of the High Representative, which is the chief peace implementation agency in Bosnia and Herzegovina and has legal authority over the country, continued to press ahead with media reforms in 2002, particularly in establishing a national public broadcasting service. That became a politically sensitive issue because of the broadcast media's role in promoting ethnic hatred during the recent war.

In May, the outgoing high representative, Wolfgang Petritsch, imposed 43 different laws, amendments, or regulations that the parliaments of Bosnia and Herzegovina, the Republika Srpska, and the Federation had failed to enact. Included was a package of laws establishing European-style public broadcasters. The statutes were imposed amid a debate within Bosnia and Herzegovina about how to find a healthy balance between public and private broadcasters. The country's broadcast regulatory body, the Communications Regulatory Agency, continued to make a determined effort to consolidate the nation's broadcast market by reissuing licenses based on program quality, financial viability, and technical capabilities. In the process, the agency reduced the number of broadcasters by nearly a third.

In a positive development, *Nezavisne Novine* opened the country's first private printing press in July, strengthening the paper's financial stability and ending the monopoly of government printing presses, which often charged independent newspapers higher printing rates.

Telephone threats and indirect pressure on journalists—particularly from influential political parties, such as the hard-line Bosnian Serb nationalist SDS party and the reformist SDP party—escalated ahead of the October 5 general elections. The Vienna-based Organization for Security and Co-operation in Europe, an election monitoring body, documented one case of physical intimidation and a number of politically motivated tax audits against journalists prior to the elections.

While Western officials had urged Bosnians to support ethnic reintegration and reforms by voting for political moderates, the poll results revealed a nationalist comeback. The three Muslim, Serb, and Croat nationalist parties that were in power when the country's civil war began in the early 1990s were all voted in to the country's three-member rotating presidency and gained strong positions in national legislatures.

Broadcast media provided relatively diverse and balanced reporting on the elections, partly due to strict monitoring and enforcement of standards by the Communications Regulatory Agency. The print media, which are subject to fewer restrictions than broadcast media, covered the electoral campaigns more aggressively and critically. Many newspapers, however, openly supported one political party or another and published stories based on spurious information that targeted their political enemies.

Bosnia's new high representative, Paddy Ashdown, has focused on reforming the judiciary and legal systems to combat lawlessness and corruption. In November, he repealed criminal penalties for defamation and enacted the Law on Protection Against Defamation to encourage greater freedom and responsibility in the press.

BULGARIA

DURING 2002, BULGARIA WAS INVITED TO JOIN NATO IN 2004, but the European Union (EU) postponed Bulgaria's admission until 2007 at the earliest. The EU's decision reflected concern about the country's economic underdevelopment, rampant corruption, weak judiciary, and politicized Prosecutor General's Office. Bulgarian journalists, meanwhile, spent much of 2002 covering local drug gangs and police attempts to control them. Bulgaria, geographically situated in the southeastern Balkans, is a major drug smuggling route into Europe.

Regulation of the state media remains politicized, and in November 2001, the Parliament approved amendments to the Media Law strengthening the Electronic Media Council, a broadcast media regulatory body, by granting it authority to elect the directors of state radio and television and increasing its power to issue licenses. In March, the council appointed Kiril Gotsev, a veteran with two decades of administrative experience at the station, to replace Liljana Popova, a supporter of former prime minister Ivan Kostov.

The NATO requirement that new members restrict access to intelligence information led the Parliament to enact some disappointing legal reforms in 2002. For instance, in April, Parliament suspended partial public access to communist-era secret-police files and adopted a Law on Classified Information, which regulates access to classified documents. As a part of these changes, a commission established in 1997 to screen senior politicians and government officials for a history of collaborating with the secret police was dismantled. This took place while the commission was preparing to open the secret-police files of senior journalists and directors of banks and insurance companies, and to publish a list of agents and informants.

In April, Parliament began wrangling over the proposed removal of Panayot Denev, director of the state news agency, BTA, for allowing the agency to publish articles that criticized state policies. Legislators dismissed Denev in October and replaced him with Stoyan Cheshmedzhiev, the director of a local radio station in the eastern city of Varna.

Politically motivated libel lawsuits and violent attacks continued to discourage reporters from covering sensitive issues, such as corruption. Katia Kassabova, a journalist with the independent newspaper *Compass*, was convicted of libeling four government officials in May and fined 4,700 levs (US$2,500). The case stemmed from an article she had written in September 2000 about corruption in the local education system. And in March, Pavel Nikolov, owner of the independent Radio Montana, received death threats and was later beaten with metal pipes by several men. Nikolov is well known for his reporting on government corruption in the northwestern city of Montana, and, according to several local sources, the attack was widely considered an attempt to discourage both him and his station from continuing to pursue such stories.

While tabloid journalism dominates much of Bulgaria's press, the launch of the Internet newspaper *Mediapool.bg*, which focuses on serious analytical news and updates its site several times a day, may change the media landscape in the future.

CROATIA

THE GRADUAL STABILIZATION OF THE WESTERN BALKANS, combined with closer bilateral ties to neighboring Yugoslavia, encouraged some increased diversity in Croatia's media during 2002. On January 7, for example, national Croatian Radio Television (HRT) broadcast a Serbian Orthodox Christmas service for the first time since the country declared independence from Yugoslavia in 1991. In May, after an 11-year hiatus, Croatia's main newspaper distribution company, Tisak, began selling Serbian dailies and weeklies from Yugoslavia at newsstands again.

And although Croatia has been invited to join the European Union in 2004, powerful far-right opposition, bitter rivalries in the ruling reformist coalition, and a judiciary in need of reform continue to frustrate the country's lively and influential press. The government's tense relations with The Hague–based U.N. International War Crimes Tribunal for the former Yugoslavia dominated the news in 2002. Fresh war crimes indictments of senior military officials stoked nationalist passions and further strained the fragile government.

Throughout 2002, HRT and its two branches—Croatian Television (HTV) and Croatian Radio—continued their lumbering transition from state to public control. HRT faced strong criticism for mismanagement and politicized decision-making. In February, the Croatian Journalists' Association and independent journalists criticized HTV editor-in-chief Jasna Ulaga-Valic for canceling an edition of the current-affairs talk show "Latinica" that dealt with the highly sensitive issue of fascist ideology in contemporary Croatian politics. And in April, the Croatian Helsinki Committee, a Zagreb-based human rights organization, criticized HTV for failing to broadcast a ceremony at the country's World War II–era concentration camp, Jasenovac, after having recently provided live coverage of a ceremony honoring World War II–era fascist collaborators. Slavko Goldstein, a prominent historian and member of HRT's oversight board, resigned in May to protest the unbalanced coverage.

In June, Forum 21, an independent association of broadcast journalists, protested that HTV was appointing editors in violation of its own nomination procedures and called for the selection process to be reviewed. Then, in late November, 10 senior

HTV editors resigned, complaining of chaos within the station and leading the Croatian Journalists' Association to call for Ulaga-Valic's resignation. In early December, HRT oversight board member Jaksa Kusan quit, frustrated with the board's inability to encourage reforms at the broadcaster.

Croatia's judiciary continued to hand down punitive verdicts in libel cases. In March, the Zagreb District Court upheld two such rulings by the Zagreb Municipal Court fining the independent Split-based weekly *Feral Tribune* a total of 200,000 kunas (US$ 25,000) in lawsuits dating back to the mid-1990s.

CYPRUS

SOME 35,000 TURKISH TROOPS ARE STATIONED in the self-proclaimed Turkish Republic of Northern Cyprus (TRNC), founded after Turkey invaded the northern half of the Mediterranean island in 1974. The island remains divided into a more prosperous ethnic Greek sector in the south and an isolated and impoverished ethnic Turkish sector in the north. Cyprus' capital, Nicosia, is also divided in two, with one side controlled by the internationally recognized Greek-Cypriot authorities and the other by the Turkish government.

During 2002, opposition Turkish-Cypriot journalists in northern Cyprus frequently criticized the TRNC. In response, authorities and their supporters harassed and intimidated those journalists.

The daily *Afrika*, based in northern Cyprus, is known for its critical reporting about senior politicians in Turkey, Turkish military officials stationed on the island, and Rauf Denktash, the leader of the northern Cypriot regime. During 2002, the newspaper reportedly received multiple threats, and two of its editors—Sener Levent and Memduh Ener—were imprisoned in August and served two months for allegedly libeling Denktash.

The prison sentences came on the heels of June 30 local elections in the north, in which Denktash's ruling party retained power but lost three key cities to the opposition. Denktash also faced growing international pressure throughout 2002 for obstructing efforts to reunify the island.

Meanwhile, the European Court of Human Rights in Strasbourg, France, opened the case of Turkish-Cypriot journalist Kutlu Adali, who was gunned down outside his home in July 1996. Adali, a left-wing opposition journalist for the Nicosia daily *Yeni Duzen*, opposed Cyprus' division and criticized the policies of Denktash and Turkey. He had received death threats prior to his assassination, and an ultranationalist group with links to Turkish security forces claimed responsibility for his killing. Turkish-Cypriot authorities failed to investigate the case.

In 1997, Adali's wife, Ilkay, filed a case against Turkey with the European Court of Human Rights, claiming that Turkish and TRNC agents were involved in the murder. The case remained pending at year's end.

CZECH REPUBLIC

DESPITE HAVING JOINED NATO IN 1999 and being a front-runner for European Union membership in 2004, many senior politicians in the Czech Republic remain hostile toward the country's feisty press and regularly obstruct critical media coverage of political scandals.

The country was shaken on July 22, when news broke that police had uncovered a plot by Karel Srba, a former senior Foreign Ministry official, to assassinate Sabina Slonkova, an investigative reporter for the Prague daily *Mlada Fronta Dnes*. Police arrested Srba and three accomplices after being tipped off by one of the would-be assassins. Srba had been forced to resign from his position as general secretary of the Foreign Ministry in March 2001 after Slonkova and a colleague published a series of articles implicating him in financial corruption at the ministry. The trial of Srba and his accomplices is set to begin in March 2003.

An October 2001 threat by Prime Minister Milos Zeman to take legal action against the independent Prague weekly *Respekt* for its sharp attacks on government corruption led to a libel lawsuit and countersuit between a Cabinet minister and *Respekt* editor-in-chief Petr Holub. The affair ended in February when police officials and prosecutors rejected both lawsuits.

In an effort to limit politicians' power to intimidate journalists, Holub sent an April 5 letter to Public Ombudsman Otakar Motejl requesting that he ask the government to amend the Criminal Code to strengthen legal protection of press freedom. Motejl did not support the proposal, and authorities took no steps to decriminalize libel.

Nova television reported that journalist Zdenek Zukal continued to fight criminal libel charges filed against him in December 1999 by police officers who claimed that he had broadcast false information about them. In June, the trial was adjourned indefinitely due to a conflict of interest between Zukal's lawyers and the plaintiffs.

On April 16, an appeals court in the capital, Prague, upheld a 2001 ruling instructing *Respekt* to apologize to Miroslav Slouf, chief adviser to Prime Minister Zeman, for writing about Slouf's links with alleged criminals. *Respekt* appealed the case to the Supreme Court, where the suit remained pending at year's end.

Members of the lower house of Parliament prevailed in their efforts to retain political influence over state-run radio. On May 9, the chamber passed a bill allowing it to nominate members to the Czech Radio Council, the body that oversees the state-run Czech Radio. President Vaclav Havel unsuccessfully vetoed the measure on April 23, arguing that the upper house of Parliament and members of civil society should also be involved in the nomination process.

Following the rebellion of journalists at the state-run Czech Television (CT) against management in late 2000 and early 2001, the broadcaster continued to struggle in 2002 with allegations of financial mismanagement and managerial interference in the editorial process. In early June, CT director Jiri Balvin was cleared of charges that he rigged a tender for broadcasting equipment to favor a former employer. Later that month, police opened an investigation after hidden microphones and cameras were discovered in CT's studios. Balvin told police that he had ordered the surveillance to determine if journalists were using CT equipment for personal business. The inquiry determined that the surveillance was legal, but the incident highlighted an atmosphere of distrust within the broadcaster.

Many journalists and intellectuals mourned the U.S. decision in September to end its financial support for the Czech-language service of Radio Free Europe/Radio Liberty and to close the station. The outlet had played a pivotal role in Czech history by providing a reliable, alternative source of news during the Cold War and the decade that followed.

GEORGIA

WHILE CORRUPTION AND CRIME CONTINUED TO OVERRUN GEORGIA IN 2002, some officials blamed the country's woes on excessive press freedom, even accusing the media of contributing to the February suicide of Security Council chief Nugzar Sadzhaya. Public figures readily chastised the press for exposing inadequacies in President Eduard Shevardnadze's government. Shevardnadze himself publicly lamented past attacks on journalists, but the perpetrators of these crimes, which included violent assaults and assassinations, were not brought to justice.

In February, and again in May, gunshots were fired at the offices of the independent television station Rustavi-2, based in Georgia's capital, Tbilisi. No one was injured. Rustavi-2 staff linked the incidents to the station's reporting on corruption and crime, though police investigations have produced no results.

In July, unidentified individuals attacked the offices of the Liberty Institute, a local nongovernmental organization that defends press freedom and human rights, destroying property and seriously injuring staff, including a Radio Free Europe/Radio Liberty correspondent. Authorities detained an extremist associated with an ultra–Christian Orthodox group in connection to the attack, but he was later released.

The inquiry into the 2001 murder of Georgy Sanaya, a popular anchor for Rustavi-2, progressed slowly. Throughout 2002, state officials, including President Shevardnadze, declared the investigation concluded, but they have released little information about the crime. Law enforcement authorities insist that the murder was not politically motivated and that Grigol Khurtsilava, a former police officer who was arrested in December 2001, committed the crime. However, the journalist's family and colleagues believe that he was killed for his work.

Journalists continue to have limited access to Georgia's lawless Pankisi Gorge, a haven for refugees and rebels from the neighboring Russian region of Chechnya who sometimes conduct incursions across the porous border. The gorge remained a point of friction between the two neighbors; Georgia accused Russia of violating its borders, while Russia accused Georgia of harboring terrorists.

Following the 2001 attacks on the World Trade Center and the Pentagon in the United States, Georgian authorities sometimes justified harassment of the press as part of an effort to combat terrorism. In late March, officials arrested Islam Saidayev, editor of the newspaper *Chechenskaya Pravda*, on suspicion of having links to neighboring Chechen and international terrorists. Saidayev's lawyer maintained that his client's contacts were professional. On June 25, a court authorized the journalist's release.

Media-related legislative efforts also made the news in Georgia during 2002. On May 20, the Civil Society Representatives of Georgia, a group of 18 representatives from local civic organizations, released a statement condemning the Justice Ministry's draft amendments to the Criminal Code, which, among other measures, impose longer jail sentences for defaming government officials. The statement also accused the government of

EUROPE AND CENTRAL ASIA

stalling public television reform. Meanwhile, the government announced plans in December to prepare a draft law on television and radio broadcasting, which would create public television, a requirement of the Council of Europe, a pan-European intergovernmental organization to which Georgia belongs.

HUNGARY

AS HUNGARY CONTINUES ITS PROGRESS TOWARD EUROPEAN UNION (EU) membership in 2004, a change in government in April led to the appointment of new officials in charge of public television. Prime Minister Viktor Orban's conservative government, defeated in April elections, had previously used its political influence to pressure the public broadcasting service to provide positive coverage of state policies by, among other things, preventing the appointment of opposition representatives to the media oversight board. Orban's government had also steered advertisements from government agencies and state-owned companies to conservative newspapers, such as the Budapest daily *Magyar Nemzet*.

Government officials, the ruling right-wing Fidesz-Hungarian Civic Party (Fidesz-MPP), and their sympathizers were highly sensitive to critical media coverage. In January, journalist Peter Kende published a controversial book criticizing Orban. A short time later, the public Hungarian Television (MTV) canceled a talk show that Kende hosted.

Foreign journalists were also singled out for their critical reporting. On January 9, *Magyar Nemzet* published a list naming Budapest-based foreign correspondents who were allegedly producing biased reports about the Orban government. A March 4 editorial by *Washington Post* columnist Jackson Diehl stating that the Bush administration had refused Orban a "White House visit" because of his highly nationalistic rhetoric caused much debate in the Hungarian media. Hungary's Foreign Ministry spokesperson strongly criticized the article and denied the allegations.

Although MTV's coverage of the April parliamentary elections was biased in favor of the Fidesz-MPP, the opposition Socialist Party won the poll and formed a ruling coalition with its liberal ally, the Alliance of Free Democrats. Socialist candidate Peter Medgyessy—a former member of Hungary's communist-era Central Committee who pledged to reduce poverty, promote an independent judiciary, and support greater press freedom—became the country's new prime minister.

On May 14, a Socialist Party spokesperson discussed the new government's plans for media reform, including amending or replacing the Media Law, which regulates public and private broadcast media, reducing funding for the bloated MTV, and calling on MTV president Karoly Mendreczky to resign from his post because of the network's biased election coverage. A week later, on May 21, Parliament appointed Socialist and Free Democrats nominees to the public broadcasting service board, ending the era of maneuvering that had kept left-wing representatives off the board. On July 9, Parliament finally amended the Media Law to conform to EU standards, establishing stricter rules for advertising and copyrights.

The new government was shaken, however, on June 18, when *Magyar Nemzet* published a front-page story alleging that Prime Minister Medgyessy had worked as a communist counterintelligence officer in the late 1970s and early 1980s. Medgyessy initially denied the allegation and threatened to sue the daily but eventually conceded that the reports were true.

Meanwhile, a panel of judges continued to investigate individuals with direct or indirect "influence on public opinion"—including senior media executives, editors, and journalists—for prior links to the communist-era secret police. At the end of 2001, the panel said it had uncovered 44 executives and 1,400 staff from the broadcast media with such connections, the popular Budapest daily *Nepszabadsag* reported. In September 2002, the panel prepared to screen some 1,500 print journalists, according to *Nepszabadsag*. By year's end, however, the panel had not released any results of its investigations.

KAZAKHSTAN

PRESS FREEDOM CONDITIONS DETERIORATED SIGNIFICANTLY in Kazakhstan during 2002. Direct criticism of the president, his family, and his associates is considered seditious, and the government's growing persecution of the media has increased self-censorship. Furthermore, President Nursultan Nazarbayev has consolidated his control over the airwaves and newsstands ahead of parliamentary and presidential elections, scheduled for 2004 and 2006, respectively.

Some local analysts say that Nazarbayev expects to face no serious international repercussions for his crackdown on the media and opposition because of his cooperation with the United States in its "war on terror." Kazakhstan has agreed to let the U.S. military use three of its airfields for refueling and emergency landings.

Facing internal threats from an increasingly cohesive and assertive opposition, as well as a pending U.S. Department of Justice investigation into allegations that the president and those close to him accepted hundreds of millions of U.S. dollars in bribes from American oil companies, Nazarbayev methodically stifled any media coverage that criticized him or his policies. Media outlets that reported on the newly formed opposition Democratic Choice of Kazakhstan (DVK) party and official corruption in the energy industry were particularly vulnerable to government persecution.

For instance, on March 5, the government suspended the broadcast license for Tan, a popular Almaty-based opposition television station, for "technical" violations. In the weeks that followed, the station went off the air several times because of damaged broadcasting equipment and was eventually forced off the air until September, when a group of pro-government managers took over the station. Local journalists say the station was harassed for its coverage of opposition activities. In early 2002, Tan had broadcast live a five-hour meeting during which opposition party members and nongovernmental organizations criticized various government policies. The station also covered a standoff between police officers and DVK leader Galmuzhan Zhakiyanov, who had sought refuge at the French Embassy in Almaty. The police were trying to arrest Zhakiyanov on politically motivated charges.

Irina Petrushova, founder and editor-in-chief of the Almaty-based opposition newspaper *Respublika* and winner of CPJ's 2002 International Press Freedom Award, endured a sustained campaign of harassment for her reporting on government corruption and criticism of officials. The newspaper was forced to change its printer numerous times after government officials intimidated printing companies into cutting off their services to the

EUROPE AND CENTRAL ASIA

publication. On May 19, *Respublika* staff found a decapitated dog's corpse hanging from an office window with an attached note that read: "There won't be a next time." Three days later, assailants threw Molotov cocktails into the office, destroying much of the building and technical equipment.

The courts, meanwhile, prosecuted *Respublika*, citing a number of legal technicalities. On July 4, an Almaty court handed Petrushova an 18-month suspended prison sentence for violating a rarely enforced labor code. And on July 24, another Almaty court ordered the liquidation of the firm PR-Consulting, which published the newspaper, because it continued printing the newspaper despite an April 10 court ruling suspending *Respublika* for a minor administrative infraction. Amid growing security risks, Petrushova fled Kazakhstan, but she continues to edit the newspaper from Moscow.

Several other journalists were targeted throughout 2002 in what appeared to be an escalating campaign against the media. On May 21, according to newspaper staff, four assailants broke into the offices of the Almaty-based opposition newspaper *SolDat*, stole expensive technical equipment, and threatened further attacks if the newspaper continued publishing.

On the evening of August 28, three unknown assailants beat and stabbed Sergei Duvanov, a prominent journalist and political commentator. According to Duvanov, the attackers told him, "If you carry on, you'll be made a total cripple." The attack occurred seven weeks after he was charged with "infringing the honor and dignity of the president" in an article about alleged official corruption. Duvanov faces a fine or a maximum three-year prison sentence if convicted.

On October 27, Duvanov's case took an ominous new turn when he was detained on charges of allegedly raping a minor. The charges came just as Duvanov was preparing to leave for the United States, where he was scheduled to give a series of talks at think tanks in Washington, D.C., and New York about political conditions in Kazakhstan. Duvanov denied the rape accusation, saying it was a government effort to discredit him. Suspicion was heightened when local journalists discovered that a press release handed out by police about Duvanov's detention had been prepared by the presidential administration hours before his arrest. Duvanov was formally charged on November 7, and his trial began at the end of December.

Authorities also actively obstructed news and information on the Internet. The online newspaper *Navigator* became inaccessible on May 20, soon after it published an interview with a Geneva-based prosecutor investigating suspicious Swiss bank accounts held by Nazarbayev and other senior Kazakh officials. The Russia-based opposition Web site *Eurasia*, meanwhile, has been forced to change its Web address often because the government has repeatedly blocked access to the site.

KYRGYZSTAN

EMBOLDENED BY THE GROWING NUMBER OF U.S. TROOPS IN THE COUNTRY, President Askar Akayev has used the threat of international terrorism as an excuse to curb political dissent and suppress the independent and opposition media in Kyrgyzstan. Compliant courts often issue exorbitant damage awards in politically motivated libel suits, driving even the country's most prominent newspapers to the brink of bankruptcy.

In early 2002, the private media continued to seek to open an independent publishing house. Currently, the state publisher, Uchkun, prints all independent publications based in the capital, Bishkek. On January 14, the government approved the Provisional Regulation on Publishing Activities, which grants the Justice Ministry licensing rights and limits printing rights to partially or wholly state-owned companies. Though officials claimed that the new statute would "prevent subversive ideological and propaganda work of various extremist religious centers," the independent press believed that the true goal of the regulation was to thwart efforts spearheaded by the international community to create an independent publisher. In late May, a wave of popular protest forced Akayev to rescind the regulation.

When officials arrested Akayev's political rival, parliamentarian Azimbek Beknazarov, in January on charges of abusing power and for official misconduct allegedly committed seven years earlier, mass protests erupted in the southern Aksy Region. After several peaceful protesters were killed during clashes with police in mid-March, the opposition called for Akayev's resignation, while the prime minister and the Cabinet quit.

During this political crisis, Kyrgyzstan's media split along political lines. Pro-government outlets blamed violence on the opposition, while the independent and opposition media faulted the government. Meanwhile, a state commission investigating the killings found that the National Broadcasting Company's "biased reporting" had in part incited unrest. In response, the president created a public council to monitor the broadcaster. In June, the case against Beknazarov was dropped.

Amid this souring political climate, the state readily muzzled the independent press. In late January, Uchkun refused to print the independent *Moya Stolitsa–Novosti*, reportedly in retaliation for its strong criticism of the Akayev government and family. After the independent weekly *Res Publica* offered to print *Moya Stolitsa–Novosti* on its pages, Uchkun suspended *Res Publica*'s publication, citing a fine owed in an earlier defamation lawsuit. Both newspapers continued to post online versions and resumed print publication in May. *Res Publica* was forced to pay the hefty fine.

Meanwhile, politicians and businessmen continued to file libel lawsuits against publications that covered official corruption. *Moya Stolitsa–Novosti* found itself embroiled in a number of politically motivated cases and in danger of bankruptcy. The newspaper's supporters rushed to create the Committee to Defend the Newspaper *Moya Stolitsa*, which protested what they believed was a political campaign to destroy the publication.

One of the most bizarre cases came after State Secretary Osmonakun Ibraimov accused *Moya Stolitsa–Novosti* of mocking the Kyrgyz people's "national sentiment" in an October 4 article that expressed doubt about the officially recognized age of Kyrgyzstan—2,200 years. The government has planned an extravagant celebration of the state's 2,200th anniversary in 2003. After Ibraimov's statement, the newspaper faced a deluge of libel lawsuits from Kyrgyz citizens seeking damages. Most notably, a man named Akin Toktaliyev, feeling that, as a Kyrgyz citizen, he was libeled by the article's disparaging tone, sued the paper, seeking 5 million soms (US$108,200) and 50,000 soms (US$1,080) from the newspaper and the author, respectively. The verdict was scheduled to be announced in early 2003.

Moya Stolitsa-Novosti also faced extensive verbal government harassment for its

EUROPE AND CENTRAL ASIA |

unyielding criticism of official corruption and abuse of power, with the Internal Affairs Ministry going so far as to say the paper contributed to interethnic strife and instability by criticizing law enforcement authorities.

MACEDONIA

LINGERING POLITICAL INSTABILITY, PERVASIVE OFFICIAL CORRUPTION, and interethnic tension kept Macedonia on edge in 2002. Sporadic clashes between the Macedonian government and ethnic Albanian rebels continued despite a peace accord signed in August 2001 to end the country's short-lived civil war, which began in January 2001. As a result, independent journalism remains a tenuous and risky profession there.

According to local media analysts, authorities influenced editorial policies by selectively placing government advertisements in publications that favor the regime. Meanwhile, biased, inaccurate, and inflammatory reporting by many journalists continued to erode public trust in the media.

In the first half of 2002, hard-line nationalist politicians, such as Interior Minister Ljube Boskovski, issued statements and leaked unverifiable terrorist threats—which journalists readily published—to legitimize the deployment of security forces in ethnic Albanian communities that are pushing for increased civil liberties.

Threats and violence against journalists escalated prior to the September 15 parliamentary elections. With the ruling Internal Macedonian Revolutionary Organization–Democratic Party for Macedonian National Unity (VMRO-DPMNE) lagging in the polls, VMRO-DPMNE supporters castigated international organizations, local nongovernmental groups, and the media in an effort to boost their party's popularity, claiming that these organizations are destabilizing and anti-Macedonian.

On September 5, Boskovski threatened to arrest newspaper editors for allegedly "preparing a scenario to destroy the reputation of the current government in the pre-election period." The threat followed the publication of a report by the International Crisis Group, a Brussels-based policy institute, highlighting "endemic" corruption in Macedonia. A week before the poll, rumors circulated in the capital, Skopje, that the police had prepared a list of journalists to arrest.

The ongoing threats and violence galvanized journalists, prompting the Association of Journalists of Macedonia (ZNM) to organize numerous protests. Several broadcast media outlets stopped work for five minutes on World Press Freedom Day, May 3, to protest government interference in the media. Journalists wore bulletproof vests and helmets at a May 20 rally to protest a recent incident where Boskovski, while testing a grenade launcher in front of an audience, injured a reporter from the Skopje daily *Dnevnik*, who was hit with shrapnel.

A week after the Social Democratic Union defeated the VMRO-DPMNE, three unidentified men brutally assaulted Radio Tumba editor-in-chief Zoran Bozinovski in the studio while he was hosting a live program, prompting some 500 journalists to protest outside the Interior Ministry on September 30. A month later, in an effort to improve ethical standards and professionalism in reporting, the ZNM announced that its Professional Standards Board would begin blacklisting journalists and editors who are on politicians' payrolls.

ROMANIA

GOVERNMENT OFFICIALS, WARY OF ANY MEDIA COVERAGE that could potentially threaten the country's efforts to join NATO and the European Union, used threats and intimidation to promote docile reporting—resulting in increased self-censorship in 2002.

In an October report, the Bucharest-based Media Monitoring Agency, a media rights group, noted that press freedom has declined significantly under the ruling Party of Social Democracy. The report pointed out that television coverage of government policies has grown less critical. "Everyone is being told to shut up at the moment, until we get into NATO," said Mircea Toma, president of Freedom of Expression, a Bucharest-based press freedom organization.

The government also harassed foreign news outlets. In May, Secretary-General Serban Mihailescu threatened to sue the Paris daily *Le Monde* for libel in connection with a May 23 article highlighting corruption in Romania and criticizing Mihailescu. Also in May, President Ion Iliescu lashed out at *The Wall Street Journal Europe* over an article questioning the trustworthiness of Romania's former Securitate, the country's communist-era secret police, many of whose members remain in sensitive intelligence positions. Romania, said the president, "does not need the advice of journalists" to deal with such issues.

The president's tongue-lashing of the *Journal* was mild, however, in comparison to an ominous government threat issued to several newspapers that republished the *Journal* article. On May 13, in a message sent to those publications, the Defense Ministry's Press Office warned that "life is short, and your health has too high a price to be endangered by debating highly emotional subjects."

Such threats undermined other efforts by Romania to convince NATO that the country is making needed reforms. In April, in response to concerns of Western military officials, the government approved the Law on Classified Information. The legislation is designed to reassure NATO officials, who are reluctant to share secrets with former members of the Securitate who remain in office.

During 2002, Parliament began debating the Law on the Right to Reply, a draft of which Defense Minister Ioan Mircea Pascu had initiated early in the year. The law would require publications to publish all letters from readers offended by an article. Failure to do so could result in a fine of up to 100 million leus (US$3,000). Those offended by an article could seek compensation through the courts even if their responses are published.

In early June, a 62-year-old reporter for the Romanian independent daily *Timisoara*, Iosif Costinas, disappeared while working on a book about local organized crime figures. Costinas' journalism focused on highly sensitive political issues, including the continued presence of communist-era secret police agents in the government. Laurian Ieremeiov, the deputy editor of *Timisoara*, said he believes that the disappearance is related to Costinas' work.

On September 12, the government's National Audiovisual Council caused a political uproar when it accused the private, Bucharest-based OTV television station of promoting racism and revoked the station's license. The decision came two days after the station, which is known for its sensationalism, broadcast an interview with ultranationalist politician Corneliu Vadim Tudor, who made anti-Semitic and anti-Roma remarks, criticized the U.S. ambassador to Romania, and accused the government of corruption.

EUROPE AND CENTRAL ASIA

Council member Rasvan Popescu criticized the closure, saying that the pro-government bias of public and private television stations makes OTV one of the few outlets that air opposition views. This was the first time the council had closed a television station, and the Center for Independent Journalism, a U.S. government–funded media training organization, called the ruling a "dangerous precedent."

Libel remains a criminal offense in Romania, punishable by imprisonment or hefty fines that can exceed a journalist's lifetime earnings. During 2002, hundreds of journalists faced charges of libeling government officials. On June 25, the lower house of Parliament passed a bill to reduce the sentence for libel from five to three years in prison, but President Iliescu vetoed the legislation on November 1.

The country's harsh media landscape led more than 300 journalists to register with the Romanian Online Editors' Association, a nongovernmental organization that publishes articles on its Web site that other media outlets have refused to print.

RUSSIA

RUSSIAN PRESIDENT VLADIMIR PUTIN, ALONG WITH HIS COTERIE of conservative former intelligence officials, pressed ahead in 2002 to impose his vision of a "dictatorship of the law" in Russia to create a "managed democracy." Putin's goal of an obedient and patriotic press meant that the Kremlin continued using various branches of the state apparatus to rein in the independent media.

Overall, the independent press continued to provide a certain plurality of views, but direct criticism of the president or other senior officials has become more restrained and less frequent than it was under President Boris Yeltsin in the 1990s. And while Putin's administration has demonstrated some sensitivity to international public opinion, this has only resulted in a shift from blatant pressures to more subtle and covert tactics. For example, instead of daylight raids by armed tax police, media outlets now are more likely to be targeted with politically motivated lawsuits and hostile corporate takeovers. Meanwhile, the murder, imprisonment, and harassment of independent journalists throughout Russia's provinces continued in 2002.

The most brazen Kremlin efforts at media management occurred in late October, when a group of heavily armed Chechen rebels seized a Moscow theater where some 700 people were attending a performance of the musical "Nord-Ost." The rebels demanded that Russian troops pull out of the war-torn region of Chechnya in southern Russia. As local journalists scrambled to cover the crisis, the Kremlin cracked down with information controls and threats to curb coverage.

During the crisis, which began on October 23 and ended on the morning of October 26, Russia's Media Ministry temporarily closed the private Moscow television station Moskoviya for allegedly promoting terrorism in their coverage of the siege. And while Anna Politkovskaya, a war correspondent for the independent Moscow-based newspaper *Novaya Gazeta*, was attempting to negotiate the hostages' releases, the Media Ministry forced the independent Moscow-based Ekho Moskvy radio station to remove from its Web site the text of a telephone interview with a hostage-taker. After Putin ordered the Federal Security Bureau (FSB) to use a narcotic gas and storm the theater—a move that resulted in the deaths of all the rebels and more than 120 hostages—the ministry issued a warning to the government-run Moscow daily *Rossiiskaya Gazeta* for publishing the photograph of the body of a woman killed by the hostage-takers.

Even after government troops stormed the theater, effectively ending the crisis, the Kremlin set its sights on a number of media outlets whose coverage had displeased officials. Kremlin chief of staff Aleksandr Voloshin and press secretary Aleksandr Gromov unsuccessfully pressured the television station NTV to fire its host and deputy head of news, Savik Shuster, for broadcasting an interview with anguished relatives of some of the hostages, according to network sources. Russian embassies throughout Europe also went on the offensive, criticizing German ARD television, Czech Television, and the Turkish media for their critical coverage of the crisis.

In November, both houses of Parliament approved amendments to the Law on the Struggle with Terrorism and the Law on Mass Media, which Parliament was considering at the time of the crisis. The amendments banned the media from printing or broadcasting information that justifies extremist activities and resistance to counterterrorist operations, hinders counterterrorist operations, or reveals anti-terrorist tactics.

In a rare display of solidarity, the managers of state and independent media, as well as two competing journalist associations, issued a joint appeal calling on Putin not to sign the amendments. The group said that the provisions were too broad and could potentially be used to ban all discussion of the war in Chechnya and to prevent the media from reporting critically on government responses to crises. CPJ also sent a letter to the president. On November 25, Putin vetoed the amendments and sent them back to Parliament for revision. While the media welcomed the veto, journalists remained concerned about what new legal restrictions for reporting on crises would follow.

The hostage crisis put the spotlight on the plight of Chechens and their ongoing war for independence, which have become nearly impossible for the media to cover. The Kremlin maintained its information embargo on the region, restricting the ability of Russian and foreign correspondents to report independently on the war's devastation. Journalists were required to travel with elaborate police escorts, which, along with the fear of being kidnapped by Chechen rebels, made it difficult to meet and interview citizens.

Novaya Gazeta's Politkovskaya covertly visited Chechnya to investigate allegations of human rights violations in February but was followed by FSB officers, arrested by Russian soldiers, detained on a military base for one night, and threatened by military officials in retaliation for her work. In October, Putin, angry with the U.S. government–funded Radio Free Europe/Radio Liberty's (RFE/RL) increased coverage of the conflict in Chechnya, revoked a special broadcast agreement with RFE/RL, making the station vulnerable to potential legal and regulatory harassment.

During 2002, the Kremlin continued to consolidate the media under the state's authority and that of powerful businesses with links to Putin. In June, Putin appointed FSB lieutenant general Aleksandr Zdanovich, who has criticized coverage of the Chechen war, to the post of senior deputy chairman of the All-Russian State Television and Radio Broadcasting, where he will oversee the state-run RTR national television network.

Meanwhile, Kremlin allies continued their campaign against the independent national television channel TV-6, owned by exiled media tycoon and Putin opponent Boris

Berezovsky. In a complicated financial maneuver on which many observers saw the Kremlin's fingerprints, the Presidium of the Highest Arbitration Court issued a ruling on January 11 upholding the liquidation of the Moscow Independent Broadcasting Company, TV-6's parent company.

On March 27, the Federal Tender Commission awarded TV-6's broadcasting license to a partnership of journalists led by NTV's former director, Yevgeny Kiselyov, who was ousted from NTV when Gazprom, the state gas monopoly, took control of the station. (Media-Most Holding Company, which was owned by exiled media magnate and Putin opponent Vladimir Gusinsky, had controlled NTV.) The new entity, renamed TVS, is overseen by two Kremlin loyalists—former prime minister and senior KGB official Yevgeny Primakov and the influential industrial lobbyist Arkady Volsky. However, Kiselyov and his team have managed to retain significant editorial autonomy and produce fairly critical news reports at TVS.

Novaya Gazeta, which specializes in investigative journalism, including high-profile cases of government corruption, also continued to face politically motivated lawsuits and physical attacks in retaliation for its reporting. The newspaper faced closure in late February when Moscow's Basmanny District Court awarded libel damages of 45 million rubles (US$1.45 million) to a judge from the Krasnodar District Court and the financial institution Mezhprombank. In June, however, the bank waived the damage awards, allowing the newspaper to continue publishing. On March 11, *Novaya Gazeta* correspondent Sergei Zolovkin, who had received death threats for his reporting on organized crime and official corruption in the Krasnodar Region, was the target of an assassination attempt in the southwestern city of Sochi.

In early March, CPJ sent a delegation to Vladivostok and Moscow to meet with military journalist Grigory Pasko, who was sentenced to four years in prison on December 25, 2001. Pasko, who had been reporting for the Russian military newspaper *Boyevaya Vakhta* (Battle Watch) on environmental damage caused by the Russian navy, was convicted of "treason in the form of espionage" for "intending" to give classified documents to Japanese news outlets. The CPJ delegation met with Pasko supporters and government officials to discuss the journalist's case but was prevented from visiting Pasko himself. Although Pasko's lawyers appealed, the Military Collegium of the Supreme Court upheld the ruling on June 25. But on January 23, 2003, Pasko was released on parole for good behavior after serving two-thirds of his sentence.

Harassment of journalists remains commonplace in Russia's provinces, where powerful local leaders and businessmen are often extremely thin-skinned about any critical reporting. When two journalists attended Putin's annual press conference in Moscow on June 24, for example, and posed questions about corruption in their regions, both faced retaliation from local authorities. Dina Oyun, an editor for the Tuva Online Web site, asked Putin about voting fraud in the Siberian republic of Tuva. Subsequently, the head of the local election commission asked the local prosecutor's office to investigate her allegations and prosecute her for spreading allegedly false information. Aleksei Vasilivetsky, a journalist for the newspaper *Nyaryana Vynder* in the northern Nenets Autonomous District, asked Putin about local corruption investigations. The following week, Vasilivetsky's paper, under pressure from local officials, fired Olga Cheburina, the paper's editor-in-chief.

State surveillance of the Internet continued via regulations requiring Russian Internet service providers to install monitoring devices that route all online traffic through servers controlled by local law enforcement agencies.

Journalists in Russia also face violent attacks in retribution for their work, and during 2002, three journalists were killed there because of their journalism. Meanwhile, in a reflection of the rampant crime and violence that prevails in Russian society, CPJ documented 14 other cases of journalists who were killed for reasons unrelated to their reporting.

On June 26, the Moscow Circuit Military Court acquitted six suspects—including five former military officers and the deputy head of a private security firm—accused in the October 1994 murder of Dmitry Kholodov, an investigative reporter for the Moscow-based independent newspaper *Moskovsky Komsomolets*. Kholodov wrote extensively about corruption in the Russian military and was killed when he opened a booby-trapped briefcase that he had been told contained secret documents exposing corruption at the military's highest levels. Journalists became outraged when the judge ruled that the evidence to convict the suspects was inconclusive, despite the fact that some of them had confessed to parts of the crime and that Defense Minister Pavel Grachev had admitted to asking subordinates to "sort things out" with journalists who reported critically on the military. (Grachev maintained that he wasn't implying murder.) This case highlighted the widespread violence against journalists and the culture of impunity that the inaction of the Kremlin and regional leaders fosters in Russia.

SLOVAKIA

SLOVAKS VOTED FOR A MODERATE, CENTER-RIGHT COALITION of reformist parties in September parliamentary elections, continuing the country's course toward NATO and European Union membership. However, during 2002, the government's limited tolerance of criticism, sluggish reform of the state media, and tentative progress toward decriminalizing libel laws reflected a lack of political will in developing a truly independent media in Slovakia.

In 2002, the Constitutional Court and Parliament suspended paragraphs 102 and 103 of the Criminal Code, which pertain to defamation of public officials and the republic in general. However, legislators upheld the constitutionality of Paragraph 156, which deals with libeling public officials for their professional performance. The suspension of the two paragraphs voided a lawsuit filed by President Rudolf Schuster in June 2001 against Alex Kratky, a reporter for the Bratislava daily *Novy Cas*, the country's largest-circulation newspaper. Kratky had written a satirical article about the president in May 2001 and faced two years in prison.

In a separate case, on May 21, a regional court in Zilna upheld a ruling issued by a lower court ordering *Novy Cas* to pay 5 million crowns (US$105,400) in damages to politician Jan Slota for a 1999 article that incorrectly claimed he had been seen intoxicated and urinating on the terrace of a restaurant in the capital, Bratislava. *Novy Cas* has yet to pay the fine and is considering appealing the ruling to the Supreme Court.

Public officials and politicians regularly admonished the media for their reporting, particularly ahead of the September elections. On February 12, Miroslav Dzurinda, a senior state railway official and brother of Prime Minister Mikulas Dzurinda, complained that

EUROPE AND CENTRAL ASIA

media coverage of an ethical conflict related to his own work was actually intended to discredit his brother and threatened to sue newspapers in retaliation for their reporting on the issue. On April 18, President Schuster scolded journalists for providing too much coverage of ultranationalist politician and former prime minister Vladimir Meciar, saying, "It would be good for you to leave him alone."

On September 13, a week before the parliamentary elections, Meciar grabbed, threatened, and tried to punch Luboslav Choluj, a reporter from the independent television station JOJ, after he had asked Meciar how the politician could afford to pay for expensive renovations of a private villa. Two days later, Meciar walked out of a live televised debate when the host asked him whether a businessman had lent him the money for the renovations.

Political influence on private media outlets remains a problem, particularly with TV Markiza, the country's most popular television station. Prior to the parliamentary elections, TV Markiza provided biased coverage in favor of its majority owner, Pavol Rusko, who heads the Alliance for New Citizens (ANO) party. Following the poll, the ruling coalition appointed ANO partisans to run the Culture Ministry—which is responsible for regulating state and private media—raising the specter of a serious conflict of interest for Rusko.

The state-run Slovak Television (STV) struggled with financial mismanagement and allegations that political considerations influence editorial decisions there. On June 2, STV journalists Beata Oravcova and Michal Dyttert resigned to protest an order from STV management to include Rusko in their weekly debate program. On August 19, during the session before the elections, Parliament fired STV director Milan Materak for granting STV managers "excessive" severance packages but failed to select a successor.

On April 1, the government transformed the bloated, state-run TASR news agency into an official government bureau, placing journalists in the awkward position of becoming civil servants who must pledge loyalty to the state. In June, revelations of financial abuses at TASR led the government to replace director Ivan Ceredejev with Peter Nedavaska, a 24-year veteran of the news agency.

In an effort to promote journalistic ethics, on April 10, the Slovak Syndicate of Journalists and the Association of Publishers of Print Media established the Press Council to examine complaints against the media. Meanwhile, on April 15, the country's first Roma news agency, Roma Press Agency (*www.rpa.sk*), was established as a civic association in the eastern city of Kosice to provide more objective coverage of Slovakia's isolated and impoverished Roma community.

SLOVENIA

PRESS FREEDOM IS GENERALLY RESPECTED IN SLOVENIA, but journalists investigating sensitive issues continue to face occasional intimidation or pressure in retaliation for their coverage.

Police have made no progress in their investigation of a brutal, February 2001 attack on Miro Petek, a journalist for *Vecer*, Slovenia's second-largest daily. Petek sustained severe skull fractures after two unknown assailants beat him outside his home in the small town of Mezica in northern Slovenia. He spent five months recovering from the near fatal assault. In March 2002, the Slovenian government created a parliamentary commission to investigate the case.

According to local sources and press reports, the attack stemmed from either Petek's coverage of financial malfeasance allegedly committed by millionaire businessman Janko Zakrsnik, or from the journalist's investigation of corruption in the trucking industry. Zakrsnik has denied any involvement in Petek's attack and has filed civil lawsuits seeking monetary damages from six journalists who have linked him to it.

Meanwhile, the Prosecutor's Office said it is preparing a new case against Blaz Zgaga, an investigative journalist with *Vecer* who was cleared in January 2002 of charges of revealing military secrets. Zgaga had been charged in October 2000 after publishing a June 2000 article that questioned the legality of a joint Slovenian-U.S. intelligence operation conducted during the 1999 NATO war against Yugoslavia.

The new case against Zgaga alleges that his article harmed Slovenia's national security by causing the termination of intelligence sharing and training programs with NATO and the United States. The Slovenian government is very sensitive about relations with the West because of the country's pending applications for NATO and European Union membership. Zgaga refused to answer questions about the case at a court hearing held on June 26 and is still waiting to hear if the prosecutor will convene a trial.

TAJIKISTAN

THE DEVASTATING LEGACY OF THE CIVIL WAR **(1992-1997)** between President Imomali Rakhmonov's government and various opposition parties for control over the country continued to haunt the Tajik media in 2002. Because of widespread poverty—a result of the war and a subsequent string of natural disasters—reporters often work in run-down offices with outdated equipment. Only a small fraction of the population can access or afford the Internet. Moreover, the media community remains small, since many of the country's leading journalists either fled during the civil war or perished in it. (Tens of thousands died during the conflict, including at least 24 journalists.) Scarred by the violent murders of their colleagues, many journalists heavily censor themselves to avoid retribution. And the government's failure to effectively investigate cases of murdered journalists only deepens the press' sense of insecurity.

During 2002, official harassment and reprisal continued to threaten journalists who dared to criticize authorities or report on sensitive issues. Journalists struggled to access information, and some ministries remained completely closed to the press. By and large, journalists avoided stories about official corruption, drug trafficking, and organized crime. Meanwhile, the Health Ministry castigated media outlets that covered a typhoid outbreak in the capital, Dushanbe, and the government criticized journalists who reported on a border agreement that yielded territory to China. In late October, military officials conscripted three independent television journalists in the northern city of Khujand, apparently in retaliation for a program they had produced that criticized the conscription of young men into military service.

In April, Parliament passed a vague Media Law amendment banning repressive treatment of the media and obstruction of journalists' work. Libel, however, remains a criminal offense in Tajikistan, carrying a five-year prison term when committed against the president.

With Tajikistan remaining a base for thousands of foreign journalists covering the

EUROPE AND CENTRAL ASIA

U.S.-led military campaign in neighboring Afghanistan, many enterprising locals have begun catering to foreigners' tastes, even selling T-shirts featuring Osama bin Laden's portrait at a price that exceeds the average Tajik's monthly income. The government's small concessions to the media may be intended to acquire greater military and economic aid by convincing the West that the country is moving toward democracy.

In April, CPJ deputy director Joel Simon and Europe and Central Asia program coordinator Alex Lupis met in New York City with Tajik foreign minister Talbak Nazarov and the country's ambassador to the United Nations, Rashid Alimov, to discuss Tajikistan's press freedom record and to protest the government's persecution of Dodojon Atovullo, exiled editor of the opposition newspaper *Charogi Ruz*. In April 2001, the Tajik government brought criminal charges against Atovullo for sedition and insulting the president in retaliation for the journalist's criticism of government officials.

In late June, in a show of goodwill, the Tajik government dropped the charges against Atovullo, paving the way for his return to Tajikistan. However, the journalist remains in exile and told CPJ that he is wary of returning. "The authorities may allow me to go back, but only in return for my silence," he said.

Meanwhile, during 2002, the State Committee for Television and Radio (SCTR) granted private radio stations Asia-Plus, Asia-FM, and Radio Vatan licenses to broadcast in Dushanbe. Previously, the SCTR routinely denied licenses to private broadcasters. Asia-Plus had been seeking the license since 1998.

TURKMENISTAN

THE MAGNITUDE OF PRESIDENT SAPARMURAT NIYAZOV'S CULT of personality might even astonish the Soviet tyrant Joseph Stalin. A golden statue in Turkmenistan's capital, Ashgabat, honors Niyazov, who is called "Turkmenbashi," or "the Father of All Turkmen," and his portrait graces the country's currency. In 2002, Niyazov's birthday was declared a national holiday, and he renamed the months of the year, dubbing January "Turkmenbashi" in his own honor.

Niyazov's authoritarian regime maintained its iron grip on Turkmenistan's politics, economy, and press. The oil- and natural gas–rich country has no free or private media; freedom of expression and political dissent are not tolerated. The state-controlled media barked and bit on command in 2002, denouncing out-of-favor officials and exiled political opponents while consistently exalting the head of state. Journalists could write freely only in overseas publications under heavily guarded aliases.

During 2002, the government tightened control of the Internet and other outside sources of information, blocking Web sites of an Azerbaijani daily, the Turkmen opposition in exile, several Russian dailies, and the Moscow-based Information Analytical Center Eurasia, an independent research organization.

The Russian press also endured Niyazov's censorship. In April, Turkmen officials seized two issues of the Moscow-based daily *Komsomolskaya Pravda* containing articles by journalist Nikolai Varsegov, who criticized Turkmenistan in writings about his recent travels there. In mid-July, authorities began blocking delivery of Russian publications to Turkmen subscribers, officially terminating those subscriptions a month later. Also in mid-July,

Niyazov closed the privately owned cable system that transmitted foreign satellite broadcasts into Turkmenistan, claiming the system operated illegally. Critics say, however, that Niyazov wanted to block critical voices and foreign and nonstate sources of information.

During 2002, Niyazov dismissed and arrested numerous state officials, including ministers and security officers, for alleged corruption and drug smuggling. He also dismissed the heads of the state's Coordination Council for Broadcasting and Turk-mentelekinofilm—the state television film production company—for unspecified "professional shortcomings."

A wave of detentions followed a November 25 assassination attempt on Niyazov. (He escaped the attack on his motorcade unharmed, although some of his entourage suffered injuries.) Niyazov charged political oppositionists living abroad and a Turkmen businessman as the main culprits in the plot. Leonid Komarovsky, a Russian journalist who was in Turkmenistan on a business trip unrelated to journalism, was detained, most likely due to his connections with opposition figures. Several international reporters and pundits have speculated that Niyazov orchestrated the attack in order to prosecute his political enemies.

International human rights and press freedom organizations lambasted Niyazov's repressive regime in 2002. A report by the Organization for Security and Co-operation in Europe noted that "the notion of freedom of speech is completely and utterly absent in Turkmenistan."

For the United States and its allies, however, with Turkmenistan becoming strategically important in the "war on terrorism"—particularly to U.S. military operations in neighboring Afghanistan—concerns about the country's human rights record took a backseat to geopolitical interests. The United States and its allies have overlooked Niyazov's atrocious human rights record in exchange for getting permission to station troops in Turkmenistan to service cargo planes en route to Afghanistan, and to build a natural-gas pipeline from Turkmenistan to South Asia via Afghanistan.

UKRAINE

DURING 2002, PRESIDENT LEONID KUCHMA'S RELATIONSHIP with the United States hit an all-time low over suspicions that he sold a sophisticated radar system to Iraq. At home, his presidency was threatened by court rulings that opened a criminal case against him (and that were later overturned) for alleged involvement in the 2000 murder of journalist Georgy Gongadze. Increasingly isolated, Kuchma lashed out at critics in the press.

In the run-up to March parliamentary elections, the government flagrantly violated press freedom and censored the media. Kuchma denied his political opponents media access, and influential state and private news outlets that supported the president turned into Kuchma mouthpieces. Journalists in the capital, Kyiv, reported receiving explicit directives, or *temnyky* (lists of topics), from the president's administration, prescribing subjects to be covered and how to report them.

With the Internet becoming an increasingly popular source of information in the country, state officials continued to call for regulation of critical Internet publications. Currently, Ukrainian legislation does not regulate Internet media, as it does other press outlets. Consequently, the Internet is significantly less vulnerable to government pressure and censorship.

Ukraine remained a dangerous place for the press in 2002. Those who dared to criticize or cover corruption or organized crime often faced persecution. For instance, in late January, an assailant threw acid at an editor from the *Berdyansk Delovoi* newspaper in southeastern Ukraine, damaging her face and eyes, in suspected retaliation for the paper's reporting. In addition, throughout 2002, tax authorities harassed, detained, and beat journalists.

The 2001 murder of journalist Igor Aleksandrov continued to make headlines. In May, a court acquitted Yuri Verdyuk, a suspect charged with committing the murder. Verdyuk died two months later of a heart attack, days before the Supreme Court ordered a new investigation into the killing. At the same time, Prosecutor General Svyatoslav Piskun announced that authorities had identified the crime's mastermind, claiming they had a photograph of him, but offered no further information.

Authorities initially made little progress in their investigation into the 2000 murder of journalist Georgy Gongadze, despite the fact that audiotapes implicating Kuchma in the killing had been released in November 2000. In fact, officials effectively blocked the creation of an international investigative commission and efforts by the U.S. Federal Bureau of Investigation to aid in the inquiry. Unable to rely on Ukraine's judiciary, Gongadze's widow, Myroslava, has filed a lawsuit against Ukraine's Prosecutor General's Office with the European Court of Human Rights.

The pace of the investigation seemed to pick up, however, after Piskun became prosecutor general in July. He assigned the case to a new investigative team and charged a regional prosecutor and an investigator for tampering with evidence and abusing their power. The case against the two officials went to court in December and remained ongoing at year's end.

On September 16, independent journalists and opposition members, along with thousands of others, commemorated the second anniversary of Gongadze's disappearance by holding nationwide anti-Kuchma rallies. A Kyiv-based state broadcaster and some regional broadcasters did not air coverage of the rallies in a timely fashion because the outlets went off the air that day for what authorities said were routine maintenance checks. Earlier in the month, Piskun announced that a headless corpse found in a forest near Kyiv was that of Gongadze. The journalist's mother, wary of the findings, demanded that a French forensic expert be allowed to conduct another autopsy. Eventually, the Prosecutor General's Office agreed to the examination. At year's end, the new forensic work was under way in Switzerland.

In October, Ukraine lost another journalist. The body of Mykhailo Kolomyets, director of Ukrayinski Novyny news agency, was found hanging from a tree in a forest in neighboring Belarus. The Prosecutor General's Office was investigating the possibility that Kolomyets had been pressured into committing suicide. The journalist's colleagues believe he may have been targeted for his work, but the official investigation was still under way at year's end.

Mounting allegations of state interference in the press prompted Parliament to hold hearings on "Society, Mass Media, Authority: Freedom of Speech and Censorship in Ukraine" on December 4. Journalists testified about the existence of censorship, including *temnyky* and intimidation tactics. An administration representative denied government improprieties but admitted to using *temnyky*, although he said they weren't directives but merely suggestions. The hearings, while providing a forum for journalists to voice their grievances, produced no corrective actions.

On a positive note, increasing government pressure seemed to unify members of the media. In October, a group of journalists produced a Manifesto of Ukrainian Journalists, which acknowledged the existence of political censorship. The group threatened a nation-wide strike and established the Kyiv Independent Media Union. To date, nearly 500 Ukrainian journalists have signed the document, and several hundred have joined the union.

UNITED KINGDOM

PRESS FREEDOM IS GENERALLY RESPECTED IN THE UNITED KINGDOM, but CPJ was alarmed by a legal case in which Interbrew, a Belgium-based brewing group, and the British Financial Services Authority (FSA), a banking and investment watchdog agency, demanded that several U.K. media outlets turn over documents that had been leaked to them. The case threatened to erode the media's ability to protect sources, and to deter whistle-blowers from talking with the press.

Interbrew claimed that news reports published in November 2001 by Reuters news agency and four daily newspapers—*The Guardian, The Financial Times, The Independent,* and *The Times*—about an imminent bid by the Belgian company for South African Breweries (SAB) were based on false information and caused Interbrew's shares to fall and SAB's stock to jump. Interbrew suggested that the anonymous source of this allegedly false information may have illegally profited from the stock market reaction. Interbrew claimed that the documents had been doctored to make the financial markets believe that a bid was imminent. The company said it needed the originals to trace the damaging leak.

The news organizations refused to hand over the documents, citing their duty to protect sources, but on December 19, 2001, the High Court ruled that Interbrew's right to seek justice trumped the media's interest in protecting sources. On July 22, Interbrew applied to the High Court for seizure of *The Guardian*'s assets. That threat receded four days later, when the brewing company handed the entire affair over to the FSA, which launched its own investigation. The FSA has statutory powers to demand compliance and, if the news organizations resist, could raid their offices to search for the documents.

By year's end, no penalties had been enforced against the media groups, and their lawyers were appealing the case to the European Court of Human Rights, in Strasbourg, France, to clarify the United Kingdom's law on the protection of journalistic sources.

UZBEKISTAN

INCREASED INTERNATIONAL AID AND THE PRESENCE OF U.S. TROOPS who use Uzbekistan as a base for the "war on terror" inspired President Islam Karimov to pay lip service to press freedom. With much fanfare, Karimov's government ended prior censorship of newspapers—one of the few systems in the world that required papers to submit copy to censors in advance of publication. Yet the change was almost completely undermined when the

EUROPE AND CENTRAL ASIA

government subsequently pressured editors to censor articles themselves. Some papers even hired the state's former censors to minimize the risk of publishing anything that might be deemed offensive.

Hopes for more freedom had been raised among journalists on May 7, when news broke that the State Press Committee had dismissed the director of its Agency for the Protection of State Secrets. A week later, government censors stopped reviewing newspapers prior to publication. During the next few weeks, local newspapers began publishing articles on previously taboo topics, such as unemployment, corruption in the education system, and past police abuses.

But the government's action soon proved hollow. At a meeting in the capital, Tashkent, shortly after the director of the state secrets agency was fired, State Press Committee head Rustam Shugalyamov warned the editors of Uzbekistan's six official newspapers that authorities would now closely monitor newspaper content after publication.

Although the consequences of editorial error were not specified, the presidential administration was quick to set an example. On July 19, the editor-in-chief of the Tashkent weekly *Mohiyat*, Abdukayum Yuldashev, was removed from his post for several weeks for publishing an article about press freedom written by Karim Bakhryev, an independent journalist whose work had not appeared in print for years because the Karimov administration had blacklisted him.

Even without official censorship, the country's highly centralized government and vigilant security service, along with the police, courts, prosecutors, inspectors, and other state agencies—all of which remain firmly under Karimov's control—engender widespread fear and self-censorship among journalists, who rarely, if ever, question or debate government policy.

In June, a CPJ delegation consisting of board member Peter Arnett, editorial and program director Richard Murphy, and Europe and Central Asia program coordinator Alex Lupis conducted a nine-day mission to Uzbekistan to investigate press freedom conditions there. After meeting with senior government officials to discuss conditions in the country, CPJ held a press conference in Tashkent to present to the government a list of recommendations for improving press freedom, including the release of imprisoned journalists and the reform or abolishment of politicized media regulatory bodies. Soon after the press conference, which was attended by about 50 international and local journalists and widely covered in the media, presidential spokesman Sherzod Kudratkhodzhayev dismissed CPJ's recommendations, saying they were based on conversations with "resentful" journalists. CPJ's findings were published in a report titled "Back in the USSR."

On July 3, Karimov decreed that the old State Press Committee should be replaced by a new state-run press agency with a mandate to monitor the media, according to local press reports. The Uzbek Press and Information Agency has the power to suspend media licenses and official certificates of registration for "systematic" breaches of Uzbekistan's restrictive media and information laws. It is also supposed to ensure that the government does not violate the rights of media outlets.

Local independent journalists are skeptical of the agency's willingness to defend them, however, considering that its new director, Rustam Shagulyamov, is a Karimov loyalist and former chairman of the State Press Committee.

Uzbekistan remains the foremost jailer of journalists in Europe and Central Asia, with three journalists in prison. Madzhid Abduraimov, a correspondent with the national weekly *Yangi Asr*, was sentenced to 13 years in August 2001 for writing about corruption. Mukhammad Bekdzhanov, editor of *Erk*, a newspaper published by the banned opposition Erk party, and Yusuf Ruzimuradov, an *Erk* employee, were sentenced to 14 years and 15 years in prison, respectively, in August 1999 for distributing *Erk* and criticizing the government. During its mission to Uzbekistan in June, CPJ uncovered reports that more journalists have been imprisoned for their work and continues to investigate those cases. Earlier in the year, however, authorities had amnestied several hundred political prisoners, including Shodi Mardiev, a 63-year-old reporter with the state-run radio station in Samarkand, who was imprisoned in 1997 for his critical stance toward government officials.

YUGOSLAVIA

DURING 2002, THE INTENSE POLITICAL AND PERSONAL RIVALRY between Yugoslav president Vojislav Kostunica, a conservative nationalist, and Serbian prime minister Zoran Djindjic, a pragmatic reformist, consumed politics in Serbia, the dominant republic in the Yugoslav federation. The conflict, which stalled government reforms, was further complicated by negotiations between the two Yugoslav republics of Serbia and Montenegro on transforming the Yugoslav federation into a union of two sovereign states. The possibility that the Yugoslav presidency would no longer exist forced Kostunica to run for the Serbian presidency in the fall against a Djindjic ally, Miroslav Labus. Voter apathy was so high that neither candidate garnered more than 50 percent of the electorate, leaving the presidency empty at year's end.

Politicians from the coalition of ruling parties, the Democratic Opposition of Serbia (DOS), were far less heavy-handed with the press than their predecessors under former Yugoslav president Slobodan Milosevic. But DOS leaders have not hesitated to use subtle forms of pressure, such as threatening phone calls and intimidating police interviews, with independent media that do not embrace their policies.

Limited progress was made in reforming outdated Milosevic-era media regulatory laws, which had allowed large pro-government media outlets to retain national broadcasting licenses. In early July, the government reformulated a draft Broadcasting Law, which would establish an independent broadcasting agency to supervise the broadcast media and transform state-run Radio Television Serbia (RTS) into a more independent public broadcasting service, in order to assert more government control over the agency's executive council. Despite protests from broadcast associations, Parliament approved the measure on July 19. Legislators, however, missed an October deadline to appoint members to the Broadcast Agency Council.

Legislative reform stalled, with the government failing to pass new laws on telecommunications, public information, and defamation. The lack of political will to pass these measures and reform institutions hampered democratization. As a result, journalists reporting on politically sensitive issues such as government corruption, organized crime, and war crimes remained vulnerable to harassment and intimidation from politicians, businessmen, and law enforcement officials.

Impunity for killing journalists also remains a serious problem. Officials made no progress in their investigations into the June 2001 murder of Milan Pantic, a crime reporter for the Belgrade daily *Vecernje Novosti*, and the April 1999 assassination of *Dnevni Telegraf* editor-in-chief Slavko Curuvija.

In May, the Independent Association of Serbian Journalists announced its support for legislation to establish a process for identifying journalists who promoted war crimes and ethnic cleansing during the wars in Croatia, Bosnia, and Kosovo in the 1990s. While the initiative is unpopular with citizens who are anxious to put the past behind them, independent journalists are frustrated that DOS has allowed most of Milosevic's war propagandists to remain in senior positions in the state broadcast and print media in exchange for their loyalty and political support.

Serbian authorities made some progress in dealing with abuses committed against the media under Milosevic. On June 21, a district court sentenced Dragoljub Milanovic, the former director of RTS, to 10 years in prison for failing to evacuate employees from the RTS building in Belgrade during NATO air strikes in April 1999, which resulted in the deaths of 16 people. Milanovic was accused of intentionally placing low-level employees at risk in an effort to increase the number of civilian casualties and discredit NATO.

The Kostunica-Djindjic rivalry spilled over into the media through the Serbian government's Communications Bureau, a public relations office created by Djindjic in the winter of 2001 to replace the notorious Information Ministry. Djindjic's propaganda chief, Vladimir "Beba" Popovic, used the office to discredit Djindjic's rivals by leaking to loyal media outlets secret-police files that contained incriminating or damaging information. In some cases, Popovic bullied journalists who criticized Djindjic. In mid-September, for example, Popovic was accused of organizing a smear campaign in the local media accusing Veran Matic, editor-in-chief of Belgrade radio station B92, of illegally privatizing the broadcaster. Two media outlets allied with Djindjic, TVBK and TV Pink, gave the story prime-time news coverage. The smear campaign against Matic and the popular B92 was seen as an effort by authorities to punish the station for maintaining an independent editorial policy and diluting the government's influence over the broadcast media.

Only foreign pressure seemed to temper the government's hostility toward B92. In response to U.S. diplomatic efforts, Serbian authorities granted B92 temporary frequencies in August, allowing it to expand its audience from greater Belgrade to just over half of Serbia. U.S. influence also forced Djindjic to fire Popovic on October 25.

In the fall, the media largely focused on Milosevic's trial at the U.N. International War Crimes Tribunal for the former Yugoslavia in The Hague. In October, two Serbian journalists—Jovan Dulovic and Dejan Anastasijevic, both of the Belgrade weekly *Vreme*—received death threats for testifying against Milosevic. In a controversial move, both revealed the sources for some of their articles in order to establish that Milosevic exercised command responsibility during a massacre in the Croatian city of Vukovar.

Meanwhile, security conditions remained dangerous in the southern Serbian province of Kosovo, which the United Nations currently administers. Journalists reported physical threats and intimidation from political parties and organized crime figures over reports on human rights abuses and corruption. As Montenegro struggled to decide whether to stay in the Yugoslav federation with Serbia or become an independent state, the media there became mouthpieces for various politicians, sabotaging the possibility of public debate. ∎

| CASES TABLE OF CONTENTS |

ARMENIA

APRIL 2

A1+ Television
LEGAL ACTION, CENSORED

The independent television channel A1+ lost its broadcast frequency and was forced off the air. The National Committee on Television and Radio (NCTR), whose members are appointed by President Robert Kocharian, awarded the A1+ frequency to the entertainment company Sharm, which has close government ties, according to Radio Free Europe/Radio Liberty.

A1+ is known for its critical stance toward the government of Kocharian, who is up for re-election in 2003. The government maintains that the NCTR's decision was impartial. Under a new press law, passed in October 2000, all television stations were required to reapply for their broadcast frequencies. In February, the NCTR announced that a public frequency tender would be held in April.

On April 1, the parent company of A1+, Meleteks, petitioned the Economic Court to block the tender, citing procedural violations. The court ruled against the channel on April 25. The company unsuccessfully appealed in May and again in June. A group of private citizens also sued the NCTR, claiming that the court's decision violated their right to information. The court rejected this lawsuit on September 2, as well as the appeal in late November.

Meanwhile, A1+ was forced off the air at midnight on April 2. That same day, several hundred A1+ supporters protested the move in the streets of the capital, Yerevan. Three days later, nearly 10,000 protesters gathered in Yerevan to demand the return of A1+. The channel remained off the air at year's end.

Mark Grigorian, free-lance
ATTACKED

Free-lance journalist Grigorian suffered serious shrapnel wounds to the head and chest from a grenade thrown at him at around 10:30 p.m. as he walked past the entrance of the Yerevan Choreography School in the capital, Yerevan. He was taken to a local hospital, where he underwent surgery to stop bleeding in his lungs. At year's end, the journalist was recovering at home.

Grigorian told Public Television of Armenia from his hospital bed that he saw "a young man running away" seconds after the grenade exploded. The journalist has been working on an article about an October 1999 attack on the Armenian Parliament that left eight high-level politicians, including the prime minister, dead.

Grigorian had recently interviewed several witnesses and politicians for the story, which he planned to publish on October 27, the third anniversary of the massacre, the U.S. government–funded Radio Free Europe/Radio Liberty reported. Since the Parliament shooting, several Armenian journalists have been harassed or attacked in retaliation for their coverage of the government's investigation into the incident.

The Yerevan Prosecutor General's Office announced that the Interior Ministry has opened an investigation into the grenade attack. Grigorian is also deputy director of the Yerevan-based Caucasus Media Institute, which conducts training courses for journalists in Armenia, Azerbaijan, and Georgia.

NOVEMBER 8

Noyan Tapan
HARASSED, LEGAL ACTION

The National Committee on Television

and Radio (NCTR), whose members are appointed by President Robert Kocharian, refused to accept independent television station Noyan Tapan's entry in a broadcasting license tender set for November 19. The commission claimed the application was prepared incorrectly.

Armenian civic and press freedom groups, as well as journalists, decried the decision as a government effort to prevent independent media from broadcasting their views. Noyan Tapan protested the NCTR's decision in court, and in early December, Armenia's Economic Court ruled in the station's favor, obliging the NCTR to accept the station's candidacy within three days. The NCTR appealed the ruling, which was pending at year's end.

DECEMBER 28

Tirgran Nagdalian, Armenia Public Television
KILLED (MOTIVE UNCONFIRMED)

For full details on this case, see page 367.

AZERBAIJAN

JUNE 4

Mubariz Djafarli, *Yeni Musavat*
ATTACKED

Two unknown assailants attacked Djafarli, a correspondent with the well-known opposition newspaper *Yeni Musavat*, near his apartment in Azerbaijan's capital, Baku, according to Azerbaijani and foreign sources. While beating the journalist, the attackers made references to his recently published articles that contained unfavorable comments about Ilham Aliyev, President Heydar Aliyev's son. However, the journalist told Azerbaijani media that he wrote his last article about the president's son more than a month prior to the beating.

JUNE 22

Elhan Kerimov, Azerbaijani News Agency
ATTACKED

Kerimov, a photo correspondent at the Azerbaijani News Agency, was hit on the back of the head by a district police chief while the journalist was filming soccer fans at the Azadlyg Square in the capital, Baku, who were celebrating the Turkish team's victory over Senegal. According to Azerbaijani news reports, although the incident took place in front of other working reporters, the police chief offered no explanation or apologies and insulted members of the press.

DECEMBER 9

Yeni Musavat
LEGAL ACTION

The Sabail District Court found the opposition daily *Yeni Musavat* guilty of defamation and fined the newspaper 3 million manats (US$600). The head of the Saatli District executive body, Hulhuseyn Ahmedov, had sued *Yeni Musavat* for defamation and sought 20 million manats (US$4,100) in damages after the newspaper published an article by Mahir Mammadov titled "In Saatly the Opposition is Beaten with Sticks."

Earlier in December, the Sabail District Court began hearing another defamation case against *Yeni Musavat*. Azerbaijan's deputy minister Mammad Beytullayev had sued the newspaper for defamation and sought 300 million manats (US$61,220) in damages after it published articles that criticized Azerbaijan's military. The case was ongoing at year's end.

Various government officials have recently filed at least 10 other libel cases against *Yeni Musavat*. The newspaper's staff and many colleagues believe that the suits are politically motivated, and that they are part of a campaign to bankrupt and silence the critical publication.

BELARUS

MARCH 24

Viktor Tolochko, ITAR-TASS
Vasily Fedosenko, Reuters
`HARASSED`

Tolochko, an ITAR-TASS photographer and Fedosenko, a Reuters photographer, were harassed when police violently dispersed an illegal opposition rally in the capital, Minsk. According to local and Russian reports, Fedosenko was forced into a police bus, and officers tore up his accreditation card and his plane ticket to Afghanistan, where he was headed for his next assignment. Meanwhile, police smashed Tolochko's camera. Most detainees were released soon after, including the journalists.

APRIL 26

NTV
`HARASSED`

The Belarusian Foreign Affairs Ministry denied accreditation to a film crew from NTV, a Moscow-based Russian television network. The crew had already arrived in the country's capital, Minsk, from Moscow. NTV's Minsk bureau explained that they needed a second television crew in Minsk so one could cover President Aleksandr Lukashenko's upcoming trip to the areas of Belarus polluted by the Chernobyl catastrophe while the second covered the traditional opposition rally known as "The Chernobyl Route." The ministry did not comment on its decision.

AUGUST 2

Mikhail Padalyak, *Nasha Svaboda*
Nasha Svaboda
`LEGAL ACTION`

The Minsk-based independent thrice-weekly *Nasha Svaboda* and its reporter, Padalyak, were convicted of defamation by Minsk's Moskovsky District Court, which fined the publication 100 million Belarusian rubles (US$55,000) and ordered Padalyak to pay a 5 million Belarusian ruble (US$2,700) fine.

The court also ordered *Nasha Svaboda* to pay for a retraction to be printed in the state newspaper *Sovetskaya Belorussiya* and in *Respublika*, a Council of Ministers publication. The lawsuit—filed by Anatol Tozik, chairman of the State Control Committee—came after *Nasha Svaboda* published a July 16 article alleging that Tozik had complained to Belarusian president Aleksandr Lukashenko about Prosecutor General Viktar Sheiman's professional conduct.

The lawsuit was filed days after Lukashenko publicly announced his distaste for what he called the media's attempts to "discredit highest-level officials" with "false information" and the president's desire to punish those who "disseminate" these "distorted facts." In 1999, *Nasha Svaboda*'s predecessor, *Naviny*, closed after the same court levied an excessive fine against the publication of US$50,000 in a defamation lawsuit filed by Prosecutor General Sheiman, who was at that time head of the Security Council.

AUGUST 31

ORT
`CENSORED`

Belarusian authorities banned the Russian network ORT (currently renamed

Pervy Kanal), which broadcasts in Belarus on the First National Channel, from airing a film titled "The Wild Hunt-2" in Belarus. The film was made by Pavel Sheremet, former head of ORT's Minsk bureau and a colleague and friend of disappeared ORT cameraman Dmitry Zavadsky. "The Wild Hunt-2" alleges government involvement in the disappearances of Zavadsky and opposition politicians in Belarus. While ORT's Russian audience saw the film, the Belarusian First National Channel aired another program.

SEPTEMBER 1

Mikola Markevich, *Pahonya*
Paval Mazheika, *Pahonya*
IMPRISONED

For full details on this case, see page 377.

SEPTEMBER 20

Irina Khalip, *For Official Use*
LEGAL ACTION

The Prosecutor's Office in the capital, Minsk, initiated a criminal libel case against Khalip, a journalist with *For Official Use*, the supplement of the leading daily *Belorusskaya Delovaya Gazeta*. The case stemmed from an article published in the supplement alleging that Belarusian prosecutor general Viktor Sheiman was involved in a bribery scheme. The case was ongoing at year's end.

SEPTEMBER 24

Andrei Pachobut, *Pahonya*
Iryna Charnyauka, *Pahonya*
Andrei Maleshka, *Pahonya*
HARASSED, LEGAL ACTION

Beginning in late September, Maleshka, Pachobut, Charnyauka, and other staff of *Pahonya* were regularly summoned to the local police office and questioned about the newspaper's online version. After the Belarusian High Economic Court shuttered *Pahonya* in November 2001 for libeling President Aleksandr Lukashenko, *Pahonya*'s staff continued to post an online version of the publication.

In September 2002, the Hrodna Prosecutor's Office opened an investigation into *Pahonya*'s online activities, accusing the newspaper of illegally distributing printed materials. However, the journalists contend that because Belarusian law does not regulate Internet publications, it is illegal to prosecute them as regular media outlets.

OCTOBER 30

Mykhailo Kolomyets, Ukrainski Novyny
KILLED (MOTIVE UNCONFIRMED)

For full details on this case, see page 368.

NOVEMBER 26

Mestnoye Vremya
HARASSED, LEGAL ACTION

The Belarusian Information Ministry rescinded the independent weekly *Mestnoye Vremya*'s registration and blocked its bank accounts. *Mestnoye Vremya* had begun publishing on November 1, 2002. Days later, the Minsk District Executive Committee annulled a decision allowing the newspaper to rent editorial offices where it was then based. This decision made it possible for the Information Ministry to rescind the registration for a regulation violation because the editorial address published on the newspaper's pages and its actual address were different. At year's end, the newspaper was suing the Minsk District Executive Committee and demanding that its registration be reinstated.

DECEMBER 16

Viktar Ivashkevich, *Rabochy*
IMPRISONED

For full details on this case, see page 377.

BOSNIA AND HERZEGOVINA

SEPTEMBER 15

Independent print media in Sarajevo
THREATENED

Foreign Minister Zlatko Lagumdzija, who is also the head of the reformist Social Democratic Party, threatened to close a number of unidentified independent newspapers in the capital, Sarajevo, after the October 5 national elections. Lagumdzija made the threat during a meeting between several Bosnian ministers and representatives of the Bosnian diaspora in New York City, the Sarajevo-daily *Oslobodjenje* reported.

Lagumdzija said that "certain papers in Bosnia-Herzegovina will cease to exist after the October 5 election" but later backtracked, explaining that after the elections there would no longer be a need for the political debates published in these newspapers during the run-up to the poll, according to a September 19 interview in the Sarajevo daily *Dnevni avaz*.

CROATIA

JANUARY 30

Srecko Jurdana, *Nacional*
Denis Latin, "Latinica"
THREATENED

Latin, editor and host of the weekly current affairs program "Latinica" on Croatian Television (HTV), was threatened with administrative charges and criminal slander

charges after an edition of the program discussed corruption and inefficiency in the country's judicial system, according to local press reports. Jurdana, a columnist for the Zagreb-based weekly *Nacional* and a guest on the program, was also threatened with slander charges. During the program, Latin had asked whether state prosecutor Radovan Ortinski should resign, resulting in a strong backlash from government officials.

On January 30, HTV acting director Marija Nemcic filed administrative charges against Latin for allegedly violating the station's ethical code. The same day, another state prosecutor, Krunoslav Canjuga, said he was considering filing slander charges against Latin and several guests on the program, including Jurdana, lawyers Anto Nobilo and Cedo Prodanovic, and Judge Vladimir Gredelj.

On February 20, the Foreign Ministry issued a statement saying that the state prosecutor would not press charges against Latin and his guests. On February 28, the Commission for Ethics of the Croatian Radio Television rejected Nemcic's complaint.

MAY 31

Sandra Krizanec, Croatian Radio and Television
THREATENED

Krizanec, a reporter at the Osijek Studio of Croatian Radio and Television (HRT), was threatened over the telephone by Parliament member Branimir Glavas, according to the local press. Krizanec had prepared a brief report for HRT's noon news show about financial irregularities committed during the privatization of state-owned companies in the 1990s. A county prosecutor interviewed for the story implied that Glavas, who was involved in the privatization of the Osijek daily *Glas Slavonije*, had been involved in corruption. Several hours later, Glavas called the journalist and physically threatened her for reporting the story.

Osjecki dom
HARASSED

Approximately 100 members of the Croatian War Veteran's Association (HVIDR) surrounded the printing house of the weekly newspaper *Osjecki dom* for several days and prevented its new edition from being distributed, according to local press reports.

Members of the far-right HVIDR were angry that the newspaper was going to publish a list of the country's 3,300 disabled war veterans, along with information about their disabilities. Disabled veterans receive generous benefits from the state, but government corruption dating from the 1990s has allowed political loyalists of the former ruling nationalist HDZ party who were not injured to receive the benefits as well. *Osjecki dom* editor-in-chief Dario Topic explained that, "We wanted the public to discuss the issue ... and gain insight into how budget funds are spent."

Osjecki dom management claimed that police knew about HVIDR's plans to block the newspaper's distribution but did not prevent the action.

CYPRUS

FEBRUARY 24

Afrika
THREATENED

An unidentified individual called the office of the opposition daily newspaper *Afrika* and made a bomb threat, the newspaper reported. The caller said, "I have placed a bomb in your printing house, but I pitied you. However, from now on I will not pity you."

AUGUST 8

Sener Levent, *Afrika*
Memduh Ener, *Afrika*
IMPRISONED, LEGAL ACTION

Levent and Ener, editor-in-chief and editor, respectively, of the opposition daily *Afrika*, were sentenced to six months in prison for libeling Turkish Cypriot leader Rauf Denktash in a July 1999 article titled "Who is the number one traitor?" The newspaper also received a suspended fine of 5 billion Turkish liras (US$3,000), which the publication will be required to pay if it repeats the offense within the next two years. The editors were arrested and jailed after the verdict was announced. On October 3, an appeals court ruled that the journalists' punishment was too severe, reduced their prison sentences to six weeks, and released the men, who had already served eight weeks in jail.

OCTOBER 14

Xavier Vidal Folchs, *El País*
HARASSED

Folchs, editor-in-chief of the Madrid daily *El País*, and 10 other unidentified Spanish journalists, were expelled from the northern breakaway region of Cyprus. The journalists were visiting the internationally recognized southern half of the island to participate in a conference on EU enlargement.

They crossed into the northern half of the island, which Turkish military forces occupy, to meet with Turkish Cypriot journalists, opposition activists, and members of nongovernmental organizations. Police officers and a Turkish Cypriot government official broke up the meeting and expelled the Spanish journalists to the island's southern sector, charging that the group had not identified themselves as journalists when they crossed into the north.

EUROPE AND CENTRAL ASIA

CZECH REPUBLIC

JULY 18

Sabina Slonkova, *Mlada Fronta Dnes*
THREATENED, HARASSED

Slonkova, an investigative reporter for the Prague daily *Mlada Fronta Dnes*, was the target of a murder plot allegedly planned by Karel Srba, the former general secretary of the Czech Foreign Ministry. Srba was arrested on July 19—in addition to three others who had been arrested on July 18—on suspicion of planning to kill the journalist.

Slonkova has written frequently about Srba in recent years. She told the Czech News Agency that she believes she was targeted because she covered controversial business deals that Srba had made while in the ministry. One of the alleged hired assassins warned police of the planned murder, and Slonkova went into hiding for 10 days while detectives searched for those behind the plot. The trial against Srba and his accomplices is set to begin in March 2003.

GEORGIA

JANUARY 25

Stereo One Television
HARASSED

Associates of Basil Mkalashvili, leader of a Christian Orthodox extremist group, arrived at the independent television station Stereo One and demanded that the station cease a daily Protestant church program about the Bible. Staff called the police, who removed the intruders. However, soon after, a group of Mkalashvili's followers gathered outside the station, threatening to destroy it. Stereo One temporarily halted the offending television program.

FEBRUARY 19

"60 Minutes," Rustavi 2
ATTACKED

Gunshots were fired in the middle of the night at the offices of the Tbilisi-based independent television station Rustavi-2. According to Georgian and international sources, a bullet was fired through the 16th floor window of the office of Rustavi-2's "60 Minutes" program. No one was injured. Rustavi-2 staff believe that the actions were intended to intimidate the station, which is known for its investigative reporting on official corruption and criticism of government authorities. The police investigation into the attack produced no results.

MARCH 31

Islam Saidayev, *Chechenskaya Pravda*
LEGAL ACTION

In late March, Georgian authorities arrested Islam Saidayev, a Chechen journalist and a naturalized Georgian citizen who is editor-in-chief of the newspaper *Chechenskaya Pravda*, on suspicion of connection to terrorists, including a Chechen field commander and al-Qaeda members. The journalist's lawyer maintains that Saidayev's contacts with Chechen rebels were related to his professional work. On June 25, Saidayev was released when a court in the capital, Tbilisi, ruled that there was insufficient evidence to warrant his detention.

MAY 14

Rustavi-2
ATTACKED

Shots were fired at the offices of the Tbilisi-based independent television station Rustavi-2, according to Georgian and international reports. A few of the station's staff were in the room when the shot was fired, but no one was hurt. Rustavi-2 staff believe that the attack was designed to intimidate the station, which is known for its investigative reporting on official corruption and criticism of government authorities. The police investigation into the attack produced no results.

THE HAGUE

DECEMBER 11

Jonathan C. Randal, *The Washington Post*
LEGAL ACTION

The U.N. International War Crimes Tribunal for the Former Yugoslavia in The Hague (ICTY) ruled to limit compelled testimony from war correspondents. The decision, announced at the tribunal's Appeals Chamber, came in response to the appeal by former *Washington Post* reporter Jonathan C. Randal, who had been subpoenaed to testify in the case of former Bosnian-Serb housing minister Radoslav Brdjanin, who is facing charges of genocide because of his alleged role in the persecution and expulsion of more than 100,000 non-Serbs during the Bosnian war. The subpoena against Randal was set aside, and he is no longer required to testify.

Randal had quoted Brdjanin in a 1993 article as saying that "those unwilling to defend [Bosnian-Serb territory] must be moved out" to create "an ethnically clean space." After Randal declined to testify voluntarily, the ICTY's Prosecutor's Office requested a subpoena to compel Randal to do so, claiming that the information he could provide was "pertinent" to the prosecution.

Randal challenged the subpoena, but the lower court upheld it on June 7. He then took his case to the Appeals Chamber,

which heard oral arguments on October 3. Lawyers for Randal, including noted U.S. First Amendment attorney Floyd Abrams, argued that routinely compelling the press to testify could undermine the ability of journalists to work in war zones. An amicus brief signed by 34 media outlets and press freedom organizations, including CPJ, argued that journalists should only be compelled to testify in circumstances where their testimony is "absolutely essential to the case" and "the information cannot be obtained by other means."

The Appeals Chamber largely agreed, noting that "if war correspondents were to be perceived as potential witnesses for the Prosecution ... war correspondents may shift from being observers of those committing human rights violations to being their targets." Because of this risk, the Appeals Chamber ruled that journalists should only be compelled to testify when "the evidence sought is of direct and important value in determining a core issue in the case ... and cannot reasonably be obtained elsewhere."

The Appeals Chamber said that the prosecutor could request that the lower court issue a new subpoena for Randal, applying the standard that they had articulated in the December 11 decision.

KAZAKHSTAN

MARCH 5

TAN TV
LEGAL ACTION, CENSORED

The Ministry of Transportation and Communications announced that it had suspended the license of the Almaty-based opposition TAN TV for six months, according to international press reports. Several days prior to the suspension, Tan TV had

EUROPE AND CENTRAL ASIA

277

broadcast a statement from several local parliamentarians who criticized President Nursultan Nazarbayev for transferring state funds to a secret Swiss bank account, the online independent newspaper *Navigator* reported.

The ministry, however, claimed that the suspension was due to the station's faulty transmitter, improper registration of equipment, poor sanitary conditions, and violations of a language law requiring media outlets to broadcast at least half of their material in Kazakh.

MARCH 6

Nachnyom s Ponedelnika
LEGAL ACTION

The Bostandyk District Court found the Almaty-based weekly *Nachnyom s Ponedelnika* guilty of not publishing a proper masthead and ordered the paper to suspend publication for three months, according to local press reports. The verdict came in retaliation for a March 1 live telephone interview the newspaper had conducted between journalists, politicians, and the exiled former prime minister Akezhan Kazhegeldin, a frequent critic of President Nursultan Nazarbayev, the BBC reported.

The state-run Kazakh telephone company cut off the interview, and all the newspaper's telephone lines stopped working. On March 13, officials from the Bostandyk District Court sealed off the paper's office.

MARCH 8

Irina Petrushova, *Delovoye Obozreniye Respublika*
THREATENED

Petrushova, founder and editor-in-chief of *Delovoye Obozreniye Respublika*, an opposition newspaper based in the southern city of Almaty, received a funeral wreath from an anonymous sender. Journalists at the newspaper, which is known for its critical coverage of the Kazakh government, believe that the threat was politically motivated.

MARCH 11

Bakhytzhan Ketebayev, Tan TV
LEGAL ACTION

Ketebayev, president of the opposition Tan TV, was found guilty of violating copyright laws and ordered to pay an 8,000 tenge (US$53) fine by the Almaty City Court, the BBC reported. The court ruled that Tan TV showed two Russian movies without copyright permission, even though Ketebayev provided documentary evidence that the station had obtained permission from a Moscow-based film distribution company. According to Kazakh sources, the verdict came in retaliation for Tan TV's critical coverage of the government.

MARCH 27

TAN TV
HARASSED

TAN TV was forced off the air in the early morning hours after unidentified individuals shot nine holes through the station's transmission cable with a rifle, according to international press reports. Journalists from TAN found several empty cartridges near the cable later that morning.

APRIL 2

Ruslan Tairov, TAN TV
ATTACKED

Tairov, a cameraman for the opposition TAN TV, was beaten by a group of unidentified individuals after he began filming police officers who were beating an unidentified cameraman from Irbis Television. Tairov was later hospitalized. The journalists were filming the arrest of the wife of an opposition leader during a standoff at the French Embassy in Almaty, according to local press reports. Officers also confiscated the Irbis cameraman's videotape and damaged his camera.

MAY 15

TAN TV
HARASSED

Unidentified vandals damaged the opposition TAN TV's newly installed transmitter and pierced the transmission cable with a nail, disrupting the station's broadcasting, the BBC reported. On June 18, TAN TV held a press conference to announce that the Ministry of Transportation and Communications had refused to reissue the station a permit to go back on the air. However, according to the online independent newspaper *Navigator*, TAN TV began broadcasting again on September 23, after a new pro-government team took over the station's management.

MAY 19

Delovoye Obozreniye Respublika
THREATENED

Staff at the opposition newspaper *Delovoye Obozreniye Respublika* found a decapitated dog's corpse hanging from an office window with an attached note that read, "There won't be a next time," according to journalists in Almaty. The following day, Irina Petrushova, the paper's founder and editor-in-chief, found the dog's head in the building's yard. Journalists at the newspaper, which is known for its critical coverage of the Kazakh govern-

ment, believe that the threats were politically motivated.

MAY 21

Bakhytgul Makinbai, *SolDat*
SolDat
ATTACKED

Makinbai, a correspondent with the Almaty opposition newspaper *SolDat*, and Kenzhe Aitpakiyev, a staff member, were assaulted by four assailants who broke into the paper's offices. According to the two victims, the assailants beat them, stole expensive technical equipment, and threatened further attacks if the newspaper continued publishing. Journalists at the newspaper, which is known for its critical coverage of the Kazakh government, believe that the attack was politically motivated. Police are investigating the incident, but no progress had been reported by year's end.

MAY 22

Delovoye Obozreniye Respublika
ATTACKED

Assailants threw Molotov cocktails into the office windows of *Delovoye Obozreniye Respublika*, an opposition newspaper based in the southern city of Almaty. No one was injured in the attack, but the resulting fire destroyed much of the office, including the publication's technical equipment. Police opened an investigation into the incident and in July claimed that *Delovoye Obozreniye Respublika* publisher, Muratbek Ketebayev, had hired two young men to set fire to his own newspaper. The Interior Ministry never charged Ketebayev, and local human rights activists have criticized the police for violating administrative procedures during the inquiry.

July 9

Sergei Duvanov, free-lance
`LEGAL ACTION`

Duvanov, who writes for several Web sites financed by Kazakhstan's political opposition, was summoned to the Almaty office of the National Security Committee, or the KNB, the successor to the KGB, where he was informed that the General Prosecutor's Office had filed criminal charges against him for "infringing the honor and dignity of the president." Under Article 318 of the Kazakh Criminal Code, the charge carries a hefty fine or a maximum three-year prison sentence.

The charges stemmed from a May 6, 2002, article titled "Silence of the Lambs," which was published on the opposition Web site *www.kub.kz*. The article repeated allegations published by other media outlets, including some in the United States, claiming that Nazarbayev and his associates were attempting to cover up illegal profits from oil deals. The report also questioned the legality of the president's actions in diverting US$1 billion to a Swiss bank account in 1996.

Following the July 9 interrogation, investigators searched Duvanov's apartment and office and confiscated two computer hard drives, along with several articles and other documents. On July 11, the journalist was summoned to the KNB office in Almaty for a second interrogation, which lasted nearly four hours. According to the opposition party Democratic Choice of Kazakhstan, authorities have not pursued these charges, though the case remained open at year's end.

July 24

Delovoye Obozreniye Respublika
`HARASSED`

The Almaty Inter-District Economic Court ordered the liquidation of the firm PR-Consulting, which publishes the opposition newspaper *Delovoye Obozreniye Respublika*. The court found that PR-Consulting had continued to publish the paper despite an April 10 court ruling that suspended the newspaper for allegedly violating administrative regulations, namely failing to display the registration date and certificate number on the weekly's pages.

August 16

Artur Platonov, KTK
`ATTACKED`

Platonov, the well-known host of the weekly television program "Portrait of the Week" on the private station KTK, was brutally assaulted by three assailants as he was driving home. The journalist was hospitalized with a broken nose and contusions. The suspected attackers, three former police officers, were detained and questioned the night of the attack but were later released.

The journalist's colleagues believe the attack is connected to Platonov's work. "Portrait of the Week" often criticizes Kazakh police and government authorities, and Platonov has received numerous threats in the past. The suspects maintain, however, that they stopped Platonov because he was driving recklessly, and that they used force after the journalist sprayed them with mace. Platonov says he used the spray in self-defense.

August 28

Sergei Duvanov, free-lance
`ATTACKED`

Duvanov, a free-lancer who writes for opposition-financed Web sites, was severely beaten while returning to his home in Almaty at around 9:45 p.m. He took the elevator to his fourth floor apartment, where he was attacked by three men with clubs as he stepped on to the landing, said CPJ sources. Because there are no lights in the stairwell, he was unable to identify his attackers. When the men left, a neighbor called an ambulance, and the journalist was taken to the hospital.

At a September 29 press conference, Duvanov's colleagues at the Kazakhstan Bureau for Human Rights and the Rule of Law—where he works as the editor-in-chief of the organization's bulletin, *Human Rights in Kazakhstan and the World*—were told that in addition to severe bruising and a concussion, Duvanov suffered light knife wounds to his arms and chest. He also had difficulty speaking and lifting his head.

Duvanov said that in response to his question, "Why are you beating me?" one of his attackers said, "You know why. And if you carry on, you'll be made a total cripple." Police, who are investigating the attack, visited the journalist in the hospital and reportedly took his notebook and cell phone. No progress in the case had been reported by year's end. Kazakh authorities have frequently harassed Duvanov, a political commentator who is well known for his critical analyses of political conditions in the country.

OCTOBER 27

Sergei Duvanov, *Prava Cheloveka v Kazakhstane i Mire*
IMPRISONED
For full details on this case, see page 401.

DECEMBER 7

Assandi Times
CENSORED
Early in the morning, a group of police officers and officials from the KNB security service confiscated 1,000 copies of the pro-opposition *Assandi Times* newspaper without explanation at the airport in the northern city of Pavlodar. The newspapers had arrived by plane from Almaty, where the paper is based. Marat Tulindinov, a local representative of Democratic Choice of Kazakhstan opposition party, arrived at the airport to pick up the newspapers, but the officials informed him that they had already taken the publication.

KYRGYZSTAN

JANUARY 19

Moya Stolitsa–Novosti
HARASSED, LEGAL ACTION, CENSORED
The Uchkun Publishing House, a state-run monopoly, ceased printing the independent daily *Moya Stolitsa–Novosti*, citing lack of contract for the year 2002. The popular newspaper is known for its criticism of official corruption and abuse of power. The newspaper sued the publisher, and on January 29, a Bishkek court ordered Uchkun to print *Moya Stolitsa–Novosti* until the legal case against Uchkun is heard in court. However, a few days later, on February 4, the same court reversed that ruling.

Another publication, the independent weekly *Res Publica*, offered to print *Moya Stolitsa–Novosti* on its pages beginning on January 22, but Uchkun soon refused to print *Res Publica*. Both newspapers continued to post online versions.

Sources at *Moya Stolitsa–Novosti* told CPJ that on May 3, Uchkun announced that it was ready to resume printing the newspaper, but only after *Moya Stolitsa–Novosti* withdrew its January lawsuit against the publisher. The newspaper refused. Uchkun began printing

EUROPE AND CENTRAL ASIA

the publication again on May 22, after reaching an agreement with *Moya Stolitsa–Novosti* editor-in-chief Aleksandr Kim.

JANUARY 21

Res Publica
HARASSED, LEGAL ACTION

After the Uchkun Publishing House refused on January 19 to print an independent daily *Moya Stolitsa–Novosti*, the independent weekly *Res Publica* offered to print the newspaper on its pages. As a result, *Moya Stolitsa–Novosti* transferred its paper stock to *Res Publica* and notified Uchkun in a letter. However, Uchkun suspended *Res Publica*'s printing, citing a fine owed in an earlier defamation lawsuit. The newspaper continued to post an online version. In early May, *Res Publica* resumed publication, after paying a hefty fine.

DECEMBER 31

Lyudmila Zholmukhamedova, *Moya Stolitsa–Novosti*
Moya Stolitsa–Novosti
LEGAL ACTION

In late December, Akin Toktaliyev, who claimed to be a private citizen with no government connections, sued *Moya Stolitsa–Novosti* for defamation. He said he was defamed by an October 4 article by Zholmukhamedova, which expressed skepticism about the officially recognized age of Kyrgyzstan's statehood—2,200 years. The government has planned an extravagant celebration of the anniversary in 2003.

Toktaliyev claimed that, as a Kyrgyz citizen, he was defamed by the article's demeaning tone. He sought 5 million soms (US$108,220) from the paper and 50,000 soms (US$1,080) from Zholmukhamedova in damages. The lawsuit came after

State Secretary Osmonakun Ibraimov accused the paper of mocking the Kyrgyz people's "national sentiment" in the October 4 article. At year's end, the case was ongoing.

MACEDONIA

JULY 16

Mare Stoilova, A1 Television
ATTACKED

Stoilova, a reporter with A1 Television, was attacked by a group of unidentified men who also damaged her car while she was in the southeastern town of Stip covering the funeral of a young man who had been beaten to death in a bar brawl, according to local press reports. The men said they were angered by A1's coverage of the bar fight, during which members of the Tigers Unit of the Special Forces Police had killed the young man. After Stoilova fled to her car, the men followed her, smashing the windows and the vehicle, according to the London-based Institute for War and Peace Reporting. Police questioned three suspects but arrested no one.

JULY 31

Simon Ilievski, *Utrinski Vestnik*, Kanal 5
ATTACKED, THREATENED

Ilievski, a reporter with the Skopje-based opposition daily *Utrinski Vestnik* and the Skopje-based Kanal 5 television station, was attacked while having dinner in a restaurant in the southern Macedonian city of Ohrid, according to local sources and the London-based Institute for War and Peace Reporting. An unknown assailant threw a full bottle of beer at Ilievski, striking him in the head, then threatened to cut the journalist's throat with the broken glass and told him never to mention the prime minister again in any of his reports. Ilievski linked the attack to his recent criticism of the ruling VMRO-DPMNE party.

SEPTEMBER 6

Marjan Djurovski, *Start*
LEGAL ACTION

The Interior Ministry filed criminal libel charges against Djurovski, a journalist with the weekly magazine *Start*, which is based in the Macedonian capital, Skopje. The ministry also stated that additional steps would be taken against other local journalists. According to the Interior Ministry, the charges stemmed from an article by Djurovski in the September 6 issue of *Start* claiming that the government was prepared to start a war to delay the September 15 parliamentary elections.

SEPTEMBER 10

Ljupco Palevski, *Global, Start*
ATTACKED

The car of Palevski, who owns the bilingual Macedonian- and Albanian-language daily *Global* and the Macedonian-language weekly *Start*, was destroyed by a Molotov cocktail late in the evening. Sources at *Global* suspect that the attack came in reprisal for an article the paper had published earlier that day claiming that the government was planning to use the "Lions," a unit of the Interior Ministry Special Forces, to disrupt campaigning for the September 15 national elections.

That same night, unknown assailants fired on the BRO printing house, which publishes *Global*. The bullets damaged the building and delayed the publication of *Global*'s next edition, but no one was injured.

SEPTEMBER 24

Redzo Balic, Radio Tumba
Zoran Bozinovski, Radio Tumba
ATTACKED, HARRASSED

Bozinovski, editor-in-chief of Radio Tumba, and Balic, a journalist at the station, were attacked by three men who forced themselves into the station's offices while the journalists were hosting a live program, the Skopje-based Macedonian Institute for the Media reported. First, the assailants put the barrel of a rifle in Balic's mouth and threatened him. Then they attacked Bozinovski, hitting him on the head with the rifle butt and a crowbar.

The three men fled the scene in an unlicensed white Volkswagen Golf. Bozinovski said the attack came in retaliation for the station's reports on alleged corruption and criminal activity committed by local authorities who belong to the right-wing nationalist VMRO-DPMNE party.

MOLDOVA

MARCH 11

Larisa Manole, Teleradio-Moldova
Dinu Rusnac, Teleradio-Moldova
HARASSED

News anchors Manole and Rusnac were dismissed from the Communist Party–controlled state broadcaster Teleradio-Moldova (TVM) because of "technical errors" and Rusnac's incomplete contract, according to TVM management. Moldovan sources indicated, however, that the journalists were fired for actively protesting state censorship at the station. Several of TVM's technical staff were also dismissed or reprimanded at the same time for protesting censorship at TVM, according to Moldovan reports.

EUROPE AND CENTRAL ASIA

MARCH 14

Ana Bradu-Josanu, Teleradio-Moldova
Aurelia Vasilica, Teleradio-Moldova
HARASSED

Bradu-Josanu and Vasilica, news anchors at the Communist Party–controlled state broadcaster Teleradio-Moldova (TVM), were suspended by the station's management. The journalists' colleagues believe that the two were fired for actively protesting state censorship on TVM, according to Moldovan sources. Both Bradu-Josanu and Vasilica had participated in a recent anti-censorship strike.

APRIL 10

Kommunist
ATTACKED

A bomb exploded just outside the editorial offices of the Communist Party newspaper *Kommunist* in the Moldovan capital, Chisinau. The bomb, which was planted near the office entrance, caused structural damage to the building and shattered its windows, as well as those in a nearby apartment building. An elderly guard sustained minor injuries but was not hospitalized. Police have opened an investigation into the incident, but no progress in the inquiry had been reported by year's end.

The bomb attack came amid rising tensions between the pro-Russian Communist Party and the ethnic Romanian nationalist opposition, which is seeking to align the country with neighboring Romania and the European Union. Opposition leaders have been organizing demonstrations calling for the resignation of the communist-dominated Parliament and government. In a statement read to Parliament, the Communist Party blamed the attack on "extremist elements who want to destabilize the country," according to The Associated Press.

JUNE 21

All parliamentary reporters
LEGAL ACTION

Moldova's Parliament approved new regulations enabling legislators to suspend the accreditation of journalists covering the legislative body. The regulations also allow Parliament members to reproach reporters publicly for printing incorrect information. A reporter's accreditation can be suspended if a demanded retraction is not published in the manner desired by the lawmaker.

AUGUST 5

Natalia Florea, The Associated Press, Flux News Agency
HARASSED

Education Minister Gheorghe Sima confiscated the audiocassette of Florea, a reporter for The Associated Press and Flux News Agency, during a speaking engagement. The minister snatched the audio recorder from the journalist and handed it to his security personnel, who took the tape and returned the recorder to Florea. The tape was not returned.

OCTOBER 9

Sergiu Afanasiu, *Accente*
Valeriu Manea, *Accente*
LEGAL ACTION

Afanasiu and Manea, editor-in-chief and journalist, respectively, at the weekly *Accente*, were detained on charges of receiving a bribe of US$1,500 in return for not publishing compromising materials about a local businessman. According to the Moscow-based Center for Journalism in Extreme Situations (CJES), the businessman offered Afanasiu bribes several times, but he never accepted them and instead published materials about the man's activities. *Accente* staff believe that the charges are spurious and came in reprisal for the paper's critical reporting.

The journalists were released on October 23, but both had to sign an agreement not to leave the capital, Chisinau, while the case remains ongoing. According to CJES, a court hearing is scheduled for January 30, 2003.

ROMANIA

Iosif Costinas, *Timisoara*
MISSING

Costinas, a 62-year-old reporter for the independent daily *Timisoara*, disappeared from the western city of Timisoara in early June. The journalist's work focused on sensitive political issues, including a number of unsolved murders that occurred during the 1989 anti-communist revolt, which began in Timisoara, as well as the continued presence of communist-era secret police agents in the government. Prior to Costinas' disappearance, he was working on a book about organized crime and government corruption in Timisoara, according to The Associated Press.

RUSSIA

DATE UNKNOWN

Sergei Kalinovsky, *Moskovsky Komsomolets—Smolensk*
KILLED (MOTIVE UNCONFIRMED)
For full details on this case, see page 372.

JANUARY 11

TV-6
LEGAL ACTION
The Presidium of the Highest Arbitration

Court upheld the liquidation of the Moscow Independent Broadcasting Company (MNVK), parent company of Russia's only independent, nationwide television channel, TV-6.

The suit was originally lodged in September 2001 by the pension fund of LUKoil-Garant, a minority shareholder in TV-6. LUKoil-Garant is a subsidiary of the giant LUKoil Corporation, which owns 15 percent of TV-6. The Russian industrial magnate Boris Berezovsky, who is a bitter opponent of President Vladimir Putin, owns 75 percent of the station, either outright or through other companies that he controls.

Originally, the Moscow Arbitration Court ruled to close MNVK, citing an obscure Russian law that prohibits companies from running a deficit for more than two years. TV-6 appealed, and though a Moscow appellate court upheld the liquidation in November 2001, another appeal from TV-6 led to a ruling in the station's favor on December 29, 2001. However, on January 1, 2002, the Russian Parliament repealed a law that allowed shareholders to liquidate their own companies, thus eliminating the legal basis for proceedings against TV-6.

But on January 4, the deputy chairman of the Highest Arbitration Court, Eduard Remov, filed a protest with the Presidium of the Highest Arbitration Court, which upheld the television company's liquidation. The Arbitration Court rejected TV-6's argument against liquidation. Instead, Judge Remov argued that since the original ruling came while the shareholder liquidation law was still in force, LUKoil's claim was valid and should be upheld.

Press Minister Mikhail Lesin ordered TV-6 off the air at midnight on January 22, 2002. The tender for TV-6 frequency was set for late

EUROPE AND CENTRAL ASIA

March 2002. On March 27, the Federal Licensing Commission unanimously awarded the tender for TV-6 broadcasting frequency to Media-Sotsium, a partnership between businessmen, politicians, and a team of journalists headed by Yevgeny Kiselyov, former director of television channel NTV. The new station was dubbed TVS.

Kiselyov and his team went back on the air as TVS on June 1 and have managed to retain significant editorial autonomy and fairly critical news reporting.

FEBRUARY 28

Marina Popova, *Moskovsky Komsomolets vo Vladivostoke*
ATTACKED

Popova, a correspondent for the popular Vladivostok daily *Moskovsky Komsomolets vo Vladivostoke*, was brutally assaulted in the middle of the afternoon by two unknown assailants while she was walking through the courtyard of a children's hospital in the city. The attackers knocked the journalist to the ground and smashed her head against the pavement. They fled the scene when someone scared them off.

Although the assailants took Popova's purse, they did not take other valuables, such as a gold watch or two other bags. She suffered head injuries, including a contusion and a concussion, as a result of the attack.

The journalist and her colleagues believe that the attack is directly linked to her investigative journalism. Specifically, Popova attributes the assault to an article she wrote in the February 28, 2002, issue of *Moskovsky Komsomolets vo Vladivostoke* alleging that some local police officers were protecting local brothels. Local police launched an investigation into the incident, but no progress had been reported by year's

end. Popova recovered from the attack and returned to work.

MARCH 9

Natalya Skryl, *Nashe Vremya*
KILLED

For full details on this case, see page 365.

MARCH 11

Sergei Zolovkin, *Novaya Gazeta*
ATTACKED

Zolovkin, a correspondent for the daily *Novaya Gazeta*, was the target of an assassination attempt in the southwestern city of Sochi. At around 10 p.m., Zolovkin and his wife had parked their car outside their apartment building and were walking to the building entrance when an unidentified gunman fired at the journalist. Zolovkin wielded his gas pistol, a nonlethal weapon that many Russians carry for self-defense, and fired it twice, missing both times. The gunman fired once more (both bullets missed) and then ran away.

After Zolovkin gave chase, a passing police patrol arrested the gunman, Artur Minasian, who later confessed to the shooting and was sentenced in September to 10 years in prison. Investigators were not able to determine if Minasian had acted alone. However, Zolovkin and his colleagues believe that the attempted murder was connected to his professional activities, and that those who masterminded the shooting have not been caught. Prior to the attack, the journalist had received several death threats stemming from his reporting on organized crime and official corruption in the Krasnodar Region. Shortly after the shooting, Zolovkin went into hiding, where he remained at year's end.

MARCH 29

Igor Zotov, *Nezavisimaya Gazeta*
LEGAL ACTION

Zotov, deputy editor-in-chief of the Moscow independent daily *Nezavisimaya Gazeta*, was charged with criminal libel. The case against Zotov is ostensibly based on a November 27, 2001, article alleging that three Moscow judges accepted bribes from the lawyers of Anatoly Bykov, a prominent businessman from the Krasnoyarsk Region who was on trial for attempted murder.

As the editor responsible for that day's edition of the newspaper, Zotov is accused of libeling Moscow City Court chairperson Olga Yegorova and two federal judges from Moscow's Meshchansky Intermunicipal Court. Zotov faces up to four years in prison if convicted.

The article cited anonymous sources in the Federal Security Service (FSB), the successor to the KGB, and other law enforcement bodies to support its claims about the three judges. On April 4, 2002, *Nezavisimaya Gazeta* published a letter from Krasnoyarsk governor Aleksandr Lebed to an undisclosed federal authority in Moscow containing similar allegations of judicial misconduct in the Bykov case.

On December 5, 2001, *Nezavisimaya Gazeta* published a letter from the businessman's attorneys repudiating the November 2001 article's allegations. According to Russia's Law on Mass Media, publishing such a letter constitutes a retraction. However, the three judges accused of bribery never contacted the newspaper seeking a retraction, according to a December 29, 2001, editorial in *Nezavisimaya Gazeta*.

In December 2001, the Moscow Prosecutor's Office launched a criminal libel investigation against *Nezavisimaya Gazeta*. However, local sources believe that the case against Zotov may have nothing to do with the stories about the judges. The charges were brought against Zotov shortly after the newspaper published his March 7, 2002, article on a film backed by Boris Berezovsky, a bitter rival of Russian president Vladimir Putin, that blamed the FSB for apartment building bombings throughout Russia in 1999. The Russian government contends that Chechen rebels perpetrated these attacks.

By year's end, the case against Zotov remained open, but prosecutors had not actively pursued it.

APRIL 10

Igor Rodionov, *Moskovsky Komsomolets na Altaye*
ATTACKED

Rodionov, editor of the daily *Moskovsky Komsomolets na Altaye*, was assaulted by three unknown assailants in the Siberian city of Barnaul between 7:30 a.m. and 8 a.m. as he was leaving his apartment. The attackers beat and stabbed him but did not take his cell phone, money, documents, or other valuables, making robbery an unlikely motive. He was rushed to the local city hospital, where he underwent surgery.

Rodionov's colleagues believe his assault may be connected to his work. *Moskovsky Komsomolets na Altaye* is well known for its investigative journalism and coverage of influential local figures. Newspaper staff met with the regional prosecutor, who plans to monitor the investigation personally. No progress on the inquiry had been reported by year's end.

APRIL 12

Yan Svider, *Vozrozhdeniye Respubliki*
ATTACKED

Svider, a journalist with the opposition

newspaper *Vozrozhdeniye Respubliki*, was attacked by two unknown assailants in the city of Cherkessk, in the southern Karachaevo-Cherkessiya Republic. Svider was assaulted in the entranceway of his apartment building while he was on his way to work. The region's deputy prosecutor told the Russian news agency RIA Novosti that the assailants beat the 55-year-old journalist with metal rods. He was hospitalized for a head injury and broken arms and legs.

Vozrozhdeniye Respubliki's editor, Vladimir Panov, and the Prosecutor's Office believe that Svider may have been attacked for his professional work. The newspaper, which began publishing in January 2001, is linked to the Vozrozheniye Respubliki political movement, which opposes Karachaevo-Cherkessiya Republic's president, Vladimir Semyonov.

APRIL 29

Valery Ivanov, *Tolyatinskoye Obozreniye*
KILLED

For full details on this case, see page 366.

JUNE 7

Novaya Gazeta
LEGAL ACTION

A bailiff from Moscow's Basmanny District Court came to the offices of the newspaper *Novaya Gazeta* and initiated proceedings for sealing the publication's property, which included conducting an inventory of the property and sequestering it.

The move came after a financial institution, Mezhprombank, sued the publication in the Basmanny Court in early 2002, claiming that one of the institution's business deals had collapsed because of a December 2001 *Novaya Gazeta* article. The newspaper had

reported that Mezhprombank was implicated in a scandal involving Russian money laundering through the Bank of New York.

Novaya Gazeta maintains that its reporting is accurate and contends that documents the paper procured demonstrate that it was not to blame for the collapse of the bank's business deal. Yet the Basmanny Court refused to accept the documents as evidence and, on February 28, ordered *Novaya Gazeta* to pay 15 million rubles (US$482,310) in damages to the bank.

To prove its innocence, the newspaper sought to open a criminal fraud case against Mezhprombank with the Moscow Prosecutor's Office. However, the case file containing all documents disappeared unexpectedly. According to the newspaper's editor-in-chief, Dmitry Muratov, the Basmanny Court claims it sent the documents to the Prosecutor's Office, which maintains that it never received the documents.

But in late June, Mezhprombank withdrew its claim and the damage award against the paper, reportedly because it did not want to "set a dangerous precedent for freedom of expression," according to the Moscow-based news agency Interfax.

JUNE 9

RTR Television
Vladimir Gerdo, *Vechernyaya Moskva*
Sergei Chirikov, EPA
Sergei Ponomaryov, *Kommersant*
Ekho Television
ATTACKED

Several journalists were attacked during soccer riots that broke out in the capital, Moscow, after the Russian team lost to the Japanese in a World Cup match. Ekho Television's technical equipment was destroyed, and its van, along with the van of the RTR Television news program "Vesti," was set on fire.

Gerdo, with the Moscow newspaper *Vechernyaya Moskva*; Chirikov, a photographer for the photo agency EPA; and Ponomaryov, with the leading Moscow daily *Kommersant*, were attacked and beaten by the soccer fans. The journalists sustained minor injuries, and Ponomaryov's camera was broken. Moscow city authorities arrested and prosecuted several people in connection to the riots.

JUNE 14

German Galkin, *Vecherny Chelyabinsk*
ATTACKED

Galkin, deputy editor of the local newspaper *Vecherny Chelyabinsk* in the Ural city of Chelyabinsk, was assaulted by two unknown assailants outside his apartment. The journalist suffered minor injuries as a result. Galkin, who is also a correspondent with the Moscow-based daily *Kommersant*, believes that the attack is connected to his critical coverage of local officials. Police are investigating the incident, but no progress had been reported by year's end.

AUGUST 14

Viktor Shamayev, *Penzenskaya Pravda, Dlya Sluzhebnogo Polzovaniya*
ATTACKED

Shamayev, a crime reporter for the daily *Penzenskaya Pravda* and editor of the newspaper *Dlya Sluzhebnogo Polzovaniya*, was abducted by several unknown assailants. The journalist was taken to a basement in an unknown building, where he was tied to a stool, beaten, and then told to give up journalism and leave town. He was released and reportedly remains in the town of Arbekov.

SEPTEMBER 26

Roddy Scott, Frontline
KILLED

For full details on this case, see page 366.

OCTOBER 24

Ekho Moskvy
HARASSED, CENSORED
Moskoviya
Rossiiskaya Gazeta
HARASSED, LEGAL ACTION, CENSORED

Media Ministry spokesman Yuri Akinshin warned media outlets not to air statements from a large group of heavily armed Chechen rebels that had seized some 700 people in a Moscow theater on October 23 to demand that Russian troops pull out of the war-torn region of Chechnya in southern Russia. The warning came after Moscow-based Ekho Moskvy radio station broadcast a brief interview on October 24 with one of the gunmen in the theater. "If this is repeated," said Akinshin, "we reserve the right to take all proper measures, up to the termination of the activity of those media," the Moscow-based Interfax news agency reported.

Ekho Moskvy editor-in-chief Aleksei Venediktov confirmed that the station had received a warning from the Media Ministry but pointed out that "in the view of our lawyers, we have not violated a single provision of Russian law." On October 25, the Media Ministry submitted a request to the Communications Ministry to shut down Ekho Moskvy's Internet site but withdrew the request after the station removed the text of the interview from the site, Russian news reports said.

At the same time, the Media Ministry closed Moskoviya, a Moscow television station, for allegedly promoting terrorism.

EUROPE AND CENTRAL ASIA |

289

However, after meeting with the director general of the station, Moskoviya resumed broadcasting the next day. Meanwhile, the Moscow daily *Rossiiskaya Gazeta* received a warning from the Media Ministry for publishing a photograph of the body of a young woman who was killed by the armed captors on October 23 as she tried to enter the theater where the hostages were being held.

NOVEMBER 1

Versiya
HARASSED, LEGAL ACTION
Andrei Soldatov, *Versiya*
Rustam Arifdzhanov, *Versiya*
HARASSED

The offices of *Versiya*, a Moscow-based independent newspaper, were searched, and computer equipment was confiscated by the Russian Federal Security Service (FSB). The FSB claimed it searched the offices because a May 27 article in paper revealed state secrets.

During the search, Soldatov, who wrote the article, and Arifdzhanov, *Versiya*'s editor-in-chief, were summoned to FSB offices for questioning. The journalists signed a standard agreement not to divulge the subjects of the interrogation. Other journalists at the publication were questioned as well.

The newspaper's staff and colleagues link the heightened FSB interest in the newspaper to material it published about the "Nord-Ost" October hostage standoff that contradicted official information. The standoff began on October 23, when a large group of heavily armed Chechen rebels seized some 700 people in a Moscow theater, demanding that Russian troops pull out of the war-torn region of Chechnya in southern Russia.

NOVEMBER 25

Irada Huseynova, *Bakinsky Bulvar*
HARASSED, LEGAL ACTION

Huseynova, a correspondent for the Azerbaijani weekly *Bakinsky Bulvar* who works for the Moscow-based Center for Journalism in Extreme Situations (CJES), was detained in Moscow and faced extradition to Azerbaijan. CJES director Oleg Panfilov told CPJ that Moscow police arrived at CJES offices and detained Huseynova at the request of Azerbaijan's Prosecutor General's Office. In Azerbaijan, she could be sentenced to prison on criminal defamation charges.

On September 4, 2001, Huseynova, along with Elmar Huseynov, founder of *Bakinsky Bulvar*, and Bella Zakirova, the paper's editor-in-chief, were convicted of civil defamation. The three were fined 80 million manats (US$17,400) each.

Baku mayor Hajibala Abutalibov had sued *Bakinsky Bulvar* for defamation and sought to close the paper after it published an article by Huseynova criticizing the mayor for closing and demolishing commercial kiosks, a move that left many unemployed. On September 6, 2001, the court forbade publishing houses and distributors from printing and circulating copies of *Bakinsky Bulvar*.

Following the paper's closure, the court launched criminal cases against Huseynov, Huseynova, and Zakirova. All three were charged with defaming the mayor, an offense punishable by one to three years in prison.

On September 20, 2001, Huseynova requested political asylum in Germany after attending a conference in Warsaw, Poland, according to local press reports. She then moved to Moscow, where she began working as an editor and analyst at CJES. On September 21, 2001, both Huseynov and

Zakirova were found guilty of criminal defamation. The court sentenced Huseynov to six months in prison and gave Zakirova a six-month suspended sentence. Azerbaijani president Heydar Aliyev later signed a pardon authorizing Huseynov's release.

Russian authorities released Huseynova on November 27, 2002, and she longer faces extradition to Azerbaijan.

DECEMBER 20

Oleg Chuguyev, *Molodoi Dalnevostochnik*
Irina Polnikova, *Molodoi Dalnevostochnik*
ATTACKED

Chuguyev, editor-in-chief of *Molodoi Dalnevostochnik* newspaper, and his wife, Polnikova, a journalist for the paper, were beaten with metal pipes by two masked men while the journalists were entering their apartment building. The assailants hit Polnikova in the face, then fractured Chuguyev's knee, broke his jaw, and knocked out several of his teeth. *Molodoi Dalnevostochnik* has consistently featured critical reporting on local politicians, organized crime figures, and neo-Nazis.

SLOVAKIA

SEPTEMBER 13

Luboslav Choluj, JoJ Television
THREATENED

Choluj, a reporter with the privately owned JoJ Television, was attacked by Slovakia's former prime minister Vladimir Meciar, who was campaigning for general elections scheduled for late September. The journalist had repeatedly asked Meciar to explain how he had paid for a $1 million renovation of his luxury villa even though the

politician claimed to own nothing more than a beat-up car and a three-bedroom apartment when he left office in 1998. According to Choluj, Meciar—who is a former amateur boxer—told the journalist, "If you ask me the same question again, I am going to give you a punch that you won't forget."

TAJIKISTAN

JULY 8

Asia-Plus
HARASSED

Independent media agency Asia-Plus was refused a broadcast license by the State Committee for Television and Radio. In 1998, Asia-Plus had applied to open a radio station in the Tajik capital, Dushanbe, where only state-run television and radio stations operated. The agency received a brief reply from the committee on July 8 stating that another radio station in Dushanbe was "unnecessary."

Asia-Plus director Umed Babakhanov told CPJ he believes that the committee's decision can be attributed to two factors. "The first is that the state doesn't want competition in this market and wishes to maintain its monopoly. The second reason is that some top officials fear the appearance of an independent station that is outside their control."

On April 19, CPJ deputy director Joel Simon and Europe and Central Asia program coordinator Alex Lupis met with Tajik foreign minister Talbak Nazarov in New York City to discuss press freedom issues. CPJ then sent a letter to Nazarov on May 8 outlining specific press freedom problems, including the inability of Asia-Plus to obtain a broadcast license.

In a July 29 meeting in Vienna, Austria, with Hamrokhon Zaripov, the Tajik ambassador to Austria, Switzerland, and Hungary,

CPJ Europe and Central Asia consultant Emma Gray raised the Asia-Plus case in a two-hour discussion on press freedom issues. On July 29, Tajik president Imomali Rakhmonov met with Asia-Plus director Babakhanov and said he would instruct the committee to issue the license. Asia-Plus began broadcasting in early September.

OCTOBER 28

Akram Azizov, SM-1
Nazim Rakhimov, SM-1
Yusuf Yunusov, TRK-Asia
HARASSED
Makhmud Dadabayev, SM-1
THREATENED

Yunusov, a 21-year-old with TRK-Asia, Azizov, 21, and Rakhimov, 20, both of SM-1, were conscripted into military service in retaliation for producing a talk show that criticized local military officials, according to local and international reports.

The program, which aired on October 24 and 27, was produced by journalists from the local, independent television stations SM-1 and TRK-Asia in the northern city of Khujand and reported that the military uses gangs to forcibly recruit young men into military service. During the show, senior military officer Faziliddin Domonov denied the use of such aggressive tactics, the New York–based Eurasianet Web site reported. The program reportedly enraged Domonov, who called the station on October 25 and threatened to conscript the journalists.

On October 28, four military officials burst into the SM-1 and TRK-Asia offices and arrested nine journalists who had produced and participated in the talk show. While the journalists were in detention, officials told them "you don't know who you're dealing with," and "we'll show you how to present us on television," the Moscow-based

press freedom group Center for Journalism in Extreme Situations reported. Six journalists were eventually released, but Yunusov, Azizov, and Rakhimov were conscripted and remained in the military at year's end.

On the evening of November 5, a military officer called SM-1 director Dadabayev and threatened to kill him and close his station, the Tajikistan office of the U.S. media training organization Internews reported.

TURKMENISTAN

APRIL 4

Komsomolskaya Pravda
HARASSED, CENSORED

Turkmen officials seized two April editions of the Moscow-based daily *Komsomolskaya Pravda*, in which journalist Nikolai Varsegov criticized Turkmenistan in writings about his recent travels there. The Turkmen government also blocked access to the newspaper's Web site.

Beginning July 16, *Komsomolskaya Pravda* subscribers stopped receiving newspapers and magazines published in Russia. According to international reports, Turkmen customs officials seized periodicals delivered from Russia. In mid-August, the Turkmenistan Communications Ministry announced it had stopped delivering Russian publications to the country.

UKRAINE

MAY 22

Yuliya Makalova, VIK
ATTACKED

Makalova, senior editor of the local radio station VIK in the city of Kherson, was assaulted and robbed while she returned to her apartment in the evening, according to international and local press reports. An unidentified assailant threw her on the ground, kicked her in the head several times, and stole her bag, which contained a tape recorder, a notebook, and a taped interview with a Kherson mayoral candidate. None of her jewelry was taken. The journalist suffered a concussion.

Anna Osolodkina, chief editor for VIK, said that she was "certain" the attack was linked to Makalova's work because the journalist was investigating allegations of corruption in the Kherson City administration at the time of the attack. Local police officials opened an investigation into the assault but consider the incident a robbery.

NOVEMBER 1

Oleksandr Panych, *Donetskiye Novosti*
MISSING

Panych, a 36-year-old journalist and manager for the daily *Donetskiye Novosti*, disappeared in late November from the southeastern city of Donetsk and has not been heard from since. *Donetskiye Novosti* editor-in-chief Ryma Fil said that Panych had written articles about drugs and business issues, The Associated Press reported. Panych disappeared several days after he sold his apartment for US$14,000. Soon after, investigators found bloodstains on the apartment's carpet. Prosecutors believe he may have been robbed but have not ruled out the possibility that his disappearance is related to his journalism.

UNITED KINGDOM

JULY 22

The Guardian
The Financial Times
The Independent

The Times
Reuters
LEGAL ACTION

Interbrew, a Belgium-based brewing company, applied to the United Kingdom's High Court to seize the assets of the London-based newspaper *The Guardian*. The company also initiated legal proceedings against three other newspapers, *The Financial Times*, *The Independent*, and *The Times*, as well as Reuters news agency, to force the outlets to hand over information about documents leaked from Interbrew.

Interbrew claimed that these news organizations' November 2001 reports about an imminent bid for South African Breweries (SAB) were based on false information and caused the company's shares to fall and SAB's stock to jump. Interbrew suggested that the anonymous sources of this allegedly false information may have illegally profited from the stock market reaction. Interbrew alleged that the documents had been doctored to make the financial markets believe that a bid was imminent and said the company needed the original documents to trace the damaging leak.

The news organizations refused to hand over the documents, citing their duty to protect journalists' sources. On December 19, 2001, however, the High Court ruled that the public interest in protecting the source of the leak was outweighed by the public interest in letting Interbrew seek justice. Seven months of legal wrangling ensued, culminating in Interbrew's July 22 decision to apply to the High Court for seizure of *The Guardian*'s assets. That threat receded four days later, when the brewing company handed the entire affair over to the U.K.'s Financial Services Authority (FSA). The FSA launched its own investigation into the affair.

The FSA has statutory powers to demand

EUROPE AND CENTRAL ASIA

compliance and, if the news organizations resist, could raid their offices for the documents. By year's end, no penalties had been enforced against the media outlets, and their lawyers were appealing the case to the European Court of Human Rights, in Strasbourg, France, to clarify the U.K.'s law on the protection of journalistic sources.

YUGOSLAVIA

JANUARY 27

Stevan Niksic, *NIN*
LEGAL ACTION

Niksic, editor-in-chief of the Belgrade-weekly *NIN*, was found guilty of criminal libel and sentenced to a five-month suspended prison sentence by the First Municipal Court in the capital, Belgrade, according to Serbian press reports. Aleksa Djilas, son of the late Milovan Djilas, a former senior communist official and later a dissident, filed the lawsuit against Niksic for publishing a letter in *NIN* in 2000 from a reader who criticized Milovan. The letter's publication followed an edition of the weekly in which Milovan was interviewed.

MARCH 11

Publika
CENSORED

Milo Djukanovic, the president of the Montenegrin republic of Yugoslavia, ordered that the entire print run of the March 11 edition of the Podgorica daily *Publika*, which is close to Djukanovic's Democratic Party of Socialists, be destroyed and replaced with a new edition after noticing an article he found offensive, according to local press reports.

Copies of the daily had been brought to a dinner at the Montenegro Hotel in the Montenegrin capital, Podgorica, and distrib-

uted to guests. Djukanovic ordered copies collected from the dinner and destroyed, according to sources there, after reading an article in the paper in which a close business associate, Veselin Barovic, said he would not support the dinner because he disagreed with the policies of U.S. ambassador William Montgomery, a co-sponsor of the evening's event. The complete run of 7,000 copies was destroyed and replaced by a new edition without the article that offended Djukanovic.

APRIL 24

Vladislav Asanin, *Dan*
LEGAL ACTION

A court in Podgorica, the capital of Montenegro, which, along with Serbia, is one of Yugoslavia's two republics, upheld the sentence and conviction of Asanin, editor-in-chief of the Podgorica daily *Dan*. The journalist was originally convicted of criminal libel and sentenced to three months in prison in December 2001, but he appealed the ruling.

In 2001, Montenegrin president Milo Djukanovic sued Asanin after *Dan* reprinted a series of articles from the Croatian weekly *Nacional* linking Djukanovic to illegal cigarette smuggling in the Balkans.

Asanin appealed the April conviction and also resigned as *Dan*'s editor-in-chief. On November 19, the High Court in Podgorica upheld the conviction and sentenced Asanin to 30 days in prison. He appealed the November conviction and remained free at year's end pending a decision on the appeal, which had not yet been heard.

MAY 15

Zeljko Bodrozic, *Kikindske Novine*
ATTACKED, LEGAL ACTION

Bodrozic, editor-in-chief of newspaper

Kikindske Novine, was convicted of libel and fined 10,000 Yugoslav dinars (US$150) by a court in the northern Serbian town of Kikinda, according to local press reports. Dmitar Segrt, general manager of the Toza Markovic construction material factory, sued Bodrozic after he wrote in the January 11, 2002, edition of *Kikindske Novine* that Segrt, once a close ally of former Yugoslav president Slobodan Milosevic, had transformed himself into a reformist with close ties to the new government.

Workers from Segrt's factory were waiting outside the courthouse when the verdict was read, and they attacked the editor when he emerged from the building. Bodrozic suffered a neck injury as a result of the incident.

Sead Krpuljevic, *Monitor*
ATTACKED

Krpuljevic, a photographer for the independent Podgorica weekly *Monitor*, was attacked by members of the pro-Belgrade Socialist People's Party (SNP) when he was standing in front of party headquarters in the central Montenegrin city of Niksic on the night of local elections, according to local press reports. SNP supporters hit Krpuljevic several times and pushed him into the building, where party officials confiscated his film and then released him.

MAY 25

Vojkan Ristic, BETA
Liljana Stojanovic, *Glas Javnosti*
Radomir Ilic, B92
HARASSED

Ilic, of the Belgrade-based independent radio station B92; Ristic, of the Belgrade-based independent news agency BETA, and Stojanovic, of the independent Belgrade daily *Glas Javnosti*, were detained by a group of ethnic Albanian men from a local militia for

an hour in the southern Serbian village of Veliki Trnovac.

The journalists were prevented from attending and reporting on a ceremony in the local stadium commemorating the first anniversary of the death of Ridvam Qazimi, commonly known as Leshi, a prominent commander of the disbanded Liberation Army of Presevo, Medvedja, and Bujanovac who had died fighting Serbian forces in 2001. The journalists were released and allowed to attend the ceremony after they called international officials and Serbian government representatives to protest their detention.

MAY 31

BK Television
HARASSED

Officials at the National Bank of Yugoslavia (NBJ) prevented BK Television journalists and cameramen from entering the NBJ building in the capital, Belgrade, to attend a bank news conference, according to local press reports. NBJ also issued a statement saying that BK Television was being denied further access to bank information because of the station's alleged lack of professionalism and bias. The incident came after a recent BK Television report criticized the policies of NBJ governor Mladjan Dinkic. NBJ changed its policy the next week, in early June, and allowed BK Television to attend its press conferences.

JUNE 13

Dan
LEGAL ACTION

The Lower Court in the Montenegrin capital, Podgorica, found the Podgorica daily *Dan* guilty of defaming Montenegrin president Milo Djukanovic in a series of articles claiming that he was involved in a Balkan tobacco smuggling ring. The paper was ordered to pay him 15,550 euros (US$14,600) in damages. The articles making the allegations, which Djukanovic has denied, originally appeared in the independent Croatian weekly *Nacional* in the summer of 2001. Other Croatian, Serbian, and Montenegrin media outlets had reported the story, while prosecutors in the Italian port city of Bari formally opened an investigation into the accusations in May 2002.

JULY 12

Vladimir Radomirovic, *Reporter*
THREATENED, HARASSED
Radomirovic, editor-in-chief of the Belgrade weekly *Reporter*, was threatened and questioned by police about his sources for an article in the July 2 edition of the paper, according to local press reports. Plainclothes detectives from the Serbian Interior Ministry arrived at the *Reporter* newsroom on July 11 with a summons requesting that Radomirovic visit the Secretariat for Internal Affairs in Belgrade the following day for questioning. When Radomirovic refused to sign the summons, the detectives threatened to arrest him. But after consulting with his lawyer, the editor agreed to be questioned.

On July 12, he went to the secretariat, where officers threatened and questioned him about an article reporting that the Serbian government's Communication Bureau had surveillance equipment that had been used to monitor the office of Yugoslav president Vojislav Kostunica. Radomirovic

told the independent Radio B92 station that he refused to reveal the story's sources.

OCTOBER 10

Dejan Anastasijevic, *Vreme*
THREATENED
Anastasijevic, a correspondent for the respected Belgrade weekly *Vreme*, received death threats by telephone after testifying against former Yugoslav president Slobodan Milosevic at the U.N. International War Crimes Tribunal for the former Yugoslavia in The Hague, according to international reports. Anastasijevic testified about a massacre of civilians committed by Yugoslav soldiers in the Croatian city of Vukovar.

OCTOBER 16

Jovan Dulovic, *Vreme*
THREATENED
Dulovic, a correspondent for the Belgrade weekly *Vreme*, and his family received death threats after Dulovic testified against former Yugoslav president Slobodan Milosevic at the U.N. International War Crimes Tribunal for the former Yugoslavia in The Hague, according to international reports. Dulovic provided detailed evidence that Yugoslav soldiers and members of Serbian paramilitary forces executed civilians in the Croatian city of Vukovar.

During the war in Croatia, Dulovic worked for the pro-Milosevic newspaper *Politika Ekspes* and, as a result, had greater access to the battlefield and was more trusted by Yugoslav soldiers and members of Serbian paramilitary units. ■

OVERVIEW: MIDDLE EAST AND NORTH AFRICA

by Joel Campagna

THE ARAB WORLD CONTINUES TO LAG BEHIND THE REST OF THE GLOBE in civil and political rights, including press freedom. Despotic regimes of varying political shades regularly limit news that they think will undermine their power. Hopes that a new generation of leaders would tolerate criticism in the press have proved illusory, with many reforms rolled back in 2002. Meanwhile, the Israeli-Palestinian conflict has been deadly for journalists and remains the dominant news story for local and Pan-Arab media, which have aggressively covered the fighting's violent twists and turns, winning influence in the Arab world and beyond.

Throughout the region, government control of the press varies from the most authoritarian regimes, where media are strictly regulated and harnessed to serve the state, to those that tolerate independent media but control journalists with carrots and sticks. With only a handful of exceptions, governments have maintained their monopoly over broadcast media, which—in a region where illiteracy remains high—are particularly influential.

In the more repressive and centralized states of the region, including Iraq and Libya, governments own or control all media. Despite the existence of private publications in authoritarian countries such as Syria and Tunisia, the heavily censored, state-controlled media remain dominant, while private papers are often indistinguishable from state-owned publications. And in the autocratic Persian Gulf monarchies of Saudi Arabia, Oman, and the United Arab Emirates, privately owned papers remain hostage to harsh political environments that do not tolerate dissent.

In Algeria, Bahrain, Egypt, Iran, Jordan, Kuwait, Lebanon, Morocco, Turkey, and Yemen, various independent and outspoken newspapers exist, but journalists must contend with a battery of official tactics that hinder their work: censorship, criminal prosecution, arrest, detention, and intimidation by security forces.

Restrictive press legislation proved once again to be among the most formidable tools to harass the independent media during 2002. Press laws allow officials to control the licensing or distribution of publications and also empower authorities to prosecute journalists, imprison them, or close their newspapers.

During 2002, authorities in Algeria and Jordan used legislation adopted in 2001 to crack down on journalists who tackled government corruption. Newspaper closures or criminal prosecutions were carried out in Algeria, Egypt, Iran, Lebanon, Mauritania, Morocco, Tunisia, Turkey, and Yemen. Media laws empowered courts to censor newspapers or bar the press from covering certain news. In Jordan, authorities imposed news blackouts on explosive political developments. Courts in Iran and Turkey continued to invoke repressive laws with vigor, prosecuting critics and closing newspapers.

Joel Campagna is a CPJ senior program coordinator who is responsible for the Middle East and North Africa. **Hani Sabra,** research associate for the Middle East and North Africa, contributed substantially to the writing and research of this section. **Nilay Karaelmas,** a CPJ consultant, provided important research on Turkey.

In addition to press laws, governments also use covert pressure to keep journalists in check. Intelligence services continue to operate with impunity, intimidating, detaining, and threatening reporters to hamper independent, investigative reporting. Other pressure has been used in Saudi Arabia, where officials fired a group of editors because of coverage deemed too liberal. In Morocco, meanwhile, authorities dissuaded companies from advertising in the muckraking weekly *Le Journal Hebdomadaire*.

In recent years, journalists have been cautiously optimistic about the rise of young, progressive-minded leaders. However, entrenched "Old Guard" forces, economic uncertainty, and fears of political instability have undermined progress, and hopes for media reform crumbled in 2002 under the weight of state crackdowns. Bashar al-Assad's ascension to power in Syria two years ago, which saw the launch of the first nonstate papers in 40 years, gave way to a government counterattack on political dissent in 2002.

In neighboring Jordan, King Abdullah II, who promised reform three years ago when he succeeded his father, the late King Hussein, oversaw a sharp decline in press freedom, including the adoption

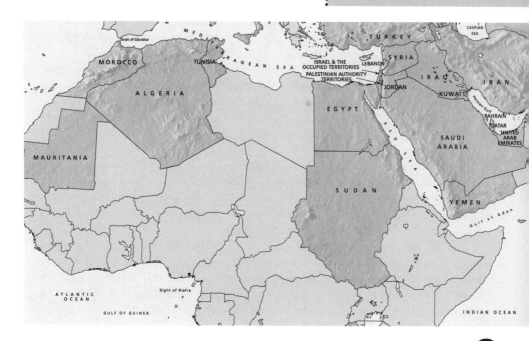

of a harsh new press law and the legal harassment of journalists. And under Morocco's young King Muhammad VI, newspapers were prosecuted, while the government passed a new media law that differed little from the repressive one that had previously been in place.

In Bahrain, political reforms launched by King Hamed Bin Issa al-Khalifa initially augured well for media freedom, but the results have so far been mixed. In a year that saw the country's first democratic elections in 30 years, the government licensed new independent newspapers but also harassed journalists, adopted restrictive press legislation, and censored the Internet.

Outside the Arab world, in Turkey and Iran, reform efforts did not result in improved media conditions. Despite a series of democratic changes in Turkey, including the softening of some repressive press statutes, prosecutors there continued to initiate criminal lawsuits against those who criticized the army or expressed pro-Kurdish or pro-Islamist political sentiments. In Iran, President Muhammed Khatami, now in his second term, has been unable to implement his political and social reform programs and rein in the conservative-controlled courts that continue to close newspapers and prosecute journalists.

Despotic rule was not the only force that fueled attacks on press freedom. Armed conflict and political violence also imperiled reporters and provided a backdrop for media restrictions. The most dangerous place in the region for journalists in 2002—and the most troubling in terms of press freedom abuses—was the West Bank. During Israel's massive military offensive there in late March, the army threatened, intimidated, and, in some cases, physically prevented journalists from covering its military operations. Israel Defense Forces fired at reporters, detained several journalists, confiscated film or press cards from others, ransacked the offices of private West Bank television and radio stations, and attacked the Palestinian National Authority's broadcasting facilities. Israeli officials also expelled foreign correspondents and refused to accredit Palestinian journalists.

On the other side, Palestinian security forces and militants harassed journalists by confiscating film and attacking reporters. Militant Jewish settlers in the West Bank also perpetrated a number of violent assaults against reporters. In neighboring Jordan, journalists felt the repercussions of Israeli-Palestinian violence. Authorities confiscated journalists' footage of pro-Palestinian demonstrations and intimidated others who tried to record the events.

Three journalists in the region were killed in the line of duty in 2002, all in the West Bank by Israeli gunfire. Several more escaped injury when Israeli troops fired upon them. Journalist safety in conflict situations became an increasing concern for the international media as they anticipated a U.S.-led attack on Iraq, where potential dangers included chemical and biological weapons and kidnappings.

The U.S.-led "war on terror" had a number of negative side effects on local media in the Arab world. Jordan invoked the need to combat "terrorism" when it enacted repressive Penal Code amendments shortly after the September 11, 2001, attacks on the United States and then used them against members of the media in 2002. In Yemen, where U.S. and Yemeni armed forces are battling suspected al-Qaeda militants, local authorities questioned journalists who reported on militant attacks against the army, while some editors said that officials advised them not to cover certain related stories.

There was, however, some cause for optimism about media freedom in the region. Iranian journalists continued to publish amid an unrelenting judicial crackdown. Some Moroccan, Lebanese, and Algerian newspapers remained feisty. When reporters and pundits found no outlets to express themselves in local media, they turned to a growing number of satellite television stations, Pan-Arab newspapers, and Web sites. Several London-based newspapers have become among the most influential in the region.

During 2002, satellite television had the most significant impact on news coverage in the Arab world. The Qatar-based satellite channel Al-Jazeera remained the most influential television station in the region. A year after drawing international scrutiny for its coverage in Afghanistan, the station continued to attract both fans and critics with its bold, uncensored news and debate programs. Al-Jazeera has spawned imitators and has even forced some Arab media to liberalize their coverage.

Eager to join the satellite boom, virtually every state in the region boasts a government satellite television station, although few offer serious news programming. Several regional channels—including United Arab Emirates–based Abu Dhabi TV and Middle East Broadcasting Centre—are widely watched for their quality news programming, even if they do not enjoy the same level of freedom as Al-Jazeera. In addition to Al-Jazeera, Abu Dhabi TV and Lebanese Hezbollah's Al-Manar TV have been particularly influential because of their extensive coverage of the Palestinian intifada.

But as alternative sources of information have become increasingly influential, states have sought to repress them. Al-Jazeera continued to enrage Arab regimes—as well as Western governments and pundits—during 2002. In what has become a familiar routine, authorities in several countries harassed the station's reporters and launched diplomatic protests against Qatar. Bahrain barred Al-Jazeera's reporters from covering the country's local elections, while Jordan and Kuwait closed the station's local bureaus. In reaction to Al-Jazeera programming, both Saudi Arabia and Jordan recalled their ambassadors from Qatar's capital, Doha. In October, information ministers from several Arab countries threatened to boycott the station.

This concerted harassment was indicative of a wider trend in which governments sought to punish those who expressed themselves on alternative electronic media. In Jordan, former parliamentarian Toujan al-Faisal was jailed for accusing the prime minister of corruption in an online newspaper. Tunisian authorities imprisoned Internet journalist Zouhair Yahyaoui, who headed a news Web site that ridiculed the oppressive policies of President Zine el-Abidine Ben Ali. Egyptian editor Ahmed Haridy, of the online daily newspaper *Al Methaq al-Araby*, was sentenced to six months in jail for libeling the editor of Egypt's *Al-Ahram* newspaper. Bahrain banned a number of political opposition Web sites, and several governments blocked undesirable content. Meanwhile, Turkey's Parliament passed a law that imposed tight restrictions on the Internet, subjecting online content to Turkey's restrictive laws governing expression.

But these harsh measures have failed to deter people from indulging in new media. There are few places in the region where satellite dishes cannot be used or Internet cafés

MIDDLE EAST AND NORTH AFRICA

found, and although cost still keeps dishes and computers beyond the grasp of most people, the technology does reach young and influential intellectual segments of the population.

Countries across the region are becoming more cognizant of the power of satellite news and electronic media. In fact, many states have attempted to harness that power to influence their own political agendas. In 2002, the Egyptian satellite channel Nile TV began airing 30 minutes a day of Hebrew-language news programming, while Israel launched an Arabic satellite service, and the United States started the Arabic-language Radio Sawa. (Hezbollah's Al-Manar TV already broadcasts news segments in Hebrew.)

Satellites and the Internet are not easily controlled, and the emergence of these alternative news outlets has eroded the information blockades of despotic regimes in the region. In the process, these sources have provided up-to-date news and platforms for open political and social debate. Ultimately, however, people will not fully reap the benefits of media until the political shackles are lifted at home. "Change will come in time from within as political culture evolves," noted one Jordanian journalist. "Media freedom will be a consequence of opening from within." ■

ALGERIA

ALGERIA'S PRIVATE PRESS HAS SURVIVED A BRUTAL, extremist-led assassination campaign that lasted from 1993 to 1996 and took the lives of 58 journalists. Since the early 1990s, it has also weathered government interference. Nevertheless, the private press has earned a reputation for tough criticism of the government and politicians.

Algerians can choose from an assortment of publications, including a number of private and state-owned dailies. Private papers, which began appearing in 1990, have actively reported on the political violence that has plagued the country for more than a decade, as well as on recent unrest in the eastern Kabylia region. Radio and television are state-owned and reflect government views. Although coverage in the private press is generally feisty, it has also occasionally been accused of having allegiances to certain politicians and political interests.

In 2001, President Abdel Aziz Bouteflika, who has had a bitter relationship with the media, signed into law a series of amendments to the country's Penal Code that prescribe prison terms of up to one year and fines of up to 250,000 dinars (US$3,200) for defaming the president. The amendments mandate similar punishments for defaming Parliament, the courts, and the military. During 2002, officials took advantage of these repressive new statutes, engendering self-censorship among many journalists.

In February, following a complaint from the Defense Ministry, the government charged Selima Tlemcani, a journalist for the French-language daily *El-Watan*, with defaming the army in a December 11, 2001, article she wrote accusing the military police of financial misconduct. *El-Watan* editor Omar Belhouchet was also named in the suit.

The Defense Ministry lodged defamation complaints against at least three other journalists—cartoonist Ali Dilem of the daily *Liberté*, *Le Matin* editor Muhammad Benchicou, and cartoonist Ahmed Hisham. Their cases were still pending at year's end.

However, in a separate case filed by the ministry against Dilem, he was fined 10,000 dinars (US$130) in December, becoming the first journalist to be convicted under the Penal Code amendments. The case stemmed from a cartoon he had drawn of former president Mohammad Boudiaf, who was assassinated in the early 1990s.

In February, prosecutors attempted to reinstate a one-year suspended prison sentence that had been handed down against *El-Watan*'s Belhouchet in 1997. The sentence stemmed from statements he had made to the French media hinting that government officials may have been responsible for the murders of some journalists during the country's civil war, between 1993 and 1996.

Journalists were also physically attacked or threatened. In July, thugs connected with local businessman Saad Garboussi in the western town of Tebessa violently assaulted *El-Watan* reporter Abdelhai Beliardouh in his home. Beliardouh had written an article alleging that the Garboussi, who heads the local chamber of commerce, had been previously arrested because of financial links with Islamist militants. The assailants subsequently brought Beliardouh to Garboussi's home, where the businessman demanded to know the journalist's sources for his story and threatened to kill his family. Beliardouh died in November from complications sustained in a suicide attempt. His colleagues at *El-Watan* believe he attempted suicide because he was distressed about the incident with Garboussi.

Beliardouh's ordeal highlights the dangers that journalists in Algeria still face. The mid-1990s murders of 58 reporters and editors—a figure that does not include numerous other media workers who were killed—remain unsolved. Islamist militants have been blamed for most of the killings, but many local journalists suspect state involvement in some of the incidents. The government has kept its investigations of the killings closed and has forbidden independent international inquiries. Officials say they have identified 20 of the killers and have sentenced 15 to death in absentia, but these claims are impossible to verify.

Meanwhile, the whereabouts of missing journalists Djamel Eddine Fahassi and Aziz Bouabdallah remain unknown. CPJ investigations have revealed that state security agents were likely responsible for their abductions, in 1995 and 1997, respectively. But Algerian authorities continue to deny involvement in the disappearances and have failed to undertake serious investigations to determine their fates.

Algeria's press is not as diverse as it was in the early 1990s. Although new publications have been licensed in recent years—including the independent dailies *Al-Jeel* and *Al-Ahdath* in 2002—some journalists complain that authorities have ignored license requests.

Fear of government reprisal, ideological prejudices, and limited information kept the media from covering sensitive topics, such as human rights, military corruption, and the military's controversial role in national politics. According to several reporters, many journalists work for or have close ties with intelligence officers.

Foreign journalists continue to encounter restrictions. The government requires bodyguards to accompany many foreign reporters—supposedly for safety reasons. Some journalists, however, contend that the escorts seek to control rather than to protect. In May, prior to parliamentary elections, the government temporarily barred foreign

MIDDLE EAST AND NORTH AFRICA |

reporters from entering the Kabylia region, where anti-government protests have lasted for more than a year.

BAHRAIN

IN 2002, BAHRAINIS WENT TO THE POLLS FOR THE FIRST TIME IN THREE DECADES. Municipal and parliamentary elections, held in May and October, respectively, were the result of King Hamed Bin Issa al-Khalifa's much anticipated political reforms, which are aimed at bringing limited democracy to this tiny Persian Gulf archipelago. Although the elections represented a breakthrough for Bahrain and the Gulf region, the press was not entirely free to cover the political process.

In March, the government, which is the country's sole Internet provider, blocked access to a number of political Internet sites—including those of opposition groups—claiming that they incite "sectarianism" and contain "offensive content."

Officials barred the Qatar-based Al-Jazeera satellite channel from covering Bahrain's May 9 local elections, stating that the station "harms Bahrain and Bahrain's citizens," "encourages violence," spreads "false news to its viewers," and is a medium for "Zionist infiltration in the Gulf region." Press reports suggested that this hard line came because the network had aired footage from anti-U.S. protests after Israel's April military offensive into the West Bank.

Bahrain's press continued to report on the country's political reforms but remained pro-government. Meanwhile, critics accused local newspapers of ignoring opposition views and practicing self-censorship.

In 2002, the government granted licenses to at least three new papers. One, the daily *Al-Wasat*, headed by a former opposition figure, began publishing in September. In its first few months, the paper cautiously staked out new terrain in local-affairs coverage.

A new, restrictive press law was introduced in October but was temporarily "frozen" after an outcry from newspapers. The law would have established a host of restrictions and would have given the information minister the power to seek court-ordered closures of newspapers and to refer journalists to courts for criminal prosecution. Officials met with editors to hear their concerns and appeared prepared for a compromise.

EGYPT

EGYPT'S POSITION AS ONE OF THE MOST POLITICALLY INFLUENTIAL COUNTRIES in the Arab world ensures its press a prominent regional standing. The country boasts some of the best-known writers and commentators in the Middle East, and newspaper columnists often pointedly criticize government officials and policies. Nonetheless, Egyptian journalists know that some topics remain sensitive—criticism of President Hosni Mubarak and his family, the army, security forces, and human rights abuses—and they tailor their reporting accordingly.

In addition to self-censorship, journalists must also contend with the infamous Press Law 96 of 1996, which prescribes a one-year prison sentence for defamation, two years if a public official files the suit. Journalists also face imprisonment under other, broader Penal Code provisions, such as those that prohibit "violating public morality" and "damaging national interest." Seven Egyptian journalists were imprisoned for libel and other criminal offenses between 1998 and 2001, and several more were prosecuted.

In March, a court in the capital, Cairo, sentenced Adel Hammouda and Essam Fahmy, both of the independent weekly *Sawt al-Umma*, to six months in prison each for defaming prominent Egyptian businessman Naguib Sawiris. The case stemmed from an article in which they had accused Sawiris of financial misconduct. Though the journalists were never jailed, the ruling may have fostered even more self-censorship among journalists trying to document alleged corruption by officials and businessmen close to the state.

According to CPJ research, in 2002 the government launched criminal prosecutions against online journalists and writers for the first time. In April, Ahmed Haridy, editor of the online publication *Al Methaq al-Araby*, was sentenced to six months in prison for defaming Ibrahim Nafie, editor-in-chief and chairman of Egypt's largest newspaper, the state-owned *Al-Ahram*. Nafie, who, like other editors of state-owned papers, is appointed to his post at the paper by the president, is an influential figure because of his close relationships with the country's top leaders.

In May, a court allowed the sister tabloid magazines *Al-Nabaa* and *Akher Khabar* to resume publication after they were banned in 2001 for running articles, accompanied by graphic photos, alleging that a Coptic monk was having sexual relations with women in a monastery and then blackmailing them with videotapes of the interludes. One of the biggest stories of 2001, the racy articles provoked riots by Coptic Christians in Egypt. Mamdouh Mahran, the magazines' publisher, is serving a three-year sentence for the stories.

In September, the ruling National Democratic Party elected President Mubarak's son, Gamal, to a top leadership post and appointed him to head a new party committee. Though some observers privately criticized the actions as part of an attempt by Mubarak to groom his son for the presidency, the media refrained from questioning Gamal's advancement, a sign that self-censorship still pervades the press when it comes to the sensitive topic of the president and his family.

In addition to legal actions, journalists also faced harassment from state officials. In June, during local elections, Egyptian police detained two journalists from United Arab Emirates–based Abu Dhabi TV and two others from German television channel ZDF in separate incidents while they tried to film at polling stations in Alexandria. The two crews were taken to a police station, where they were briefly held and their tapes were confiscated. Also during the elections, police barred an Associated Press reporter from entering a polling station in Alexandria.

The state owns and operates most of Egypt's broadcast media, but four private television stations are now on the air. Al-Mehwar, owned by a group of businessmen, has been operating since late 2001, while Dream 1 and Dream 2, owned by Egyptian tycoon Ahmed Bahgat, who is said to have close relations with high-level government officials, have been broadcasting since November 2001. The channels are accessible only via satellite, which few Egyptians have, and Al-Mehwar, the only one to offer news segments, uses reports from state-owned TV stations. However, observers say that one program on Dream 2 does tackle politically sensitive topics more aggressively than state television. Though the station has not yet suffered any reprisals for its political coverage, the government did send the channel a warning after it hosted a program on masturbation.

Meanwhile, censors still have the last word on state-run television. In May, the popular political talk show "Rais El Tahrir" (Editor-in-Chief) was briefly taken off the air after host Hamdi Kandil began criticizing Arab regimes and the Arab Summit, which was held in Beirut in the spring.

In the late 1990s, the government created a "media city" outside of Cairo where media outlets can rent facilities to produce commercial films, as well as news broadcasts and feeds. Journalists who use the facilities have said that officials have not meddled in the content of their productions.

The government strictly controls the newspaper licensing process, making it difficult to launch new publications without official consent. To circumvent these restrictions, some independent publishers register their papers as foreign publications in countries such as Cyprus and then print them inside Egypt or abroad. However, these publications are subject to an Egyptian foreign-publications censor, who reports directly to the minister of information and can ban publications that contain objectionable material. To avoid censorship and financial loss from suspensions, some papers have informal arrangements with the censors, who agree to review publications before printing.

IRAN

LIBERAL NEWSPAPERS THAT HAVE EMERGED IN IRAN since reformist president Muhammed Khatami took office six years ago serve as an important platform for his agenda of social and political reform. But the reformist media continue to face repression from the conservative-controlled judiciary, which has closed publications, prosecuted and arrested journalists, and fostered a climate of intimidation and fear in the press.

Iran's conservatives, backed by Supreme Leader Ayatollah Ali Khamenei, used their control over key state institutions, especially the courts, to target the media and block the president's reforms. The Press Court suspended or closed at least eight publications during 2002 on charges including publishing "propaganda" or "lies."

Overall, 55 publications have been closed since a conservative crackdown began in April 2000, according to CPJ research. In July, for example, an appellate court upheld a May decision banning leading reformist daily *Norooz* for six months and sentencing the paper's editor to six months in jail. Both were accused of publishing lies and insulting the state and Islamic institutions.

Throughout 2002, officials barred coverage of explosive or embarrassing political issues. In May, after reformist papers alleged that Iranian officials were secretly negotiating with U.S. diplomats to re-establish formal relations between the two countries, the judiciary warned that journalists who expressed support for such talks would face criminal prosecution. In July, the Supreme National Security Council banned press commentary about the resignation of prominent cleric Ayatollah Jalaleddin Taheri as the leader of the Friday prayers in the southern city of Isfahan. Taheri had cited the failure and corruption of the Islamic Republic as his reasons for quitting. A few days later, the Press Court suspended the pro-reform daily *Azad* for violating the ban.

The government also detained, questioned, and charged several journalists for their work. In late September, the Press Court questioned Abdolah Naseri, managing director of the state news agency, IRNA, after the agency ran a story about a poll indicating that most Iranians support resuming relations with the United States. At year's end, it was unclear whether a formal indictment would be issued against Naseri, but the three men involved in conducting the poll, including well-known reformist Abbas Abdi, were arrested in October and November and are being prosecuted on several charges, including publishing false information and "espionage."

Meanwhile, some journalists have been physically attacked with impunity. Said Asghar, who was sentenced to 15 years in prison in 2000 for attempting to assassinate reformist and journalist Saeed Hajjarian, was inexplicably freed in 2002. Hajjarian, publisher of the newspaper *Sobh-e-Emrooz* and an important Khatami adviser who had printed investigative articles linking Intelligence Ministry officials to the late 1998 murders of several leading intellectuals and dissidents, was shot twice in the face outside the offices of the Tehran City Council in March 2000. Today, Hajjarian is severely disabled and, though active in the reform movement, is no longer a journalist.

In November, amid public frustration with reformists' inability to overcome conservative resistance to change, the pro-Khatami Parliament passed two laws designed to weaken conservative authority. The first law empowers the president to overrule the judiciary if he deems their decisions unconstitutional, which could allow Khatami to reverse future newspaper closures. The second law reduces the influence of the Guardians Council, a conservative clerical body charged with approving electoral candidates and parliamentary legislation, by limiting its veto power over candidates for elected office. Both laws are currently awaiting council approval, but observers say that the council may not accept the laws since the second one restricts council authority.

In recent years, several jailed journalists have been released on parole. But at year's end, at least two remained behind bars for their work: investigative reporters Akbar Ganji and Emadeddin Baghi, who were both imprisoned in 2000. In October, Ayatollah Khamenei pardoned prominent Iranian journalist and reform politician Abdullah Nouri, editor of the now defunct daily *Khordad*, who had been imprisoned in 1999 for religious dissent. Numerous other prison sentences against editors and writers are pending appeal, though the journalists remain free.

State television and radio remains under conservative control, but satellite dishes are available, allowing many to access international news and programming. In a brief show of force in 2001, authorities confiscated hundreds of dishes after secular, U.S.-based Iranian opposition groups aired anti-government broadcasts on their satellite channels. But authorities soon stopped pursuing dish owners, and the use of dishes remains widespread. In mid-December, Parliament passed a bill overturning a largely ignored 1995 ban on satellite dishes and permitting their regulated use. The conservative Guardians Council has not yet approved the law.

Today, the Internet in Iran is censorship-free and has become increasingly popular among youth. The Web is available at universities, in a number of high schools, and in hundreds of cybercafés across the country. According to the government, Iran had 400,000 Internet users in 2001. Because the Web has become a popular forum to discuss sensitive social and political issues, conservative officials have issued warnings about the need to regulate or censor immoral or "political" content. However, no concrete actions have yet been taken.

Iranian students have fervently supported President Khatami, particularly his bid to expand press freedom. For several days in November, students across the country protested ongoing state restrictions on freedom of expression after a scholar convicted of apostasy for challenging clerical rule was sentenced to death. More broadly, the protests revealed popular disappointment with the ongoing conservative crackdown and the president's failure to effect reform.

IRAQ

WITH THE THREAT OF U.S. MILITARY ACTION LOOMING, President Saddam Hussein invited the foreign press to cover a sham election in October, in which the government reported that he took 100 percent of the vote, extending his rule another seven years. A few days later, the media covered demonstrations that followed Hussein's order to empty Iraq's prisons. The U.S. news channel CNN reported that Iraqi officials ordered CNN's Baghdad bureau chief, Jane Arraf, and five other non-Iraqi reporters and staff members to leave the country because of overly critical reporting on the protests. But Iraq denied the move and said that the journalists could work freely after leaving the country to renew their visas. In late December, Iraqi officials banned Arraf from the country without explanation.

Though clearly a political charade, the October election further demonstrated the Iraqi leader's unyielding grip on power. For decades, Hussein and his Baath Party have quashed all internal dissent, using the press as a propaganda tool.

Predictably, Iraqi media—which are owned or controlled by the government, the Baath Party, or Hussein's eldest son, Uday—display uncritical support for the regime, frequently offering garish praise for Hussein while heaping scorn on his enemies. Journalists are well aware of the consequences of negative reporting; according to Max van der Stoel, the former U.N. human rights rapporteur for Iraq, "the mere suggestion that someone is not a supporter of the president carries the prospect of the death penalty."

But even state-controlled media can encounter problems. The influential daily *Babel*, founded by Uday Hussein, was suspended for 30 days in November. No reason was given for the move. The influence of the paper's owner, however, gives it some leeway to question certain government policies. For example, the paper has criticized the government's heavy-handed dealings with foreign media outlets.

The government, which is the country's sole Internet service provider, heavily censors online content. Satellite dishes, modems, and fax machines are banned. However, Iraqis seeking alternative information often tune in to regional or foreign radio stations. The government has recently allowed restricted access to satellite television on a subscription basis, but the service does not offer news channels such as the Qatar-based Al-Jazeera or the United Arab Emirates–based Abu Dhabi TV. Moreover, the cost is beyond the reach of most Iraqis.

Foreign correspondents continue to face a variety of restrictions. Obtaining visas to enter the country can take months and when granted only allow short stays—10 days to two weeks—and require leaving the country for renewal. Once inside Iraq, foreign journalists are constantly shadowed by government minders from the Information Ministry, who make reporting difficult to impossible. Some journalists, however, have managed limited reporting outside the presence of minders by conducting spot interviews during lunches or sightseeing. In rare cases, reporters have slipped through the cracks and worked without being assigned a minder. Still, there are reports that unattended journalists are "secretly" monitored.

The government frequently takes journalists on organized trips, which many say are little more than propaganda sideshows. Access to areas beyond the capital, Baghdad, is even more restricted. Against the wishes of the United Nations, however, the Iraqi government has allowed news media to follow U.N. weapons inspectors on site visits in an apparent attempt to bolster the country's contention that it is not developing weapons of mass destruction.

Meanwhile, locally based foreign correspondents live under the constant threat of expulsion or of being blacklisted for future visas if they offend officials. In July, for example, Iraq banned a correspondent from Al-Jazeera for 10 days because of his use of language, including referring to President Hussein without his full title.

In the U.N.-mandated Kurdish enclaves in northern Iraq, local media operate freely, and rival Kurdish factions have established television stations and newspapers. While they tend to be partisan in nature, media outlets there are not subject to state censorship. The Internet is also available in the north.

By early winter, a U.S. military strike to topple Hussein's regime seemed inevitable, and foreign media outlets began discussing the potential dangers of covering the conflict, including biological or chemical attacks and kidnappings. Some journalists expressed additional fears that the U.S. government might limit media access, as it did during the 1991 Gulf War and more recently in Afghanistan.

U.S. editors have held discussions with Defense Department officials about media access in the event of war. In November, the Pentagon announced that it would attempt to "embed" news reporters and photographers with front-line troops. At year's end, however, questions remained about whether the policy would be implemented, and, if it were, whether troops would still restrict the media. It was also unclear whether journalists not working with troops would be given the same access and freedom of movement.

ISRAEL AND THE OCCUPIED TERRITORIES (INCLUDING THE PALESTINIAN AUTHORITY TERRITORIES)

WHILE THE PRESS IS LARGELY FREE WITHIN ISRAEL PROPER, the country's military assault on the Occupied Territories fueled a sharp deterioration in press freedom in the West Bank and Gaza during much of 2002. Despite vocal international protest, the Israel Defense Forces (IDF) committed an assortment of press freedom abuses, ranging from banning press access in the West Bank to opening fire on journalists covering events.

MIDDLE EAST AND NORTH AFRICA |

309

In late March, following a string of deadly Palestinian suicide bombings in Israel, Prime Minister Ariel Sharon launched the country's largest military offensive in the West Bank since 1967, when the army captured the area from Jordan. In the initial days of the six-week operation—code-named Operation Defensive Shield—the IDF declared nearly all of the West Bank's main cities "closed military areas" and off-limits to the press. Journalists attempting to cover the action were frequently thwarted at checkpoints by troops and forced to take alternate routes into cities through orchards, back roads, or dirt paths. Israeli officials maintained that the ban was instituted for safety reasons. However, the hard-line approach against journalists trying to defy the closed military zones indicated otherwise.

CPJ documented numerous instances in which troops fired on or in the direction of clearly identified journalists. Authorities also detained and threatened members of the press, confiscated their credentials and film, and in some cases expelled them from the country. Troops raided, and at times temporarily occupied, media offices in the West Bank. In an April case that drew widespread international media coverage, IDF troops hurled stun grenades and fired rubber bullets at reporters waiting outside the besieged Ramallah compound of Palestinian leader Yasser Arafat.

Foreign journalists who covered the events said that they had never witnessed such harsh treatment from Israeli government forces. In one particularly disturbing incident on April 1, NBC correspondent Dana Lewis and his two-person camera crew came under IDF fire in Ramallah while driving in an armored car clearly marked as press. A soldier fired two rounds at their car and then a third round, after the journalists had stopped the vehicle, turned on an interior light to make themselves visible, and placed their hands on the windshield.

Throughout the operation, at least three journalists were wounded by suspected IDF gunfire. Several more had shots fired in their direction. In one case, it was unclear whether Palestinians or Israelis were responsible for opening fire. CPJ wrote numerous letters to the Israeli government protesting the army's rough treatment of the press.

The Israeli army also detained several journalists—sometimes for weeks or months at a time—without charge. Three of the longest held were Hossam Abu Alan, a veteran photographer for Agence France-Presse; Youssry al-Jamal, a soundman for Reuters; and Kamel Jbeil, a reporter for the Palestinian daily *Al-Quds*. IDF troops detained the journalists in April, held them in administrative detention, and accused them of having contacts with armed Palestinian groups. All three were released in the fall without charge.

Local Palestinian media infrastructure was heavily damaged as a result of the IDF's military operation. In January, Israeli forces dynamited the offices of the Palestinian National Authority's Voice of Palestine radio station and Palestine Television, which the Israeli government has accused of "incitement." Israeli troops also raided or occupied and ransacked several private Palestinian stations during 2002.

Even in the weeks after Operation Defensive Shield, members of the press continued to face movement restrictions in the West Bank. The Israeli army intermittently imposed the closed military zones, shutting out the press, during brief incursions into Palestinian areas. On June 19, the military barred journalists from covering the latest operation, Operation

Determined Path, which resulted in Israel's reoccupation of most major West Bank towns.

During 2002, the number of checkpoints increased across the West Bank, and the army blocked alternate routes that journalists had used to evade roadblocks. Journalists often waited for hours at checkpoints, and some were still denied entry.

Many foreign correspondents believe that the restrictive measures were an attempt by Israel, unhappy with what it perceived as unfair treatment in the international media, to dictate the conflict's coverage. These reporters maintain that army constraints on the press made it difficult to verify rumors and unsubstantiated reports. In April, for example, the Israeli order prohibiting journalists from entering the West Bank town of Jenin fed confusion about the human and material toll of the IDF's incursion and battle with Palestinian militants there.

But even when the IDF was not in the midst of a major operation, troops harassed the press, confiscating film, verbally abusing, or physically assaulting journalists. Gunfire from troops continued to pose a mortal danger. During 2002, three journalists were killed in the line of duty by Israeli gunfire. Imad Abu Zahra, a Palestinian fixer and free-lance photographer, was shot in Jenin (and later died as a result of his wounds) at a time when no clashes appeared to be taking place.

As in previous years, the army failed to conduct thorough investigations in 2002 and has punished troops in only a handful of incidents in which journalists were wounded by gunfire or attacked by troops since the second intifada began in September 2000. In late August 2002, the IDF announced that it had concluded an inquiry into the March shooting death of Italian photographer Rafaelle Ciriello and reported that there was "no evidence and no knowledge of an [army] force that fired in the direction of the photographer," despite eyewitness testimony to the contrary.

The army was not the only obstacle to the media. Militant Jewish settlers in the West Bank and Gaza continued to perpetrate violent attacks against journalists. In October, settlers punched and assaulted reporters with stones while they covered the dismantling of the West Bank settlement Havat Gilad.

Many international media outlets employ Palestinian stringers or fixers, who serve as essential, front-line personnel at foreign news organizations. But only a handful of these media workers have received their accreditation, or GPO card, which facilitates movement through checkpoints. These new, more restrictive regulations affecting Palestinian journalists have handicapped media organizations' ability to operate in the Occupied Territories.

Today, only a few Israeli journalists venture into the territories because of army restrictions barring them and due to threats from Palestinian militants. The few who go must sign a waiver absolving the army of responsibility for their safety. The army has arranged trips to the West Bank for Israeli reporters. In March, the practice was temporarily stopped after Israel's Channel 2 television allegedly broke a pool agreement and bypassed military censors to air disturbing footage of an IDF raid on a Palestinian home, during which a mother died while her children watched.

The Israeli daily *Ha'aretz* reported in April that government-run Israel Radio's Arabic-language department had implemented new guidelines restricting language used in news broadcasts, including forbidding the use of the word "victim" when referring to

MIDDLE EAST AND NORTH AFRICA

Palestinian civilians killed in the conflict. *Ha'aretz* also cited complaints from journalists about other official interference in news content.

Meanwhile, Israel's Supreme Court dismissed a high-profile libel case launched nearly a decade ago by then defense minister Ariel Sharon against *Ha'aretz* and journalist Uzi Benziman. In 1991, Sharon sued over an article in which Benziman alleged that Sharon had misled then prime minister Menachem Begin about his true war aims in Israel's 1982 invasion of Lebanon, arguing that Sharon had failed to disclose his intent to move into the Lebanese capital, Beirut.

Although Israel's Hebrew-, Arabic-, and English-language press are mostly free, government and military officials can censor media outlets if authorities deem certain news—such as troop buildups and death counts—harmful to the country's security interests. Journalists, however, have the option of appealing to the High Court of Justice. Most media can circumvent the restrictions by attributing sensitive stories to foreign news outlets. In December, the government closed the Islamist weekly *Sawt al-Haq wal Huriyya*, maintaining that it posed a threat to public peace.

IN THE PALESTINIAN AUTHORITY TERRITORIES, PALESTINIAN LEADER Yasser Arafat maintained a tenuous hold on power in 2002, despite Israel's massive spring military offensive into the West Bank and pressure from both Israel and the Bush administration to resign as head of the Palestinian National Authority (PNA). As the conflict intensified during the year, the PNA's power weakened.

That weakness appeared to significantly reduce the PNA's ability to restrict press freedom. Nevertheless, officials managed to impose constraints on the media, if not with the same intensity and breadth of past years, while militant groups and Palestinian civilians also harassed members of the press. In at least one case, a Palestinian gunman opened fire, on an Associated Press armored vehicle in Ramallah.

In January, Palestinian security authorities in the West Bank city of Hebron closed the weekly newspaper *Akhbar al-Khalil* without explanation. Newspaper staff alleged that the PNA was responding to Israeli and U.S. pressure to shutter the publication, which frequently criticized those countries' Middle East policies.

PNA officials also confiscated journalists' film and intimidated reporters covering sensitive news stories. In February, Palestinian police took footage from photojournalists who had filmed a Palestinian mob at a Jenin courthouse killing three defendants who had just been convicted of murder. In June, officers from Arafat's security force seized videotapes from a France 2 television crew of a demonstration led by Hamas spiritual leader Ahmed Yassin, who was supposed to be under PNA house arrest at the time.

In March, Palestinian information minister Yasser Abed Rabbo urged the Qatar-based satellite channel Al-Jazeera not to air a live interview with Israeli prime minister Ariel Sharon because of his aggressive attitude toward Palestinians. The interview was eventually canceled because, according to Al-Jazeera, Sharon failed to cooperate with the station's terms, which required a Doha-based interviewer rather than an Israel-based one.

In August, the pro-PNA Palestinian Journalists' Association barred journalists from photographing Palestinian children wearing military uniforms or carrying weapons, arguing that such footage violated children's rights and served "the interests of Israel and its propaganda against the Palestinian people." However, the group has no legal power over the media and did not say what the consequences would be for those who violate the ban. The order was rescinded a few days later amid local and international protest.

In September, Israeli authorities arrested an aide to Palestinian Legislative Council speaker Ahmed Qurei for allegedly threatening a *Jerusalem Post* reporter. The newspaper reported that its correspondent Khaled Abu Toameh had received threatening phone calls after writing that Qurei had spoken with Sharon to request a meeting to discuss the siege on Arafat's Ramallah compound.

Meanwhile, Palestinian militiamen and demonstrators repeatedly attacked reporters and occasionally prevented them from covering stories. In one April incident in the West Bank town of Bethlehem, Palestinian militants threatened journalists working for international media outlets and forced them to hand over footage of the body of an alleged Palestinian collaborator who had been murdered. In October, also in Bethlehem, a group of Palestinians assaulted photographers covering the funeral of a militant killed by Israeli forces. A Reuters photographer was seriously injured in the incident. That same month, another group of Palestinians assaulted several journalists covering a Gaza City explosion in which three Hamas members had died, apparently while making bombs.

The escalating Israeli-Palestinian conflict has made the mainstream Palestinian press—already staunchly pro-PNA—more loyalist, while years of physical attacks, arbitrary detentions, threats, newspapers closures, and official censorship have increased self-censorship. The media avoid criticizing Arafat and the security services, as well as reporting news that reflects negatively on PNA leadership. Indirect pressure, such as phone calls, are said to be common. Two of the three main daily newspapers—*Al-Ayyam* and *Al Hayat al-Jadida*—have direct or indirect relations with the PNA and its officials, either because the editor is an aide to Arafat or because the PNA finances the paper's payroll. (The third main daily, *Al-Quds*, is privately owned but avoids criticizing the PNA.)

In an effort to crack down on militants, in late 2001, authorities closed the opposition Islamist weeklies *Al-Risala* and *Al-Istiqlal*—Gaza-based publications affiliated with the Khalas Party, which comprises former Hamas members, and the Islamic Jihad group, respectively. But in April, the Palestinian High Court of Justice ruled that *Al-Risala*'s closure was illegal and ordered it reopened. The PNA at first refused to comply but in early November gave the paper permission to resume publishing. *Al-Istiqlal* remained closed at year's end.

Some Palestinian journalists criticize the Palestinian media's failure to discuss important issues affecting the Palestinian community, such as the movement for PNA leadership and structure reform, which gained momentum after the siege on Arafat's compound was lifted in May. After the PNA shuffled its Cabinet and security chiefs in June, one Palestinian journalist lamented in the online publication *Amin.org* that "it was not the Palestinian media who carried out news about the reform; instead, non-Palestinian media like Arab satellite channels, the foreign media, and the Israeli press [did,]" and that "it was not Palestinian journalists who started the debate but Palestinian academics and political analysts."

MIDDLE EAST AND NORTH AFRICA |

The PNA controls the official Palestine TV and Voice of Palestine radio, which loyally reflect PNA views. These stations operated under extreme duress after Israeli forces destroyed their offices. Israel has repeatedly accused the stations of inciting Palestinians to commit violence against Israelis. But these official outlets garner few viewers among Palestinians, who prefer local news from the popular Al-Jazeera satellite channel, Abu Dhabi TV, or even Lebanese Hezbollah's Al-Manar TV. For example, during Israel's March and April West Bank offensive, Al-Jazeera provided local information about emergency services available to citizens there.

To some extent, private Palestinian broadcast stations have served a similar role during the second intifada, but during Israel's 2002 offensive, several were forced off the air or had their studios destroyed or vandalized by Israeli troops. Some of those unable to broadcast beamed Al-Jazeera on their frequencies.

As discussions about reform intensified in May, Arafat signed the Palestinian Basic Law, which, among other statutes, guarantees press freedom. Legislators had originally adopted the law in 1997. At year's end, amid the chaos of the renewed conflict in the West Bank and Gaza, it was too early to tell what impact the law would have. While it prohibits censorship and other restrictive practices against the press, the law leaves open the possibility of imposing future constraints on the media.

JORDAN

AFTER ASSUMING THE HASHEMITE THRONE THREE YEARS AGO, King Abdullah II stirred hopes that he would introduce greater political openness in Jordan. But although Abdullah has expressed support for democracy and freedom of expression, human rights in the country have deteriorated.

During 2002, the government of Prime Minister Ali Abou al-Ragheb continued to undermine basic liberties. In a case that had a chilling effect on the press, a state security court in May convicted former member of Parliament Toujan al-Faisal of publishing "false information," inciting unrest, and harming the "dignity" of the state and of government officials. The case stemmed from an open letter al-Faisal had written to Abou al-Ragheb in the Houston-based online publication *Arab Times* accusing him of corruption. Al-Faisal was sentenced to 18 months in jail without appeal. In June, King Abdullah pardoned her, but not before al-Faisal went on a hunger strike and her case generated international protest.

Al-Faisal was one of several Jordanian journalists detained, prosecuted, or investigated under the country's harsh new Penal Code amendments, which Abou al-Ragheb's government instituted in October 2001, ostensibly as part of an anti-terrorism effort. The amendments grant authorities sweeping powers to jail and fine journalists and to close publications. Some observers assailed the laws as an attempt not to combat terrorism but to muzzle dissent. In fact, by the end of 2002, it was government critics—not individuals suspected of terrorism—who were being sent before the courts.

On top of threatening legal action, officials continued to exert both direct and indirect pressure on journalists. The General Intelligence Directorate, the country's powerful security agency, continued to monitor the media diligently. Agents questioned, detained, and threatened journalists in retaliation for their work. Reporters and editors, meanwhile, raised concerns about security forces infiltrating newspapers and using journalists as agents. Members of the media also spoke of editorial censorship, fear of dismissal for reporting on contentious issues, and increased self-censorship.

The government bullied reporters, editors, and camera crews on several occasions in an effort to block negative news. In March, security forces confiscated the film of television crews attempting to cover pro-Palestinian demonstrations and denied the journalists access to facilities to relay their footage abroad. The government closed the Amman bureau of the Qatar-based satellite television channel Al-Jazeera in August after a talk show guest criticized Jordan's relationship with Israel and poked fun at King Abdullah's limited knowledge of Arabic. Throughout the year, security officials harassed and questioned Al-Jazeera staff, at one point confiscating equipment from the network's Amman-based production company.

Authorities also employed crude censorship tactics. As in the past, the government and state prosecutors imposed news blackouts on sensitive political stories. In March, a state prosecutor barred the media from reporting on the state's investigation into a massive bank defrauding scheme involving a Jordanian businessman with alleged ties to the security services. That month, officials interrupted the print run of the weekly *Al-Majd* and ordered it to remove stories about the alleged scandal. The weekly *Al-Hadath* received the same order. When the businessman, Majd al-Shamaylah, was extradited from Australia in November, prosecutors reimposed the blackout.

Also in November, the government launched military operations in the southern city of Maan to root out what it called a "gang of outlaws" that had taken control of the town. The army declared the city a closed military area and barred local and international media from entering, except at selected times by official escort. In the capital, Amman, authorities detained Al-Jazeera's former bureau chief and a local Jordanian reporter for their coverage of the incident.

Nonetheless, compared to its neighbors, such as Iraq and Syria, Jordan boasts a lively print media. Still, the country's three main dailies practice self-censorship. The daily *Al Arab al-Youm* ceased being the force it once was when its chairman resigned two years ago, apparently due partly to government pressure. Several privately owned weeklies often criticize the government, but they have few readers.

The pro-government Jordan Press Association (JPA), a representative body for journalists, has at times restricted press freedoms by pressuring or expelling journalists who violate its regulations. By law, all journalists must belong to the organization to work in Jordan. The JPA's bylaws also bar members from having direct contact with Israel; violators face suspension or expulsion. In January, the JPA threatened action against Abdullah Etoum, editor of the weekly *Al-Hilal*, for traveling to Israel to interview Israeli foreign minister Shimon Peres. The case was dropped after Etoum apologized and pledged to have no more contacts with Israel.

Since assuming the throne, King Abdullah has promised a number of initiatives aimed at modernizing the local media. In 2001, he called for the abolishment of the Information Ministry, which has regulated the media and enforced press restrictions. The ministry was to be replaced by the High Media Council, a 12-member supervisory body with an

MIDDLE EAST AND NORTH AFRICA |

ambiguous mandate, including recommending media policy to the government. The council has so far floundered, however, marred by resignations and an uncertain role, and the Information Ministry remains in place.

In 2002, the government opened a media investment zone in hopes of attracting international news organizations to the country—an idea that has been long in the offing. So far, only one production company operates in the zone, providing studio space and media equipment for potential clients.

The government maintains its monopoly over radio and television, despite amending a law in 2000 that paves the way for private stations. Authorities have yet to issue the guidelines for such stations. Satellite dishes are relatively widespread, and many Jordanians enjoy access to regional and international news channels. The Internet, meanwhile, has become increasingly popular, accessible in schools, homes, and Internet cafés.

KUWAIT

KUWAIT'S PRESS HAS LONG BEEN RECOGNIZED AS THE MOST LIBERAL in the Persian Gulf. Kuwaiti newspapers, all of which are privately owned, are known for outspoken and critical coverage of the government and its policies. Nonetheless, the country's press laws prohibit "subjecting the person of the emir to criticism" and empower authorities to suspend newspapers and jail journalists for "tarnishing public morals," "disparaging God [and] the prophets," "violating the national interest," or "creating divisions among people."

In early January, the Cabinet approved the draft of a new press statute, which contains strict measures opposed by journalists, including a cap on the number of newspapers that can be licensed every year and increased government authority to close publications. Parliament had not considered the law by year's end.

In early 2002, the Interior Ministry prosecuted Muhammad al-Melaify, a contributor to the local daily *Al-Watan* and an employee at the Kuwaiti Ministry of Religious Endowments (which oversees the country's religious land) because he claimed during an Al-Jazeera satellite channel talk show that the Kuwaiti government had a passive stance toward the United States' detention of Kuwaiti nationals in Afghanistan and Guantánamo Bay, Cuba. The ministry alleged that al-Melaify's comments "aimed to create strife among the people and threatened Kuwaiti national interests." *Al-Watan* later said it would no longer publish al-Melaify's work. In a separate case, he was prosecuted in November after appearing on Al-Jazeera and praising an armed attack on U.S. Marines in Kuwait that killed one in October.

In November, one month after information ministers of the Gulf Cooperation Council, a regional organization that promotes security and economic cooperation, had threatened to boycott Al-Jazeera for "insulting and slandering" their countries, Kuwaiti authorities closed the channel's Kuwait bureau because the station was "biased" against the country. The bureau remained closed at year's end.

In June, an appellate court upheld the murder conviction of Kuwaiti police officer Khaled al-Azmi, who was found guilty in February of killing Hidaya Sultan al-Salem, the owner and editor of the weekly magazine *Al-Majales*. Al-Salem was shot in March 2001 on her way to work in the capital, Kuwait City, in what her lawyers and the government said was retribution for an *Al-Majales* article that had allegedly insulted the women of al-Azmi's tribe. However, two Kuwaiti journalists say that al-Azmi may have killed al-Salem because of a personal dispute. Al-Azmi appealed the case to Kuwait's highest court, which had not heard the case by year's end.

Ibtisam Berto Sulaiman al-Dakhil and Fawwaz Muhammad al-Awadi Bessisso, both of whom were jailed in June 1991 and later sentenced to life in prison because they worked for *Al-Nida'*—the collaborationist newspaper published under the Iraqi occupation of Kuwait—were pardoned in 2002. But because Bessisso is not a citizen of any country, no nation is willing to accept him as a refugee, according to his brother, who lives in the United States. Al-Dakhil, a naturalized Kuwaiti citizen from Iraq, lost her citizenship as a result of her conviction and is also awaiting deportation. Both are currently being held in Kuwaiti jails while they try to find countries of residence. Since 1996, some 15 *Al-Nida'* journalists have been released, many by royal decree, and all have been deported.

LEBANON

ALTHOUGH LEBANON'S PRIVATE MEDIA ARE KNOWN FOR THEIR INTENSE DEBATES over local politics and criticism of government officials, Lebanese authorities do not hesitate to use censorship, legal harassment, and intimidation against journalists or media outlets that the government believes go too far.

In September, Lebanese security forces closed the offices of Murr Television (MTV) and Radio Mount Lebanon, owned by Christian opposition Parliament member Gabriel Murr. Armed security forces roughed up staff and ordered them to leave the offices. The Publications Court accused the stations of violating a law that prohibits airing propaganda during elections, which were held in June. Some observers suspect that the closure was partly triggered by MTV's criticism of the Lebanese government and of Syria—which posts some 20,000 troops in Lebanon and plays a significant role in the country's politics. Right before the June poll, prosecutors had accused the station of harming Lebanon's ties with Syria through its coverage. During the elections, station staff claimed that they were prohibited from covering the poll because they work for MTV. Both outlets remained closed at year's end.

MTV was not the only television station subjected to state harassment. Prosecutors began investigating the other main Christian-owned station, Lebanese Broadcasting Corporation International (LBCI), after it ran a report in late August about a Muslim government employee who had killed eight people at the Ministry of Education building. Officials objected to LBCI's news anchor pointing out that the majority of the victims shared the same religion. Witnesses interviewed in the report accused the suspected murderer, who is Muslim, of targeting Christians. Because the Lebanese government fears sectarian violence, officials are extremely sensitive to any coverage of religious differences in the country. Lebanon's information minister, Ghazi Aridi, has warned journalists repeatedly against provoking sectarian strife. Officials are still investigating LBCI, but the station had not been officially charged at year's end.

The state also went after print media in 2002. In January, authorities imposed prior censorship on the influential London-based daily *Al Sharq al-Awsat* after it carried a front-page report in late December 2001 detailing an alleged assassination attempt on Lebanese president Emile Lahoud. The restriction was lifted a few days later. In April, a court dismissed the cases against *Al Sharq al-Awsat*'s editor-in-chief and Beirut bureau chief, both of whom had been prosecuted in connection with the article.

The English-language *Daily Star* faced the threat of prosecution when the *International Herald Tribune*, which is distributed with the *Daily Star*, ran an advertisement from the New York–based Anti-Defamation League in early April expressing support for Israel. Lebanon and Israel technically remain at war, and showing public support for Israel can be illegal in Lebanon. The distribution agreement between the *Tribune* and the *Daily Star* does not give the *Daily Star* any editorial control over *Tribune* content, but *Daily Star* publisher, Jamil Mroue, could have been prosecuted as the *Tribune*'s Beirut representative. Ultimately, Mroue, who faced jail time, was not charged, and the *Daily Star* chose not to distribute the *Tribune* on a later occasion when it carried the same advertisement.

Even though newspaper editorials regularly criticize government policies and many television channels feature lively call-in shows, the press continues to censor itself, avoiding tough criticism of the president, the army, and security forces, as well as stories that authorities believe might inflame sectarian tensions. Criticism of Syria and its controversial role in Lebanese politics remains highly constrained.

MAURITANIA

MAURITANIAN AUTHORITIES CONTINUE TO USE THE COUNTRY'S harsh 1991 press law to punish journalists who run afoul of the regime. Article 11 of the law allows the interior minister to ban the sale of publications that commit such vague offenses as "insulting Islamic principles or the credibility of the state," harming "the public interest," or disturbing "peace and security." Under the law, distribution or sale of offending publications is punishable by up to one year in prison and a fine. Publishers are required to submit copies of publications to the Interior Ministry prior to distribution.

Authorities banned numerous publications in 2002, including an issue of the bimonthly French-language *Le Rénovateur* in July. The paper's editor told the local press that the ban stemmed from an article about foreign exchange and price increases of basic goods. In August, the Interior Ministry halted printing of an edition of the weekly *Le Calame*, which carried a report about protests in France against Mauritanian president Maaouya Ould Sid Ahmed Taya, who was on a state visit there at the time.

Journalists who angered the government were arbitrarily detained during 2002. Authorities held Mohammed Fall Ould Oumere, editor of the weekly French-language *La Tribune*, for 10 days in April after accusing him of belonging to an anti-government group called Conscience and Resistance. Oumere had written an article about the group in a March issue of *La Tribune*. Mohamed Mahmoud Ould Bakkar, publisher of the monthly *Al-Khaima* and the weekly *Assahafa,* was held for two days in September for allegedly belonging to the same group.

MOROCCO

AFTER MOROCCO'S KING MUHAMMAD ASSUMED THE THRONE IN 1999, the press continued a trend toward aggressive reporting that had begun during the final two years of the rule of his father, the late King Hassan II. However, a number of official restrictions imposed on the press during the last three years have tempered optimism about a new era of liberal media reform. Morocco's press, which has established independent, influential publications that push the government's boundaries of free speech, still operates with the fear of criminal prosecution and harassment.

The new Moroccan Press Code, which was approved in March 2002 but had not gone into effect by year's end, differs little from the previous one. The new statute slightly reduces prison terms for defaming public officials or members of the royal family, but sentences remain lengthy. Authorities also retain the power to revoke publication licenses or to confiscate and suspend publications deemed threatening to public order.

In February, a Casablanca court of appeals convicted Aboubakr Jamai, publications director of the French-language weekly *Le Journal Hebdomadaire*, and Ali Ammar, the newspaper's general director, of defaming Foreign Minister Muhammad Ben Aissa. The charges stemmed from articles published in 2000 in the weekly's now defunct predecessor, *Le Journal*, alleging that Ben Aissa had profited from the purchase of an official residence during his tenure as Morocco's ambassador to the United States in the late 1990s. The court sentenced the journalists to three-month and two-month suspended prison sentences, respectively. Both men were also ordered to pay fines and damages totaling 510,000 dirhams (about US$44,000) each. The case was appealed to Morocco's highest court, the Court of Cassation. By year's end, no date had been set for the hearing, and it is unclear whether the journalists will be required to pay damages before the high court hears the case.

Le Journal Hebdomadaire and its sister publication, the Arabic-language *Assahifa*, are not the first private publications in the country, but they are considered the first truly independent ones since they are not aligned with any political party or ideology. Television and radio outlets, meanwhile, avoid criticizing the government.

Moroccan authorities also targeted other independent publications, such as the small circulation *Wijhat Nadhar*, which appears on an irregular basis. In May, secret service agents confiscated all 8,000 copies of the magazine before distribution, without explanation. The issue contained the text of a speech by Moulay Hichem, the cousin of King Muhammad and a frequent critic of the monarchy, who is third in line to the throne.

Authorities also harassed *Rissalit al-Futuwwa* and *Al-Adl wil Ihsan*, papers published by the Islamist group Justice and Charity. Both have resorted to publishing and distributing their papers independently because printers refuse to work with them. Also in 2002, the March issue of the French magazine *VSD* was confiscated and barred from distribution because of an article that criticized King Muhammad.

On February 12, José Luis Percebal, a Morocco-based Spanish journalist for the Spanish radio station Cadena Cope, was found dead in his home in the capital, Rabat.

MIDDLE EAST AND NORTH AFRICA |

Percebal had been stabbed in the back. Sources at Cadena Cope told CPJ that there was no sign of forced entry, but that his cell phone was missing from the crime scene. At year's end, an official at Cadena Cope said the station believes that the murder was not connected to Percebal's journalistic work. The official said that authorities had made some arrests but that a trial had not yet begun.

QATAR

OPERATING FROM THE TINY, GAS-RICH PERSIAN GULF MONARCHY OF QATAR, the 24-hour satellite news channel Al-Jazeera continued to break news and spark controversy in 2002. During the last six years, the station has helped transform television news in the Arab world through bold, uncensored programming and raucous political debates that reach millions in the Middle East and beyond.

A year after making headlines across the globe with its coverage from Afghanistan and its broadcasts of Osama bin Laden's taped messages, the network remained the most influential news channel in the region.

As in previous years, Al-Jazeera continued to trigger official complaints and reprisals from governments across the Middle East for its provocative coverage. In May, Bahraini authorities barred the station's reporters from covering the country's municipal elections, alleging that the station "harms Bahrain and Bahrain's citizens" and is a medium for "Zionist infiltration in the Gulf region." In Jordan, the government closed the station's Amman bureau after a guest on a talk show criticized the country's relationship with Israel and mocked King Abdullah's limited knowledge of Arabic. Jordan also pulled its ambassador from Qatar's capital, Doha, in August for four months in protest. Saudi Arabia did the same in late September because of coverage it deemed anti-Saudi. Meanwhile, governments throughout the region issued formal protests, while their own domestic media launched acerbic attacks against the channel.

For all of Al-Jazeera's successes, critics in the Arab world highlight the station's soft coverage of Qatari affairs and its failure to criticize the country's ruling family with the same zeal it uses for other leaders.

In 2001, the station's US$140 million start-up grant from the Qatari government expired, and station officials announced that the channel would begin operating independent of government financing. It is unclear whether the government still provides money, or if the station can survive without government backing.

Other broadcast and print media in Qatar do not display the same flair as Al-Jazeera, although some papers are considered more liberal than their counterparts elsewhere in the Gulf. Authorities have taken a number of encouraging steps to free the media since Qatar's emir, Hamed bin Khalifa al-Thani, deposed his father in a bloodless 1995 coup, including abolishing the Information Ministry and ending formal censorship. Nevertheless, self-censorship remains common, and the local media avoid direct criticism of the emir and other sensitive political topics.

Although the print media are in private hands, ownership is closely linked with the government through personal relations. The government is responsible for licensing publications, and several criminal statutes exist that can be employed against critics. Under the

Press Law, for example, it is prohibited to "criticize" the emir or to publish news that "harms supreme national interests." Foreign publications can be censored, and the state controls Internet access.

In October, Feras al-Majalli, a Jordanian national working for Qatar State Television, was sentenced to death for spying. It remains unclear how credible the charges against him are. Many observers, however, suspect that al-Majalli is being used as a pawn in the building tensions between Qatar and Jordan. According to al-Majalli's lawyer, his client's trial was plagued by irregularities, including the state's appointment of new judges prior to the verdict. Al-Majalli has appealed the case.

SAUDI ARABIA

THE KINGDOM OF SAUDI ARABIA IS ONE OF THE MOST POLITICALLY CLOSED SOCIETIES in the world. The country's ruling al-Saud family tolerates no internal dissent, prohibits political parties and democratic elections, and closely supervises the media.

Although privately owned, Saudi newspapers are largely toothless. The government approves the hiring of editors and can dismiss them at will. Newspapers receive generous state subsidies as well as guidelines from the Information Ministry about how to cover certain political news. Saudi editors avoid criticizing the ruling family and official policies, as well as reporting on any material that might be interpreted as morally objectionable. Criticism of Islam is off-limits.

However, since 2001, some Saudi newspapers have been tackling previously taboo topics, such as crime and unemployment, and have even criticized the government for its lack of accountability. In March 2002, the dailies *Al-Watan* and *Al-Madina* took on the country's influential religious police, lambasting them for allegedly hindering the rescue of Saudi schoolgirls during a fire because the students were not wearing the proper headscarves and clothing. (More than 15 died in the blaze.) The papers also challenged extremism in the kingdom and called for religious reform.

The government has shown little patience for this new display of daring, dismissing several editors in retaliation for their coverage. In March, the Information Ministry forced Muhammad Mukhtar al-Fal, *Al-Madina*'s editor, to resign after he published a poem accusing the country's conservative judiciary of corruption. The poet, Abdel Mohsen Mosallam, was detained and questioned for several days. *Al-Watan*'s editor-in-chief, Qanan al-Ghamdi, was fired from his post in May because officials felt that the paper's tone had become too liberal. And in July, the Information Ministry forced the director of *Al-Madina*'s publishing house, Ahmed Muhammad Mahmud, to resign, most likely because he allowed al-Fal to pen a column for the paper and wrote a critical article about the authorities' demolition of a poor neighborhood in the city of Jeddah.

In the past, authorities have pressured journalists and other critics by withdrawing their passports or barring them from traveling abroad. The London-based daily *Al Quds al-Arabi* reported in June that the Saudi government barred opposition figure Mohsen al-Awaji from traveling to Qatar to appear on the satellite television station Al-Jazeera's talk show "Without Borders." The show was slated to discuss U.S. government pressure on Saudi Arabia in the aftermath of the September 11, 2001, attacks on the United States.

MIDDLE EAST AND NORTH AFRICA |

321

Foreign media continue to face a variety of barriers in Saudi Arabia. The government censors foreign publications before they enter the country, barring distribution of issues and excising articles that reflect negatively on the regime or that contain objectionable moral or political content. In early 2002, authorities reimposed censorship on the London-based *Al-Hayat* daily, from which the paper had been previously exempted by presidential decree, after it published an article criticizing the Information Ministry. In October, censors banned an edition of the daily that contained an open letter from U.S. intellectuals urging their Saudi counterparts to denounce Islamist extremism.

Following September 11, 2001, the Saudi government relaxed its formerly stringent policy on issuing visas to foreign journalists and allowed several to report from the country. However, some correspondents complained that their telephone conversations were monitored, that government agents intimidated sources, and that officials threatened to withdraw visas because of investigative reports. In April 2002, authorities confiscated videotapes and a laptop computer from Bob Arnot, a reporter with the U.S.-based cable channel MSNBC, while he was boarding a plane to leave the country. The journalist had conducted interviews with Saudi youths who had expressed anti-U.S. views. His tapes and the laptop were returned about a month later.

Saudi Arabia began allowing public access to the Internet in 1999, but officials heavily restrict content. The government has invested millions of dollars in a filtering system that blocks morally and politically objectionable material. Banned political sites include those of Amnesty International and Saudi opposition and human rights groups. Some Saudis are able to bypass state controls by dialing into service providers outside the country.

Saudi Arabia has one of the highest penetration rates for home satellite dish usage in the region, and much of the population can readily access Pan-Arab and international satellite stations. Cell phones, as well as text messaging, are omnipresent and allow citizens to distribute and share news and information. Saudi citizens frequently call talk shows on satellite channels such as Al-Jazeera to participate in debates about Saudi Arabia. This has infuriated the government, which recalled its ambassador to Qatar in late September to protest programs on Al-Jazeera that criticized Crown Prince Abdullah's Middle East peace plan and accused the government of not supporting Palestinians.

SUDAN

THE SUDANESE PUBLIC HAS ACCESS TO SEVERAL HIGH-PROFILE INDEPENDENT NEWSPAPERS that criticize government authorities and policies. But that criticism comes at a price, especially when it relates to the Muslim government's nearly 20-year-old civil war with Christian and animist rebels in the south of the country.

In early September, the government suspended negotiations that were being held in Machakos, Kenya, with the rebels, and many independent journalists and newspaper editorials criticized the move. Authorities took swift action, detaining columnist Osman Merghani, of the daily *Al Rai al-Aam*, who had lambasted the Sudanese government's action on a program broadcast by the Qatar-based satellite channel Al-Jazeera. The government also confiscated three independent dailies for their coverage of the controversy: *Al-Horiyah*, *Al-Sahafa*, and the English-language *Khartoum Monitor*. Officials later questioned the papers' editors.

Sudanese journalists say they have some freedom in their daily reporting and that restrictions, including prior censorship, occur less often today than in previous years. Nonetheless, members of the press maintain that the government's eagerness to crack down on its critics engenders self-censorship and fear.

The ubiquitous National Press Council (NPC), which includes pro-government journalists, Parliament members, and presidential appointees, enforces Sudan's harsh press laws and has the power to ban and confiscate publications deemed offensive.

In August, the NPC suspended the independent *Al-Ayam* for one day after the paper used "explicit" language in a story about female circumcision. The *Khartoum Monitor* was suspended for two days in November after it ran a story about AIDS that the council deemed "too sexual." Journalists complain that the suspensions place hefty financial burdens on publications, since they often have already paid printing fees and lose advertising revenue.

Authorities regularly call journalists and tell them not to cover certain topics. Many independent reporters ignore these instructions, often without government reprisal. But in November, officials suspended three independent newspapers, *Al-Sahafa*, *Al-Horiyah*, and *Al-Watan*, for alleging that police had violently dispersed opposition student protesters at Khartoum University the previous month. Authorities questioned the editors of the publications and detained *Al-Watan* editor Sidahmed Khalifa for three days. Khalifa had held a press conference the day the newspapers were confiscated criticizing the action. He was released without charge.

In January, a Khartoum court ordered *Khartoum Monitor* editor Nial Bol to pay a 5 million pound (US$2,000) fine after he wrote an article about the slave trade in Sudan. The paper itself was fined 15 million pounds (US$6,000). The court ruled that Bol would have to spend six months in prison if he did not pay. Shortly after the ruling, Bol paid the fine, and he remained free at year's end.

SYRIA

AN ONGOING STATE CRACKDOWN AGAINST PRO-DEMOCRACY ACTIVISTS CONTINUED to stunt what were once promising media reforms introduced in 2000 by Syria's young president, Bashar al-Assad. For a short time, it appeared that Bashar, who replaced his authoritarian father, the late Hafez al-Assad, in 2000, would inspire a more liberal media and greater government transparency. After taking office, Bashar authorized the country's first private and non–Baath Party newspapers in nearly 40 years. In 2000 and 2001, three new party papers and two private papers were introduced in the country.

But a crackdown that began in early 2001 continued and has derailed much of the progress. During 2002, the government prosecuted and jailed several pro-democracy activists who criticized the government and advocated political reform. One of them, 71-year-old Communist Party leader Riyadh al-Turk, who had previously served 18 years

MIDDLE EAST AND NORTH AFRICA

in solitary confinement for his opposition views, was sentenced to 30 months in prison for "attacking the constitution" and "inciting insurrection" in statements he made criticizing Hafez al-Assad's rule.

The state-owned papers that had exhibited uncharacteristic panache in their opinion pages in 2000 today reflect the rigid style of previous years, displaying unwavering support for the government. Although the satirical weekly *Al-Domari* has mocked officials and some government policies, it, like all newly licensed private and party papers, largely avoids criticizing the regime.

In 2002, the government licensed at least three additional private publications—an insurance magazine, an advertising publication, and a political-cultural magazine called *Abyad wa Aswad* (Black and White), which is run by the son of the country's army chief of staff. Yet no publication appeared poised to practice hard-hitting journalism. In January, the Cabinet approved a regulation allowing private radio stations to broadcast, but they are barred from airing news or political programming.

The passage of a new press law, first announced by Bashar in 2001, dashed all hopes of a media revival. The law maps out an array of restrictions against media professionals, including requiring periodicals to obtain licenses from the prime minister, who can deny any application not in the "public interest." Publications can be suspended for up to six months for violating content bans, and the prime minister can revoke the licenses of repeat offenders. The new legislation also prohibits publishing "falsehoods" and "fabricated reports"—crimes punishable by one to three years in prison and by fines of between 500,000 and 1 million lira (US$9,500 and US$18,900). Those charged with libel or defamation face fines and up to one year in jail. The law also allows authorities to censor foreign publications and force journalists to divulge their sources.

Authorities harassed journalists on numerous occasions during 2002. Haytham Maaleh, a human rights activist and lawyer, was charged in September before a military court, along with three others, for distributing unauthorized copies of a human rights magazine. Authorities accused the men, all members of a Syrian human rights group, of belonging to an illegal organization and of spreading "false information." In July, the London-based *Al Quds al-Arabi* reported that intelligence agents summoned Marwan Habash, a writer and former minister of the Baath Party's regional leadership, for questioning after he had published an article calling for strengthened civil society in Syria. And in December, Ibrahim Hemaidi, Damascus bureau chief for the London-based Pan-Arab daily *Al-Hayat*, was arrested for an article he wrote alleging that Syrian officials were preparing for an influx of Iraqi refugees in the event of a U.S.-led attack on Iraq.

While local media remain restricted, an increasing number of Syrians have access to satellite dishes, enabling them to watch international and Pan-Arab news channels. Internet access continues to expand; the country boasts dozens of Internet cafés. The government is Syria's sole Internet provider and blocks content about Israel, sex, and Syria's human rights record, as well as sites that allow access to free Internet e-mail. Still, Web surfers appear to have little trouble evading the restrictions by using proxy sites or dialing into Internet service providers outside the country.

into Internet service providers outside the country.

TUNISIA

IN MAY, PRESIDENT ZINE EL-ABIDINE BEN ALI WON 99.52 PERCENT APPROVAL for constitutional changes that allow him to run for a fourth term in 2004. The poll—condemned by
human rights groups inside and outside the country as rigged—did not surprise those
familiar with Ben Ali's 15-year, strongman rule of Tunisia.

Through a combination of censorship and intimidation, Tunisian authorities have all
but stamped out independent voices in the country's media, with the exception of a few
courageous dissident journalists who publish their work underground, on the Internet, or
in Western newspapers.

Those who write critically about political affairs have faced an array of official
reprisals: physical attacks, imprisonment, the banning of their publications, the withholding of state advertising, anonymous telephone threats, cut phone and fax lines, the
removal of accreditation, and travel restrictions. The result is a press that—although
mostly privately owned—is almost completely subservient to the regime. In April, when
19 people were killed after suspected al-Qaeda operatives drove a gas-filled truck into a
synagogue on Tunisia's Djerba Island, the local media described the incident as a traffic
accident, even when foreign media correctly speculated that terrorism was the cause.

While officials have long censored critical Internet content (including CPJ's Web
site), during 2002, authorities prosecuted and imprisoned an Internet journalist for the
first time. In June, Zouhair Yahyaoui, editor of the online newspaper *TUNeZINE*
(*www.tunezine.com*), was sentenced to 28 months in prison on charges of publishing
false information and using stolen communication lines to post his Web site, which
had been functioning for nearly a year before his prosecution. He remained in jail
at year's end.

Tunisian authorities had regularly blocked the site to users inside Tunisia, but
TUNeZINE circumvented these barriers by establishing alternate addresses. Observers
believe that authorities targeted Yahyaoui because many young Tunisians were visiting the
site and learning how to access other blocked addresses. In addition, Yahyaoui regularly
published content that criticized the Tunisian regime, including a satirical poll mocking
the May referendum.

Tunisian officials are beginning to realize just how powerful the Internet is for the
clandestine press. Many independent journalists who have left the country during the last
few years communicate via the Internet with activists and journalists in Tunisia. These
exiled members of the media complain that they regularly receive e-mail viruses that may
come from the government.

When human rights activist and journalist Sihem Bensedrine applied for a publication
license in 2002, officials ignored her request. She then established *Kalima*, an online journal that carries articles in Arabic and French from such noted independent journalists as
Taoufik Ben Brik. Authorities began blocking access to the site, so she and her staff
resorted to secretly printing and distributing the paper to individual readers.

In addition to restricting local print, broadcast, and electronic media, Tunisian authori-

MIDDLE EAST AND NORTH AFRICA

Pierre Tuquoi, a reporter with the French newspaper *Le Monde*, was refused entry into Tunisia while en route to cover the referendum because, authorities said, he had "ill will" toward the country. In 1999, Tuquoi co-authored the book *Our Friend Ben Ali*, which lambasted Tunisia's human rights record.

While publications affiliated with legally sanctioned opposition parties exist, they do not receive government subsidies as do other papers, and as a result do not publish regularly.

Although Tunisian newspapers and government television stations have lost credibility among much of the public, satellite television has become very popular, especially Arabic-language stations such as the Qatar-based Al-Jazeera and the private, London-based El Zeitouna, which is affiliated with Tunisia's banned Al-Nahda Party.

TURKEY

IN NOVEMBER, THE ISLAMIST-ORIENTED JUSTICE AND DEVELOPMENT PARTY WON parliamentary elections in Turkey. The new prime minister, Abdullah Gul, and influential party head Recep Tayyip Erdogan affirmed that joining the European Union would be a top government priority. To that end, they promised greater democratic reform, including an easing of long-standing restrictions on freedom of expression that remain in place despite changes implemented by the outgoing government of Prime Minister Bulent Ecevit.

In early February, the National Assembly passed what officials called a "minidemocracy package," consisting of amendments to repressive laws that have been used to punish journalists, writers, and intellectuals. The amendments, adopted in accordance with changes made to the constitution in 2001, restrict the application of Penal Code Article 312, which outlaws "incitement to hatred on the basis of differences of social class, race, religion, sect, or region." Another amendment, to Penal Code Article 159, which penalizes "insult" to state institutions such as the military, reduces prison penalties from six years to three. Minor penalty changes were made to articles 7 and 8 of the Anti-Terror Law, which bans terrorist and separatist propaganda. In August, the National Assembly further amended Article 159, limiting its application to cases where "insult" is done with "intent," and modified the Press Law to replace prison sentences with fines. Nevertheless, the amended laws still contain restrictive provisions that can land journalists in jail. And other repressive laws and Penal Code articles remain on the books, unchanged.

Following Parliament's passage of the reform legislation, free expression advocates had hoped that Turkish courts, particularly the Court of Appeals, would use the new statutes to dismiss convictions of journalists and intellectuals. But by year's end, some courts, including the Court of Appeals, had acquitted journalists in criminal cases or had dismissed prosecutions, while others had handed down convictions or had launched new prosecutions. The Turkish Human Rights Foundation, a local nongovernmental organization, reported that authorities in the first half of 2002 launched more than 2,000 freedom of expression–related prosecutions.

While the number of journalists imprisoned in Turkey has steadily dropped in recent years—13 were in jail at year's end, mostly for being affiliated with outlawed groups' publications—legal harassment of the media continued. Those who criticized the army and judiciary, or who wrote critically about sensitive political issues, such as the struggle of the country's Kurdish minority for greater cultural rights or the role of Islam in politics and society, remained the most vulnerable. Journalists in the pro-Kurdish, leftist, and Islamist media were the primary targets, but members of the mainstream media also faced legal action.

In a case that attracted widespread international media coverage, Turkish publisher Abdullah Keskin was convicted in July of "separatist propaganda"—a crime under Article 8 of the Anti-Terror Law—for publishing a Turkish-language edition of former *Washington Post* reporter Jonathan Randal's book about the Kurds, *After Such Knowledge, What Forgiveness? My Encounters in Kurdistan.* A State Security Court sentenced Keskin to six months in prison, which was converted to a fine of about US$500. State prosecutors had objected to passages in the book referring to "Kurdistan." The book, which was confiscated on January 15, 2002, remained banned after the trial.

Because the judiciary dictates prosecutions, the new government will likely have little effect on Islamist newspapers, which continue to be singled out for legal action. In October, a State Security Court convicted Mehmet Sevki Eygi and Selami Caliskan, columnist and managing editor, respectively, at the daily *Milli Gazete,* of "inciting hatred" in connection with a November 2000 column that criticized the Turkish courts for barring religious headscarves in government offices and universities. Both men were sentenced to 20 months in prison, and *Milli Gazete* was closed for three days. (Caliskan's prison sentence was converted into a US$1,200 fine soon after the conviction. Sevki Eygi's sentence remained in force, but he was free at year's end pending appeal.)

The government continued to confiscate books and newspapers and to ban distribution of leftist and pro-Kurdish publications. In November, however, authorities lifted a 15-year-old state of emergency in the country's southeast region, home to much of the Kurdish population. By December, several previously prohibited papers had appeared on local newsstands.

The number of private radio and television stations has grown since the mid-1990s, when the government first authorized them, but stations must contend with an array of tough laws and regulations. The Supreme Radio and Television Board (RTUK), the main regulatory body for broadcast media, can sanction broadcast outlets and suspend television and radio stations for airing violent, sensational, or politically controversial programming. Dozens of closures were ordered during 2002, including that of CNN-Turk, which was shuttered for one day in April after broadcasting a speech in January by a labor union figure who had accused the Nationalist Movement Party of interfering in union affairs. Smaller, pro-Kurdish outlets have historically received the stiffest penalties. In March, the RTUK banned the small, private Gun TV for one year because it had broadcast a Kurdish-language music video. Gun TV has appealed the ruling.

In August, as a part of one of its democratic reform packages, Parliament voted to allow the use of the previously banned Kurdish language (as well as other regional languages) in radio and television broadcasts. The RTUK formalized the measure in November, drafting regulations that permit the broadcasts to air only on state stations for no longer than 30 minutes a day on television and 45 minutes a day on radio.

MIDDLE EAST AND NORTH AFRICA

But even as the government introduced liberalizing measures, it also created new, restrictive ones. In May, President Ahmet Necdet Sezer was forced to sign a highly restrictive radio and television broadcasting law that he had vetoed a year earlier but that the Ecevit government later resubmitted to Parliament. The new legislation outlaws, among other things, broadcasts that "violate the existence and independence of the Turkish Republic, the territorial and national integrity of the State, the reforms and principles of Atatürk," or that "instigate the community to violence, terror, or ethnic discrimination." Fines for violators range from 5 billion lira (US$4,000) to 250 billion lira (US$190,000), with a 50 percent increase for repeat offenders. Broadcasters convicted three times within a single year can have their licenses revoked. More troubling, the legislation subjects online content to Turkey's restrictive laws governing freedom of expression.

After signing the law, Sezer referred it to Turkey's Constitutional Court, which ruled in June to temporarily freeze certain articles, including one that enhances the concentration of media ownership. However, censorship and other punitive provisions remain in effect.

Turkish journalists argue that because only a handful of large companies dominate the country's mainstream media, opinions and coverage of sensitive political issues are limited. The Dogan Medya group remained the most powerful media force in the country at year's end. Dogan owns eight newspapers and two television stations and reportedly controls roughly 40 percent of advertising revenue and 80 percent of newspaper distribution in Turkey.

UNITED ARAB EMIRATES

IN THE AUTOCRATIC CITY-STATES THAT COMPRISE THE UNITED ARAB EMIRATES (U.A.E.), local media face both the promise of new technology and the burdens of long-standing state restrictions.

The country boasts a number of private newspapers that offer decent coverage of regional and business news. However, reporting on domestic matters is decidedly tame, and journalists steer clear of any news that might irritate local authorities. The 1980 Press Law prohibits, among other things, any speech that "criticizes the head of state or leaders of the Emirates," "harms Islam or the regime," "threatens the supreme national interests," or "shames leaders of friendly Arab or Islamic states." Offenders can be fined, imprisoned, or have their newspapers suspended.

The government also licenses publications, authorizes the establishment of private printing presses, and monitors both local and foreign publications, which are subject to confiscation if they contain objectionable moral or political content. Journalists say that officials give newspapers and television stations guidelines on how to cover certain news stories, while editors and reporters often receive admonishing phone calls from officials. In past years, CPJ has received reports that United Arab Emirate journalists have been barred from writing or detained by authorities in response to their published criticisms.

Despite these restrictions, local media have flourished in recent years, due in large part to substantial government expenditures on services and infrastructure. The emirate of Dubai, already the region's leading commercial hub, has aggressively positioned itself as a media center to attract more investment.

In January 2001, the first phase of the much-hyped Dubai Media City—a 200 hectare (500 acre) plot of sparkling media offices, state-of-the-art production facilities, restaurants, and handsome apartments for media professionals—was completed. With incentives such as lower operating costs compared to Europe and full ownership for noncitizens, the media city has already succeeded in luring several prominent regional and international media organizations. In April, the Saudi-owned Middle East Broadcasting Centre officially opened its offices there after relocating from London. Other companies now operating from the media city include CNN Arabic, Reuters, and the leading Saudi-owned daily *Al Sharq al-Awsat*.

The government has vowed to respect freedom of expression for those operating in the media city. According to its own promotional literature, the media city is working with the government on draft regulations "guaranteeing freedom of expression within the dimensions of responsibility and accuracy." It remains unclear, however, how this will translate into practice.

Government authorities own or finance nearly all domestic broadcast media. One bright spot in the U.A.E. media landscape has been the meteoric rise of the semiofficial Abu Dhabi TV, which was relaunched in 2000 as a regional channel following a multimillion-dollar makeover. The channel's news coverage, especially of the Palestinian intifada, has rivaled that of the Qatar-based Al-Jazeera satellite channel. But while some viewers seem to prefer Abu Dhabi TV's less sensational political talk shows, most observers agree that the channel does not enjoy the same editorial freedom as Al-Jazeera when it comes to political news and debate.

Satellite dishes are widespread in the U.A.E., allowing access to international and Pan-Arab news channels. The Internet is also increasingly prevalent, with the U.A.E. ranking among the highest per capita users in the Arab world. Authorities in Dubai have attempted to establish the emirate as a leading Internet hub following the 2000 launch of an Internet City, designed as a base for companies looking to tap into emerging telecommunications markets in the region, and the start in 2001 of a program making certain government services available online. The U.A.E. government, which is the country's main Internet service provider, employs Web-filtering technology to block sexually explicit content and some political sites.

YEMEN

IN A REGION WHERE OIL-RICH MONARCHIES ABHOR DISSENT, Yemen's press is relatively open and diverse, with numerous opposition and independent publications and journalists who do not avoid criticizing government officials or policies. However, the Yemeni press still faces criminal prosecutions, newspaper closures, arbitrary detentions, and threats from security forces.

The 1990 Press Law prohibits criticism of the president. Article 103, frequently used to prosecute journalists, bars the media from publishing material that "prejudices religion," "jeopardizes the supreme interests of the country," and may "raise tribal or sectarian divisions." Penalties include up to a year in prison, a ban on practicing journalism, and publication closure.

In July, state prosecutors summoned three Yemeni journalists working for the foreign press—Faisal Mukarram of the London-based daily *Al-Hayat*, Ahmed al-Hajj of The Associated Press, and Khaled al-Mahdi of Deutsche Presse-Agentur—for violating Article 103 of the Press Law after they reported that the deputy army chief of staff was injured when local tribes in the northern al-Jouf region, a hotbed for Islamist militants, fired on his helicopter.

Soon after the prosecutors questioned the men, President Ali Abdullah Saleh issued a decree halting legal proceedings against all journalists in the country. Initially, the move was considered a positive step for press freedom. But to be amnestied, reporters were required to sign a pledge that they would no longer violate the law. Mukarram, al-Hajj, and al-Mahdi refused, saying that to do so was an admission of guilt that would set a dangerous precedent. The cases against the three journalists remained open at year's end.

In another case, authorities used Article 103 to prosecute two opposition journalists, Abdel Rahim Mohsen and Ibrahim Hussein, who write for the weeklies *Al-Osboa* and *Al-Thawri*, respectively. Mohsen and Hussein were detained separately and held incommunicado until they were both charged on July 2. Although the presidential amnesty applied to them, they also refused to sign the pledge. Their case also remained open at year's end.

As in previous years, the government closed several publications in 2002. In February, the Information Ministry shuttered the weekly *Al-Shumou*. The paper's editor-in-chief said that the ministry provided no explanation for its action, and that officials have refused to discuss the matter with him. He reasoned that the closure came in response to *Al-Shumou*'s various "criticisms of government ministers." Mahboob Ali, head of the Yemeni Journalists' Syndicate, said that Information Ministry officials informed him that the paper was suspended for failing to comply with licensing procedures. The weekly reopened in the fall, after fulfilling the licensing requirements.

Since September 11, 2001, Yemen has emerged as an important strategic ally to the United States in its "war on terror." Yemeni journalists disagree on whether their government's efforts to subdue suspected al-Qaeda militants have had a negative effect on the media. Some said that authorities were too busy battling militants to pay much attention to the press, which was allowed unusual freedom for several months during 2002. Others, however, said that self-censorship has increased, especially on issues such as military operations and the status of government detainees. According to a Yemeni editor, the Information Ministry issued a directive in March instructing his paper not to cover events in Marib, Al-Jouf, and Shabwa provinces, where authorities are fighting anti-government militants allegedly linked to al-Qaeda. Other correspondents reportedly received warnings from officials about their coverage of military matters.

When a French tanker was attacked off the coast of Yemen in October, authorities maintained for 10 days that the attack was an accident before admitting that it was an act of terrorism. However, Yemeni journalists said that the government allowed coverage of the incident, including speculation that it was a terrorist attack.

Television is an important source of news in Yemen, where only half the population is literate. Two government-owned television stations broadcast, but many Yemenis, especially those in urban areas, have access to satellite television. Arabic stations such as the Qatar-based Al-Jazeera are increasingly popular. ■

| CASES TABLE OF CONTENTS |

ALGERIA

FEBRUARY 25

Selima Tlemcani, *El-Watan*
Omar Belhouchet, *El-Watan*
LEGAL ACTION

Tlemcani, a journalist at the French-language daily *El-Watan*, was charged with defaming the army following a complaint filed by the Defense Ministry. The case stemmed from a December 11, 2001, *El-Watan* article she had written accusing the military police of financial misconduct.

El-Watan editor Belhouchet accompanied her to court. Although Belhouchet was not named in the original complaint against Tlemcani, the presiding judge added the editor's name to the charges during the course of the proceedings.

A trial date for the two was set for March 18, but by year's end, no trial had taken place.

A week before Tlemcani appeared in court with her editor, prosecutors had attempted to reinstate a 1997 judgment against Belhouchet. That case stemmed from statements Belhouchet had made to the French media hinting that Algerian government officials may have been responsible for the murders of some journalists during the country's civil war, between 1993 and 1996.

In November 1997, Belhouchet received a one-year suspended sentence, a conviction that he later appealed. He told CPJ that authorities never pursued the case after his appeal, and that he was surprised that the government had revived the case.

A court was expected to rule on the 1997 case before March 4, but by year's end, no decision had been announced.

BAHRAIN

MAY 9

Al-Jazeera
CENSORED

Correspondents from the Qatar-based satellite channel Al-Jazeera were barred from Bahrain by Minster of Information Nabil al-Hamr, who claimed that the station "harms Bahrain and Bahrain's citizens," "encourages violence," spreads "false news to its viewers," and is a medium for "Zionist infiltration in the Gulf region." Prior to al-Hamr's announcement, Bahraini authorities had ignored visa and accreditation requests from an Al-Jazeera correspondent who had tried to visit the country from Doha, Qatar, in early May, according to Al-Jazeera staff. Al-Jazeera reporters were supposed to be in Bahrain to cover the country's May 9 municipal elections.

EGYPT

MARCH 5

Mohamed Eid Galal, Al-Jazeera
Mohamed Ezzedine El-Najjar, Al-Jazeera
HARASSED

Galal and El-Najjar were filming a pro-Palestinian student protest at the campus of Alexandria University in the morning, according to sources at the Cairo bureau of Al-Jazeera, the Qatar-based satellite channel, when Egyptian security officers approached the journalists as they were loading equipment into their car. Galal and El-Najjar displayed their press credentials but were told they did not have permission to film and would be taken in for questioning at the Bab Sharq Police Station.

After several hours of questioning, El-Najjar was released, but Galal spent the night at the station. The next morning, he appeared before a judge, who ordered him released. Al-Jazeera retrieved its equipment undamaged, but the tape that contained footage of the protest was not returned.

MARCH 21

Essam Fahmy, *Sawt al-Umma*
Adel Hammouda, *Sawt al-Umma*
LEGAL ACTION

The Abdeen Misdemeanor Court convicted Hammouda, editor of the independent weekly *Sawt al-Umma*, and Fahmy, head of the paper's board of directors, of defaming prominent Egyptian businessman Naguib Sawiris and sentenced them to six months in prison each. The charges stemmed from a series of articles published in 2001 detailing alleged financial misconduct by Sawiris and his telecommunications company, Orascom Telecom.

According to Hammouda, since the articles appeared, Sawiris has filed more than 20 suits in different localities against the journalists, all of which remain pending. On March 24, the journalists posted a 500 Egyptian pound (US$107) bail fee and filed an appeal. The case was postponed until January 29, 2003.

APRIL 28

Ahmed Haridy, *Al Methaq al-Araby*
LEGAL ACTION

Haridy, editor of the online publication *Al Methaq al-Araby*, was sentenced to six months in prison after the Boulaq Abu al-Aila Misdemeanor Court in the capital, Cairo, found him guilty of defaming Ibrahim Nafie, editor-in-chief and chairman of Egypt's largest newspaper, the semiofficial *Al-Ahram*.

The charges stem from a series of articles published in *Al Methaq al-Araby* in May and June 2001 alleging that Nafie and several other senior *Al-Ahram* managers were involved in financial malfeasance. According to Haridy, Nafie filed suit against him in July 2001. Haridy told CPJ that he posted bail of 1,000 Egyptian pounds (US$215) and appealed the court's decision. The case was postponed until February 1, 2003.

JUNE 27

Gihan Rushdy, ZDF
Ayman Atef, ZDF
HARASSED

Rushdy, a correspondent with the ZDF news agency, told CPJ that she and her cameraman, Atef, were detained, along with their driver, and held for about an hour at a police station after officers saw them filming physical confrontations between police and voters trying to reach a polling station during runoff parliamentary elections in the northern city of Alexandria. Officials confiscated the journalists' film.

Sarah al-Deeb, The Associated Press
HARASSED, ATTACKED

Al-Deeb, of The Associated Press, was prevented by police from entering a polling station during the runoff parliamentary elections in the northern city of Alexandria. She told CPJ that, at the time, voters trying to get to the polling station were clashing with police who appeared to be barring them from entry. As al-Deeb was speaking to three would-be voters who could not reach the station, three women attacked her, one of them pulling her hair and hitting her on the back of the neck. Al-Deeb said that police, who were close by, did not intervene.

MIDDLE EAST AND NORTH AFRICA

Rida al-Shafie, Abu Dhabi TV
Hany Emara, Abu Dhabi TV
HARASSED

Emara, a reporter for Abu Dhabi TV, told CPJ that he and his cameraman, al-Shafie, were setting up their equipment near a police barricade when they asked a police officer for permission to film in the polling station during the runoff parliamentary elections in the northern city of Alexandria. The officer took the two journalists to a police station, where officials confiscated the tape from the journalists' camera and held them at the station for about six hours. They were released just as the polling stations were closing.

IRAN

APRIL 16

Ali-Hamed Imam, *Shams-e Tabriz*
LEGAL ACTION
Shams-e Tabriz
CENSORED

Imam, editor of the local weekly *Shams-e Tabriz*, was sentenced to 74 lashes and seven months in prison by a court in Tabriz, 350 miles (560 kilometers) northwest of the capital, Tehran. According to Iran's state news agency, IRNA, the court also revoked Imam's publishing license and suspended the paper. Although it was impossible to verify which articles may have prompted the ruling, IRNA reported that 17 charges had been filed against Imam stemming from "repeated press offenses."

APRIL 29

Ahmed Zeidabadi, *Hamshahri*
LEGAL ACTION

Zeidabadi, a reformist journalist for the newspaper *Hamshahri*, was sentenced to 23 months in prison. On April 29, The

Associated Press quoted Zeidabadi's wife as saying that he was originally charged in August 2000 with "insulting Supreme Leader Ayatollah Ali Khamanei and publishing lies against the Islamic establishment for the purpose of disturbing public opinion." The charges came after he gave a series of critical lectures at several Iranian universities, according to a CPJ source. He was not convicted in the original case but spent seven months in prison before being released on bail. Authorities did not pursue the case against him until late April 2002.

The verdict seemed prompted by a recent interview that Zeidabadi had given in the daily newspaper *Bonyan*, in which he condemned Palestinian suicide bombings. He also said that he supported U.N. Security Council resolutions 242 and 338, the so-called land-for-peace resolutions regarding the Israeli-Palestinian conflict, which the Iranian government opposes, a local source told CPJ. Zeidabadi has previously written for the reformist daily *Azad*, which was closed in April 2000, and the newspaper *Ettelaat*. He appealed the court's verdict and remained free at year's end.

MAY 4

Iran
CENSORED

The daily *Iran*, which is published by the official Islamic Republic News Agency, was banned by Tehran's conservative Press Court after the paper ran an article in April saying that the Prophet Mohammed enjoyed listening to female singers. The ban was lifted the next day.

Bonyan
CENSORED

Iran's Press Court banned the daily *Bonyan*. According to a CPJ source, the court cited the Precautionary Measures Law, a prerevolutionary statute that allows courts to seize "instruments used for committing crimes." The court said that *Bonyan*, widely known for its critical reporting, had stolen its name and logo from a provincial weekly. But a source told CPJ that the charge appeared to be a pretext to punish the paper for its reformist editorial stance.

MAY 8

Mohsen Mirdamadi, *Norooz*
LEGAL ACTION
Norooz
CENSORED

Mirdamadi, a member of Parliament and director of leading reformist daily *Norooz*, was convicted by Iran's conservative Press Court of insulting the state, publishing lies, and insulting Islamic institutions in articles the paper had published. The court sentenced Mirdamadi to six months in prison, banned him from practicing journalism for four years, and ordered him to pay a 2 million riyal (US$1,150) fine. The court also banned *Norooz* from publishing for six months.

The prosecutor general had originally filed the charges against the paper in December 2001. Mirdamadi appealed the decision, and the paper continued to publish until July 24, when a Tehran appeals court confirmed the earlier sentences. Mirdamadi remained free at year's end.

JULY 11

Azad
LEGAL ACTION

The pro-reform daily *Azad* was ordered by Tehran's conservative Press Court to cease publishing indefinitely because the paper had violated a government directive banning media commentary about the resignation of prominent cleric Ayatollah Jalaleddin Taheri. Iran's Supreme National Security Council, which is headed by President Muhammad Khatami and includes other top government officials, had issued the directive a day earlier, on Wednesday, July 10, instructing publishers not to take a position "for or against" Taheri.

On Thursday, July 11, *Azad* published a front-page story discussing Taheri's resignation and supporting critical statements the cleric had made about the government. The paper was banned later that day and has not appeared on newsstands since.

Taheri, a prominent cleric and associate of Ayatollah Khomeini, the leader of Iran's 1979 Islamic revolution, resigned on July 9 as the leader of the Friday prayers in the city of Isfahan, about 250 miles (400 kilometers) south of the capital, Tehran. In his resignation letter, published in some reformist newspapers on July 10, Taheri accused the government of corruption and said that the promises of the revolution had not been realized.

AUGUST 8

Ayineh-e-Jonoub
CENSORED

The newly launched daily *Ayineh-e-Jonoub* (formerly a weekly) was banned by Tehran's conservative Press Court, which cited a dozen unspecified complaints in its ruling. In addition, Press Court judge Said Mortazavi pointed to a recent Appeals Court ruling that had convicted the paper's publisher, reformist member of Parliament Mohammed Dadfar, of anti-regime "propaganda" as another reason for the ban.

Rouz-e-No
LEGAL ACTION

Publication of the new daily *Rouz-e-No*, which was to hit newsstands the week of August 12, was barred by Tehran's conservative Press Court. The court ruled that the paper was a continuation of the recently banned *Norooz*. In July, a court had upheld a six-month suspension of reformist-leaning *Norooz*, which remained closed at year's end.

SEPTEMBER 15

Golestan-e-Iran
Vaqt
LEGAL ACTION

The *Golestan-e-Iran* daily newspaper was closed by Tehran's conservative Press Court for allegedly publishing lies and rumors. In the same ruling, the court also announced the suspension of the weekly *Vaqt*. A source in Iran said that the paper was accused of publishing photos and articles considered to be "immoral." Both papers have small circulations and are reformist-leaning.

ISRAEL AND THE OCCUPIED TERRITORIES (INCLUDING THE PALESTINIAN AUTHORITY TERRITORIES)

JANUARY 3

Akhbar al-Khalil
CENSORED

The offices of the weekly newspaper *Akhbar al-Khalil*, in the West Bank city of Hebron, were raided by Palestinian security authorities. The officials ordered the paper's immediate closure but gave no reason for the move. According to an editor at the paper, however, a Palestinian National Authority (PNA) security officer told him that the PNA was responding to Israeli and U.S. pressure

to close the paper, which frequently criticized those countries' Middle East policies.

JANUARY 19

Voice of Palestine
ATTACKED

In the early morning hours, Israeli forces entered a five-story building that houses administrative offices and broadcasting facilities for the Palestinian National Authority's (PNA) Voice of Palestine (VOP) radio station, as well as studios for the PNA's Palestine Television. The forces confiscated equipment and detonated explosives, setting the building on fire and causing half of it to collapse.

VOP resumed broadcasting at the facilities of a private West Bank Palestinian radio station. The Gaza-based Palestine Television also continued to broadcast through its main facility. The Israel Defense Forces described the action as a response to a Palestinian gunman's attack on a banquet hall in the Israeli city of Hadera two days earlier, which killed six Israelis and wounded dozens.

FEBRUARY 2

Several journalists
HARASSED

Palestinian police harassed and confiscated the tapes of camera crews who were filming riots outside a courtroom in the West Bank city of Jenin, where a Palestinian mob had stormed the courtroom and killed three defendants who had just been convicted of murder, according to the Foreign Press Association of Israel, which is based in Tel Aviv.

FEBRUARY 13

Several journalists
CENSORED

Israel Defense Forces (IDF) denied journalists access to the Gaza Strip during military operations, according to the Foreign Press Association of Israel (FPA). In a statement, the FPA said, "We understand possible concerns for the safety of journalists in a conflict zone. But the IDF's sweeping closure went well beyond what is justifiable under these circumstances." The statement added that journalists were also denied access to areas where no conflict was occurring. A single press pool was created for print journalists, the FPA said.

FEBRUARY 14

Sagui Bashan, Channel 2 Television
`ATTACKED`

Bashan, a reporter with Israel's Channel 2 television station, was shot by one or more Israel Defense Forces (IDF) soldiers while the journalist was driving his car toward the Karni border crossing near the Gaza Strip. Bashan was trying to retrieve film footage from his cameraman, who was covering the aftermath of a bomb attack against an Israeli tank that had killed three soldiers.

Moments before the incident, a soldier at an IDF roadblock located in Israel proper, about one-half mile (1 kilometer) from the Karni crossing, tried to prevent Bashan from entering the area. Bashan asked the soldier to produce an official military order to justify barring him access as a journalist, which the soldier could not do. Bashan then told the soldier that he intended to approach the Karni crossing. He re-entered his car, put the vehicle in reverse, and headed for the crossing via a side road.

Moments later, several rounds of live gunfire struck his car. Ricocheted bullets grazed Bashan in the arm and leg, and he was later treated at a hospital. An IDF spokesperson contacted by CPJ said that the incident was "under investigation."

FEBRUARY 21

Voice of Palestine
`ATTACKED`

Israel Defense Forces (IDF) entered a two-story building housing offices and studios used by the Palestinian National Authority's Voice of Palestine radio and Palestine Television. Khaled Al-Siam, director of both outlets, told Agence France-Presse that the IDF soldiers confiscated equipment and later detonated explosives, setting the building on fire and causing it to collapse.

MARCH 12

Several journalists
`ATTACKED`

Israeli forces directed heavy machine gun fire at the City Inn Hotel, where about 30 to 40 reporters and cameramen, most of them from Western media outlets, were filming an Israeli army operation against the Al-Amari refugee camp near the West Bank city of Ramallah.

Israeli forces fired on the hotel, which is located some 300 yards (275 meters) from the Al-Amari camp, for about 15 minutes, according to press reports and journalists on the scene. Israeli forces gave no prior warning of the attack. Journalists said the gunfire smashed windows and damaged the interior and exterior of the building. There were no injuries. However, gunfire destroyed an ABC camera after the fleeing crew left it on its tripod.

An Israel Defense Forces (IDF) spokesman told CPJ that the army was responding to Palestinian gunfire coming from the hotel's upper floors and other nearby buildings. The spokesman added that the army was unaware that journalists were in the hotel, and that Israeli forces ceased fire after news agencies alerted the IDF to the situation.

Several journalists who spoke with CPJ

MIDDLE EAST AND NORTH AFRICA |

vehemently denied that a gunman was in the hotel, which was located away from cross fire and provided a good vantage point on the refugee camp. Journalists argued that the army should have been aware that media representatives were inside the hotel because some 20 clearly marked press vehicles were parked outside. Several Israeli tanks drove by the hotel before the attack, they said.

March 13

Raffaele Ciriello, free-lance
KILLED
For full details on this case, see page 362.

Al-Jazeera
ATTACKED
The central Ramallah offices of the Qatar-based satellite channel Al-Jazeera came under Israeli gunfire shortly after the station finished an interview with Palestinian National Authority information minister Yasser Abed Rabbo, Al-Jazeera correspondents told CPJ.

The gunfire came from a tank stationed about 111 yards (100 meters) away from the office and struck a window where a second staff cameraman was filming Israeli-Palestinian clashes occurring some 333 yards (300 meters) away from the station. Another round entered the fifth floor office and hit a wall, narrowly missing a cameraman's head. Other staff members ducked for cover, while some rounds hit the outside of various floors of the building, Al-Jazeera sources said.

Tareq Abdel Jaber, Egyptian TV
ATTACKED
Abdel Jaber, a reporter for Egyptian TV, told CPJ that he and his cameraman were driving on a main street in Ramallah when

their car, which was clearly marked as a press vehicle, came under fire. There was no fighting in the area at the time, the journalist said. Bullets penetrated the car and struck Abdel Jaber's flak jacket, but he was not seriously hurt. The journalist could not identify the shooter but said that Israeli tanks and military personnel were surrounding the area at the time.

March 14

Several journalists
ATTACKED
A group of journalists traveling in an Associated Press (AP) armored car came under fire from Palestinian gunmen in the West Bank city of Ramallah, according to international wire reports. According to the AP, gunmen fired on the car for about 30 seconds, puncturing the vehicle's tires. No one was injured in the attack. The gunmen later told the reporters that they had opened fire on the vehicle after hearing a report that Israeli soldiers were driving around in a vehicle marked "TV," a rumor Israeli officials vehemently denied.

March 29

Carlos Handal, Nile TV, Abu Dhabi TV
ATTACKED
Handal, a Palestinian cameraman who works for Egypt's Nile TV and the United Arab Emirates' Abu Dhabi TV, was shot in the mouth after his car came under attack in Ramallah, according to international press reports. Handal was hospitalized in stable condition. It is unclear who fired the shot at him.

Anthony Shadid, *Boston Globe*
ATTACKED
Shadid, a reporter for the *Boston Globe*,

was wounded by a single gunshot in Ramallah. The journalist told CPJ that he and his colleague, *Boston Globe* stringer Said Ghazali, were walking away from Palestinian National Authority chairman Yasser Arafat's besieged compound in Ramallah when a bullet entered Shadid's left shoulder. The area was completely quiet at the time, and both journalists were wearing flak jackets marked "TV" in red tape. Shadid told CPJ that he did not see who shot him, but that Israeli tanks and soldiers were surrounding the area. He was taken to a Palestinian hospital after a group of Israeli soldiers gave him first aid.

APRIL 1

Majdi Banura, Al-Jazeera
ATTACKED

Banura, a cameraman with the Qatar-based satellite channel Al-Jazeera, was injured when Israeli troops fired at the Star Hotel in Bethlehem, where most journalists covering the Israeli army's offensive into the West Bank were staying. Two of Banura's colleagues told CPJ that he and several journalists were standing on the fifth floor of the hotel when Israeli troops began firing into the hotel. Both journalists said that there was heavy Israeli-Palestinian cross fire outside at the time. As bullets punctured the window, Banura was struck in the head by broken glass but was not seriously injured.

Ismail Khader, Reuters
Mark Mina, Middle East Broadcasting Centre
HARASSED

Khader, a cameramen for Reuters, and Mina, a cameraman for the Middle East Broadcasting Centre, were forced to strip down to their underwear by Israeli troops on the fourth day of the Israeli army's offensive into Ramallah, which began on March 29. Khader and Mina told CPJ that they were in an armored car owned by Reuters, which was clearly identified as a press vehicle. Israeli troops signaled the journalists to stop as they neared Al Manara Square, which had been secured by Israeli forces at the time.

Both men said that there was no exchange of fire in the area that morning. The soldiers ordered the men out of the car and motioned for Khader to approach. When he was about 20 meters (66 feet) away, the soldiers ordered Khader to place his camera and cell phone on the ground and to remove his flak jacket, shirt, and pants. Mina was ordered to do the same. When he refused to remove his pants, Khader said a soldier threatened to shoot Mina. The journalists were forced to kneel in their underwear for about 25 minutes before being allowed to leave.

Dana Lewis, NBC
ATTACKED

Lewis, a correspondent with the U.S. TV station NBC, and his two-person camera crew came under fire from the Israel Defense Forces (IDF) in Ramallah at dusk while driving in an armored car that was clearly identified as a press vehicle. After an initial burst of gunfire hit the car, a lone IDF soldier opened fire with a second burst from a range of about 50 to 100 feet (15 to 30 meters). The journalists then stopped the car, turned on an interior light to make themselves visible, and placed their hands on the windshield. After 15 to 20 seconds, the soldier fired a third burst, hitting the windshield. The NBC crew escaped by driving away in reverse.

Orla Guerin, BBC News
ATTACKED

Guerin, a BBC correspondent, and her

television crew came under Israeli fire while covering peaceful protesters walking through the streets of Bethlehem. Video footage of the incident shows the camera panning on the demonstrators and then focusing on an Israeli tank, which then fires machine gun rounds at the camera. The crew took cover behind a car that was clearly marked as a press vehicle. No one was injured in the attack.

The Associated Press
Reuters
Palestine TV
`THREATENED, HARASSED`

Journalists working for The Associated Press, Reuters, and Palestine TV in Bethlehem were threatened by Palestinian militants and forced to hand over footage, shot the night before, of the body of an alleged Palestinian collaborator who had been shot in a parking lot.

APRIL 2

Marc Innaro, RAI
Mauro Mauritzi, RAI
Fernando Pelligrini, RAI
Toni Capuozzo, TG5
Garu Nalbandian, TG5
Luciano Gulli, *Il Giornale*
`ATTACKED`

Israeli troops in the West Bank town of Bethlehem opened fire on a car carrying journalists Innaro, Mauritzi, and Pellegrini, of Italy's television and radio station RAI; Capuozzo and Nalbandian, of the Italian television station TG5; and Gulli, of the Italian daily *Il Giornale*. The journalists had gone to Bethlehem to cover the Israeli army's military offensive in the West Bank and were traveling in a white armored car marked "TV." According to Innaro, Israeli troops had allowed the journalists into the

town at about 10 a.m. Shortly after they arrived, the journalists heard gunfire in the vicinity of Manger Square.

As they approached the square, the group decided to leave because it was too dangerous. They turned their car around and began to leave the city center. After traveling about 220 yards (200 meters), they encountered two Israeli armored vehicles.

The journalists spoke through a loudspeaker to inform the troops that they were journalists who were attempting to leave. The soldiers did not respond but motioned for the journalists to leave the area. Some of the journalists exited the car, raised their hands in the air, and walked toward the vehicles, identifying themselves as journalists. The journalists told CPJ that the immediate area was clear of fighting.

As the journalists approached, the troops opened fire at the car with four journalists inside. "One of the soldiers aimed his weapon at us and other soldiers shot at the car," Innaro told Israel's daily *Ha'aretz*. "The photographers got back in the car. We turned around and headed for the church." Innaro telephoned a Franciscan monk at the Church of the Nativity compound and asked him to open the door to the monastery so they could take refuge.

"We parked the car by the monastery and ran, under fire, to the door of the monastery," Innaro said. Because they were running, he said, it was not possible to determine whether the fire came from Israeli troops or Palestinian militants.

Atta Oweisat, Gamma
`ATTACKED`

Oweisat, a photographer for the photo agency Gamma, was detained by Israeli troops in Ramallah and held for nearly six hours. He and other journalists were ordered out of their car and forced to take off their flak jackets and put their personal possessions on the ground. The troops detained Oweisat when they found that his press card had expired. He was blindfolded and handcuffed during his detention.

Magnus Johansson, Reuters
ATTACKED

An Israeli soldier fired one round toward the car of Reuters photographer Johansson, which was clearly identified as a press vehicle, while he was reporting in Bethlehem. Before the incident occurred, Johansson had heard soldiers shouting at him and exited his car. The soldiers ordered him back in the vehicle, and the shot was fired as he attempted to drive away.

Al-Quds Educational TV
CENSORED

Al-Quds Educational TV offices near Ramallah were occupied by Israeli troops early in the evening. Two staffers were detained briefly, and the station was forced off the air. Al-Quds Educational TV is a project affiliated with Al-Quds University. Recent programming on the station has included health information, public service announcements, and programming designed to help children deal with trauma. The soldiers occupied the offices until April 21, when staff returned to find the premises damaged, according to CPJ sources.

Layleh Odeh, Abu Dhabi TV
HARASSED
Jasem al-Azawi, Abu Dhabi TV
HARASSED, EXPELLED

Israeli authorities expelled al-Azawi, a journalist and talk show host for the United Arab Emirate television station Abu Dhabi TV, after revoking his press credentials along with those of Odeh, a Ramallah-based correspondent for the channel.

On April 2, Israeli government press spokesman Daniel Seaman ordered the journalists to turn over their press credentials, and al-Azawi was given two days to leave the country. No specific reason was cited for the deportation. Before al-Azawi's accreditation was revoked, he and Odeh had reported a story on March 31 alleging that Israeli troops had executed surrendering Palestinian police officers in Ramallah. Police took al-Azawi from a Jerusalem press building and escorted him to a police station and then to his East Jerusalem hotel to pack his belongings before going to the airport.

APRIL 3

Maher Rumani, Al-Manara, Nasser TV
IMPRISONED

Rumani, a news presenter for Ramallah-based Al-Manara radio station and Nasser TV, was detained by Israeli forces on or about April 3 during the Israeli offensive into Ramallah. The journalist was detained when troops entered the building that houses both stations. Rumani was the only staff member there at the time. He had been broadcasting emergency information on the radio station and keeping watch over the offices. According to station director Ammar Ammar, Rumani was held for 20 days, and Israeli forces blindfolded and beat him during his detention.

Ashraf Faraj, Al-Roa
Jalal Ehmad, Al-Roa
IMPRISONED

Faraj, an editor at the private, Bethlehem-based television station Al-Roa, and Ehmad, a cameraman at the station, were detained by Israeli troops in downtown Bethlehem. Several other journalists who were detained with them were released later that day. The group had opened a makeshift media center in Manger Square to cover events unfolding in the town. Troops confiscated cameras, tapes, and other equipment. Faraj and Ehmad were held at a facility near Beitunia in the West Bank before being released several days later, according to CPJ sources.

APRIL 5

Several journalists
ATTACKED

Israel Defense Forces (IDF) fired stun grenades and rubber bullets at a group of at least 24 reporters attempting to cover the pending arrival of U.S. Middle East envoy Anthony Zinni at Palestinian National Authority leader Yasser Arafat's Ramallah compound.

Eyewitnesses told CPJ that the journalists had driven to the compound in several armored press cars. Shortly after they arrived and exited the vehicles, IDF troops arrived and hurled about six stun grenades in their direction. According to CNN, the grenades "produce a blinding flash and a very loud explosion, designed to disorient those targeted." One grenade exploded under CNN reporter Michael Holmes' foot. The IDF troops ordered the journalists to leave and then fired rubber bullets at their armored vehicles, CNN reported. The journalists regrouped and tried to return to the area, but Israeli troops turned them away.

Some journalists had their press accreditation confiscated, CPJ sources said.

APRIL 8

Nile TV
Abu Dhabi TV
HARASSED

A building in Ramallah housing Egyptian television channel Nile TV and United Arab Emirate channel Abu Dhabi TV was raided by several Israeli soldiers. A witness reported that troops forced the journalists in the office to lie on the ground and knocked Nile TV cameraman Raed al-Helw to the ground. Soldiers dismantled journalists' cell phones and threw the parts around the room. Troops also fired live rounds at a locked office door to gain access to the room, according to the same witness. After 45 minutes, the soldiers left and searched the rest of the building, which houses several other foreign television stations.

APRIL 9

Gilles Jaquier, France 2
ATTACKED

Jaquier, a cameraman with television channel France 2, was wounded by a single gunshot near his shoulder while reporting outside the West Bank city of Nablus, an eyewitness told CPJ. Jaquier, who was wearing a bulletproof vest, was transported to a Jerusalem hospital after having the bullet removed at a hospital in Nablus. It is unclear who fired the shot, and the witness said the area was quiet at the time of the shooting.

Vincent Benhamou, free-lance
HARASSED

Benhamou, a French free-lance cameraman, had a tape confiscated by Israel Defense Forces. He told The Associated Press that after he turned to walk away from the soldiers, he heard two shots fired in the air.

APRIL 16

Mohammed Daraghmeh,
The Associated Press
HARASSED

Daraghmeh, an Associated Press (AP)

correspondent, was detained by Israeli forces early in the morning and released that evening. According to the AP, the journalist did not arrive home until the next day. Daraghmeh, who was rounded up along with 50 other men during a sweep in the West Bank town of Nablus, was released from an Israeli army base 6 miles (10 kilometers) away from his home. As Daraghmeh made his trek back, Israeli soldiers threatened him, harassed him, and forced him to take unsafe roads by foot to his house, he told the AP. Daraghmeh has been covering the northern West Bank for the AP since 1996. He also writes for the Palestinian daily *Al-Ayam*.

APRIL 18

Kamel Jbeil, *Al-Quds*
Maher al-Dessouki, Al-Quds
Educational TV
IMPRISONED

Jbeil, a reporter for the Palestinian daily *Al-Quds*, and al-Dessouki, a talk show host with Al-Quds Educational TV, were detained on or about April 18 at al-Dessouki's brother-in-law's residence in Ramallah. Al-Dessouki was released on June 27 after being held for more than two months in administrative detention without charge. Jbeil was held, also without charge, until September 15.

Jbeil's lawyer told CPJ that in early July, an Israeli military judge had extended the journalist's administrative detention for another three months. In a June 23 letter to CPJ, Prime Minister Ariel Sharon's adviser Ranaan Gissin wrote that Jbeil and other detained journalists were "arrested on suspicion of having contact (unrelated to their journalistic work) with a terrorist organization." The letter provided no details supporting those allegations.

APRIL 20

Mahfouz Abu Turk, Reuters
HARASSED

Veteran Reuters photographer Abu Turk was detained by Israeli troops at an army checkpoint while he and two colleagues were leaving the Jenin refugee camp. After examining the journalists' press cards, the soldiers blindfolded Abu Turk and took him away in an armored personnel carrier. When one of the journalists asked why Abu Turk had been detained, a soldier told them that the photographer was on a "list" and had to be "questioned." Abu Turk later told CPJ that he was handcuffed and put on a bus, where he was held for 22 hours without food or water before being released. He was never questioned.

APRIL 24

Hussam Abu Alan, Agence France-Presse
IMPRISONED
Mazen Dana, Reuters
HARASSED

Abu Alan, a veteran, Hebron-based photographer for Agence France-Presse (AFP), and Dana, a Reuters cameraman, were detained by Israel Defense Forces troops. Soldiers stopped the two men at the Beit Einun checkpoint north of Hebron when they tried to reach a nearby village to cover the funeral of Palestinian militants killed by Israeli forces.

The soldiers detained the two journalists for about three hours and confiscated their cameras. Dana was released and his camera was later returned, but Abu Alan was handcuffed, blindfolded, and taken to an undisclosed location.

After repeated protests from AFP, the army said in a May 3 letter that it suspected Abu Alan of "assisting the terrorist Tanzim organization." AFP repeatedly asked Israeli authorities, including Foreign Minister Shimon Peres during a Paris press conference, to furnish proof of Abu Alan's involvement in wrongdoing but received none.

AFP quoted lawyer Mohammed Burghal as saying that on July 24, a military judge had extended Abu Alan's detention for three months. He was then moved from Ofer Prison to Ketziot Prison, in Israel's southern Negev desert. On October 22, Abu Alan was released without charge.

APRIL 30

Youssry al-Jamal, Reuters
IMPRISONED
Mazen Dana, Reuters
HARASSED

Al-Jamal, a soundman for Reuters news agency, and Dana, a Reuters cameraman, were detained by Israel Defense Forces troops in the West Bank town of Hebron. The two journalists were filming near the Al-Ahli Hospital when soldiers demanded to see their identification cards and arrested them. The journalists were blindfolded, handcuffed, and taken to an outdoor holding area, where they spent the night without food or water. Dana was released the next day, but al-Jamal remained in custody.

Reuters told CPJ that according to a June 18 military court decision, al-Jamal was to be released on July 10. But sources at Reuters said that the detention was later extended for three months. On July 11, Reuters protested to Israeli authorities and noted that it had been denied access to information about its employee's detention.

Israeli officials accused al-Jamal of having contacts with Palestinian militant groups but provided no evidence to support the allegations. On October 9, al-Jamal was released without charge.

MAY 22

Suhaib Jadallah Salem, Reuters
IMPRISONED

Salem, a Reuters photographer, was detained by Israeli authorities for five days. According to Reuters news reports, no charges were ever filed against him. Israeli authorities took Salem into custody at the Abu Holi checkpoint in the Gaza Strip. Reuters reported that Salem was attempting to enter the town of Rafah, en route to Egypt, where he was scheduled to fly to Japan to cover the World Cup soccer tournament. He was traveling in a Reuters armored car, clearly identified as a press vehicle, with a driver and two other passengers.

Reuters reported that Israeli soldiers produced a plastic bag containing a grenade while they were searching Salem's car. "I had never seen it before," said Salem when he was released. "I don't know where it came from."

JUNE 24

Hamouda Hassan, Reuters
Abdel Karim Khadr, Reuters
ATTACKED

The armored car of Reuters cameraman Hassan and Reuters soundman Khadr, which was clearly marked as a press vehicle, came under Israel Defense Forces gunfire at the entrance to the al-Amari refugee camp in Ramallah. Israeli soldiers then ordered the two journalists out of the car at gunpoint and detained them for about an hour-and-a-half, said Hassan.

JUNE 26

Mazen Dana, Reuters
ATTACKED

Dana, a Reuters television cameraman, came under gunfire in the West Bank town of Hebron when a single bullet pierced the side of his video recorder as he was filming from a window on the top floor of a three-story apartment building. The journalist was filming the Israeli army's destruction of a Palestinian National Authority security forces building about 330 yards (300 meters) away. Several Israeli soldiers were stationed about 165 yards (150 meters) from his location.

Dana did not see who fired the shot but said there was no exchange of gunfire in the vicinity of the building at the time of the shooting. He added that he had been filming from the same window for about 40 minutes without incident. Other Palestinian residents had been watching the demolition from a window one floor below where Dana was stationed, also without incident. The Israel Defense Forces spokesman's office did not respond to a request for comment.

JULY 12

Imad Abu Zahra, free-lance
KILLED

For full details on this case, see page 363.

AUGUST 11

Gideon Levy, *Ha'aretz*
Miki Kratsman, *Ha'aretz*
ATTACKED

Levy, a reporter with the Israeli daily *Ha'aretz*, and Kratsman, his photographer, came under Israel Defense Forces (IDF) gunfire in the West Bank town of Tulkarem while they were traveling in a taxi with a representative from an international human rights organization. As they approached the IDF's District Coordination Office, a soldier at a lookout post about 165 yards (150 meters) away fired at them. Three

bullets hit the armor-plated taxi's windshield, but no one was injured.

The journalists, who were in the area with IDF permission, were traveling in a white armored Mercedes with Israeli license plates. The army apologized for the incident and said the unit that opened fire had not been informed that the journalists had permission to be in the area.

An army spokesman told CPJ that the soldier responsible for firing the shot was not punished, but that his commanding officer received a suspended 21-day jail sentence. In addition, the IDF ordered a second soldier confined to base for 35 days for failing to alert the unit that the journalists had permission to be in the area.

AUGUST 27

All journalists
HARASSED

The Palestinian Journalists' Syndicate, a professional press association based in the Gaza Strip, attempted to prevent Palestinian and foreign journalists from photographing images of Palestinian children wearing military uniforms or carrying weapons by "banning" such images. However, the group has no legal power over the media and did not say what the consequences would be for those who violate the ban.

The syndicate's statement said that such footage serves "the interests of Israel and its propaganda against the Palestinian people," reported The Associated Press (AP). The AP also quoted syndicate deputy chairman Tawfik Abu Khosa as saying that photographs of children in these situations violates children's rights and has "negative effects" on Palestinians. The ban was reversed a few days later after local and international protests.

SEPTEMBER 22

Issam Tillawi, Voice of Palestine
`KILLED`

For full details on this case, see page 363.

JORDAN

JANUARY 13

Fahd al-Rimawi, *Al-Majd*
`LEGAL ACTION`

Al-Rimawi, editor of the independent weekly *Al-Majd*, was summoned by a State Security Court prosecutor in the capital, Amman, and accused of publishing "false information." He was subsequently ordered detained for 15 days. The arrest stemmed from several *Al-Majd* articles that criticized Prime Minister Ali Abou al-Ragheb's government. Al-Rimawi was held in Amman's Juwaydeh Prison until his release on January 16.

MARCH 3

Al-Majd
`CENSORED`

The State Security Court banned the March 4 issue of *Al-Majd* unless the paper's management removed two articles about alleged government corruption, one detailing a large-scale financial scandal, and the other criticizing former internal security chief Samih el-Bateekhi.

According to *Al-Majd* editor Fahd al-Rimawi, the March 4 issue had already been sent out for printing when officials ordered the ban. Another local newspaper, *Al-Rai*, handles *Al-Majd*'s printing. Before *Al-Majd* could be printed, *Al-Rai* staffers received a fax from the State Security Court prosecutor general ordering them not to print *Al-Majd*. When al-Rimawi contacted the State Security

Court, he was told that the paper could only be published if he agreed to remove the two offending articles.

Under Penal Code amendments passed in 2001, publications can be suspended or permanently banned if they print information that may "undermine national unity or the country's reputation," "violate basic social norms," "sow the seeds of hatred," or "harm the honor or reputation of individuals," among numerous other restrictions. Offending journalists face prison sentences of up to six months and fines of up to 5,000 Jordanian dinars (US$7,000).

MARCH 5

Reuters TV
Associated Press Television News
Al-Jazeera
`HARASSED`

Reuters TV, Associated Press Television News, and Al-Jazeera were barred by state-run Jordan TV from using its facilities to relay footage of pro-Palestinian students demonstrating at Jordan University, according to sources at Al-Jazeera.

Reuters TV
`HARASSED`

Jordanian authorities confiscated footage of pro-Palestinian students demonstrating at Jordan University from a Reuters TV crew at the King Hussein Bridge, which links Jordan with the West Bank, according to CPJ sources.

MARCH 8

Al-Jazeera
Abu Dhabi TV
Al Manar TV
`HARASSED`

State-owned Jordan TV (JTV) refused to

let journalists from Lebanon's Al Manar TV, Al-Jazeera, and Abu Dhabi TV use JTV facilities to feed film of pro-Palestinian rallies at the Baqa'a refugee camp outside of the capital, Amman, unless they agreed to make major content edits to the footage, according to sources at Al-Jazeera. The stations agreed to the changes and were eventually allowed to use JTV's facilities.

MARCH 10

**Associated Press Television News
Reuters TV
Abu Dhabi TV
HARASSED**

Security forces confiscated the camera equipment of journalists working with Associated Press Television News, Reuters TV, and Abu Dhabi TV after they filmed a pro-Palestinian rally at Jordan University, according to CPJ sources. Officials returned the cameras without the tapes approximately 45 minutes later.

MAY 16

Toujan al-Faisal, free-lance
IMPRISONED

Al-Faisal, a writer and former member of Jordan's Parliament, was sentenced to 18 months in prison. A State Security Court in the capital, Amman, convicted al-Faisal of publishing "false information abroad," "harming the dignity of the state and undermining the reputation of the state and its individuals," and "incitement to unrest," a source at the hearing told CPJ.

The case against al-Faisal came after she penned an open letter in March to King Abdullah in the Houston-based online publication *Arab Times* accusing Prime Minister Ali Abou al-Ragheb of corruption. She had also recently criticized the Jordanian govern-

ment on a number of satellite television stations, including the Qatar-based satellite channel Al-Jazeera.

Zayd al-Radaydeh, one of al-Faisal's lawyers, said that the team was prevented from mounting a proper defense when the judges refused their requests to call Prime Minister Abou al-Ragheb as a witness. Al-Faisal was detained on March 16. On June 26, the king pardoned the journalist but did not overturn her conviction.

AUGUST 7

**Al-Jazeera
CENSORED**

The Qatar-based satellite channel Al-Jazeera had its license to operate in Jordan revoked by Information Minister Muhammad Adwan, who also barred staff from working for the station in the country. The move came after a guest on the August 7 broadcast of the debate program "Opposite Direction" criticized Jordan's relationship with Israel and poked fun at King Abdullah's limited knowledge of Arabic. According to international reports, Adwan accused the station of inciting "sedition" in Jordan and of "defaming" the royal family.

Station staff said they only learned about the closure after the official news agency Petra reported the minister's statements. In 1998, Al-Jazeera's Amman bureau was closed for several weeks after participants in another show criticized Jordan.

DECEMBER 23

Hisham Bustani, *Al-Arab*
IMPRISONED
Al-Arab
CENSORED

Bustani, an activist who penned an article in the bimonthly Lebanese magazine *Al-*

Arab, was arrested for an article he penned titled, "The Mechanisms of Violation and Oppression: The case of [Jordan's] Juweidah Prison." Bustani told CPJ that he was held for six days without charge and was only questioned by intelligence agents on his first day of detention. He also said that intelligence officers threatened him, telling him that he could be turned over to the State Security Court at any time. Bustani said that the issue of *Al-Arab*, which has a small circulation in Jordan, was banned.

LEBANON

AUGUST 6

Jean Feghali, Lebanese Broadcasting Corporation International
Pierre Daher, Lebanese Broadcasting Corporation International
LEGAL ACTION

A state prosecutor ordered an investigation into charges that Feghali, news editor at the private television station Lebanese Broadcasting Corporation International (LBCI), and Daher, LBCI chairman, are responsible for "inciting sectarian strife" and "disturbing general peace." The men face up to three years in prison and a fine of up to 100 million Lebanese pounds (US$66,100).

The accusations stemmed from a July 31 report the station broadcast about eight government employees who had been murdered by a disgruntled colleague in the Ministry of Education building. The government objected to the fact that LBCI's news anchor pointed out that the majority of the victims shared the same religion. Witnesses interviewed in the report accused the killer, who is Muslim, of targeting Christians.

The Lebanese government is extremely sensitive to any coverage of sectarian differences in the country, and Lebanese information min-

ister Ghazi Aridi has warned journalists repeatedly against provoking sectarian strife.

SEPTEMBER 5

Murr Television
Mount Lebanon Radio
CENSORED

The private Lebanese television station Murr TV (MTV) and Mount Lebanon Radio were raided by Lebanese Internal Security Forces who forcibly closed the stations and roughed up employees. According to sources familiar with the case, the closures were based on a Beirut court ruling that MTV had violated a law prohibiting news stations from broadcasting propaganda during elections.

The television and radio stations are owned by Gabriel Murr, a Christian opposition Parliament member who opposes Syria's political influence in Lebanon. Although the Lebanese press often avoids criticizing Syria, both stations have criticized the Syrian and Lebanese governments.

The court decision was not based on a particular political advertisement but on promotional spots aired on the station during the June elections urging citizens to register to vote, said a source at the station. The advertisements did not mention Murr by name. State prosecutors originally brought the case against MTV in August on charges that included harming relations with Syria and violating election laws.

MAURITANIA

APRIL 10

Mohammed Lemine Ould Bah, Radio Monte Carlo Middle East, Radio France International
HARASSED

Bah, a correspondent for Radio Monte

Carlo Middle East and Radio France International, was temporarily banned from practicing journalism after the minister of communications objected to his reports on the state of relations between Senegal and Mauritania.

MOROCCO

FEBRUARY 14

Ali Ammar, *Le Journal Hebdomadaire*
Aboubakr Jamai, *Le Journal Hebdomadaire*
`LEGAL ACTION`

Jamai, publications director of the weekly newspaper *Le Journal Hebdomadaire*, and Ammar, the paper's general director, were convicted by a Casablanca court of appeals of defaming Foreign Minister Muhammed Ben Aissa. The charges stemmed from articles published in 2000 in *Le Journal Hebdomadaire*'s now defunct predecessor, *Le Journal*, alleging that Ben Aissa had profited from the purchase of an official residence during his tenure as Morocco's ambassador to the United States in the late 1990s. The journalists argued that in the original trial, held in a lower court, the judge used procedural grounds to prevent them from presenting a defense.

The court sentenced Jamai and Ammar to three-month and two-month suspended prison sentences, respectively. Both men were also ordered to pay fines and damages totaling 510,000 dirhams (US$44,000) each. The case was appealed to Morocco's highest court, the Court of Cassation. By year's end, no date had been set for the hearing. It is unclear whether the journalists will be required to pay damages before the high court hears the case. Staff at *Le Journal Hebdomadaire* told CPJ

that the fines and other penalties could bankrupt the publication.

SAUDI ARABIA

MARCH 16

Abdel Mohsen Mosallam, *Al-Madina*
`LEGAL ACTION`
Muhammad Mukhtar al-Fal, *Al-Madina*
`CENSORED`

Mosallam, a Saudi poet and journalist, was detained for six days after the daily *Al-Madina* published a poem of his that strongly criticized the Saudi judiciary. At year's end, it remained unclear whether Mosallam had been charged with any offense. According to press reports, two days later, Saudi authorities ordered the dismissal of *Al-Madina*'s editor, al-Fal, apparently because of Mosallam's poem.

APRIL 21

Bob Arnot, MSNBC
`HARASSED`

Arnot, a reporter with U.S. cable channel MSNBC, was escorted off a flight to Dubai, United Arab Emirates, by security officials at Riyadh Airport. The officials demanded video footage that Arnot had gathered during his trip to Saudi Arabia, which the journalist took with Saudi government permission. After Arnot refused to surrender his footage, the officials confiscated 18 videotapes and a laptop computer from him. Arnot and the other passengers were delayed for five hours before being allowed to board the plane and continue the flight.

Saudi authorities gave no reason for the confiscation. However, the journalist had worked on several sensitive stories, including one in which Saudi schoolboys expressed anti-American sentiments. Officials at the school had asked Arnot to hand over the tapes after those interviews, but the journalist refused. Government officials returned the tapes and the computer a month later.

SUDAN

SEPTEMBER 3

Osman Merghani, *Al Rai al-Aam*
`IMPRISONED`

Merghani, a columnist for the Khartoum-based daily *Al Rai al-Aam*, was ordered by authorities to report to the General Security Office, where he was detained. A day earlier, Merghani had appeared on a program on the Qatar-based satellite channel Al-Jazeera that dealt with the suspension of peace talks between the Sudanese government and rebels. Merghani criticized the government for quitting the negotiations, which are aimed at ending the country's 20-year-old civil war. Merghani was released without charge on September 5.

DECEMBER 28

Al-Horiyah
Al-Sahafa
Al-Watan
`CENSORED`

The independent, Arabic-language daily *Al-Watan* was banned by the Internal Security Service. Sources at the paper, which repeatedly came under government pressure in 2002, told CPJ that the ban was issued because of the paper's coverage of topics considered a threat to state security. Editors at the paper plan to mount a legal challenge, claiming that the order is unconstitutional.

On December 27, the Internal Security service also questioned the editors of two other independent papers, *Al-Horiyah* and *Al-Sahafa*, about articles that had appeared in their pages. The two papers did not publish on December 28.

SYRIA

DECEMBER 23

Ibrahim Hemaidi, *Al-Hayat*
`IMPRISONED`

For full details on this case, see page 408.

TUNISIA

JUNE 4

Zouhair Yahyaoui, *TUNeZINE*
`IMPRISONED`

For full details on this case, see page 409.

AUGUST 23

Abdullah Zouari, *Al-Fajr*
`IMPRISONED`

Zouari, formerly with the banned Islamist weekly *Al-Fajr*, was sentenced to eight months in prison for defying a July 15 Interior Ministry order banishing him to the small southern Tunisian village of Khariba Hassi Jerbi, about 370 miles (600 kilometers) outside the capital, Tunis. The journalist unsuccessfully contested the decision and was arrested on August 19 for defying the order.

Zouari's arrest came nearly three months after he was released from prison on June 6, when he completed an 11-year sentence for "association with an unrecognized organization." Zouari had been tried by a military court in 1991, along with 279 other individuals, for belonging to the banned Al-Nahda party, of which *Al-Fajr* was the mouthpiece.

Zouari again appealed the order, but a court in the small southern town of Medenine ruled against him on September 4, 2002. The president pardoned Zouari in November, and he was released soon after.

TURKEY

July 31

Abdullah Keskin, free-lance
LEGAL ACTION

Keskin, a Turkish publisher charged with "separatist propaganda" for publishing a U.S. journalist's book about Turkey's Kurdish minority population, was convicted and sentenced to a six-month prison sentence, which the court converted to a fine of about US$500.

An Istanbul State Security Court ruled that Keskin had violated Article 8 of Turkey's Anti-Terror Law when his publishing house, Avesta, printed a Turkish edition of *After Such Knowledge, What Forgiveness? My Encounters in Kurdistan*, a book about the Kurds written by retired *Washington Post* correspondent Jonathan Randal. Keskin, who was out of the country and did not attend the hearing, appealed the verdict, which remained pending at year's end.

State prosecutors based the charges against Keskin on several passages from the book that contained references to "Kurdistan," which literally means "land of the Kurds." Turkish courts often cite such references to justify prosecuting journalists and intellectuals for allegedly supporting the separatist ambitions of Turkey's Kurdish minority population.

Randal's book, originally published in 1997, was later translated into several lan-

guages. The Turkish edition, which Avesta published in 2001, was confiscated on January 15, 2002, and remains banned. Keskin was charged with violating the Anti-Terror Law in January 2002. His trial began on April 3.

December 25

Sinan Kara, *Datca Haber*
IMPRISONED

For full details on this case, see page 414.

YEMEN

February 3

Al-Shumou
CENSORED

The daily newspaper *Al-Shumou* was closed indefinitely by the Ministry of Information. *Al-Shumou* editor-in-chief Seif al-Hadheri told CPJ that he suspected the closure came in response to *Al-Shumou*'s "criticisms of government ministers." Mahboob Ali, head of the Yemeni Journalists' Syndicate, said that Ministry of Information officials informed him that the paper was suspended for allegedly failing to comply with licensing procedures. Yemeni journalists and government officials have often criticized the paper for being "unprofessional" in its news coverage. The weekly reopened in the fall, after fulfilling the licensing requirements.

June 21

Ibrahim Hussein, free-lance
Abdel Rahim Mohsen, free-lance
IMPRISONED

Hussein, a free-lance journalist who writes for opposition newspapers (including the daily *Al-Thawri*, an organ of the Yemeni Socialist Party), was arrested at the office of the Yemeni Unionist Party, according to CPJ sources. Mohsen, also a free-lance journalist who writes for opposition publications, had been arrested at his home on May 23. The two men were held incommunicado and were only allowed to meet with their lawyer on Monday, July 1, at the office of a state prosecutor in charge of handling press cases. They were released the next day.

The journalists were detained for several newspaper articles they wrote in the months before their arrests. According to the journalists' lawyer, Jamal al-Jaabi, at the July 1 meeting, the prosecutor displayed files containing dozens of articles published in the weekly newspapers *Al-Osboa* and *Al-Thawri*, including some that criticized alleged government corruption, human rights abuses, and restrictions on civil liberties.

Al-Jaabi said that the two were charged on July 2 in a court in the capital, Sana'a, with "harming national unity" and " inciting racial, sectarian, or tribal discrimination." But al-Jaabi told CPJ that he was not able to attend the hearing because he was never notified of the proceedings. If convicted, the journalists each face up to one year in prison. The case was adjourned until July 7 but remained pending at year's end.

JULY 9

Faisal Mukarram, *Al-Hayat*
Ahmed al-Hajj, The Associated Press
Khaled al-Mahdi, Deutsche Presse-Agentur
LEGAL ACTION

Mukarram, a reporter for the London-based daily *Al-Hayat*; al-Hajj, a reporter with The Associated Press; and al-Mahdi, a correspondent for Deutsche Presse-Agentur, were summoned by a state prosecutor and charged with violating Article 103 of the Press Law, which bans journalists from publishing "any secret document or information that might jeopardize the supreme interests of the country or expose any of its security or defense secrets."

The charge stemmed from articles that the three wrote about a July 4 incident in which Deputy Army Chief of Staff Ali Salah was injured when local tribes in the al-Jouf region, in northern Yemen, fired on his helicopter. According to the journalists' lawyer, Khalid al-Ansi, the prosecutor alleged that the published articles "revealed military and security secrets." Although the story was covered in several Yemeni newspapers, only Mukarram, al-Hajj, and al-Mahdi were charged. If convicted, they each face up to a year in prison. Authorities have not actively pursued the charges against the writers, but the cases against them have not been officially dropped. ■

HOW CPJ INVESTIGATES AND CLASSIFIES ATTACKS ON THE PRESS

CPJ CLASSIFIES THE CASES IN THIS BOOK according to the following categories:

ATTACKED
In the case of journalists, wounded or assaulted. In the case of news facilities, damaged, raided, or searched; non-journalist employees attacked because of news coverage or commentary.

CENSORED
Officially suppressed or banned; editions confiscated; news outlets closed.

EXPELLED
Forced to leave a country because of news coverage or commentary.

HARASSED
Access denied or limited; materials confiscated or damaged; entry or exit denied; family members attacked or threatened; dismissed or demoted (when it is clearly the result of political or outside pressure); freedom of movement impeded; detained for less than 48 hours.

IMPRISONED
Arrested or detained by a government for at least 48 hours.

KILLED
Murdered, or missing and presumed dead, with evidence that the motive was retribution for news coverage or commentary. Includes journalists killed in cross fire.

LEGAL ACTION
Credentials denied or suspended; fined; sentenced to prison; visas denied or canceled; passage of a restrictive law; libel suit intended to inhibit coverage.

MISSING
Kidnapped or detained by nongovernment forces for at least 48 hours; disappeared.

THREATENED
Menaced with physical harm or some other type of retribution.

CPJ DOCUMENTED THE CASES OF 19 JOURNALISTS who were killed for their work in 2002. An analysis of this alarming death toll is included in the introduction to this book on page x.

The number of journalists killed in the line of duty each year is probably the world's most frequently cited press freedom statistic. CPJ thoroughly investigates each report of a journalist killed to determine whether the journalist was targeted because of his or her profession. Those caught in cross fire while covering conflict are included along with journalists singled out for assassination. We define journalists as those who cover the news or comment on public affairs in print, in photographs, on radio, on television, or online. Reporters, writers, editors, publishers, and directors of news organizations are all included. We do not classify a case as confirmed until we are sure that the death was related to the victim's journalistic work.

When the motive for a journalist's murder is unclear but there is reason to suspect that it was related to the journalist's profession, CPJ classifies that death as "motive unconfirmed" and includes it on a separate list. CPJ then continues to investigate the crime. CPJ documented 13 "motive unconfirmed" cases in 2002. They are described beginning on page 367. With regard to both lists, CPJ continues to press for official investigations of the killings, as well as for the apprehension and punishment of the perpetrators.

JOURNALISTS KILLED:
MOTIVE CONFIRMED

BANGLADESH: 1

HARUNUR RASHID
Dainik Purbanchal, March 2, 2002, Khulna

Rashid, a reporter for the Bengali-language newspaper *Dainik Purbanchal*, was ambushed by gunmen while he was riding his motorcycle to work in the southwestern city of Khulna, according to Bangladeshi and international news reports. *Dainik Purbanchal*, which is published in Khulna, is a well-regarded regional daily.

Three unidentified young men brought Rashid to a hospital, told doctors he had been injured in a car accident, and then disappeared. A doctor at the hospital told the Dhaka-based newspaper *The Independent* that Rashid had suffered a fatal bullet wound to his chest.

Rashid, also known as Rashid Khukon, was a crime reporter who had written several stories about official corruption and links between criminal syndicates and outlawed Maoist guerrilla groups, including the Purbo Bangla Communist Party (PBCP). Rashid's relatives told reporters that he was on a PBCP hit list. Though the PBCP issued a statement denying responsibility for Rashid's murder, some colleagues said a splinter faction of the group may be behind the killing.

The reporter had received anonymous death threats throughout his career and, for the last year, had been provided with police protection. However, he did not always travel with security guards.

Local journalists believe Rashid was killed for his reporting. Amiya Kanti Pal, a former colleague, told Reuters that,

"Rashid was a brave reporter. We suspect that the criminals he wrote about might be behind his murder."

The Criminal Investigation Department, a federal law enforcement body, is investigating the case.

BRAZIL: 1

TIM LOPES
TV Globo, June 3, 2002, Rio de Janeiro

Lopes, an award-winning investigative reporter with TV Globo, was brutally murdered by drug traffickers.

He had disappeared the day before while working on assignment in the suburbs of Rio de Janeiro in a favela, an impoverished community on the outskirts of the city.

On June 2, the 50-year-old Lopes traveled to the favela of Vila Cruzeiro. His driver met him there at around 8 p.m., but the journalist said he needed more time to finish his work. They agreed to meet again at 10 p.m., but Lopes never arrived. This was Lopes' fourth visit to Vila Cruzeiro, and he was carrying a hidden camera.

According to TV Globo, Lopes was working on a report about parties hosted by drug traffickers in Vila Cruzeiro that allegedly involved drugs and the sexual exploitation of minors. Favela residents had told Lopes that they were powerless against the traffickers and complained about the lack of police action.

On June 3, TV Globo reported Lopes' disappearance to the authorities.

According to the Rio de Janeiro Civil Police, two suspects, both members of a gang headed by local drug trafficker Elias Pereira da Silva, also known as "Crazy Elias," were arrested on the morning of June 9. Both men claimed that they had heard how Lopes was murdered but denied any involvement in his killing.

According to the suspects' depositions, details of which the police released, drug traffickers close to Pereira da Silva kidnapped Lopes in Vila Cruzeiro at around midnight on June 2. After Lopes told the traffickers that he was a TV Globo reporter, they called Pereira da Silva, who was in a nearby favela. The traffickers tied Lopes' hands, forced him into a car, and took him to the favela where Pereira da Silva was staying. There, they beat the reporter and shot him in the feet to keep him from escaping. They then held a mock trial and sentenced Lopes to death.

Pereira da Silva killed Lopes with a sword, and the journalist's body was burned and put in a hidden burial ground, the suspects said.

On June 12, police found badly decomposed human remains, along with Lopes' camera and watch, in Favela da Grota. After DNA tests, police confirmed on July 5 that the remains belonged to Lopes. Two days later, they were officially buried.

Lopes had received Brazil's most important journalism award in December 2001 for a TV Globo report on drug trafficking. The report, titled "Drug Fair" and broadcast in August 2001, was filmed with a hidden camera and showed how traffickers sold drugs in a makeshift open drug market in a favela outside Rio de Janeiro. Reporter Cristina Guimarães, who co-produced the piece with Lopes and two other colleagues, received death threats in September 2001 and had to leave Rio de Janeiro State, according to the daily *O Estado de S. Paulo*. The daily *Jornal do Brasil* reported that Lopes had also received threats for the report.

On September 19, after a two-day search, police apprehended Pereira da Silva.

In early August, several members of his gang who had also been charged with murdering the journalist were either arrested or killed in a shoot-out with police.

At year's end, Pereira da Silva and his accomplices remained in jail. No date had been set for trial.

ORLANDO SIERRA HERNÁNDEZ
La Patria, February 1, 2002, Manizales

Sierra, a deputy editor and columnist for *La Patria* newspaper in Manizales, a town in Colombia's coffee-growing region, was shot while walking to work on January 30. He died on February 1.

Authorities believe that one of any number of local political bosses whom Sierra had denounced in his columns hired an assassin to kill the journalist. "The most likely hypothesis points to politicians, and that's the angle our investigators are continuing to pursue," a spokesperson from the Public Prosecutor's Office told CPJ in mid-December.

Sierra wrote a Sunday column for the 80-year-old newspaper in which he frequently highlighted political corruption and human rights abuses committed by leftist guerrillas, a rival right-wing paramilitary army, and state security agents, said Álvaro Segura López, editor of *La Patria*.

However, the 42-year-old journalist was most critical of local political bosses who, according to a March 6 editorial in *El Tiempo*, Colombia's top daily newspaper, "run the department like a feudal colony." Sierra frequently accused prominent politicians from the local Liberal and Conservative parties of nepotism, vote buying, and looting public coffers.

After receiving death threats in 1998,

the government assigned Sierra bodyguards for a short period, but he later stopped using them, according to a report from a joint investigation into the murder by seven of Colombia's leading newspapers and newsmagazines, published in late February and early March.

The threats came after regional assemblyman Ferney Tapasco González was removed from office because authorities had discovered that he had been convicted in the 1970s of selling military ration cards while serving as the mayor of Supia, Caldas Department, according to the report.

Sierra publicly backed the legal process to remove Tapasco González and also used his column to revisit another incident, in which the lawmaker was convicted of concealing information about the 1991 murder of a schoolteacher in Caldas, the report said.

Since April 2001, Sierra had also been investigating possible links between Tapasco González and a gang of assassins. The former politician has denied involvement in the killing, and authorities said he is not under formal investigation.

On the same day that Sierra was shot, police arrested 21-year-old Luis Fernando Soto Zapata, who later confessed to the killing and was sentenced on May 8 to 19-and-a-half years in prison.

Soto told the court that he shot Sierra on a whim after mistaking him for a man who had allegedly killed a relative several years ago. However, a public prosecutor told CPJ that he doubts the claim, pointing out that footage from a hidden police camera shows Soto lingering for more than two hours before the shooting at the spot where Sierra was killed.

Police also arrested Luis Arley Ortiz on the day Sierra was shot. Authorities released Ortiz soon after but issued a warrant for his arrest again in May, alleging that he had acted as a middleman between a gang of assassins and the person or people who allegedly ordered Sierra's death. Authorities said they have not been able to find him and believe he has been killed.

On July 17, authorities charged Francisco Antonio Quintero Tabares with homicide for Sierra's killing. Quintero is believed to be the boss of the gang of hit men that allegedly included Soto. Authorities have been questioning Quintero but have yet to learn anything new, the spokesperson from the Public Prosecutor's Office said.

HÉCTOR SANDOVAL
RCN Televisión, April 12, 2002
outside of Cali

Sandoval, a cameraman with RCN Televisión, died of gunshot wounds sustained while covering an April 11 firefight between the Colombian army and leftist rebels.

Walter López, who was driving Sandoval and his crew, was also shot and killed during the firefight, said Rocío Arias, executive producer of RCN Televisión news.

The journalists came under fire on April 11 at around 1:45 p.m. in a mountainous region outside the southwestern city of Cali, where the army was pursuing fighters from the Revolutionary Armed Forces of Colombia (FARC). The rebels had just kidnapped 13 provincial lawmakers and four aides and were apparently seeking refuge when the army launched an operation to free the captives.

The crew had decided to leave when an army helicopter hovering above opened fire on their vehicle, said Juan Bautista Díaz, a free-lance photographer working for *Semana* newsmagazine. The letters "RCN" were marked in large, bright colors on the roof and both sides of the vehicle, according to Arias and Bautista.

A bullet pierced the roof and tore through López's arm and into his body. According to Bautista, he appeared to have died instantly, but his colleagues were trying to apply a tourniquet when the army helicopter resumed fire. They were forced to flee for cover in a nearby ravine, said Bautista.

The journalists then tried to signal the helicopter for help by waving white T-shirts in the air. Fifteen minutes after López was shot, a bullet from the helicopter ripped through Sandoval's left leg, said Bautista.

Continued fighting forced Bautista, Sandoval, and RCN correspondent Luz Estela Arroyave to hide in the ravine for about two hours before journalists from a local newspaper who had also come to cover the fighting took them to a hospital. Sandoval died several hours after arriving at the hospital due to significant blood loss from the bullet wound.

Though the army has opened an investigation into the killings, no progress had been reported by year's end, according to an army spokesperson in Cali.

The FARC later freed one of the lawmakers and four aides.

EFRAÍN VARELA NORIEGA
Radio Meridiano-70, June 28, 2002, Arauca

Varela, the owner of Radio Meridiano-70, was shot and killed in northeastern Colombia.

The journalist, who had recently alerted the public to the presence of paramilitary fighters in the region, was driving home from a university graduation in Arauca

Department in the afternoon when gunmen yanked him from his car and shot him in the face and chest, said Col. Jorge Caro, acting commander of Arauca's police.

Varela hosted two polemical programs for the station, based in the town of Arauca, during which he criticized all sides fighting in Colombia's civil conflict, according to José Gutiérrez, who co-hosted one of the shows, called "Let's Talk Politics," with Varela.

A few days before the killing, Varela had told listeners during the morning news program that fighters from the paramilitary United Self-Defense Forces of Colombia (AUC) had arrived in Arauca, which is on the border with Venezuela, and were patrolling the town's streets, according to Gutiérrez.

Tensions have been building in the oil-rich region since early June, when the leftist Revolutionary Armed Forces of Colombia (FARC) began threatening to kill civil servants there who refused to resign. The rebels are battling the paramilitary army for control over lucrative territory in Arauca and throughout the country.

Three years ago, Varela's name appeared on a list of people that the paramilitary army had declared military targets, said acting police commander Caro, adding that authorities were investigating rumors that the AUC was responsible for the killing. Caro, a frequent listener of the station, said that Varela seemed to reserve his sharpest criticism for the paramilitaries.

A spokesperson for the Public Prosecutor's Office told CPJ in mid-December that authorities have issued an arrest warrant for a paramilitary commander believed to have been involved in the killing. The spokesperson said it wasn't known when the warrant was issued and refused to reveal the name of the paramilitary leader for fear of jeopardizing the search for him.

Varela, who was in his early 50s, was also the secretary of a provincial peace commission, as well as its former president, said Evelyn Varela, his 28-year-old daughter and Radio Meridiano-70's manager. In recent months, Varela had begun warning his only child that his life could be in danger. "He had us prepared for the worst," his daughter said.

INDIA: 1

RAM CHANDER CHATERPATTI
Poora Sach, November 21, 2002, Sirsa

Chaterpatti, editor of the Hindi-language newspaper *Poora Sach*, died in a New Delhi hospital of injuries sustained in an assassination attempt made a month earlier.

On October 24, a gunman fired several shots at Chaterpatti, a journalist based in Sirsa, a town in the northern state of Haryana. Chaterpatti was taken to an area hospital but was later transferred to the Apollo Hospital in New Delhi.

Police arrested three suspects, including the alleged gunman and a leader of the Sirsa-based religious sect Dera Sacha Sauda, according to the Press Trust of India news agency. Officials said they believe that Dera Sacha Sauda members ordered Chaterpatti's murder in reprisal for the journalist's reporting on sexual abuse and other crimes allegedly committed at the group's compound in Sirsa.

A delegation of journalists, including the president of the regional journalists' group Haryana Patrakar Sangh and representatives of India's National Union of Journalists, met with the director general of police in Haryana on the day of Chaterpatti's death, November 21, to press authorities to bring the perpetrators to justice. The delegation also complained that several journalists in the area have received death threats for reporting on the activities of Dera Sacha Sauda.

NEPAL: 1

NAVA RAJ SHARMA
Kadam, June 1, 2002, Kalikot
～

Sharma, editor of the Nepali-language weekly *Kadam*, was kidnapped by Maoist rebels on June 1 and later killed, according to a team of journalists and human rights activists organized by the government's National Human Rights Commission (NHRC). The NHRC group visited Kalikot District, where Sharma lived, as part of an August mission to Nepal's remote midwestern region. While there, they learned of Sharma's murder from local residents and police.

Nepal's Maoist rebels, who have been fighting a guerrilla war since 1996 to overthrow the country's constitutional monarchy, control portions of the country, including much of Kalikot and neighboring districts.

Rebels kidnapped Sharma from the village of Syuna on June 1, according to members of the NHRC team. The national English-language newspaper *The Kathmandu Post* reported that police recovered Sharma's badly mutilated body from the area in mid-August. Rebels had gouged out his eyes, cut his hands and legs, and shot him in the chest, police told the NHRC team.

Sharma, who lived in the village of Sipkhana, which is adjacent to Syuna, was known as an independent journalist. He had

been working at *Kadam* since 1998 and was formerly the editor of the local newspaper *Karnali Sandesh*, according to the Kathmandu-based Center for Human Rights and Democratic Studies (CEHURDES). A CEHURDES representative was part of the NHRC team that visited the area.

Sharma was also a schoolteacher, but local press sources said it appeared that he was targeted for his journalism. Rebels later claimed that they had murdered him because he was a government spy. But one journalist said that Sharma had resisted pressure from the rebels to turn *Kadam* into a Maoist propaganda organ.

PAKISTAN: 2

DANIEL PEARL
The Wall Street Journal, date unknown
Karachi
～

U.S. government officials confirmed on February 21 that Pearl, kidnapped South Asia correspondent for *The Wall Street Journal*, had been killed by his captors.

The exact date of his murder was uncertain, but authorities announced his death after receiving a graphic, three-and-a-half minute digital videotape containing scenes in which one of the killers slits Pearl's throat, and then someone holds his severed head. The faces of the assailants are not visible on the video, according to news reports.

Pearl, 38, went missing on January 23 in the port city of Karachi, Pakistan, and was last seen on his way to an interview at the Village Restaurant, downtown near the Metropole Hotel. According to *The Wall Street Journal*, Pearl had been reporting on Richard Reid, a suspected terrorist who allegedly tried to blow up an airplane during a trans-Atlantic flight with a bomb in his shoe.

Four days after Pearl's disappearance, a group calling itself "The National Movement for the Restoration of Pakistani Sovereignty" sent an e-mail to several U.S.- and Pakistan-based news organizations claiming responsibility for kidnapping Pearl and accusing him of being an American spy. The e-mail also contained four photographs of the journalist, including one in which he is held at gunpoint and another in which he is holding a copy of the January 24 issue of Pakistan's *Dawn* newspaper.

The e-mail contained a series of demands, including the repatriation of Pakistani detainees held by the U.S. Army in Guantanamo Bay, Cuba. The sender or senders, who used a Hotmail e-mail account under the name "Kidnapperguy," said Pearl was "at present being kept in very inhuman circumstances quite similar infact [sic] to the way that Pakistanis and nationals of other sovereign countries are being kept in Cuba by the American Army."

Another e-mail was sent on January 30, also including photographs of Pearl held captive. This e-mail accused him of being an agent of Mossad, Israel's spy agency, and said he would be killed within 24 hours unless the group's demands were met.

After scrutinizing the videotape that officials received weeks later, authorities believe that Pearl may have been murdered before the second e-mail was sent. During that footage, Pearl is forced to identify himself as Jewish and to deliver scripted lines reiterating some of the demands made in the e-mails, according to an FBI analysis of the tape that was provided to the *Journal*.

On February 12, before Pearl's murder was discovered, Pakistani police announced the arrest of Ahmed Omar Saeed Sheikh, whom they identified as the prime suspect behind the journalist's kidnapping.

On March 14, a U.S. grand jury indicted Saeed, charging him with hostage-taking and conspiracy to commit hostage-taking resulting in Pearl's murder. U.S. prosecutors also unsealed a secret indictment filed against Saeed in November 2001 accusing him of participating in the 1994 kidnapping of U.S. tourist Bela Nuss in India. Pakistan refused to extradite Saeed, possibly to avoid damaging disclosures of links between the country's intelligence agencies and militant Islamist groups that the United States wants to see eliminated.

In April, Saeed and three accomplices—Salman Saqib, Fahad Naseem, and Shaikh Adil—were charged with Pearl's kidnapping and murder before Pakistan's special anti-terrorism court. The trial, initially convened at Karachi's Central Jail and later moved to a heavily guarded prison in Hyderabad due to security concerns, was closed to journalists and the public.

In mid-May, as the trial was under way, police found a dismembered body believed to be Pearl's buried in the outskirts of Karachi on property owned by the Al-Rashid Trust, an Islamic charity that the United States has accused of funneling money to al-Qaeda. Police were reportedly led to the shallow grave by Fazal Karim, a member of the banned militant Sunni Muslim group Lashkar-e-Jhangvi. At year's end, Karim had not been charged, and though it has been widely reported that he was detained, authorities have never officially acknowledged his arrest.

On July 15, the anti-terrorism court announced that Saeed and his accomplices were guilty of Pearl's kidnapping and murder. Saeed, who was accused of masterminding the crime, was sentenced to death by hanging; Saqib, Naseem, and Adil each received 25-year prison sentences. All four have appealed the ruling, and the case remained pending at year's end.

Shortly after the ruling, U.S. officials announced DNA test results confirming that the body found in May was indeed Pearl's.

In mid-August, The Associated Press (AP) published a detailed account of Pearl's kidnapping, citing two investigators who spoke on condition of anonymity. The officials said that, according to Karim (who had led police to the journalist's body in May) and two others held in unofficial custody, Pearl was shot and wounded on the sixth day of his capture when he tried to escape and was murdered on the ninth day. The AP identified the two other detainees as Zubair Chishti and Naeem Bukhari, who is also known as Attaur Rehman and is a leader of the sectarian group Lashkar-e-Jhangvi. The men also said that three Arabs, possibly from Yemen, were brought to the hideout on the ninth day and that they were involved in filming and carrying out the execution.

Karim later identified one of the Yemenis among those arrested in a September 11, 2002, raid in Karachi, during which U.S. and Pakistani authorities detained several suspected al-Qaeda members, including Ramzi Binalshibh, allegedly a senior al-Qaeda leader who has claimed a central role in coordinating the September 11, 2001, attacks on the United States.

The Washington Post reported that Karim and Bukhari "have told police that the man who slit Pearl's throat was Khalid Sheik Mohammed," whom U.S. intelligence officials have identified as the current head of al-Qaeda's military operations. U.S. officials have told journalists that Mohammed was not among those captured in the Karachi raids, and that his current status is unclear. He had appeared with Binalshibh in a pre-recorded inter-

view broadcast by the Qatar-based Arabic-language satellite channel Al-Jazeera to coincide with the anniversary of the September 11 attacks.

A former U.S. intelligence officer, Robert Baer, told the United Press International (UPI) news agency that he had given Pearl information about Mohammed, and that he believes it was the journalist's investigations of Mohammed that may have cost him his life. Baer, who worked for the Central Intelligence Agency for more than 20 years in Asia and the Middle East and wrote the book *See No Evil*, which criticizes the CIA, told UPI, "I have heard from [intelligence] people who follow this closely that it was people close to Mohammed that killed him, if it wasn't Mohammed himself."

UPI quoted a *Wall Street Journal* spokesperson as saying that, "Everything we know from before and after Danny's murder indicates his reporting effort focused on Richard Reid."

SHAHID SOOMRO
Kawish, October 20, 2002, Kandhkot

Soomro, a correspondent for the Sindhi-language newspaper *Kawish*, was assassinated in the town of Kandhkot, Sindh Province, apparently in reprisal for his reporting on abuses committed during general elections held on October 10.

At around midnight on October 20, three men went to Soomro's home and tried to abduct him, according to his younger brother Aziz, who witnessed the crime. When Soomro resisted, the men shot him dead. *Kawish* editor Ali Kazi said that Soomro had at least nine bullet wounds and died almost instantly.

The gunmen escaped with two accomplices in a white car waiting outside Soomro's house, said local news reports.

Aziz filed a case with police identifying three of the assailants by name, Wahid Ali Bijarani, Mohammad Ali Bijarani, and Mohammad Siddiq.

Wahid Ali and Mohammad Ali, who are brothers, are members of the powerful Bijarani family, which owns much land in the area around Kandhkot and exercises considerable influence through the feudal system still prevalent in much of Pakistan. A third brother, Mir Mehboob Bijarani, was elected to the Sindh Provincial Assembly in the October 10 poll, while an uncle, Mir Hazzar Khan Bijarani, won a seat in the National Assembly. (Both represent exiled former prime minister Benazir Bhutto's Pakistan People's Party.)

Soomro's colleagues suspect that he was killed for his reporting about alleged abuses committed by Bijarani family members and supporters during the elections. Soomro had a reputation for courageous, independent reporting, and his publication, *Kawish*, is one of the most influential newspapers in Sindh Province.

On October 24, police announced that Wahid Ali Bijarani, Mohammad Ali Bijarani, and Mohammad Siddiq, the three suspects identified by the journalist's family, had been detained for questioning. At year's end, the men remained in custody but had not been charged.

The Bijarani family has not commented publicly on the allegations.

PALESTINIAN AUTHORITY TERRITORIES: 3

RAFFAELE CIRIELLO
free-lance, March 13, 2002, Ramallah
≈

Ciriello, an Italian free-lance photographer who was on assignment for the Italian daily *Corriere della Sera*, was killed by Israeli gunfire in the West Bank city of Ramallah, according to press reports and eyewitness testimony. Ciriello was the first foreign journalist killed while covering the current Palestinian uprising, which began in September 2000. The photographer died after being hit by a burst of machine-gun fire from the direction of an Israeli tank during an Israeli military offensive in the West Bank and Gaza Strip.

Amedeo Ricucci, of the Italian television station Rai Uno, told CPJ that he and his cameraman were accompanying Ciriello and trailing a group of Palestinian gunmen at the time of the shooting. Ricucci said the area was quiet and was located less than a half-mile (0.8 kilometers) from a nearby refugee camp where fighting between Israelis and Palestinians was taking place.

According to Ricucci, the three journalists were standing inside a building off an alleyway when a tank emerged at one end of the street 150 to 200 yards (135 to 180 meters) away. Ciriello left the building and pointed his camera at the tank. He then came under fire without warning. Ciriello was shot six times and died of his wounds soon after.

At least one Palestinian gunman was in Ciriello's vicinity at the time of the shooting, according to press reports. The Italian government has demanded a full investigation into the attack.

After Ciriello's death, an Israel Defense Forces (IDF) spokesperson was unable to provide details about the circumstances of the shooting and claimed to have no information about the presence of journalists in Ramallah, which the IDF said was a closed military area at the time. The IDF added that journalists who entered the area were "endangering" themselves.

In late August, the IDF announced that,

based on an investigation it had conducted into the incident, there was "no evidence and no knowledge of an [army] force that fired in the direction of the photographer."

IMAD ABU ZAHRA
free-lance, July 12, 2002, Jenin

Abu Zahra, a Palestinian free-lance photographer who also worked as a fixer and interpreter for foreign journalists, died after being hit by Israel Defense Forces (IDF) gunfire in the West Bank town of Jenin.

According to sources in Jenin, residents had gone into the city center on July 11 after Israeli forces lifted a curfew that had been in effect since June 21. Abu Zahra's colleague Said Dahla, a photographer for the official Palestinian news agency WAFA, told CPJ that at around 2 p.m., the sound of tanks coming toward the area led residents to flee or take cover inside nearby businesses or residences.

Together, Dahla and Abu Zahra went into the middle of Faisal Street to photograph an Israeli armored personnel carrier (APC) that had slammed into an electricity pole there. Dahla said that he and Abu Zahra were alone in the street at this point, facing two Israeli tanks (near the APC), which he estimated to be about 40 meters (45 yards) in front of them.

Both men were holding cameras, according to Dahla, and Dahla wore a flak jacket clearly marked "press." Dahla said that Abu Zahra also wore a cloth vest that identified him as a member of the press.

According to Dahla, moments after the two began taking photographs, gunfire erupted from the tanks. Dahla, who was hit in the leg with bullet shrapnel, said that he looked over and saw that Abu Zahra had been injured in his thigh and was bleeding profusely.

Dahla said that as they tried to take shelter in a nearby building, the tanks continued to fire on them. Dahla told CPJ that they remained in the building entrance, unable to get to a hospital. He estimated that more than 25 minutes passed before Abu Zahra was helped into a taxi and taken to Jenin Hospital, where he died on July 12.

According to an Israeli army spokesperson, after the APC hit the electricity pole on the afternoon of July 11, a mob attacked the personnel carrier with Molotov cocktails and rocks, and people in the crowd fired on the tanks. The spokesperson said the soldiers in the tanks responded by firing back at the source of the gunfire.

However, witnesses told CPJ that residents did not attack the tanks until after the two journalists had been shot. Photos of the stranded APC taken by Dahla before the shooting show no signs of clashes or hostile action near the carrier. Moreover, there were no other reports of people injured by gunfire in Jenin that day.

ISSAM TILLAWI
Voice of Palestine, September 22, 2002
Ramallah

Tillawi, a journalist and program host for the official Palestinian National Authority radio station, Voice of Palestine (VOP), died after being shot in the head by Israeli gunfire during protests in the West Bank city of Ramallah. The incident occurred late in the evening near Ramallah's Manara Square.

According to Palestinian sources, Tillawi was both covering and participating in Palestinian demonstrations that had erupted there in protest of the Israeli army's siege of Palestinian leader Yasser Arafat's headquarters. Journalists and VOP officials said that Tillawi was equipped with a tape recorder and a jacket marked "press."

An Israel Defense Forces spokesperson said at the time that Tillawi was among the rioters and was not distinguishable as a reporter.

EDGAR DAMALERIO
Zamboanga Scribe, DXKP Radio
May 13, 2002, Pagadian City
≈

Damalerio, managing editor of the weekly newspaper *Zamboanga Scribe* and a commentator on DXKP radio station in Pagadian City, on the island of Mindanao, was shot and killed at about 8 p.m. by a single bullet to his left torso while he was driving home from a press conference in Pagadian City. He was 32.

Two witnesses riding in Damalerio's jeep identified the gunman as local police officer Guillermo Wapili. Although an investigator from the National Bureau of Investigation said his office had recommended as early as May 17 that local prosecutors arrest Wapili, the suspect was only briefly detained and was never charged. Wapili, who remained at large in Pagadian City at year's end, has not commented publicly on the allegations and could not be reached by CPJ.

CPJ believes that Damalerio, known for his critiques of corruption among local politicians and the police, was killed for his journalistic work.

The day of Damalerio's murder, his wife told him that she had noticed two men "casing the house," according to a report in the *Philippine Daily Inquirer* by Hernan de la Cruz, publisher of the *Zamboanga Scribe*. Damalerio called his wife 30 minutes before he was killed to let her know that he was on his way home, the report said. The jour-

nalist advised her to "just close the door and lock the gate. Be careful."

A few hours before Damalerio was shot, an employee of the *Zamboanga Scribe* reported receiving a number of mysterious anonymous telephone calls. On May 14, the day after the journalist's death, an unidentified male made threatening phone calls to the newspaper warning that publisher de la Cruz may be next. (De la Cruz now has a uniformed army soldier as his bodyguard.)

On August 10, a possible third witness in the case, a member of a local civilian militia named Juvy Lovitaño, was murdered. He had recently contacted the National Bureau of Investigation to report that a local police officer had approached him to take out a contract on Damalerio's life.

The two witnesses riding in the car with Damalerio when he was shot are afraid for their lives. Fearing threats against her and her baby boy, Damalerio's widow, Gemma, went into hiding in another province.

In August, CPJ conducted an in-depth investigation into Damalerio's murder and met with government officials, including Interior Secretary Joey Lina, to try to move prosecution efforts forward. Lina, who dismissed Pagadian police chief Asuri Hawani after Damalerio's assassination for "covering up the crimes of his men," he said, has ordered a special investigation into the murder.

SONNY ALCANTARA
"Quo Vadis San Pablo," *Kokus*
August 22, 2002, San Pablo
≈

Alcantara, a newspaper publisher and cable-TV commentator, was shot dead in the city of San Pablo, south of the capital, Manila.

A lone gunman shot the journalist in the

forehead while he was riding a motorcycle near his home, police investigators told CPJ. Investigators said they believe that at least one accomplice informed the gunman by cell phone of Alcantara's departure from his home at about 10 a.m.

San Pablo journalists told CPJ that Alcantara had recently broken a story on his cable-TV program, "Quo Vadis San Pablo," implicating a local politician in a corrupt land deal. Alcantara was also the publisher of *Kokus*, a weekly newspaper covering politics and community affairs. According to Alcantara's wife, colleagues had warned the journalist to be careful in his reporting on local government officials.

Police agree that Alcantara, 51, may have been killed because of his work as a journalist. "He was a very vocal commentator," San Pablo police chief Ernesto Cuizon told CPJ. "We can't discount that he was killed because of his journalism." Though investigators told CPJ that they have identified a suspect and have circulated a sketch of the man, who is believed to be a hired killer, no one had been charged with the murder by year's end.

RUSSIA: 3

NATALYA SKRYL
Nashe Vremya, March 9, 2002
Rostov-on-Don

Skryl, a business reporter for *Nashe Vremya*, a newspaper in the southwestern city of Rostov-on-Don, died from head injuries sustained during an attack the previous evening.

Late on the night of March 8, Skryl was returning to her home in the town of Taganrog, just outside Rostov-on-Don, when she was attacked from behind and struck in the head about a dozen times with a heavy, blunt object, according to press reports. Neighbors called an ambulance and the police after hearing her scream. Skryl was found unconscious and taken to Taganrog Hospital, where she died the following day.

Skryl, 29, reported on local business issues for the newspaper, which is owned by Rostov regional authorities. Just before her death, she was investigating an ongoing struggle for control of Tagmet, a local metallurgical plant. *Nashe Vremya* editor-in-chief Vera Yuzhanskaya believes that Skryl's death was related to her professional activities, the ITAR-TASS news agency reported.

Since opening an investigation shortly after the murder, officials have changed their theory several times. Initially, the prosecutor's office said that because Skryl was carrying jewelry and a large sum of cash that were not taken at the time of her murder, robbery could be ruled out as a motive.

But on July 24, the Taganrog Directorate of Internal Affairs announced that robbery was the motive, and that the crime was unrelated to her journalistic activities, the Ekho Rosotova radio station reported.

Taganrog authorities switched their story yet again on September 5, *Nashe Vremya* editor-in-chief Vera Yuzhanskaya told CPJ, when they closed the murder investigation without officially identifying the reason for the murder.

Grigory Bochkarov, an analyst in Rostov-on-Don for the Moscow-based Center for Journalism in Extreme Situations, told CPJ that the only credible motive for Skryl's murder was her reporting about Tagmet and that police had emphasized the robbery motive in an effort to play down the significance of the case.

Just prior to her death, Skryl reportedly told several colleagues that she had recently obtained sensitive information about the Tagmet story and was planning to reveal the material in an upcoming article.

VALERY IVANOV
Tolyatinskoye Obozreniye, April 29, 2002
Togliatti
☙

Ivanov, editor of the *Tolyatinskoye Obozreniye* newspaper in the southern city of Togliatti, was shot dead outside his home at approximately 11 p.m.

The 32-year-old was shot eight times in the head at point-blank range while entering his car, a colleague at the newspaper told CPJ.

Eyewitnesses said the killer was 25 to 30 years old, used a pistol with a silencer, and fled the scene on foot, according to local press reports and CPJ sources.

Ivanov's colleagues believe the killing was connected to his work. *Tolyatinskoye Obozreniye* is well known for its reports on local organized crime, drug trafficking, and official corruption.

Ivanov also served as a deputy in the local Legislative Assembly.

Local police have opened a criminal investigation into the murder and are considering several possible motives, though the primary theory is that he was killed in retaliation for his writing. At year's end, no further progress in the investigation had been reported.

RODDY SCOTT
Frontline, September 26, 2002
Galashki Region, Ingushetia
☙

Roddy Scott, 31, a British free-lance cameraman working for Britain's Frontline television news agency, was killed in the republic of Ingushetia. Russian soldiers found his body in Ingushetia's Galashki

Region, near the border with Chechnya, following clashes between Russian forces and a group of Chechen fighters.

Scott had accompanied the Chechens as they crossed from Georgia into Russia, United Press International reported.

UGANDA: 1

JIMMY HIGENYI
United Media Consultants and Trainers
January 12, 2002, Kampala
☙

Higenyi, a student at United Media Consultants and Trainers, was killed while covering a rally in the capital, Kampala, organized by the opposition Uganda People's Congress. He had been assigned the story as part of his journalism coursework.

The government had banned the gathering under Article 269 of the constitution, which outlaws all political activity in the country. A few moments after a large group of people gathered at the rally's venue, the police fired into the crowd, hitting Higenyi. He died instantly.

The inspector general of police, Maj. Gen. Katumba Wamala, apologized for Higenyi's death and said that the police take full responsibility. But by year's end, no disciplinary action had been taken against the officers involved in the shooting.

VENEZUELA: 1

JORGE IBRAÍN TORTOZA CRUZ
2001, April 11, 2002, Caracas
☙

Tortoza, 48, a photographer for the daily *2001*, was shot on the afternoon of April 11 while covering violent clashes between opposition demonstrators and government supporters in the capital, Caracas. He died later that evening.

The journalist, who was carrying his camera and wearing a vest identifying him as a member of the press, was standing on a corner near Caracas City Hall when he was shot in the head at around 4 p.m. He was then taken to José María Vargas Hospital, where he died at around 6 p.m., according to press reports.

The clashes came on the third day of a nationwide strike leading to a short-lived coup that ousted President Hugo Chávez Frías on April 11. He returned to power on April 14.

Several videos made public the following week did not show conclusively where the shots that killed the journalist had come from, or who fired them, according to local press reports. However, the Caracas Metropolitan Police released a video revealing that five gunmen were on the roof of the City Hall at the time of Tortoza's shooting.

None of the gunmen were in uniform, but two of them had on bulletproof vests. Other amateur videos show more unidentified gunmen in adjacent buildings. Eyewitness accounts and videos implicate both the Venezuelan National Guard and the Caracas Metropolitan Police in the shooting.

Eurídice Ledezma, a Venezuelan journalist and political analyst, told CPJ that Tortoza was shot by a gunman she saw firing from the roof of City Hall.

Tortoza, a veteran photographer, had worked for *2001* since 1991. On April 25, about 300 reporters, photographers, and cameramen from both the private and state media held a march to pay homage to him. The journalists, who carried posters with Tortoza's picture, demanded that those responsible for his death be punished, and that journalists be allowed to do their job without fear of reprisal.

During the events of April 11, at least 15 people were killed and dozens were injured, including four journalists.

By late October, the investigation into Tortoza's killing had stalled. According to the Venezuelan human rights organization PROVEA, there were conflicting reports about the kind of weapon used and the direction from which the bullet came. By year's end, no one had been charged with the murder.

JOURNALISTS KILLED: MOTIVE UNCONFIRMED

ARMENIA: 1

TIRGRAN NAGDALIAN
Armenian Public Television
December 28, 2002, Yerevan

Nagdalian, the 36-year-old head of state-owned Armenian Public Television, was shot in the head as he was leaving his parents' home in Armenia's capital, Yerevan, on December 28. The journalist was rushed to a hospital, where he died during emergency surgery, according to press reports.

The motive for the murder remained unclear at year's end. Nagdalian, who also hosted a weekly news program on the station and worked for the U.S. government–funded Radio Free Europe/Radio Liberty from 1995 to 1997, was a strong supporter and friend of Armenian president Robert Kocharian.

Government officials believe that the murder was politically motivated, but some local media experts pointed to Nagdalian's lavish lifestyle and business interests as a possible explanation for his killing.

Armenian authorities have launched an investigation into the murder.

BANGLADESH: 1

SYED FARROQUE AHMED
Pubali Barta, August 3, 2002, Srimangal

Police found the mutilated body of Ahmed, 50, on August 3, more than two months after he had disappeared, according to the press freedom groups Reporters Sans Frontières and the Bangladesh Center for Development Journalism and Communication (BCDJC). Ahmed was editor of the local Bengali-language newspaper *Pubali Barta*, published in the southeastern town of Srimangal. Police had no leads in the case, according to the BCDJC.

BELARUS: 1

MYKHAILO KOLOMYETS
Ukrainski Novyny, October 30, 2002
Maladzechna

The body of Kolomyets, co-owner and director of the Kyiv, Ukraine–based Ukrainski Novyny news agency, was found on October 30 hanging from a tree in a forest in northwestern Belarus, near the city of Maladzechna, according to Ukrainski Novyny.

Kolomyets' colleagues said that they reported the journalist missing on October 28, after he had failed to come to work a week earlier. According to Ukrainian police, the journalist had traveled to neighboring Belarus on October 22. Lyubov Ruban, a friend of Kolomyets', said the journalist called her that day and informed her that he was planning to commit suicide.

Although Kolomyets had received no known threats for his work, colleagues say he may have been targeted because of the agency's reputation for independent reporting, or because of the large financial stake he held in the company. Ukrainian authorities are investigating the case.

BRAZIL: 1

DOMINGOS SÁVIO BRANDÃO
LIMA JÚNIOR
Folha do Estado, September 30, 2002
Cuiabá

Brandão, owner, publisher, and columnist of the daily *Folha do Estado*, based in the city of Cuiabá, in the central Brazilian state of Mato Grosso, was shot at least five times by two unidentified men on a motorcycle, according to several news reports. The two men had been waiting for Brandão near the paper's new offices, which were under construction.

As Brandão was surveying the exterior of the building with an engineer from the construction company, the gunmen approached the journalist, shot him in the chest and head with a 9 mm handgun, and then fled on the motorcycle. Several people witnessed the murder.

In an October 1 editorial, the paper blamed the murder on a "parallel power," a reference to organized crime groups that have taken over Mato Grosso. The paper attributed Brandão's death to the paper's extensive coverage of drug trafficking, illegal gambling, and government corruption but also mentioned that the journalist was a businessman who owned construction and publishing companies. Brandão had not received any threats, according to the newspaper.

On October 2, police arrested two retired military police officers and accused them of murdering Brandão and several others. During a raid of the suspects' homes, police confiscated several weapons, ammunition, and four motorcycles. On October 4, police announced that tests confirmed that the suspects' weapons were used in Brandão's murder, and that their fingerprints matched those found near the construction site where the journalist was killed.

On December 5, a federal judge ordered that businessman João Arcanjo Ribeiro, a former police officer, be held in temporary detention after federal and state prosecutors identified him as the head of an organized crime group in Mato Grosso and linked him to several homicides. The same day, federal and state law enforcement agencies raided Arcanjo's properties and confiscated documents, computer hard drives, and weapons. However, Arcanjo had fled and is currently being sought by federal police, who have alerted the international police agency Interpol.

On December 11, federal and state prosecutors formally indicted Arcanjo on charges of homicide, smuggling, money laundering, tax evasion, illegal gambling, and racketeering. According to local press reports, Arcanjo is also suspected of ordering the murder of Brandão in retaliation for his denunciations in *Folha do Estado* against organized crime.

Seven other men, including the two retired military police officers who were arrested on October 2 and subsequently jailed, were identified in the indictment as members of the criminal organization allegedly led by Arcanjo, according to local news reports. The two suspects, who have been in jail since October in connection with Brandão's killing, were also indicted.

COLOMBIA: 5

MARCO ANTONIO AYALA
CÁRDENAS
El Caleño, January 23, 2002, Cali
◆

Ayala, a photographer for *El Caleño*

newspaper, was shot and killed by two assassins on a motorcycle while he was leaving a photo shop near the newspaper's offices, authorities said. The 43-year-old died instantly after being shot in the head six times. He had worked at the newspaper in Cali, Colombia's third-largest city, for four years.

Even though Capt. Mónica Quiroz of the Cali Police Department said that there was no known motive for the attack, an *El Caleño* editor suggested that Ayala might have been killed because of a photo published in December 2001.

The editor, Luis Fernando García, reported that Ayala had taken a photo at the annual Cali Fair that inadvertently showed a local criminal figure with his mistress. Following the photograph's publication on December 23, 2001, the man's wife allegedly called Ayala requesting a copy. Ayala was leaving the developing shop with the photograph when he was gunned down, according to García.

Blanca María Torres, *El Caleño*'s managing editor, told CPJ that the identity of the man in the photo is not clear.

In December 2002, spokespersons for the Public Prosecutor's offices in Cali and Bogotá declined to discuss the case beyond saying that it was still under investigation.

OSCAR JAVIER HOYOS NARVÁEZ
Radio Súper, June 6, 2002
outside Popayán
◆

Hoyos, a Radio Súper correspondent, was riding with his brother in a car outside Popayán, the capital of Cauca Department, when unidentified men in another vehicle stopped them and shot Hoyos twice in the chest, according to a bulletin from the Cauca Department Police. He died while being driven to a nearby hospital.

Hoyos had worked for Radio Súper for five months, covering the township of Sotará, about 12 miles (20 kilometers) south of Popayán, said John Jairo Uribe, a correspondent for the station. Hoyos had reported on violence, legislative and presidential elections, and community news, according to Uribe. He said Hoyos had received no known threats and described the journalist's reports as "impartial and positive."

An official at the Cauca Prosecutor's Office said that the crime is under investigation and declined to comment. According to Uribe, some of his colleagues at the radio station suspect the gunmen might have been attempting to rob Hoyos. The journalist's brother could not be reached for comment.

MARIO PRADA DÍAZ
Horizonte del Magdalena Medio
July 12, 2002, Santander Department
⤜

The body of Prada, publisher of the monthly *Horizonte del Magdalena Medio*, in northeastern Colombia's Santander Department, was found riddled with bullet wounds near his home in the municipality of Sabana de Torres on July 12. A source told CPJ that Prada, 44, had been abducted from his house at 11 p.m. the night before. The source said that it was not clear who killed Prada or why.

Prada had apparently received no threats. He had run the monthly *Horizonte Sabanero* for several years before changing its name to *Horizonte del Magdalena Medio* in June. The publication, which covered social and cultural issues, was not considered controversial.

But according to the daily *Vanguardia Liberal*, based in Bucaramanga, the capital of Santander Department, Prada had

written an editorial in *Horizonte del Magdalena Medio*'s June issue criticizing the local government. *Vanguardia Liberal* also quoted a town representative as saying that Prada had held office in the local council at a time when the left-wing Patriotic Union (UP) ruled Sabana de Torres. Right-wing paramilitaries have killed thousands of UP members.

JOSÉ ELI ESCALANTE
La Voz de Cinaruco, October 28, 2002
Esmeralda
⤜

Escalante, a correspondent for the radio station La Voz de Cinaruco (Voice of Cinaruco) in the town of Esmeralda, Arauca Department, was shot and killed while returning home from his mother's grave site, authorities told CPJ. A spokesperson for the Arauca Department Police confirmed that the journalist was shot three times but provided no further details about the murder because officials had lost the crime report.

Escalante had worked for eight years as a part-time correspondent for the station, said station news director José Domingo Pitta. The journalist, 55, covered community news in Esmeralda but, according to Domingo, tried to avoid reporting on sensitive political topics and Colombia's civil conflict.

Escalante resigned from his position as an Esmeralda town councilman in July after the leftist Revolutionary Armed Forces of Colombia (FARC) threatened to kill all of Colombia's elected municipal leaders unless they resigned, said Domingo. He told CPJ that Escalante had never been threatened personally.

According to Domingo, there are no suspects or motives in the killing. Local investigators could not be reached for comment.

Both the FARC and the smaller leftist National Liberation Army, or ELN, are active in the region, but no armed group has taken responsibility for the killing.

GIMBLER PERDOMO ZAMORA
Panorama Estéreo, December 1, 2002
Gigante

Perdomo, news director and general manager of FM radio station Panorama Estéreo, in the town of Gigante, was shot and killed while walking home with his wife, authorities told CPJ. The journalist was shot six times at 10 p.m. and died instantly. A bullet grazed his wife's face, but she was not seriously injured.

A police spokesperson said that two men and a woman were involved in the shooting but offered no motive. The murder is under investigation.

Perdomo, 32, hosted two news programs at the station but rarely commented on Colombia's civil conflict, political corruption, or other sensitive topics, said colleague Andres Garzón. Most of the station's other programming is devoted to music.

Perdomo occasionally received calls during his broadcasts from listeners complaining about problems with municipal services and sometimes publicly encouraged local politicians to act, said Garzón.

According to sources, neither Perdomo nor the station had received threats before the killing. The journalist had been a town councilman in Gigante for 10 years, beginning in 1990. He chose not to run for re-election in 2001, according to Garzón.

Perdomo was also an administrator at a hotel and restaurant in Gigante.

The leftist Revolutionary Armed Forces of Colombia (FARC) is reportedly active in the region.

INDIA: 2

PARITOSH PANDEY
Jansatta Express, April 14, 2002, Lucknow

Pandey, a crime reporter for the Hindi-language daily *Jansatta Express*, was shot dead at point-blank range at around 10:30 p.m. in his home in the residential neighborhood of Gomtinagar, in Lucknow, according to police. At least six shots were fired at Pandey's head and chest, and he apparently died instantly.

Jansatta Express editor Ghanshyam Pankaj told CPJ that because Pandey was reporting regularly on criminal gangs, it is likely he was targeted because of his work. However, Pankaj was uncertain which articles might have prompted the assassination.

Local journalists complained that Gomtinagar police responded slowly to Pandey's murder. Dozens of journalists staged an angry demonstration in the early-morning hours of April 15, carrying Pandey's body to Raj Bhawan, the official residence of Uttar Pradesh governor Vishnu Kant Shastri.

During the demonstration, a security official hit *Dainik Jagran* newspaper reporter Manish Srivastava with a rifle butt, causing serious injuries.

In July, the national English-language daily *Times of India* reported that a suspect arrested in connection with a separate murder had admitted to helping arrange Pandey's assassination because the journalist had information about the crime for which the gunman was originally detained. In late September, police arrested another individual who confessed involvement in Pandey's murder, but this person suggested that the killing was prompted by a personal dispute.

The motive behind the journalist's murder remained unclear at year's end.

YAMBEM MEGHAJIT SINGH
Northeast Vision, October 13, 2002
Manipur State

Late in the evening, Meghajit, chief correspondent in Imphal for the television production company Northeast Vision, was found dead, blindfolded with his hands tied. He had been beaten with bamboo sticks and shot in the head, according to local journalists. Imphal is the capital of Manipur State, in India's conflict-ridden northeast region.

The local newspaper *Manipur Mail* reported that two men had summoned Meghajit at his home at around 8:30 p.m. No group has claimed responsibility for the murder.

Local journalists said they do not know what might have motivated the killing. Meghajit was the chief correspondent in charge of filming in Manipur for Northeast Vision, which provides footage for channels including Imphal Cable Television and the national network Doordarshan. However, colleagues at the Manipur Electronic Media Journalists Union, of which Meghajit was vice president, said his work had not been particularly controversial.

Meghajit was also a dealer in semiprecious stones, and some journalists speculated that he was killed in connection with this business.

NEPAL: 1

AMBIKA TIMSINA
Janadesh, date unknown, Morang

Timsina's corpse was found on December 12 about a half-mile (1 kilometer) from his house in eastern Nepal's Morang District, according to the Kathmandu-based Center for Human Rights and Democratic Studies. His body had bullet wounds.

Timsina had worked for the pro-Maoist weekly *Janadesh* before going underground soon after the government declared a state of emergency in November 2001. In fall 2002, he surrendered to government security forces.

Although the motive for Timsina's murder is not clear, CPJ sources in Nepal believe he may have been killed by Maoist rebels who suspected him of acting as an informant to the government after his surrender.

RUSSIA: 1

SERGEI KALINOVSKY
Moskovsky Komsomolets–Smolensk
date unknown, Smolensk

The body of 26-year-old Kalinovsky, editor-in-chief of the Smolensk edition of the Moscow daily *Moskovsky Komsomolets*, was found on April 1 beside a lake outside the city of Smolensk, in central Russia.

Kalinovsky, who reported on local politics and crime for the paper and for the local SCS television station, had disappeared on the evening of December 14, 2001.

Local police have opened a criminal investigation and are considering several possible motives for the murder, but no suspects had been detained by year's end.

In March 2001, Kalinovsky's apartment was damaged by a fire that he suspected was set in retaliation for his work, according to the online news service *NTVRU.COM*. Local investigators, however, ruled out arson as a cause. ■

JOURNALISTS IN PRISON IN 2002

136 journalists in prison as of December 31, 2002

THERE WERE **136** JOURNALISTS IN PRISON AROUND THE WORLD at the end of 2002 who were jailed for practicing their profession. The number is up significantly from the previous year, when 118 journalists were in jail. An analysis of the reasons behind this increase is contained in the introduction on page x.

At the beginning of 2003, CPJ sent letters of inquiry to the heads of state of every country on the list below requesting information about each jailed journalist. Readers are encouraged to add their voices to CPJ's by writing directly to the heads of state, whose names and addresses can be found at *www.cpj.org*.

This list represents a snapshot of all the journalists who were incarcerated when the clock struck midnight on December 31, 2002. It does not include the many journalists who were imprisoned and released throughout the year; accounts of those cases can be found in the regional sections of this book.

A word about how this list is compiled: In totalitarian societies where independent journalism is forbidden, CPJ often defends persecuted writers whose governments view them as political dissidents rather than as journalists. This category would embrace the samizdat publishers of the former Soviet Union and the wall-poster essayists of the pre-Tiananmen period in China. We also include political analysts, human rights activists, and others who were prosecuted because of their written or broadcast work.

We consider any journalist who is deprived of his or her liberty by a government to be imprisoned. Journalists remain on this list until we receive positive confirmation that they have been released. In some cases, we have received reports that a journalist was killed in government custody. One example is Nepalese journalist Krishna Sen, who was arrested by government forces in Nepal on May 20, 2002, and has not been heard from since. We keep Sen on this list as a way of holding the Nepalese government accountable for his fate.

Journalists who either disappear or are abducted by nonstate entities, including criminal gangs, rebels, or militant groups, are not included on the imprisoned list. Their cases are classified as "missing." CPJ documented four such cases in 2002. Details are available on CPJ's Web site. ∎

ALGERIA: 2

Djamel Eddine Fahassi, Alger Chaîne III
Imprisoned: May 6, 1995

Fahassi, a reporter for the state-run radio station Alger Chaîne III and a contributor to several Algerian newspapers, including the now banned weekly of the Islamic Salvation Front, *Al-Forqane*, was abducted near his home in the al-Harrache suburb of the capital, Algiers, by four well-dressed men carrying walkie-talkies. According to eyewitnesses who later spoke with his wife, the men called out Fahassi's name and then pushed him into a waiting car. He has not been seen since, and Algerian authorities have denied any knowledge of his arrest.

Prior to Fahassi's "disappearance," Algerian authorities had targeted him on at least two occasions because his writing criticized the government. In late 1991, he was arrested after an article in *Al-Forqane* criticized a raid conducted by security forces on an Algiers neighborhood. On January 1, 1992, the Blida Military Court convicted him of disseminating false information, attacking a state institution, and disseminating information that could harm national unity.

He received a one-year suspended sentence and was released after five months. On February 17, 1992, he was arrested a second time for allegedly attacking state institutions and spreading false information. He was transferred to the Ain Salah Detention Center in southern Algeria, where hundreds of Islamic suspects were detained in the months following the cancellation of the January 1992 elections.

In late January 2002, Algerian ambassador to the United States Idriss Jazairy responded to a CPJ query, saying a government investigation did not find those responsible for Fahassi's abduction. The ambassador added that there was no evidence of state involvement.

Aziz Bouabdallah, *Al-Alam al-Siyassi*
Imprisoned: April 12, 1997

Bouabdallah, a reporter for the daily *Al-Alam al-Siyassi*, was abducted by three armed men from his home in the capital, Algiers. According to Bouabdallah's family, the men stormed into their home and, after identifying the journalist, grabbed him, put his hands behind his back, and pushed him out the door and into a waiting car. An article published in the daily *El-Watan* a few days after his abduction reported that Bouabdallah was in police custody and was expected to be released soon.

In July 1997, CPJ received credible information that Bouabdallah was being held at the Châteauneuf detention facility in Algiers, where he had reportedly been tortured. But Bouabdallah's whereabouts are currently unknown, and authorities have denied any knowledge of his abduction.

In late January 2002, Algerian ambassador to the United States Idriss Jazairy responded to a CPJ query, saying a government investigation did not find those responsible. The ambassador added that there was no evidence of state involvement.

BANGLADESH: 4

Saleem Samad, Reporters Sans Frontières
Imprisoned: November 29, 2002

Police arrested Samad, a well-known free-lance journalist and press freedom activist, for his work with a documentary crew that was preparing a report about Bangladesh for the "Unreported World" series on Britain's Channel 4. Samad, who is the Bangladesh representative for the Paris-based press freedom group Reporters Sans Frontières, had worked for the documentary team as an interpreter.

On November 25, police had arrested Zaiba Malik, the reporter for the documentary; Bruno Sorrentino, the film's director and cameraman; and Priscilla Raj, a free-lance Bangladeshi journalist who also worked for the documentary team as an interpreter. Samad had gone into hiding after his colleagues' arrests but was found and detained on November 29. All four journalists were accused of sedition.

Police arrested the journalists for their alleged involvement in "clandestine activities as journalists with an apparent and malicious intent of portraying Bangladesh as an Islamic fanatical country," said a statement issued by the Bangladeshi government, as reported by the Agence France-Presse news agency.

On December 11, authorities released Malik and Sorrentino and deported them to Britain. The two foreign journalists signed a statement saying they would not produce any reports from their footage gathered in Bangladesh and "expressing regret for the unfortunate situation arising since their arrival in Bangladesh." However, the Bangladeshi journalists remained in jail. Raj was not released until December 23.

On December 4, while being transport-ed back to prison after attending a court hearing, Samad shouted to journalists out of the window of his van, "I have been subjected to inhuman torture," according to Bangladeshi press reports.

On December 23, the High Court ordered Samad's release on bail within 24 hours. However, the next day, government authorities ordered that Samad remain in custody for 30 more days under the Special Powers Act, which allows for the preventive detention of anyone suspected of anti-state activities. On January 14, 2003, the High Court ruled that the gov-ernment's order to extend Samad's detention was illegal and that he should be released. Samad was finally freed from Kashimpur Jail, which is just outside of Dhaka, on January 18.

Shahriar Kabir, free-lance
Imprisoned: December 8, 2002

Kabir, a free-lance journalist and human rights activist, was detained in the capital, Dhaka, as part of a police sweep during which about 40 opposition figures were arrested. Authorities initially said that Kabir was being held in connection with a sedition case against journalists working on a documentary about the political situation in Bangladesh for Britain's Channel 4. The government had accused the Channel 4 team of having the "malicious intent of portraying Bangladesh as an Islamic fanatical coun-try." Kabir was among those interviewed for the film.

During a December 12, 2002, court hearing, Kabir told investigators that he had been tortured in police custody and denied food for more than 24 hours, according to Bangladeshi press reports. He was trans-ferred to three different jails and was last imprisoned in the southern city of Chittagong, about 160 miles (260 kilome-ters) from Dhaka, a move that made it difficult for his relatives and lawyers to visit.

On January 4, 2003, the High Court declared Kabir's detention illegal and ordered his release within 24 hours. On January 5, the government ignored the rul-ing and ordered Kabir to remain in detention for 90 more days under the Special Powers Act, which allows for the preventive detention of anyone suspected of anti-state activities. He was finally freed on the afternoon of January 7.

This was the second time in a year that Kabir was imprisoned. An outspoken crit-ic of the government, Kabir was arrested in November 2001 and accused by the Home Ministry of being "involved in a heinous bid to tarnish the image of Bangladesh and its government." The charge stemmed from his reporting on the ruling party's responsibility for a wave of attacks against Bangladesh's Hindu minor-ity that followed the October 2001 parliamentary elections. He was first detained under the provisions of the Special Powers Act and was later charged with treason. He was freed on January 20, 2002, following two separate High Court orders for his release.

Muntasir Mamun, free-lance
Imprisoned: December 8, 2002

Mamun, a writer and historian, was among several prominent government critics and opposition members arrested in a series of police raids on December 8 and 9 in the capital, Dhaka. He was held under the provisions of Bangladesh's Special Powers Act (SPA), which allows for the preventive detention of anyone suspected of anti-state activities, on suspicion of trying to destabilize the government.

Mamun, the author of several books about Bangladesh, is a professor of history at Dhaka University. He also regularly contributes columns to several Bengali-language newspapers and had recently written articles about alleged abuses committed by the army during the government's recent anti-crime drive, Operation Clean Heart.

On December 12, the Chief Metropolitan Magistrate's Court in Dhaka rejected Mamun's bail petition and ordered him to be held for 30 days in preventive detention, under the SPA, while his case was being investigated. Mamun was imprisoned at the remote Dinajpur Jail, located about 250 miles (400 kilometers) from Dhaka in northern Bangladesh, making it both difficult and expensive for lawyers and family members to visit him.

On January 5, 2003, the High Court declared Mamun's detention illegal and ordered the government to release him within 24 hours. The court ruled that the government had failed to demonstrate sufficient grounds for Mamun's detention. However, Dinajpur Jail officials claimed that they did not receive the court order promptly and only released Mamun on January 9.

Enamul Hoque Chowdhury, Bangladesh Sangbad Sangstha
Imprisoned: December 13, 2002

Police arrested Chowdhury, a senior reporter for the government-controlled news agency Bangladesh Sangbad Sangstha (BSS) and a stringer for Reuters news agency, for allegedly fabricating comments, attributed to the home minister, that al-Qaeda may have been responsible for a series of bombings on December 7, 2002, that killed at least 17 people in the northern town of Mymensingh. Reuters' coverage of the attacks quoted the statements.

Home Minister Altaf Hossain Chowdhury (no relation to the journalist) denied making the statements. Reuters later withdrew five stories regarding the explosions that ran on December 7 and 8, saying it could "no longer vouch for the accuracy of the remarks," and that it was conducting an internal investigation into its coverage of the attacks. BSS dismissed Enamul Hoque Chowdhury on December 14.

A police statement issued after the journalist's arrest said that his reporting had "tarnished the country's image internationally and threatened its relations with powerful and friendly countries." Police later filed a case against the journalist for complicity in the Mymensingh bomb attacks, which the government claims were part of a conspiracy by the political opposition to destroy the administration's reputation. He is being held under Bangladesh's Special Powers Act, which allows for preventive detention of anyone suspected of anti-state activities.

"We permit a free press," Communications Minister Nazmul Huda told London's *Financial Times*. "But we will not allow reporters to besmirch our reputation internationally by making unsubstantiated allegations about Islamic extremism or the presence of an al-Qaeda cell."

Chowdhury admitted to colleagues that he mistakenly attributed comments about al-Qaeda's possible role in the blasts to the home minister. However, the journalist has denied any criminal wrongdoing. Legal challenges to his detention were ongoing in January 2003. The High Court ordered a medical board to examine Chowdhury for evidence that he was tortured while in police custody. As this book went to press, Chowdhury was imprisoned at Dhaka Central Jail.

BELARUS: 3

Mikola Markevich, *Pahonya*
Paval Mazheika, *Pahonya*
Imprisoned: September 1, 2002

Markevich and Mazheika, both of the independent weekly newspaper *Pahonya*, were convicted on June 24, 2002, by the Leninsky District Court in the city of Hrodna, in western Belarus, of libeling President Aleksandr Lukashenko. The journalists were sentenced to two-and-a-half and two years, respectively, of corrective labor. The case stemmed from two September 2001 editions of *Pahonya* that criticized the president ahead of the widely disputed September 9, 2001, presidential elections.

The sentences were later reduced to 18 months for Markevich and 12 months for Mazheika. They began serving their corrective labor terms on September 1, 2002. The two men live in detention centers under police supervision and perform compulsory labor. They were the first journalists convicted under a criminal libel law passed in 1999, which carries a maximum sentence of five years in prison for libeling the president.

During a 10-day research mission to Belarus in the fall of 2002, CPJ visited both journalists and brought them supplies and also lobbied the government for their releases. In August 2002, Markevich reported that the Hrodna City Executive Council had denied a petition to register his new publication, *Holos*. Previously, Markevich had submitted four other prospective newspapers for the council's approval, all of which were denied.

Viktar Ivashkevich, *Rabochy*
Imprisoned: December 16, 2002

Ivashkevich, editor-in-chief of the independent newspaper *Rabochy*, was convicted by a court in the capital, Minsk, of libeling President Aleksandr Lukashenko and sentenced to two years' hard labor. Under Belarus' Criminal Code, libeling the president is punishable by up to five years in prison.

The case stemmed from an article in a special August 2001 issue of the newspaper titled "A Thief Belongs in Prison," which accused Lukashenko's administration of corruption. *Rabochy*'s special issue never reached its readers because prosecutors seized 40,000 copies of it and submitted them as evidence in the case.

A Minsk District Prosecutor's Office charged Ivashkevich with criminal libel almost a year later, on June 20, 2002.

The journalist's trial began on September 11, 2002, and he was convicted five days later, on September 16. Ivashkevich appealed the verdict, but on October 15, the Criminal Cases Collegium of the Minsk City Court upheld his sentence. In early December, prosecutors rejected a request by the journalist to serve his corrective labor in Minsk. On December 16, he left the capital for Baranovichy, a city 85 miles (136 kilometers) southwest of Minsk, where he is serving his term.

During a 10-day research mission to Belarus in the fall of 2002, CPJ met with Ivashkevich to discuss his case, his publication's dire financial situation, and press freedom conditions in Belarus.

BURMA: 9

U Win Tin, free-lance
Imprisoned: July 4, 1989

U Win Tin, former editor-in-chief of the daily *Hanthawati* and vice chairman of Burma's Writers Association, was arrested and sentenced to three years of hard labor on the false charge of arranging a "forced abortion" for a member of the opposition National League for Democracy (NLD). One of Burma's most well-known and influential journalists, U Win Tin helped establish independent publications during the 1988 student democracy movement. He was also a senior leader of the NLD and a close adviser to opposition leader Daw Aung San Suu Kyi.

In 1992, he was sentenced to an additional 10 years for "writing and publishing pamphlets to incite treason against the State" and "giving seditious talks," according to a May 2000 report by the Defense Ministry's Office of Strategic Studies. On March 28, 1996, prison authorities extended U Win Tin's sentence by another seven years after they convicted him, along with at least 22 others, of producing clandestine publications—including a report describing the horrific conditions at Rangoon's Insein Prison to Yozo Yokota, the U.N. special rapporteur for human rights in Burma.

U Win Tin was charged under Section 5(e) of the Emergency Provisions Act for having "secretly published anti-government propaganda to create riots in jail,"

according to the Defense Ministry report. His cumulative sentence is, therefore, 20 years of hard labor and imprisonment.

Now 72 years old, the veteran journalist is said to be in extremely poor health after years of maltreatment in Burma's prisons—including a period when he was kept in solitary confinement in one of Insein Prison's notorious "dog cells," formerly used as kennels for the facility's guard dogs. He suffers from spondylitis, a degenerative spine disease, as well as a prostate gland disorder and hemorrhoids. The journalist has had at least two heart attacks, and in 2002, he spent several months at Rangoon General Hospital following a hernia operation.

In July 2002, reports emerged that U Win Tin's health had deteriorated even further, and many international groups, including CPJ, called for his immediate and unconditional release. In November 2002, authorities again transferred U Win Tin to Rangoon General Hospital, this time for medical treatment in connection with a heart ailment.

Ohn Kyaing, free-lance
Thein Tan, free-lance
Imprisoned: September 6, 1990

On September 7, 1990, Col. Than Tun, Burma's deputy chief of military intelligence, announced at a press conference that Ohn Kyaing and Thein Tan were among six leaders of the opposition National League for Democracy (NLD) arrested on the previous day, according to international news reports.

On October 19, 1990, the Information Committee of the junta (then known as the State Law and Order Restoration Council and later renamed the State Peace and Development Council) announced at a press conference that

Ohn Kyaing and Thein Tan "had been sentenced to seven years imprisonment by a military tribunal for inciting unrest by writing false reports about the unrest, which occurred in Mandalay on 8 August 1990," according to the BBC's translation of a state radio broadcast.

The Mandalay "unrest" the committee referred to involved the killing of four pro-democracy demonstrators by the military. Government troops fired on protestors—who were commemorating the democracy rallies of August 8, 1988, during which hundreds were shot dead—killing two monks and two students.

Ohn Kyaing, who also uses the name Aung Wint, is the former editor of the newspaper *Botahtaung* and one of Burma's most prominent journalists. He retired from *Botahtaung* in December 1988 to become more involved in the pro-democracy movement, according to the PEN American Center. In 1990, Ohn Kyaing was elected to Parliament for the NLD, representing a district in Mandalay. (The results of the elections, which the NLD won, were never honored by the military junta.) A leading intellectual, he continued to write. Thein Tan, whose name is sometimes written as Thein Dan, is also a free-lance writer and political activist associated with the NLD.

PEN reported that in mid-1991, Ohn Kyaing received an additional sentence of 10 years in prison under the 1950 Emergency Provisions Act for his involvement in drafting a pamphlet for the NLD titled "The Three Paths to Power." Thein Tan also received an additional 10-year sentence, according to Amnesty International, presumably for the same reason.

In a list of Burmese political prisoners published in April 2001, Amnesty International reported that the sentences of both men were reduced to 10 years on January 1, 1993. However, Ohn Kyaing and Thein Tan remained in prison at the end of 2002. Ohn Kyaing was jailed at Taungoo Prison, and Thein Tan was jailed at Thayet Prison, according to the Thailand-based Assistance Association for Political Prisoners in Burma.

Maung Maung Lay Ngwe, *Pe-Tin-Than*
Imprisoned: September 1990

Maung Maung Lay Ngwe was arrested and charged with writing and distributing publications that "make people lose respect for the government." The publications were titled, collectively, *Pe-Tin-Than* (Echoes). CPJ believes he may have been released but has not been able to confirm his legal status or find records of his sentencing.

Sein Hla Oo, free-lance
Imprisoned: August 5, 1994

Sein Hla Oo, a free-lance journalist and former editor of the newspaper *Botahtaung*, was arrested along with dissident writer San San Nwe on charges of contacting anti-government groups and spreading information damaging to the state. On October 6, 1994, Sein Hla Oo was sentenced to seven years in prison. San San Nwe and three other dissidents, including a former UNICEF worker, received sentences ranging from seven to 15 years in prison on similar charges.

Officials said the five had "fabricated and sent anti-government reports" to diplomats in foreign embassies, foreign radio stations, and foreign journalists. Sein Hla Oo, elected in 1990 to Parliament representing the National League for Democracy (NLD), had been imprisoned previously for his political activities.

Though San San Nwe was granted an early release in July 2001 along with 10 other political prisoners associated with the NLD, Sein Hla Oo remained in jail. He was held at Myitkyina Prison, according to the Thailand-based Assistance Association for Political Prisoners in Burma.

Though Sein Hla Oo's sentence should have expired in August 2001, he is now being forced to serve the remainder of an earlier 10-year prison sentence, issued by a military court in Insein Prison in March 1991, according to his wife, Shwe Zin. Authorities had arrested Sein Hla Oo in August 1990 along with several other NLD members but released him under an amnesty order in April 1992. Shwe Zin told the Oslo-based opposition radio station Democratic Voice of Burma in an interview that her husband had signed a document in October 2001 agreeing to abide by Article 401 of the Criminal Procedure Code, which allows prisoners' sentences to be suspended if they pledge not to engage in activities that threaten public order.

Aung Htun, free-lance
Tha Ban, free-lance
Imprisoned: February 1998

Aung Htun, a writer and activist with the All Burma Federation of Student Unions, was arrested in February 1998 for writing a seven-volume book documenting the history of the Burmese student movement. He was sentenced to a total of 17 years' imprisonment, according to a joint report published in December 2001 by the Thailand-based Assistance Association for Political Prisoners in Burma and the Burma Lawyers Council. Aung Htun was sentenced to three years for allegedly violating the 1962 Printer and Publishers Registration Act, seven years under the 1950 Emergency Provisions Act, and another seven years under the 1908

Unlawful Associations Act. He is jailed at Tharawaddy Prison.

In April 1998, the All Burma Students Democratic Front announced that five others were also prosecuted for contributing to the books, including journalist Tha Ban, a former editor at *Kyemon* newspaper and a prominent Arakanese activist. Tha Ban, whose name is sometimes written as Thar Ban, was sentenced to seven years in prison. He is being held at Insein Prison.

In August 2002, the human rights group Amnesty International issued an urgent appeal on behalf of Aung Htun and Tha Ban, saying that both journalists required immediate medical attention. Amnesty reported that Aung Htun "has growths on his feet which require investigation, is unable to walk, and suffers from asthma," and that Tha Ban's eyesight has "seriously deteriorated."

Aung Pwint, free-lance
Thaung Tun, free-lance
Imprisoned: October 1999

Aung Pwint, a videographer, editor, and poet, and Thaung Tun, an editor, reporter, and poet better known by his pen name Nyein Thit, were arrested separately in early October 1999. CPJ sources said they were arrested for making independent video documentaries that portrayed "real life" in Burma, including footage of forced labor and hardship in rural areas. Aung Pwint worked at a private media company that produced videos for tourism and educational purposes, but he also worked with Thaung Tun on documentary-style projects. Their videotapes circulated through underground networks.

The military government had prohibited Aung Pwint from making videos in 1996 "because they were considered to show too negative a picture of Burmese society and living standards," according to Human Rights Watch, which awarded Aung Pwint a Hellman-Hammett grant in 2001. A notable poet, he has also written under the name Maung Aung Pwint.

The two men were tried together, and each was sentenced to eight years in prison, according to CPJ sources. Aung Pwint was initially jailed at Insein Prison but was later transferred to Tharawaddy Prison, according to CPJ sources. Thaung Tun was jailed at Moulmein Prison, according to the Thailand-based Assistance Association for Political Prisoners in Burma.

CHINA: 39

Chen Renjie, "Ziyou Bao"
Lin Youping, "Ziyou Bao"
Imprisoned: July 1983

In September 1982, Chen, Lin, and Chen Biling wrote and published a pamphlet titled "Ziyou Bao" (Freedom Report), distributing around 300 copies in Fuzhou, Fujian Province. They were arrested in July 1983, and authorities accused them of making contact with Taiwanese spy organizations and publishing a counterrevolutionary pamphlet. According to official government records of the case, the men used "propaganda and incitement to encourage the overthrow of the people's democratic dictatorship and the socialist system." In August 1983, Chen Renjie was sentenced to life in prison, and Lin Youping was sentenced to death with reprieve. Chen Biling was sentenced to death and later executed.

Hu Liping, *Beijing Ribao*
Imprisoned: April 7, 1990

Hu, a staff member of *Beijing Ribao* (Beijing Daily), was arrested and charged with "counterrevolutionary incitement and propaganda" and "trafficking in state

secrets," according to a rare release of information on his case from the Chinese Ministry of Justice in 1998. The Beijing Intermediate People's Court sentenced him to 10 years in prison on August 15, 1990. Under the terms of his original sentence, Hu should have been released in 2000, but CPJ has been unable to obtain information about his legal status.

Chen Yanbin, *Tieliu*
Imprisoned: September 1990

Chen and Zhang Yafei, both university students, were arrested and charged with counterrevolutionary incitement and propaganda for publishing *Tieliu* (Iron Currents), an underground publication about the 1989 crackdown at Tiananmen Square. Several hundred mimeographed copies of the publication were distributed. Chen was sentenced to 15 years in prison and four years without political rights after his release. Zhang was sentenced to 11 years in prison and two years without political rights after his release. However, Zhang was freed on January 6, 2000, after showing "genuine repentance and a willingness to reform." In September 2000, the Justice Ministry announced that Chen's sentence had been reduced by three months for good behavior.

Liu Jingsheng, free-lance
Imprisoned: May 28, 1992

Liu was arrested and charged with "organizing and leading a counterrevolutionary group and spreading counterrevolutionary propaganda." He was sentenced to 15 years in prison after being tried secretly in July 1994.

Liu had belonged to labor and pro-democracy groups, including the Liberal Democratic Party of China, the Free Labor Union of China, and the Chinese

Progressive Alliance, and had written articles supporting the 1989 pro-democracy demonstrations. During the Democracy Wall movement in 1979, Liu co-edited the pro-democracy journal *Tansuo* (Explorations) with dissident Wei Jingsheng.

Court documents stated that Liu was involved in organizing and leading anti-government and pro-democracy activities. Prosecutors also accused him and other dissidents who were tried on similar charges of writing and printing political leaflets that were distributed in June 1992, during the third anniversary of the Tiananmen Square demonstrations. Liu has had his sentence reduced three times for good behavior, by a total of one year and eight months. In May 2002, on the 10th anniversary of her husband's arrest, Liu's wife, Jin Yanming, wrote an account of his imprisonment, trial, and the subsequent harassment of her family by security officials. The document was distributed online.

Kang Yuchun, *Freedom Forum*
Imprisoned: May 1992

Kang disappeared on May 6, 1992, and was presumed arrested, according to the New York–based advocacy organization Human Rights Watch. In October 1993, in response to an inquiry from the U.N. Working Group on Disappearances, Chinese authorities said Kang was arrested on May 27, 1992. On July 14, 1994, he was one of 16 individuals tried in a Chinese court for alleged involvement with underground pro-democracy groups. Kang was accused, among other charges, of launching *Freedom Forum*, the magazine of the Chinese Progressive Alliance, and of commissioning people to write articles for the magazine. On December 16, 1994, he was sentenced to 17 years in prison for "disseminating counterrevolu-

tionary propaganda" and for "organizing and leading a counterrevolutionary group." His sentence has been reduced three times, by a total of three years and eight months, for good behavior.

Wu Shishen,
Xinhua News Agency
Ma Tao, *Zhongguo Jiankang Jiaoyu Bao*
Imprisoned: November 6, 1992

Wu, an editor for China's state news agency, Xinhua, was arrested for allegedly leaking an advance copy of President Jiang Zemin's 14th Communist Party Congress address to a journalist from the now defunct Hong Kong newspaper *Kuai Bao* (Express). His wife, Ma, editor of *Zhongguo Jiankang Jiaoyu Bao* (China Health Education News), was arrested on the same day and accused of acting as Wu's accomplice. The Beijing Municipal Intermediate People's Court held a closed trial, and on August 30, 1993, sentenced Wu to life imprisonment for "illegally supplying state secrets to foreigners." Ma was sentenced to six years in prison. According to the terms of her original sentence, Ma should have been released in November 1998, but CPJ has been unable to obtain information on her legal status.

Fan Yingshang, *Remen Huati*
Sentenced: February 7, 1996

In 1994, Fan and Yang Jianguo printed more than 60,000 copies of a magazine called *Remen Huati* (Popular Topics). The men had allegedly purchased fake printing authorizations from an editor of the *Journal of European Research* at the Chinese Academy of Social Sciences, according to official Chinese news sources. CPJ was unable to determine the date of Fan's arrest, but on February 7, 1996, the Chang'an District Court in Shijiazhuang

City sentenced him to 15 years in prison for "engaging in speculation and profiteering." Authorities termed *Remen Huati* a "reactionary" publication. Yang escaped arrest and was not sentenced.

Hua Di, free-lance
Imprisoned: January 5, 1998

Hua, a permanent resident of the United States, was arrested while visiting China and charged with revealing state secrets. The charge is believed to stem from articles that Hua, a scientist at Stanford University, had written about China's missile defense system.

On November 25, 1999, the Beijing No. 1 Intermediate People's Court held a closed trial and sentenced Hua to 15 years in prison, according to the Hong Kong–based Information Center for Human Rights and Democracy. In March 2000, the Beijing High People's Court overturned Hua's conviction and ordered that the case be retried. This judicial reversal was extraordinary, particularly for a high-profile political case. Nevertheless, in April 2000, the Beijing State Security Bureau rejected a request for Hua to be released on medical parole; he suffers from a rare form of male breast cancer.

On November 23, 2000, after a retrial, the Beijing No. 1 Intermediate People's Court issued a slightly modified verdict, sentencing Hua to 10 years in prison. News of Hua's sentencing broke in February 2001, when a relative gave the information to foreign correspondents based in Beijing. In late 2001, Hua was moved to Tilanqiao Prison in Shanghai, according to CPJ sources.

Gao Qinrong, Xinhua News Agency
Imprisoned: December 4, 1998

Gao, a reporter for China's state news

agency, Xinhua, was jailed for reporting on a corrupt irrigation scheme in drought-plagued Yuncheng, Shanxi Province. Xinhua never carried Gao's article, which was finally published on May 27, 1998, in an internal reference edition of the official *People's Daily* that is distributed only among a select group of party leaders. But by fall 1998, the irrigation scandal had become national news, with reports appearing in the Guangzhou-based *Nanfang Zhoumo* (Southern Weekend) and on China Central Television. Gao's wife, Duan Maoying, said that local officials blamed Gao for the flurry of media interest and arranged for his prosecution on false charges.

Gao was arrested on December 4, 1998, and eventually charged with crimes including bribery, embezzlement, and pimping, according to Duan. On April 28, 1999, he was sentenced to 13 years in prison after a closed, one-day trial. He is being held in a prison in Qixian, Shanxi Province, according to CPJ sources.

In September 2001, Gao wrote to Mary Robinson, then the U.N. high commissioner for human rights, and asked her to intercede with the Chinese government on his behalf. Gao has received support from several members of the Chinese People's Political Consultative Conference of the National People's Congress, who issued a motion at its annual parliamentary meeting in March 2001 urging the Central Discipline Committee and Supreme People's Court to reopen his case. But by the end of 2002, there had been no change in his legal status.

Yue Tianxiang,
Zhongguo Gongren Guancha
Imprisoned: January 1999

The Tianshui People's Intermediate

Court in Gansu Province sentenced Yue to 10 years in prison on July 5, 1999. The journalist was charged with "subverting state power," according to the Hong Kong–based Information Center for Human Rights and Democracy. Yue was arrested along with two colleagues—Wang Fengshan and Guo Xinmin—both of whom were sentenced to two years' imprisonment and have since been released. According to the Hong Kong–based daily *South China Morning Post*, Yue, Guo, and Wang were arrested in January 1999 for publishing *Zhongguo Gongren Guancha* (China Workers' Monitor), a journal that campaigned for workers' rights.

With help from Wang, Yue and Guo started the journal after they were unable to get compensation from the Tianshui City Transport Agency following their dismissal from the company in 1995. All three men were reportedly members of the outlawed China Democracy Party, a dissident group, and were forming an organization to protect the rights of laid-off workers. The first issue of *Zhongguo Gongren Guancha* exposed extensive corruption among officials at the Tianshui City Transport Agency. Only two issues were ever published.

Wang Yingzheng, free-lance
Imprisoned: February 26, 1999

Police arrested Wang in the city of Xuzhou, in eastern Jiangsu Province, as he was photocopying an article he had written about political reform. The article was based on an open letter that the 19-year-old Wang had addressed to Chinese president Jiang Zemin. In the letter, Wang wrote—as translated by Agence France-Presse—"Many Chinese are discontented with the government's inability to squash corruption. This

is largely due to a lack of opposition parties and a lack of press freedom."

About five months earlier, in September 1998, Wang had been imprisoned for two weeks, during which time authorities questioned him about his association with Qin Yongmin, a key leader of the China Democracy Party who received a 12-year prison sentence in December 1998.

On December 10, 1999, Wang was convicted of subversion and sentenced to three years in prison. His trial was closed, but his family was notified of the verdict by letter, according to the Hong Kong–based Information Center for Human Rights and Democracy. According to the original terms of his sentence, Wang should have been released in February 2002, but CPJ has been unable to determine his legal status.

Wu Yilong, *Zaiye Dang*
Imprisoned: April 26, 1999
Mao Qingxiang, *Zaiye Dang*
Zhu Yufu, *Zaiye Dang*
Xu Guang, *Zaiye Dang*
Imprisoned: June 1999

Wu, an organizer for the banned China Democracy Party (CDP), was detained by police in Guangzhou on April 26, 1999. Mao, Zhu, and Xu, also leading CDP activists, were reportedly detained sometime around June 4, the 10th anniversary of the brutal crackdown on pro-democracy demonstrations in Tiananmen Square. The four were later charged with subversion for, among other things, establishing a magazine called *Zaiye Dang* (Opposition Party) and circulating pro-democracy writings online.

On October 25, 1999, the Hangzhou Intermediate People's Court in Zhejiang Province conducted what *The New York Times* described as a "sham trial." On

November 9, 1999, all four journalists were convicted of subversion. Wu was sentenced to 11 years in prison. Mao was sentenced to eight years in prison; Zhu, to seven years; and Xu, to five years.

In December 2002, Mao was transferred to a convalescence hospital after his health had sharply declined as a result of being confined to his cell. Zhu, who has also been confined to his cell and forbidden from reading newspapers, had been placed under tightened restrictions at year's end after refusing to express regret for his actions, according to the New York–based advocacy group Human Rights in China.

Liu Xianli, free-lance
Imprisoned: May 11, 1999

The Beijing Intermediate Court found writer Liu guilty of subversion and sentenced him to four years in prison, according to a report by the Hong Kong–based Information Center for Human Rights and Democracy.

Liu's "crime" was attempting to publish a book on Chinese dissidents, including Xu Wenli, one of China's most prominent political prisoners and a leading figure in the China Democracy Party. In December 1998, Xu was himself convicted of subversion and sentenced to 13 years in prison. On December 24, 2002, Xu was released on medical parole and deported to the United States.

Jiang Qisheng, free-lance
Imprisoned: May 18, 1999

Police arrested Jiang in the late evening and searched his home, seizing his computer, several documents, and articles he had written for *Beijing zhi Chun* (Beijing Spring), a New York–based pro-democracy publication. The arrest came after Jiang published a series of essays and open letters related to the 10th anniversary of the government's violent suppression of student-led demonstrations in Tiananmen Square. One essay called for a candlelight vigil on June 4, 1999; another urged the government to conduct a full investigation into the massacre; and a third protested the police's brutal treatment of Cao Jiahe, an editor of *Dongfang* (Orient) magazine who was detained on May 10, 1999, and tortured while in police custody. Cao had been detained for allegedly circulating a petition to remember the hundreds killed by government troops during the Tiananmen crackdown.

During Jiang's two-and-a-half-hour trial, held on November 1, 1999, prosecutors cited an April essay calling for a protest vigil, "Light a Thousand Candles," as evidence of his anti-state activities. Prosecutors also accused him of circulating an article on political reform, though Jiang said he showed the piece to only three friends. On December 27, 2000, thirteen months after his trial, the Beijing No. 1 Intermediate People's Court sentenced Jiang to four years in prison.

An Jun, free-lance
Imprisoned: July 1999

An, an anti-corruption campaigner, was sentenced to four years in prison on subversion charges. The Intermediate People's Court in Xinyang, Henan Province, announced the verdict on April 19, 2000, citing An's essays and articles on corruption as evidence of his anti-state activities.

A former manager of an export trading company, An founded the civic group Zhongguo Fubai Xingwei Guancha (China Corruption Monitor) in 1998 and was arrested in July 1999. The group reportedly exposed more than 100 cases of corruption. During his November 1999 trial, An "said he was only trying to help the government end rampant corruption," according to Agence France-Presse.

In November 2001, An's family sent a letter to President Jiang Zemin appealing for the journalist's release for medical reasons. An suffers from heart problems and has not received adequate treatment while in prison, according to Agence France-Presse.

On December 7, 2002, An began a hunger strike to protest prison conditions, according to the New York–based advocacy group Human Rights in China. At the end of the year, he was in critical condition after having refused food for more than three weeks.

Qi Yanchen, free-lance
Imprisoned: September 2, 1999

Police arrested Qi at his home in Cangzhou, Hebei Province. His wife told reporters that officers confiscated his computer, printer, fax machine, and a number of documents. Qi, an economist, has published many articles in intellectual journals and online publications calling for economic and political reforms. He was also associated with the online magazine *Canzhao* (Consultations), a publication linked to the banned China Development Union.

On May 30, 2000, Qi was prosecuted for subversion before the Cangzhou People's Court in a closed, half-day trial. He was sentenced to four years in prison on September 19, 2000. His sentencing papers cited as evidence articles he had written for Hong Kong magazines and overseas Web sites.

Zhang Ji, free-lance
Imprisoned: October 1999

Zhang, a student at Qiqihar University in the northeastern province of

Heilongjiang, was charged on November 8, 1999, with "disseminating reactionary documents via the Internet," according to the Hong Kong–based Information Center for Human Rights and Democracy.

Zhang had allegedly distributed news and information about the banned spiritual movement Falun Gong. He was arrested sometime in October as part of the Chinese government's crackdown on the sect.

Using the Internet, Zhang reportedly transmitted news of the crackdown to Falun Gong members in the United States and Canada and also received reports from abroad, which he then circulated among practitioners in China. Before Zhang's arrest, Chinese authorities had increased Internet surveillance as part of their effort to crush Falun Gong.

Huang Qi, Tianwang Web site
Imprisoned: June 3, 2000

Public security officials came to Huang's office and arrested him for articles that had appeared on the Tianwang Web site, which he published. In January 2001, he was charged with subversion.

In October 1998, Huang and his wife, Zeng Li, launched Tianwang (*www.6-4tianwang.com*), a missing-persons search service based in Chengdu, Sichuan Province. The site soon became a forum for users to publicize abuses of power by local officials and to post articles about a variety of topics, including the June 4, 1989, military crackdown on peaceful demonstrations in Tiananmen Square, the independence movement in the Xinjiang Uighur Autonomous Region, and the banned spiritual group Falun Gong.

In December 1999, Huang published an investigative report about labor abuses committed against workers whom the Sichuan provincial government had sent abroad.

While several domestic newspapers subsequently investigated and published stories on the case, authorities in Chengdu began threatening Huang and repeatedly interrogated him about his reporting.

Huang has been beaten in prison and has tried to commit suicide, according to an open letter he wrote from prison in February 2001 that was published on the Tianwang site. His family members, including his wife and young son, have not been allowed to visit or communicate with him since his arrest two years ago.

The Chengdu Intermediate Court in Sichuan Province held a secret trial on August 14, 2001. Family members were not allowed to attend, and no verdict or sentencing date was released. Huang's trial had been postponed several times throughout 2001 in an apparent effort to deflect international attention from China's human rights practices during the country's campaign to host the 2008 Olympic Games. (Two of the trial delays—on February 23 and June 27—coincided with important dates in Beijing's Olympics bid.)

Overseas supporters of Huang regularly post updates on his case to the Tianwang Web site, which is now hosted on a server outside China.

Xu Zerong, free-lance
Imprisoned: June 24, 2000

Xu was arrested in the city of Guangzhou and held incommunicado for 19 months before being tried by the Shenzhen Intermediate Court in January 2002. He was sentenced to 10 years in prison on charges of "leaking state secrets" and to an additional three years on charges of committing "economic crimes."

Xu, an associate research professor in the Institute of Southeast Asian Studies at Zhongshan University in Guangzhou, has

written several free-lance articles about China's foreign policy and co-founded a Hong Kong–based academic journal, *Zhongguo Shehui Kexue Jikan* (China Social Sciences Quarterly). Xu is a permanent resident of Hong Kong.

Chinese officials have said that the "state secrets" charges against Xu stem from his use of historical materials for his academic research. In 1992, Xu photocopied four books published in the 1950s about China's role in the Korean War, which he then sent to a colleague in South Korea, according to a letter from the Chinese government to St. Antony's College, Oxford University. (Xu earned his Ph.D. at St. Antony's College, and since his arrest, college personnel have actively researched and protested his case.) The Security Committee of the People's Liberation Army in Guangzhou later determined that these documents should be labeled "top secret."

The "economic crimes" charges are related to the "illegal publication" of more than 60,000 copies of 25 books and periodicals since 1993, including several books about Chinese politics and Beijing's relations with Taiwan, according to official government documents.

Some observers believe that the charges against Xu are more likely related to an article he wrote for the Hong Kong–based *Yazhou Zhoukan* (Asia Weekly) newsmagazine revealing clandestine Chinese Communist Party support for Malaysian communist insurgency groups. Xu was arrested only days before the article appeared in the June 26, 2000, issue. In the article, Xu accused the Chinese Communist Party of hypocrisy for condemning the United States and other countries for interfering in China's internal affairs by criticizing its human rights record. "China's support of world revolution is based on the concept of 'class above sovereignty'…which is equivalent to the idea of 'human rights above sovereignty,' which the U.S. promotes today," Xu wrote.

Xu's family has filed an appeal, which was pending at press time. They have not been allowed to visit him since his arrest.

Guo Qinghai, free-lance
Imprisoned: September 15, 2000

Guo was arrested after posting numerous essays on overseas online bulletin boards calling for political reforms in China. In almost 40 essays posted under the pen name Qing Song, Guo covered a variety of topics, including political prisoners, environmental problems, and corruption. In one essay, Guo discussed the importance of a free press, saying, "Those who oppose lifting media censorship argue that it will negatively influence social stability. But according to what I have seen … countries that control speech may be able to maintain stability in the short term, but the end result is often violent upheaval, coup d'états, or war."

Guo, who worked in a bank, also wrote articles for Taiwanese newspapers. He was a friend and classmate of writer Qi Yanchen, who was sentenced to four years in prison on subversion charges just four days after Guo's arrest (see above). One of Guo's last online essays appealed for Qi's release. On April 3, 2001, a court in Cangzhou, Hebei Province, tried Guo on subversion charges. On April 26, he was sentenced to four years in prison.

Liu Weifang, free-lance
Imprisoned: October 2000

Liu was arrested sometime after September 26, 2000, when security officials from the Ninth Agricultural Brigade District, in the Xinjiang Uighur Autonomous Region, came to his house, confiscated his computer, and announced that he was being officially investigated, according to an account that Liu posted online. His most recent essay was dated October 20, 2000.

Liu had recently posted a number of essays criticizing China's leaders and political system in Internet chat rooms. The essays, which the author signed either with his real name or with the initials "lgwf," covered topics such as official corruption, development policies in China's western regions, and environmental issues. At press time, the articles were available online at *http://liuweifang.ipfox.com*.

"The reasons for my actions are all above-board," Liu wrote in one essay. "They are not aimed at any one person or any organization; rather, they are directed at any behavior in society that harms humanity. The goal is to speed up humanity's progress and development." The official *Xinjiang Daily* characterized Liu's work as "a major threat to national security." According to a June 15, 2001, report in the *Xinjiang Daily*, the Ninth Agricultural Brigade District's Intermediate People's Court had sentenced Liu to three years in prison.

Jiang Weiping, free-lance
Imprisoned: December 4, 2000

Jiang was arrested after publishing a number of articles in the Hong Kong magazine *Qianshao* (Frontline), a monthly Chinese-language magazine focusing on mainland affairs, revealing corruption scandals in northeastern China.

Jiang wrote the *Qianshao* articles, which were published between June and September 1999, under various pen names. His coverage exposed several major corruption scandals involving high-level officials. Notably, Jiang reported that

Shenyang vice mayor Ma Xiangdong had lost nearly 30 million yuan (US$3.6 million) in public funds gambling in Macau casinos. Jiang also revealed that Liaoning provincial governor Bo Xilai had covered up corruption among his friends and family during his years as Dalian mayor.

Soon after these cases were publicized in *Qianshao* and other Hong Kong media, central authorities detained Ma. He was accused of taking bribes, embezzling public funds, and gambling overseas and was executed for these crimes in December 2001. After Ma's arrest, his case was widely reported in the domestic press and used as an example in the government's ongoing fight against corruption. However, in May 2001, Jiang was indicted for "revealing state secrets."

The Dalian Intermediate Court held a secret trial in September 2001. On January 25, 2002, the court formally sentenced Jiang to eight years in prison on charges including "inciting to subvert state power" and "illegally providing state secrets overseas." This judgment amended an earlier decision to sentence Jiang to nine years. During the January sentencing, Jiang proclaimed his innocence and told the court that the verdict "trampled on the law," according to CPJ sources. He has since appealed the verdict, but the case remained pending at year's end.

According to CPJ sources, Jiang has a serious stomach disorder and has been denied medical treatment. Jiang's wife and daughter have not been allowed to see or speak with him in the two years since his arrest. His wife, Li Yanling, has been repeatedly interrogated and threatened since her husband's arrest. In March 2002, the local public security bureau brought her in for questioning and detained her for several weeks.

An experienced journalist, Jiang had worked until May 2000 as the northeastern China bureau chief for the Hong Kong paper *Wen Hui Bao*. He contributed freelance articles to *Qianshao*. In the 1980s, he worked as a Dalian-based correspondent for Xinhua News Agency.

In November 2001, CPJ honored Jiang with its annual International Press Freedom Award. In February 2002, CPJ sent appeals to Chinese president Jiang Zemin from almost 600 supporters—including CBS news anchor Dan Rather, civil rights leader Jesse Jackson, and former U.S. ambassador to China Winston Lord—demanding Jiang's unconditional release. That month, U.S. president George W. Bush highlighted Jiang's case in meetings with Jiang Zemin during a state visit to China. No progress had been made in the case by the end of 2002.

Lu Xinhua, free-lance
Imprisoned: March 10, 2001

Lu was arrested in Wuhan, Hubei Province, after articles he had written about rural unrest and official corruption appeared on various Internet news sites based overseas. On April 20, 2001, he was charged with "inciting to subvert state power," a charge frequently used against journalists who write about politically sensitive subjects. Lu's trial began on September 18. On December 30, 2001, he was sentenced to four years in prison.

Yang Zili, *Yangzi de Sixiang Jiayuan* Web site
Xu Wei, *Xiaofei Ribao*
Jin Haike, free-lance
Zhang Honghai, free-lance
Imprisoned: March 13, 2001

Yang, Xu, Jin, and Zhang were detained on March 13 and charged with subversion on April 20. The four were active participants in the Xin Qingnian Xuehui (New Youth Study Group), an informal gathering of individuals who explored topics related to political and social reform and used the Internet to circulate relevant articles.

Yang, the group's most prominent member, published a Web site, Yangzi de Sixiang Jiayuan (Yangzi's Garden of Ideas), which featured poems, essays, and reports by various authors on subjects such as the shortcomings of rural elections. Authorities closed the site after Yang's arrest.

When Xu, a reporter with *Xiaofei Ribao* (Consumer Daily), was detained on March 13, authorities confiscated his computer, other professional equipment, and books, according to an account published online by his girlfriend, Wang Ying. Wang reported that public security officials also ordered *Xiaofei Ribao* to fire Xu. The newspaper has refused to discuss his case with reporters, according to The Associated Press.

The Beijing No. 1 Intermediate People's Court tried all four on September 28, 2001. Prosecutors focused predominately on the group's writings, including two essays circulated on the Internet called "Be a new citizen, reform China" and "What's to be done?" According to the indictment papers, these articles demonstrated the group's intention "to overthrow the Chinese Communist Party's leadership and the socialist system and subvert the regime of the people's democratic dictatorship." No verdict had been announced in the case by the end of 2002.

Liu Haofeng, free-lance
Imprisoned: March 2001

Liu was secretly arrested in Shanghai in mid-March while conducting research on

social conditions in rural China for the dissident China Democracy Party (CDP). On May 16, 2001, Liu was sentenced to "re-education through labor," a form of administrative detention that allows officials to send individuals to labor camps for up to three years without trial or formal charges.

After Liu's arrest, friends and family were not informed of his whereabouts, and CDP members say they only found out what had happened to him when they received news of his sentence in August 2001.

Sentencing papers issued by the Shanghai Re-education Through Labor Committee cited several alleged offenses, including a policy paper and an essay written by Liu that were published under different pen names on the CDP's Web site. The essay focused on the current situation of China's peasants. The committee also accused Liu of trying to form an illegal organization, the "China Democracy Party Joint Headquarters, Second Front."

The journalist had previously worked as an editor and reporter for various publications, including the magazine *Jishu Jingji Yu Guanli* (Technology, Economy, and Management), run by the Fujian Province Economic and Trade Committee, and *Zhongguo Shichang Jingji Bao* (China Market Economy News), run by the Central Party School in the capital, Beijing. Beginning in 1999, he worked for Univillage, a research organization focusing on rural democratization, and managed its Web site. He was working as a free-lance journalist at the time of his arrest.

Wang Jinbo, free-lance
Imprisoned: May 2001

Wang, a free-lance journalist, was arrested in early May 2001 for e-mailing essays to overseas organizations arguing that the government should change its official view that the 1989 protests in Tiananmen Square were "counterrevolutionary." In October 2001, Wang was formally charged with "inciting to subvert state power." On November 14, the Junan County Court in Shandong Province held a closed trial; only the journalists' relatives were allowed to attend. On December 13, 2001, Wang was sentenced to four years in prison.

Wang, a member of the banned China Democracy Party, had been detained several times in the past for his political activities. In February 2001, days before the International Olympic Committee (IOC) visited Beijing, he was briefly taken into custody after signing an open letter calling on the IOC to pressure China to release political prisoners. A number of Wang's essays have been posted on various Internet sites. One, titled "My Account of Police Violations of Civil Rights," describes his January 2001 detention, during which police interrogated him and held him for 20 hours with no food or heat after he signed an open letter calling for the release of political prisoners.

Wang Daqi, *Shengtai Yanjiu*
Imprisoned: January 24, 2002

Wang, editor of *Shengtai Yanjiu* (Ecology Research) magazine, was arrested after leaving his house to go grocery shopping, according to the New York–based advocacy group Human Rights in China. Several state security officers also searched his home and confiscated copies of the magazine, his journal, and other personal items.

Soon after his arrest, authorities said Wang was being detained under Article 109 of the Criminal Code, which covers the crime of defection to another country. However, on December 19, 2002, the Hefei Intermediate Court, in Anhui Province, sentenced Wang to one year in prison on subversion charges. Prosecutors cited as evidence articles Wang had written for *Shengtai Yanjiu,* including one titled "On the 35th Anniversary of the Cultural Revolution."

Wang, 70, has repeatedly angered authorities by publishing articles and editorials that blame the government for China's ecological problems. In 1997, state security officers ordered him to stop publishing *Shengtai Yanjiu*, but he refused. Wang's sentence accounts for time served since February 7, 2002, when his wife was notified of his arrest. He is due to be released on February 6, 2003.

Tao Haidong, free-lance
Imprisoned: July 9, 2002

Tao, an Internet essayist and pro-democracy activist, was arrested in Urumqi, the capital of the Xinjiang Uighur Autonomous Region, and charged with "incitement to subvert state power." According to the Minzhu Luntan (Democracy Forum) Web site, which had published Tao's recent writing, his articles focused on political and legal reform. In one essay, titled "Strategies for China's Social Reforms," Tao wrote that "the Chinese Communist Party and democracy activists throughout society should unite to push forward China's freedom and democratic development or else stand condemned through the ages."

Previously, in 1999, Tao was sentenced to three years of "re-education through labor" in Xi'an, Shaanxi Province, according to the New York–based advocacy group Human Rights in China, because of his essays and his work on a book titled *Xin Renlei Shexiang* (Imaginings of a New Human Race). After his early release in

2001, Tao began writing essays and articles and publishing them on various domestic and overseas Web sites.

In early January 2003, the Urumqi Intermediate Court tried Tao, but no sentence had been announced by press time.

Zhang Wei, *Shishi Zixun, Redian Jiyao*
Imprisoned: July 19, 2002

Zhang was arrested and charged with illegal publishing after producing and selling two underground newspapers in Chongqing, in central China. According to an account published on the Web site of the Chongqing Press and Publishing Administration, a provincial government body that governs all local publications, beginning in April 2001, Zhang edited two newspapers, *Shishi Zixun* (Current Events) and *Redian Jiyao* (Summary of the Main Points), which included articles and graphics he had downloaded from the Internet.

Two of Zhang's business associates, Zuo Shangwen and Ou Yan, were also arrested on July 19, 2002, and indicted for their involvement with the publications. Zuo printed the publications in neighboring Sichuan Province while Ou managed the publications' finances. At the time of their arrests, police confiscated 9,700 copies of *Shishi Zixun*.

The official account of their arrests stated that the two publications had "flooded" Chongqing's publishing market. The government declared that "the political rumors, shocking 'military reports,' and other articles in these illegal publications misled the public, poisoned the youth, negatively influenced society and sparked public indignation." Zhang, Zuo, and Ou printed more than 1.5 million copies of the publications and sold them in Chongqing, Chengdu, and other cities.

On December 25, 2002, the Yuzhong District Court in Chongqing sentenced Zhang to six years in prison and fined him 100,000 yuan (US$12,000), the amount that police said he had earned in profits from the publications. Zuo was sentenced to five years and fined 50,000 yuan (US$6,000), while Ou was sentenced to two years in prison.

Chen Shaowen, free-lance
Imprisoned: August 2002

Chen, a free-lance writer, was arrested on suspicion of "using the Internet to subvert state power," according to a September 14 report in the official *Hunan Daily*. The article did not give the date of Chen's arrest, although Boxun News, an overseas online news service, reported that he was arrested on August 6.

Chen, who lives in Lianyuan, Hunan Province, has written numerous essays and articles for various overseas Chinese-language Web sites, including the online magazine *Huang Hua Gang* and Minzhu Luntan (Democracy Forum). According to his biography on the Minzhu Luntan Web site (*asiademo.org*), Chen's essays covered topics including China's unemployment problem, social inequalities, and flaws in the legal system.

The *Hunan Daily* article accused Chen of "repeatedly browsing reactionary websites ... sending in numerous articles of all sorts, fabricating, distorting and exaggerating relevant facts, and vilifying the Chinese Communist Party and the socialist system." The report stated that Chen had published more than 40 articles on overseas "reactionary" Web sites. Chen is still under investigation, and it is not clear whether he has been formally charged. His family has not been allowed to visit him in detention.

Liu Di, free-lance
Imprisoned: November 7, 2002

Liu disappeared on November 7. The following day, security officials came to her house, which she shares with her 80-year-old grandmother, and confiscated Liu's computer, several books, and other personal belongings. Officials told her family that Liu was being investigated for "participating in an illegal organization." Authorities have not offered her family any further explanation as to her whereabouts.

Liu, 22, is a fourth-year student in the psychology department at Beijing Teacher's University. Using the pseudonym Buxiugang Laoshu (Stainless Steel Mouse), she wrote several online essays criticizing the Chinese government.

In one essay, Liu wrote that, "My ideals are the ideals of an open society... In my view, freedom does not just include external freedom, but freedom within our hearts and minds." In another essay, Liu called on Chinese citizens to stop reading official news and to read only "reactionary" materials. She also wrote in support of Huang Qi and Yang Zili, Web site publishers who have been arrested and charged with subversion.

Liu had expressed fears of being arrested and said that school authorities had called her in for questioning several times prior to her disappearance, according to online accounts written by her friends and acquaintances.

Liu's arrest became a rallying point for Chinese Internet users worldwide, and in December her supporters created a Web site (*http://171.64.233.179*) and launched a global petition demanding her release. By year's end, the petition had gathered more than 700 signatures from inside and outside China.

Liu's disappearance came one day before the opening of the 16th Communist Party Congress. During the run-up to the congress, Chinese authorities escalated a crackdown on free expression by arresting government critics, closing Web sites, and tightening already stringent control over the official media.

CUBA: 1

Bernardo Rogelio Arévalo Padrón,
Línea Sur Press
Imprisoned: November 18, 1997

Arévalo Padrón, founder of the Línea Sur Press news agency, remains in prison despite being eligible for parole, and his health has suffered as a result of his prolonged imprisonment.

On October 31, 1997, a provincial court sentenced Arévalo Padrón to six years in prison for "lack of respect" for President Fidel Castro Ruz and Cuban State Council member Carlos Lage. The charges stemmed from a series of interviews Arévalo Padrón gave in late 1997 to Miami-based radio stations in which he alleged that while Cuban farmers starved, helicopters were taking fresh meat from the countryside to President Castro, Lage, and other Communist Party officials in the capital, Havana.

The journalist began his sentence on November 18, 1997, in a maximum-security prison. On April 11, 1998, State Security officers beat Arévalo Padrón and placed him in solitary confinement after accusing him of making anti-government posters. Later, another prisoner was found to have made the posters.

Arévalo Padrón has also suffered bouts of bronchitis and was reportedly treated twice for high blood pressure in the prison infirmary. On January 8, 2000, the journalist was transferred to Labor Camp No. 20, where he served four months.

On April 6, 2000, the journalist was sent to the overcrowded and unsanitary San Marcos Labor Camp, where he worked chopping weeds with a machete in sugarcane fields. Prison authorities constantly watched Arévalo Padrón, censored his incoming and outgoing mail, and threatened to send him back to a maximum-security prison if he did not meet his production quota.

Because of his strenuous work at the labor camps, Arévalo Padrón developed lower back pain and coronary blockage. After ignoring Arévalo Padrón's pain for weeks, in September 2000 prison authorities allowed him to see a doctor, who determined that Arévalo Padrón's poor health disqualified him from physical work, and that he should permanently wear an orthopedic brace.

In October 2000, prison authorities informed Arévalo Padrón that his parole had been approved. But he remained in the labor camp, a violation of Cuban law.

Early in 2001, Arévalo Padrón was transferred to the El Diamante Labor Camp, where prison officers continued to harass him. In February 2001, the journalist's colleagues reported that he had again developed high blood pressure. In early March, Arévalo Padrón complained that officials refused to take him to a hospital outside the labor camp for treatment. On March 21, prison authorities relented after pressure from friends, family, and press freedom organizations. A heart specialist recommended that Arévalo Padrón check his blood pressure daily, take medication, avoid tension, and stop smoking.

In May 2001, prison officers routinely ignored the journalist's requests to have his blood pressure checked and often withheld his medication. During the same period, a court again denied him parole despite his poor health.

On June 30, 2001, the journalist was transferred to another labor camp. For the prison transfer, he had to walk several miles in the heat carrying his belongings, the journalist said in a letter to colleagues. In the new labor camp, he was assigned to a cell for chronically ill prisoners. He was exempt from physical work but lacked adequate medical attention and food. Despite his legal right to be paroled, his jailers told him that he would serve his entire sentence. In October 2001, judges ignored his request for parole, and the journalist continued to report constant harassment.

In November 2001, the European Union requested that Arévalo Padrón be released and allowed to travel to Spain, but authorities did not respond. The journalist's request to attend a January 2002 appointment with the U.S. Interests Section Refugee Unit in Havana was also ignored.

In July 2002, Arévalo Padrón was transferred back to the maximum-security Ariza Prison. In December 2002, he suffered from a severe fever and was treated with antibiotics. According to his colleagues, Arévalo Padrón's wife, Libertad Acosta, suspects he contracted a severe bacterial infection. In addition, he suffers from migraines and high blood pressure, and his family and friends say his mental health has deteriorated. Arévalo Padrón's six-year sentence ends in October 2003.

DEMOCRATIC REPUBLIC OF CONGO: 2

Raymond Kabala, *Alerte Plus*
Imprisoned: July 19, 2002

Kabala, publication director of the independent daily *Alerte Plus*, based in the capital, Kinshasa, was arrested by plainclothes police officers and detained at the provincial police department. The next day, he was transferred to Kinshasa's Penitentiary and Reeducation Center (CPRK).

According to local sources, Kabala's arrest stemmed from a July 11 *Alerte Plus* article reporting that Minister of Public Order and Security Mwenze Kongolo had allegedly been poisoned. The newspaper learned that the information was false and published a correction the next day.

According to the local press freedom group Journaliste En Danger (JED), Kabala claims that authorities repeatedly questioned him about the article's sources and tortured him during his detention.

On the afternoon of July 22, officers of the Kinshasa/Matete Appeals Court Prosecutor's Office arrested Delly Bonsange, the journalist who had written the offending article. He spent the night in police custody, and authorities questioned him about the report the next day. He was later transferred to the CPRK.

On September 6, a Kinshasa court convicted Kabala and Bonsange of "harmful accusations," "writing falsehoods," and "falsification of a public document." Kabala was sentenced to 12 months in prison and fined US$200,000. Bonsange was sentenced to six months and fined US$100,000.

According to a JED representative who attended the court proceedings, the "falsification of a public document" charge came because the actual address of *Alerte Plus*' office differs from the one listed in the paper.

On September 26, Bonsange was transferred to Kinshasa's General Hospital after a doctor found his blood sugar levels unusually high. The journalist told JED that, during the first days of his detention, officials had barred him from taking his diabetes medication and following his usual diet.

According to JED, on November 21, a Kinshasa appeals court ruled that the charge against Bonsange of "writing falsehoods" was unfounded but upheld the charge of "falsification of a public document." The journalist's six-month prison sentence was dropped, and he was released on December 3. He was, however, fined US$750.

The court upheld the charges and the fine against Kabala but reduced his prison sentence from 12 to seven months.

Kadima Mukombe, Radio Kilimandjaro
Imprisoned: December 31, 2002

Mukombe, a journalist for the private Tshikapa-based Radio Kilimandjaro, was arrested by agents of the Congolese Armed Forces (FAC) Military Intelligence Branch (DEMIAP).

Mukombe hosts a local-language radio program that focuses on development issues in Tshikapa and the surrounding region of the diamond-rich West Kasai Province. According to the local press freedom group Journaliste En Danger (JED), on his December 30 program, Mukombe criticized several local military officials who have allegedly become diamond traders and have allowed their soldiers to steal from the local population. On the program, Mukombe interviewed diamond miners who denounced harassment by these military officials.

Mukombe was accused of "insulting the army." He was held at the local DEMIAP station until January 2, 2003, when he was transferred to the Tshikapa Central Prison. Eyewitnesses said FAC agents beat Mukombe at the time of his arrest, according to JED.

CPJ was unable to confirm whether

authorities intended to prosecute Mukombe. Local sources said it is possible that Mukombe could be tried for the offense in the military court system, which has been known to hand down heavier sentences than civilian courts.

Journalists in the capital, Kinshasa, said that Mukombe had also been arrested on December 23 following the broadcast of a program during which he denounced the poverty endured by the local population while valuable diamonds are mined on a daily basis in the city. Mukombe was released that day after signing an agreement to no longer "set the population against the established authorities," only to be re-arrested days later. He remained in prison at press time.

EGYPT: 1

Mamdouh Mahran, *Al-Nabaa*
Imprisoned: September 30, 2001

Mahran, editor of the controversial weekly newspaper *Al-Nabaa*, was sentenced to three years in prison and fined 200 Egyptian pounds (about US$50) on September 16, 2001, for allegedly undermining public security, publishing scandalous photos, insulting religion, and causing civil turmoil.

The charges stemmed from a June 17, 2001, *Al-Nabaa* cover story alleging that a Coptic Christian monk had sex with several women in a Coptic monastery in southern Egypt and filmed the encounters to blackmail the women. The piece was accompanied by provocative photos. The *Al-Nabaa* article led to demonstrations and riots among Egypt's Coptic minority, who viewed the story as insulting to their religion.

Coptic Church officials vehemently denied that sexual acts had occurred in the monastery and pointed out that the

monk in question had been defrocked five years earlier, a fact omitted from *Al-Nabaa*'s account.

Mahran was to begin his sentence on October 1, 2001, but he allegedly suffered a heart attack the day before. He was taken, under guard, to a private heart trauma center in the capital, Cairo, where he remained hospitalized under guard at the end of 2002.

ERITREA: 18

Zemenfes Haile, *Tsigenay*
Imprisoned: January 1999

Sometime in early 1999, Haile, founder and manager of the private weekly *Tsigenay*, was detained by Eritrean authorities and sent to Zara Labor Camp in the country's lowland desert. Authorities accused Haile of failing to complete the National Service Program, but sources told CPJ that the journalist completed the program in 1994.

Near the end of 2000, Haile was transferred to an unknown location, and friends and relatives have not seen or heard from him since. CPJ sources in Eritrea believe that Haile's continued detention is part of the government's general crackdown on the press, which began in September 2001.

Ghebrehiwet Keleta, *Tsigenay*
Imprisoned: July 2000

Keleta, reporter for the private weekly *Tsigenay*, was kidnapped by security agents on his way to work sometime in July 2000 and has not been seen since. The reasons for Keleta's arrest remain unclear, but CPJ sources in Eritrea believe that Keleta's continued detention is part of the government's general crackdown on the press, which began in September 2001.

Selamyinghes Beyene, *MeQaleh*
Binyam Haile, *Haddas Eritrea*
Imprisoned: Fall 2001

Beyene, reporter for the independent weekly *MeQaleh*, and Haile, a journalist at the pro-government *Haddas Eritrea*, were arrested some time in the fall of 2001 and have been missing since. CPJ was unable to confirm the reasons for their arrests, but Eritrean sources believe that the detention of the journalists is part of the government's general crackdown on the press, which began in September 2001.

Amanuel Asrat, *Zemen*
Imprisoned: September 2001
Medhanie Haile, *Keste Debena*
Imprisoned: September 18, 2001
Yusuf Mohamed Ali, *Tsigenay*
Mattewos Habteab, *MeQaleh*
Imprisoned: September 19, 2001
Temesken Ghebreyesus, *Keste Debena*
Said Abdelkader, *Admas*
Imprisoned: September 20, 2001
Dawit Isaac, *Setit*
Seyoum Fsehaye, free-lance
Imprisoned: September 21, 2001
Dawit Habtemichael, *MeQaleh*
Imprisoned: on or about September 21, 2001
Fesshaye "Joshua" Yohannes, *Setit*
Imprisoned: September 27, 2001

Beginning September 18, 2001, Eritrean security forces arrested at least 10 local journalists. Two others fled the country. The arrests came less than a week after authorities abruptly closed all privately owned newspapers, allegedly to safeguard national unity in the face of growing political turmoil in the tiny Horn of Africa nation.

International news reports quoted presidential adviser Yemane Gebremeskel as saying that the journalists could have been arrested for avoiding military service. Sources in the capital, Asmara, however, say that at least two of the detained journalists, free-lance photographer Fsehaye and Mohamed Ali, editor of *Tsigenay*, are legally exempt from national service. Fsehaye is reportedly exempt because he is an independence war veteran, while Mohamed Ali is apparently well over the maximum age for military service.

CPJ sources in Asmara maintain that the suspension and subsequent arrests of independent journalists were part of a full-scale government effort to suppress political dissent in advance of December 2001 elections, which the government canceled without explanation.

On March 31, 2002, the 10 jailed reporters began a hunger strike to protest their continued detention without charge, according to local and international sources. In a message smuggled from inside the Police Station One detention center in Asmara, the journalists said they would refuse food until they were either released or charged and given a fair trial. Three days later, nine of the hunger strikers were transferred to an undisclosed detention facility. According to CPJ sources, the 10th journalist, Swedish national Isaac, was sent to a hospital, where he is being treated for posttraumatic stress disorder, a result of alleged torture while in police custody. His health condition remained unspecified at the end of 2002.

During a July 2002 fact-finding mission to Asmara, a presidential official told a CPJ delegation that only "about eight" news professionals were being held in detention facilities, whose whereabouts he refused to disclose.

Simret Seyoum, *Setit*
Imprisoned: January 6, 2002

During a July 2002 fact-finding mission to the capital, Asmara, CPJ delegates confirmed that Seyoum, a writer and general manager at the banned private weekly *Setit*, was arrested while trying to cross Eritrea's border with Sudan. The driver of the minivan carrying Seyoum and others was also arrested, after border patrol agents opened fire on his vehicle, chased it, and captured some of its passengers. At least one of the fugitives, an Eritrean journalist who chose to remain anonymous, survived the incident and reached the Sudanese capital, Khartoum, days later.

Seyoum, a hero of Eritrea's 30-year independence war against Ethiopia, is being held in solitary confinement at the Hadish Maaskar detention facility near the town of Gyrmayka on the border with Sudan, according to CPJ sources in Eritrea.

Hamid Mohammed Said, Eritrean State Television
Saadia, Eritrean State Television
Saleh Aljezeeri, Eritrean State Radio
Imprisoned: February 15, 2002

During a July 2002 fact-finding mission to the capital, Asmara, CPJ delegates confirmed that around February 15, Eritrean authorities arrested Said, a journalist for the state-run Eritrean State Television (ETV), Saadia (full name unknown), a female journalist with the Arabic-language service of ETV, and Aljezeeri, a journalist for Eritrean State Radio. All three were still in government custody at the end of 2002.

The reasons for their arrests are unclear, but CPJ sources in Eritrea believe their continued detention is related to the government's general crackdown on the press, which began in September 2001.

Tewodros Kassa, *Ethiop*
Imprisoned: July 7, 2002

Kassa, former editor-in-chief of the Amharic-language weekly *Ethiop*, was sentenced to two years in prison on two counts of violating Ethiopia's restrictive Press Proclamation No. 34 of 1992 in three articles published in *Ethiop* in 1997.

The first charge, "disseminating false information that could incite people to political violence," stemmed from two stories: The first reported that the ruling Ethiopian People's Revolutionary Democratic Front (EPRDF) had fired personnel at the Debre Zeit air force base who previously worked for the former regime of Mengistu Haile Mariam and replaced them with pro-EPRDF workers; the second article alleged that unidentified individuals had failed in an attempt to bomb a popular hotel in the capital, Addis Ababa.

The second charge, "defamation," resulted from another 1997 article in *Ethiop*, which alleged that a private investment company specializing in natural-resource development had connections in the EPRDF government. According to a source at *Ethiop*, Kassa was charged even after the newspaper complied with a government order forcing the publication to print a letter of apology.

At the time of his conviction, Kassa was already in jail. In mid-May, he was imprisoned for missing a court hearing related to the charges. Sources in Addis Ababa said Kassa had mistaken the date of the hearing.

Boubacar Yacine Diallo, *L'Enquêteur*
Imprisoned: December 19, 2002

Diallo, founding publisher, owner, and columnist of the independent bimonthly

L'Enquêteur, was arrested by gendarmes in the capital, Conakry. The arrest followed the publication of an article in that day's edition of *L'Enquêteur* alleging that army inspector general Col. Mamadou Baldé had resigned. Baldé denied the allegation and accused his detractors of "wanting to do him in," Agence France-Presse reported.

Diallo was charged with defamation, and on December 20, he was transferred from the gendarmerie to Conakry's Central Prison to await trial. On January 3, 2003, Diallo was provisionally released from prison. On January 7, he was convicted of defamation and sentenced to a year in prison. However, shortly after the sentence was announced, President Lansana Conté pardoned Diallo.

INDIA: 1

Iftikhar Gilani, *Kashmir Times*
Imprisoned: June 9, 2002

Police arrested Gilani, New Delhi bureau chief for the Jammu-based newspaper *Kashmir Times*, following a raid on his home earlier that day by various agencies, including the Intelligence Bureau, the Special Branch of Police, and the Income Tax Department. Authorities confiscated the journalist's computer and several documents, including bank statements, according to his wife. Gilani, who is a well-regarded independent journalist, also reports for the German broadcaster Deutsche Welle and the Pakistani newspapers *The Friday Times* and *The Nation*. The journalist's detention coincided with the arrest the same day of his father-in-law, Syed Ali Shah Geelani, a senior separatist leader in Kashmir.

Authorities accused Gilani of possessing classified documents "prejudicial to the safety and security of the country." He was charged under India's Official Secrets Act, a draconian, colonial-era law. However, the document cited by investigators as central to the case had been published in a Pakistani journal and was readily available on the Internet. Though journalists and international organizations, including CPJ, highlighted this information in the days immediately following Gilani's arrest, military intelligence officials conceded the point only in December.

In a December 12 evaluation of the document in question, intelligence officials admitted that the paper was "easily available" and of "negligible security value." The government, however, did not withdraw the case against Gilani until January 10, 2003. The Metropolitan Magistrate's Court in Delhi ordered Gilani's release on January 13.

INDONESIA: 1

Lesley McCulloch, free-lance
Imprisoned: September 11, 2002

Indonesian troops arrested McCulloch, an academic and free-lance journalist, along with her friend, Joy Lee Sadler, while conducting security operations in Keuleut District in restive Aceh Province. The two were taken to the South Aceh District Police Station.

Soldiers also arrested the women's Acehnese interpreter, Fitrah bin Amin, but she was soon released without charge.

Spokesman Maj. Taufik Sugiono told The Associated Press (AP) that the women were carrying a computer disk with digital images and documents relating to the rebel Free Aceh Movement, known by its Indonesian acronym, GAM. "We questioned them as they were foreigners carrying rebel documents in a conflict-area," Sugiono told the AP. "We just wanted to know what are they doing here." In interviews with journalists, McCulloch and Sadler later claimed that during their detention in South Aceh, they were sexually harassed, beaten, and threatened at knifepoint.

GAM rebels have been fighting for Aceh's independence from Indonesia since 1976 in a conflict that has killed more than 12,000 people during the last decade alone. McCulloch, a British national who most recently worked as a lecturer at the University of Tasmania in Australia, has written frequently on Aceh, specifically about the military's alleged profiteering from the resource-rich province. Sadler, a U.S. national, is a nurse who has treated refugees in conflict zones.

On September 17, police transferred McCulloch and Sadler to a detention center in the provincial capital, Banda Aceh, and announced that the two were formally under investigation. Police threatened to accuse them of espionage but ultimately charged them with carrying out "activities incompatible with tourist visas" under Article 50 of the Immigration Law, punishable by up to five years' imprisonment. Though foreign correspondents accused of visa infractions in Indonesia have generally been deported, police expressed their intention to use this case as a stern warning. "Police will make strong efforts to intensively investigate so this can become a lesson for foreigners who violate the law in Aceh and Indonesia," Aceh police spokesman Taufik Sutiyono told the Agence France-Presse news agency.

McCulloch, who maintains that she was visiting friends in Aceh, told journalists that she believes she was targeted because of her critical writings about

alleged abuses committed by Indonesian security forces in Aceh.

Trial proceedings began in Banda Aceh on November 25, and on December 30, McCulloch and Sadler were sentenced to five months and four months in prison, respectively. While announcing his decision, Judge Asril Marwan said that McCulloch received the harsher sentence because her actions "could have threatened national security and the territorial integrity of the Republic of Indonesia," according to London's *Guardian* newspaper.

Both women will receive credit for time served, which means that McCulloch's sentence is due to expire in February 2003. Sadler was freed on January 10, 2003.

IRAN: 2

Akbar Ganji, *Sobh-e-Emrooz, Fath*
Imprisoned: April 22, 2000

Ganji, a leading investigative reporter for the reformist daily *Sobh-e-Emrooz* and a member of the editorial board of the pro-reform daily *Fath*, was arrested and prosecuted in both Iran's Press Court and Revolutionary Court.

The case in the Press Court stemmed from Ganji's investigative articles about the 1998 killings of several dissidents and intellectuals that implicated top intelligence officials and former president Hashemi Rafsanjani. In the Revolutionary Court, Ganji was accused of making propaganda against the Islamic regime and threatening national security in comments he made at an April 2000 conference in Berlin on the future of the reform movement in Iran.

The Press Court case remained pending at the end of 2002, but on January 13, 2001, the Revolutionary Court sentenced Ganji to 10 years in prison, followed by five years of internal exile. In May 2001, after Ganji had already served more than a year in prison, an appellate court reduced his punishment to six months.

The Iranian Justice Department then appealed that ruling to the Supreme Court, arguing that the appellate court had committed errors in commuting the original 10-year sentence. The Supreme Court overturned the appellate court's decision and referred the case to a different appeals court. On July 16, 2001, that court sentenced Ganji to six years in jail. According to the state news agency IRNA, the ruling is "definitive," meaning that it cannot be appealed.

The legal situation was not clear, however. IRNA quoted an official with the Tehran-based Society for Defending Press Freedom in August 2001 as saying, "No one as yet knows which judge or which officials of the judiciary have made this latest decision." The case's outcome was still unclear at the end of 2002.

Emadeddin Baghi, *Fath, Neshat*
Imprisoned: May 29, 2000

Baghi, a contributor to the banned daily *Neshat* who was on the editorial board of another outlawed daily, *Fath*, was detained during a closed-door trial. On July 17, 2001, Tehran's Press Court sentenced him to five-and-a-half years in prison.

According to the state news agency IRNA, Baghi was charged with publishing articles that "questioned the validity of ... Islamic law," "threatening national security," and "spreading unsubstantiated news stories" about the role of "agents of the Intelligence Ministry in the serial murder of intellectuals and dissidents in 1998."

The charges were based on complaints from a number of government agencies, including the Intelligence Ministry, the conservative-controlled Islamic Republic of Iran Broadcasting, and former security officials.

The charges also mentioned a 1999 piece Baghi had published in *Neshat* responding to another article criticizing the death penalty that had itself landed *Neshat* editor Mashallah Shamsolvaezin in jail. The closed-door trial began on May 1, 2000. In late October 2001, an appeals court reduced the sentence to three years. Baghi remains in Tehran's Evin Prison.

KAZAKHSTAN: 1

Sergei Duvanov, *Prava Cheloveka v Kazakhstane i Mire*
Imprisoned: October 27, 2002

Duvanov, a prominent 49-year-old journalist known for his criticism of Kazakh authorities, was arrested on suspicion of raping a minor. The journalist was officially charged on November 6.

Duvanov denied the rape accusation, saying it was a government effort to discredit him. The charges came just as Duvanov was preparing to leave for the United States, where he was scheduled to give a series of talks at Washington, D.C.– and New York–based think tanks about political conditions in Kazakhstan.

Shortly after his arrest, Duvanov went on a hunger strike to protest his detention. He ended the strike after 13 days, when prison authorities began to force-feed him. His trial, which began on December 24, was ongoing at year's end.

Duvanov, who writes for opposition-financed Web sites and is the editor-in-chief of a bulletin published by the Almaty-based Kazakhstan Bureau for Human Rights and the Rule of Law, is known for his biting criticism of Kazakhstan's political system and high-level officials, including Kazakh president Nursultan Nazarbayev. Authorities have frequently harassed him in reprisal for his work.

On the evening of August 28, 2002, three unknown assailants beat and stabbed Duvanov in the stairwell of his apartment building, saying of his work, "If you carry on, you'll be made a total cripple."

On July 9, 2002, the General Prosecutor's Office charged him with "infringing the honor and dignity of the president"—a criminal offense punishable by a fine or up to three years in prison—after he accused Nazarbayev of corruption in an article. Authorities later dropped that criminal case against him without any explanation.

KUWAIT: 2

Ibtisam Berto Sulaiman al-Dakhil, *Al-Nida'*

Fawwaz Muhammad al-Awadi Bessisso, *Al-Nida'*

Imprisoned: June 1991

Bessisso and al-Dakhil were sentenced to life in prison for their work with *Al-Nida'*, a newspaper that Iraqi authorities launched during Iraq's occupation of Kuwait in 1990. At the end of 2002, they were the last remaining imprisoned journalists in Kuwait, which jailed 17 reporters and editors for their work with *Al-Nida'* following the Gulf War, charging them with collaboration.

The defendants were reportedly tortured during their interrogations. Their trial, which began on May 19, 1991, in a martial-law court, failed to meet international standards of justice. In particular, prosecutors failed to rebut the journalists' defense that they had been forced to work for the Iraqi newspaper.

On June 16, 1991, the journalists were sentenced to death. Ten days later, following international protests, all martial-law death sentences were commuted to life

imprisonment. The other 15 journalists were freed gradually starting in 1996, most on the occasion of Kuwaiti emir Sheikh Jaber al-Ahmed al-Sabah's annual prisoner amnesties in February.

In 2002, the emir pardoned Bessisso and al-Dakhil. But because Bessisso is not a citizen of any country, no nation is willing to accept him as a refugee, according to his brother, who lives in the United States. Al-Dakhil, a naturalized Kuwaiti citizen from Iraq, lost her citizenship as a result of her conviction and is also awaiting deportation. Both are currently being held in Kuwaiti jails while they try to find countries of residence.

NEPAL: 16

Om Sharma, *Janadisha*
Khil Bahadur Bhandari, *Janadesh*

Imprisoned: November 26, 2001

Police raided the offices of three publications closely associated with Nepal's Maoist movement: the daily *Janadisha*, the weekly *Janadesh*, and the monthly *Dishabodh*. Officers arrested nine staff members, including seven journalists, and also confiscated equipment and written materials. The arrested journalists included Om Sharma, an editor for *Janadisha*; Khil Bahadur Bhandari, executive editor of *Janadesh*; Govinda Acharya, an editor of *Janadesh*; Dipendra Rokaya, an editorial assistant at *Janadesh*; Deepak Sapkota, a reporter for *Janadesh*; Ishwarchandra Gyawali, executive editor of *Dishabodh*; and Manarishi Dhital, an editorial assistant for *Dishabodh*.

All were arrested about two hours before the government announced a state of emergency and issued a sweeping anti-terrorism ordinance that criminalized any contact with or support for Maoist rebels.

On November 5, 2002, nearly one year after their arrests, authorities released Rokaya, Sapkota, Gyawali, and Dhital without charge. Acharya was released on December 16, 2002, along with Chandraman Shrestha, the managing editor of *Janadesh*, who had been arrested separately.

Sharma, a veteran journalist who is known as an outspoken supporter of the radical left, and Bhandari, also a longtime journalist associated with pro-Maoist papers, remained imprisoned in Kathmandu's Central Jail at the end of 2002.

Dev Kumar Yadav, *Janadesh*
Imprisoned: November 28, 2001

Yadav, a reporter for the weekly *Janadesh* and daily *Janadisha,* was arrested in the southeastern district of Siraha. Authorities arrested him under the provisions of a sweeping anti-terrorism ordinance introduced in November 2001 allowing for the arrest of anyone suspected of supporting Maoist rebels. Authorities released him without charge on January 7, 2003, according to the Kathmandu-based Center for Human Rights and Democratic Studies.

Chitra Choudhary, *Nawa Paricharcha, Yugayan*
Imprisoned: December 6, 2001

Choudhary was an advising editor at the weekly *Nawa Paricharcha* and the former editor-in-chief of *Yugayan*, both published in Tikapur, a town in the far-western district of Kailali. He was also the principal of the National Lower Secondary School in Patharaiya School. He was arrested at the school on the morning of December 6, 2001, and brought to the Tikapur police station, where Sama Thapa, editor of *Yugayan*, was also detained. Both journalists were later transferred to the regional police station in Shangadhi, the district headquarters of Kailali.

Authorities arrested them under the provisions of a sweeping anti-terrorism ordinance introduced in November 2001 that criminalized any contact with or support for the Maoist rebels. Choudhary, who had written articles supportive of the Maoist rebels, also spent time detained at the army barracks in Dhangadhi, according to a local human rights monitoring group.

Thapa was released without charge on April 4, 2002, "because they could not get any proof of his affiliation with the Maoists," said one journalist. Choudhary was still detained at the end of 2002 at an undisclosed location, according to the Center for Human Rights and Democratic Studies, a Kathmandu-based press freedom group.

Komal Nath Baral, *Swaviman*
Imprisoned: December 21, 2001
Janardan Biyogi, *Swaviman*
Imprisoned: December 27, 2001

Army soldiers arrested Baral, an editor at *Swaviman* weekly, in Pokhara, the capital of Kaski District. *Swaviman*, which is published from Pokhara, was a small newspaper characterized by local journalists as supportive of the Maoist rebel movement. Several days after Baral's arrest, on December 27, soldiers arrested Biyogi, subeditor of *Swaviman.*

Authorities arrested the two under the provisions of a sweeping anti-terrorism ordinance introduced in November 2001 that criminalized any contact with or support for Maoist rebels. Both men were originally held in army custody in Kaski, then transferred to a jail in neighboring Tanahu District, and ultimately imprisoned at Kaski Jail.

Badri Prasad Sharma, *Baglung Weekly*
Imprisoned: December 25, 2001
Security forces arrested Sharma, editor and publisher of *Baglung Weekly*, at his home in the midwestern town of Baglung. Authorities arrested him under the provisions of a sweeping anti-terrorism ordinance introduced in November 2001 that criminalized any contact with or support for Maoist rebels.

Local journalists and human rights activists said that Sharma was viewed as an independent journalist, though the paper often covered news about the Maoist rebels.

"Security persons suspect his newspaper is close to the Maoists because his newspaper covers pro-Maoist news," one journalist from Baglung told CPJ. A delegation from the Baglung chapter of the Federation of Nepalese Journalists visited local administrative officials and vouched for Sharma's journalistic credentials. However, he remained imprisoned in Baglung Jail at the end of 2002.

Debram Yadav, *Blast Times, Jana Aastha*
Imprisoned: January 1, 2002
Yadav, a reporter for the popular regional tabloid *Blast Times* and the Kathmandu-based paper *Jana Aastha,* was arrested in the southeastern district of Saptari. He was arrested under the provisions of a sweeping anti-terrorism ordinance introduced in November 2001 that criminalized any contact with or support for Maoist rebels. He was imprisoned at Saptari Jail. Yadav was released on January 17, 2003, according to news reports.

Posh Raj Poudel, *Chure Sandesh*
Imprisoned: January 23, 2002
Police arrested Poudel, executive editor of the newspaper *Chure Sandesh*, in the capital, Kathmandu, along with his colleague Suresh Chandra Adhikari, the paper's editor-in-chief. Police initially detained them at the Hanuman Dhoka Police Detention Center in Kathmandu but later transferred them to southern Chitwan District, along the Indian border. *Chure Sandesh* was a pro-Maoist newspaper published from Chitwan.

On November 26, 2001, the government declared a state of emergency and issued sweeping anti-terrorism legislation that criminalized any contact with or support for Maoist rebels. Two days later, police raided the offices of *Chure Sandesh*, as well as the home of the weekly's publisher, where they seized documents and copies of the paper, according to the Kathmandu-based Center for Human Rights and Democratic Studies.

Adhikari was released on November 8, 2002, but Poudel remained imprisoned at Bharatpur Jail in Chitwan at year's end.

Bhim Sapkota, *Narayani Khabar Weekly, Adarsha Samaj*
Imprisoned: May 6, 2002
Sapkota, a subeditor for *Narayani Khabar Weekly* and reporter for the newspaper *Adarsha Samaj*, was arrested in the southern district of Chitwan. Authorities detained him under the provisions of a sweeping anti-terrorism ordinance introduced in November 2001 that criminalized any contact with or support for Maoist rebels. Sapkota, who is also a schoolteacher, had previously contributed articles to the pro-Maoist publications *Janadesh* and *Mahima*. He

was imprisoned at Bharatpur Jail in Chitwan.

Shiva Tiwari, *Janadisha*
Bharat Sigdel, *Janadisha*
Imprisoned: May 19, 2002
Krishna Sen, *Janadisha*
Atindra Neupane, *Janadisha*
Sangeeta Khadka, *Jana Ahwan*
Imprisoned: May 20, 2002

Tiwari, executive editor of the daily *Janadisha*, and Sigdel, a reporter for *Janadisha*, were arrested on May 19, according to sources close to the paper. The next day, police arrested Sen, editor of *Janadisha* and former editor of the weekly *Janadesh*; Neupane, a reporter for *Janadisha*; and Khadka, a reporter for the weekly *Jana Ahwan*. The journalists, all of whom worked for publications closely associated with the Maoist rebels, were detained under the provisions of a sweeping anti-terrorism ordinance introduced in November 2001 that criminalized any contact with or support for Maoist rebels.

The journalists' arrests were widely reported in the local press. However, after news reports emerged in late June 2002 that Sen may have been killed in police custody, a government-appointed commission said it found no evidence that he had ever been detained. Officials have since denied responsibility for Sen's fate. Because Sen's body has not been recovered and no credible investigation has been undertaken to determine his status, CPJ holds the government accountable for his fate.

At the end of 2002, Tiwari was imprisoned at Bhadra Bandi Jail, Sigdel and Neupane were imprisoned at Central Jail, and Khadka was imprisoned at the Women's Jail—all in the capital, Kathmandu.

Dinesh Chaudhari, *Spacetime Daily*
Imprisoned: November 3, 2002

Security forces arrested Chaudhari, Jajarkot-based reporter for the national newspaper *Spacetime Daily*. Jajarkot is a remote district in western Nepal. Local journalists say that Chaudhari was targeted for reporting on the alleged torture of area villagers by government security forces. Chaudhari had recently taken photographs of the victims for his newspaper. He was arrested under the provisions of a sweeping anti-terrorism ordinance introduced in November 2001 that criminalized any contact with or support for Maoist rebels. At the end of 2002, he was being held at a police detention center in Jajarkot.

NIGER: 1

Abdoulaye Tiémogo, *Le Canard Déchaîné*
Imprisoned: June 18, 2002

Tiémogo, publisher and editor-in-chief of the satirical weekly *Le Canard Déchaîné*, was arrested for allegedly defaming Prime Minister Hama Amadou in a series of unflattering opinion pieces. Tiémogo accused the prime minister of attempting to bribe Mahamane Ousmane, the head of Niger's Parliament, in a bid to retain his position. According to Tiémogo's stories, Amadou offered 6 million CFA francs (US$9,000), which Ousmane reportedly refused. Tiémogo appeared in court on June 19 and was ordered held without bail, said sources in the capital, Niamey.

On June 28, the journalist was convicted of libel and sentenced to eight months in prison. He was also ordered to pay a 50,000 CFA franc (US$75) fine. In addition, Tiémogo was ordered to pay Amadou 1 million CFA francs (US$1,500) in damages.

According to CPJ sources, after his conviction, Tiémogo sent a letter of apology to the judge conceding that the articles' allegations were unfounded. Though Tiémogo appealed the conviction, on November 11, the Niamey Appeals Court upheld his sentence.

PAKISTAN: 1

Munawwar Mohsin, *The Frontier Post*
Imprisoned: January 29, 2001

Police in Peshawar arrested Mohsin and four colleagues from *The Frontier Post* after the newspaper published a letter to the editor titled "Why Muslims Hate Jews," which included derogatory references to the Prophet Mohammed.

Although the newspaper's senior management claimed that the letter was inserted into the copy by mistake and apologized for failing to stop its publication, district officials responded to complaints from local religious leaders by closing the paper and ordering the immediate arrest of seven staff members on blasphemy charges. In Pakistan, anyone accused of blasphemy is subject to immediate arrest without due process; those found guilty may be sentenced to death.

At the end of 2002, the blasphemy case was still pending, though Mohsin was the only journalist from *The Frontier Post* who remained in prison. (Two of the journalists charged in the case immediately went into hiding and were never arrested. The other four were eventually released on bail.) Mohsin, who was working as the newspaper's subeditor, admitted responsibility for publishing the letter, which he says he had not read carefully. He told *The New York Times* that he "could never think of abusing our Holy Prophet" but confessed that, having only recently completed a drug

rehabilitation program, his mind may have been slightly addled. Mohsin is imprisoned in Peshawar Central Jail.

RUSSIA: 1

Grigory Pasko, *Boyevaya Vakhta*
Imprisoned: December 25, 2001

Pasko, an investigative reporter with *Boyevaya Vakhta* (Battle Watch), a newspaper published by the Pacific Fleet, was convicted of treason on December 25, 2001, and sentenced to four years in prison by the Military Court of the Pacific Fleet in Vladivostok. The ruling also stripped Pasko of his military rank and state decorations.

The journalist was taken into custody in the courtroom and then jailed. Pasko's attorney, Anatoly Pyshkin, filed an appeal with the Military Collegium of the Russian Supreme Court seeking full acquittal.

Pasko was first arrested in November 1997 and charged with passing classified documents to Japanese news outlets. He had been reporting on environmental damage caused by the Russian navy. asko spent 20 months in prison while awaiting trial.

In July 1999, he was acquitted of treason but found guilty of abusing his authority as an officer. He was immediately amnestied, but four months later, the Military Collegium of the Russian Supreme Court canceled the Vladivostok court's verdict and ordered a new trial. Pasko's second trial began on July 11, 2001, after having been postponed three times since March.

During the trial, Pasko's defense argued that the proceedings lacked a basis in Russian law. Article 7 of the Federal Law on State Secrets, which stipulates that information about environmental dangers cannot be classified, protects Pasko's work on sensitive issues, such as unlawful dumping of radioactive waste. The prosecution relied on a secret Ministry of Defense decree (No. 055) even though the Russian Constitution bars the use of secret legislation in criminal cases.

The defense also challenged the veracity of many of the witnesses, several of whom acknowledged that the Federal Security Service (FSB) falsified their statements or tried to persuade them to give false testimony. An FSB investigator was reprimanded for falsifying evidence in the first trial, and the signatures of two people who witnessed a search of the reporter's apartment were allegedly forged.

Throughout 2001, CPJ issued numerous statements calling attention to Pasko's ordeal, and in early June, a CPJ delegation traveled to Vladivostok before Pasko's trial to publicize concerns over the charges.

In early 2002, in a ruling that seemed to bode well for Pasko, the Military Collegium of the Russian Supreme Court annulled a clause of Defense Ministry Decree No. 010, a relic from the Soviet period, which prohibited "nonprofessional" contacts between Russian military personnel and foreign citizens. A CPJ delegation conducted a four-day mission to Vladivostok and Moscow in early March 2002 to meet with Pasko supporters, politicians, and government officials to discuss the case but was prevented from visiting Pasko.

At the same time, the Military Collegium nullified Defense Ministry Decree No. 055 after Pasko's lawyers had filed a complaint challenging its legality. This decree listed various categories of military information as state secrets. Three months later, however, the Appeals Board of the Supreme Court reinstated the decree.

Pasko was held in a temporary detention facility in Vladivostok until October 2002, when he was transferred to a prison, as required by Russian law. On January 23, 2003, a court in the city of Ussuriisk, in the Russian Far East, granted Pasko parole. He was released immediately and traveled to his home in Vladivostok.

Under Russian law, Pasko, who had served two-thirds of his four-year sentence, was eligible for parole based on good behavior. State prosecutors are contemplating protesting the parole decision, Russian and international news reported.

Pasko and his defense attorneys plan to seek the reversal of the journalist's guilty verdict. According to Russian news reports, Pasko's lawyer Ivan Pavlov said a petition has already been filed with the chairman of the Russian Supreme Court and should be heard in February 2003. "We are going to work to achieve the full exoneration of my good name. We're going to do everything to ensure that this criminal case is recognized as falsification," said Pasko, following his release, according to The Associated Press.

SIERRA LEONE: 1

Paul Kamara, *For Di People*
Imprisoned: November 12, 2002

Kamara, the founding editor of one of Sierra Leone's leading newspapers, *For Di People*, was sentenced to six months in prison for defaming a local judge.

Kamara was taken to Pa Demba Road Prison in the capital, Freetown, after the High Court convicted him on 18 counts of criminal libel under sections 26 and 27 of Sierra Leone's Public Order Act. The journalist was also fined US$2,100 on nine of the 18 counts, sources reported. On the remaining counts, Kamara has the choice of either paying a US$1,350 fine or serving an additional three months in jail. The court also recommended that the government ban his newspaper for six months.

The verdict against Kamara came almost a year after prominent appeals court judge Tolla Thompson, who also heads the Sierra Leone soccer association, accused Kamara of writing libelous articles in *For Di People* criticizing the judge's management of the association. Kamara owns a popular local soccer team.

According to staff members at *For Di People*, Kamara appealed the ruling to the Supreme Court, where he will dispute the legality of the charges against him, as well as the High Court's authority to try the case. At year's end, the Supreme Court had not yet considered the appeal.

Meanwhile, Kamara's staff has vowed to defy any ban and to continue publishing the award-winning daily. The paper was still appearing at the end of 2002.

SYRIA: 1

Ibrahim Hemaidi, *Al-Hayat*
Imprisoned: December 23, 2002

Hemaidi, the Damascus bureau chief for the influential London-based Pan-Arab daily *Al-Hayat*, was detained by Syrian police in connection with a December 20 article he wrote discussing the Syrian government's alleged preparations for a possible influx of Iraqi refugees in the event of a U.S.-led attack on Iraq. The Syrian government denied the report, and *Al-Hayat* published a statement from the authorities to that effect on December 24.

On December 27, the official Syrian news agency, SANA, acknowledged Hemaidi's detention and said that he is accused of "publishing false information,"

which carries a penalty of up to three years in prison and a fine of up to 1 million Syrian pounds (US$19,500).

TOGO: 2

Julien Ayi, *Nouvel Echo*
Imprisoned: August 8, 2002

Ayi, publication director for the independent daily *Nouvel Echo*, was arrested and jailed at police headquarters in the capital, Lomé, on charges of "defamation of the president" and "disturbing public order." Alphonse Nevamé Klu, the paper's editor-in-chief, was likewise charged but went into hiding to avoid arrest.

The charges against the two journalists stemmed from an August 2 *Nouvel Echo* article claiming that President Gnassingbé Eyadéma had amassed a US$4.5 billion fortune, and that he is one of the world's 497 wealthiest people, according to a list published in the American financial magazine *Forbes*. The article also alleged that Faure Gnassingbé, Eyadéma's son and a National Assembly member, had control over the fortune and that the riches were "ill-gotten," the French news agency Agence France-Presse (AFP) reported.

Following the article's publication, the government informed the journalists that it was lodging a complaint with police against the newspaper. A government statement, meanwhile, verified that Eyadéma had not appeared on *Forbes*' list of 497 names. On August 3, the state television channel broadcast the *Forbes* list, pointing out that no Africans appeared in the document. When contacted by AFP, Interior Minister Sizing Walla said, "The publication of these lies is a way of inciting the population to rebellion."

Walla also said that when questioned by police before his arrest, Ayi had revealed that Claude Améganvi, a trade unionist and chair of the opposition Workers Party, was the article's source. Améganvi was arrested by authorities on August 6 and faces the same charges as Ayi. Though Améganvi also edits the trade union newspaper *Nyawo*, local journalists said his arrest was most likely not related to his journalistic activities.

On September 13, Ayi and Améganvi were convicted and sentenced to four months in prison and a fine of 100,000 CFA francs (US$150) each. Klu was sentenced in absentia to six months in prison and the same fine.

According to the news Web sites *Diastode.com* and *letogolais.com*, in early December, an appeals court extended Ayi and Améganvi's sentences by two months. *Nouvel Echo* has not appeared since early August.

Sylvestre Djahlin Nicoué, *Courrier du Citoyen*
Imprisoned: December 26, 2002

Nicoué, director of the private weekly *Courrier du Citoyen*, was arrested in the capital, Lomé, after he published an editorial in that day's edition of the newspaper arguing that if the government did not take swift measures to institute democratic reforms in the country, the Togolese people would rebel in 2003. Nicoué was accused of "inciting armed rebellion against the state" and was detained at police headquarters.

Local sources said that representatives of Togolese journalists' organizations attempted to intervene on Nicoué's behalf by meeting with President Gnassingbé Eyadéma. Hopes for negotiating the journalist's release were dashed, however, when the *Courrier du Citoyen* published a critical article in its January 2, 2003, edition titled "Kill Us All and Reign Over Our

Dead Bodies." The following day, authorities transferred Nicoué to Lomé Prison.

TUNISIA: 2
Hamadi Jebali, *Al-Fajr*
Imprisoned: January 1991

On August 28, 1992, a military court sentenced Jebali, editor of *Al-Fajr*, the weekly newspaper of the banned Islamic Al-Nahda Party, to 16 years in prison. He was tried along with 279 other individuals accused of belonging to Al-Nahda. Jebali was convicted of "aggression with the intention of changing the nature of the state" and "membership in an illegal organization."

During his testimony, Jebali denied the charges and presented evidence that he had been tortured while in custody. Jebali has been in jail since January 1991, when he was sentenced to one year in prison after *Al-Fajr* published an article calling for the abolition of military courts in Tunisia. International human rights groups monitoring the mass trial concluded that the proceedings fell far below international standards of justice.

Zouhair Yahyaoui, *TUNeZINE*
Imprisoned: June 4, 2002

Yahyaoui, editor of the online publication *TUNeZINE*, was arrested at the Internet café where he worked in the capital, Tunis, and detained. He was sentenced two weeks later to 28 months in prison.

A Tunis court found Yahyaoui guilty of intentionally publishing false information, a violation of Article 306 of the country's Penal Code. The charge stemmed from a number of articles posted on *TUNeZINE*, including a piece criticizing the May 26, 2002, constitutional referendum in which 99.52 percent of voters approved constitutional changes allowing President Zine el-Abidine Ben Ali to run for a fourth term. Yahyaoui was also found guilty of using stolen communication lines to post his Web site, a violation of Section 84 of the Telecommunications Code.

Since Yahyaoui established *TUNeZINE* in July 2001 using a pseudonym, the site has frequently published articles and commentary—including the views of leading Tunisian dissidents—that harshly criticize the Tunisian government. Authorities have blocked the Web site to users inside Tunisia, but *TUNeZINE* has often circumvented these barriers by establishing alternate addresses.

TURKEY: 13

Huseyin Solak, *Mucadele*
Imprisoned: October 27, 1993

Solak, the Gaziantep bureau chief of the now banned socialist magazine *Mucadele,* was arrested and charged under Article 168/2 of the Penal Code with membership in Devrimci Sol (also known as Dev Sol), an outlawed underground leftist organization responsible for numerous terrorist operations in Turkey. Solak was convicted on testimony from a witness who said he had seen the journalist distributing copies of *Mucadele.*

According to the trial transcript, the prosecution witness also testified that Solak had hung unspecified banners in public and had served as a lookout while members of Devrimci Sol threw a Molotov cocktail at a bank in the town of Gaziantep. The prosecution also cited "illegal" documents found after searches of Solak's home and office. Solak confessed to the charges while in police custody but recanted in court.

On November 24, 1994, Solak was

sentenced to 12 years and six months in prison. At the end of 2002, he was being held in Sincan F-type Prison.

Hasan Ozgun, *Ozgur Gundem*
Imprisoned: December 9, 1993

Ozgun, a Diyarbakir correspondent for the now banned pro-Kurdish daily *Ozgur Gundem,* was arrested during a December 9, 1993, police raid on the paper's Diyarbakir bureau. He was charged with being a member of the outlawed Kurdistan Workers' Party (PKK), under Article 168/2 of the Penal Code.

Trial transcripts show that the prosecution based its case on what it described as *Ozgur Gundem*'s pro-PKK slant, following a Turkish-government pattern of harassing journalists affiliated with the publication. The prosecution also submitted copies of the banned PKK publications *Serkhabun* and *Berxehun,* found in Ozgun's possession, as well as photographs and biographical sketches of PKK members from the newspaper's archive. The state also cited Ozgun's possession of an unlicensed handgun as evidence of his PKK membership.

Ozgun maintained that the PKK publications were used as sources of information for newspaper articles, and that the photos of PKK members were in the archive because of interviews the newspaper had conducted in the past. Ozgun admitted to having purchased the gun on the black market but denied all other charges. At the end of 2002, Ozgun was being held in Aydin Prison.

Serdar Gelir, *Mucadele*
Imprisoned: April 26, 1994

Gelir, Ankara bureau chief for the now banned weekly socialist magazine *Mucadele,* was detained on April 16, 1994. He was formally arrested and imprisoned 10 days later on the charge of belonging to an illegal organization.

The Ministry of Justice informed CPJ that Gelir was charged and convicted under Article 168/2 of the Penal Code and Article 5 of the Anti-Terror Law 3713 and sentenced to 15 years in prison by the Ankara State Security Court for being a member of the armed, illegal leftist organization Devrimci Sol (also known as Dev Sol). Court records, however, indicate that he was sentenced to 12 years and six months. At the end of 2002, Gelir was being held in Sincan F-type Prison.

Utku Deniz Sirkeci, *Tavir*
Imprisoned: August 6, 1994

Sirkeci, the Ankara bureau chief of the leftist cultural magazine *Tavir*, was arrested and charged with belonging to the outlawed organization Devrimci Sol (also known as Dev Sol), under Article 168/2 of the Penal Code.

Court records from Sirkeci's trial show that the state accused him of throwing a Molotov cocktail at a bank in Ankara, but the documents do not state what evidence was introduced to support the allegation. Prosecutors also cited Sirkeci's attendance at the funeral of a Devrimci Sol activist to support the charge that he belonged to the organization.

Sirkeci said he had attended the funeral in his capacity as a journalist. He provided detailed testimony of his torture by police, who, he alleged, coerced him to confess. He was convicted and sentenced to 12 years and six months in prison and is currently jailed in Sincan F-type Prison.

Aysel Bolucek, *Mucadele*
Imprisoned: October 11, 1994

Bolucek, an Ankara correspondent for the now banned weekly socialist magazine

Mucadele, was arrested at her home and charged with belonging to an outlawed organization under Article 168/2 of the Penal Code, partly on the basis of a hand-written document that allegedly linked her to the banned leftist group Devrimci Sol (also known as Dev Sol). She has been in prison since her arrest.

Court documents from her trial show that the state also cited the October 8, 1994, issue of *Mucadele* to support its argument that the magazine is a Devrimci Sol publication. The prosecutor claimed that the October 8 edition insulted security forces and state officials and praised Devrimci Sol guerrillas who had been killed in clashes with security forces.

Earlier in 1994, Bolucek had been acquitted of the same charges, so the defense argued that it was illegal for the defendant to be tried twice for the same crime. The defense accepted the prosecution's claim that Bolucek had written the document but said that the police forced her to write it under torture while she was in custody. The defense also argued that a legal publication could not be used as evidence, and that the individuals who made incriminating statements about Bolucek to the police had done so under torture and had subsequently recanted. On December 23, 1994, Bolucek was convicted and sentenced to 12 years and six months in jail. At the end of 2002, she was being held in Kutahya Prison.

Burhan Gardas, *Mucadele*
Imprisoned: March 23, 1995

Gardas, the Ankara bureau chief for the now banned weekly socialist magazine *Mucadele*, was prosecuted several times beginning in 1994. Court records state that Gardas was arrested on January 12,

1994, at his office and charged with violating Article 168/2 of the Penal Code. During a search of the premises, police reportedly found four copies of "news bulletins" of the outlawed organization Devrimci Sol (also known as Dev Sol).

During the trial, the prosecution claimed that police also found banners with left-wing slogans, along with photographs of Devrimci Sol militants who had been killed in clashes with government security forces. The prosecution a lso claimed that Gardas shouted anti-state slogans during his arrest, and that he was using *Mucadele*'s office for Devrimci Sol activities.

Gardas denied all the charges. His attorney argued that the illegal publications were part of the magazine's archive and that Gardas had been tortured in prison, submitting a medical report to prove the allegation. On May 14, 1994, Gardas was released pending his trial's outcome.

While awaiting the verdict in the 1994 prosecution, Gardas was arrested on March 23, 1995, when police raided the office of the successor to *Mucadele*, the weekly socialist magazine *Kurtulus*, for which he was also the Ankara bureau chief. Officials said he had violated Article 168/2 of the Penal Code because of his alleged membership in the banned organization Devrimci Sol. During the raid, police seized three copies of *Kurtulus* "news bulletins" and six *Kurtulus* articles discussing illegal rallies.

Court documents from his second trial, held at the Number 2 State Security Court of Ankara, reveal that the prosecution's evidence against Gardas consisted of his refusal to talk during a police interrogation—allegedly a Devrimci Sol policy—and his possession of publica-tions that the prosecution contended were the mouthpieces of outlawed organizations. In addition, Ali Han, an employee at *Kurtulus*' Ankara bureau, testified that Gardas was a Devrimci Sol member. Gardas denied the claim, and his lawyer argued that his client had the constitutional right to remain silent during police interrogations.

On July 4, 1995, the Number 1 State Security Court of Ankara sentenced Gardas to 15 years in prison on the 1994 charge. In 1996, he was convicted and sentenced to an additional 15 years for the second set of charges. At the end of 2002, Gardas was serving his term at Kirsehir Prison.

Ozgur Gudenoglu, *Mucadele*
Imprisoned: May 24, 1995

Gudenoglu, Konya bureau chief of the now banned socialist weekly magazine *Mucadele*, was arrested, charged, tried, and convicted under Article 168/2 of the Penal Code for belonging to an illegal organization. He was sentenced to 12 years and six months in prison for alleged membership in the outlawed leftist organization Devrimci Sol (also known as Dev Sol). Gudenoglu was reportedly jailed in Konya Prison.

Fatma Harman, *Atilim*
Imprisoned: June 24, 1995

Harman, a reporter for the now banned socialist weekly *Atilim*, was detained during a June 15, 1995, police raid on the newspaper's Mersin bureau.

On June 24, 1995, Harman was formally arrested and charged under Article 168/2 of the Penal Code for allegedly belonging to the outlawed Marxist-Leninist Communist Party (MLKP). *Atilim*'s lawyer reported that the prosecution based its case on the argument that the MKLP published *Atilim*. The prosecution introduced copies of *Atilim* found in Harman's possession as evidence of her affiliation with the MLKP and claimed that several unspecified "banners" were found in the *Atilim* office. The prosecution also alleged that Harman lived in a house belonging to the MLKP. On January 26, 1996, Harman was sentenced to 12 years and six months in prison and jailed in Adana Prison. She is currently in Nidge Prison.

Erdal Dogan, *Alinteri*
Imprisoned: July 10, 1995

Dogan, an Ankara reporter for the now banned socialist weekly *Alinteri*, was arrested and later charged under Article 168/2 of the Penal Code for allegedly belonging to the outlawed Turkish Revolutionary Communist Union (TIKB).

According to the trial transcript, the prosecution argued that the TIKB published *Alinteri*. The case against Dogan was based on the following evidence: (1) a photograph of Dogan, taken at a 1992 May Day parade, allegedly showing him standing underneath a United Revolutionary Trade Union banner; (2) a photograph of Dogan taken on the anniversary of a TIKB militant's death; (3) a photograph allegedly showing Dogan attending an illegal demonstration in the capital, Ankara; (4) a statement of an alleged member of the TIKB who claimed that Dogan belonged to the organization.

The defense argued that the incriminating statement was invalid because it had been extracted under torture. Dogan's lawyer told CPJ that the photograph from the militant's memorial was blurry, and Dogan testified in court that he had attended the May Day parade in

his capacity as a journalist. He was convicted, sentenced to 12 years and six months in prison, and jailed in Bursa Prison. At the end of 2002, he was being held in Bolu Prison.

Sadik Celik, *Kurtulus*
Imprisoned: December 23, 1995

Celik, Zonguldak bureau chief for the now banned leftist weekly *Kurtulus*, was detained and charged with violating Article 168/2 of the Penal Code for allegedly belonging to the outlawed Revolutionary People's Liberation Party-Front (DHKP-C).

The prosecution claimed that the DHKP-C published *Kurtulus*, and that Celik's position with the magazine proved he was a member of the group. Celik was accused of conducting "seminars" for the DHKP-C at the magazine's office, propagandizing for the organization, transporting copies of the magazine from Istanbul to Zonguldak by bus, and organizing the magazine's distribution in Zonguldak. The prosecution also stated that Celik's name appeared in a document written by a DHKP-C leader. (It is not clear whether the document was introduced as material evidence.)

The prosecution claimed that Celik's refusal to speak while in police custody proved his guilt. The defense argued that the prosecution could not substantiate any of its claims. Celik acknowledged having distributed the magazine in his capacity as *Kurtulus*' bureau chief. He said that he had held meetings in the office to discuss the magazine's affairs. The defense presented the statements of two *Kurtulus* reporters to corroborate Celik's statements. On October 17, 1996, Celik was sentenced to 12 years and six months in prison.

Mustafa Benli, *Hedef, Alevi Halk Gercegi*
Imprisoned: May 11, 1998

Benli, owner and editor of the leftist publications *Hedef* and *Alevi Halk Gercegi*, was arrested on or about May 11, 1998, and later charged with "membership in an illegal organization," a crime under Article 168/2 of the Penal Code. According to court documents, the prosecution charged that *Hedef* was the mouthpiece of the Turkish Revolutionary Party, and that authorities had found copies of illegal magazines in Benli's possession. That, along with articles published in *Hedef* and *Alevi Halk Gercegi*, was cited as partial proof of Benli's membership in the organization. He was sentenced to 12 years and six months in prison and is currently in Edirne Prison.

Memik Horuz, *Ozgur Gelecek, Isci Koylu*
Imprisoned: June 18, 2001

Horuz, editor of the leftist publications *Ozgur Gelecek* and *Isci Koylu*, was arrested and later charged with "membership in an illegal organization," a crime under Article 168/2 of the Penal Code. Prosecutors based the case against Horuz on interviews he had allegedly conducted with leftist guerrillas in Topcam, which *Ozgur Gelecek* later published in 2000 and 2001. The state also based its case on the testimony of an alleged former militant who claimed that the journalist belonged to the outlawed Marxist-Leninist Communist Party. Horuz was convicted on June 12, 2002, and sentenced to 15 years in prison. He is currently in Sincan F-type Prison.

Sinan Kara, *Datca Haber*
Imprisoned: December 25, 2002

Kara, publisher of the weekly *Datca Haber*, was sentenced by a criminal court in the southwestern province of Mugla to three months in prison in April 2001 for violating the Press Law, which requires that newspapers distribute two copies of each edition to a local government district office. However, after the Turkish government amended the law in August 2002, Kara's penalty was converted in September 2002 to a 30 billion lira (US$18,000) fine, which the journalist was unable to pay.

As a result, a local prosecutor ordered him to serve three months and eight days in prison for not paying the fine. He was jailed on December 25, 2002, and was in Ula Prison at year's end. Local Turkish journalists believe the original suit was intended to antagonize Kara, whose publication has angered provincial authorities with its critical coverage, and who has been targeted with several lawsuits.

UZBEKISTAN: 3

Mukhammad Bekdzhanov, *Erk*
Yusuf Ruzimuradov, *Erk*
Imprisoned: March 15, 1999

Bekjanov, editor of *Erk*, a newspaper published by the banned opposition Erk party, and Ruzimuradov, an employee of the paper, were sentenced to 14 years and 15 years in prison, respectively, at an August 1999 trial in the capital, Tashkent. They were convicted for distributing a banned newspaper containing slanderous criticism of President Islam Karimov, participating in a banned political protest, and attempting to overthrow the regime. In addition, the court found them guilty of illegally leaving the country and damaging their Uzbek passports.

Both men were tortured during their six-month pretrial detentions in the Tashkent City Prison. Their health has deteriorated as a result of conditions in the prison.

According to human rights activists in Tashkent, Bekjanov was transferred on November 27, 1999, to "strict-regime" Penal Colony 64/46 in the city of Navoi in central Uzbekistan. He has lost considerable weight and, like many prisoners in Uzbek camps, suffers from malnutrition. Local sources have informed CPJ that Ruzimuradov is being held in "strict-regime" Penal Colony 64/33 in the village of Shakhali near the town of Karshi.

Madzhid Abduraimov, *Yangi Asr*
Imprisoned: August 1, 2001

Abduraimov, a correspondent with the national weekly *Yangi Asr*, was convicted of extortion and sentenced to 13 years in prison. In a January 15, 2001, article in *Yangi Asr*, Abduraimov charged that Nusrat Radzhabov, head of the Boysunsky District grain production company Zagotzerno, had misappropriated state funds and falsified documents. Abduraimov also accused the businessman of killing a 12-year-old in a car accident and alleged that Radzhabov's teenage son was part of a group that had beaten and raped a 13-year-old boy.

Radzhabov claims that Abduraimov asked him for money and threatened to publish more accusations unless he was paid. According to the Institute for War and Peace Reporting (IWPR), Radzhabov tried to sue Abduraimov for slander but dropped the suit after a local prosecutor's investigation confirmed the facts in the article.

Authorities arrested Abduraimov and accused him of receiving a US$6,000 bribe. He and a witness quoted by the IWPR claimed that a man threw the money into the back seat of his car immediately before police stopped his vehicle, searched it, and arrested him. Abduraimov was held in the Termez Regional Police Department jail until his trial began in Termez City Court on July 4, 2001.

According to Abduraimov, the court proceedings were influenced by local officials who objected to his reporting on corruption in the oil business. His request for a change of venue was not granted. He refused to attend the hearings and was sentenced in absentia.

Abduraimov is known for his investigative reporting and critical stance toward local law enforcement bodies and authorities. The journalist and his family have been persecuted for several years with threatening phone calls, and his son was reportedly beaten by police and sentenced to four months in jail for disorderly conduct. Supporters say Abduraimov was most likely framed, and it is not known where he is being held.

VIETNAM: 7

Ha Sy Phu, free-lance
Imprisoned: May 12, 2000

Nguyen Xuan Tu, a scientist and political essayist better known by his pen name, Ha Sy Phu, was placed under house arrest and charged with treason. The arrest came after an April 28, 2000, raid on Ha Sy Phu's home in Dalat, Lam Dong Province, during which police confiscated a computer, a printer, and several diskettes. They returned on May 12 with orders for his arrest signed by Col. Nguyen Van Do, police chief of Lam Dong Province.

Officials suspected that Ha Sy Phu had helped draft a pro-democracy declaration, according to CPJ sources, and his arrest followed the government's longstanding harassment of the writer. Ha Sy Phu was held under Administrative Detention Directive 31/CP, which allows two years of house arrest without due process, and was required to report daily to the Dalat police for interrogation.

In January 2002, police searched Ha Sy Phu's home and again confiscated his computer. The raid came during a period of escalating harassment of dissidents in Vietnam. Though the treason charge against Ha Sy Phu was withdrawn in January 2001, authorities have renewed his administrative detention order, and he remained under house arrest at the end of 2002.

Tran Khue, free-lance
Imprisoned: October 9, 2001

On October 22, 2002, the Foreign Ministry announced that writer Tran Khue, also known as Tran Van Khue, had been placed under administrative detention, or house arrest, for two years, and that his term had begun on October 9, 2001. Administrative Detention Directive 31/CP allows two years of house arrest without due process.

In September 2001, Khue had been active in failed efforts to legally register the independent National Association to Fight Corruption. He had also established online publications, called *Dialogue 2000* and *Dialogue 2001*, which included articles by himself and others advocating political reform. In January 2002, the government ordered local officials to confiscate and destroy all printed copies of the publications.

On March 8, 2002, seven police officers entered and searched Khue's home in Ho Chi Minh City and confiscated his computer equipment and several documents, according to CPJ sources. On March 10, Khue sent a message via cell phone to a friend indicating that he was in danger. Immediately after the message was sent, all means of communication with Khue were cut.

According to CPJ sources, police had searched Khue's house for materials relating to an open letter that he sent to Chinese president Jiang Zemin during Jiang's visit to Vietnam in late February 2002. The letter, which was distributed over the Internet, protested recent border accords between the two countries.

On December 29, 2002, about 20 security officials came to Khue's home and detained him for meeting with Hanoi-based democracy activist Pham Que Duong and his wife. The officers also confiscated his computer and computer disks. The day before, Duong was arrested at the Ho Chi Minh City train station as he was returning to Hanoi. A government official stated that the two men had been "caught red-handed while carrying out activities that seriously violate Vietnamese laws." She said that Khue and Duong will be tried but did not clarify on what charges or when.

Nguyen Khac Toan, free-lance
Imprisoned: January 8, 2002

Toan was arrested in an Internet café in the capital, Hanoi. He had reported on protests by disgruntled farmers and then transmitted his reports via the Internet to overseas pro-democracy groups. Authorities later charged him with espionage. On December 20, 2002, Toan was sentenced to 12 years in prison, one of the harshest sentences given to a Vietnamese democracy activist in recent years.

Toan, 47, served in the North Vietnamese army in the 1970s. After becoming active in Vietnam's pro-democracy movement, he began to write articles using the pen name Veteran Tran Minh Tam.

During the National Assembly's December 2001 and January 2002 meeting, large numbers of peasants gathered in front of the meeting hall to demand compensation for land that the government had wrongfully confiscated from them during recent redevelopment efforts. Toan helped the protesters write their grievances to present to government officials. He also wrote several news reports about the demonstrations and sent the articles to overseas pro-democracy publications.

Toan's trial took less than one day, and his lawyer was not allowed to meet with him alone until the day before proceedings began. The day after Toan was sentenced, the official Vietnamese press carried reports stating that he had "slandered and denigrated executives of the party and the state by sending electronic letters and by providing information to certain exiled Vietnamese reactionaries in France." He is currently being held in B14 Prison, in Thanh Tri District, outside Hanoi.

Bui Minh Quoc, free-lance
Imprisoned: January 14, 2002

Free-lance journalist Bui Minh Quoc was charged with "possessing anti-government literature," including his own writings, and put under administrative detention, or house arrest, for two years in Dalat District. Administrative Detention Directive 31/CP allows two years of house arrest without due process. Prior to his arrest, he had conducted extensive research on Vietnam's territorial concessions to China, according to international news reports.

A Foreign Ministry spokesperson told journalists that, "The competent authorities told me that Quoc had violated Vietnamese law and they will provide more specifics on his violations in the coming time." Quoc, a poet and journal-ist who was a North Vietnamese Radio correspondent during the Vietnam War, was also under house arrest between 1997 and 1999.

Le Chi Quang, free-lance
Imprisoned: February 21, 2002

Le Chi Quang, 32, was detained at an Internet café in the capital, Hanoi. He had written and posted several articles online criticizing government policy. According to Vietnamese authorities, officials at a popular domestic Internet service provider notified the Public Security Bureau that Quang had used computers at a specific Internet café in Hanoi to communicate with "reactionaries" living abroad. Security officials then tracked him down at the café.

On September 24, the state prosecutor's office, known as the Supreme People's Organ of Control, issued a document outlining specific charges against Quang. The document cites several articles by Quang as evidence of his "anti-government" activities, including an essay titled "Beware of Imperialist China," which criticized land and sea border agreements between China and Vietnam; essays praising well-known dissidents Nguyen Thanh Giang and Vu Cao Quan; and an article about the U.S.-Vietnam bilateral trade agreement.

On November 8, following a three-hour trial on national-security charges, the Hanoi People's Court sentenced Quang to four years in prison followed by three years of house arrest. Quang was charged under articles 88 and 92 of the Criminal Code, which ban the distribution of information that opposes the government. Quang's parents were the only observers allowed into the courtroom, and his lawyer was not allowed to present a defense before the court, according to CPJ sources. While the chief judge in the case told foreign reporters that Quang had pleaded guilty, CPJ sources said that he admitted in court to having written the articles mentioned by the prosecution but denied committing any crime.

During Quang's trial, about 100 family members and supporters gathered outside the courthouse. In December 2002, he was transferred to Sao Do Prison in Phu Ly, south of Hanoi.

Pham Hong Son, free-lance
Imprisoned: March 27, 2002

Son, a medical doctor, was arrested after he posted an essay online about democracy. Authorities also searched his home and confiscated his computer and several documents, according to the Democracy Club for Vietnam, an organization based in both California and Hanoi, Vietnam's capital.

Prior to his arrest, Son translated into Vietnamese and posted an essay titled "What is Democracy?" (The article first appeared on the U.S. State Department Web site.) Son had previously written several essays promoting democracy and human rights, all of which appeared on Vietnamese-language online forums.

After Son's arrest, the government issued a statement claiming that his work was "anti-state and anti-Vietnam Communist Party," according to international press reports. At the end of 2002, Son was being held in B14 Prison, in Thanh Liet Village, Thanh Tri District, outside Hanoi. By year's end, authorities had not formally charged Son or announced his trial date.

Nguyen Vu Binh, free-lance
Imprisoned: September 25, 2002

Security officials searched Binh's home in Vietnam's capital, Hanoi, before arresting him, according to CPJ sources. Police did not disclose the reasons for the writer's arrest, although CPJ sources believe it may be linked to an essay he had written criticizing border agreements between China and Vietnam.

In late July, Binh was briefly detained after submitting written testimony to a U.S. Congressional Human Rights Caucus briefing on freedom of expression in Vietnam. Authorities then required him to report to the local police station daily. He was also subjected to frequent, day-long interrogation sessions.

Binh, a former journalist, worked for almost 10 years at *Tap Chi Cong San* (Journal of Communism), an official publication of Vietnam's Communist Party. In January 2001, he left his position there after applying to form an independent opposition group called the Liberal Democratic Party.

Since then, Binh has written several articles calling for political reform and criticizing current government policy. In August, he wrote an article titled "Some Thoughts on the China-Vietnam Border Agreement," which was distributed online.

In 2002, Vietnamese authorities cracked down on critics of land and sea border agreements signed by China and Vietnam as part of a rapprochement following the 1979 war between the two countries. Several writers have criticized the government for agreeing to border concessions without consulting the Vietnamese people.

By the end of 2002, authorities had not filed formal charges against Binh or announced a trial date. ∎

CPJ INTERNATIONAL PRESS FREEDOM AWARDS

SINCE 1991, CPJ HAS HONORED SEVERAL JOURNALISTS EACH YEAR from around the world with its International Press Freedom Awards. Recipients have shown extraordinary courage in the face of enormous risks, bravely standing up to tyrants who refuse to allow free discussion in order to hide corruption or keep the world from witnessing their deeds. These journalists have endured terrible difficulties, including jail or physical violence, simply for working to uncover and report the truth, or because they have expressed opinions that the leaders of their countries deem to be dangerous.

INTERNATIONAL PRESS FREEDOM AWARD RECIPIENTS 1991-2002

1991
Pius Njawe, *Le Messager*, Cameroon
Bill Foley and Cary Vaughan, United States
Tatyana Mitkova, TSN, former Soviet Union
Byron Barrera, *La Época*, Guatemala
Imprisoned: Wang Juntao and Chen Ziming, *Economics Weekly*, China

1992
David Kaplan, ABC News, United States
Muhammad al-Saqr, *Al-Qabas*, Kuwait
Sony Esteus, Radio Tropic FM, Haiti
Gwendolyn Lister, *The Namibian*, Namibia
Thepchai Yong, *The Nation*, Thailand

1993
Omar Belhouchet, *El-Watan*, Algeria
Nosa Igiebor, *Tell*, Nigeria
Veran Matic, Radio B92, Yugoslavia
Ricardo Uceda, *Sí*, Peru
Imprisoned: Doan Viet Hoat, *Freedom Forum*, Vietnam

1994
Iqbal Athas, *The Sunday Leader*, Sri Lanka
Aziz Nesin, *Aydinlik*, Turkey
Daisy Li Yuet-wah, Hong Kong Journalists Association, Hong Kong
In memory of staff journalists, *Navidi Vakhsh*, Tajikistan
Imprisoned: Yndamiro Restano, free-lance, Cuba

1995
Yevgeny Kiselyov, NTV, Russia
José Rubén Zamora Marroquín, *Siglo Veintiuno*, Guatemala
Fred M'membe, *The Post*, Zambia
Veronica Guerin, *Sunday Independent*, Ireland
Imprisoned: Ahmad Taufik, Alliance of Independent Journalists, Indonesia

1996
Yusuf Jameel, *Asian Age*, India
J. Jesús Blancornelas, *Zeta*, Mexico
Daoud Kuttab, Internews Middle East, Palestinian Authority Territories
Imprisoned: Ocak Isik Yurtcu, *Ozgur Gundem*, Turkey

1997
Ying Chan, *Yazhou Zhoukan*, United States
Shieh Chung-liang, *Yazhou Zhoukan*, Taiwan
Victor Ivancic, *Feral Tribune*, Croatia
Freedom Neruda, *La Voie*, Ivory Coast
Yelena Masyuk, NTV, Russia
Imprisoned: Christine Anyanwu, *The Sunday Magazine*, Nigeria

1998
Grémah Boucar, Radio Anfani, Nigeria
Gustavo Gorriti, *La Prensa*, Panama
Goenawan Mohamad, *Tempo*, Indonesia
Pavel Sheremet, ORT, *Belorusskaya Delovaya Gazeta*, Belarus
Imprisoned: Ruth Simon, Agence France-Presse, Eritrea

1999
Baton Haxhiu, *Koha Ditore*, Kosovo
Jugnu Mohsin and Najam Sethi, *The Friday Times*, Pakistan
María Cristina Caballero, *Semana*, Colombia
Imprisoned: Jesús Joel Díaz Hernández, Cooperativa Avileña de Periodistas Independientes, Cuba

2000
Steven Gan, *Malaysiakini*, Malaysia
Modeste Mutinga, *Le Potentiel*, Democratic Republic of the Congo
Zeljko Kopanja, *Nezavine Novine*, Bosnia-Herzegovina
Imprisoned: Mashallah Shamsolvaezin, *Asr-e-Azadegan, Neshat*, Iran

2001
Geoff Nyarota, *The Daily News*, Zimbabwe
Mazen Dana, Reuters, Palestinian Authority Territories
Horacio Verbitsky, free-lance, Argentina
Imprisoned: Jiang Weiping, *Qianshao*, China

2002
Irina Petrushova, *Respublika*, Kazakhstan
Tipu Sultan, free-lance, Bangladesh
Ignacio Gómez, "Noticias Uno," Colombia
Imprisoned: Fesshaye Yohannes, *Setit*, Eritrea

CPJ BURTON BENJAMIN AWARDS

Since 1991, CPJ has given the Burton Benjamin Memorial Award to an individual in recognition of a lifetime of distinguished achievement for the cause of press freedom. The award honors Burton Benjamin, the late CBS News senior producer and former CPJ chairman, who died in 1988.

BURTON BENJAMIN MEMORIAL AWARD RECIPIENTS 1991–2002

1991
Walter Cronkite
CBS News

1992
Katherine Graham
The Washington Post Company

1993
R.E. (Ted) Turner
CNN

1994
George Soros
Open Society Institute

1995
Benjamin C. Bradlee
The Washington Post

1996
Arthur Ochs Sulzberger
The New York Times

1997
Ted Koppel
ABC News

1998
Brian Lamb
C-SPAN

1999
Don Hewitt
CBS News

2000
Otis Chandler
The Los Angeles Times
Times Mirror Company

2001
Joseph Lelyveld
The New York Times

2002
Daniel Pearl
The Wall Street Journal

CONTRIBUTORS

THE COMMITTEE TO PROTECT JOURNALISTS IS EXTREMELY GRATEFUL to the following foundations, corporations, and individuals for their invaluable support during 2002:

ABC, Inc.
The Abernathy MacGregor Group, Inc.
Advance Publications
Helen Alexander
Allen & Company Incorporated
Marcia and Franz Allina
American Express Company
American Institute of CPAs
Deborah Amos and Rick Davis
Andrews McMeel Universal
Terry Anderson
The Annenberg Foundation
AOL–Time Warner Inc.
Ken Auletta
Peter Arnett
Around Foundation
The Associated Press
The Baltimore Sun
Bankrate Financial News
Eva and Tobias J. Bermant
H. Claire and Thomas R. Bettag
Bloomberg
BP America Inc.
British Airways
Meredith and Tom Brokaw
Business Week
Camera Planet
Canary Wharf Group plc
CBS News
Cisco Systems Inc.
Citigroup
Walter Cronkite
Cleary, Gottlieb, Steen & Hamilton
CNBC Europe
CNN
Columbia University Graduate
  School of Journalism
Murray Cohen
Continental Airlines
Community Counselling Services
Frank N. Cooper

The Copley Press
Catherine Cosman
Cynthia Crossen and James Gleick
Crowell & Moring LLP
Daily News
Debevoise & Plimpton
Dow Jones & Company, Inc.
Drue Heinz Trust
Richard Edelman
Factiva
Forbes Inc.
The Ford Foundation
Forstmann Little & Co.
Fortune
Fox News Channel
Freedom Forum/Newseum
Freshfields Bruckhaus Deringer LLP
Fried, Frank, Harris, Shriver & Jacobson
Josh Friedman and Carol Ash
The Gannett Foundation
Gannett Co., Inc.
Anne Garrels and Vint Lawrence
Goldman Sachs
James C. and Toni K. Goodale
Cheryl Gould
Philip Graf
The Philip L. Graham Fund
GVA Williams
Ruth Ann and William Harnisch
Harper's Magazine
The Heinz Endowment
Hogan & Hartson L.L.P.
Charlayne Hunter-Gault
Kathleen E. Hunt
Alberto Ibargüen
Instinet Corporation
Walter Isaacson
Steven L. Isenberg
The JKW Foundation
John S. and James L. Knight Foundation
Johnson & Johnson

Jonathan M. Tisch Foundation
Alex S. Jones
Mr. and Mrs. George M. Keller
Bill Kovach
Killfee.com
Jane Kramer
Henry R. Kravis
David Laventhol
Lazard
Richard A. Leibner
Anthony Lewis
Lexis-Nexis
Stuart H. Loory
The Los Angeles Times
John R. MacArthur
Robert and Donna MacNeil
Makinson Cowell
Markle Foundation
Kati Marton
Michael Massing
The McClatchy Co.
The Robert R. McCormick Tribune Foundation
Media News Group
Merrill Lynch & Co., Inc.
Metropolitan Philanthropic Fund
Geraldine Fabrikant Metz and Robert T. Metz
The Miami Herald/Knight Ridder
Middleberg Euro RSCG
Persephone Miel
Miramax
Morgan Stanley
Anne and Victor Navasky
NBC
The New York Times
The New York Times Foundation
The Samuel I. Newhouse Foundation
Newsday
The New Yorker
The Nieman Foundation for Journalism
   at Harvard University
Frank del Olmo
Orrick, Herrington & Sutcliffe LLP
Open Society Institute
James Ottaway
Burl Osborne

Clarence Page
Patterson, Belknap, Webb & Tyler LLP
Philip Morris
Erwin Potts
PublicAffairs
The Pulitzer Foundation
Joyce Purnick and Max Frankel
Sir William Purves
Radianz Inc.
Dan Rather
The Record
RealNetworks
The Reebok Human Rights Foundation
Reuters Group PLC
Susan and Gene Roberts
Ruben and Elisabeth Rausing Trust
The Rudin Foundation, Inc.
Tim Russert
RVC Europe Ltd.
Diane Sawyer
Schulte Roth & Zabel LLP
The Scripps Howard Foundation
Simpson Thatcher & Bartlett
Sony Corporation of America
Jerry Speyer
The St. Petersburg Times
Stanley Eisenberg Charitable Gift Fund
Sullivan & Cromwell
Matthew V. Storin
Paul C. Tash
Time Inc.
TIME Magazine
The Times Mirror Foundation
The Tinker Foundation
Tishman Real Estate Services
Tribune Company
Viacom
Verizon Foundation
Wachtell, Lipton, Rosen & Katz
Mary Ellen and Robert C. Waggoner
The Washington Post Company
Weil, Gotshal & Manges LLP
Bob Woodward
William Zabel

We also extend our gratitude to the individuals and organizations that made contributions in memory of *Wall Street Journal* reporter Daniel Pearl.

Laura M. Abbott	Richard and Mary Lou Homan
Krishnan Anantharaman	Alibeth Howell
Eva and Tobias J. Bermant	Mark and Mary Jean Isenberg
Bloomberg News	Faun Miller Kiddle
Martha Ann Clark	The Medill Club of Greater New York
Terrie Clifford	David B. Michels
Laura Corwin	Karl Putnam
Cynthia W. Cross	Nathan's Restaurant
Peter and Erica Eisinger	Fleming Rutledge
Financial Times	*Seattle Post-Intelligencer*
Arnold Freedman	Susannah H. Skyer
Peter Gall	Susanne Stout Smith
Jon Hallett	Society of Professional Journalists,
Helping.org	Central Ohio Chapter
Thomas & Carolyn Langfitt Family Foundation	Kris Spadaccia
Michael J. Hirschhorn and Jimena P. Martinez	Gayle Vezina

Some of the vital resources that help make the work of CPJ possible are in-kind services and contributions. We thank the following for their support during the last year:

The Associated Press	NBC
Freedom Forum	Reuters
IDT	

CPJ is grateful to Lexis-Nexis for its continued in-kind contribution of information technology services.

 LEXIS·NEXIS
A member of the Reed Elsevier plc group

Continental Airlines is the Preferred Airline for the Committee to Protect Journalists.

Continental Airlines

CPJ AT A GLANCE

The Committee to Protect Journalists is an independent, nonprofit organization founded in 1981. We promote press freedom worldwide by defending the right of journalists to report the news without fear of reprisal.

HOW DID CPJ GET STARTED?
A group of U.S. foreign correspondents created CPJ in response to the often brutal treatment of their foreign colleagues by authoritarian governments and other enemies of independent journalism.

WHO RUNS CPJ?
CPJ has a full-time staff of 22 at its New York headquarters, including area specialists for each major world region. CPJ also has a Washington, D.C., representative and an Asia program consultant based in Bangkok, Thailand. A 35-member board of prominent U.S. journalists directs CPJ's activities.

HOW IS CPJ FUNDED?
CPJ is funded solely by contributions from individuals, corporations, and foundations. CPJ does not accept government funding.

WHY IS PRESS FREEDOM IMPORTANT?
Without a free press, few other human rights are attainable. A strong press freedom environment encourages the growth of a robust civil society, which leads to stable, sustainable democracies and healthy social, political, and economic development. CPJ works in more than 120 countries, many of which suffer under repressive regimes, debilitating civil war, or other problems that harm press freedom and democracy.

HOW DOES CPJ PROTECT JOURNALISTS?
By publicly revealing abuses against the press and by acting on behalf of imprisoned and threatened journalists, CPJ effectively warns journalists and news organizations where attacks on press freedom are occurring. CPJ organizes vigorous protest at all levels—ranging from local governments to the United Nations—and, when necessary, works behind the scenes through other diplomatic channels to effect change. CPJ also publishes articles and news releases, special reports, a biannual magazine, and the most comprehensive survey of attacks against the press worldwide.

WHERE DOES CPJ GET ITS INFORMATION?
CPJ has full-time program coordinators monitoring the press in Africa, the Americas, Asia, Europe and Central Asia, and the Middle East and North Africa. They track developments through their own independent research, fact-finding missions, and firsthand contacts in the field, including reports from other journalists. CPJ shares information on breaking cases with other press freedom organizations worldwide through the International Freedom of Expression Exchange, a global e-mail network.

WHEN WOULD A JOURNALIST CALL UPON CPJ?
- *In an emergency.* Using local and foreign contacts, CPJ can intervene whenever foreign correspondents are in trouble. CPJ is also prepared to notify news organizations, government officials, and human rights organizations immediately of press freedom violations.
- *When traveling on assignment.* CPJ can advise journalists covering dangerous assignments.
- *When covering the news.* Attacks against the press are news, and they often serve as the first signal of a crackdown on all freedoms. CPJ is uniquely situated to provide journalists with information and insight into press conditions around the world.
- *When becoming a member.* A basic membership costs only US$45, and each donation helps CPJ defend journalists. Members receive CPJ's magazine, *Dangerous Assignments*, and its e-newsletter, *CPJ Update*. If you are interested in becoming a member, please visit CPJ's Web site, *www.cpj.org*.

HOW TO REPORT AN ATTACK ON THE PRESS

CPJ needs accurate, detailed information in order to document abuses of press freedom and help journalists in trouble. CPJ corroborates the information and takes appropriate action on behalf of the journalists and news organizations involved.

What to report:
Journalists who are:
- Arrested
- Assaulted
- Censored
- Denied credentials
- Harassed
- Kidnapped
- Killed
- Missing
- Threatened

- Wounded
- Wrongfully expelled
- Wrongfully sued for libel or defamation

News organizations that are:
- Attacked or illegally searched
- Censored
- Closed by force
- Editions confiscated or transmissions jammed
- Materials confiscated or damaged
- Wrongfully sued for libel or defamation

Information needed:
CPJ needs accurate, detailed information about:
- Journalists and news organizations involved
- Date and circumstances of incident
- Background information

Anyone with information about an attack on the press should call CPJ.
Call collect if necessary: (212) 465-1004, or send us a fax at (212) 465-9568.

Contact information for regional programs:
Africa: (212) 465-9344, ext. 112
E-mail: africa@cpj.org
Americas: (212) 465-9344, ext. 120
E-mail: americas@cpj.org
Asia: (212) 465-9344, ext. 140
E-mail: asia@cpj.org
Europe and Central Asia: (212) 465-9344, ext. 101
E-mail: europe@cpj.org
Middle East and North Africa: (212) 465-9344, ext. 104
E-mail: mideast@cpj.org

What happens next:
Depending on the case, CPJ will:
- Investigate and confirm the report
- Pressure authorities to respond
- Notify human rights groups and press organizations around the world
- Increase public awareness through the press
- Publish advisories to warn other journalists about potential dangers
- Send a fact-finding mission to investigate